D1573273

American
Women Leaders

American Women Leaders

1,560 Current Biographies

CAROL HOOKS HAWKINS

Foreword by Walter L. Hawkins

McFarland & Company, Inc., Publishers
Jefferson, North Carolina, and London

LIBRARY OF CONGRESS CATALOGUING-IN-PUBLICATION DATA

Hawkins, Carol Hooks, 1949–
American women leaders: 1,560 current biographies / Carol Hooks Hawkins ; foreword by Walter L. Hawkins.
p. cm.

ISBN 978-0-7864-3847-1
illustrated case binding : 50# alkaline paper 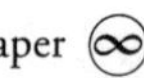

1. Women — United States — Biography.
2. Leadership — United States. 3. United States — Biography.
I. Title.
CT3260.H39 2009 920.72 — dc22 2008037474

British Library cataloguing data are available

Cover photograph: Oprah Winfrey,
guest of honor at the United Nations Association,
Waldorf Astoria, New York, September 30, 2004.
(AP Photo/Amy Sussman/Graylock.com)

Manufactured in the United States of America

McFarland & Company, Inc., Publishers
Box 611, Jefferson, North Carolina 28640
www.mcfarlandpub.com

To my daughter,
Whitney Leann Hawkins

You have the power to reach beyond.
Commit to the Lord in whatever you do,
and you will succeed (Proverbs 16:3)

Acknowledgments

First and foremost, I thank God.

This book could not have been written without the love and support of my husband, Walter Lee Hawkins. Thank you, thank you, thank you for your constant strength and guidance. Also to my children Winter, Donta, Whitney and Faheem (son-in-law). To my grandgirls, Kailyn and Hay-Lei. Thanks to my mother, Sylvia Hooks; my father, Ephriam Hooks; my mother-in-law, Helen Hawkins and my brothers and sister, Melvin Hooks, Alvin Hooks and Sheryl Hooks. To all of you: "you're the best."

Special thanks goes to a few of the many family and friends whose love has always encouraged me and contributed to me being who I am: Sheryl Hooks Grayson, Lillian Hooks, Sharon Arnold, Michelle Barnett, Andrea Beasley, Juanita Brady, Gloria Carter, Yvette Clarke, Patricia June Clay, Minyon Conley, Warrkesha R. Conyers, Karen Duckett, Janice Gates Garrett, Brenda Procter Grant, Katherine Gregory, Carla Simmons Harris, Gwendolyn Harris, Olga G. Harris, Carol J. Harvey, Andrea H. Johnson, Rita Johnson, Beverly (Beaver) McKinney, Beverly Medlock, Linda Morris, Alice Faye Parker, Marcia Tucker Roberts, Annie Roberson, Maria Veliz, Altonia Walker and Rose Marie Walton.

Table of Contents

Preface

American Women Leaders provides profiles of 1,560 notable women in the United States, with all individuals meeting two general criteria for inclusion. First, they were born or spent their childhood years in the United States. (A few exceptions were made where some foreign-born individuals have resided most of their adult lives in the United States.) Second, they have played an important role in the development of American children by serving as a role model.

The standards used to measure contribution and accomplishments include membership in professional and community organizations; notable athletic achievements and records; career successes; national, state, city or community leadership; being the first American woman in a profession, field or position; major honors; Olympic medals or selection to any hall of fame.

American Women Leaders provides the reference librarian, the student or any researcher with brief, objective, accurate and well-researched biographical articles about living American women. Although some of the names are familiar, it is expected that the reader will learn of several women whose names are not well known but whose accomplishments are obviously deserving of recognition.

This book does not attempt to chronicle the full range of American women's contributions in the United States; instead its intent is to identify some individuals who have served as role models and insure that their achievements are noted and recorded historically to be made readily available for generations to follow.

Foreword

The individuals in this book prompt a strong reaction from almost everyone who reads their biographical information. These women understand, define, and display the essence of leadership. Their personal qualities and skills have focused not only on personal achievements, but also on improving society at large. The American people have benefited from their personal sacrifices, education, training and values.

I believe everyone living in the United States, where diversity is about empowering people and promoting the human spirit, will be inspired by these leaders. These women leaders have shown their competitive edge by using the full potential of their individual abilities which will inspire all. The long-held belief of a glass ceiling does not appear to be unbreakable.

An individual acting alone can accomplish much; but a group of people acting together in a unified force can accomplish great wonders. I hope this book removes the bias and prejudiced beliefs that have been deeply rooted within this country about the ability of women to serve in key positions.

Walter L. Hawkins

AMERICAN WOMEN LEADERS

Cynthia Aaron

JUDGE. Justice Cynthia Aaron received a Bachelor of Arts degree in psychology with distinction and departmental honors from Stanford University in 1979. She earned her Juris Doctor degree (cum laude) from Harvard Law School in 1984.

After graduating from law school, she served as a trial attorney at Federal Defenders of San Diego, Inc. In 1988, she served in private law practice. In 1994, she was appointed to the position of United States magistrate judge in the United States District Court of the Southern District of California. She also served as an adjunct professor of law at both the University of San Diego School of Law and California Western School of Law. In January 2003, Governor Gray Davis appointed her an associate justice to the California Court of Appeal Fourth District, Division One.

Sharon A. M. Aarons

JUDGE. Judge Sharon A.M. Aarons received her undergraduate degree from New York University and earned her Juris Doctor from the City University School of Law at Queens College. Her professional career includes serving as a staff attorney with Legal Aid, as principal law clerk to Supreme Court Justice Alexander W. Hunter, Jr., in private law practice, and as principal law clerk to Surrogate of Bronx County Justice Lee L. Holzman.

She was elected judge to the New York City Civil Court, in King County, New York, and began her first term on January 1, 2004.

Juanita Jones Abernathy

NONPROFIT EXECUTIVE. Juanita Jones Abernathy is a native of Uniontown, Alabama. She received her elementary and high school education at Selma University, a boarding school in Selma, Alabama. She received a Bachelor of Science degree in business education from Tennessee State University.

A former high school teacher specializing in a business curriculum, her business acumen has yielded her success in numerous entrepreneurial ventures. She rose to become senior sales director in Mary Kay Cosmetics and successfully maintained a top position in the corporation for many years. As wife and widow of the later Rev. Dr. Ralph David Abernathy, she became pivotally involved in the civil rights movement at its inception in 1955 and has traveled around the world working for justice and equality. She serves as the president and CEO of the Ralph David Abernathy Foundation.

Peggy L. Ableman

JUDGE. Judge Peggy L. Ableman received a bachelor's degree with honors from Simmons College in Boston, Massachusetts, and she earned her Juris Doctor degree from Emory University School of Law.

From 1979 to 1983, she served as an assistant United States attorney for the District of Delaware; from 1983 until her appointment to the Superior Court, she served as an associate judge of the Family Court of the State of Delaware. In 1995, she was the first recipient of the chief justice's Award for Outstanding Judicial Service.

Shirley S. Abrahamson

JUDGE. Justice Shirley S. Abrahamson is a native of the City of New York. She received a bachelor's degree from New York University in 1953. She earned a Juris Doctor degree from Indiana University Law School in 1956, and a doctorate of law in American legal history from University of Wisconsin in 1962.

Before joining the Wisconsin Supreme Court, she was in private practice in Madison for 14 years and was a professor at the University of Wisconsin Law School. She was appointed justice to the Supreme Court by Governor Patrick Lucey in 1976. She won election in 1979 and re-election in 1989 and 1999.

Arlene Ackerman

EDUCATION. Arlene Ackerman received a Bachelor of Arts degree in elementary education from Harris Stowe Teachers College, St. Louis, Missouri, and a Master of Arts degree in educational administration and policy. She earned a Master of Arts degree in education from Harvard University, and her doctorate in education administration, planning and social policy, urban superintendent's program.

Her professional career includes serving as a teacher at both the elementary and middle school levels; as principal at the middle school level; as director, Upward Bound Program for first generation college-bound students; as director, Basic Skills Academy for at-risk high school youth; as assistant superintendent, special services, assistant superintendent for curriculum, instruction and academic achievement and deputy superintendent/chief academic officer for the Washington, D.C., public school system; and as superintendent of the District of Columbia Public Schools.

Dr. Ackerman serves as superintendent of the San Francisco Unified School District.

Val Ackerman

SPORTS. Val Ackerman received a bachelor's degree from the University of Virginia in 1981, where she was a four-year starter for the women's basketball team and a two-time Academic All-American. She played one season of professional basketball in France before attending University of California at Los Angeles School of Law, from which she earned her Juris Doctor degree in 1985.

She joined the National Basketball Association (NBA) in 1988 as a staff attorney and served as special assistant to Commissioner David Stern from 1990 to 1992. She was named director of business affairs in 1992 and vice president of business affairs in 1994. As a member of the Board of Directors of USA Basketball, she helped create the 1995–1996 USA Basketball Women's National Team program which culminated with a gold medal performance at the 1996 Summer Olympics in Atlanta, Georgia.

Ms. Ackerman serves as president of the Women's National Basketball Association (WNBA).

Carolyn Adams

GOVERNMENT OFFICIAL. Carolyn Adams is a native of Chicago, Illinois. She spent two years at Illinois State University then returned to the Chicago area to earn her Bachelor of Arts degree in communication at Columbia College.

Her professional career includes serving eight years as senior account manager for Clearchannel Commu-

nications. There, she successfully sold radio and outdoor advertising and oversaw event marketing for several multi-million dollar corporations and state agencies. She served in similar roles for WGN Radio and Chicago's WVON radio before working for Clearchannel.

On May 25, 2003, Governor Rod Blagojevich appointed Carolyn Adams as lottery superintendent for the State of Illinois.

Cheryl Adams

MILITARY. Cheryl Adams was born in St. Louis, Missouri. She enlisted in the Air Force on October 15, 1977. She earned an associate degree in personnel administration from the Community College of the Air Force. Her military education includes the United States Air Force Non Commissioned Officer Academy, United States Air Forces Senior Non Commissioned Officer Academy, Senior Non Commissioned Officer Leadership Development, and Medical Service Specialist School.

She graduated from basic training at Lackland AFB and attended Medical Service Specialist School at Sheppard AFB, Texas. Following an active duty training tour, she returned to fulfill her Reserve commitment with the former 52nd Medical Services Squadron, now the 932nd Aeromedical Staging Squadron (ASTS) in August 1978.

Her career progression included assignments as staff technician, section supervisor, and superintendent of nursing services. In 1991, during Operation Desert Shield/Desert Storm, she served as facility nursing superintendent at Al Jubail, Saudi Arabia. In May 1995, she became the senior enlisted advisor, subsequently command chief master sergeant for the 932nd Airlift Wing, at Scott Air Force Base, Illinois. In February 2001, she was selected to serve as the command chief master sergeant for the Air Force Reserve Command at Robins Air Base in Georgia, where she advises the commander on matters influencing the health, morale, welfare and effective utilization of more than 70,000 active duty and reserve members within the command and serves as the commander's representative to numerous committees, councils, boards and military and civilian functions.

She is the first African American female in the history of the Air Force Reserves to be selected for this position.

Karen S. Adams

MILITARY. Karen S. Adams received a Bachelor of Arts degree in political science from California State Polytechnic University, Pomona, in 1977. She earned a Master of Science degree in human resource management and organizational development from Chapman University in 1991 and a Master of Science degree in national resource strategy from the Industrial College of the Armed Forces in 2003.

Her military career include numerous command and staff assignments that include serving as the deputy director, strategic communications, office of the Army Chief Information Officer G-5 at the Pentagon; as the chief, training and mission support branch, operations division, Installation Management Agency, Crystal City, Virginia; as the United States Army garrison commander at Fort Gordon, Georgia.

Upon relinquishment of command, Colonel Adams assumed duties as the deputy region director, Installation Management Agency, Heidelberg, Germany.

Valencia Adams

BUSINESS EXECUTIVE. Valencia Adams received a bachelor's degree in business administration from Georgia State University. She continued her education by completing management courses at Columbia University and Emory University.

Her professional career includes serving for over 37 years with BellSouth Corporation. She has served as chief operating officer of BellSouth's Consumer Services division, responsible for planning, developing, and implementing strategies to service the residential market in BellSouth's nine-state territory. She serves as vice president and chief diversity officer for BellSouth Corporation. She has oversight for diversity and inclu-

sion strategy development and implementation across BellSouth Corporation.

Vickee Jordan Adams

COMMUNICATIONS. Vickee Jordan Adams received a Bachelor of Arts in English from the University of Pennsylvania. She has served as vice president and manager of communications training for public relations firm Burson-Marsteller. She served as senior vice president at Ketchum Public Relations where she oversaw a team of international communications specialists. At Dow Jones & Company she was director of corporate communications. As a spokesperson for the company, she had media relations responsibility for *The Wall Street Journal.*

Ms. Adams currently serves as United States director of media communication and senior vice president of Hill & Knowlton. She is responsible for leading Hill & Knowlton's media communications strategy for clients.

Clara Adams-Ender

MILITARY. Clara Adams-Ender is a native of Wake County, North Carolina. She received her bachelor's degree in nursing from North Carolina Agricultural and Technical State University in Greensboro, North Carolina. She earned her masters of science in nursing from the University of Minnesota and a master of military art and science from the United States Army Command General Staff College at Fort Leavenworth, Kansas. Her military education includes graduation from the United States Army War College and the United States Army Medical Office Advanced Course. While attending North Carolina A&T State University in Greensboro she worked as a domestic and beautician to earn extra money.

She joined the Army because she had an important goal in mind: She wanted to finish her education and she needed money to do it. A veteran of over 30 years in the Army, General Adams-Ender has held such diverse assignments as chief nurse of two medical centers, assistant professor of nursing, inspector general, and chief Army nurse recruiter. During the Vietnam War, Adams-Ender served as a staff nurse with the 121st Evacuation Hospital

Kim T. Adamson

JUDGE. Judge Kim T. Adamson received a Bachelor of Science degree from Westminster College of Salt Lake City in 1979. She later earned her masters of professional communication from Westminster and currently serves on the alumni board.

Her professional career includes serving as a law enforcement officer for over 20 years and as a chief warrant officer-5 with the United States Marine Corps Reserves. In October 2001, while stationed at Marine Corps Base at Quantico, she served as a G-3 action officer, the staff secretary for Marine Corps Base Quantico and as the anti-terrorism force protection officer for the 2004 Marine Corps Marathon. In February 2005, she joined the 4th Civil Affairs Group, where she deployed to Iraq as a civil affairs officer, and the Anti-Terrorism Force Protection Unit as the platoon commander for personnel retrieval processing.

Judge Adamson is a senior Justice Court judge in Salt Lake City, Utah.

Rebecca L. Adamson

BUSINESS EXECUTIVE. Rebecca L. Adamson received a bachelor's degree in humane letters from Dartmouth College and a Master of Science degree in economic development from Southern New Hampshire University.

Ms. Adamson, a Cherokee, is founder and president of First Nations Development Institute (1980) and founder of First Peoples Worldwide (1997). She has worked directly with grassroots tribal issues since 1970. Her work established a new field of culturally appropriate, values-driven development which created the first reservation-based micro-enterprise loan fund in the

United States, the first tribal investment model, a national movement for reservation land reform, and legislation that established new standards of accountability regarding federal trust responsibility for Native Americans.

She was selected by the National Women's History Project as one of the 2003 honorees and in 2002 was selected by the Virginia Foundation for Women as one of eight Virginia Women in History honorees.

Mary M. Adolf

NONPROFIT EXECUTIVE. Mary M. Adolf received a Bachelor of Science degree in food and nutrition from the University of Nebraska and a Master of Science degree in food science/meat science from the University of Nebraska. She completed a dietetic internship at Oklahoma State University and is a registered dietitian.

During her professional career from 1981 to 2000, she held four senior positions with the National Livestock and Meat Board/National Cattlemen's Beef Association and served as senior vice president/associate director of Ketchum's Global Food and Nutrition Practice. Ketchum is the world's leading food public relations agency.

Ms. Adolf serves as the president and chief operating officer of the National Restaurant Association Educational Foundation (NRAEF), a not-for-profit organization.

Susan C. Aldridge

EDUCATION. Susan C. Aldridge received a bachelor's degree from Colorado Women's College. She earned her master's degree and doctorate degree in public administration from the University of Colorado.

Her professional career includes serving as a faculty member of the National University of Singapore, as a lecturer at Hong Kong University, as a division director for the Denver Regional Council of Governments, and as vice president of Aldridge and Associates, Inc. In 2001, she served as vice chancellor for Troy University's College and eCampus in Alabama.

Dr. Aldridge was appointed president of Maryland University College on February 1, 2006.

Ellen Alemany

FINANCE. Ellen Alemany received a master's of business administration with a specialization in finance from Fordham University in 1980.

Her professional career includes serving from 1977 to 1987 with Chase Manhattan Bank in operations, structured trade, and the media and electronics department as a senior lender. She joined Citibank in 1987 and in 1988 was appointed area head of Citibank's New York Leveraged Capital Group. In 1991, she was appointed a senior credit officer of the bank. She has held a number of positions in the global corporate bank including customer group executive of North American markets, global industry head of media and communications, and U.S. industry head of consumer products. In November 1999, she was appointed executive vice president of Citibank and the customer group executive for the Global Relationship Bank in Europe. Her other roles have included chairman and chief executive officer for Citibank International PLC, Citibank's pan-European Bank, and country corporate officer for the United Kingdom. She was the executive vice president for the Commercial Business Group, which includes CitiCapital, the Commercial Markets Group, and the Commercial Real Estate Group.

She was appointed chief executive officer, global transaction services, Citigroup corporate and investment banking in 2006.

Pamela G. Alexander

JUDGE. Judge Pamela G. Alexander received a Bachelor of Arts from Augsburg College in 1974 and earned her Juris Doctor degree from the University of Minnesota Law School in 1977.

Her first assignment after law school was serving

as a law clerk at the Neighborhood Justice Center and the Legal Rights Center. She served in private law practice from 1977 to 1983. She was appointed judge to the municipal court, Minneapolis, in 1983. She was assigned as a judge of the district court in 1986. She has been continually re-elected for the past twenty years.

Yvette M. Alexander

JUDGE. Judge Yvette M. Alexander is a native of Grambling, Louisiana. She received a Bachelor of Arts degree in political science from Grambling State University and earned a Juris Doctor degree from the Louisiana State University Law Center in 1979. Her professional career includes serving as counsel for the Louisiana state legislature and for the Louisiana State Senate. She served at the East Baton Rouge Parish public defender's office and as an assistant attorney general for the Louisiana attorney general's office. From 1988 to 1995, she served as chief legal counsel for the secretary of state of Louisiana; in 1995, she was elected judge for Division "D" of Baton Rouge City Court, in Louisiana.

Laila Ali

SPORTS. Laila Ali is a native of Miami Beach, Florida, and is the daughter of Muhammad Ali and Veronica Porsche Ali.

She served as a personal trainer in Los Angeles before she entered women's boxing in 1999. She made her debut on October 8, 1999, and knocked out April Fowler in the first round. She won her next eight fights and on June 8, 2001, she won an eight-round majority decision over Jackie Frazier-Lyde, Joe Frazier's daughter. A year later she beat Shirvelle Williams by a six-round decision. She won the IBA title with a two-round knockout of Suzzette Taylor, on August 17, 2002, in Las Vegas, and on November 9, 2002, she retained that title and added the WIBA and IWBF belts by unifying the crown with an eight-round knockout win over her division's other world champion, Valerie Mahfood in Las Vegas, Nevada. On June 21, 2003, she retained her titles in a rematch with Mahfood, knocking her out in six rounds. In 2004, she fought Nikki Eplion on July 17, 2004, and retained her world title, knocking out Eplion in the fourth round. On September 24, 2004, she added the IWBF Light Heavyweight title to her collection by beating Gwendolyn O'Neal by a knockout in three rounds in Atlanta, Georgia. On February 11, 2005, she won an eight round technical knockout over Cassandra Geigger in a scheduled 10-round fight. On June 11, 2005, she beat Erin Toughill to remain undefeated. On December 17, 2005, she defeated Asa Sandell in Berlin, Germany. On November 11, 2006, she defeated Shelley Burton by a TKO. On February 3, 2007, in Cape Town, South Africa, she knockout Gwendolyn O'Neil out in the first round. Ms. Ali, whose nickname is "She-bee-Stingin," has never lost a professional fight.

Bernadette Allen

GOVERNMENT OFFICIAL. Bernadette M. Allen is a native of Washington, D.C., and was raised in Seat Pleasant, Prince George's County, Maryland. She received a Bachelor of Arts degree in French civilization and linguistics from Central College in Pella, Iowa, in 1978. In a study year abroad (1977), she earned a certificate in French civilization from the Sorbonne University in Paris, France. During the years 1987–1989 she completed a Master of Arts in human resources management from George Washington University. She speaks French and Mandarin Chinese.

Her professional career includes a commission into the United States diplomatic service in January 1980. She served as desk officer in the Africa Bureau's Regional Affairs Office (1985–1987), as visa officer in the Visa Office Coordination Division (1985–1989), as deputy director of consular training at the National Foreign Affairs Training Center (NFATC) (1994–1996), as a legislative management officer (1996–1998); as director of the visa office coordination division (1998–2000), and as chief of the Montreal Consular Section (2000–2002). From 2002 to 2005, she served as consul general at the U.S. Consulate General in Montréal. She was nominated by President George Bush on October 26, 2005, to serve as United States ambassador to the Republic of Niger. She was confirmed by the United States Senate on February 16, 2006, and sworn in as ambassador on March 28, 2006.

Carla H. Allen

MINISTRY. Carla H. Allen holds a Bachelor of Science degree in political science and a master's degree in public administration. She is also a certified personal trainer and aerobics instructor.

Ms. Allen is the founder of FIT4ANEWLIFE Health and Fitness Ministry, a health ministry birthed out of New Orleans, Louisiana, and strategically relocated to Atlanta after Hurricane Katrina. She also served as host of the first Christian health and fitness broadcast on WHNO-TV 20 in the southern region that reached 850,000 households every morning. She is the copastor of New Life Family Worship Center in Fayetteville, Georgia, with her husband Pastor Glenn B. Allen, Sr., the founder and senior pastor. She appears with her husband on Atlanta Interfaith Broadcast. She also wrote a column on "Health and Fitness God's Way" in the *Data News Weekly*, a local newspaper in New Orleans.

Debbie Allen

ENTERTAINMENT. Debbie Allen is a native of Houston, Texas. She received a Bachelor of Arts degree cum laude from Howard University in Washington, D.C.

She began taking dance lessons at the age of three, training at the Ballet National de Mexico and was admitted to the Houston Foundation for Ballet at 14. She was given a full scholarship, becoming the only black in the company. She was refused admission to the North Carolina School of the Arts, despite being asked to demonstrate technique to the other auditioners, because, according to the dance director, she was "built wrong." After this stinging blow, she stopped dancing for a year. She enrolled at Howard University in Washington, D.C., where she began studying Greek classics, speech, and theater arts. During her career she has performed in many musicals, television variety series, movies, commercials, choreography and directed several variety series. She produced the critically acclaimed film *Amistad* with Steven Spielberg and Colin Wilson and has choreographed the annual Academy Awards for five years. Her musicals include *Purlie*, and in 1973, she was cast in *Raisin*. Her first variety series was a comedy called *3 Girls 3*. In 1977, she appeared as Ben Vereen's dancing partner in the television special "Stompin." In February 1979, she starred in *The Next Generation*, in March she starred in *Ain't Misbehavin*. In 1980, she was in Broadway's *West Side Story* and in 1981, she took a role in the movie *Ragtime*. In 1984, Ms. Allen was named one of the producers of "Fame," and she directed several of its episodes. The show won five Emmy awards, and Ms. Allen won one for best choreography. She played a tough prison guard in the movie *Women of San Quentin*. In 1984, she co-wrote, choreographed, and performed in *Dancin' in the Wings*. In 1986, she was cast in Richard Pryor's movie *Jo Jo Dancer* and was back on Broadway in *Sweet Charity*. In 1991, she was the singer, dancer, actor, choreographer, and director of the hit TV series "A Different World" on NBC. She has also directed episodes of "The Fresh Prince of Bel-Air," "Family Ties," and "Quantum Leap." Ms. Allen has written two children's books, *Brothers of the Knight* and *Dancing with Wings*. She is the founder of the Debbie Allen Institute, which promotes dance as a foundation to nurture the creative spirit within each student while stressing the importance of all art disciplines for lifelong success in academic and personal achievements.

Fannie L. Allen

GOVERNMENT OFFICIAL. Fannie L. Allen received a bachelor's degree from Morris Brown College and a master's degree in business administration from Averett College. She is a graduate of the Protocol School of Washington — the nation's leading school of protocol.

Allen is a 30-year veteran of the United States Army Reserve, currently serving at the rank of lieutenant col-

onel. She is chief of the grants division in the Bureau of Educational and Cultural Affairs. She joined the foreign affairs community in the early 1980s and has traveled to approximately 30 countries in the course of her work. She is responsible for the management of personnel in the department. Since 1988, her team has been a leader in the government in meeting the mandates of the Grants, Gov and E-Grants initiatives. She provides seminars, workshops and dining tutorials on business etiquette, dining skills, and international protocol, including dining like a diplomat.

Faye Allen

JUDGE. Judge Faye Allen received a Bachelor of Arts degree in criminology from Florida A&M University in 1986 and earned her Juris Doctor degree from Florida State University in 1990. She has served in private law practice.

In 2005, she was appointed judge for Orange County Criminal Court.

Sharon Allen

FINANCE. Sharon Allen received a bachelor's degree in accounting from the University of Idaho and received an honorary doctorate degree in administrative science from the University of Idaho.

She is the chairman of the board at Deloitte & Touche USA LLP (D&T USA). Prior to assuming the board chair, she was a member of the D&T USA Board of Directors and managing partner of the Deloitte U.S. Firms' Pacific Southwest practice based in Los Angeles. She is the first woman ever elected as board chair.

Susan Au Allen

BUSINESS EXECUTIVE. Susan Au Allen received a Juris Doctor degree from the Antioch School of Law and an LL.M. in international law from Georgetown University Law Center.

In 1984, she founded the US Pan Asian American Chamber of Commerce (USPAACC) with a group of civic and business leaders in Washington, D.C., and became full time president and chief executive officer in 2001. A strong and effective advocate for Asian American issues on Capitol Hill and in the White House, her achievements reached a new level in Washington, D.C., when President George H.W. Bush appointed her to the Council of the Administrative Conference of the United States (1991–1996). She was also appointed vice chair of the Republican National Committee's New Majority Council organized to reach out to minority communities across the nation and served as its surrogate speaker from 1997 to 2000.

Sharon Allison-Ottey

MEDICINE. Sharon Allison-Ottey received a bachelor's degree from North Carolina University in Durham, North Carolina, and earned her Medical Doctor from East Carolina University School of Medicine in Greenville, North Carolina.

Dr. Allison-Ottey was named the American Geriatric Society's 1999 Investigator of the Year for her pioneering work in AIDS in the elderly. She is one of the first in the world to publish on this topic. She served as scientific consultant in neurobehavioral toxicology to the United States Environmental Protection Agency.

Dr. Allison-Ottey serves as chief executive officer at COSHAR Inc., and is the founder and the director of health and community initiatives at COSHAR Foundation .

Jenny Alonzo

ENTERTAINMENT EXECUTIVE. Jenny Alonzo received a Bachelor of Science degree in communications from St. John's University in New York.

She has served as administrator of on-air promotion at WNBC-TV and on-air coordinator for NBC Network's advertising and promotion department. She was manager of on-air promotion at WNBC-TV in New York. She joined Lifetime Entertainment Services and served from January 1994 to May 1996 as Lifetime's director of operations for on-air promotion. She was named vice president of production and operations in May 1996. In September 2004, Ms. Alonzo was named senior vice president, production planning and multi-

cultural strategies, Lifetime Entertainment Service. She also oversees all production and operation of on- and off-air creative services and marketing, handles resource allocations including budgeting and personnel, on-location print and video shooting, talent coordination and pre- and post-production scheduling. In addition, she supervises the scheduling and strategic planning of Lifetime's on-air promotion inventory.

Becky Alseth

BUSINESS EXECUTIVE. Becky Alseth received a Bachelor of Science degree from Montana Tech and a master of business administration from the University of Washington in Seattle.

Her professional career includes serving in numerous positions at Therasense, Inc., move.com, United Distillers & Vintners, and Nestle. In 2003, she joined Avis Budget Group as vice president brand marketing where she oversees all marketing activities for Avis Rent A Car System, LLC, and Budget Rent A Car System, Inc.

Diane R. Alshouse

JUDGE. Judge Diane R. Alshouse received a Bachelor of Arts degree from Luther College in Decorah, Iowa, in 1970, and earned her Juris Doctor degree from Hamline University School of Law in 1984.

She served as an assistant attorney for Hennepin County and as managing attorney for Ramsey County Public Defender's office. She was appointed judge on August 18, 2005, by Governor Tim Pawlenty for the Second Judicial District, Ramsey County, Minnesota.

Cecilia Maria Altonaga

JUDGE. Judge Cecilia Maria Altonaga is a native of Baltimore, Maryland. She received a Bachelor of Arts degree from Florida International University in 1983 and earned her Juris Doctor degree from Yale Law School in 1986.

Her professional career includes serving as an attorney with the Miami Dade County Attorney's office, Florida, 1986–1987; as law clerk for Judge Edward B. Davis at the United States District Court for the Southern District of Florida, 1987–1988; as assistant county attorney for the Miami Dade County Attorney's office, Florida, 1988–1996. In May 1996, Governor Lawton Chiles appointed her judge, County Court, Eleventh Judicial Circuit Court, in Florida; in September 1999, Governor Jeb Bush appointed her circuit court judge, Eleventh Judicial Circuit Court in Florida.

On January 15, 2003, she was nominated by President George W. Bush to a seat on the United States District Court in the Southern District of Florida which was vacated by Shelby Highsmith. Judge Altonaga was confirmed by the Senate on May 6, 2003, and received her commission on May 7, 2003.

Blanca Alvarado

ELECTED OFFICIAL (FIRST). Blanca Alvarado is a native of Cokedale, Colorado. She is a long-time resident of Santa Clara County. She has served the public in a variety of capacities since her youth. In the early 1970s, she worked for the Department of Social Services and later at the Center for Employment Training. In 1980, she was elected to the city council representing the community of East San Jose. She was elected to the Board of Supervisors

in March 1996. In January 1998, she served as the first Latina chairperson in the county's history. She was elected to her second term in 2000, and in 2003, she once again served as the chairperson of the board. Blanca was re-elected for her third and final term in March 2004.

Carol Alvarado

ELECTED OFFICIAL. Carol Alvarado is a native of Houston, Texas. She received a Bachelor of Arts degree in political science, from the University of Houston.

Her professional career includes serving as a legislative assistant to Congressman Gene Green in Washington, D.C. She also worked as senior executive assistant to Houston Mayor Lee P. Brown. In 2001, she was elected to the Houston City Council to represent District I.

Aida Alvarez

GOVERNMENT OFFICIAL (FIRST). Aida Alvarez is a native of Aquadilla, Puerto Rico. She received a Bachelor of Arts degree cum laude from Harvard College and in 1985 she was awarded an honorary doctorate of Laws from Lona College.

Her professional career includes serving as a journalist for the New York *Post*; she served as an investment banker at the First Boston Corporation and at Bear Stearns; as a public servant, she spent two years at the New York City Health and Hospitals Corp; she served as a commissioner on the New York City Charter Revision Commission and was a member of the Mayor's (NYC) Committee on Appointments. In June 1993, she was named director of the Office of Federal Housing Enterprise Oversight; in 1997, she was appointed by President Bill Clinton as administrator of the Small Business Administration, thus becoming the first Hispanic woman and Puerto Rican to serve as an executive officer in a president's cabinet.

During the 2004 presidential election, Ms. Alvarez was named official spokeswoman for Senator John Kerry.

Theresa Alvillar-Speake

GOVERNMENT OFFICIAL. Theresa Alvillar-Speake received a bachelor's degree from California State University and earned her Master of Business Administration from Golden Gate University.

Her professional career includes serving from 1991 to 1993 as the assistant director for program development in the Minority Business Development Agency; from 1994 to 1997 she was founder and executive director of NEDA San Joaquin Valley, a non-profit business development organization; from 1997 to 2000, she served as assistant director of business relations for the California Employment Development Department; she served as the manager of small business and disabled veteran business enterprise programs for the State of California Department of Transportation.

Ms. Alvillar-Speake was appointed director of the office of Minority Economic Impact, Department of Energy.

Carmen Twillie Ambar

EDUCATION. Carmen Twillie Ambar is a native of Little Rock, Arkansas. She received a Bachelor of Science degree in foreign service from the Edmund A. Walsh School at Georgetown University, and a master's degree in public affairs from the Woodrow Wilson School of Public and International Affairs at Princeton University and earned her Juris Doctor from Columbia School of Law.

Her professional career includes a private law practice. She served as assistant dean for graduate education at the Woodrow Wilson School, at Princeton University, overseeing the operation of its three graduate programs.

Ms. Ambar was appointed the ninth woman to lead Douglass College and the youngest dean appointed in its history.

Belinda C. Anderson

EDUCATION. Belinda C. Anderson received a Bachelor of Science degree and a Master of Science in his-

tory from Radford University. She earned a doctorate of education in higher education Administration from Virginia Tech.

Her professional career includes serving as a classroom teacher in Portsmouth and Norfolk for Virginia Public School Systems, as director of academic advising services at Radford University in Radford, Virginia, as dean and professor of the School of General and Continuing Education at Norfolk State University. She joined Virginia Union University in August 2000 as vice president of academic student affairs.

Dr. Anderson was named interim president of Virginia Union University in August 2003.

Chandra Y. Anderson

BUSINESS EXECUTIVE. Chandra Y. Anderson received a bachelor's degree from Indiana University Center on Philanthropy.

Her professional career includes serving as senior vice president of development for the United Way. She was with United Way for ten years and was responsible for raising nearly $350 million in the annual campaign. During her tenure, United Way of New York City achieved double-digit growth in the local campaign for the first time in history for two consecutive years. As senior vice president of resource development for Apollo Theater Foundation, Inc., she was responsible for oversight of the $65 million capital campaign and instituting the Apollo's first annual campaign since the organization became a not-for-profit in 1991.

Ms. Anderson serves as senior vice president of development for the National Urban League. She joined the Urban League in July 2005.

Michelle J. Anderson

EDUCATION. Michelle J. Anderson received a Bachelor of Arts degree in community studies with honors from the University of California at Santa Cruz in 1989 and the Chancellor's Award for outstanding academic achievement. She earned a Juris Doctor degree from Yale University Law School in 1994, where she was notes editor of the *Yale Law Journal* and editor of the *Yale Journal of Law & Feminism*. She also earned an LL.M. in advocacy and represented clients pursuing a range of civil rights claims and criminal appeals from Georgetown University.

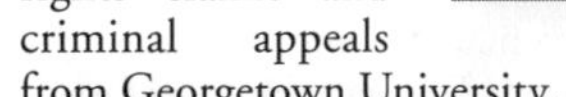

Her professional career includes serving as a law clerk at the United States Court of Appeals for the Ninth Circuit for Judge William A. Norris and as a fellow and visiting professor at Georgetown University Law Center in the Appellate Litigation Program and the Institute for Public Representation, respectively. She served as co-chair of the Pennsylvania assessment team of the American Bar Association's Death Penalty Moratorium Project. She is a member of the Board of Directors and policy chair for National Alliance to End Sexual Violence.

Dr. Anderson serves as dean of the City University of New York Law School and professor.

Silvia Signars Anderson

MILITARY. Silvia Signars Anderson entered the United States Air Force in May 1979 after receiving her commission as a second lieutenant through the Reserve Officer Training Corps at Indiana University.

Her military and civilian education includes Squadron Officer School, Air Command and Staff College, and Air War College at Maxwell Air Force Base in Alabama. She holds a bachelor in business administration and management from Indiana University, in Bloomington, Indiana; a master in logistics systems from the Air Force Institute of Technology at Wright-Paterson Air Force Base in Ohio; she earned a master in national resource strategy from the Industrial College of the Armed Forces at Fort McNair in Washington, D.C.

She has served in a variety of support, major command, education, and joint duty assignments throughout her career: August 1992, commander, 438th Aerial Port Squadron at McGuire Air Force Base in New Jersey; July 1994, transportation coordinator at the United States Atlantic Command in Norfolk, Virginia; July 1997, commander of the 86th Logistics Support Squadron at Ramstein Air Base in Germany; July 1998, deputy commander at the 86th Logistics

Group at Ramstein Air Base; June 2000, assistant for air transportation policy in the office of the Secretary of Defense at the Pentagon, in Washington, D.C.; June 2002, deputy chief of staff for passenger and personnel property at Headquarters Military Traffic Management Command in Alexandria, Virginia; June 2003, commander of the 78th Mission Support Group at Robins Air Force Base in Georgia. As commander of the 78th Mission Support Group, she manages and leads 1,800 military and civilian personnel. She operates all support functions required to maintain the combat readiness and effectiveness of the Warner Robins Air Logistics Center, 78th Air Base Wing, and more than 60 tenant units. She also oversees a $45 million annual budget for the operation of communications, mission support, security forces, logistics readiness, civilian personnel, and services, including the commissary and base exchange.

Tina Anderson

AVIATION. Tina Anderson received a bachelor's degree in aeronautical studies from the University of North Dakota. She also completed her flight instructions at the University of North Dakota. She holds certificates in Airline Transport Pilot (ATP) and is a Certified Flight Instructor (CFII, MEI).

Her professional career includes serving as a first officer with Horizon on the Dash-8 based out of Portland, Oregon. In the spring of 2001, she was hired as a first officer on the DC-9 for Northwest Airlines, based out of both Detroit and Minneapolis. She also serves as an aviation lecturer.

Tina Anderson

EDUCATION. Tina Anderson received a bachelor's degree in mental retardation from the University of Georgia and a master's degree in learning disabilities and behavior disorders from Augusta State University. She earned her doctorate degree in early childhood special education and special education technology from the University of Georgia.

She has worked in the field of special education for over 20 years as a teacher, behavior specialist, educational therapist, and educational consultant. She is currently a part-time assistant professor for the Department of Special Education at the University of Georgia in addition to being a private educational consultant.

Annie Andrews

MILITARY. Captain Annie Andrews is a native of Midway, Georgia. She received a Bachelor of Science degree in criminal justice from Savannah State University in 1983 and earned a Master of Science degree in management from Troy State University in 1986. Her military education includes a master's degree in national security and strategic studies from the College of Naval Command and Staff, Naval War College, in 1999. She also graduated from the Joint Forces Staff College, and in April 2000, she was designated a joint specialty officer.

Captain Andrews has served in a variety of assignments to include serving in December 1992 at the Bureau of Naval Personnel, Washington, D.C., where she served as branch head, Deserter Branch/Deserter Apprehension Program (PER-842). In June 1995, she served as the commander, Boston Military Entrance Processing Station in Boston, Massachusetts. In September 1999, she was assigned to the Pentagon where she served as chief, requirements branch, and joint manpower planner, Manpower and Personnel Directorate J-1, the Joint Staff in Washington, D.C. From October 2001 to March 2002, she served on the OPNAV (N13) staff in Washington, D.C., as the assistant human resources community manager assisting in the transformation of the fleet support community. She reported to Navy Recruiting District San Francisco in June 2002 as executive officer and assumed the duties as commanding officer of Navy Recruiting District San Francisco in December 2003. During her tenure, Team San Francisco earned both the Officer and Enlisted Recruiting "R" Excellent Awards for three consecutive years. Captain Andrews reported for duties as executive officer, Recruit Training Command in April 2005. She assumed the duties as commanding officer of Recruit Training Command in June 2006.

Maya Angelou

AUTHOR/ENTERTAINER (FIRST). Maya Angelou (born Marguerite Johnson) is a native of Saint Louis, Missouri. She began her career as a dancer in bars, such as the Purple Onion, and appeared at the Blue Angel and Mr. Kelly's in Chicago, and at the Village Vanguard in New York. From 1954 to 1955, she toured Europe and Africa in *Porgy and Bess*. After returning to the United States, Ms. Angelou resumed her career as a nightclub performer. In May 1961 she played the queen in Jean Genet's Off Broadway *The Blacks* at the

Saint Mark's Playhouse in New York. In 1966 she had a part in Jean Anouilh's *Medea,* produced in Hollywood. In 1972, she achieved the distinction of being the first black woman to have a screenplay, *Georgia, Georgia,* produced. In 1973 she acted in the play *Look Away,* a short-lived drama, and in 1974 she appeared in her first full-length film, *Sister, Sister.* In 1976 she directed an episode of the series "Visions." She was the first black woman admitted to the Directors Guild of America. She appeared in 1977 in "The Richard Pryor Special." President Gerald Ford appointed Ms. Angelou to the Bicentennial Commission, and President Jimmy Carter appointed her to the Commission of International Woman's Year. In 1977 she performed in the television production of Alex Haley's *Roots,* which earned her an Emmy nomination. In 1979 her first volume of autobiography (written in 1970) *I Know Why the Caged Bird Sings,* was made into a television movie, for which she wrote the script and music. Since 1981 Ms. Angelou has held a life-time appointment as Reynolds professor of American studies at Wake Forest University in Winston-Salem, North Carolina. On January 20, 1993, she became the first black American to recite a poem at a presidential swearing-in ceremony. President-elect Bill Clinton asked her to compose an inaugural poem and to recite it at his swearing-in. In 1998 she directed the feature film *Down in the Delta* and was on the children's television show, *Sesame Street.* She also appeared in Tyler Perry's *Madea's Family Reunion* in 2006. She has received several honorary doctorates.

Collette Appolito

BUSINESS EXECUTIVE. Collette Appolito received a bachelor's business administration degree in finance from Cleveland State University.

Her professional career includes serving with NationalCity, working her way up the ranks from revenue clerk to manager/lending officer; serving as marketing director for Springhouse ManorCare Health Services in Westlake, Ohio; serving as project coordinator in the City of Cleveland's Department of Economic Development. She was appointed director of the City of Cleveland's Office of Equal Opportunity in May 2004.

Ms. Appolito serves as executive director of the Presidents' Council Foundation, an advocacy group for business development in Greater Cleveland's African American community.

LaRita A. Aragon

MILITARY (FIRST). LaRita A. Aragon received a Bachelor of Science degree in education from Central State College, and a master's degree in guidance and counseling from Central State College in Edmond, Oklahoma. She has completed numerous military schools including Air Command and Staff College, Air War College, Reserve Officer National Defense Security Course, Russian General Officer Security Course, Professional Military Comptroller Course, and Senior Leader Depot Course.

She enlisted in the Oklahoma Air National Guard on September 9, 1979, as an airman basic in the 219th Engineering Installation Squadron, Oklahoma City, Oklahoma. She received her commission through the Academy of Military Science at Knoxville, Tennessee, in October 1981. She returned to the 219th Engineering Installation Squadron as an administrative officer. In February 1989 General Aragon became the first female commander in the Oklahoma Air National Guard when she assumed command of the 137th Service Flight at Will Rogers Air National Guard Base. She became the first female to hold the rank of brigadier general in Oklahoma National Guard and the first female commander of the Oklahoma Air National Guard in March 2003.

She was promoted to major general on November 18, 2005, becoming the first female in the Oklahoma National Guard to receive the two-star rank. From September 2005 to September 2006, she served as the Air National Guard assistant to the commander, air education and training command at Randolph Air Force Base, Texas; in September 2006, she was assigned as the Air National Guard assistant to the deputy chief of staff manpower and personnel, at the Pentagon, in Washington, D.C.

Shellye Archambeau

TECHNOLOGY EXECUTIVE. Shellye Archambeau received a Bachelor of Science degree from the University of Pennsylvania, Wharton School of Business.

Her professional career includes serving 15 years at IBM, holding several domestic and international exec-

utive positions. She served as president of Blockbuster, Inc.'s e-commerce division, as chief marketing officer of NorthPoint Communications, as chief marketing officer and executive vice president of sales for Loudcloud, Inc., and as chief executive officer for Zaplet.

Ms. Archambeau serves as chief executive officer of MetricStream, a leading technology firm located in the Silicon Valley.

Vicki Ariyasu

ENTERTAINMENT EXECUTIVE. Vicki Ariyasu received a master's degree in education, technology in education and children's literature from Harvard University.

Her professional career includes serving at Amblin Entertainment working as a creative development associate to Steven Spielberg; she served as vice president of development for Klasky-Csupo. She oversaw motion picture and television development through to production; she is currently working for Walt Disney Television Animation in creative development as a curriculum consultant.

Mary Armstrong

BUSINESS EXECUTIVE. Mary Armstrong received a Bachelor of Science degree from the University of Washington and a master's degree in chemical engineering from the University of Rochester, in New York.

Ms. Armstrong worked as a process engineer for Chevron Research Company, in Richmond, California, before she began her Boeing career in 1984 as a process engineer for manufacturing research and development. She also served as an equipment engineer and held management positions in environmental management at the Montana Aviation Research Company subsidiary and facilities. Her earlier leadership assignments included serving as vice president and general manager of the Boeing Aircraft Systems & Interiors Division, vice president of Boeing Facilities Services for the Puget Sound area and Wichita, Kansas. She has served as vice president and general manager of the Commercial Airplanes Fabrication division headquartered in Auburn, Washington. In December 2004, Ms. Armstrong was named president of Boeing Shared Services Group. In this assignment, she reports to the Boeing chief financial officer and leads a 10,000 person, multi-billion business unit that provides cost-effective services across Boeing's global enterprise.

Saundra Brown Armstrong

JUDGE. Judge Saundra Brown Armstrong is a native of Oakland, California. She received a Bachelor of Arts from California State University, Fresno, in 1969, and earned her Juris Doctor degree from the University of San Francisco School of Law in 1977.

Her career began as a police officer with the Oakland Police Department, Oakland, California (1970–1977). She then served as a deputy district attorney in Alameda County, California; as senior consultant for the California Assembly Committee on Criminal Justice; as trial attorney in the Public Integrity Section, U. S. Department of Justice; commissioner for the Consumer Product Safety Commission; commissioner for the U.S. Parole Commission. She also served as a judge at the Alameda Superior Court, California.

She was nominated by George H. W. Bush on April 25, 1991, to a seat vacated by William A. Ingram, was confirmed by the U.S. Senate on June 14, 1991, and received commission on June 18, 1991, as judge, U.S. District Court, Northern District of California.

Susan E. Arnold

BUSINESS EXECUTIVE (FIRST). Susan E. Arnold is a native of Pittsburgh, Pennsylvania. She received a Bachelor of Arts from the University of Pennsylvania in 1976 and earned a Masters of Business Administration from the University of Pittsburgh in 1980.

Her professional career includes serving with Procter & Gamble Company for more than 25 years. She joined Procter & Gamble Company in 1980 in the U.S. laundry and cleaning products sector. She served as general manager of the deodorant business in the U.S. in 1993 and was appointed an officer of the company in 1996. In July 1999, she was appointed president of Global Personal Beauty Care which made her the first woman president of a Procter & Gamble line division.

Ms. Arnold was appointed president of the Procter & Gamble Company's global personal beauty care and feminine care businesses in 2002.

Janice Arouh

ENTERTAINMENT EXECUTIVE. Janice Arouh received a Bachelor of Arts degree in communications from John Carroll University.

Her professional career includes serving as vice president of affiliate sales and marketing, Western region at *TV Guide*; from 1994 to 1999, she held various positions at Fox Channels Group, spanning the launch of Fox's first-ever basic cable network, FX, through the Fox/Liberty merger; serving as senior vice president of affiliate sales and marketing at Fox Family where she primarily focused on distribution growth in the Western region.

Ms. Arouh currently serves as senior vice president of network distribution and service for Hallmark Channel.

Leslye A. Arsht

GOVERNMENT OFFICIAL. Leslye A. Arsht is a native of Houston, Texas. She received a bachelor's degree from the University of Houston in Texas.

Her professional career includes serving as an associate vice chancellor for news and public affairs at Vanderbilt University and from 1987 to 1989 as a deputy press secretary and deputy assistant to President Ronald Reagan. In June 2004, she was selected to serve as a member of the under secretary of defense for personnel and readiness team.

Ms. Arsht was appointed deputy under secretary of defense for military community and family policy in February 2006.

Sepideh "Sepi" Asefnia

BUSINESS EXECUTIVE. Sepideh "Sepi" Asefnia is a native of Tehran, Iran. She came to the United States when she was 15. She received a bachelor's degree from North Carolina State University.

Her professional career includes serving with the North Carolina Department of Transportation and then working as a highway department manager with a private engineering firm for four years. She established SEPI Engineering Group in 2001 with three employees and currently employs 48.

Jodie Asel

JUDGE. Judge Jodie Asel received a bachelor's degree from the University of Missouri and earned her Juris Doctor degree from Columbia School of Law. Her professional career includes serving as an assistant prosecuting attorney for Boone County, Missouri, and as assistant public defender. She was then engaged in private law practice. In 1991, she was appointed an associate circuit judge to the Missouri Division IV Circuit Court.

Sylvia G. Ash

JUDGE. Judge Sylvia G. Ash received her undergraduate degree from Stony Brook University and earned her

Juris Doctor degree from Howard University School of Law. Her professional career includes serving as a judicial law clerk, Superior Court of New Jersey, Chancery Division; and as supervising attorney for the District Council 37 Municipal Employees Legal Services. In 2006, she was elected judge, New York Civil Court, in Kings, County, New York.

Diane T. Ashley

FINANCE. Diane T. Ashley received a Bachelor of Arts degree in French (with a year of study at the Sorbonne in Paris) from Yale University and a master's of Education degree in human resources from Boston University. She earned a Juris Doctor degree from Rutgers University School of Law. She was elected in 2001 and continues to serve as the first female chair of the Board of Trustees of New York Theological Seminary.

Her professional career includes serving as Citigroup's executive-on-loan to the Rev. Jesse Jackson and the Rainbow PUSH Coalition. She serves as senior vice president and director of Citigroup Supplier Diversity, responsible for leading the company in increasing business development opportunities for minority, women, veteran, and disabled-owned enterprises across all business of Citigroup.

Judith Ashmann-Gerst

JUDGE. Judge Judith Ashmann-Gerst received a Bachelor of Arts degree from UCLA in 1965 and earned her Juris Doctor from Whittier Law School (magna cum laude) in 1972.

Her professional career includes serving with the State Attorney General's office in Los Angeles and as a special counsel to the City Attorney of Los Angeles. In 1979, she joined the United States Attorney's office as the executive assistant. She was appointed judge to the Los Angeles Municipal Court in 1981, and was elected judge to the Superior Court in 1986 in San Fernando Valley where she served for 18 years. She served as the supervising judge of the North Valley District of the Superior Court, then transferred downtown presiding over a fast track civil caseload; she was appointed to the California Court of Appeals, 2nd District, in December 2001.

Kim J. Askew

LAW. Kim J. Askew received a bachelor's degree summa cum laude from Knoxville College and earned her Juris Doctor degree from Georgetown University Law School.

She served as an attorney at Hughes & Luce, LLP, in Dallas, Texas, representing clients in complex commercial and employment litigation. She served as chair of the Board of Directors of the State Bar of Texas from 2003 to 2004. She has been named one of the "Best Lawyers in America" for her commercial litigation practice and a "Best Lawyer in Dallas," for her labor and employment practice. She became the first African-American lawyer to hold the prestigious national position of chair of the American Bar Association's Section of Litigation. She was sworn in at the 2006 American Bar Association's annual meeting on August 4, 2006.

Sharon B. Atack

JUDGE. Judge Sharon B. Atack earned an undergraduate degree from the College of William and Mary and a Juris Doctor degree from the University of Florida. Before receiving an appointment to judge, she served as an assistant public defender and was in private law practice.

In 1995, she received an appointment to judge for the Flagler County Court where she presides over criminal, civil, juvenile, and child support cases.

Judith S.H. Atherton

JUDGE. Judge Judith S.H. Atherton received her Juris Doctor degree from the University of Utah College of Law in 1983. Her professional career includes serving in private law practice, serving as an assistant administrative law judge and as an assistant attorney general.

She has also taught at the University of Utah College of Law.

In 1992, she was appointed commissioner to the Third District. In July 1995, she was appointed judge to the Third District Court in Utah.

Marylin E. Atkins

JUDGE. Chief Judge Marylin E. Atkins received a Bachelor of Arts degree in psychology from Saginaw Valley State University in 1973. She earned her Juris Doctor from the University of Detroit School of Law.

Her professional career includes serving with the Michigan Employment Security Commission from 1973 to 1980. She then served as an assistant attorney general for the State of Michigan, as a member of the Worker's Compensation Appeal Board, and as a magistrate judge in the Michigan's 36th Judicial District Court. In March 1994, she was appointed judge to the Michigan's 36th District Court in Detroit. She was appointed chief judge pro tem May 1, 1999, serving until December 31, 1999. She was appointed chief judge effective January 1, 2000.

Debra Austin

PERFORMING ARTS. Debra Austin received a scholarship to the School of American Ballet when she was 12. At 16, she was hand-picked by Georgia Balanchine to join the New York City Ballet. While at New York City Ballet, she danced many principal roles by both Balanchine and Jerome Robbins, one of which was filmed for a PBS television special, "Live from Lincoln Center."

Her professional career includes joining the Zurich Ballet in Switzerland where she danced principal roles in works by all of the major choreographers. She toured with the company as a principal dancer; back in the U.S. she danced at a gala performance at the Academy of Music hosted by Bill Cosby where Grover Washington played the saxophone; she has taught in many schools in Florida including the American Cultural Center in Miami, the Palm Beach Dance Center and the Miami City Ballet School; in 1998, she moved to North Carolina and joined the faculty of the Cary Ballet Conservatory directed by Suzanne Clark and also served as the "ballet master" for the Carolina Ballet.

Debra Austin

EDUCATION. Debra Austin received a bachelor's degree in English from Michigan State University and earned a master's degree in English from the University of Florida. She earned a Master of Business Administration degree from Florida State University and her doctorate in higher education from Florida State University. She holds an honorary degree from Flagler College in St. Augustine.

Her professional career includes serving as an English instructor at Lake Sumter Community College in Leesburg. She has served in numerous academic administrative positions, from division head to chief academic officer to the acting president at Tallahassee Community College; she also served as assistant vice president for academic affairs at Florida State University.

Dr. Austin was named as Florida's chancellor of colleges and universities.

Judith Ayres

GOVERNMENT OFFICIAL. Judith Ayres received a bachelor's degree in zoology and physiology from Miami University and she earned a master's of public administration from the John F. Kennedy School of Government at Harvard University.

Her professional career includes serving as principal of the Environmental Group, a nonprofit environmental research organization. She served with William D. Ruckelshaus Associates, an international environmental consulting firm and from 1983 to 1988, she served as regional administrator for the Environmental Protection Agency for Region 9. She was appointed assistant administrator of environmental protection for international activities.

Ronda E. Babb

JUDGE. Judge Ronda E. Babb is a native of Trinidad. She and her family immigrated to the United States in 1971, settling in Brooklyn, New York. She graduated from Tilden High School in Brooklyn, New York, and received a Bachelor of Arts degree from Wellesley Col-

lege in Massachusetts in 1979. She earned her Juris Doctor degree from Brooklyn Law School in 1984.

Her professional career includes serving in private law practice and as an administrative law judge for the City of New York Environmental Control Board. In 2002, she was appointed judge by Governor Jeb Bush to Brevard County, Florida's Eighteenth Judicial Circuit in Viera, Florida. In 2004, Brevard's county court judges unanimously elected Judge Babb to serve as administrative judge.

Claire Babrowski

BUSINESS EXECUTIVE. Claire Babrowski received a bachelor's degree from the University of Illinois at Urbana-Champaign and earned her Master's of Business Administration from the University of North Carolina in 1995.

Her professional career includes serving with the McDonald's Corporation from 1974 to 2005, where her last position was senior executive vice president and chief restaurant operations officer. From June 2005 to February 2006, she served as executive vice president and chief operating officer of RadioShack.

Ms. Babrowski was named president, chief operating officer and acting chief executive officer of RadioShack, an American consumer electronic specialty retailer with more than 7,000 stores.

MaryAnn Baenninger

EDUCATION. MaryAnn Baenninger attended Montgomery County Community College and received her bachelor's degree in psychology summa cum laude from Temple University's Ambler campus in Philadelphia. She also earned her doctorate degree from Temple University.

Her professional career includes serving as a tenured associate professor in the Department of Psychology at the College of New Jersey in Ewing, N.J., serving as a professor at Washington College in Chestertown, Maryland and at Philadelphia University in Philadelphia, Pa.

Dr. Baenninger was appointed the 14th president of the College of Saint Benedict.

Katherine Baicker

GOVERNMENT OFFICIAL. Katherine Baicker received a Bachelor of Arts in economics from Yale in 1993 and earned her doctorate in economics from Harvard in 1998.

Her professional career includes serving as an associate professor in the Department of Public Policy at the School of Public Affairs at the University of California at Los Angeles and as a research associate at the National Bureau of Economic Research in the public economics program. From 2001 to 2002, she served as senior economist at the Council of Economic Advisers.

President George W. Bush nominated Dr. Katherine Baicker on September 22, 2005, and she was confirmed by the Senate on November 4, 2005, to serve as a member of the Council of Economic Advisers.

Catherine Todd Bailey

GOVERNMENT OFFICIAL. Catherine Todd Bailey is a native of Indiana. She received a bachelor's degree from Franklin College.

Her professional career includes serving as a first grade teacher in Louisville, Kentucky. She was the cofounder in 1984 of the Louisville Ronald McDonald House and from 2000 through 2004, she served as Republican National Committee (RNC) member from Kentucky.

President George W. Bush nominated Catherine Todd Bailey to become U.S. Ambassador to Latvia on September 8, 2004. She was confirmed by the Senate on November 21 and was sworn in as ambassador by U.S. Secretary of State Colin Powell on January 1, 2005. She presented her credentials to President Vaira Vike-Freiberga as ambassador extraordinary and plenipotentiary of the United States of America to the Republic of Latvia on February 4, 2005.

Darlyne Bailey

GOVERNMENT OFFICIAL. Darlyne Bailey is a native of Harlem in New York City. She received a bachelor's degree from Lafayette College in Pennsylvania. She received a master's degree in psychiatric social work from Columbia University and earned her doctorate in organizational behavior from Case Western Reserve University.

Her professional career includes serving thirteen years at the Mandel School of Applied Social Sciences at Case Western Reserve University as a professor and seven years as dean of the Mandel School. She is the first nonwhite woman to hold the dean's position at the Mandel School; she served as vice president for academic affairs at Teachers College, Columbia University.

Dr. Bailey was appointed dean of the University of Minnesota College of Education and Human Development (CEHD) in 2006. She became the first female dean and the first African-American dean at CEHD.

Rosanne Bailey

MILITARY. General Rosanne Bailey received a Bachelor of Science degree in economics from Purdue University in West Lafayette, Indiana. She earned a Master of Science degree in engineering management from the Air Force Institute of Technology at Wright-Patterson Air Force Base in Ohio. She is a distinguished graduate of Squadron Officer School at Maxwell Air Force Base in Alabama, 1980; a distinguished graduate of Air Command and Staff College at Maxwell Air Force Base, 1988; a distinguished graduate of Senior Acquisition Course and Industrial College of the Armed Forces at Fort Lesley J. McNair in Washington, D.C.; and a graduate of the National Security Management Course, Syracuse University, Syracuse, New York, 2000.

She has held a wide variety of assignments including commander of the 435th Air Base Wing at Ramstein Air Base and commander of the Kaiserslautern Military Community in Germany. In her dual role as wing and KMC commander, she leads the largest American community outside the United States. The wing is comprised of seven groups, 26 squadrons and approximately 5,000 personnel in 27 geographically separated units, including the air base group at Rhein-Main Air Base in Germany. She served as the commander of Cheyenne Mountain Operations Center, United States Northern Command, Cheyenne Mountain Air Station, Colorado. She was promoted to brigadier general on January 1, 2002.

Stephanie Bailey

MEDICINE. Stephanie Bailey received a Bachelor of Science degree in psychology from Clark University and a Master of Science in health services administration from College of St. Francis. She earned her Medical Doctor degree from Meharry Medical College.

Her professional career includes serving as a physician and medical advisor for the East Nashville Clinic, Nashville Health Department. From that post she advanced to medical director/director of health services administration in 1988 and then as acting director of health in 1995. She was first to convene a group of health care providers to address an estimated 60,000 uninsured Davidson County residents.

Dr. Bailey was appointed director of health for the Metro Nashville Public Health Department.

Lisa Baird

SPORTS EXECUTIVE. Lisa Baird received a Bachelor of Arts degree and earned a Masters of Business Administration degree from Pennsylvania State University. Her professional career includes serving at General Motors in Detroit where

she held various marketing positions including serving as brand manager of the Pontiac Grand Am, regional marketing manager in the northeast sales division, and marketing lead for the company's consumer internet activities. She was a senior-level marketing and advertising executive with IBM, General Motors and the Procter & Gamble Company. At IBM, she served as the vice president of world wide integrated marketing communications, heading up a division that provided services in over 70 countries.

The National Football League named Lisa Baird senior vice president of marketing in August 2005. She is responsible for the NFL's marketing, brand development, advertising and fan development programs, including the research, direct marketing and database functions.

Ellen S. Baker

ASTRONAUT. Ellen S. Baker is a native of New York City and graduated from Bayside High School in New York in 1970. She received a Bachelor of Arts degree in geology from the State University of New York in Buffalo in 1974, and a doctorate of Medicine degree from Cornell University in 1978. She also earned a masters in public health from University of Texas School of Public Health in 1994.

In 1981, following her residency, she joined NASA as a medical officer at the Lyndon B. Johnson Space Center. That same year she graduated from the Air Force Aerospace Medicine Course at Brooks Air Force Base in San Antonio, Texas. She served as a physician in the Flight Medicine Clinic at the Johnson Space Center.

Dr. Baker was selected by the National Aeronautics and Space Administration (NASA) in May 1984 and became an astronaut in June 1985. Since then, she has worked a variety of jobs at NASA in support of the Space Shuttle and space station programs and development of the exploration program. A veteran of three space flights, she has logged over 686 hours in space. She was a mission specialist on STS-34 in 1989, STS-50 in 1992, and STS-71 in 1995. She now serves as the lead astronaut for medical issues and education programs.

Karen R. Baker

JUDGE. Justice Karen R. Baker is a native of Clinton, Arkansas, and graduated from Clinton High School in 1981. She received a Bachelor of Science degree from Arkansas Tech University and earned her Juris Doctor degree from the University of Arkansas at Little Rock Law School in January of 1987.

She was engaged in private law practice for eight years prior to taking the bench. In 1995, she was appointed to serve as Second Division, circuit/chancery/juvenile judge for the Twentieth Judicial District which includes Faulkner, Searcy, and Van Buren counties. In 1996, she was elected to the position of Fourth Division, circuit/chancery judge for the Twentieth Judicial District. She was elected associate judge to the Arkansas Court of Appeals, District Two, Position Two. District Two is a large district which includes nineteen counties in central and north-central Arkansas.

Sari M. Baldauf

BUSINESS EXECUTIVE. Sari M. Baldauf is a native of Kotka, Finland. She received a master's degree in business administration from Helsinki School of Economics and Business Administration. She holds an honorary doctorate in technology from Helsinki University of Technology.

Her professional career includes serving as director at Sanoma WSOY, F-Secure, and the Savonlinna Opera Festival and on the global board of the International Youth Foundation. She previously held various positions at Nokia Corp. since 1983.

In 1998, she was named president of Nokia Networks. She was a member of the Group Executive Board of Nokia from 1994 until 2005. She currently serves as a director of Hewlitt-Packard Company.

Cynthia Baldwin

JUDGE. Justice Cynthia Baldwin received her Bachelor of Arts degree and a Master's of Arts degree from the Pennsylvania State University in English and American literature. She earned her Juris Doctor degree from Duquesne University.

Her professional career includes serving in private law practice and as attorney-in-charge, Commonwealth of Pennsylvania, Office of Attorney General, Bureau of Consumer Protection. She served as president of Pennsylvania State University international alumni association and is a gubernatorial appointee to the Board of Trustees. She has served in both visiting and adjunct professorships and still retains the latter.

She was nominated by Governor Ed Rendell in December 2005 to fill a vacancy on the court when Justice Russell M. Nigro was rejected by voters. She is the first African-American female judge of Allegheny County Court of Common Pleas. In February 2006, she was confirmed as a justice of the Supreme Court of Pennsylvania. She is the second African-American female to ever hold the position of Pennsylvania Supreme Court justice. She was confirmed by a 46–1 vote on February 17, 2006. She joined the state's highest court on Monday, February 27, 2006. Her ceremonial swearing in was in March 2006.

Elizabeth Ballard

ELECTED OFFICIAL. Elizabeth Ballard received an Associate of Arts degree from Indian Hills Community College and a Bachelor of Science degree in psychology from Missouri Western State College. She earned her Juris Doctor degree from the University of Oregon School of Law. She serves as the deputy district attorney for Morrow County, Oregon.

Tina Ballard

GOVERNMENT OFFICIAL. Tina Ballard received her Bachelor of Arts degree in English. She has earned a Master of Science degree in management and a Master of Science degree in national resource strategy. She completed the Industrial College of the Armed Forces Senior Acquisition Course and the Leadership for a Democratic Society Federal Executive Institute.

Prior to her current appointment as the deputy assistant secretary, Ms. Ballard served as the director of combat support operations and the deputy executive director of contract management operations in the Defense Contract Management Agency. In these positions her responsibilities included agency policy to accomplish contingency contract administration services in multiple theatres of military operations, supplier risk management, quality assurance and engineering support, delivery management, pricing/modification actions, business and financial systems, payment and financial management, contract closeout and industrial base analysis.

She is the deputy assistant secretary of the Army (policy and procurement). She directly supports the Army acquisition executive and the assistant secretary of the Army (acquisition, logistics and technology), serving as the Army's principal acquisition and procurement policy authority for all Army acquisition programs. She is responsible for the management and execution of the Army's contracting function.

Elizabeth K. Balraj

ELECTED OFFICIAL. Elizabeth K. Balraj is native of Salem, India. Upon immigrating to the United States in 1966, she trained in anatomic pathology at Akron General Hospital and St. Luke's Hospital, Cleveland, Ohio. She did her fellowship in forensic pathology at Cuyahoga County Coroner's office in 1972. She is board certified in anatomic pathology and forensic pathology.

In 1972, Dr. Balraj began her work in the Cuyahoga County Coroner's office as deputy coroner and pathologist. In 1987, she was appointed coroner of Cuyahoga County after the retirement of Samuel R. Gerber, M.D. She was elected coroner of Cuyahoga County on November 1, 1988, and has been re-elected continuously.

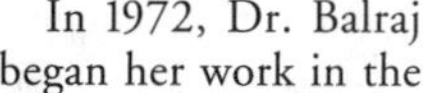

Patricia Bamattre-Manoukian

JUDGE. Justice Patricia Bamattre-Manoukian received a Bachelor of Arts degree in political science and psychology in 1972. She earned her Juris Doctor degree from Loyola Law School in Los Angeles in 1977. She also received a master's degree of public administration in 1974 and a Ph.D. in public administration in 1989 with a specialization in the administration of justice from the University of Southern California.

Her professional career includes serving as a deputy district attorney in the Orange County district attorney's office from 1977 to 1983; in October 1983, Governor George Deukmejian appointed her judge to the Orange County Municipal Court; in 1985, she relocated to Northern California to join her husband who was practicing law in Santa Clara County. Governor Deukmejian appointed her to the Santa Clara County Municipal Court and elevated her to the Santa Clara County Superior Court in March 1988. In 1989, she served as the family law supervising judge.

In October 1989, she was appointed associate justice to the California Court of Appeal Sixth District. From September 2001 to January 2003 she served as the acting administrative presiding justice.

Evelyn P. Banks

MILITARY. Command Master Chief Evelyn P. Banks is a native of Memphis, Tennessee, and an honor graduate of Byhalia High School. Mindful of the privilege to serve her fellow Americans, she enlisted in the United States Navy on January 28, 1984 and completed recruit training in Orlando, Florida.

Her first tour of duty was onboard USS *Samuel Gompers* (AD 37). During this tour she attended Mess Management Specialist "A" School and graduated with honors. Her following tours included Navy Recruiting District in Memphis, Tennessee, and Naval Air Station, Adak, Arkansas. While in Adak, she advanced to chief petty officer and qualified as an enlisted aviation warfare specialist. Following Adak, Master Chief Banks executed orders to USS *Acadia* (ad 42). Before the decommissioning of *Acadia* and her transfer to Naval Recruiting District Jacksonville, Florida, she advanced to senior chief petty officer.

She attended the Air Force Senior Non-Commissioned Officer Academy at Montgomery, Alabama, prior to arriving to the Precommissioning Unit *Decatur* (PCU). At PCU *Decatur*, she advanced to master chief petty officer. Her first command master chief billet was Navy Support Facility Diego Garcia. During this highly successful tour, she accomplished unprecedented milestones in leadership for the command and the 27 tenant commands under her cognizance.

She is a graduate of the United States Navy Senior Enlisted Academy; she served on the academy staff as a faculty advisor prior to assuming her current position as the command master chief of Carrie Air Wing *Fourteen* in Lemoor, Louisiana. She is the first African American female to serve as the command master chief of a Carrie Air Wing.

Paula Banks

BUSINESS EXECUTIVE. Paula Banks is a native of Chicago, Illinois. She received a bachelor's degree from Loyola University and completed post-graduate study at the University of Illinois. She is also a graduate of the International Advanced Management Program at Harvard University.

Her professional career includes serving as director of public relations; human resources director; manager, labor relations; and store operations and merchandising manager at Sears, Roebuck and Company. She joined BP in 1996 after more than 24 years with Sears, Roebuck and Co.

Ms. Banks serves as vice president of Global Social Investment at BP, one of the world's largest energy companies.

Tyra Lynne Banks

ENTERTAINMENT. Tyra Lynne Banks is a native of Los Angeles, California. She attended Immaculate Heart High School, an all-girl, independent Catholic private school in Los Angeles. She attended Loyola Marymount University.

She received her first modeling job in 1991 at the age of 17, while attending Loyola Marymount University. That same year she was featured in a Tina Turner music video for the song "Love Thing." She was the first black woman to be featured with a white woman on the cover of the *Sports Illustrated* swimsuit issue. She was one of the original Victoria's Secret Angels. In 1997 she won the prestigious Michael Award for "Supermodel of the Year." She has done runway shows in London, Paris, Tokyo, Milan, and the United States. She has been featured in many magazines, television commercials, and billboard advertisements. She has appeared in numerous music videos that include Michael Jackson's "Black or White" and Tiara Summers' "Wild

Girls." Ms. Banks' movie appearances include the 2000 Disney film *Life-Size*, *Love Stinks* in 1999, *Coyote Ugly* in 2000, and the 2002 movie *Halloween: Resurrection*. She went on to host the reality television show *America's Next Top Model* and is currently hosting her own daytime talk show, *The Tyra Banks Show*.

Amy L. Banse

BUSINESS EXECUTIVE. Amy L. Banse received a Bachelor of Arts degree from Harvard University and a Juris Doctor degree from Temple University Law School.

Her professional career includes serving as an associate attorney in private law practice. She joined Comcast Corporation as an in-house attorney responsible for programming acquisition. In 1997, she was made a vice president of Comcast Corporation and head of the then newly created programming investments department. Ms. Banse serves as president of Comcast Interactive Media, a division of Comcast that is responsible for the development and growth of the company's Internet businesses, including the Comcast.net portal.

Vivian Banta

FINANCE. Vivian Banta was born and raised overseas. She lived in Lebanon, Iraq, and Libya until she was 18 years old. She attended Marymount International School in Rome, Italy, and the University of the Pacific in Stockton, California.

She began her career at Chase as vice president of global custody, international operations and systems in 1987. She was named executive vice president in charge of global investor services at the Chase Manhattan Corporation and its principal subsidiary, the Chase Manhattan Bank, N.A. In this capacity, she grew revenue five-fold and assets under administration to over $3.5 trillion. She joined Prudential in 1998 as chief administrative officer of individual financial service. In March 2000, she was appointed chief executive officer of the former U.S. Consumer Group and executive vice president of Prudential Financial. In August 2002, Ms. Banta was named a member of Prudential Financial office of the chairman with responsibility for the insurance division.

Juanita Powell Baranco

BUSINESS EXECUTIVE. Juanita Powell Baranco is a native of Washington, D.C., and was raised in Shreveport, Louisiana. She received a Bachelor of Science degree and her Juris degree from Louisiana State University.

She served in private law practice and was appointed as an assistant attorney general for the state of Georgia. She serves as executive vice president and chief operating officer of Baranco Automotive Group consisting of Baranco Pontiac-GMC Trucks in Lilburn, Georgia, Baranco Lincoln-Mercury in Duluth, Georgia, and Baranco Acura in Morrow, Georgia. On June 2, 2003, Mrs. Baranco and her husband, along with former Atlanta mayor and U.S. Ambassador Andrew Young, opened Mercedes-Benz of Buckhead in Atlanta, Georgia.

Esther L. Barazzone

EDUCATION. Esther L. Barazzone received a Bachelor of Arts degree in philosophy and history as a member of the first graduating class of New College. She received a Master of Arts degree and earned a Ph.D. in European intellectual history from Columbia University where she was a fellow of the faculty.

She has traveled extensively throughout her career and joined several international delegations including the World Affairs Council's U.S. Delegation to Egypt (2005), for which she was one of ten leaders selected among World Affairs Council's member cities; German Marshal Fund's Pittsburgh delegation to Turin, Italy and Lyon, France (2004); United Nations Women's Conference in Beijing, representing a delegation of students and faculty from U.S. Women Colleges (1995). She has visited Cuba, Europe, Guatemala, Haiti, India, Japan, Korea, Mexico and Pakistan. She now

serves as the 18th president of Chatham College, Women's Undergraduate/Coed Graduate College in Pittsburgh, Pennsylvania.

Anne Elizabeth Barnes

JUDGE. Judge Anne Elizabeth Barnes is a native of Dekalb County, Georgia. After attending Dekalb County public schools she received a Bachelor of Arts degree (magna cum laude) from Georgia State University in 1979. She earned her Juris Doctor from the University of Georgia in 1983 and received her Master of Laws in the judicial process from the University of Virginia in 2004.

She served in private practice in Atlanta and Savannah. In 1998, she won election to the Georgia Court of Appeals and took office January 1, 1999. She was the first woman to be elected in a state-wide judicial race without having been first appointed to the bench and was re-elected without opposition to a second term in 2004.

Kay Barnes

ELECTED OFFICIAL (FIRST). Mayor Kay Barnes received a Bachelor of Science degree in secondary education from the University of Kansas and master's degree in secondary education and in public administration and organizational behavior from the University of Missouri in Kansas City.

Her professional career includes serving for 23 years as president of Kay Waldo, Inc., a human resources development firm and co-hosting and producing a cable television talk show, "Let's Talk." In 1974 she became one of two women on the Jackson County legislature; in 1979 she was elected to a four-year term on the city council serving the Fourth District At-Large; she also served as chairwoman of the Tax Increment Financing Commission from 1996 to 1998. In March 1999, she was elected mayor of Kansas City and became the first woman mayor of the city. She was re-elected to a second term in March 2003.

Colleen C. Barrett

BUSINESS EXECUTIVE. Colleen C. Barrett is a native of Vermont. She graduated from junior college in Worchester, Massachusetts. In 1968, she worked as a legal secretary for Heb Kelleher. She became very involved with one of Kelleher's clients, Southwest Airlines, which Kelleher had co-founded in 1967. In 1978, she became corporate secretary to Southwest's Board of Directors. She was named president and COO in 2001 and today serves as president and corporate secretary at Southwest Airlines in Dallas, Texas.

Charlene Barshefsky

BUSINESS EXECUTIVE. Charlene Barshefsky received her Juris Doctor degree from Catholic University School of Law.

Her professional career includes private law practice. She served as deputy United States trade representative and acting United States trade representative from 1993 to 1996 and served as a United States ambassador and chief trade negotiator and principal trade policy maker for the United States from 1996 to 2001. As the United States trade representative and member of the president's cabinet, she was a central figure in an historic and tumultuous period of trade expansion and globalization and a central figure for international business.

Former Ambassador Barshefsky has been a director of Intel since January 2004 and is a senior international partner in private practice.

Jacqueline K. Barton

TECHNOLOGY EXECUTIVE. Jacqueline K. Baton received a Bachelor of Arts degree (summa cum laude) at Barnard College in 1974 and went on to receive a Ph.D. in inorganic chemistry at Columbia University in 1979 after a post-doctoral fellowship at Bell Laboratories at Yale University.

She has pioneered the application of transition metal complexes as tools to probe recognition and reactions of double helical DNA. Using chiral coordination com-

plexes, matching their shapes, symmetries, and functionalities to sites along the strand, she has designed octahedral metal complexes which recognize nucleic acid sites with affinities and specificities rivaling DNA-binding proteins. She is known as a national expert on DNA. She has served as a professor of chemistry and biochemistry at Hunter College, Columbia University, California Institute of Technology, and the University of New York. She was elected to the Dow Board of Directors in 1993 and currently serves as chair of the environment, health and safety committee and as a member of the committee on directors and governance and the compensation committee.

Carol Bartz

TECHNOLOGY EXECUTIVE. Carol Bartz received a Bachelor of Science degree with honors in computer science from the University of Wisconsin. She received an honorary Doctor of Humane Letters from the New Jersey Institute of Technology, an honorary Doctor of Science degree from Worcester Polytechnic Institute and an honorary Doctor of Letters degree from William Woods University.

Her professional career includes serving in product line and sales management positions at Digital Equipment Corporation and 3M Corporation. She served as vice president of worldwide field operation at Sun Microsystems. She was appointed executive chairman of the board of Autodesk, Inc. Ms. Bartz was chairman, president and chief executive officer of Autodesk for 14 years. Ms. Bartz was appointed to President Bush's Council of Advisors on Science and Technology.

Lezli Baskerville

GOVERNMENT OFFICIAL. Lezli Baskerville received a bachelor's degree from Douglass College and earned a Juris Doctor cum laude from Howard University School of Law.

Ms. Baskerville served in private law practice. From 1999 to 2003, she served as vice president for government relations for the College Board, where she was chief executive officer of the Washington office and provided leadership to the board's federal and state government relations teams, the EOC, Upward Bound, and sponsored-scholarship programs. She was named the fifth president and chief executive officer of the National Association for Equal Opportunity in Higher Education, the national membership and advocacy association for the nation's 120 historically and predominately black colleges and universities.

Alice Moore Batchelder

JUDGE. Judge Alice Moore Batchelder is a native of Wilmington, Delaware. She received a Bachelor of Arts degree from Ohio Wesleyan University in 1964 and earned her Juris Doctor degree from Akron University School of Law in 1971. She also received an LL.M degree from the University of Virginia School of Law.

Her professional career includes serving in private law practice from 1971 to 1983. From 1983 to 1985, she served as a judge with the United States Bankruptcy Court for the Northern District of Ohio. On February 28, 1985, she was nominated as a judge to the United States District Court for the Northern District of Ohio by President Ronald Reagan. She was confirmed by the United States Senate on April 3, 1985, and received commission on April 4, 1985. On June 12, 1991, she was nominated as a judge to the United States Court of Appeals for the Sixth Circuit by President George H. W. Bush. She was confirmed by the United States Senate on November 27, 1991, and received her commission on December 2, 1991.

Patricia E. Bath

MEDICINE (FIRST). Patricia E. Bath is a native of New York. She received a bachelor's degree in chemistry and physics from Hunter College in New York. She received her Medical Doctor degree from Howard University College of Medicine in Washington, D.C. She completed her internship at Harlem Hospital in 1969 and a fellowship in ophthalmology at Columbia University in 1970. She completed training at New York University in 1973, where she was the first African American resident in ophthalmology.

In 1975, she was the first woman to be called to join the Department of Ophthalmology at the University of California at Los Angeles (UCLA); in 1983, she co-founded the student National Medical Association and became the first woman in the history of the United States to hold the position of chair of ophthalmology residency training program at Drew-UCLA. She also founded the American Institute for the Prevention of Blindness (AIPB).

Dr. Bath holds patents from the United States, Japan, Canada, and five European countries. She is the first African American woman doctor to receive a patent for a medical invention. Her patent (no. 4,744,360), a method for removing cataract lenses, transformed eye surgery by using a laser device, making the procedure more accurate.

Lynne A. Battaglia

JUDGE. Lynne A. Battaglia is a native of Buffalo, New York. She received a Bachelor of Arts degree from American University in 1967 and received a Master of Arts degree from American University in 1968. She earned her Juris Doctor degree from the University of Maryland School of Law in 1974.

Her professional career includes serving as an assistant United States attorney, District of Maryland, 1978 to 1982; as senior trial attorney, Office of Special Litigation, U.S. Department of Justice, from 1984 to 1988; as the chief, criminal investigations division, Office of Attorney General, 1988 to 1991; as chief of staff to U.S. Senator Barbara A. Mikulski, 1991 to 1993. She was appointed U.S. Attorney, District of Maryland, 1993 to 2001. Since January 26, 2001, she has served as judge, Maryland Court of Appeals, 3rd Appellate Circuit.

Maureen Beal

BUSINESS EXECUTIVE. Maureen Beal is a native of Chicago, Illinois, and moved to Los Angeles when she was 13 years old.

After completing school she began working for National Van Lines for ten years then went into the manufacturing field in sales and customer service management. In 1981 she opened a sales office for National Van Lines in California and then returned to Chicago in 1982 to help her father in his business. She was appointed vice president of the international division and treasurer of the company. In 1993, she became chairman and chief executive officer for National Van Lines after her father's passing.

Melissa L. Bean

ELECTED OFFICIAL. Melissa L. Bean is a native of Chicago, Illinois, and a graduate of Maine East High School in Park Ridge, Illinois. She received an Associate of Arts degree from Oakton Community College in Des Plaines, Illinois, in 1982, and a Bachelor of Arts from Roosevelt University in Chicago, Illinois, in 2002. Her professional career includes serving in the private business sector. She was elected a United States representative to the 109th Congress on January 3, 2005.

Lillian M. Beard

MEDICINE. Lillian M. Beard received both a bachelor's degree and her Medical Doctor degree from Howard University.

Her professional career includes serving as a practicing pediatrician in Silver Spring, Maryland. She is an associate clinical professor of pediatrics at the George Washington University School of Medicine and Health Sciences and served as an assistant professor at the Howard University College of Medicine. She is a frequent guest expert and spokesperson on national television programs such as *Good Morning America*, CNN's *Health Accent*, ABC's *Home Show*, and *Fox After Breakfast*, discussing issues related to children's health; she

served as editor of Health Power Teen and Parent Channels.

Teresa Beasley

LAW. Teresa Beasley received a Bachelor of Arts degree from the University of Alabama and earned her Juris Doctor degree from Cleveland-Marshall College of Law. She is a graduate of the 2004 class of Cleveland Bridge Builders and is a member of the Kaleidoscope's Class of 2005 40 under 40.

Prior to October 2002, she was engaged in private law practice; in 2002 she served the City of Cleveland Department of Law as chief counsel. She was appointed director of the City's Department of Law where she advised the mayor and city council of Cleveland on critical legal issues facing the city and its citizens. She led the litigation, prosecutorial, and transactional work of a department of 85 lawyers in both criminal and civil divisions. In 2006, she returned to private law practice.

Jill Beck

EDUCATION. Jill Beck is a native of Worcester, Massachusetts. She received a Bachelor of Arts in philosophy and art history from Clark University and a Master of Arts in history and music from McGill University. She earned her doctorate degree in theatre history and criticism from the City University of New York.

Her professional career includes serving on the faculties of the City College of the City University of New York, the Juilliard School, Connecticut College, Southern Methodist University, and the University of California, Irvine. She served as dean of the School of the Arts at the University of California in Irvine from 1995 to 2003.

Dr. Beck was appointed Lawrence University's 15th president in January 2004 and assumed office on July 1, 2004.

G. Valerie Beckles

MEDICINE. G. Valerie Beckles is a native of Trinidad. She graduated from medical school in Jamaica and then trained in Nassau and London.

For two decades, she has cared for the health of communities near and far and leads free medical missions to Haiti and Honduras. She serves as Aetna's medical director for South Florida.

Charlene Begley

BUSINESS EXECUTIVE. Charlene Begley received a Bachelor of Science in business administration from the University of Vermont.

Her professional career began at General Electric (GE) in 1988. She has held a variety of leadership roles within the company including vice president of operations at General Electric Capital Mortgage Services, quality leader and later chief financial officer at GE Transportation Systems; as director of finance for GE Plastics-Europe; as vice president of the corporate audit staff; and as chief executive officer at GE Fanuc Automation. In January 2003, she was named president and chief executive officer of GE Transportation's rail business.

Ms. Begley was appointed president and chief executive officer of General Electric Plastic which has its headquarters at Pittsfield, Massachusetts, in July 2005.

Carol A. Beier

JUDGE. Justice Carol A. Beier is a native of Kansas City, Kansas. She received a Bachelor of Science degree in journalism from the University of Kansas in Lawrence. She earned her Juris Doctor degree from the University of Kansas in 1985. She graduated from the University of Virginia School of Law, receiving a LL.M. Master's of Law in the judicial process.

Her professional career includes serving eleven years in private law practice. She spent one year teaching at the University of Kansas School of Law and served as

law clerk for the United States Court of Appeals for the Tenth Circuit.

In February 2000, she was appointed judge to the Kansas Court of Appeals. On September 5, 2003, she was appointed justice to the Kansas Supreme Court.

April D. Beldo

MILITARY. April D. Beldo's military assignments include serving at Naval Hospital ARD in Corpus Christi, Texas; at HS-6 Naval Air Station at North Island, California, where she deployed on the USS *Abraham Lincoln* (CVN 72) and USS *Kitty Hawk* (CV 63); at the Recruit Training Command in Great Lakes, Illinois; as commander, naval force, United States Atlantic Fleet, AMMT at Norfolk, Virginia; and on USS *George Washington* (CVN 73) at Norfolk, Virginia.

She was selected into the command master chief program in November 2002. She is a graduate of the Senior Enlisted Academy (class 100 Gold), Newport, Rhode Island. In February 2005, she was serving as the command master chief of USS *Bulkeley* (DDG-84).

Eve Belfance

JUDGE. Judge Eve Belfance is a native of Akron, Ohio, where she attended the Akron public schools and graduated from Firestone High School. She is a graduate of Yale University and earned her Juris Doctor degree at Case Western Reserve School of Law. She has served as a federal judicial clerk in Washington, D.C.; she was engaged in private law practice until November 2005 when she was elected judge to the Akron Municipal Court.

Diane L. Bell

NONPROFIT EXECUTIVE. Diane L. Bell received a Bachelor of Arts in social work from the University of Maryland and received a master's degree in social work from the School of Social Work and Community Planning at the University of Maryland.

In July 2003, Ms. Bell was appointed to the Baltimore City Board of Commissioners. She serves as the president and chief executive officer of Empower Baltimore Management Corporation (EBMC), the non-profit organization that manages the empowerment zone in Baltimore City.

Ella B. Bell

ELECTED OFFICIAL. Ella B. Bell received a Bachelor of Science degree from Tuskegee University in 1969, a master's degree in education supervision from Alabama State University, and earned a doctoral in educational leadership from the University of Alabama.

She has served with the Drop Out Prevention Center at Alabama State University. She was elected to the Alabama State Board of Education in 2001 and re-elected in 2005.

Stephanie W. Bell

EDUCATION. Stephanie W. Bell graduated from Jefferson Davis High School in Montgomery, Alabama. She received a bachelor's degree in English/journalism from Auburn University in Auburn, Alabama.

Her professional career includes serving as an English teacher to

Chinese adults in Taichung, Taiwan; as a reporter at the *Montgomery Advertiser/Alabama Journal*; and as executive director, SCORE 100 (Statewide Committee on Reforming Education). Since her election in 1995 she has served as a commissioner, Alabama State Board of Education.

Stephanie Bell-Rose

NONPROFIT EXECUTIVE. Stephanie Bell-Rose is a native of New York. She received her Bachelor of Arts degree with honors from Harvard University. She received her masters of public administration from the Kennedy School of Government and earned a Juris Doctor from Harvard Law School. She also studied urban development for a year in Venezuela and Mexico as a Harvard University Rockefeller Scholar.

She has served as counsel and program officer for public affairs at the Andrew W. Mellon Foundation. She now serves as president of the Goldman Sachs Foundation in New York, N.Y.

Patricia Bell-Scott

EDUCATION. Patricia Bell-Scott serves as a professor of child and family development and women's studies and adjunct of psychology at the University of Georgia. She received her Ph.D. from the University of Tennessee at Knoxville and has been involved in women's studies for nearly three decades. She teaches an undergraduate course on women in the family and society and a graduate seminar on black women's narratives. She specializes in black women's autobiographical writing and women's developmental issues.

Patricia D. Benke

JUDGE. Justice Patricia D. Benke received a Bachelor of Arts degree in political science from California State University, San Diego, in 1971 and earned her Juris Doctor degree from the University of San Diego School of Law in 1974.

Her professional career includes serving as a deputy attorney general in the San Diego Office of the State Attorney General from 1974 to 1983; as a judge of the Municipal Court, San Diego County; and as a judge of the Superior Court, San Diego County. In June 1987 she was appointed justice to the California Court of Appeal. She was elected to this seat which she currently serves.

Angela M. Bennett

ELECTED OFFICIAL. Angela M. Bennett received two Bachelor of Arts degrees in political science and in radio, TV and film in 1974 and earned a Juris Doctor from the University of Missouri–Kansas City in 1977.

Her professional career includes serving as chief environmental attorney, assistant district counsel for the United States Army Corps of Engineers; as assistant attorney general for the state of Missouri; as an assistant county counselor for Jackson County, Missouri; and as complaint officer, human relations and citizens complaints for Jackson County. She serves as director of the United States Department of Education's Office of Civil Rights, Kansas City office. She was appointed to the University of Missouri Board of Curators in 2001 by Governor Bob Holden. She serves as vice president of the board of curators. She is chair of the executive committee and a member of the academic and student affairs committee.

Valerie D. Benton

MILITARY. Chief Master Sergeant Valerie D. Benton is the eighth command chief master sergeant for the director, Air National Guard, at the National Guard Bureau in Washington, D.C. She is responsible for all affairs concerned with the enlisted personnel of the Air National Guard. She was promoted to chief master sergeant on October 1, 2000.

She was an active duty Air Force enlisted member for twelve years. She served as an active guard/reserve member of the Kansas Air National Guard. She then served as the Air National Guard first sergeant functional manager, United States Air Force First Sergeant Academy, at Maxwell Air Force Base in Alabama until her current assignment.

Kathleen F. Berg

MILITARY. Kathleen F. Berg received a bachelor's degree in mathematics education with distinction from the University of Hawaii in 1973 and a professional diploma, secondary mathematics education from the University of Hawaii. She earned a master's degree of education, secondary education, from the University of Hawaii and a doctorate of philosophy degree in education psychology from the University of Hawaii.

Her military schools attended include the Air National Guard Academy of Military Science Distinguished Graduate Award in 1977; the Air Command & Staff College in 1993; the Air War College in 1997.

Her professional endeavors include serving from May 1987 to May 1993 as chief of operations, 293rd Combat Communication Squadron; from May 1993 to May 2000, as the commander, 293rd Combat Communications Squadron; from May 2000 to August 2004 as director of communications and information at Headquarters Hawaii Air National Guard.

Brigadier General Berg was assigned as the assistant adjutant general for the Air Headquarters Hawaii Air National Guard in August 2004. She was promoted to brigadier general on July 29, 2005.

Carolyn Berger

JUDGE. Judge Carolyn Berger received a Bachelor of Arts degree from the University of Rochester in 1969 and received a masters' in elementary education from Boston University in 1971. She earned her Juris Doctor degree from Boston University School of Law in 1976. She also received an honorary Doctor of Laws from Widener University School of Law in 1996.

Her professional career includes serving as a deputy attorney general with the Delaware Department of Justice from 1976 to 1979. She was engaged in private law practice from 1979 to 1984 and in 1984 she was appointed a vice chancellor for the Delaware Court of Chancery. On July 22, 1994, she was appointed justice to the Delaware Supreme Court.

Terry Bergeson

ELECTED OFFICIAL. Terry Bergeson is a native of Massachusetts. She received a Bachelor of Arts degree in English from Emmanuel College in Boston in 1964 and earned a master's degree in counseling and guidance from Western Michigan University. She received a doctorate from the University of Washington.

Her professional career includes serving as a public school teacher and counselor, first in her home state of Massachusetts and then in Alaska; she served as a counselor at Lincoln High School in Tacoma; and was selected to serve as chair of the National Education Association's Women's Caucus and implemented a national women's leadership training project. In 1989 she was hired as the executive director of the Central Kitsap School District where she supervised nine schools and several special programs. In 1993 she was appointed executive director of the Washington State Commission on Student Learning. She served as executive director until 1996 when she ran for and was elected as state superintendent of public instruction. She took office in January 1997.

Dr. Bergeson was re-elected to her term of office as Washington State superintendent of public instruction in 2004.

Nomi Bergman

BUSINESS EXECUTIVE. Nomi Bergman received a Bachelor of Arts degree in economics and statistics from the University of Rochester.

Her professional career includes doing computer programming and consulting with Arthur Andersen & Co. management information consulting division. Her next position was with Advance Publications Systems Group where she did similar consulting work with the Newhouse properties; after the Time Warner/Advance Newhouse partnership, she worked in Time Warner Cable's Charlotte division in several capacities, including oversight of the division's high speed data deploy-

ment as vice president and general manager of high speed data services.

In 2002, she assumed the position of executive vice president of strategy and development for Advance/Newhouse Communications, corporate headquarters for Bright House Networks.

Shelley Berkley

ELECTED OFFICIAL. Shelley Berkley was born in New York and grew up in Las Vegas, Nevada. She graduated from Valley High School in Las Vegas and became the first member of her family to attend college. She received a bachelor's degree with honors from the University of Las Vegas. She earned a Juris Doctor degree from the University of San Diego Law School, California.

She served in the Nevada state assembly from 1982 through 1984. From 1983 to 1985 she served as vice chair of the Nevada University and Community College System Board of Regents. She was elected a United States representative in 1998 and began serving in the United States House of Representatives in January 1999. She represents the First Congressional District of Nevada which includes Las Vegas, North Las Vegas, and unincorporated areas in Clark County.

Gail Berman

ENTERTAINMENT EXECUTIVE. Gail Berman received a bachelor's degree from the University of Maryland in College Park (1978).

Her professional career includes serving as president of Fox Entertainment at FOX Broadcasting Company since May 2000. At Fox she headed the network's program development, scheduling, marketing, and business affairs functions. She now serves as president of Paramount Pictures' annual slate of films including the acquisition of literary properties, development, budgeting, casting and production of motion pictures.

Margaret Bernal

JUDGE. Judge Margaret Miller Bernal was engaged in private law practice until 1992 when she was appointed a commissioner (judge) of the Whittler Municipal Court. Within six years she was appointed a judge of the municipal court. In 2000, Judge Bernal was elevated to Superior Court judge when the municipal and superior courts were consolidated.

Marielsa Bernard

JUDGE (FIRST). Judge Marielsa Bernard was born in Washington, D.C., and grew up in the Silver Spring and Rockville areas of Maryland. She graduated in 1973 from Thomas S. Wootton High School in Rockville, Maryland. She received a Bachelor of Arts degree in political science/English from Loyola College in 1977 and earned her Juris Doctor degree from the Columbus School of Law at Catholic University of America in 1980.

Her legal career began in 1978 as a law clerk in private practice; from 1984 to 1986, she was engaged in private law practice. While in private practice, she also served as a criminal justice act misdemeanor panel attorney for the United States District Court.

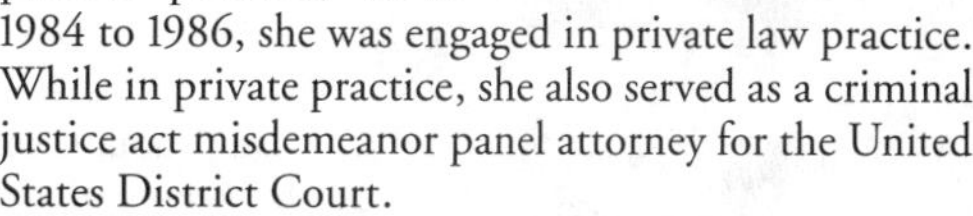

In September 1998, Maryland Governor Parris N. Glendening appointed her judge to the District Court of Maryland for Montgomery County, District 6. In March 2002, she was elevated to judge on the circuit court for Montgomery County, Maryland. She is the first Hispanic to serve in the Montgomery County judiciary.

Debra Bernes

JUDGE. Judge Debra Bernes is a native of Atlanta, Georgia. She attended the City of Atlanta public

schools, graduating from Atlanta's Henry Grady High School in 1973. Following high school, she attended the University of Florida where she received a Bachelor of Arts degree in education in 1979 with high honors. She earned her Juris doctorate from the University of Florida's Fredric G. Levin College of Law in 1978 and became a member of the Georgia bar in 1979.

In 1979, Judge Bernes began a twenty-year career as an assistant district attorney for the Cobb Judicial Circuit, Marietta, Georgia, where she concentrated in felony prosecutions and appellate law. In 2000, she entered private practice. On November 23, 2004, she was elected as the seventieth judge to the Georgia Court of Appeals. Her term of office began on January 1, 2005.

Bertice Berry

ENTERTAINMENT. Bertice Berry received a bachelor's degree magna cum laude from Jacksonville University where she was awarded the President's Cup for leadership and earned a Ph.D. in sociology from Kent State University.

After teaching at Kent State, she left to become an award-winning entertainer, lecturer and comedienne. From 1991 through 1994 she won the coveted national Comedian of the Year award. She has appeared on *The Oprah Winfrey Show* and *The Tonight Show with Jay Leno*. Among her best-selling publications are the inspirational memoir, *I'm on My Way, but Your Foot Is on My Head*. She served as host and co-executive producer of her own nationally syndicated talk show, "The Bertice Berry Show," and hosted "USA Live," a four-hour live interview and entertainment show on the USA cable network.

Cherie Killian Berry

ELECTED OFFICIAL (FIRST). Cherie Killian Berry is a native of Catawba County, North Carolina. She served in the North Carolina House of Representatives from 1993 to 2000, representing the state's 45th district. She is the former business owner of LGM Ltd., a company that produces spark plug wires for the automotive industry.

On January 6, 2001, she was sworn in as North Carolina's first female labor commissioner. She was elected to a second term in November 2004.

Janet J. Berry

JUDGE. Janet J. Berry received her undergraduate degree and her Juris Doctor degree from Tulane University. Her professional career includes serving as law clerk at the United States District Court for the Eastern District of Louisiana and as law clerk at the Nevada Supreme Court. She was engaged in private law practice when she was appointed judge to the Reno Municipal Court in 1992. In 1996 she was appointed judge to the Nevada Second Judicial District Court.

Judith Borg Biggert

ELECTED OFFICIAL. Judith Borg Biggert is a native of Chicago, Illinois, and attended New Trier High School in Winnetka, Illinois. She received a Bachelor of Arts from Stanford University, Stanford, California, in 1959 and earned her Juris Doctor degree from Northwestern University Law School in Evanston, Illinois, in 1963.

Her professional career includes serving as a clerk to Judge Luther M. Swygert at the United States Court of Appeals, 7th Circuit, from 1963 to 1964 and as a

member of the Illinois State General Assembly, 1993 to 1998. She was elected a United States representative to the 106th Congress and to the three succeeding Congresses since January 3, 1999.

J. Veronica Biggins

FINANCE. J. Veronica Biggins is a native of Belmont, North Carolina. She received Bachelor of Science degree from Spelman College and earned a Master of Arts degree from Georgia State University.

Her professional career includes serving for over 20 years in the banking industry. She joined NationsBank, now Bank of America, as a management trainee. She received several promotions and was one of the highest-ranking females in banking in the country when she left the industry as executive vice president for Corporate Community Relations. In 1994, she was appointed director of presidential personnel for President Bill Clinton. Ms. Biggins was selected to serve as vice chairman of the United States delegation in Beijing, China, during the fourth world conference on women of the United Nations in 1995. She serves as a senior partner at Heidrick & Struggles, an international executive consulting firm, and managing partner of the company's diversity services practice and is an active member of the board of directors and the global financial services industry practice.

Judith M. Billings

JUDGE. Judith M. Billings earned her Juris Doctor degree from the University of Utah College of Law in 1977, and an LLM from the University of Virginia Law School in 1990. Her professional career includes serving in private law practice. In January 1987, she was appointed judge to the Utah Court of Appeals.

Laura Carpenter Bingham

EDUCATION. Laura Carpenter Bingham is a native of a King's Mountain, North Carolina. She received an Associate of Arts degree from Peace College and a Bachelor of Arts degree in political science from the University of North Carolina at Chapel Hill. She earned a Master of Arts degree in philanthropic studies at Indiana University.

Her professional career includes serving as senior vice president for philanthropy at Covenant Health in Knoxville, Tennessee, and as vice president for development and external relations at Hollins University in Roanoke, Virginia. She also served in several North Carolina legislative and executive government posts including assistant for policy for former Lt. Gov. Robert B. Jordan.

Ms. Bingham was appointed the ninth president of Peace College on July 1, 1998. She is the first alumna and the second woman in the college's nearly 150-year history to hold the post.

Nancy Bingham

AEROSPACE. Nancy Bingham received a Bachelor of Art degree in bioengineering from the University of California in San Diego. She earned a Master of Science degree in bioengineering/fluid mechanics from the University of California in San Diego and a Master of Science in management from the Graduate School of Business Stanford University.

She began her career at the National Aeronautics and Space Administration (NASA) in 1982 at the Ames Research Center. She has worked as a design engineer for control systems at the Numerical Aerodynamic Simulation Facility, the Fluid Mechanics Laboratory, and the High Reynolds Number Channel II. She has also served as the design engineer for electronic, telemetry, and computer systems in support of the life sciences flight

experiments program for the Space Shuttle. She was the experiment manager for the autogenic feedback training experiment on flight 51C of the Space Shuttle. This experiment was successfully flown in 1984. From 1987 to 1993, she served as the project manager for the 12-foot pressure wind tunnel restoration project, responsible for the design, demolition, reconstruction and test of the restored facility. She has held various director positions at NASA, and served as acting director for research and development services until 1998. She currently serves as associate director for systems management and planning.

Patricia Martin Bishop

JUDGE. Patricia Martin Bishop attended summer school at the University of Nairobi in Kenya, East Africa in 1979. She received a Bachelor of Science degree from Middlebury College in Middlebury, Vermont, in 1981. She earned her Juris Doctor degree from the Northern Illinois University College of Law in 1985.

Her professional career includes serving in the office of the Cook County Public Defender for ten years as an assistant public defender in the Sixth District, as attorney supervisor in early entry unit in the Sixth District, and as deputy chief of the Fifth District. In 1996, she was elected judge to the Illinois Circuit Court of Cook County in Chicago, Illinois.

Carolyn Vesper Bivens

SPORTS EXECUTIVE (FIRST). Carolyn Vesper Bivens has worked for six years in various sales and marketing positions for Xerox Corporation in Dallas and Washington, D.C. She served in key positions at *USA Today*, where she was a member of the original launch team for the "Nation's Newspaper." In 1985, she was named vice president of national circulation sales. She was appointed president and chief operating officer of Initiative Media North America, the largest media services agency in the United States and part of the Interpublic Group of Companies.

Ms. Bivens was named commissioner of the Ladies Professional Golf Association (LPGA) on June 16, 2005, and became the first female and seventh commissioner in the organization's 55-year history when she assumed the position in July 2005.

Cathleen Black

BUSINESS EXECUTIVE. Cathleen Black received a bachelor's degree from Trinity College in Washington, D.C., and holds eight honorary degrees.

Ms. Black began her career in advertising sales with several magazines, including during the launch of *Ms.* She made publishing history in 1979 when she became the first woman publisher of a weekly consumer magazine: *New York*. She is widely credited for the success of *USA Today*, where she served as first president for eight years, then as publisher, board member and executive vice president/marketing of Gannett, its parent company. In 1991, she was selected to serve as president and chief executive officer of the Newspaper Association of America, the industry's largest trade group where she served for five years.

Ms. Black serves as president of the Hearst Magazines, a division of the Hearst Corporation and one of the world's largest publishers of monthly magazines. She manages the financial performance and development of nineteen magazines, some of which are the industry's best known titles: *Cosmopolitan*, *Esquire*, *Good Housekeeping*, *O, The Oprah Magazine*, *Marie Claire*, *Popular Mechanics*, *Harper's BAZAAR*, *Redbook*, and *Town & Country*. She also oversees 142 international editions of those magazines selling on newsstands in more than 100 countries. She has overseen eleven magazine launches and acquisitions in the last six years, most recently launching *SHOP Etc.*, *Weekend* and *Quick & Simple*, Hearst's first weekly magazine in the United States.

Susan Harrell Black

JUDGE. Susan Harrell Black is a native of Valdosta, Georgia. She received a Bachelor of Arts degree from Florida State University in 1964 and earned her Juris Doctor degree from the University of Florida College of Law in 1967. She also received a LL.M. degree from the University of Virginia in 1984.

Her career experience includes serving as a high school teacher in Jacksonville, Florida; as an attorney with the United States Army Corps of Engineers in Jacksonville, Florida; as an assistant state attorney in

Jacksonville, Florida; as an assistant general counsel for the City of Jacksonville, Florida; as a judge, Duval County Court, Florida; as a judge, Circuit of Florida, Fourth Judicial Circuit.

She was nominated by Jimmy Carter on May 23, 1979, was confirmed by the Senate on July 23, 1979, and received commission on July 24, 1979, as a judge, U.S. District Court, Middle District of Florida. She served as chief judge from 1990 to 1992.

Judge Black was nominated by George H.W. Bush on March 10, 1992, to a seat vacated by Thomas Alonzo Clark, was confirmed by the Senate on August 11, 1992, and received commission on August 12, 1992, as a judge on the U.S. Court of Appeals for the Eleventh Circuit.

Katie Blackburn

SPORTS EXECUTIVE. Katie Blackburn received a bachelor's degree from Bethel College in St. Paul, Minnesota. She majored in theatre while in college and joined the "Lamb's Players Theatre" in San Diego. She was a "founding mother" of SAK Theatre, an improvisational theatre company which performed at Renaissance festivals and was a major entertainment company for Disney's Epcot Center in Orlando, Florida.

Ms. Blackburn's grandfather, the legendary coach Paul Brown, founded the Cincinnati Bengals when she was three. She currently serves as executive vice president of the Cincinnati Bengals. She is responsible for negotiating player contracts and overseeing the team's radio and television networks.

Marsha Blackburn

ELECTED OFFICIAL. Marsha Blackburn is a native of Laurel, Mississippi. She graduated from Northeast Jones High School in Laurel, Mississippi, and received a Bachelor of Science degree from Mississippi State University in 1973.

Her political career began in 1977 as a founding member of the Williamson County Young Republicans. She served as chairwoman of the Williamson County Republican Party from 1989 to 1991. In 1992 she was an unsuccessful candidate for the 103rd Congress; in 1995 she was appointed chairwoman of the Tennessee Film, Entertainment and Music Commission; and in 1998 she won elective office for the first time when she was elected to the Tennessee State Senate representing Williamson County and part of Davidson County.

Carolyn Wade Blackett

JUDGE. Carolyn Wade Blackett received a Bachelor of Arts degree from Brown University in Providence, Rhode Island, and a Doctor of Jurisprudence degree from St. Louis University School of Law in St. Louis, Missouri, in 1982. Upon graduation, she was a practicing attorney at the National Labor Relations Board, Federal Express Corporation, and Warning Cox law firm.

In September 1994, the governor of Tennessee appointed her judge of Division IV of the Shelby County Criminal Court. Judge Blackett has stood successfully for re-election twice in Shelby County and was most recently unopposed for an eight year term. She was the first female criminal court judge in Shelby County and the first African American female criminal court state judge in the state of Tennessee.

Patricia Ann Blackmon

JUDGE. Patricia Ann Blackmon is a native of Mississippi and graduated from Lanier High School in 1968. She graduated from Mississippi's Tougaloo with a bachelor's degree (magna cum laude) in 1975. She earned her Juris Doctor degree from Cleveland-Marshall College of Law at Cleveland State University.

Her professional career includes serving as a chief prosecutor for the city of Cleveland where she was the

city's first night prosecutor, as an assistant director of victims/witness program, and as a professor at Dyke College. Judge Blackmon serves as judge on the Ohio Court of Appeals, Eighth District Court, in Cuyahoga County, Ohio.

Norma E. Blake

LIBRARIAN. Norma E. Blake has had over 25 years experience in New Jersey libraries including the directorship of both the Burlington County and Gloucester County library systems. She serves as the New Jersey state librarian.

She has served as president of the state library association and was named the New Jersey Library Association's Librarian of the Year.

Shirley A. Blakely

MILITARY. Shirley A. Blakely became a registered dietitian following completion of a dietetic internship in the United States Army at the Fitzsimons General Hospital, Denver, Colorado, and worked as a dietitian in the United States Army. She later obtained her Master of Science and Ph.D. degrees in nutritional sciences.

She was selected as the chief professional officer for the dietitian category effective September 1, 2000. As chief dietitian officer, she is responsible for providing leadership and coordination of Public Health Service (PHS) dietitian professional affairs for the Office of the Surgeon General and the Dietitian Professional Advisory Committee on matters such as recruitment, retention, and career development of PHS dietitians.

Kathleen B. Blanco

ELECTED OFFICIAL (FIRST). Kathleen B. Blanco is a native of Coteau, Louisiana. She received a Bachelor of Science degree in business education from the University of Louisiana at Lafayette.

Her professional career includes serving as a teacher at Breaux Bridge High School, a public school in Southwest Louisiana. In 1984 she became the first woman elected to represent the people of Lafayette in the state legislature. Five years later she was elected to the Public Service Commission where she became the first woman to serve as a commissioner and, later became the first woman to chair the commission (1993–1994). In 1995 she became the first woman ever elected to serve as lieutenant governor for the State of Louisiana. She was overwhelmingly re-elected to her second term in 1999, winning 80 percent of the vote.

Ms. Blanco was elected governor for the State of Louisiana on January 12, 2004, the first woman to serve as such.

Sharon Jackson Bland

BUSINESS EXECUTIVE. Sharon Jackson Bland received a Bachelor of Arts degree in political science and African-American studies with a minor in education from the University of Massachusetts in 1988, and received a masters of public and business administration coursework from the University of the District of Columbia, Washington, D.C. She also holds a Juris Doctor degree from Georgetown University Law Center, Washington, D.C., 1992. She completed the certified public manager pro-

gram at George Washington University in Washington, D.C.

In 1992 she began working for the Clear Solution in Bethesda, Maryland, as a management consultant. In 1995, she worked for University of the District of Columbia, serving as the director of university affairs and community programs. She also taught employment law, political science courses and civil rights law. From 2000 to 2004, she worked for the executive office of the mayor in Washington, D.C. Presently, she serves as vice president, corporate business development and government relations for McKissack & McKissack, located in Washington, D.C.

Deb S. Blechman

JUDGE. Deb S. Blechman received a Bachelor of Arts from the University of Central Florida in 1976 and earned her Juris Doctor degree from the University of Florida in 1980.

Her judicial career includes serving as a judge of the Orange County Traffic Court from 1995 to 1997 and as a judge of the Orange County Criminal Court from 1998 to 2002. In 2003 she served as a judge in Orange County Traffic Court; from 2004 to 2005, she served as judge for Orange County Criminal Court; in 2006 she was assigned judge, Orange County Civil Court in Orange County, Florida.

Nancy M. Blount

JUDGE. Nancy M. Blount received her undergraduate degree from the University of Michigan and earned her Juris Doctor degree from the University of Michigan Law School. Her professional career includes serving in private law practice. On January 1, 1983, she was elected judge to the Michigan's 36th Judicial District Court in Detroit.

Paula Blunt

GOVERNMENT OFFICIAL. Paula Blunt has worked at the United States Department of Housing and Urban Development for over 20 years in various senior executive, senior management and supervisory positions. Positions Ms. Blunt has held at HUD include deputy director for program operations and director of economic development and supportive services, both in the office of Public and Indian Housing. Prior to joining HUD, Ms. Blunt worked for the Washington, D.C., Housing Authority and also worked at the U.S. Departments of Energy and Justice. She was also a faculty member at Lincoln University in Pennsylvania and the University of the District of Columbia.

Ms. Blunt serves as the general deputy assistant secretary for the office of Public and Indian Housing at the United States Department of Housing and Urban Development, where she participates with the assistant secretary for public and Indian housing in the planning, management, direction and policy formulation for all activities pertaining to the operation of public and Indian housing programs. This includes the administration of all public housing, housing choice vouchers (Section 8 rental assistance) and Native American programs that benefit more than 3,400 housing agencies across the country, and comprises well over 60 percent of HUD's annual operating budget.

Ms. Blunt is recipient of the 2004 "Presidential Rank Award" in recognition of her exceptional long-term accomplishments in the federal government.

Susan Bodine

GOVERNMENT OFFICIAL. Susan Bodine received a bachelor's degree from Princeton University and earned her Juris Doctor degree from the University of Pennsylvania.

Her professional career includes serving six years in private law practice; in January 1995, she served as staff director and senior counsel of the Water Resources and Environment subcommittee of the House Committee on Transportation and Infrastructure where she worked primarily on Clean Water Act, Wetlands, Superfund, Brownfields, and Army Corps of Engineers civil works legislation and oversight.

Ms. Bodine serves as assistant administrator of U.S. Environmental Protection Agency Office of Solid Waste and Emergency Response.

Barbaranette T. Bolden

MILITARY. Barbaranette T. Bolden received a Bachelor of Arts degree in history from Arkansas State University in 1974 and a Master of Arts degree in history from Arkansas State University in 1975. She earned a Juris Doctor degree from Howard University School of Law and also the United States Army War College.

Her professional career began when she enlisted in the Arkansas Army National Guard on May 15, 1975, in the 567th Engineer Battalion. After moving to Washington, D.C., to attend school, she joined the District of Columbia Army National Guard. She received her commission in 1978 from the District of Columbia Army National Guard Officer Candidate School. She has served in numerous positions of increasing authority and responsibility to include company commander, Battalion S-1 and S-3, Brigade S-1; personnel management officer, Headquarters DARC; battalion commander, director of personnel, director of plans, operations, training and military support, the Joint Chief of Staff for the District of Columbia National Guard; land military support to civilian authorities branch chief, US Northern Command; and most recently as the J3 operations for the Joint Task Force–Armed Forces Inaugural Committee.

Brigadier General Bolden serves as the commander for the 260th Military Police Command and commander of the Joint Task Force for the District of Columbia National Guard. She is responsible for the planning, coordination and integration of operations for the federal agencies for homeland defense and homeland security. She was promoted to brigadier general on September 9, 2005.

Melissa L. Bondy

MEDICINE. Melissa L. Bondy received a Bachelor of Arts degree in psychology from the University of Texas in Austin in 1975 and a master of public health in epidemiology and environmental science from the University of Texas School of Public Health in 1982. She also earned a Ph.D. in epidemiology from the University of Texas School of Public Health.

Dr. Bondy serves as professor of epidemiology at the University of Texas M.D. Anderson Cancer Center and director of the Childhood Cancer Epidemiology and Prevention Center. She is also associate professor at Baylor College of Medicine Department of Pediatrics, Hematology/Oncology Section, in Houston, Texas. Dr. Bondy's epidemiological research primarily focuses on understanding multiple risk factors such as genetic susceptibility and heredity associated with development of brain gliomas and breast cancer. She is also known for insightful research involving families of glioma patients and for studies that evaluate genetic susceptibility and environmental determinants in breast and colorectal cancer.

Dr. Bondy is a scientific review advisor for the Susan G. Komen Breast Cancer Research Foundation and has served as a permanent member of the epidemiology group for the Department of Veterans Affairs. She is chair of the epidemiology committee of the Radiation Therapy Oncology Group.

Gwendolyn Boney-Harris

MILITARY. Gwendolyn Boney-Harris is a native of Georgia and grew up in Miami, Florida, where she graduated from high school. She entered Saint Augustine's College in Raleigh, North Carolina, to study criminal justice and political science. While there she joined the Reserve Officers Training Corps (ROTC).

She was commissioned into the United States Army in May 1980 following graduation from Saint Augustine's College with a bachelor's degree in criminal justice and a graduate degree in national strategic studies from the United States Army War College. Her military education includes completion of the Quartermaster Officer Basic and Advanced Courses, Fort Lee, Virginia; United States Army Command and General Staff College, Fort Leavenworth, Kansas; and the United States Army War College, Carlisle Barracks, Pennsylvania.

She has held key leadership and staff positions to include serving as the technical supply officer, 597th Maintenance Company, 68th Transportation Battalion at Fort Carson, Colorado; as deputy division property officer, 24th Infantry Division, Support Command,

Fort Stewart, Georgia; as commander, Supply Company, 299th Support Battalion, 1st Infantry Division (Forward), United States Army Europe, Germany; as support operations officer, 224th Forward Support Battalion, Fort Stewart, Georgia; as commander, Logistic Task Force for 1-64 Armor Battalion, Somalia; as assistant division G-4, 24th Infantry Division, Fort Stewart, Georgia; as logistic officer, G-4, United States Army Europe, Germany; as commander, 47th Forward Support Battalion, 1st Armored Division, United States Army Europe; as the special assistant to the Army chief of staff, Pentagon, Washington, D.C.; as garrison commander, Installation Management Agency, European Region, Army Garrison Stuttgart in 2005.

Mary Bono

ELECTED OFFICIAL. Mary Bono is a native of Cleveland, Ohio. She received a Bachelor of Arts degree from the University of Southern California, Los Angeles, California.

Her professional career includes serving as a restaurant business manager; as a personal fitness instructor; as a member of the Board of the Palm Springs, California, International Film Festival.

Ms. Bono was elected as a Republican to the 105th Congress by special election to fill the vacancy caused by the death of her husband, United States Representative Sonny Bono. She has been reelected to the four succeeding Congresses (April 7, 1998 to the present).

Lisa Borders

ELECTED OFFICIAL. Lisa Borders received a bachelor's degree from Duke University in Durham, North Carolina and a Masters of Science in health administration from the University of Colorado in Denver, Colorado.

Ms. Borders serves as president of the Atlanta City Council, having been elected in a citywide special election on August 10, 2004. She was reelected by an overwhelming margin in 2005's regular citywide election cycle.

She also serves as a senior vice president with Cousins Properties Incorporated, an Atlanta-based real estate investment trust (REIT). She worked as the chief administrator for Atlanta Women's Specialists and also served as vice president for operations for Healthcap Atlanta.

Dana H. Born

MILITARY. Dana H. Born graduated with distinction from the United States Air Force Academy in 1983 with a Bachelor of Science degree in behavioral science. She earned a Masters of Science degree in experimental psychology from Trinity University at San Antonio, Texas, in 1985, and a received a Master of Arts degree in research psychology from the University of Melbourne, Australia, in 1991. She earned a Doctor of Philosophy degree in industrial and organizational psychology from Pennsylvania State University, University Park, in 1994. She is a graduate of Squadron Officer School at Maxwell Air Force Base in Alabama; of Air Command and Staff College in 1996; and of the Air War College in 2000.

Her staff assignments include serving as assistant director for recruiting research and analysis in the office of assistant secretary of defense for force management policy and aide to the secretary of the Air Force and deputy chief of the personnel issues team in the office of the deputy chief of staff for personnel. She commanded the 11th Mission Support Squadron at Bolling Air Force Base, in Washington, D.C.; from June 2002 to September 2004, she served as a permanent professor and head of the United States Air Force Academy's behavioral sciences and leadership department, at United States Air Force Academy, Colorado Springs, Colorado. In September 2004, she was selected to serve as the dean of the faculty at the United States Air Force Academy. She commands the 700-member faculty mission element and oversees the annual design and instruction of more than 500 undergraduate courses for 4,000 cadets in 32 academic disciplines. She also directs the operation of five support staff agencies and faculty resources involving more than $250 million.

Lisa M. Boscola

ELECTED OFFICIAL. Lisa M. Boscola is a native of Bethlehem, Pennsylvania. She received a Bachelor of Arts in political science (cum laude) in 1984 and earned her Master of Arts political science in 1985 from Villanova University.

Her professional career includes serving as a deputy county administrator from 1987 to 1993. In 1993 she

was elected a Pennsylvania state representative serving in the House of Representatives from 1994 to 1998. In 1997 she was elected a Pennsylvania state senator and has served in Pennsylvania State Senate since 1998.

Chris Boskin

MEDIA EXECUTIVE. Chris Boskin received a Bachelor of Arts degree in art history and English from the University of California in Berkeley and also studied at the Academia in Florence, Italy.

Ms. Boskin joined Knapp Communications in 1972 as San Francisco manager for *Architectural Digest*, and later helped develop and launch *Bon Appetit*. In 1975, she joined East West Network as San Francisco manager. From 1977 to 1987, she was the Pacific and Asia manager for the *New Yorker* magazine. From 1988 to 1990, she was San Francisco, Pacific Northwest, and Asia manager for Hearst Magazines, responsible for *Esquire*, *Harpers Bazaar*, *House Beautiful*, and *Connoisseur*. She served as advertising director and publisher for *Countryside* prior to joining *Town & Country* in 1991. In 1992, Ms. Boskin joined *Worth* magazine as publisher and helped develop and launch other Worth Media titles including: *Equity*, *Civilization*, and *American Benefactor*.

Ms. Boskin currently serves as a consultant to several media companies and as a member of the board for the Corporation for Public Broadcasting.

Gina Boswell

BUSINESS EXECUTIVE. Gina Boswell received a Bachelor of Science in business administration summa cum laude from Boston University and a Masters of Public and Private Management (MPPM) from the Yale School of Management. She is a former certified public accountant (CPA).

Her professional career includes serving for seven years with Estee Lauder Companies, most recently as vice president for new business development. From 1999 to 2003 she worked for Ford Motor Company where she launched multiple eBusiness platforms, headed the company's vehicle personalization business unit and eventually led the business strategy for Ford's global enterprise. She joined Avon Products in 2003 as senior vice president, corporate strategy and business development.

In January 2005, Ms. Boswell was appointed senior vice president and chief operating officer of Avon North America, Avon Products, Inc.

Sheryl J. Bourbeau

MILITARY. Sheryl J. Bourbeau received a Bachelor of Science degree in pre-law/political science magna cum laude from James Madison University in Virginia in 1979. In 1983, she entered a Department of the Army intern program for contract specialists at Fort Gordon, Georgia. She was selected for the NAVSEA Commander's Development Program in May 1996.

Her professional career includes serving with the United States Army as a contract specialist and with the United States Navy as a contract specialist at the Naval Supply Center at Bremerton, Washington. She was assigned to Naval Sea Systems Command (NAVSEA) Headquarters in Washington, D.C. While on this assignment she was responsible for the negotiation and administration of major shipbuilding contracts for both new construction and overhauls; in 1992 she was appointed sole procuring contracting officer for all amphibious assault ships; in 1995 her responsibilities were expanded to include the coastal minehunter and mine counter measure ships and the LPD 17 Class Amphibious ship; in 1997, she became the deputy supervisor of shipbuilding, conversion and repair, USN, New Orleans; in May 2000, she was selected into the Senior Executive Service as the deputy commander for surface ships for the Naval Sea Systems Command; in September 2001 she was appointed the NAVSEA chief information officer.

Ms. Bourbeau serves as deputy director, command, control, communication and computer and deputy chief information officer of the Marine Corps.

Margretta Jeffers Bowen

FINANCE. Margretta Jeffers Bowen received a Bachelor of Arts degree from Morgan State University and earned a Juris Doctor degree from Ohio State University of College of Law. She has over 30 years experience, specializing in Securities and Exchange Commission. In 1980 she joined the Equitable Life Assurance

Society, now AXA Financial Inc. She now serves as vice president and associate general counsel for AXA Financial Inc./ Equitable Life in New York.

Kathleen M. Bowers

JUDGE. Kathleen M. Bowers received her undergraduate degree from Miami University of Ohio in 1971 and earned her Juris Doctor degree from the University of Denver in 1977. Her professional career includes serving as an assistant city attorney for the Denver City Airport, city attorney's office; as an attorney at the Massachusetts Attorney General's office; and in the natural resources section and appellate division of the Colorado Attorney General's office. On August 1, 1988, she was appointed judge to the Colorado 2nd Judicial District, Denver County Court.

Barbara L. Bowies

BUSINESS EXECUTIVE. Barbara L. Bowies received a Bachelor of Arts degree in mathematics (with honors) from Fisk University and earned a Master of Business Administration in finance from the University of Chicago School of Business.

Her professional career includes serving as director for Black & Decker Corporation, Dollar General Corporation, and Georgia-Pacific Corporation. She was appointed a director of Wisconsin Energy Corporation and Wisconsin Electric Power Company in 1998. She has served as the founder and chief executive officer of the Kenwood Group, Inc., since 1989.

Kathleen Gill Bowman

EDUCATION. Kathleen Gill Bowman is a graduate of the University of Minnesota where she also earned her Ph.D. in English education. Her professional career includes serving as a faculty member and special assistant to the president of Reed College where she also directed the development of program for gifted precollegiate studies and two graduate programs. She served as vice provost for international affairs at the University of Oregon from 1989 to 1994 and as associate vice president for research from 1985 to 1989.

On May 16, 1994, she became the eighth president of Randolph-Macon Woman's College in Lynchburg, Virginia. She retired in the summer of 2006.

Linda Bowman

EDUCATION. Linda Bowman received a bachelor's degree in English and Spanish and earned a master's degree in public administration and English from the University of Colorado. She also holds a doctorate in public administration from the University of Colorado.

She serves as president of Community College of Aurora in Colorado. She also represents the 13 presidents in the Colorado Community College System to the Education Foundation Board that supports Colorado Community College System.

Barbara Boxer

ELECTED OFFICIAL. Barbara Boxer is a native of Brooklyn, in Kings County, New York, and attended public schools, graduating from Wingate High School in 1958. She received a Bachelor of Arts degree from Brooklyn College in 1962.

Her professional career includes serving as a stockbroker from 1962 to 1965; as a newspaper editor from

1972 to 1974; and as a congressional aide in 1974–1976. She was elected to the Board of Supervisors of Marin County, California, and served from 1976 to 1982; she was a delegate, California State Democratic Convention in 1983; she was elected a United States representative to the 98th and to the four succeeding Congresses from January 3, 1983, to January 3, 1993; she was elected to the United States Senate in 1992 and reelected in 1998 and 2004, which term ends January 3, 2011.

Ann Boyden

JUDGE. Ann Boyden received her Juris Doctor degree from the University of Utah College of Law in 1987. She served as a deputy district attorney for Salt Lake County from 1987 to 1997. In October 1997 she was appointed judge by Governor Michael O. Leavitt to the Utah Third District Court in Salt Lake, Utah.

Edna J. Boyle

JUDGE. Edna J. Boyle received a Bachelor of Arts degree in political science with a dual emphasis in international government and politics and she earned her Juris Doctor degree from the University of Akron. Her professional career includes serving as an assistant Summit County prosecuting attorney, as director of the Summit County Board of Elections, as magistrate for the Summit County Juvenile Court, and as magistrate for the Summit County Probate Court, and as a judge for the Akron Municipal Court. In 2006 she began serving as judge on the Court of Appeals of Ohio, Ninth Appellate District.

Patricia Jean E. P. Boyle

JUDGE. Patricia Jean E. P. Boyle is a native of Detroit, Michigan. She received a Bachelor of Arts degree from Wayne State University and earned her Juris Doctor degree from Wayne State University Law School in 1963 as the first-ranked in her class and the only woman in her class. Her professional career includes serving as a law clerk in private practice 1963 to 1964; as a law clerk at the United States District Court, Eastern District of Michigan from 1964 to 1965; as an assistant United States attorney, U.S. Attorney's office, Department of Justice from 1965 to 1970; as a deputy prosecutor at the Wayne County Prosecutor's office; as judge in the recorders' court in the city of Detroit from 1976 to 1978. On July 25, 1978, she was nominated judge to the United States District Court, Eastern District Michigan, by President Jimmy Carter. She was confirmed by the United States Senate on September 22, 1978, and received her commission on September 23, 1978. She resigned her seat on the district court to accept an appointment as associate justice to the Michigan Supreme Court. She was elected to her position in 1986 and re-elected in 1990 to an eight-year term.

Ann Walsh Bradley

JUDGE. Ann Walsh Bradley was born in Richland Center, Wisconsin. She received a bachelor's degree from Webster College in St. Louis and earned her Juris Doctor from the University of Wisconsin Law School in 1976.

Her professional career includes serving as a high school teacher before entering law school. After law school she served in practice and in 1985 she was appointed a judge on the Circuit Court in Marathon County. She was elected justice on the Wisconsin Supreme Court and was reelected in 2005.

Jennette B. Bradley

ELECTED OFFICIAL (FIRST). Jennette B. Bradley served as a member of Columbus City Council for 11 years, as vice president and public funds manager for a large bank headquartered in Ohio, and as senior vice president and public finance banker for a national securities firm. She has also served as executive director of the Columbus Metropolitan Housing Authority and as director of the Ohio Department of Commerce. She made history when she became the first African-American woman to be elected lieutenant governor for the state

of Ohio; in January 2005 she was sworn in as Ohio's 45th treasurer of state.

M. Jane Brady

ELECTED OFFICIAL (FIRST). M. Jane Brady, a native of Delaware, graduated from Christiana High School. She received a bachelor degree from the University of Delaware and earned her Juris Doctor degree from Villanova University School of Law. From 1977 to 1990 she served as a prosecutor with the Department of Justice culminating with three years of service as chief prosecutor in Sussex County. She entered private law practice in 1990 where she remained until her election as attorney general in 1994. She is the first woman to serve as attorney general of the state of Delaware.

Barbara C. Brannon

MILITARY. Barbara C. Brannon received a Bachelor of Science degree in nursing (cum laude), from San Francisco State University, San Francisco, California. She earned a Masters of Science degree in cardiovascular nursing from the University of California in San Francisco, California. Her military education includes graduating from Squadron Officer School, then the Air Command and Staff College in 1981. She was an outstanding graduate of the Air War College.

She has held a wide variety of command and staff assignments including serving as chief nurse executive, 90th Medical Group, Francis E. Warren Air Force Base, Wyoming, from June 1992 to June 1995. She was promoted to colonel on September 1, 1994; she served as commander, 382nd Technical Training Squadron, Sheppard Air Force Base in Texas, June 1995 to August 1996; from August 1996 to October 1998 she was assigned as the commander, 31st Medical Group at Aviano Air Base in Italy; from October 1999 to July 2000 she served as the director of the Air Force medical readiness and nursing and services in the Office of the Surgeon General at headquarters of the United States Air Force at Bolling Air Force Base in Washington, D.C. She was promoted to brigadier general on December 1, 1999; from July 2000 to June 2003 she was assigned as commander, 89th Medical Group at Andrews Air Force Base in Maryland; and then as assistant Air Force surgeon general at Headquarters United States Air Force, Bolling Air Force Base in Washington, D.C.; in June 2003 she was assigned as the assistant Air Force surgeon general, medical force development and assistant Air Force surgeon general, nursing services, in the Office of the Surgeon General at Headquarters United States Air Force, Bolling Air Force Base in Washington, D.C. She was promoted to major general on August 1, 2003.

Tanya Mozell Bransford

JUDGE. Tanya Mozell Bransford received a Bachelor of Arts degree from Gustavus Adolphus College in 1980 and earned a Juris Doctor degree from Hamline University School of Law in 1983.

After graduation from law school she served in private practice from 1983 to 1987. She began her judicial career as a worker's compensation judge in the office of administrative hearings. Judge Bransford was the first African-American female worker's compensation judge in the state of Minnesota from 1987 to 1990. She has served as a Hennepin County District Court judge in the juvenile division since 1990.

Laurell A. Brault

MILITARY. Laurell A. Brault is originally from Nassau, Bahamas. She enlisted in the United States Navy in December 1974 and served as a hospital corpsman for ten years. She graduated from Officer Candidate School in Newport, Rhode Island, in February 1985 as an ensign in the General Unrestricted Line (1100) community. Her enlisted duty stations included Naval Hospital Great Lakes, Illinois; Portsmouth, Virginia; Subic Bay, Republic of Philippines; and Marine Corps Officer Selection Office, New York, New York.

Following her commission she was assigned to the comptroller's office on the staff of commander, United States Atlantic Fleet in Norfolk, Virginia; in 1988 she graduated from Oceanographic Watch Officer School and was later designated as an integrated undersea surveillance officer. Subsequent duty assignments included Naval Facility Bermuda, where she served as the current operations officer; commander, Area ASW Forces Sixth Fleet, Naples, Italy; and officer-in-charge, Operations Research Detachment, Okinawa, Japan. In 1994 she returned to Naples as the operations officer for commander, Military Sealift Command Mediterranean.

In September 1996 she became the Navy element commander at Headquarters, Allied Forces Southern Europe for United States Navy personnel assigned to NATO in the Mediterranean theater. Following her executive officer assignment, she transferred to the Office of the Chief of Naval Operations, Shore Installation Management, and was subsequently selected as a legislative fellow. In 1999, she served as a defense fellow on the staff of Senator Olympia Snowe (R–Maine), where she was responsible for providing staff support on national security and foreign affairs issues. She was assigned as a congressional liaison officer for appropriation matters on the staff of the Assistant Secretary of the Navy (financial management and budget); she reported to the Navy Personnel Command in April 2000, where she served initially as the director of staff support and strategic communications and later as the fleet support officer community manager and head detailer. In October 2004 she was serving as the commander of Naval Ocean Processing Facility at Navy Air Station, Whidbey Island.

Carol Moseley Braun

GOVERNMENT OFFICIAL (FIRST). Carol Moseley Braun is a native of Chicago, Illinois. She attended Chicago public schools before receiving a Bachelor of Arts degree from the University of Illinois. She earned her Juris Doctor degree from the University of Chicago. She has received eight honorary degrees.

Her professional career includes serving in private law practice. She was appointed an assistant United States attorney in Chicago and served from 1972 to 1977. In 1978 she was elected a representative in the Illinois General Assembly as an independent Democrat. While in the general assembly she served as assistant majority leader. She left the legislature in 1987 to run for countywide office in Cook County and became the first woman of color to do so in Illinois. She was elected the first African American woman to hold an elective office in Cook County Government, serving as the recorder of deeds. In 1992, she made history when she was elected the first African American woman and the first African American Democrat ever elected to the United States Senate. In 1998, she was appointed United States ambassador to New Zealand. As ambassador, her portfolio included New Zealand, Samoa, Antarctica and the Cook Islands. She is the first United States ambassador to be made an honorary member of the Te Atiawa Maori tribe. After returning from her ambassadorial posting to New Zealand in 2001, she taught law and political science at Morris Brown College in Atlanta, Georgia, and at DePaul University. She now serves in private law practice in Chicago, Illinois.

Donna Brazile

POLITICS. Donna Brazile is a native of New Orleans, Louisiana. She received a bachelor's degree from Louisiana State University in Baton Rouge.

Her professional career includes serving in several presidential campaigns: first for Carter-Mondale in 1976 and 1980, for the Rev. Jesse Jackson's first historic bid for the presidency in 1984, for Mondale-Ferraro in 1984, and for Clinton-Gore in 1992 and 1996. Prior to joining the Gore campaign, she was chief of staff and press secretary to Congresswoman Eleanor Holmes Norton of the District of Columbia where she helped guide the district's budget and local legislation on Capitol Hill; she is a weekly contributor and political commentator on CNN's *Inside Politics* and *American Morning*. In addition, she is a columnist for *Roll Call Newspaper* and appears regularly on MSNBC's *Hardball* and Fox's *Hannity and Colmes*.

Ms. Brazile is chair of the Democratic National Committee's Voting Rights Institute (VRI) and is an adjunct professor at Georgetown University in Washington, D.C. The Voting Rights Institute was established in 2001 to help protect and promote the rights of all Americans to participate in the political process.

Cora Smith Breckenridge

EDUCATION. Cora Smith Breckenridge earned her undergraduate degree from Indiana University in 1959 and a master's degree from Indiana University in 1963. She is a retired speech/language pathologist for Elkhart Community Schools. Among other activities, she was elected as a mem-

ber of the national Board of Directors of the NAACP in 2000 and is the membership chairperson.

She was first elected to the Indiana University Board of Trustees in 1997. She is the first African American to serve on Indiana University's governing body.

Jody A. Breckenridge

MILITARY. Jody A. Breckenridge received a Bachelor of Science degree in biology from Virginia Tech and was commissioned upon graduation from Officer Candidate School in 1976. She earned a master's degree in public policy from the University of Maryland and a master's degree of science in national resource strategy from the Industrial College of the Armed Forces.

Admiral Breckenridge has served as Group Seattle operations officer and Group/COPT Seattle assistant port safety officer, Headquarters Marine Environmental Protection Division and National Response Center. While serving at Headquarters, Rear Admiral Breckenridge also served as a White House social aide. She was assigned on March 31, 2006, as commander of District Eleven of the United States Coast Guard.

Rear Admiral Breckenridge assumed duties as the director, Strategic Transformation Team, on July 16, 2007. She is responsible for aligning and synchronizing the efforts to transform and modernize the Coast Guard.

Sharon Brehm

EDUCATION. Sharon Brehm received a bachelor's degree from Duke University and earned a master's degree in social relations from Harvard University. She holds a Ph.D. in clinical psychology from Duke University.

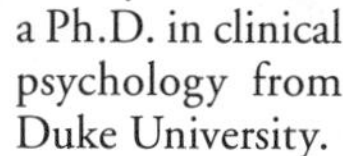

Her professional career includes serving as an associate dean of the Harpur College of Liberal Arts and Sciences, as associate dean of liberal arts and sciences at Kansas University, as the provost at Ohio University, and as vice president for academic affairs and chancellor at Indiana University, the Bloomington campus. She was selected to serve as vice president for academic affairs and chancellor of the Indiana University Bloomington campus.

Maria E. Brennan

NONPROFIT EXECUTIVE. Maria E. Brennan is a native of Washington, D.C. She has nearly 20 years of non-profit executive management experience, with non-profits ranging in size from 2,000 to 33,000 members. She has particular expertise in the areas of strategic planning, branding strategies and resource development and has been instrumental in the growth and success of the American Women in Radio and Television's (AWRT) key franchises including the Gracie Allen Awards, the AWRT Leadership Summit and its numerous public service campaigns. She was selected to serve on the women's leadership board at the John F. Kennedy School of Government at Harvard University and is a member of its strategic planning and communications sub-committee. She serves on the diversity board of the Federal Communications Commission and is the appointed liaison for American Women in Radio and Television to Women Impacting Public Policy (WIPP).

Ms. Brennan was elected president of American Women in Radio and Television and its sister foundation. She has served as its chief executive since 2002.

Shirley M. Brennan

JUDGE. Shirley M. Brennan received a Bachelor of Arts degree in criminal justice, Florida Atlantic University in 1977 and earned her Juris Doctor degree from Nova Law School in 1980.

Her professional career includes serving as an assistant public defender from Okeechobee, Florida. She was engaged in private law practice, then served as an assistant state attorney, chief juvenile prosecutor for Okeechobee, Florida, from 1991 to 1995. Since 1996, she has served as a judge of the Florida 19th Judicial Circuit Court in Okeechobee County.

Rosalind Brewer

BUSINESS EXECUTIVE. Rosalind Brewer received a Bachelor of Science degree in chemistry from Spelman College in Atlanta, Georgia. She has also completed the advanced management program at the Wharton School of Business.

She serves as president and corporate officer of Kimberly-Clark Corporation. She currently leads the global nonwovens sector which includes research and development, engineering, and manufacturing. The sector operates 27 nonwoven base machines in the U.S., Great Britain and South Korea.

Sally Brice-O'Hara

MILITARY. Sally Brice-O'Hara is a native of Annapolis, Maryland. She received a Bachelor of Arts degree in sociology from Goucher College. She received her Coast Guard commission from Officer Candidate School the following year. She holds a Master of Arts degree in public administration from Harvard University, John F. Kennedy School of Government, a Master of Science degree in national security strategy from the National War College and an honorary doctorate of humane letters awarded by Goucher College in 2002.

Her professional career includes serving a wide variety of assignments. Most recently, she served as the director of personnel management administering an extensive range of service-wide human resource programs. At the time of selection to flag rank, she was commanding officer of Training Center Cape May, site of the Coast Guard's only recruit training program. She assumed command of the Fifth Coast Guard District in April 2003. This middle Atlantic region spans 156,000 square miles of ocean, bays, rivers, and wetlands from New Jersey to North Carolina. She was selected to serve as the commander of the Fourteenth Coast Guard District and Pacific Area deputy commander for East Asia Pacific engagement on May 3, 2006.

Bobbe J. Bridges

JUDGE. Bobbe J. Bridges received her bachelor's degree (magna cum laude) from the University of Washington and received a Master of Arts and Ph.D. in political science at the University of Michigan. She earned her Juris doctorate degree from the University of Washington School of Law in 1976.

Her professional career includes serving as chief judge of King County Juvenile Court from 1994 to 1997. She served as a judge for King County Superior Court for ten years; from 1998 to January 2000 she served as the presiding judge. In 1999 she was appointed justice to the Washington State Supreme Court by Governor Gary Locke, and was seated in January 2000.

Pamela E. Bridgewater

GOVERNMENT OFFICIAL. Pamela E. Bridgewater, a native of Fredericksburg, Virginia, graduated from Walker-Grant High School. She received a bachelor's degree in political science from Virginia State University in 1968 and earned a master's degree in political science from the University of Cincinnati. In addition, she was awarded an honorary Doctor of Law degree from Virginia State University.

She entered the U.S. Foreign Service in 1980 after a teaching career that included Morgan State University and Bowie State University in Maryland and Voorhees College in South Carolina. She is the longest-serving U.S. diplomat in South Africa and the first African-American woman to be appointed consul general in Durban, South Africa. Her service has included stints in Brussels, Belgium; Kingston, Jamaica; the Bahamas; and Cotonou, Benin. In 2002 she was appointed U.S. deputy assistant secretary for African affairs. She manages the African bureau's relationships with sixteen countries in West Africa, economic/commercial policies and programs, and public diplomacy program.

Rita Marie Broadway

MILITARY. Rita Marie Broadway is a native of Wichita, Kansas. She received a Bachelor of Science degree in chemical science from Kansas State University. She is the first female cadet to receive an Army Reserve Officer Training (ROTC) commission from Kansas State University. She is a graduate of the United States Army Command and General Staff College, Adjutant

General Officer Branch Qualification Course and United States Army War College.

She has held numerous key military assignments including serving as the commander, 387th Replacement Battalion, 326th Area Support Group, 89th Regional Support Command, at Wichita, Kansas; as assistant deputy chief of staff for operations and training, 89th Regional Support Command, Wichita, Kansas; as commander, 561st Corps Support Group; as deputy commander, 89th Regional Support Command; as commander, 89th Regional Readiness Command (Provisional), Wichita, Kansas.

Roslyn McCallister Brock

BUSINESS EXECUTIVE. Roslyn Brock received a bachelor's degree magna cum laude from Virginia Union University. She earned a master's degree in health services administration from George Washington University and Master of Business Administration from Kellogg School of Management at Northwestern University.

Her professional career includes serving at W.K. Kellogg Foundation in Battle Creek, Michigan, as first responsible liaison, then as program associate for health programs and as the program officer for health programs. Ms. Brock served as chief executive officer of Mfume and director of business and community development at Bon Secours Health System, Inc., Marriottsville, Maryland.

Ms. Brock was elected vice chairman of the NAACP national Board of Directors at the age of 35, the youngest person and the first woman elected to the post. She also serves on the NAACP national Board of Trustees.

Rovenia Brock

HEALTH. Rovenia Brock received a Bachelor of Science degree in foods and nutrition from Virginia State University. She received a Master of Science in community nutrition and journalism and earned her Ph.D. in nutritional science from Howard University in Washington, D.C.

Her professional career includes serving as an assistant professor of nutrition, Department of Nutritional Sciences, University of the District of Columbia, Washington, D.C.; she has served as a co-host of *Heart and Soul TV*, Black Educational Television (BET), and is a former broadcast nutrition consultant, NBC 4 TV, Washington, D.C.

Rebecca Snyder Bromley

JUDGE. Rebecca Snyder Bromley received a Bachelor of Arts degree from Smith College and earned her Juris Doctor degree from the University of Virginia in 1971. She also received a master's in judicial studies from the University of Nevada–Reno.

Her professional career includes serving in private law practice from 1973 to 1981. She served as a district judge referee from 1981 to 1984 then as presiding judge of the El Paso County Court. In June 2001 she was appointed judge to the Colorado Fourth Judicial District Court by Governor Owens.

Fabienne Brooks

LAW ENFORCEMENT. Fabienne Brooks attended Western Washington University and is a 1996 Atlantic fellow in public policy. She is a 1995 graduate of the FBI National Academy and a 1999 graduate of the Pacific Northwest Command College.

Her professional career includes serving in every rank in the King County Sheriff's office: She served as a patrol officer, field training officer, media relations officer, major crimes investigator, supervisor, and precinct commander; she spent five years as the chief of detectives. She retired in August 2004 as chief of the criminal investigations division after over 26 years. She is now president of Brooks S-A-

C, Inc., a consulting practice specializing in training, expert witness evaluations and motivational speaking.

Janice M. Brooks

MILITARY. Janice M. Brooks is a native Baltimore, Maryland. She attended College at Frostburg State University in Maryland where she earned a Bachelor of Science degree in health and physical education. After teaching high school in the Baltimore City Public School System, she enlisted into the United States Marine Corps in December 1974. She attended boot camp at Marine Corps Recruit Depot, Parris Island, South Carolina.

She served on active duty from June 1975 to April 1997. Taking advantage of off-duty educational opportunities, she earned a Master of Arts from Webster University while stationed at Marine Corps Recruit Depot, Parris Island, South Carolina.

During her 22-year Marine Corps career, her primary military occupational specialty (MOS) was that of contract specialist. She also held two secondary occupational specialties as health and fitness instructor and drill instructor. She has been assigned to Marine Air Ground Task Force Training Center, Twenty-nine Palms, California; Marine Corps Logistics Base, Barstow, California; Marine Corps Base Smedley D. Butler, Okinawa, Japan; Marine Barracks "8th & I," Washington, D.C.; Marine Corps Recruit Depot, Parris Island, South Carolina; and Marine Corps Base Camp Lejeune, North Carolina. Her final duty station was Camp Butler, Okinawa, Japan, where she served two "in-place consecutive overseas tours" for a total of seven years.

After retirement from the military, she served as naval science instructor for Naval JROTC at Curtis High School in Washington State.

Adriane M. Brown

BUSINESS EXECUTIVE. Adriane M. Brown received a Bachelor of Science degree in environmental health from Old Dominion University and she earned a master's degree in management when she completed the Alfred P. Sloan fellow program at Massachusetts Institute of Technology (MIT).

Her professional career includes serving in 1980 as a shift supervisor at the Electronic Products plant in Raleigh, North Carolina. In 1984 she moved to Santa Clara, California, as an electronic product senior sales representative; in 1991 she was appointed manager of new business development for environmental products, business director—automotive substrates in 1993; and in 1996 was named division vice president and business director—automotive substrates. After 19 years with Corning, Inc., she joined Honeywell in 1999 as vice president and general manager of aircraft landing systems in South Bend, Indiana.

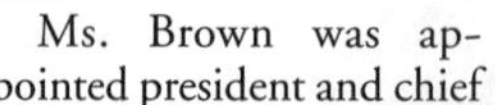

Ms. Brown was appointed president and chief executive officer of Honeywell Transportation Systems in January 2005. She serves also as president of Honeywell Turbo Technologies, a division of Transportation Systems.

Beth A. Brown

AEROSPACE. Beth A. Brown received a Bachelor of Science in astrophysics summa cum laude from Howard University. She earned a Master of Science degree in astronomy from the University of Michigan and a Ph.D. in astronomy from the University of Michigan.

Dr. Brown was the first black woman to capitalize on her Ph.D. in astronomy, finding employment outside of academe. She works in the Astrophysics Data Facility at the NASA Goddard Space Flight Center in Greenbelt, Maryland, devoting her time to multiwavelength research on elliptical galaxies, with data from the ROSAT X-ray satellite and the Chandra X-ray Observatory. Dr. Brown is also engaged in astrophysics educational outreach targeting middle and high school students. She is the National Space Science Data Center (NSSDC) principal astrophysics acquisition scientist. In this role she is NSSDC's primary interface to such Science Archive Research Centers (SARCs) as the High Energy Astrophysics SARC at Goddard, the Multi-Mission Archive at STScl (MAST) and the Infrared Science Archive (IRSA) at Caltech.

Corrine Brown

ELECTED OFFICIAL. Corrine Brown is a native of Jacksonville, Florida. She received a Bachelor of Science degree from Florida Agricultural and Mechanical University in Tallahassee, Florida. She earned a Master of Arts from Florida Agricultural and Mechanical University, Tallahassee, Florida, in 1971.

Her professional career includes serving as an edu-

cator at the University of Florida, Edward Waters College, and Florida Community College in Jacksonville, Florida. She served as a Florida state representative from 1983 to 1993 and in 1992 she was elected a United States representative to the 103rd and to the six succeeding Congresses.

Dorothy Brown

ELECTED OFFICIAL (FIRST). Dorothy Brown graduated magna cum laude from Southern University in Louisiana and received a Master's in Business Administration with honors from DePaul University. She earned her Juris Doctor degree with honors from Chicago-Kent College of Law and she is also a certified public accountant.

She made history when she was elected as the clerk of the circuit court of Cook County in 2000, becoming the first African-American to hold that position. She was re-elected to a second term in 2004. As the official keeper of records for all judicial matters brought into one of the largest unified court systems in the world, she is responsible for managing an annual operating budget of more than $100 million and has a workforce of over 2,300 employees.

Gayleatha B. Brown

GOVERNMENT OFFICIAL. Gayleatha B. Brown received a Bachelor of Arts degree and Master of Arts degree from Howard University and conducted post-graduate work in international relations at the John Hopkins University School of Advanced International Studies, both in Washington, D.C. She is pursuing a doctorate at the University of South Africa in Pretoria, South Africa.

Her professional career includes serving as a special assistant to the United States Agency for International Development (USAID) as assistant administration for Africa and a legislative assistant in the United States Congress (House of Representatives). She joined the Department of State and has represented the Department of State at the Organization of Economic Cooperation and Development Export Credit Arrangement negotiations as desk officer for the U.S. Export-Import Bank in the Department's Bureau of Economic and Business Affairs. She served as representative, regional United States Agency for International Development (USAID), and finance and development officer at the United States embassies in Paris and Abidjan. She has served as chief of the economic and commercial sections at the United State embassies in Harare, Zimbabwe, and Dar es Salaam, Tanzania.

Ms. Brown was selected to serve as the United States consul general at the American Consulate General and concurrently as the United States deputy permanent observer to the Council of Europe in Strasbourg, France.

Irma Hunter Brown

ELECTED OFFICIAL (FIRST). Irma Hunter Brown is a native of Tampa, Florida. She received an associate degree from Shorter College in North Little Rock, Arkansas, and a bachelor's degree in history and elementary education magna cum laude from the University of Arkansas at Pine Bluff. She attended the Memphis State University, now the University of Memphis and D.C. Teachers College in Washington, D.C.

Her professional career includes serving in the Washington, D.C., and Memphis, Tennessee, public school systems; as president of Shorter College; and as vice chairman, Arkansas Educational Television Network Foundation. In 1980 she was the first African American woman elected to the Arkansas House of Representatives and served that body until 1998.

Ms. Brown was elected state senator representing Little Rock in the Arkansas Senate in 2002, becoming the first African American woman to serve as a state senator in the history of the Arkansas Senate.

Janice Rogers Brown

JUDGE. Janice Rogers Brown is a native of Greenville, Alabama. She received a Bachelor of Arts degree from California State University; in 1977 she earned her Jurist Doctor degree from University of California School of Law; in 2004 she received an LL.M. degree from the University of Virginia School of Law.

Her experience includes serving as a deputy attorney general, California Department of Justice, Attorney General office; as secretary and general counsel, State of California Business, Transportation and Housing Agency; in private practice; as the legal affairs secretary for Governor Pete Wilson's office; as an associate justice on the California Court of Appeals for the Third District; and as an adjunct professor at the University of the Pacific McGeorge School of Law. Since 1996 she has served as an associate justice on the California Supreme Court.

Kay Stanfield Brown

JUDGE. A. Kay Stanfield Brown received her Juris Doctor degree from the University of Michigan School of Law in 1977. Her professional career includes serving as senior assistant general counsel for the Southeastern Michigan Transportation Authority in Detroit. In 1981 she was engaged in private law practice and in May 1987 she was appointed magistrate by the judges of the Michigan 46th District Court.

Leilani Brown

FINANCE. Leilani Brown received a Bachelor of Arts degree in international studies from Middlebury College and a master's degree in public administration and management from New York University.

Her professional career includes serving at NatWest Bank where at 23, she was said to be the youngest officer company-wide. She served with Chubb and Son, Inc. and joined AIG as vice president and corporate markets profit center executive. Ms. Brown directs the growth and profitability of the division's core employer/employee portfolio. AIG is the world's leading global insurance and financial services organization.

Lisa L. Brown

EDUCATION. Lisa L. Brown received her undergraduate degree in aerospace engineering from the University of Colorado at Boulder and her doctorate in geosciences from Penn State University where she worked with Dr. James Kasting using computer models to study the chemistry and climate of the primitive atmospheres of Earth and Mars.

She serves as the director of the Pennsylvania Space Grant Consortium, a NASA–funded research, education and outreach program at Pennsylvania State University with affiliates across Pennsylvania

Lucy Chernow Brown

JUDGE. Lucy Chernow Brown received a Bachelor of Arts degree from the University of Rochester in Rochester, New York, and earned a Masters of Art degree from Columbia University in New York City. She received her Juris Doctor (magna cum laude) from Nova University Law Center, Ft. Lauderdale, Florida.

She was engaged in private law practice prior to serving as judge in the civil, family and probate division of the State of Florida 15th Judicial Circuit. Since January 1991 she has served as circuit judge for the State of Florida, 15th Circuit.

Nancy E. Brown

MILITARY. Nancy E. Brown is a native of Glen Gove, New York, and was raised in Marion, Illinois. She received a bachelor's degree from Stephens College in Columbia, Missouri, and a Master of Science degree in communications systems management from the Naval Postgraduate School in Monterey, California. She earned a Master of Arts degree in national security

and strategic studies from Naval War College in Newport.

Her professional career includes serving in numerous positions of increased authority and responsibility to include serving in 1993 as commander of the Naval Computer and Telecommunications Station Cutler, Downeast, Maine; she was selected for assignment to the National Security Council staff at the White House where she reported for duty in August 1995; in July 1997 she assumed command of the Naval Computer and Telecommunications Area Master Station Atlantic headquartered in Norfolk; in June 1999 she returned to the White House as the deputy director, White House Military office. It was during this tour she was selected for rear admiral. In October 2000 she reported to the chief of naval operations as deputy director and Fleet Liaison, Space, Information Warfare, Command and Control (N6B); in August 2002 she assumed duties as vice director for command, control, communications, and computer systems (J6), the Joint Staff; in August 2004 she deployed to Iraq becoming the first Multi-National Force-Iraq C6 headquartered in Baghdad. She returned to the Joint Staff in April 2005.

Vice Admiral Brown has served as the director, command, control, communications and computer systems (C4 Systems), the Joint Staff. She is the principal advisor to the chairman, Joint Chiefs of Staff on all C4 systems matters within the Department of Defense.

Renee Brown

SPORTS EXECUTIVE. Renee Brown received a bachelor's degree from the University of Nevada in Las Vegas. While at college she was a three-sport superstar and she co-captained the 1973-74 Lady Wolves basketball team to the Southern Nevada–area championship, leading the team and division in scoring. She was also a starting pitcher for the softball team and a star (offensive) hitter for the volleyball team.

She served as an assistant coach for the women's basketball teams at the University of Kansas, Sanford University, and San Jose State University. Her Sanford team won the NCAA tournament in 1990 and earned a trip to the Final Four in 1991. During the 1995–96 seasons, she served as an assistant coach to Tara VanDerveer for the gold medal–winning USA Basketball Women's National Team in Colorado Springs, where she helped with game preparation, player conditioning and scouting. She joined the Women National Basketball Association (WNBA) in September 1996 as director of player personnel and was promoted to senior director in October 1999. She was named vice president of player personnel in March 2000.

Shona Brown

TECHNOLOGY EXECUTIVE. Shona Brown received a Bachelor of Science degree in computer systems engineering from Carleton University in Canada and a master's degree in economics and philosophy as a Rhodes Scholar from Oxford University. She earned a doctorate degree from Stanford University's Department of Industrial Engineering and Engineering Management.

Dr. Brown has taught in the Department of Industrial Engineering and Graduate School of Business at Stanford University and within McKinsey's mini–MBA program. Her experience includes extensive work in consumer software and hardware technology, online consumer services, and Internet media markets. She served as a partner at McKinsey and Company where she was a leader of the global strategy practice. In 2003, she joined Google, Inc., as vice president for business operations.

Yvette McGee Brown

JUDGE (FIRST). Yvette McGee Brown received her Juris Doctor degree from Ohio State University College of Law in 1985. Her professional career includes serving as chief legal counsel for the Ohio Department of Rehabilitation and Corrections and the Ohio Department of Youth Services. She serves as lead judge of Franklin County Court of Common Pleas, domestic

relations division in Columbus, Ohio. At 32, she became the youngest elected judge in Ohio and the first African American to serve on the Franklin County Court of Domestic Relations.

Yvonne Brown

ELECTED OFFICIAL. Yvonne Brown is a native of Toledo, Ohio. She received a bachelor's degree from Jackson State University in Jackson, Mississippi. She was elected as the second female mayor of the City of Tchula, Mississippi. She serves as the only black female Republican mayor in the state of Mississippi. She was the Republican candidate in the Second Congressional District against Congressman Bennie G. Thompson (D–Miss).

Virginia Brown-Waite

ELECTED OFFICIAL. Virginia Brown-Waite is a native of Albany, New York. She received a Bachelor of Science degree from State University of New York in Albany, New York, in 1976, and earned a Masters of Science from Russell State College in Troy, New York, in 1984.

Her professional career includes serving as the legislative director, New York State Senate; as a commissioner for Hernando County, Florida, from 1990 to 1992; as a Florida state senator from 1992 to 2002. She was elected as a United States representative to the 108th Congress and to the succeeding Congress.

Kim A. Browne

JUDGE. Kim A. Browne received a Bachelor of Arts degree in economics from the University of Cincinnati and earned her Juris Doctor from the Ohio State University in 1993.

Her professional career includes serving as a special assistant to DAS human resources deputy director (1994–1996); as a mediator; in private law practice; and as an adjunct professor. In January 1994, Governor Bob Taft appointed her judge, Ohio's Franklin County Court of Common Pleas of the Domestic Relations Court and Juvenile Branch in Columbus, Ohio.

Nora Brownell

GOVERNMENT OFFICIAL. Nora Brownell is a native of Erie, Pennsylvania, and attended Syracuse University.

Her professional career includes serving as the deputy executive assistant to former Pennsylvania Governor Richard Thornburgh. In 1987 she joined Meridian Bancorp, Inc. as the senior vice president of corporate affairs unit. From 1997 to 2001 she served as a member of the Pennsylvania Public Utility Commission (PUC). She was a leader in the administration of Pennsylvania's Electric Choice Consumer Education Program.

Ms. Brownell was nominated by President George W. Bush to the Federal Energy Regulatory Commission (FERC) on April 30, 2001. She was confirmed by the United States Senate on May 25, 2001, for a term that expired June 30, 2006.

Ruth E. Bruch

BUSINESS EXECUTIVE. Ruth E. Bruch received a bachelor's degree in finance from the University of Iowa.

Her professional career includes serving as president and chief operating officer of Zonetrader.com, a Chicago-based start-up, now part of Dovebid, which implemented Web-based asset management and exchange programs; as a principal with JGA Consulting in Chicago; as vice president and chief information officer (CIO) at Visteon Corporation of Dearborn, Michigan, one of the world's largest automotive suppliers.

Since April 2002, Ms. Bruch has served as senior vice president and CIO of Lucent Technologies.

Cindy H. Bruner

JUDGE. Cindy H. Bruner received her Juris Doctor degree from the University of Colorado School of Law. She served as a deputy district attorney with the Adams County District Attorney's office. In 1991 she was appointed judge to the Colorado 17th Judicial District, Adams County.

Catherine M. Brunson

JUDGE. Catherine M. Brunson received a Bachelor of Science from Florida State University and earned her Juris Doctor degree from Florida State University's College of Law.

Her professional career includes serving with the Office of Public Defender, 1st Judicial Circuit in 1975; on the State Retirement Commission from 1975 to 1976; and as an assistant county attorney in the office of the County Attorney in Palm Beach County for seven years. Since 1994 she has served as a judge in the Fifteenth Judicial Circuit.

Christine M. Bruzek-Kohler

MILITARY. Christine M. Bruzek-Kohler is a native of Camden, New Jersey. She received a Bachelor of Science in nursing from Villanova University and her commission as an ensign in 1974. She received a master's of education from Providence College. She earned a Master of Arts degree and doctorate degree in education from George Washington University. She is a fellow in the American College of Healthcare Executives.

Her professional career includes serving as charge nurse, National Naval Medical Center, Bethesda, Maryland; as staff nurse, United States Naval Regional Medical Center, Naples, Italy; as ambulatory care coordinator, Naval Hospital Newport, Rhode Island; as director of academic support department, Naval School of Health Sciences, Bethesda; as head of enlisted training programs, Naval Health Sciences Education and Training Center; as director of nursing/acting executive officer, Naval Hospital Great Lake, Illinois; as director of nursing, United States Naval Hospital, Guam; as executive officer, Naval Hospital, at Pensacola, Florida; as commanding officer, Naval Hospital, Lemoore, California; as assistant deputy chief for medical operations support, Bureau of Medicine and Surgery, in Washington, D.C.

Rear Admiral Bruzek-Kohler serves as the 21st director of the Navy Nurse Corps and the Naval medical inspector general in Bethesda, Maryland.

Beth Ann Bryan

GOVERNMENT OFFICIAL. Beth Ann Bryan received a bachelor's degree in elementary education and English from Houston Baptist University in 1969 and earned a masters in education guidance and counseling from the University of Houston.

She served as education policy director for then Texas Governor George W. Bush during the first year of his administration in 1995. Thereafter, she served as advisor to the Texas Governor's Business Council and was a key leader in the Governor's Reading Initiative. She also served as program director for the First Lady's Family Literacy Initiative for Texas. On Mach 8, 2001, she was appointed senior advisor to the U.S. Secretary of Education, in Washington, D.C.

T. J. Bryan

EDUCATION. T. J. Bryan is a native of Maryland. She received bachelor's and master's degrees in English from Morgan State College in Baltimore, Maryland. She earned a doctoral degree in English language literature, specializing in modern American literature, early American literature, and Victorian literature. She is also a graduate of the Harvard University Management Development Program and Leadership Maryland.

Her professional career includes serving from 1982 with

the English faculty of Coppin State College in Baltimore, rising to the rank of dean of arts and sciences in 1991. While at Coppin State, she also served as chair of the Department of Languages, Literature, and Journalism; as director of the honors program; and as founding dean of the honors division. In 1998, she was named associate vice chancellor for academic affairs for the 13-campus University System of Maryland. She was the primary author of two major research studies on educational equity in Maryland that led to legislation in 2000 and 2001 and the creation of a governor's task force and the passage of legislation in 2002 that provided a college-intervention program and guaranteed financial assistance to low-income students. In 2002, she was selected to serve as the chief academic officer and chief student affairs for the Pennsylvania State System of Higher Education.

Ms. Bryan was elected chancellor of Fayetteville State by the Board of Governors of the 16-campus University of North Carolina. She assumed this office on July 1, 2003.

Castell Vaughn Bryant

EDUCATION. Castell Vaughn Bryant is a native of Jasper, Florida. She received a bachelor's degree in library science and a master's degree in adult education administration from Florida A&M University. She earned a doctorate in vocational/adult education from Nova Southeastern University. She has done further study at Harvard University's Management Development program, Florida International University, and Lewis College of Business, Detroit, Michigan.

Her professional career includes serving as interim chief executive officer of Florida Memorial College; as interim president of the Wolfson Campus, and from 1981 to 1985 as dean of Students at Wolfson Campus; as president of Miami Dade's North Campus where she supervised two centers, the School of Justice, the School of Entertainment Technologies and the School of Fire and Environmental Sciences; and as president of the Medical Center Campus of Miami Dade College in Miami, where she was responsible for overseeing more than 5,000 students, the Center for Homeland Security, the School of Nursing and the School and Allied Health Technologies.

Dr. Bryant was appointed interim president of Florida A&M University (FAMU). She is the first woman to hold this post in the 117-year history of the university.

Peggy Bryant

JUDGE. Peggy Bryant received a Bachelor of Arts (magna cum laude) from Miami University in Oxford, Ohio, and earned her Juris Doctor degree (cum laude) from the Ohio State University College of Law in Columbus, Ohio. She served in private law practice in Ohio. She was appointed judge to the Franklin County Municipal Court in 1985. In 1987 she was appointed judge to the Ohio Tenth District Court of Appeals.

Wanda G. Bryant

JUDGE. Wanda G. Bryant is a native of Southport, North Carolina. She is a product of Brunswick County Public Schools and received a Bachelor of Arts degree from Duke University in 1977. During her time at Duke, she was chosen to study for a summer at Oxford University in England. She earned her Juris Doctor degree from North Carolina Central University in Durham, North Carolina.

Her professional career includes serving as the first female and first African-American prosecutor of the Thirteenth Prosecutorial District of North Carolina in 1983. From 1983 to 1988, she served as the first staff attorney for the police executive research forum in Washington, D.C.; in 1989, she became an assistant United States attorney in the Office for the District of Columbia; in 1993, she served as a senior deputy attorney general for the Office of the Attorney General. She also served as the first director of the newly established citizen's rights division of the Department of Justice. In 2001 she was appointed judge by Governor Mike Easley to the North Carolina Court of Appeals.

Claire Buchan

GOVERNMENT OFFICIAL. Claire Buchan received a bachelor's degree from Michigan State University.

Her professional career includes serving as the press secretary for Congressman H. James Saxton. During the Reagan administration she worked for the Department of Commerce in the International Trade Administration; she served as deputy communications director at the Republican National Committee; and served as press secretary for the U.S. trade representative. She served in President George H.W. Bush's administration as the deputy assistant secretary of public affairs at the Treasury Department. After leaving the government, she served as vice president for communication at ServiceMaster in Chicago.

Ms. Buchan returned to the White House during President George W. Bush's administration to serve as assistant secretary at the White House. She was appointed chief of staff at the Department of Commerce.

Mary Kate Buckley

BUSINESS EXECUTIVE. Mary Kate Buckley is a native of Massena, New York. She received a Bachelor of Arts in economics and English from College of the Holy Cross in 1982 and earned a Master of Business Administration from Stern School of Business Administration at New York University in 1991.

Her professional career includes serving with the financial advertising and public relations company Doremus & Co. and for Grey Advertising, both in New York; she worked for the Walt Disney Company for eleven years in New York, Hong Kong and Paris where she held several different positions in finance, marketing and strategic planning. Her last position at Disney was director of new ventures for Disney consumer products in Paris, where she managed the design, production, marketing and distribution of Disney's European licensed catalogues. In 1998 she joined Nike as director of new business development; from 1998 to 1999, she served as director of nike.com; from 1999 to 2001, she served as vice president of nike.com.

Ms. Buckley was appointed vice president and general manager of Americas & NIKE Bauer Hockey.

Christine B. Bucklin

BUSINESS EXECUTIVE. Christine B. Bucklin received a Bachelor of Arts degree in mathematics summa cum laude from Dartmouth College and earned a Master of Business Administration from the Stanford Graduate School of Business where she was the first woman to graduate first in her class.

Her professional career includes serving for ten years with McKinsey & Company as management consultant and partner. Ms. Bucklin serves as chief operating officer of Internet Brands, Inc., a leading operator of media and e-commerce sites for "large ticket" consumer purchases such as cars and mortgages. Founded as CarsDirect.com, the company also operates other websites including Autos.com, LoanStore.com, LoanApp.com and BestRate.com

Elaine Bucklo

JUDGE. Elaine Bucklo received her Juris Doctor degree from Northwestern University School of Law in 1972. She then served as a clerk for the Honorable Robert Sprecher of the United States Circuit Court of Appeals for the 7th Circuit. She worked in private law practice from 1974 to 1979. From 1978 to 1980, she taught at the University of California at Davis School of Law. She returned to private practice in 1980.

She served as a magistrate judge in Chicago from 1985 to 1994 and is the first United States magistrate judge to become a federal judge in Chicago. She is judge of the United States District Court for the Northern District of Illinois.

L. Gail Buckner

GOVERNMENT OFFICIAL. L. Gail Buckner received a bachelor's degree from Georgia State University, and earned a master's degree from Brenau University. She is a graduate of the 169th session of the FBI National Academy. She began her service with the Georgia Bureau of Investigation in 1981 as an undercover operative and specialized in corruption and white-collar crime cases. She has served as director of personnel facilitating overseeing the modernization of human resource projects and as director of legislative and intergovernmental affairs coordinating legislative activities both with the Georgia General Assembly and with the U.S. Congress.

She was appointed as a board member to the Georgia Board of Pardons and Paroles by Governor Sonny Perdue on January 1, 2005.

Sarah Buel

EDUCATION. Sarah Buel received a Bachelor of Arts degree from Harvard University in 1987 and earned her Juris Doctor degree Harvard Law School in 1990. After escaping domestic violence in her own life and finding very little support and laws to help her, she became an advocate for the legal rights of battered women and abused children. She is co-founder and co-direc-

tor of the National Training Center on Domestic and Sexual Violence. Her work and the work of hundreds of other victims and advocates helped create the Violence Against Women Act in 1994. This act and the 1996 additions to the act recognize that domestic violence is a crime. She serves as a clinical professor at the University of Texas Law School. She has served battered women and abused children for 27 years as a lawyer, advocate, educator, author and lecturer.

Ella Bully-Cummings

LAW ENFORCEMENT (FIRST). Ella M. Bully-Cummings received a bachelor's degree with honors in public administration from Madonna University in December 1993, and earned her Juris Doctor degree (cum laude) from the Detroit College of Law at Michigan State University in January 1998.

Chief Bully-Cummings began her career with the Detroit Police Department at 19 in July 1977. She has served in all but one rank within the Detroit Police Department. She has served as the commanding officer of the crime prevention section, the public information section, and the 8th precinct; served as acting deputy chief of the western operations bureau; commanded the department's special response team, tactical services section, housing section, and the traffic enforcement, mounted and aviation units. She retired from the Detroit Police Department in July 1999 and then pursued a law practice.

She rejoined the Detroit Police Department on May 13, 2002, when Mayor Kwame M. Kilpatrick appointed her as the department's first female assistant chief. On November 3, 2003, she was appointed chief of the Detroit Police Department by Mayor Kwame M. Kilpatrick. She is the first female to serve as chief in the department's history.

A'Lelia Bundles

JOURNALISM. A'Lelia Bundles received a bachelor's degree magna cum laude from Harvard/Radcliffe College and earned her masters degree from Columbia University School of Journalism.

Her professional career includes serving with NBC News from 1976 to 1989 in New York, Washington, Atlanta, and Houston. During that time she covered the the Rev. Jesse Jackson's 1984 presidential campaign, the 1984 Democratic Convention, the Atlanta child murders, and several hurricanes. She served as deputy bureau chief of ABC News in Washington from 1996 to 1999 after working 20 years as a network television producer at ABC News and NBC News. She was appointed the director of talent development for ABC News in Washington and New York.

Ms. Bundles is the great-great-granddaughter of Madam C.J. Walker. She penned a best-selling biography of Mrs. Walker titled *On Her Own Ground: The Life and Times of Madam C.J. Walker*.

Leslie Burger

LIBRARIAN. Leslie Burger attended library school at the University of Maryland in College Park and also has a master's degree in organizational behavior from the University of Hartford.

In 1991 Ms. Burger founded her consulting firm, Library Development Solutions. In her consulting practice, Ms. Burger has guided more than 100 urban, suburban, and rural public libraries, academic and special libraries, state libraries, and single and multi-type library cooperatives across the United States in strategic planning, space needs assessments, evaluating, and program implementation. She has directed the Princeton Public Library since 1999. From 1999 to 2004, she planned and funded the new 58,000 square foot Princeton Public Library which opened to great community excitement in April 2004. Ms. Burger served as president of the American Library Association from July 2006 to June 2007.

Anne M. Burke

JUDGE. Anne M. Burke is a native of Chicago and received her Bachelor of Art degree in education from DePaul University in 1976 and her J.D. degree from IIT/Chicago-Kent College of Law in 1983. She was admitted to the Federal Court, Northern District of Illinois in 1983, the U. S. Court of Appeals for the Seventh Circuit in 1985, and certified for the trial bar, Federal District Court in 1987.

That same year, Governor James Thompson appointed her to the Court of Claims and she was reappointed to the court in 1991 by Governor Jim Edgar. She was appointed special counsel to the governor for child welfare service in 1994 and in 1995 she was appointed to the Appellate Court, First District. Judge Burke was elected to the Appellate Court, First District for a full term in 1996 and is currently serving in that position.

Rossatte Y. Burke

MILITARY (FIRST). Rossatte Y. Burke is a native of Pittsburgh, Pennsylvania. She graduated from high school in Pittsburgh; she then completed Harlem Hospital School of Nursing in the City of New York. She received a Bachelor of Science degree in nursing from Aldelphi University, Garden City, New York. She earned a Master's of Science degree in health care administration from C.W. Post College, Long Island University, New York. Her military schools attended include Academy of Health Science, Army Medical Department Officer Basic Course; Academy of Health Sciences, Army Medical Department; Reserve Component General Staff College; Academy of Health Sciences, Chief Nurse Orientation Course; National Defense University, Reserve Component National Security Course; Army War College. She was appointed a first lieutenant in the United States Army Reserves on February 12, 1962.

From April 1962 to December 1966, she was assigned as general duty nurse and later as supervisor and instructor with the 808th Station Hospital. In February 1967, she was assigned supervisor and instructor, 912th Surgical Hospital. From February 1972 to February 1975, she was assigned as medical surgical nurse, 912th Surgical Hospital. In February 1975, she was selected as chief nurse, 74th Field Hospital. On September 15, 1978, she was promoted to lieutenant colonel in the United States Army Reserves.

From December 1980 to May 1983, she served as chief nurse, 815th Station Hospital. In May 1983, she was selected as deputy chief nurse, 364th General Hospital, as assistant chief nurse for the 364th General Hospital. On September 14, 1983, she was promoted to colonel in the United States Army Reserves. In May 1985, she was assigned as the chief nurse, 364th General Hospital and later as chief of nursing service. From February 1993 to April 1994, she was assigned as chief nurse at Headquarters, State Area Command and New York Army National Guard. On February 12, 1993, she was selected colonel in the New York National Guard.

In April 1994, Major General Burke was selected adjutant general, Headquarters and Headquarters Detachment, State Area Command, New York Army National Guard. She was promoted to brigadier general on July 28, 1995, the first woman general in the 220-year history of the New York Army National Guard. She is the first female assistant adjutant general in New York State and of the Army National Guard.

She was the first female to receive the brevet promotion to major general in the history of the New York Army National Guard and in the Army National Guard. She retired from the New York Army National Guard in February 1997.

Sheila P. Burke

GOVERNMENT OFFICIAL. Sheila P. Burke holds a master of public administrative from Harvard University. Her professional career includes serving as deputy staff director of the Senate Committee on Finance from 1982 to 1985; as deputy chief of staff to the majority leader from 1985 to 1986; as the chief of staff to former Majority Leader Bob Dole from 1986 to 1996. She was executive dean and lecturer at the John F. Kennedy School of Government at Harvard University. In June 2000, she was appointed Smithsonian's Under Secretary for American Museums and National Programs.

She is an adjunct faculty member of Georgetown University Public Policy Institute. She also serves as an adjunct lecturer at the John F. Kennedy School of Government at Harvard.

Yvonne B. Burke

ELECTED OFFICIAL (FIRST). Yvonne B. Burke is a native of Los Angeles, California. She attended the University of California at Berkeley and received her undergraduate degree from UCLA. She earned her Juris Doctor degree from USC's School of Law where she became the first black woman to be accepted to a sorority.

Her professional career includes serving as a state deputy corporations commissioner in 1964 and as a hearing officer for the Los Angeles Police Commission. After the Watts riots in 1965, she was active in efforts to secure legal representation for persons arrested during the riot and became an attorney for the McCone Commission, which investigated the causes of the riots. In 1966 she was elected to the state assembly, becoming the first African-American female elected to the state assembly; in 1972 she was elected to the United States Congress. She became the first female elected to the House from California in 20 years and the first African-American congresswoman from California. In 1979 she was appointed a Los Angeles County supervisor for the Fourth District. She served as chair of the board of supervisors from 1993 to 2002 and has served as a member of the Los Angeles County Board of Supervisors, Second District, since 1992.

Elizabeth Burmaster

EDUCATION. Elizabeth Burmaster received both her bachelor's degree and master's degree from the University of Wisconsin. She has served as both a teacher and administrator at every level from elementary, middle, and high school. She taught music in Madison elementary and middle schools before becoming choral and drama director at Madison East High School. She also served Marquette Middle School as assistant principal, as Madison school district fine arts coordinator, and Hawthome Elementary principal. She served as principal of Madison West High School for nearly a decade.

In April 2001 she was elected to the nonpartisan constitutional office of superintendent of public instruction and was reelected in April 2005 to a second term.

Ursula M. Burns

BUSINESS EXECUTIVE. Ursula M. Burns received a Bachelor of Science degree from Polytechnic Institute of New York in 1980 and a Master of Science degree in mechanical engineering from Columbus University in 1981.

She joined Xerox in 1980 as a mechanical engineering summer intern. She subsequently held several positions in engineering, including product development and planning. In June 1991 she became the executive assistant to Paul A. Allaire, then Xerox chairman and chief executive officer. From 1992 through 2000 she led several business teams including the office color and fax business, office network copying business and the departmental business. In May 2000 she was named senior vice president, corporate strategic services and president of the document systems and solutions group.

Ms. Burns serves as president of business group operations at Xerox Corporation in Stamford, Connecticut. She was named to this position in December 2002. She is also a corporate senior vice president appointed April 2000.

Columba Bush

FIRST LADY (STATE). Columba Bush, formerly Columba Garnica Gallo, was born in Leon, Guanajato, Mexico. She met Governor Jeb Bush in Leon, Mexico, while he was teaching English in an exchange program with his high school.

As Florida's first lady, she dedicates her time and energy to promoting art appreciation among Florida's young people. In 2000 she started the

Arts Recognition Program which honors high school seniors who have demonstrated exemplary talents in music, media, dance, theater or visual arts. She is also the co-founder of the Children's Cultural Education Fund of the Ballet Folklorico, which raises money for the national dance troupe of Mexico. The foundation sponsors free performances of the Ballet Folklorico to school-aged children across the United States.

Laura Bush

FIRST LADY (U.S.). Laura Bush is a native of Midland, Texas. She received a Bachelor of Science degree in education from Southern Methodist University in 1968. She earned her Master of Library Science degree from the University of Texas.

Her professional career includes serving as a public school teacher in Dallas and Houston, Texas. She also served as a public school librarian in Dallas, Houston, and Austin, Texas. In 1977, she met and married George Walker Bush. She has served as the first lady of the state of Texas and now as the First Lady of the United States.

Ms. Bush serves as an honorary ambassador for the United Nations Literacy Decade, serving as an international spokesperson for efforts to educate people throughout the world, especially women and girls. She serves as the leader of President Bush's Helping America's Youth initiative. She works with teacher recruitment programs like Teach For America, the New Teacher Project, and Troops to Teachers. She joined with the Library of Congress to launch the first National Book Festival in Washington, D.C., in September 2001. She supports education campaigns for breast cancer and heart disease.

Patricia A. Butenis

GOVERNMENT OFFICIAL. Patricia A. Butenis is a native of New Jersey. She received a Bachelor of Arts in anthropology from the University of Pennsylvania and earned a Master of Arts in international relations from Columbia University. She also completed the National War College.

Her professional career includes serving at the visa office, field liaison, in the Department of State from 1994 to 1997; as consul general in Warsaw from 1998 to 2001; as consul general in Bogota, Colombia, from 2001 to 2004; as deputy chief of mission at the United States Embassy in Islamabad from 2004 to 2006. On February 16, 2006, she was confirmed by the United States Senate as ambassador to Bangladesh and was sworn in on March 17, 2006.

Gloria Butler

MEDICINE. Gloria Butler received her undergraduate degree at Jackson State University, and later received her medical degree from the Howard University School of Medicine. She then completed the residency program at the University of Alabama–Tuscaloosa Family Practice. She serves as a board certified physician specializing in family medicine at the Vicksburg Clinic.

Kathleen Butler-Hopkins

PERFORMING ARTS. Kathleen Butler-Hopkins received both a bachelor's and master's of music degrees from the Juilliard School and has attended the Curtis Institute of Music in Philadelphia. She holds a Doctor of Musical Arts degree from Yale University School of Music where she was a scholarship student of Broadus Erle, Syoko Aki and Joseph Silverstein, former concertmaster of the Boston Symphony Orchestra. At Yale she was chosen as the School of Music student marshal in the year of her graduation for outstanding work done during the course of her doctoral program.

She is a violinist who has concertized in major forums in the United States and Europe. She is a veteran of both the Tanglewood festival and the "Yale in Norfolk" summer music programs, and her many concert credits include performances in both Carnegie Hall's Weill Recital Hall and Merkin Concert Hall in New York. In addition to her activities as soloist and chamber musician, she has served as assistant concertmaster for the Boston Civic Symphony and as concertmaster for other regional orchestras along the east coast. Since joining the faculty of the University of Alaska–Fairbanks, she has served as concertmaster and soloist with the Fairbanks Symphony and the Arctic Chamber Orchestra and as a member of the Alaska Trio, the Alaska Chamber Ensemble, and the Alaska Chamber Players.

M. Kathleen Butz

JUDGE. M. Kathleen Butz is a native of Auburn, California. She received a Bachelor of Arts degree from the University of California at Davis and earned her Juris Doctor degree from King Hall School of Law at the University of California at Davis in 1981.

She served in private law practice from 1982 to 1996. On November 5, 1996, she was elected to the Nevada County Superior Court. She was reelected to a second term in 2002. She served as presiding judge of the Nevada County Superior Court in 2001–2002 and presiding judge of the family and juvenile court for Nevada County in 2003. In October 2003 she was appointed associate justice by Governor Gray Davis to the California Court of Appeals 3rd District.

Cora Byrd

MILITARY. Cora Byrd is a native of Alabama and joined the New Jersey Army National Guard in 1977. She served as enlisted personnel manager in the directorate of personnel and community services at the New Jersey National Guard Headquarters at Fort Dix, New Jersey. In November 2004, she began serving as the command sergeant major for the 50th Personnel Support Battalion at the National Guard Armory in Lawrenceville, New Jersey. She is the first female command sergeant major in the New Jersey Army National Guard's history.

Susan Bysiewicz

ELECTED OFFICIAL. Susan Bysiewicz is a native of Middletown, where she grew up on a farm and attended public schools. She received a bachelor's degree from Yale University in 1983 and earned her Juris Doctor from Duke University School of Law in 1986.

She served in private law practicing corporate international law at a New York City firm, and at a law firm in Connecticut where she specialized in corporate and banking law. In 1992, she joined the law department of Aetna Insurance Company where she practiced health care and pension law until 1994. She was also elected in 1992 to the Connecticut State Legislature where she served until 1998. In 1998, Ms. Bysiewicz was elected the 72nd Secretary of the State for Connecticut and was re-elected in 2002 and 2006.

Andrea J. Cabral

ELECTED OFFICIAL. Andrea J. Cabral is a native of Providence, Rhode Island. She received a bachelor's degree from Boston College and earned her Juris Doctor from Suffolk University Law School.

Her professional career includes serving as a staff attorney at the Suffolk County Sheriff's office. From 1987 to 1991, she served as an assistant district attorney at the Middlesex County District Attorney's office. In 1991, she served as an assistant attorney general in the Office of the Attorney General including work in the torts division/government bureau and the civil rights/public protection bureau. From 1993 to 1994, she was director of Roxbury District Court Family Violence Project. She became chief of the domestic violence unit at the Suffolk County District Attorney's office in 1994. In 1998, she was promoted to chief of district courts and community prosecutions. On November 2, 2004, she was elected sheriff of Suffolk County, Massachusetts. She was sworn in on January 5,

2005, as the 30th sheriff of Suffolk County, and is the first woman and second black American ever elected in the commonwealth's history to serve as sheriff.

Anna Escobedo Cabral

GOVERNMENT OFFICIAL. Anna Escobedo Cabral is a native of California. She received a bachelor's degree in political science from the University of California and earned a master's degree in public administration with an emphasis in international trade and finance from the John F. Kennedy School of Government at Harvard University.

Her professional career includes serving from 1993 to 1999 as deputy staff director for the United States Senates Judiciary Committee under Chairman Orrin G. Hatch and as executive staff director of the U.S. Senate Republican Conference Task Force on Hispanic Affairs, a position she held since 1991. From 1999 to 2003 she served as president and chief executive officer of the Hispanic Association on Corporate Responsibility, a non-profit organization headquartered in Washington, D.C.

Ms. Cabral was nominated on July 22, 2004, by President Bush to serve as treasurer of the United States. She was confirmed by the United States Senate on November 20, 2004.

Yvonne Darlene Cagle

ASTRONAUT. Yvonne Darlene Cagle is a native of West Point, New York, but considers Novato, California, to be her hometown. Her civilian and military education includes a diploma from Novato High School in Novato, California, in 1977; a Bachelor of Arts degree in biochemistry from San Francisco State University in 1981 and a doctorate in medicine from the University of Washington in 1985; a transitional internship at Highland General Hospital, Oakland, California, in 1985; a certification in aerospace medicine from the School of Aerospace Medicine at Brooks Air Force Base, Texas, in 1988; residency in family practice and Ghent FP at Eastern Virginia Medical School in 1992; certification as a senior aviation medical examiner from the Federal Aviation Administration in 1995. She is a certified FAA aviation medical examiner and ACLS instructor-qualified and has taught fitness courses. She is a clinical assistant professor at UTMB, Galveston. While a United States Air Force Reservist, she was assigned to the Pentagon Flight Medicine/Special Mission Clinic.

Her medical training was sponsored by the Health Professions Scholarship Program through which she received her commission as an officer with the United States Air Force and subsequently was awarded her board certification in family practice. During her initial active duty tour at Royal Air Force Lakenheath, United Kingdom, she was selected to attend the School of Aerospace Medicine at Brooks Air Force Base, Texas. In April 1988, she became certified as a flight surgeon logging numerous hours in a diversity of aircraft. She was actively involved in mission support of aircraft providing medical support and rescue in a variety of aeromedical missions.

From 1994 to 1996, she served as the deputy project manager for Kelsey-Seybold Clinics, practicing as an occupational physician at the NASA–JSC Occupational Health Clinic. In addition to conducting job-related exams, routine health screenings, and providing acute care for on-site injuries and illness, she designed the medical protocols and conducted the screenings for selected NASA remote duty operations. In May 1989, while a flight surgeon assigned to the 48th Tactical Hospital, United Kingdom, she volunteered to serve as the Air Force medical liaison officer for the STS-30 *Atlantis* Shuttle mission to test the Magellan Spacecraft. She was assigned to the Trans Atlantic Landing (TAL) site at Banjul in West Africa to provide emergency rescue and evacuation of the Shuttle crew should it have been required. She has contributed ongoing data to the Longitudinal Study on Astronaut Health and served as a consultant for space telemedicine. She was a member of the NASA working group and traveled to Russia to establish international medical standards and procedures for astronauts. She also conducted health screenings of Mir-18 consultants from the Russian Federation.

Selected by NASA in April 1996, she reported to the Johnson Space Center in August 1996. Having completed two years of training and evaluation, she is qualified for flight assignment as a mission specialist. Currently, she is assigned technical duties in the astronaut office operations planning branch supporting Shuttle and space station.

Mary Beth CaHill

POLITICS. Mary Beth CaHill is a native of Dorchester, Massachusetts, and was raised in Framingham, Massachusetts. She received a Bachelor of Arts degree in political science from Emmanuel College.

Her professional career began as a staff associate and receptionist for former Congressman Robert F. Drinan (D–Mass); she successfully managed Edward J. Markey's campaign for a seat in the United States House of Representatives; she managed the Senate campaigns for Patrick Leahy in Vermont, Claiborne Pell in Rhode Island and Les AuCoin in Oregon; she has served in various positions for the governor of the Commonwealth of Massachusetts including director of federal-state relations under Governor Michael Dukakis from June 1987 to May 1989 and director of the governor's personnel office from May 1988 to April 1990; served as assistant to the president and director of public liaison in Bill Clinton's White House; she served as chief of staff to Senator Edward Kennedy. She has served as campaign manager for John Kerry for President.

Ann Marie Calabria

JUDGE. Ann Marie Calabria is a native of Bryn Mawr, Pennsylvania. She received a Bachelor of Arts degree summa cum laude from Fairleigh Dickinson University in 1977. She earned her Juris Doctor degree from Campbell University School of Law.

Her professional career includes serving in private law practice and with the United States Department of Housing and Urban Development. From 1996 to 2002 she served a judge at Wake County District Court.

She was elected in November 2002 for an eight-year term to the North Carolina Court of Appeals.

Tracy E. Caldwell

ASTRONAUT. Tracy E. Caldwell is a native in Arcadia, California, and graduated from Beaumont High School in Beaumont, California, in 1987. She received a Bachelor of Science degree in chemistry from the California State University at Fullerton in 1993 and a doctorate in physical chemistry from the University of California at Davis in 1997.

Her professional career includes working as an electrician/inside wireman for her father's electrical contracting company doing commercial and light industrial type construction. At the University of California she taught general chemistry laboratory and began her graduate research.

She was selected by NASA in June 1998 and reported for training in August 1998. After completion of her training and evaluation, she qualified for flight assignment as a mission specialist. In 1999 she was first assigned to the Astronaut Office International Space Station (ISS) Operations Branch as a Russian Crusader, participating in the testing and integration of Russian hardware and software products developed for ISS. In 2000, she was assigned prime crew support astronaut for the 5th ISS Expedition crew serving as their representative on technical and operational issues throughout the training and on-orbit phase of their mission. During ISS Increments 4–6, Dr. Caldwell also served as an International Space Station (ISS) spacecraft communicator (CAPCOM) inside Mission Control. In 2003 she transitioned to the Astronaut Shuttle Operations Branch and was assigned to flight software verification in the Shuttle Avionics Integration Laboratory (SAIL) and also worked supporting launch and landing operations at Kennedy Space Center, Florida. She served as lead CAPCOM for Increment 11. Dr. Caldwell is assigned to the crew of STS-118 targeted for launch in 2007. STS-118 will deliver to the station the third starboard truss segment, an external stowage platform, and logistics and supplies in a SPACEHAB single cargo module.

Essie L. Calhoun

BUSINESS EXECUTIVE. Essie L. Calhoun received a bachelor's degree in education, social science from the University of Toledo and a Master of Science degree in administration and supervision from Bowie State University. She holds an honorary doctorate from Roberts Wesleyan College.

Her professional career includes serving in 1982 as a sales representative of Eastman Kodak Company; she has held positions in marketing, sales and public affairs with Eastman Kodak. She was appointed vice president in 1999 and was elected a corporate vice president by the Kodak Board of Directors in July 2000.

Ms. Calhoun serves as chief diversity

officer of Eastman Kodak. She also serves on the senior executive diversity and inclusion council and works with the company's senior leadership as champion of a winning and inclusive culture at Kodak.

Lynne S. Callahan

JUDGE. Lynne S. Callahan is a graduate of the University of Akron and earned her Juris Doctor from the University of Akron School of Law. She served as an Akron police officer; as an assistant director of law and an assistant Summit County prosecutor. She was appointed judge in May 1997 and was elected to the bench in November 1997.

Lynn Calpeter

BUSINESS EXECUTIVE. Lynn Calpeter received a Bachelor of Science degree in business management and applied economics.

Her professional career includes serving in 1993 with GE Plastics where she held a number of positions of increasing responsibility, culminating in her appointment in 1998 as manager, GE Plastics Global PSI; she served as vice president of the GE corporate audit staff in Fairfield, Connecticut. She joined NBC Television Stations division as chief financial officer from 1999 to 2001.

Ms. Calpeter was appointed executive vice president and chief financial officer, NBC Universal in July 2003.

Jane L. Campbell

ELECTED OFFICIAL. Jane L. Campbell received a bachelor's degree from the University of Michigan and has earned a masters degree from Cleveland State University.

Her political career includes serving as a member of the Ohio House of Representatives where she served 12 years and was president of the National Conference of State Legislatures. In 1996 she was elected as a Cuyahoga County commissioner. In November 2001 she was elected as the 55th mayor of the city of Cleveland, Ohio.

Jill Campbell

COMMUNICATIONS. Jill Campbell received a bachelor's degree from the University of Nevada, Las Vegas, and earned her Master of Business Administration degree from Oklahoma City University.

She joined Cox Communications in 1982 as director of communications in Oklahoma City where she also served as customer service manager and acting general manager. She later served in several roles for Cox operations including vice president and general manager for Cox's Bakersfield and Santa Barbara, California, operations; vice president of customer operations for Cox in Phoenix; and vice president and general manager of Cox's Las Vegas operation. In 2001 she was promoted to vice president of Cox's central division.

Ms. Campbell serves as senior vice president of operations for Cox Communications, Inc.

Phyllis C. Campbell

GOVERNMENT OFFICIAL. Phyllis C. Campbell is a native of Steelton, Pennsylvania. She entered the federal service in the transportation division at Defense Distribution Depot in Ogden, Utah, with selection in 1973 into the Depot's management intern program. In 1979 she became a supply systems analyst in the newly formed Defense System Automation Center which later became the DLA System Design Center. In 1982 she returned to the Ogden installation becoming chief with responsibility for all operations and administrative systems and procedures. In 1985 she was promoted to division chief, assuming additional responsibility for a $30 million depot modernization program. In 1989 she reached a career benchmark with her selection as deputy director office of technology and information services.

In 1990 she was selected by the Office of Secretary of Defense to be the deputy for the Corporate Information Management Distribution Prototype Group. This group was chartered to develop a standard distribution system for use throughout the Department of Defense. In 1991 she was reassigned to DLA's Defense Distribution Systems Center as its business manager. In 1993 she returned to the Office of the Secretary of Defense Comptroller's Officer of Financial Review and Analysis. Until her appointment to deputy commander she served as director, distribution operations with the Defense Distribution Center. In January 2005 she was serving as deputy commander, Defense Distribution Center.

Donna A. Caniano

MEDICINE. Donna A. Caniano is a native of Albany, New York. She received a bachelor's degree from Vassar College in Poughkeepsie, New York, in 1972 and earned her Medical Doctor degree from Albany Medical School in Albany, New York, in 1976.

Her professional career includes serving as a professor of surgery and pediatrics at the Ohio State University College of Medicine and Public Health; and as program director of the medical humanities program at the Ohio State University from 1993 to 1997. Dr. Caniano expanded curriculum offerings to include cultural diversity, gender issues, spousal and child abuse, spirituality and disabilities. The medical humanities program at the Ohio State University was recognized as one of four such exemplary programs in the United States by the National Institute of Medicine.

Dr. Caniano serves as surgeon-in-chief at Columbus Children's Hospital and professor of surgery and pediatrics at the Ohio State University College of Medicine and Public Health.

Evelyn Omega Cannon

JUDGE. Evelyn Omega Cannon is a native of New Orleans, Louisiana. She received a Bachelor of Arts degree in history from the University of New Orleans in 1971 and earned her Juris Doctor degree from Duke University School of Law in 1974. She also received a Master of Law from the University of Maryland School of Law in 1983.

Her professional career includes serving as a staff attorney for the public defender service for the District of Columbia, 1976–1977; as an assistant state's attorney, Office of the Attorney General, 1983–1996 (chief of litigation 1991–1996). On December 6, 1996, she was appointed associate judge, Baltimore City Circuit Court, Maryland 8th Judicial Circuit. In 2005 she was appointed judge-in-charge of civil docket.

Tani Gorre Cantil-Sakauye

JUDGE. Tani Gorre Cantil-Sakauye is a second generation Asian-American who grew up in Sacramento, California. She received an associate degree from Sacramento City College and received her bachelor's degree from the University of California at Davis. She earned her Juris Doctor degree from King Hall.

Her professional career includes serving as a deputy district attorney; as the deputy legal affairs counsel to Governor Deukmejian in 1988; in 1990 she was appointed to the Sacramento Municipal Court as the youngest judge to sit on the bench. She has received an appointment as justice on the Third District Court of Appeal in Sacramento, California.

Nancy Cantor

EDUCATION. Nancy Cantor is a native of New York. She received a Bachelor of Arts degree from Sarah Lawrence College in 1974 and earned her doctorate in psychology from Stanford University in 1978.

Her professional career includes serving in a variety of administrative positions encompassing all aspects of a research university from chair of the Department of Psychology at Princeton to dean of the graduate school; and then provost and executive vice president for academic affairs at the University of Michigan. She served as chancellor for the University of Illinois at Urbana-Champaign.

Dr. Cantor serves as the 11th chancellor

and president of Syracuse University as well as distinguished professor of psychology and women's studies in the College of Arts and Sciences.

Maria E. Cantwell

ELECTED OFFICIAL. Maria E. Cantwell was born in Indianapolis, Indiana, and attended public schools in Indianapolis. She received a Bachelor of Arts from Miami University of Ohio in 1980 and pursed an academic course at the Miami University European Center in Luxembourg.

Her professional career includes serving as a public relations consultant; as a Washington state representative 1987–1993. She was elected as a Democrat to the 103rd Congress (January 3, 1993–January 3, 1995) and was an unsuccessful candidate for re-election to the 104th Congress; she was elected as a Democrat to the United States Senate on November 7, 2000.

Shelley Moore Capito

ELECTED OFFICIAL. Shelley Moore Capito is a native of Glendale, West Virginia. She received a bachelor's degree from Duke University in Durham, North Carolina, and a Masters of Education from the University of Virginia in Charlottesville, Virginia.

Ms. Moore has served as a college counselor and was elected to the West Virginia State House of Delegates. In 2000 she was elected a United States Representative from West Virginia and assumed her position on January 3, 2001. She was elected as a Republican to the 107th and to the succeeding Congresses.

Nancy Caplinger

JUDGE. Nancy Caplinger received a bachelor's degree from Washburn University in 1982 and earned her Juris Doctor degree from Washburn Law School in 1985.

Her professional career includes serving as a research attorney at Kansas Supreme Court from 1985 to 1987; as a law clerk at the United State District Court; and in private law practice. She returned to public service in 1995 when she became an assistant United States attorney in Kansas City, Kansas. She also served as the appellate coordinator for the United States Attorney's office, a position she held until she was appointed by Governor Kathleen Sebelius to the Kansas Court of Appeals in October 2004.

Lois Capps

ELECTED OFFICIAL. Lois Capps is a native of Ladysmith, Rusk County, Wisconsin. She received a Bachelor of Science degree from Pacific Lutheran University in Tacoma, Washington and earned a Master of Arts degree from the University of California, Santa Barbara, in 1990.

Her professional career includes serving as a nursing instructor; as a nurse administrator, Yale Hospital, New Haven, Conn.; as director, Teenage Pregnancy and Parenting Project and the Parent and Child Enrichment Center, Santa Barbara County, California; and as an instructor of Santa Barbara City College, Santa Barbara, California.

Ms. Capps was elected a Democrat to the 105th Congress by special election to fill the vacancy caused by the death of her husband, United States Representative Walter Capps, and reelected to the four succeeding Congresses (March 10, 1998 to present).

Blandina Cardenas

EDUCATION (FIRST). Blandina Cardenas is a native of Del Rio, Texas. She received a bachelor's degree in journalism from the University of Texas at Austin and earned a Ph.D. degree in education administration from the University of Massachusetts at Amherst.

She began her career in the public school system in her hometown of Del Rio in 1968, teaching at both the pre-school and high school levels. Her first national recognition came while serving as director of innovative program development for the Edgewood Independent School District. In 1977, President Jimmy Carter

appointed her to serve as commissioner of the administration for children, youth and families in the Department of Health, Education and Welfare where she led the nation's Head Start Program. In 1980, Dr. Cardenas was appointed to the U.S. Commission on Civil Rights where she served for 13 years. Also in 1980, she was an official delegate to the United Nations World Conference of Women in Copenhagen, Denmark. She was an early spokeswoman for the Mexican American civil rights movement and in 1992, was awarded "El Orden del Aguila Azteca," the highest honor bestowed by the Mexican government of a non-citizen. In August 2004, Dr. Cardenas was named president of the University of Texas Pan American in Edinburg, Texas.

Joan B. Carey

JUDGE. Joan B. Carey received a Bachelor of Arts degree from St. Joseph's College in 1961 and earned her Juris Doctor degree from New York Law School in 1966. Her professional career includes serving as a social worker and a public school teacher. She began her legal career as a prosecutor and bureau chief in the Queens County district attorney's office, and later in the Office of the Special Anti-Corruption Prosecutor. In 1978 she was appointed judge by Mayor Edward I. Koch to the New York City Criminal Court; she served as supervising judge of the Criminal Court, New York County, and as an acting justice of the Supreme Court, Criminal Term, New York County. In 1986, Governor Mario Cuomo appointed her to the New York State Court of Claims.

Elaine Carlisle

JUDGE. Elaine Carlisle received a Bachelor of Arts degree in communication from Howard University. She earned her Juris Doctor degree magna cum laude from John Marshall Law School, Atlanta, Georgia.

Her professional career includes serving as an assistant city solicitor at the Municipal Court from 1983 to 1989. In 1989, she was appointed a judge to the Atlanta Municipal Court.

Jean Carnahan

ELECTED OFFICIAL. Jean Carnahan is a native of Washington, D.C. She received a Bachelor of Arts degree in business and public administration from George Washington University in 1955.

Her professional career includes serving as the first lady of Missouri from 1993 to 2000. She was appointed to the United States Senate effective January 2, 2001, to fill the vacancy caused by the death of her husband, Mel Carnahan, who was elected posthumously on November 7, 2000. She served from January 3, 2001, to November 25, 2002, when an elected successor for the remainder of the term took office.

Robin Carnahan

ELECTED OFFICIAL. Robin Carnahan is a native of Rolla, Missouri. She received a bachelor's degree in economics magna cum laude from William Jewell College in Liberty, Missouri. She also studied at Southampton in England. She earned her Juris Doctor degree from the University of Virginia Law School where she served as executive editor of the *Virginia Journal of International Law*.

Her professional career included serving in private law practice. She served as an executive at the Export-Import Bank of the United States where she explored innovative ways to help American companies increase their sale of goods and services abroad. In 1990 she joined the National Democratic Institute in central and Eastern Europe, where she helped rebuild the region's democracies and economics. Ms. Carnahan was elected Missouri's 38th secretary of state in 2004.

Christine Carpenter

JUDGE. Christine Carpenter received her undergraduate degree from the University of Missouri and earned her Juris Doctor degree from Columbia School of Law. Her professional career includes private law practice and being a faculty member of the National Drug

Court. In 1999 she was appointed an associate circuit judge to the Missouri Division IX, Circuit Court.

Dolores Carr

JUDGE. Dolores Carr was the first deputy district attorney in California to specialize in prosecuting sex offenders who fail to register with local authorities. She served in the district attorney's office from 1985 to 2000.

In 2002 she was appointed judge for the family division of Santa Clara County Court. In 2005 she was serving as supervising judge of the Unified Family Court in the Superior Court of Santa Clara County, California.

Helen Carr

EDUCATION. Helen Carr received a Bachelor of Science degree in English and Spanish from Bishop College. She earned a master's degree in education and a doctorate degree from Texas Women's University in Denton, Texas.

She began her professional career in education in 1971 as a public school teacher in Dallas, Texas. She has served with the Contra Costa Community College District as dean of language arts and humanistic studies and related occupations at Los Medanos College and vice chancellor of educational programs and services at the district office.

Dr. Carr was appointed president of Contra Costa Community College in January 1998.

Jovita Carranza

BUSINESS EXECUTIVE. Jovita Carranza received both her bachelor's degree and master's degree from the University of Miami.

She began her career at United Parcel Service in 1976 as a hub clerk. She has served in numerous assignments of increased responsibly and authority. She has served as manager United Parcel Service Central Florida District and as the district manager for Wisconsin. In 1999 she was assigned as district manager for the American region. She was selected to serve as president for Latin America, United Parcel Services. In June 2000, she was assigned as president of international region at United Parcel Service. She has served as vice president for air operations of United Parcel Service since April 2003.

Audrey J. S. Carrion

JUDGE. Audrey J. S. Carrion is a native of New York. She attended Colegio Espiritu Santo in Puerto Rico and received a Bachelor of Arts degree from College of Notre Dame of Maryland in 1981. She earned her Juris Doctor degree from the University of Baltimore School of Law 1984.

She served as assistant attorney general, correctional litigation unit; and as a member, Mayor's Committee on Hispanic Affairs in Baltimore City. On January 11, 1996, she was named associate judge, District Court of Maryland, District 1, Baltimore City; since November 10, 1999, she has served as an associate judge, Baltimore City Court, 8th Judicial Circuit. Since November 2003, she has served as judge-in-charge of family division, 8th Judicial Circuit, Baltimore City.

Julia May Carson

ELECTED OFFICIAL. Julia May Carson is a native of Louisville, Kentucky, and is a graduate of Crispus Attucks High School in Indianapolis, Indiana. She attended Martin University, Indianapolis, Indiana, and Indiana University–Purdue University in Fort Wayne, Indiana.

Her professional career includes serving as a staff assistant to United States Representative Andrew Jacobs, Jr., of Indiana from 1965 to 1972. She was elected a Indiana state representative in 1971 and served in that office from 1972 to 1976; she served as a Indiana state

senator from 1976 to 1990; from 1990 to 1996 she served with the Indianapolis, Indiana, center township trustee. Since January 3, 1997, she served as a United States representative to the 105th and to the four succeeding Congresses.

Majora Carter

COMMUNITY ACTIVIST. Majora Carter received a Bachelor of Arts degree from Wesleyan University and a master's degree from New York University.

She co-designed the proposal for CityRiver, a job-creation, economic and ecological development for the Bronx River. She is a member of the board of the New York City Environmental Justice Alliance and a representative for the Organization of Waterfront Neighborhoods. She co-founded the group Greening for Breathing, dedicated to increasing the number of street trees in the South Bronx. She is an advocate for healthy infrastructure and making connections between green spaces and health. Her most recent project was coordinating the installation of "green roof" technology at the offices of Sustainable South Bronx.

Ms. Carter has been instrumental in coordinating pedestrian- and bicycle-friendly street ends and corridors including the ambitious South Bronx Greenway and the Hunts Point Riverfront Park Plan.

Normia E. Carter

MILITARY. Normia E. Carter entered the United States Air Force in 1974, beginning her successful career as an administration specialist at Plattsburgh Air Force Base in New York.

During her first tour she competed in the Air Force "Tops in Blue" Competition, winning "Best Female Vocalist Award" in 1976 and Best of the Show. In 1977 she cross-trained to the social actions career fields as a drug abuse counselor. After another "Tops in Blue" competition and another "Best Female Vocalist Award," she auditioned for the band career field.

Command Master Chief Carter's assignments include the 590th Air Force Band at McGuire Air Force Base, New Jersey. She served with the United States Air Force Europe Band at Einsiedlerhof Air Station in Germany. She was assigned to Scott Air Force Base in Illinois with the Headquarters Air Mobility Command Band.

She returned to Europe and the United States Air Force Europe Band in 1991 to serve as the first sergeant and vocalist. In 1997 she spearheaded the move of the United States Air Force Europe Band from Einsiedlerhof Air Station to its present duty station, Sembach Air Base, Germany. During her extended tour she also served as regional band superintendent resource advisory and interim band manager. In August 1998 she became the band director of the Band of the Pacific–Hawaii.

Rosalynn Carter

FIRST LADY (U.S.). Rosalynn Carter is a native of Plains, Georgia, and a graduate of Plains High School. She received a bachelor's degree from Georgia Southwestern College in 1946. She holds honorary degrees from Tift College and Morehouse College.

She has served as the first lady of the state of Georgia and as the first lady of the United States. She is married to the former Georgia Governor and President Jimmy Carter. A mother of four, Mrs. Carter has maintained a lifelong dedication to issues affecting women and children. In 1991 she and Betty Bumpers, wife of U.S. Senator Dale Bumpers of Arkansas, launched "Every Child by Two," a nationwide campaign to publicize the need for early childhood immunizations.

Mrs. Carter is president of the Board of Directors for the Rosalynn Carter Institute for Caregiving at Georgia Southwestern State University.

Patricia L. Caruso

GOVERNMENT OFFICIAL. Patricia L. Caruso received a bachelor's degree in political science and sociology from Lake Superior State University and earned her master's degree from the University of Michigan.

Ms. Caruso joined the Michigan Department of Corrections in 1988 as assistant business manager of Kinross Correctional Facility in Michigan. She served as business manager at Hiawatha Correctional Facility

and as correctional facility manager for the Chippewa Correction Facilities where she was in charge of facility accounting, prisoner accounting, procurement, the warehouse, prisoner stores and other business functions. In 1991, she was selected to serve as warden of the Chippewa Correctional Facility, a multi-level prison and the Straits Correctional Facility, a minimum-security prison. She held that position for more than nine years and in 2000 was appointed as one of three regional prison administrators for the Correctional Facilities Administration, overseeing 13 prisons and eight camps from Saginaw to the tip of the Upper Peninsula. Prior to her appointment as director, she held the post of correctional facilities administration deputy director.

Ms. Caruso serves as director of the Michigan Department of Correction which houses more than 48,000 prisoners in 43 prisons and 11 camps across the state.

Kimberly Casiano

MEDIA EXECUTIVE. Kimberly Casiano is a native of New York. She received a bachelor's degree magna cum laude from Princeton University and a Master of Business Administration from Harvard Business School.

In 1981, she founded Caribbean Marketing Overseas Corporation, a consulting firm specializing in import/export, financing, trade, and investment promotion between the United States, the Caribbean and Central America. She joined her family's business, Casiano Communications, Inc., as vice president in 1988.

Ms. Casiano has served as president and chief operating officer of Casiano Communications, Inc., America's largest and most experienced Hispanic publisher of periodicals and magazines since 1994. She also serves as president of Direct ResponseSource, Inc., a division of Casiano Communications, Inc.

Vanessa Castagna

BUSINESS EXECUTIVE. Vanessa Castagna received a Bachelor of Science degree in psychology and speech communication from Purdue University in 1971.

Her professional career includes serving with Lazarus, a division of Federated Department Stores, where she rose to senior vice president and general merchandising manager. From 1985 to 1992 she served as vice president, merchandising—women's at Target Stores; she served as senior vice president, general merchandising manager for women's and juniors for Marshalls Stores; from 1994 to 1996 she served as senior vice president and general merchandising manager for home décor, domestics, furniture, crafts and children's apparel at Wal-Mart.

Ms. Castagna joined JC Penney in 1999 and was appointed executive vice president, then president and chief operating officer for JC Penney in 2001. She serves as executive vice president, chairman and chief executive officer of JC Penney Stores, Catalog and Internet.

Susan Castillo

ELECTED OFFICIAL. Susan Castillo is a native of Los Angeles, California. She received a Bachelor of Arts degree in communications from Oregon State University.

Her professional career includes serving as a reporter for KVAL-TV in Eugene, Oregon. She served as the first Hispanic woman in the Oregon Legislative Assembly as a senator from 1997 to 2002 where she was vice chair of the Senate Education Committee. She was also elected as assistant Democratic leader for the 1999 and 2001 legislative sessions.

Ms. Castillo was elected Oregon's state superintendent of public instruction in May 2002 and was sworn into office on January 6, 2003. She is the first Hispanic and second woman to serve in this post.

Ida L. Castro

GOVERNMENT OFFICIAL. Ida L. Castro received a Bachelor of Arts degree from the University of Puerto Rico. She earned a Master of Arts degree and Juris Doctor degrees, both from Rutgers University.

Her professional career includes serving in private law practice; and as the special counsel to the president and director of labor relations, Hostos Community College, City University of New York. She was the first Hispanic woman to earn tenure as an associate professor at Rutgers University, Institute for Management

and Labor Relations. From 1994 to 1996 she served at the Department of Labor as deputy assistant secretary and director of the Office of Workers Compensation Programs; from 1996 to 1998 she served as the acting director of the Women's Bureau at the United States Department of Labor (DOL).

Ms. Castro was nominated by President Bill Clinton as the eleventh chair of the U.S. Equal Employment Opportunity Commission (EEOC) on April 22, 1998, and unanimously confirmed by the United States Senate on October 21, 1998. She was sworn in as the chairwoman of the EEOC on October 23, 1998.

Susan P. Caswell

JUDGE. Susan P. Caswell received a bachelor's degree in criminal justice administration from Central Missouri State University and earned her Juris Doctorate from Oklahoma City University School of Law in 1978.

She began her legal career as a legal intern and later as an assistant district attorney for the Oklahoma County district attorney's office. She left the district attorney's office for approximately six years where she served in private practice. She served as a government lawyer as director of the enforcement division of the Oklahoma Tax Commission. In 1989 she returned to the Oklahoma County district attorney's office and specialized in the prosecution of sex crimes and homicides.

In 1999 she was elected a district judge for the Seventh Judicial District of Oklahoma.

Deritha M. Ceaser

MILITARY. Deritha M. Ceaser is a native of New Orleans, Louisiana, and holds a Bachelor of Arts degree in sociology from the University of Texas at Arlington.

Her military assignments include Wing's Human Resources Office (HRO) remote designee with primary responsibility for all the wing's fulltime manning issues. From December 1983 to 2004, she served in various fulltime roles within the Military Personnel Flight including retention office manager (ROM), base education and training manager, NCOIC customer support, noncommissioned officer in charge of career enhancement. In 2004, she was serving as the senior noncommissioned officer in the personnel career field and representative on the Air National (ANG) Advisory Council to the Air Force Association. She has over 22 years of experience in the personnel field and serves as an AGR assigned as the personnel superintendent for the 136th Airlift Wing, at Fort Worth, Texas.

Gwen Chan

EDUCATION. Gwen Chan is a native of San Francisco's Chinatown and is a graduate of the San Francisco Unified School District.

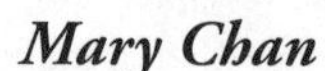

She has served as an educator in San Francisco for over 38 years. Her career includes serving as a teacher, principal, associate superintendent for high schools, chief development officer, and as deputy superintendent.

She was appointed interim superintendent of schools by the San Francisco Board of Education, effective February 1, 2006. She is the first Asian woman to serve in this office.

Mary Chan

TECHNOLOGY EXECUTIVE. Mary Chan received a Bachelor of Science degree and Master of Science degree in electrical engineering from Columbia University.

She began her career in 1985 at AT&T Bell Labs. She has served as director of business and financial management for Lucent, responsible for financial and strategic business planning, operations, and bids and proposals. She was named vice president of mobility access research and development for Lucent Technologies, where she led a diverse global R&D organization with teams in the United States, Europe, China and India. Ms. Chan was selected to lead the wireless group of Alcatel-Lucent.

Cassandra M. Chandler

GOVERNMENT OFFICIAL. Cassandra M. Chandler received a bachelor's degree in English and journalism from Louisiana State University in 1979 and earned her Juris Doctor degree from Loyola University School of Law in New Orleans, Louisiana. She is a graduate of the FBI Academy.

Her professional career includes serving as a television anchor, reporter, and talk show host for WVLA-TV in Baton Rouge. She began her Federal Bureau Investigation (FBI) career as a special agent in 1985. She has served in the FBI's New Orleans, Los Angeles, San Diego, and San Francisco field offices. In April 2000, she was assigned as section chief in the investigative services division at FBI headquarters, overseeing the FBI's analytical program for matters of criminal and domestic terrorism. In February 2001, she was appointed assistant director for all training programs for new employees and the continuing education for all Federal Bureau Investigation employees. Ms. Chandler is the first African-American woman to preside over the training division in the FBI Academy's 30-year existence.

Lisa Chang

MEDIA EXECUTIVE. Lisa Chang received a Bachelor of Arts in communications from the University of Virginia and has a Master of Business Administration in international business from Mercer University's Stetson School of Business.

She joined the Weather Channel in 1998 as director of compensation and benefits. In 1999, she was promoted to director of employment and rewards. She served as vice president of human resources supporting weather.com. Her most recent human resources position was that of vice president of human resources for the Weather Channel and the Weather Channel Interactive. She served as vice president of desktop weather following advancements in the human resources group during her first five years at the Weather Channel. Ms. Chang is executive vice president of human resources for the Weather Channel.

Shelleyanne W.L. Chang

JUDGE. Shelleyanne W.L. Chang is a native of Hawaii, born to third generation Chinese-Americans from Guangchou, South China. She grew up predominantly in the San Fernando Valley of Los Angeles. She received her bachelor's degree from the University of Washington and earned a Juris Doctor degree from McGeorge Law School.

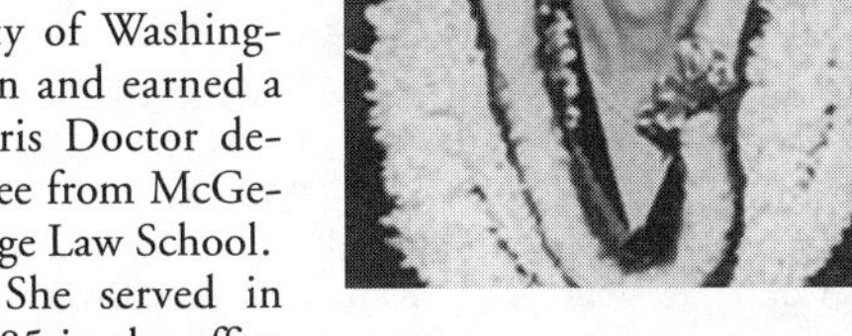

She served in 1985 in the office of chief counsel of the Internal Revenue Service; as a deputy attorney general from 1993 to 1999; and as the chief deputy legal affairs secretary for Governor Gray Davis.

On December 19, 2002, she was appointed judge on the Sacramento Superior Court in California.

Elaine L. Chao

GOVERNMENT OFFICIAL. Elaine L. Chao received a bachelor's degree from Mount Holyoke College and earned her Masters of Business Administration from the Harvard Business School. She also studied at M.I.T., Dartmouth College and Columbia University.

Ms. Chao is the nation's 24th secretary of labor and the first Asian American woman appointed to a president's cabinet in U.S. history. She is the first Kentuckian named to the president's cabinet since 1945. She was confirmed by the United States Senate on January 29, 2001.

Beth Chapman

ELECTED OFFICIAL. Beth Chapman is a native of Greenville, Alabama. She received a Bachelor of Sci-

ence degree from the University of Montevallo and earned her master's degree magna cum laude from the University of Alabama at Birmingham.

She was a private business owner in Alabama when in 1995, she became the first woman in Alabama's history to serve as appointments secretary, when she was named as a cabinet member for Governor Fob James. In 2000, she served as press secretary for Lieutenant Governor Steve Windom. In 2001, she was elected state auditor for the state of Alabama.

Micheline Chau

ENTERTAINMENT EXECUTIVE. Micheline Chau is a native of Singapore. She received a bachelor's degree in English from Wellesley College and a Master of Business Administration degree from Stanford University.

She has been an accomplished business executive with experience in several industries, and most recently was chief financial/administrative officer for Bell Atlantic Healthcare Systems. Ms. Chau began her Lucasfilm career in 1991 as chief financial officer and was named to her current position in 2003. She serves as president and chief operating officer for Lucasfilm, overseeing the daily operations of one of the world's leading film and entertainment companies. In addition to Lucasfilm's motion-picture and television productions, which have garnered 19 Oscars and 12 Emmy Awards, she guides the activities of Industrial Light & Magic and Skywalker Sound.

Lynne V. Cheney

AUTHOR. Lynne V. Cheney received a Bachelor of Arts degree with highest honors from Colorado College and earned her Ph.D. with a specialization in 19th-century British literature from the University of Wisconsin. She holds honorary degrees from numerous colleges and universities.

Her professional career includes serving as chairman of the National Endowment for the Humanities from 1986 to 1993; she published *American Memory*, a report that warned about the failure of schools to transmit knowledge of the past to upcoming generations. "A system of education that fails to nurture memory of the past denies its students a great deal"; Dr. Cheney announced a new initiative to encourage historical knowledge in April 2003. She launched the James Madison Book Award Fund which presents a yearly award of $10,000 to the book that best represents excellence in bringing knowledge and understanding of American history to young people. Dr. Cheney has written articles about history for numerous publications on topics ranging from woman's suffrage in the West and the way Americans celebrated the country's centennial. She has also written three books of American history for children.

Dr. Cheney is the wife of Vice President Dick Cheney.

Peggy Tsiang Cherng

BUSINESS EXECUTIVE. Peggy Tsiang Cherng received a Bachelor of Science degree in applied mathematics from Oregon State University. She earned a master's degree in computer science and a doctorate in electrical engineering from the University of Missouri.

Her professional career includes serving at McDonnell Douglas as a member of the technical team. Later she worked at Comtal-3M, where her highly technical background quickly led her up the corporate ladder to become software development manager. During this time her husband, Andrew Cherng, and father-in-law, Master Chef Ming Tsai Cherng, opened Panda Inn in Pasadena, California, a unique restaurant featuring gourmet Mandarin and Szechuan cuisine. The Panda business steadily grew, and in 1982, Cherng decided to join the family business. As executive vice president she created the vision, mission and value statements for Panda Restaurant Group, Inc., helping to set a solid corporate foundation for further growth.

Ms. Cherng was named president and chief executive officer of Panda Management Company, Inc. (PMC).

Laura Chick

ELECTED OFFICIAL (FIRST). Laura Chick has called Los Angeles home since 1952; she received her bache-

lor's degree in history from UCLA and a masters in social work from the University of Southern California.

Her professional career includes serving as a manager of a family owned business; as a social worker; as council member, Third District, in the West San Fernando Valley from 1993 to 2001. She served as the first woman to chair the city council's public safety committee; she was elected the 17th controller of the city of Los Angeles and was re-elected on March 8, 2005. She is the first and only woman in the history of Los Angeles to hold a citywide office.

Joan K. Chow

BUSINESS EXECUTIVE. Joan K. Chow received a bachelor's degree in linguistics from Cornell University and earned a Master of Business Administration from the Wharton School of the University of Pennsylvania.

She began her career in 1986 at Johnson & Johnson Products, Inc. where she brought strong results and market share gains as a leader of several product lines. She spent seven years at Information Resources, Inc. Until January 2007, Ms. Chow was senior vice president and chief marketing officer of Sears, Roebuck & Co. ConAgra Foods named her executive vice president and chief marketing officer in January 2007. ConAgra Foods Inc. is one of North America's leading packaged food companies, serving grocery retailers as well as restaurants and other foodservice establishments.

Uma Chowdhry

BUSINESS EXECUTIVE. Uma Chowdhry is a native of Mumbai, India; she came to the United States in 1968. She received a Bachelor of Science degree in physics from Indian Institute of Science, Mumbai University, and a Master of Science degree from Caltech in engineering science in 1970. She earned a doctorate in materials science from Massachusetts Institute of Technology in 1976.

Her professional career began in 1977 when she joined DuPont as a research scientist in Wilmington, Delaware. She spent the first 11 years of her career in CR&D in various research and management roles. From 1988 to 1992, she served as lab director and business manager in the electronics department before she moved to the chemicals sector as lab director of Jackson Lab. From 1993 to 1995, she served as research and development director for specialty chemicals and was appointed business director for the DuPont "Terathane" business in 1995. In 1997, she moved back to specialty chemicals as business planning and research and development director. In 1999 she was appointed director of DuPont Engineering's technology division and was named vice president central research and development in August 2002. In December 2004, she assumed responsibility for the company's core research programs and the DuPont "APEX" research program.

Dr. Chowdhry was named vice president and chief technology officer for DuPont in June 2006.

Cindy Christy

TECHNOLOGY EXECUTIVE. Cindy Christy received a bachelor's degree in business administration from the American University in Washington, D.C.

She began her career in 1988 at AT&T Network Systems where she held a variety of management positions in market research, market management, sales, product planning, project management and product management. In 1995 she became director, CDMA/PCS project management and led the development, execution and product realization of the CDMA digital technology platform. She was named vice president of AMPS/PCS product management, project management and product marketing in 1998. She was appointed chief operating officer of CDMA and TDMA Networks in 2000, responsible for the operational performance and strategic direction of the global CDMA and TDMA business. She served as president of Universal Mobile Telecommunications Systems (UMTS) Officer Management for Lucent's wireless networks group. She served as chief operating officer for the mobility business. She served as president of the company's mobility solutions group and was responsible for driving business operations to bring end-to-end mobile networking solutions to service providers worldwide.

Ms. Christy serves as president of Lucent Technologies' network solutions group.

Mary A. Chrzanowski

JUDGE. Mary A. Chrzanowski received a Bachelor of Science degree in criminal justice (graduating "with distinction") from Wayne State University and earned Juris Doctor degree from the University of Detroit School of Law in 1985.

She served as an assistant prosecuting attorney in Macomb County and was engaged in private law practice prior to her election. In November 1992, she was elected judge to the Michigan Macomb County Circuit Court.

Regina M. Chu

JUDGE. Regina M. Chu received a Bachelor of Arts degree from the University of Minnesota in 1975 and earned her Juris Doctor from William Mitchell College of Law in 1980. Her professional career includes serving as a law clerk at Hennepin County District Court in 1977; as a law clerk at the Minnesota Supreme Court in 1980; and as a special assistant attorney general, Minnesota Attorney General's office in 1981. From 1985 to 2002 she was engaged in private law practice. In 2002, she was appointed judge to the Minnesota Hennepin County Judicial District.

Shinae Chun

GOVERNMENT OFFICIAL. Shinae Chun received a bachelor's degree from Ewha Women's University in Seoul, Korea, and a master's degree in education and social policy from Northwestern University. She was also a fellow in the state and local government program at Harvard University John F. Kennedy School of Government.

Her professional career includes serving from 1984 to 1989 as special assistant to the governor of Illinois for Asian American affairs; from 1989 to 1991, she served as director of the Illinois Department of Financial Institutions; from 1991 to 1999, she was the director of the Illinois Department of Labor; in 1999, she was named managing director of the ITR Corporation in Chicago, Illinois.

Ms. Chun serves as director of the women's bureau of the Department of Labor.

Maria Cino

GOVERNMENT OFFICIAL. Maria Cino received a bachelor's degree from St. John Fisher College. Her professional career includes serving as a public policy and government affairs consultant for the Washington, D.C., law firm of Wiley, Rein and Fielding; as national political director for the Bush for President Campaign; as deputy chairman for political and congressional relations at the Republican National Committee; and as assistant secretary and director general of the United States and Foreign Commercial Service at the Department of Commerce.

Ms. Cino serves as the deputy secretary of transportation at the Department of Transportation.

Carolyn M. Clancy

MEDICINE. Carolyn M. Clancy received a bachelor's degree from Boston College and earned a Medical Doctor degree from the University of Massachusetts Medical School.

Her professional career includes serving as the Henry J. Kaiser Family Foundation fellow at the University of Pennsylvania; as an assistant professor in the Department of Internal Medicine at the Medical College of Virginia in Richmond; and as director of the Agency for Healthcare Research and Quality (AHRQ) Center for Outcomes and Effectiveness Research. She served as acting director of the Agency for Healthcare Research and Quality since March 2002. She holds an academic appointment at George Washington University School of Medicine (clinical associate professor, Department of Medicine).

Dr. Clancy was appointed director of the AHRQ on February 5, 2003.

Patricia Clarey

GOVERNMENT OFFICIAL. Patricia Clarey graduated from Maine-Endwell High School and received a Bachelor of Science degree from Union College. She earned a master degree of public administration from Harvard University John F. Kennedy School of Government.

Her professional career includes serving from 1986 to 1989 in the Reagan-Bush administration in several senior level positions in the Department of Interior and as director of legislative affairs for the United States National Park Services. She also served as deputy chief of staff for Governor Pete Wilson for seven years.

Ms. Clarey was appointed the first chief of staff to Governor Arnold Schwarzenegger of California.

Linda Clark

AEROSPACE. Linda Clark is a native of Birmingham, Alabama. She received bachelor's degree in engineering from the University of Alabama in Birmingham and a master's degree in management from the Florida Institute of Technology in Melbourne.

She serves as a NASA engineer in the Safety and Mission Assurance Directorate at NASA's Marshall Space Flight Center in Huntsville, Alabama. She and her team have spent two years developing non-invasive technologies to evaluate the Shuttle external tank's thermal protection system. The 154-foot long tank is covered with insulating spray-on foam, which maintains the tank's interior temperature and prevents buildup of ice on the exterior. Ms. Clark is a 17-year NASA veteran, is a key player in helping NASA to ensure safe, reliable flight operations for STS-114, Space Shuttle Return to Flight.

Nancy L. Clark

JUDGE. Nancy L. Clark received a Bachelor of Arts degree from the University of Florida in 1983. She earned her Juris Doctor degree from the University of Florida in 1986. From 1990 to 1997, she served as a certified instructor for the Commission on Criminal Justice Standards and Training.

She was appointed judge, Traffic Court, Orange County, in 2000. From 2003 to 2004, she served as a judge in Criminal Court of Orange County. In 2006, she was serving as judge in Civil Court of Orange County, Florida.

Nikki Clark

JUDGE (FIRST). Nikki Clark is a native of Detroit, Michigan. She received her undergraduate degree from Wayne State University and earned her Juris Doctor degree from Florida State University in 1977.

Her professional career includes serving as an assistant attorney general for Florida from 1981 to 1991; as director of legislation and policy development for the Florida Department of Environmental Protection Agency; and as the director of cabinet affairs for Governor Lawton Chiles. In 1993, Governor Chiles appointed her judge to the Florida's Leon County Circuit Court, making her the first African American and first woman to sit on that circuit.

Patrina Clark

GOVERNMENT OFFICIAL. Patrina Clark assumed the position of regional executive director for Naval District Washington on June 28, 2004. As regional executive director, she serves as one of two principal deputies to the commandant, Naval District Washington and is Naval District Washington's senior civilian.

She attended the University of Texas, where she began her undergraduate studies as a National Merit Scholar and University of Texas Presidential Scholar majoring in electrical engineering. She completed her undergraduate studies at Thomas Edison State College with an emphasis in communications and human resources management. She has undertaken graduate studies at Cornell University in Ithaca, New York, and George Washington University in the District of Columbia. She has a graduate certificate from Cornell's School of Industrial Labor Relations in human resources management and a master's certificate in project management from George Washington University.

She began her federal career with the Internal Revenue Service in 1986. With the exception of a one-year assignment with the Veteran's Administration, her entire federal career has been with the Internal Revenue Service. She has held leadership positions in both tax administration and human resources/support, with an emphasis in training and labor/employee relations.

Rena Clark

SPORTS EXECUTIVE. Rena Clark received a bachelor's degree in mechanical engineering from Lamar University and earned a Master of Business Administration from Harvard University.

Ms. Clark has served in both the for-profit and not-for-profit sectors. She spent four years at General Electric and a year at Bain & Company in Boston before returning to Harvard University's Graduate School of Business in 1991. While there she served as managing director of MBA program administration and chief operating officer. She also acquired, built and operated two middle-market manufacturing companies.

Ms. Clark joined the Kraft Group and the New England Patriots on May 1, 2003, as vice president of community affairs and corporate philanthropy. In her first three seasons with the organization, she has enjoyed the most successful years in franchise history with three consecutive division titles, including back-to-back 17-win seasons and two Super Bowl championships. In her role, she is responsible for all team-related community affairs and outreach programs.

Trudy H. Clark

MILITARY. Trudy H. Clark received a Bachelor of Arts degree in sociology with honors from University of Maryland and a Master of Science degree in guidance and counseling from Troy State University, Montgomery, Alabama.

Her military education includes: in 1980, she was a distinguished graduate, Squadron Officer school, Maxwell Air Force Base in Alabama; in 1987, Air Command and Staff College, Maxwell AFB, Alabama; in 1992, Armed Forces Staff College; in 1993, Air War College; in 2001, Senior Information Warfare Applications Course; in 2002, National Security Leadership Course, Syracuse University; in 2003, National Security Decision-Making Seminar, School of Advanced International Studies, John Hopkins University, Washington, D.C.; in 2004, U.S.–Russia Executive Security Program, John F. Kennedy School of Government, Harvard University.

She received her commission in 1973. She has served in staff, command and executive officer positions at the base, major command and staff levels. She has commanded three communications squadrons, a communications group, and a support group. She has served as a presidential communications officer and as the commandant of Squadron Officer School. She was also the director for command, control, communications and computer systems at U.S. Strategic Command. She served as the deputy chief information officer at Headquarters United States Air Force in Washington, D.C. She was promoted to brigadier general on August 1, 1999.

Major General Clark serves as deputy director, Defense Threat Reduction Agency, Washington, D.C. She was promoted to major general on March 1, 2003.

Cathleen B. Clarke

JUDGE. Cathleen B. Clarke is a native of Florida and was raised in the Tampa Bay area, where she graduated from Notre Dame Academy, known today as St. Petersburg Catholic High School. She received a bachelor's degree from the University of Florida in 1975 and earned her Juris Doctor from the University of Florida School of Law in 1979.

Her professional career includes serving as an assistant state attorney, state of Florida; a public defender; and as a part-time instructor at Brevard Community College's Law Enforcement Academy. In 1998, she was appointed judge by Governor Lawton Chiles to the County Court, Eighteenth Judicial Circuit in Viera, Florida; in 2001, she was elected administrative judge.

Kathleen Clarke

GOVERNMENT OFFICIAL. Kathleen Clarke is a native of Bountiful, Utah. She received a Bachelor of Arts degree in political science cum laude from Utah State University in Logan, Utah.

Her professional career includes serving from 1987 to 1993 in the office of Congressman James V. Hansen, first as director of constituent services and then as executive director. From 1993 to 1998, she served as the deputy director and then as executive director of the Utah Department of Natural Resources. Ms. Clarke was appointed director of the United States Bureau of Land Management.

Yvette Diane Clarke

ELECTED OFFICIAL. Yvette Diane Clarke is a native of Brooklyn, New York. She attended Oberlin College in Oberlin, New York. She was elected to the New York City Council in November 2001 as the representative for the 40th District in Brooklyn. She was overwhelmingly re-elected to office in November 2003 and November 2005.

Ms. Clarke was elected in 2006 as a United States representative as a Democrat to the 110th Congress. She began to serve on January 7, 2007, as a member of Congress from New York.

Patricia Clay

MILITARY. Patricia Clay received a Bachelor of Science degree in nursing from Tuskegee Institute, Tuskegee, Alabama, and earned a Master of Science in nursing from the Medical College of Virginia in Richmond, Virginia. She is a graduate of the Army Command and General Staff College. She has attended numerous military medical courses, such as the Executive Skills Course, the Intensive Care Nursing Course, Clinical Head Nurse Course, and the Combat Casualty Care Course.

She has held a variety of positions which includes two ICU head nurse positions, one at Kenner Army Community Hospital at Fort Lee, Virginia, and the other one as FORSCOM Nurse assigned to the 85th Evacuation Hospital at Fort Lee, Virginia. She has been a critical care and cardiac clinical nurse specialist/case manager at Dwight David Eisenhower Army Medical Center, Fort Gordon, Georgia. She was the chief of nursing administration days, at Keller Community Hospital, West Point, New York, before being assigned to Fort Benning in August 1998. Prior to her current position, she served as the chief, inpatient nursing section/chief, of nursing administration days. On June 2, 2000, she was assigned as the deputy commander for nursing at Martin Army Community Hospital at Fort Benning, Georgia.

Annette Clayton

BUSINESS EXECUTIVE. Annette Clayton received a bachelor's degree in general engineering from Wright State University in 1986 and earned a master's degree in engineering management from the University of Dayton in 1992. She completed the London Business School Executive Program in 1997.

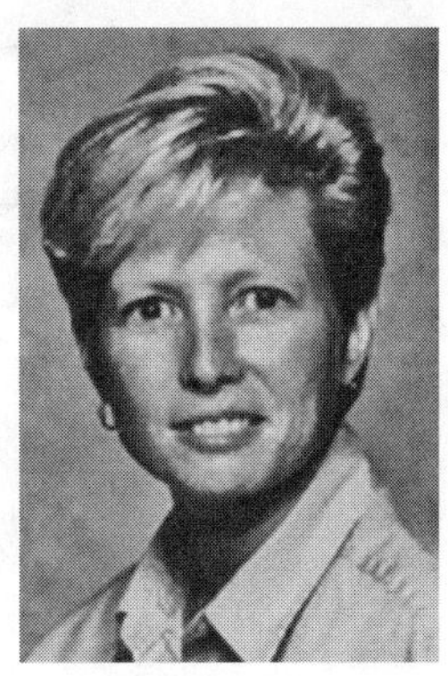

She served as the executive director of global manufacturing systems quality of General Motors Corporation from April 2000 to 2001; she served as vice president manufacturing for the Americas of Dell Corporation. In 2006, she was serving as president of Saturn Corporation, responsible for Saturn's Spring Hill, Tennessee, and Wilmington, Delaware, operations.

Eva M. Clayton

ELECTED OFFICIAL. Eva M. Clayton is a native of Savannah, Georgia. She received a Bachelor of Science degree from Johnson C. Smith University in Charlotte, North Carolina, and a Masters of Science from North Carolina Central University in Durham, North Carolina, in 1962.

Her professional career includes serving as director of the University of North Carolina health manpower development programs; as assistant secretary for community development at North Carolina Department of Natural Resources and Community Development from 1977 to 1981; and as chair of the Warren County, North Carolina, Board of Commissioners from 1982 to 1992. She was elected as a Democrat to the 102nd Congress by special election and was re-elected to the four succeeding Congresses from November 1992 to January 2003.

Mary L. Cleave

ASTRONAUT. Mary L. Cleave is a native of Southampton, New York, and graduated from Great Neck North High School in Great Neck, New York, in 1965. She received a Bachelor of Science degree in biological sciences from Colorado State University in 1969. She earned a Master of Science in microbial ecology and a doctorate in civil and environmental engineering from Utah State University in 1975 and 1979, respectively.

She was selected as an astronaut with NASA in May 1980. Her technical assignments have included flight software verification in the Shuttle Avionics Integration Laboratory (SAIL); CAPCOM on five Space Shuttle fights; malfunctions procedures book; crew equipment design. A veteran of two space flights, Dr. Cleave has logged a total of 10 days, 22 hours, 2 minutes, 24 seconds in space, orbited the earth 172 times and traveled 3.94 million miles. She was a mission specialist on STS 61-B (November 26–December 3, 1985) and STS-30 (May 4–8, 1989). She left Johnson Space Center in May 1991 to join NASA's Goddard Space Flight Center in Greenbelt, Maryland. She worked in the Laboratory for Hydrospheric Processes as the project manager for SeaWiFS (Sea-viewing, Wide-Field-of-view-Sensor), an ocean color sensor which is monitoring vegetation globally. She served as the deputy associate administrator (advanced planning), in the Office of Earth Science, NASA Headquarters in Washington, D.C. She now serves as the associate administrator for NASA's Science Mission Directorate, guides an array of research and scientific exploration programs for planet Earth, space weather, the solar system and the universe beyond.

Julia J. Cleckley

MILITARY. Julia J. Cleckley is a native of Aliquippa, Pennsylvania. She holds a bachelor's degree in psychology and education from Hunter College in New York. She earned a master's degree in human resource management from Golden Gate University in San Francisco.

She was selected to attend the United States War College in 1992 and studied at the Fletcher School of Law and Diplomacy at Tufts University in Boston.

She enlisted in the Women's Army Corps after finishing high school. She then joined the New York National Guard and received her commission in the Adjutant General Corps with the 42nd Infantry Division in 1976 while she was a schoolteacher. She has served full-time with the National Guard Bureau in northern Virginia since 1987.

After serving in the military for 26 years, on July 1, 2002, she was promoted to brigadier general. Lieutenant General Roger Schultz, the Army Guard's director, promoted the pioneering career officer from New York to one-rank during the National Guard's Year of Diversity. She became the first woman to be assigned as special assistant to the chief of the National Guard for human resources readiness (G-1) in the history of the Army National Guard.

General Cleckley's became the third one-star general among the 42,000 women serving in the Army Guard. Her accomplishments include being the first minority woman to become a branch chief at the National Guard Bureau, the first African-American woman to be promoted to colonel in the active Guard and the first woman or minority member to serve on the Army Guard director's special staff as chief of human resources. She has also served as professor of military science at Hampton University's ROTC program in Virginia.

Edith Brown Clement

JUDGE. Edith Brown Clement is a native of Birmingham, Alabama. She received a Bachelor of Arts degree from the University of Alabama in 1969 and earned her Juris Doctor degree from Tulane Law School in 1972.

Her professional career includes serving as law clerk for Hon. Herbert W. Christenberry, U.S. District Court of Eastern District of Louisiana from 1973 to 1975. She served in private law practice from 1975 to 1991. On October 1, 1991, President George H. W. Bush nominated her judge, U. S. District Court of Eastern District of Louisiana and she was confirmed by the Senate on November 21, 1991. She was commissioned on November 25, 1991. Judge Clement has served as chief judge in 2001. She was appointed to the U.S. Court of Appeals for

the Fifth Circuit by President George W. Bush and commissioned on November 26, 2001.

Hillary Clinton

ELECTED OFFICIAL. Hillary Clinton is a native of Chicago, Illinois, and attended public school in Park Ridge, Illinois. She received a Bachelor of Arts degree from Wellesley College in 1969 and earned her Juris Doctor degree from Yale Law School in 1973.

Her professional career includes private law practice, serving as an advisor to the Children's Defense Fund in Cambridge; she served as counsel for the impeachment inquiry staff, House Judiciary Committee 1974; in 1975 she joined the faculty of the University of Arkansas Law School; and in 1978 President Jimmy Carter appointed her to the Board of the Legal Services Corporation. She served as the first lady of Arkansas from 1979 to 1981 and from 1983 to 1993; and served as the first lady of the United States from 1993 to 2001. President Bill Clinton asked her to chair the task force on national health care reform. She continued to be a leading advocate for expanding health insurance coverage ensuring children are properly immunized and raising public awareness of health issues.

Ms. Clinton was elected United States Senator from New York on November 7, 2000. She is the first first lady elected to the United States Senate and the first woman elected statewide in New York. On January 20, 2007, Senator Clinton announced the formation of a presidential exploratory committee for the United States presidential election of 2008. During the 2008 presidential nomination race, she won more primaries and delegates than any other woman in American history. She collected 18 million votes during her campaign, but lost the nomination to Senator Barack Obama in June 2008.

Rosemary R. Cloud

GOVERNMENT OFFICIAL (FIRST). Rosemary R. Cloud is a native of East Point, Georgia. She is the youngest of 14 children. In 1978 she joined the Atlanta Fire Department as a fireman. In 1980 she was assigned to the Atlanta Fire Department airport unit. She worked her way up the ranks to assistant fire chief in charge of Atlanta Fire Department's airport operations.

Chief Cloud was appointed by the mayor of City of East Point on March 14, 2002, to serve as the city's fire chief. She became the first black woman ever to serve as a city fire chief anywhere in the history of the United States.

Velva D. Coaxum

MILITARY. Velva D. Coaxum holds an Associate of Science degree in business and a Bachelor of Science degree with distinction in management finance.

She enlisted into the Marine Corps in November 1979 and completed recruit training in January 1980. Upon completion of recruit training she returned to St. Louis, Missouri, where she worked as a recruiter assistant. She reported to MATSG NTTC Naval Air Station Meridian, Mississippi, for the basic Aviation Supply course in March 1980. Upon completion of Aviation Supply School as a supply clerk, she reported to her first duty station 3rd Marine Aircraft Wing, Marine Corps Air Station, El Toro, California, where she was joined for duty with H&S-13, MAG-13, transferred to VMA (AW) 242 for a 6-month overseas deployment to 1st MAW, MAG-12, in Iwakuni, Japan.

In January 1984, she was transferred to 2nd Marine Aircraft Wing H&S-31, Marine Aircraft Group 31, Marine Corps Air Station at Beaufort, South Carolina; she was then transferred to 1st Marine Aircraft Wing H&MS-36, Marine Aircraft Group-36, in Okinawa, Japan, assigned as the consumables material chief. In September 1989, she was transferred to the 2nd Marine Aircraft Wing, MALS-31, MAG-31, Marine Corps Air Station, at Beaufort, South Carolina, for duty as the repairable management chief until January 1991 when she was transferred to Drill Instructor School. Upon completion of Drill Instructor School, she was assigned to the 4th Recruit Training Battalion.

In March 1993, upon completion of drill instructor duty, she was transferred to 3rd Marine Aircraft Wing MALS-39, MAG-39, Marine Corps Air Station, at Camp Pendleton, California, where she served as the consumables management chief. Upon return, she was transferred to Reserve Unit, 4th MAW MAG-46, DETA Marine Corps Air Station at Camp Pendleton, California, as the supply/fiscal chief. In July 1999, Sergeant Major Coaxum was transferred to III MEF 7th Communication Battalion where she was assigned to Headquarters Company. During this tour she transferred to Alpha Company and served in operations Ulchi Focus Lens '00 Pohang, Korea; Tandem Thrust 2001 in Rock Hampton, Australia; and the Kingdom of Thailand, in support of Freedom Banner #5 and Cobra Gold 2002.

In August 2002, she was assigned as the sergeant major of the 2nd Medical Battalion. During this tour she deployed to Kuwait in support of Operation Enduring Freedom. Upon her return in June 2004, she was reassigned to 2nd Transportation Support Battalion.

Kay Beevers Cobb

JUDGE. Judge Kay Beevers Cobb is a native of Mississippi and was reared in Cleveland, Mississippi. She received a bachelor's degree from Mississippi University for Women where she was class president. She earned her Juris Doctor degree from the University of Mississippi School of Law in January 1978.

Her professional career includes serving in private law practice; as director of the Mississippi prosecutors programs at the University of Mississippi Law School; and as attorney for the Mississippi Bureau of Narcotics. In 1988 she joined the staff of the attorney general; in 1992 she was elected to the Mississippi Senate; in 1996 she returned to private law practice; on April 1, 1999, she was appointed to the Mississippi Supreme Court.

Sharon Cobb

AEROSPACE. Sharon Cobb is a native of Birmingham, Alabama. She received a bachelor's degree and a master's degree in materials engineering from the University of Alabama at Birmingham. She earned a doctorate degree in materials science and engineering from the University of Florida in Gainesville.

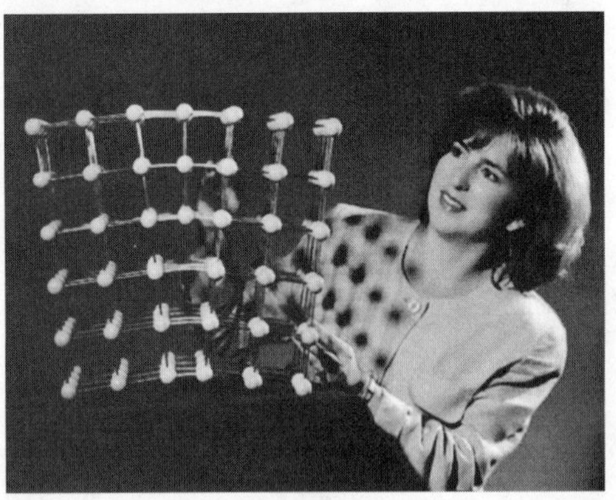

She has worked at NASA for 18 years at the Marshall Center, and has participated in several materials science experiments flown on NASA's Space Shuttle. She is using that experience as lead scientist for the materials science research rack, soon to be the main facility on the International Space Station for materials science investigations. Astronauts will install the floor-to-ceiling, 40-inch (1-meter) wide rack in the station's Destiny laboratory. She is working with Marshall Center engineers who are developing the first materials science research rack and integrating the first two experiment modules that will fit inside the rack.

Gloria Grace Coco

JUDGE. Gloria Grace Coco received a bachelor's degree from Mundelein in 1972 and earned her Juris Doctor from NIU College of Law in 1978. Her professional career includes serving as special assistant state attorney general, as deputy chief of the Illinois Attorney General's Consumer Protection division, and as an attorney with the city of Chicago Department of Building. In 1991 she was appointed judge to the First Municipal District, Circuit Court of Cook County in Chicago, Illinois. She has served in the domestic violence division since 1995 and was appointed supervising judge in 1997.

Mary Day Coker

JUDGE. Mary Day Coker received a Bachelor of Science in political science in Florida State University in 1980 and earned her Juris Doctor degree from Georgetown University Law Center in 1983.

She has served as county court judge since 2004 and also serves as the administrative judge of the county court.

Melonie Colaianne

NONPROFIT EXECUTIVE. Melonie Colaianne holds a bachelor of business administration degree and a Master's of Business Administration degree from Eastern Michigan University. She has served as vice`president and corporate secretary for Cranbrook Education Community. In 2005 she was appointed president of Masco Corporation Foundation. She represents the corporation and the foundation in their charitable engagements.

Brenda Hill Cole

JUDGE. Brenda Hill Cole is a native of Texas where she was the valedictorian of Weldon High School in Gladewater, Texas. She received a Bachelor of Arts in English from Spelman College and a Master of Science from Atlanta University. She earned her Juris Doctor from Emory University in Atlanta, Georgia.

After her admission to the state bar of Georgia, she began her law career as an assistant attorney general in the fiscal affairs division of the Georgia State Law Department, a position she held for five years. After moving to West Virginia, she was employed as counsel for the West Virginia Department of Corrections in Charleston, West Virginia, and was admitted to the West Virginia State Bar. She served as an assistant attorney general in the tax division of the West Virginia Attorney General's office and as deputy attorney general of the West Virginia Environmental and Energy division. After returning to Atlanta, Georgia, she rejoined the Georgia State Law Department serving as senior assistant attorney general heading the business and professional regulations division, and later, as deputy attorney general. She was appointed a state court judge to the State Court of Fulton County, Georgia.

Johnnetta Betsch Cole

EDUCATION. Johnnetta Betsch Cole is a native of Jacksonville, Florida. She received a Bachelor of Arts degree from Oberlin. She earned a Master of Arts degree and a doctorate degree in anthropology from Northwestern University. She received an LL.D. from Bates College in 1989.

Her professional career includes serving as an associate provost for undergraduate education at the University of Massachusetts, where she taught anthropology and African-American studies. She served as a professor of anthropology at Hunter College and as a member of the graduate faculty of the City University of New York where she directed the Latin American and Caribbean studies program. She has also taught at Washington State University and the University of California at Los Angeles at the Williams and Oberlin. In 1987 she was named president of Spelman College, becoming the first black woman to hold this position in the history of the college. She retired from the presidency in 1997. She served as a professor at Emory University in Atlanta, Georgia. She served on President-elect Bill Clinton's transition team as cluster coordination for education, labor and arts and humanities. She is the first woman ever elected to serve on the Board of Coca-Cola Enterprises. She serves as president emerita of Spelman and professor emerita of Emory. In May 2004 she became the first African American woman to serve as chair of the board of United Way of America. She holds 51 honorary degrees.

Dr. Cole serves as the 14th president of Bennett College for Women in Greensboro, North Carolina.

Sheryl Cole

ELECTED OFFICIAL. Sheryl Cole is a 25-year resident of Austin, Texas. She received a Bachelor of Arts degree from the University of Texas in accounting and earned her Juris Doctor degree from the University of Texas in 1991.

She served as an accountant in Austin, Texas, and now serves in private law practice. She also serves as a member of the Austin City Council in the City of Austin, Texas.

Carolyn Coleman

GOVERNMENT OFFICIAL. Carolyn Coleman received a bachelor's degree from the University of Kansas in 1983 and earned her Juris Doctor degree cum laude from the Indiana University School of Law in 1997.

Her professional career includes serving for 11 years with AT&T in a variety of sales management positions.

She was also engaged in private law practice and as director of the city of Indianapolis Department of Metropolitan development.

Ms. Coleman was appointed deputy mayor for neighborhoods for the city of Indianapolis, Indiana, on June 25, 2001, and serves as the chief liaison between the mayor and neighborhood residents, associations and leaders. She also coordinates the mayor's initiatives dealing with housing, metropolitan development, public works and parks.

Carolyn Quilloin Coleman

ELECTED OFFICIAL. Carolyn Quilloin Coleman is a native of Savannah, Georgia. She received a Bachelor of Science degree in history with a minor in economics and sociology from Savannah State College. She has done further study at Memphis Theological Seminary and earned a Master of Science degree in adult education from North Carolina A&T State University.

Her professional career includes serving as special assistant to Governor James B. Hunt for eight years, and as the secretary to the NAACP national Board of Directors and the vice president of the North Carolina State NAACP. She was elected to serve as the District 9 commissioner to the Guilford County Board of Commissioners in 2002; she served as the board's vice chair in 2004 and was elected chair of the board in December 2005.

Catherine G. Coleman

ASTRONAUT. Catherine G. Coleman is a native of Charleston, South Carolina, and was a graduate of W.T. Woodson High School in Fairfax, Virginia, in 1978. She received a Bachelor of Science degree in chemistry from Massachusetts Institute of Technology in 1983 and a doctorate in polymer science and engineering from the University of Massachusetts in 1991.

Coleman is a colonel in the United States Air Force who was commissioned as a 2nd lieutenant in the Air Force in 1983 and was selected by NASA in March 1992. She reported to the Johnson Space Center in August 1992. She served in the astronaut office payloads and habitability branch, working with experiment designers to insure that payloads can be operated successfully in the microgravity environment of low earth orbit. As the lead astronaut for long term space flight habitability issues, she led the effort to label the Russian segments of the International Space Station in English and also tracked issues such as acoustics and living accommodations aboard the station. A veteran of two space missions, Colonel Coleman has logged over 500 hours in space. She was a mission specialist on STS-73, trained as a backup mission specialist for an injured crew member on STS-83 and was lead mission specialist on STS-93.

Mary Sue Coleman

EDUCATION. Mary Sue Coleman received a bachelor's degree in chemistry from Grinnell College and earned her doctorate in biochemistry from the University of North Carolina. She holds honorary doctorates from Grinnell College, Luther College, the University of Kentucky, Albion College, Dartmouth College, Shanghai Jiao Tong University and Northeastern University, and a distinguished alumnus award from the University of North Carolina.

Her professional career includes serving for 19 years as a member of the biochemistry faculty at the University of Kentucky. Her work in the sciences led her to administrative appointments at the University of North Carolina at Chapel Hill and the University of New Mexico, where she served as provost and vice president for academic affairs. From 1995 to 2002 Dr. Coleman was president of the University of Iowa.

Dr. Coleman was appointed the 13th president of the University of Michigan in August 2002.

Kate Coler

GOVERNMENT OFFICIAL. Kate Coler is a native of Minnesota and received a Bachelor of Arts degree in political science from the University of Illinois at Urbana-Champaign.

Her professional career includes serving as federal legislative representative for the American Bankers Association where she was the organization's primary liaison to members of the House and Senate Agriculture Committees and United States Department Agriculture (USDA) officials. She served as the director of government relations for the Food Marketing Institute, a trade association representing grocery stores and food wholesalers. She joined USDA's Food and Nutrition Service on June 24, 2002, as deputy administrator, food stamp program. Ms. Coler was appointed deputy under secretary for Food, Nutrition and Consumer Services (FNCS) on December 1, 2003.

Barbara-Rose Collins

ELECTED OFFICIAL. Barbara-Rose Collins is a native of Detroit, Michigan. She is a graduate of public schools and attended Wayne State University. She served as a member of Detroit Region I Public School Board from 1971 to 1973; as a member of Michigan House of Representatives from 1975 to 1981; as a member of Detroit City Council, 1982 to 1991. She was elected as a Democrat to the 102nd and to the two succeeding Congresses from January 3, 1991 to January 3, 1997.

Earlean Collins

ELECTED OFFICIAL. Earlean Collins received a bachelor's degree from the University of Illinois. Her professional career includes serving as an Illinois state senator and an assistant administrator of children and family services. Ms. Collins was elected a commissioner for the 1st District of Cook County, Illinois, on the west side of Chicago.

Eileen Marie Collins

ASTRONAUT. Eileen Marie Collins is a native of Elmira, New York, and a graduate of Elmira Free Academy in Elmira, New York. She received an Associate in Science degree in mathematics/science from Corning Community College in 1976 and received a Bachelor of Arts degree in mathematics and economics from Syracuse University in 1978. She earned a Master of Science degree in operations research from Stanford University in 1986 and her second Master of Arts degree in space systems management from Webster University in 1989.

Eileen Marie Collins served as a colonel and pilot with the United States Air Force and an astronaut with NASA. She graduated in 1979 from Air Force Undergraduate Pilot Training at Vance Air Force Base in Oklahoma where she was a T-38 instructor until 1982. From 1982 to 1985 she was a C-141 aircraft commander and instructor pilot at Travis Air Force Base in California. From 1986 to 1989, she was assigned to the United States Air Force Academy in Colorado, where she was an assistant professor in mathematics and a T-41 instructor pilot. She was selected for the astronaut program while attending the Air Force Test Pilot School at Edwards Air Force Base, California, from which she graduated in 1990. She has logged over 6,280 hours in 30 different types of aircraft. She retired from the Air Force in January 2005.

She became an astronaut in July 1991. Initially assigned to orbiter engineering support, Colonel Collins has also served on the astronaut support team responsible for orbiter pre-launch checkout, final launch configuration, crew ingress/egress, and landing/recovery; she also worked in Mission Control as a space craft communicator (CAPCOM) and served as the Astronaut Office Safety Branch chief. A veteran of three space flights, Collins has logged over 537 hours in space. She served as pilot on STS-63 (February 3–11, 1995) and STS-84 (May 15–24, 1997), and was the commander on STS-93 (July 22–27, 1999). She was assigned as crew commander on STS-114.

Susan Margaret Collins

ELECTED OFFICIAL. Susan Margaret Collins is a native of Caribou, Aroostook County, Maine. She received a bachelor's degree from St. Lawrence University in Canton, New York, in 1975.

Her professional career includes serving as a member of U.S. Senator William S. Cohen's staff from 1975 to 1987, and serving as staff director of the Senate Gov-

ernmental Affairs Subcommittee on the Oversight of Government Management from 1981 to 1987. She served as commissioner of the Maine Department of Professional and Financial Regulation from 1987 to 1992; as the New England regional director, United States Small Business Administration in 1992; and as deputy state treasurer of Massachusetts in 1993. She was the first woman to win a nomination for governor of Maine in 1994, but lost the general election. She was elected a United States senator in 1996, and re-elected in 2002 for a term ending in January 3, 2009.

Rosemary M. Collyer

JUDGE. Rosemary M. Collyer is a graduate of Trinity College in Washington, D.C. (1968) and the University of Denver College of Law in 1977. She served in private law practice in Denver, Colorado, before her government service.

From 1981 to 1984, she served as chairman of the Federal Mine Safety and Health Review Commission; as general counsel of the National Labor Relations Board (1984–1989); and in private law practice in Washington, D.C.

She was appointed judge to the United States District Court in January 2003.

Sandy Colony

COMMUNICATIONS. Sandy Colony received a Bachelor of Arts degree from Skidmore College and a Master of Arts from the New School for Social Research in New York City.

Her professional career includes serving as executive director of NARAL in New York state and as vice president, corporate communications, at StarBand Communications Inc. She began her career in cable at Time Warner Cable of New York City in 1985 where she served in a number of positions, ultimately became vice president, corporate communications. She was a member of the team that launched Time Warner Cable's high-speed data service, Road Runner, in 1996; she also served as vice president, communications, for Mystor TV, a business unit of Time Warner formed to create advanced competitive services.

She serves as senior vice president of corporate communications for Insight Communications, the nation's ninth largest cable operator.

Marlene M. Colucci

BUSINESS EXECUTIVE. Marlene M. Colucci is a native of California. She received a bachelor's degree from the University of California, Los Angeles, and a Juris Doctor degree from the Georgetown University Law Center in Washington, D.C.

Her professional career includes private law practice and serving as both the deputy assistant secretary in the Office of Congressional and Intergovernmental Affairs and as counsel to the deputy secretary of labor. She was appointed by the president to serve at the U.S. Department of Labor in Washington, D.C., and she served as a special assistant to President George W. Bush in the Office of Domestic Policy.

Ms. Colucci serves as executive vice president of public policy for the American Hotel & Lodging Association (AH&LA). Ms. Colucci is responsible for setting the policy agenda and implementing the lobbying efforts of the association, providing guidance on all legislative and regulatory matters impacting AH&LA members and directing the association's political activity.

Ann L. Combs

GOVERNMENT OFFICIAL. Ann L. Combs received a bachelor's degree from the University of Notre Dame and earned her Juris Doctor degree from the George Washington University Law School in Washington, D.C.

Her professional career includes serving with the Advisory Council on Social Security, in private law practice, and as vice president and chief counsel for the retirement and pension issues for the American Council of Life Insurers. She serves as deputy assistant secretary of labor for Employee Benefits Security Administration.

Sara W. Combs

JUDGE. Sara W. Combs is a native of Louisville, Kentucky. She received her Bachelor of Arts in 1970; her Master's of Art in 1971; and a J.D. in 1979 from the University of Louisville. The Law School has honored Judge Combs by naming her among its distinguished alumni; the University of Louisville's College of Arts and Sciences named her an alumni fellow.

After serving in private practice, she was appointed by Governor Brereton Jones on July 16, 1993, as the first woman to serve on the Kentucky Supreme Court. Subsequently appointed to the Kentucky Court of Appeals, she has served in this position since her election in November 1994. On July 1, 2002, she became chief judge pro tempore of the Court of Appeals.

Beth Comstock

BUSINESS EXECUTIVE. Beth Comstock is a native of Virginia and she received a bachelor's degree from the College of William and Mary.

Her professional career includes serving as a journalist covering the Virginia legislature for a local news service, then at NBC she led media relations first in Washington, then in New York. In 1990 she moved to Turner Broadcasting where her duties involved overseeing communications for CNN, TNT, and TBS; this was followed by a stint at CBS. By the mid-1990s she was back at GE-owned NBC where she served as chief spokesperson before moving to vice president of NBC News communications. Ms. Comstock began working for GE in 1998 as head of communications. She served as vice president of corporate communication.

Ms. Comstock was appointed chief marketing officer for GE's marketing department.

Linda Conlin

GOVERNMENT OFFICIAL. Linda Conlin received a bachelor's degree from the University of Massachusetts. Her professional career includes serving from 1986 to 1989 at the United States Information Agency, first as a corporate liaison officer for the U.S./USSR Cultural Exchange Exhibit and then as associate director in the Office of Private Sector Committees. From 1989 to 1993 she served as assistant secretary of commerce for marketing; from 1994 to 1999 she served as the executive director of the New Jersey Commerce and Economic Growth Commission and director of the Officer of Travel and Tourism; in 1999 she served as a consultant with the Conlin Group in Cherry Hill, New Jersey.

Ms. Conlin served as the first vice president of the Export-Import Bank of the United States.

Patricia N. Conlon

JUDGE. Patricia N. Conlon received a Bachelor of Arts degree from the University of Dayton and earned her Juris Doctor degree from Wayne State University. Her professional career includes serving as an assistant prosecuting attorney and being engaged in private law practice. In 1996 she was elected Michigan's Kalamazoo county probate judge. In 2006 she was serving as a judge of the Michigan's 9th Judicial Circuit Court, Kalamazoo County.

Ellen Engleman Conners

BUSINESS EXECUTIVE. Ellen Engleman Conners received both her bachelor's degree and Juris Doctor degree from Indiana University. She earned a masters in public administration from Harvard University.

Her professional career includes serving as the administrator of the Research and Special Programs Administration at the U.S. Department of Transportation; in March 2003 she joined the National Transportation Safety Board in Washington, D.C., as chair.

Ms. Conners in June 2006 became the executive vice president and chief executive officer of the Indiana Association of Realtors.

Kathlene Contres

MILITARY. Kathlene Contres is a native of Spangler, Pennsylvania. She received a Bachelor of Science degree in health education with an emphasis in sports medicine from Slippery Rock University, Pennsylvania, and has earned a master's degree while serving in the Navy. She received her Navy commission at Officer Candidate School at Newport, Rhode Island.

Her professional career includes serving as quality assurance and safety officer in 1984; in Hawaii as the fleet retention officer; at the Recruit Training Command in San Diego in 1989; she was the officer in charge of personnel support detachment at Naval Station Long Beach from 1992 to 1994; she was assigned to the chief of naval operations, Navy Training Directorate, at the Pentagon; she served as the director, diversity recruiting programs.

Captain Contres is the Navy's highest-ranking female Hispanic line officer on active duty; is the commander of the Defense Equal Opportunity Management Institute (DEOMI) Department of Defense and U.S. Coast Guard equal opportunity and equal employment opportunity (EO/EEO) program requirements.

Cynthia Coogan

MILITARY. Cynthia Coogan received a Bachelor of Science degree from the University of Delaware and a Master of Business Administration degree from George Washington University. She has earned a Master of Science degree in national resource strategy from the National Defense University, and completed the Massachusetts Institute of Technology Seminar XXXI concentrating on foreign politics, international relations and the national interest.

She was commissioned into the Coast Guard through the Coast Guard Officer Candidate School in Yorktown, Virginia. Admiral Coogan has served in a wide variety of operational command and staff assignments, including chief of operations for the First Coast Guard District in Boston, Massachusetts; as commander of Group Portland in South Portland, Maine; as commander of Group Fort Macon in Atlantic Beach in North Carolina; and as commanding officer of Station San Francisco and as operations officer at Group San Francisco. In October 2006, she was assigned as director of reserve and training of the Coast Guard Reserve.

Colleen Conway Cooney

JUDGE. Colleen Conway Cooney is a native of Cleveland. She received a Bachelor of Arts degree from Western Reserve College in 1978 and earned her Juris Doctor from Case Western Reserve University Law School in 1981.

Prior to her election, she served nine years as a Cleveland municipal judge, eight years as an assistant prosecuting attorney for Cuyahoga County, and two years as a judicial law clerk at the Eighth District Court of Appeals. In 2000 she was elected judge to the Ohio Eighth District Court of Appeals in Cleveland, Ohio.

Cynthia Cooper

SPORTS. Cynthia Cooper is a native of Chicago, Illinois, and grew up in Watts, South Central Los Angeles, California. She is a graduate of Locke High School and received a bachelor's degree from the University of Southern California.

She played basketball while in college with the USC Trojans and with the United States National Team. She also played professional basketball in the Women's National Basketball Association (WNBA). She was signed by the Houston Comets, and became the team leader. She won back-to-back MVPs, was the league's leading scorer for three of the four years —1997, 1998, and 1999 and with Sheryl Swoopes, Tina Thompson and Janeth Arcain, dominated the first four years of the WNBA by winning four consecutive championships (1997, 1998, 1999, and 2000). Ms. Cooper was named finals MVP each of those years and was also named All–WNBA First-Team member through those same years (1997, 1998, 1999, and 2000). She retired as a player in July 2000 and went to coach the Phoenix

Mercury for one and a half seasons. She returned as an active player to the WNBA on April 29, 2003. She announced her final retirement from basketball on May 2, 2004. In May 2005, Cooper was selected to serve as coach of the Prairie View A&M University women's basketball team.

Jessica R. Cooper

JUDGE. Jessica R. Cooper earned her Juris Doctor from Wayne State University Law School. She began her career as an assistant defender in the Michigan State Appellate Defenders office until she entered the private practice of law. She has served as an adjunct professor of law at Michigan State University and the University of Michigan Law School.

Judge Cooper presently sits as a judge of the Michigan Court of Appeals.

LaDoris Hazzard Cordell

JUDGE (FIRST). LaDoris Hazzard Cordell is a native of Bryn Mawr, Pennsylvania. She received a Bachelor of Arts degree from Antioch College in 1971 and earned her Juris Doctor degree from Stanford Law School in 1974.

She was engaged in private law practice, then in April 1982, Governor Jerry Brown appointed her judge to the municipal court of Santa Clara County, making her the first African-American woman judge in all of northern California. During her tenure in municipal court, she served as the presiding judge and as justice pro-tem on the State Court of Appeals. On June 7, 1988, she overwhelmingly won election to the superior court of Santa Clara County. She is the first African-American woman to sit on the superior court in northern California. In December 1988, Judge Cordell traveled to South Africa to participate in that country's first human rights conference. She received international attention when she was detained by the South African police during her visit to a black township. From 1989 to 1991, she served as the supervisor of the family court. She served as a trial judge in the Juvenile Dependency Court. On February 28, 2001, after almost 19 years, she retired from the court. She began her new career as vice provost and special counselor to the president for campus relations at Stanford University. On November 4, 2003, she won election to the Palo Alto City Council.

Carolyn Corvi

BUSINESS EXECUTIVE. Carolyn Corvi is a native of Seattle, Washington. She received a bachelor's degree from the University of Washington and a master's degree in management from Massachusetts Institute of Technology.

She began her career at Boeing in 1974 and has held a variety of key leadership assignments including vice president of aircraft systems and interiors, the division that designs and produces assemblies for all airplane programs, spares and aftermarket support. She was assigned as vice president of the propulsion systems division, which develops propulsions systems and auxiliary power units for the entire Boeing family of commercial airplanes. She served as director of quality assurance for the fabrication division, which produces a diverse range of parts, tools and assemblies used in the production of every Boeing jetliner. She also served as director of program management for the 737 and 757 programs. Ms. Corvi was appointed vice president and general manager of airplane programs, commercial airplanes, a fully integrated production system. The airplane programs organization has more than 30,000 employees and includes all airplane production activities in Everett and Renton, Washington.

Lynne Costantini

MEDIA EXECUTIVE. Lynne Costantini is a native of New York. She received a bachelor's degree magna cum laude from Manhattanville College and earned her Juris Doctor degree magna cum laude from New York Law School in 1984. She completed the CTAM University Executive Education Program at the Kellogg Graduate School of Management at Northwestern University as well as the Columbia University Executive Education Program in finance and accounting.

Her professional career includes serving in

private law practice for ten years specializing in mergers and acquisitions with two major New York firms. In 1996 she joined Time Warner Cable. In her current role she negotiates national and local programming agreements with broadcast and cable networks and analyzes the financial, legal and technical aspects of each project and reviews new programming opportunities based on market trends and field research.

Patricia O'Brien Cotter

JUDGE. Patricia O'Brien Cotter received a Bachelor of Science degree in political science from Western Michigan University with honors in 1972. She earned her Juris Doctor degree from Notre Dame Law School in 1977.

Her professional career includes serving in private law practice. In 1998 she was chosen as one of five Ninth Circuit lawyers to serve on the executive committee for the Ninth Circuit Judicial Conference. On November 7, 2000, she won election to the Montana Supreme Court and assumed the position previously held by retiring Justice William Hunt.

Carol Cottrell

ELECTED OFFICIAL. Carol Cottrell received a bachelor's degree in audiology and speech science from Michigan State University in 1975 and earned a masters degree in audiology and speech science in 1976.

Her professional career includes serving as a speech pathologist for the Saginaw Public Schools from 1976 to 2001. She was elected to Saginaw City Council in November 1995; she served as mayor pro tem from 2003 to 2005; she was elected mayor of Saginaw, Michigan, in 2005.

Millicent S. Counts

BUSINESS EXECUTIVE. Millicent S. Counts received a Bachelor of Arts degree from Youngstown State University.

She serves as executive director of the United Methodist Community Center. She also serves on the bishop's initiative on children and poverty of the East Ohio Conference of the United Methodist Church. She represented the general board of global ministries of the United Methodist Church in developing a plan for the involvement of the church in relief aid for refugees fleeing Rwanda.

Katie Couric

JOURNALISM. Katie Couric is a native of Arlington, Virginia. She received a bachelor's degree in English with honors from the University of Virginia.

Her professional career includes joining NBC News in 1989 and the *Today Show* in 1990, becoming permanent co-anchor in 1991. She announced to *Today Show* viewers on April 5, 2006, that she would leave the show at the end of May to become the anchor of the *CBS Evening News*. She made her debut on the evening news broadcast on September 5, 2006.

Judith A. Cowin

JUDGE. Judith A. Cowin is a native of Boston, Massachusetts. She received her undergraduate degree from Wellesley College and earned her Juris Doctor from Harvard Law School in 1970. Her professional career includes serving as an assistant legal counsel to the Massachusetts Department of Mental Health, as legal counsel for the Office of the Chief Justice of the District Court, and as an assistant district attorney in Norfolk County from 1979 to 1991. In 1991, she was appointed an associate justice of the Superior Court where she served until Governor Paul Cellucci appointed her as an associate justice of the Supreme Judicial Court in October 1999.

Darlene L. Cox

MEDICINE. Darlene L. Cox received a bachelor's degree in nursing from Cornell University's New York

Hospital School of Nursing and a master's degree of nursing from the University of Michigan Graduate School of Rackham.

Her professional career includes serving as chief nurse and administrator of patient care services at University Hospital from 1986 to 1994. During her tenure at University Hospital, she took a one-year leave of absence to join the highly prestigious White House Fellows program where she worked on health care policy issues. She served as vice president of patient care services and chief nursing officer at Columbia-Presbyterian Medical Center. She was appointed president and chief executive officer of Essex Valley Health Care (East Orange General Hospital).

Ms. Cox was named president and chief executive officer of the University Hospital.

Susan Crawford

JUDGE. Susan Crawford received her undergraduate degree from Georgia State University in 1979 and earned her Juris Doctor degree from Georgia State University in 1987. Her professional career includes serving in private law practice, as a part-time Gainesville city solicitor, and as a part-time Hall County state court judge. She joined the Office of State Administrative Hearing in 2000 as an administrative law judge in Georgia.

Sharon Creer

SPORTS EXECUTIVE. Sharon Creer received a bachelor's degree from California State University East Bay and earned her master's degree in sports/organizational psychology from John F. Kennedy University in Orinda, California.

Her professional career includes serving as a sports psychology consultant at Richmond High School and as a recording engineer at the Plant Studio and Starlight Sound where she worked on recording projects by Miles Davis, En Vogue, and the WNBA (Women's National Basketball Association), WBCA (Women's Basketball Coach's Association), NAFE (National Association of Female Executives), JLAC Board of Directors (Jack London Aquatic Center). She now serves as one of the few elite African-American female sports agents representing a cadre of top professional athletes in the United States.

Donna L. Crisp

MILITARY. Donna L. Crisp is a native of Bay Shore, New York, and was raised in Redlands, California. She received a bachelor's degree from California State University at Long Beach.

In October 1974 she was commissioned an ensign at Officer Candidate School in Newport, Rhode Island.

Admiral Crisp has held numerous positions of increased authority during her military career, to include serving as director of manpower, personnel, and quality, United States Transportation Command, Scott Air Force Base, Illinois, where she was also selected by the deputy commander in chief to be his executive assistant with the additional duty of director of staff. She served as deputy chief of staff for shore installation management on the staff of commander, United States Pacific Fleet. In September 2004, she was assigned as the director for manpower and personnel, Joint Staff, Pentagon, Washington, D.C.

Linda Washington Cropp

ELECTED OFFICIAL (FIRST). Linda Washington Cropp received bachelor's and master's degrees from Howard University in Washington, D.C. Her professional career includes serving as a teacher and later as a guidance counselor with the District of Columbia Public School System. She was elected to the Board of Education as the Ward 4 representative; in 1990 she was elected as an at-large member of the Council of the District of Columbia and reelected in 1994 to her at-large seat; in 1997 her colleagues chose her as acting chairman and was elected to the chair in a special election and was sworn in on August 8, 1997, as the first woman to chair the Council of the District of Columbia. She was re-elected in 1998 to a full four-year term as chairman of the council.

Barbara L. Cubin

ELECTED OFFICIAL. Barbara L. Cubin is a native of Salinas, California, and grew up in Casper, Wyoming. She graduated from Natrona County High School in Casper and received a Bachelor of Science degree from Creighton University, Omaha, Nebraska.

Ms. Cubin worked as a chemist at the Wyoming Machinery Company and then as office manager for her husband's medical office. In 1979 she became a Realtor. In 1986 she was elected to the Wyoming House of Representatives from Natrona County, Wyoming. After serving six years in the House she was elected in November 1992 to the Wyoming State Senate representing part of Casper, Wyoming. In 1994 she was elected a United States Representative as a Republican to the 104th and to the succeeding Congresses.

Nancy Cuffney

LAW ENFORCEMENT. Nancy Cuffney is the highest-ranking female officer at the Monterey County Sheriff's Office. She started her career in 1977 as a deputy in the jail and throughout most of her career she worked for the corrections division. She served as a bailiff and deputy at the Monterey County Jail.

She was promoted to sergeant in corrections and worked in recruitment before becoming a commander. In 2003, she was promoted to chief deputy of the Administration Bureau and in January 2005 she was appointed the first female undersheriff with the Monterey County Sheriff's Office in Salinas, California.

Anna Culley

JUDGE. Anna Culley received a Bachelor of Arts degree from St. John's University and earned her Juris degree from St. John's University School of Law. Her professional career includes serving as an assistant district attorney for Queens County, as senior court attorney for Judge Anthony Gazzara, and as principal law clerk for the administrative judge of Queens County from 2000 to 2004. In 2004 she was appointed judge to the Civil Court of the City of New York, Queens County.

Angela M. Cummings

MILITARY. Angela M. Cummings is a native of Jacksonville, Florida. She graduated from Bennett College in Greensboro, North Carolina, with a Bachelor of Arts degree in recreation with a concentration in therapeutics for the handicapped and was commissioned in the Adjutant General Corps through ROTC. She holds a Master of Arts degree in human resource development from Webster University. Her military education includes the Adjutant General Corps Officer Basic and Advanced Courses; Systems Automation and Command; and General Staff College.

She has served in a wide variety of Adjutant General Corps assignments that include serving as a platoon leader; executive officer; officer in charge of both the Personnel Systems Branch (SIDPERS) and Personnel Services division and ID Card and Passport Section of the Wiesbaden Regional Personnel Center (RPC)–22nd Personnel and Administrative Battalion, Wiesbaden, Germany; operations officer and adjutant, Harrisburg Recruiting Battalion, New Cumberland, Pennsylvania; company commander, Student Company United States Army Element, School of Music (Army) Bandsman — Advanced Individual Training, Little Creek Naval Amphibious Base, Norfolk, Virginia; information management/systems automation staff officer for C2/J2/G2, United States Forces, Korea (USFK), Combined Forces Command (CFC), Republic of Korea, Yongsan, Korea; operations officer, Casualty and Memorial Affairs Operations Center, PERSCOM, Alexandria, Virginia; Adjutant General Corps — Advanced Individual Training School director, battalion executive officer, 369th Adjutant General Battalion, Fort Jackson, Columbia, South Carolina; chief officer management division, G1, 18th ABN Corps and ACofS, G1, 1st COSCOM, Fort Bragg, North Carolina; in October 2004, she was serving as the battalion commander, AFNORTH, United States Army with NATO.

Andy Cunningham

COMMUNICATIONS. Andy Cunningham received a Bachelor of Arts degree in English from Northwestern University.

Her professional career includes serving as chairman

and chief executive officer of Citigate Cunningham, a public relations agency she founded in 1985. She serves as the chairman, president and chief executive officer of CXO Communication, a privately held strategic communication consultancy in Palo Alto, California.

Paula D. Cunningham

FINANCE. Paula D. Cunningham received a Bachelor of Science degree in journalism from Michigan State University and a Master of Science degree in labor and industrial relations from Michigan State University.

Her professional career includes serving as owner and principal of the Mason Hills Golf Course; as keynote speaker, panel member and facilitator for a myriad of local and national organizations; and as host of a weekly talk radio program for more than six years.

She served for 25 years at Lansing Community College (LLC), where she served as vice president of planning and college relations; as executive director of marketing, community, and board relations; as director of professional development; and associate professor in the management and marketing department.

Ms. Cunningham was appointed president of Lansing Community College in 2000. She has also served on the Michigan Education Trust Board of Directors. She serves on the Lieutenant Governor's Commission on Higher Education and Economic Growth and on the Advisory Board of Sparrow Hospital. She is a member of the Tax Increment Finance Authority, a board member of community organizations such as Cristo Rey and the Capital Area United Way where she served as campaign chair in 2002. She also served as a board member of Capitol National Bank.

Ms. Cunningham was appointed by Governor Granholm to serve as head of the Michigan Department of Labor and Economic Growth. On November 1, 2006, she assumed the position of president of Capitol National Bank in Lansing.

Pauline W. Cunningham

MILITARY. Pauline W. Cunningham is native of Los Angeles, California, and is a graduate of George Washington High School.

Command Sergeant Major Cunningham is a graduate of the Army Noncommissioned Officer Academy, Finance Basic and Advance Courses; the First Sergeant Course; the United States Army Sergeants Major Academy; and the Command Sergeants Major Course. She is a graduate of Saint Leo's College with a bachelor's degree in human resource management.

She enlisted in the military in the summer of 1976 during the Woman's Army Corps era. She attended basic training at Fort McClellan, Alabama, and advance individual training at Fort Benjamin Harrison, Indiana. Upon completion of AIT she was awarded the finance MOS of 73C.

She has held leadership positions from squad leader to command sergeant major and also served as an instructor for the First Sergeants Course at Fort Bliss, Texas.

Sheree Davis Cunningham

JUDGE. Sheree Davis Cunningham received her Juris Doctor degree from Howard University School of Law in Washington, D.C. She was engaged in private law practice prior to her appointment in November 1993 as judge to the 15th Judicial Circuit Court in West Palm Beach, Florida.

Norma J. Curby

BUSINESS EXECUTIVE. Norma J. Curby is a native of St. Louis, Missouri. She received a Bachelor of Science degree in civil engineering in 1972 and a Master of Science degree in engineering management in 1978, both from the University of Missouri.

Her professional career includes serving from 1973 to 1996 as a structural engineer with Monsanto. During her employment with Monsanto, she held several product and brand management positions before she was named director, equal opportunity affairs. She subsequently held the positions of architectural commercial and market development director, as well as worldwide business director for Monsanto's polymer modifiers and process chemicals businesses. In 1997 she joined Solutia, Inc., a specialty chemicals company spun off from Monsanto, as vice president and general manager of phosphorous and derivatives.

Ms. Curby joined Air Products and Chemicals, Inc., in 2001 as vice president of global customer engagement.

Deborah B. Cureton

EDUCATION. Deborah B. Cureton received bachelor's and master's degrees from the University of South Carolina. She earned her Ph.D. in curriculum and instruction from the University of Wisconsin in Madison.

She serves as dean and chief executive officer of the University of Wisconsin–Richland. Upon her arrival, she guided a team effort to develop and submit a proposal to the United States Department of Education for a Talent Search Grant, a Trio program targeting minority and disadvantaged pre-college youth to encourage and support preparation for college.

Patricia S. Curley

JUDGE. Patricia S. Curley is a native of Milwaukee, Wisconsin. She received her undergraduate degree from Marquette University in 1969 and earned her Juris Doctor from Marquette University in 1973.

Her professional career began with a position as an assistant district attorney for Milwaukee County from 1973 to 1978. In 1978, she was appointed judge to the circuit court. In 1996, she was appointed judge on the Wisconsin Court of Appeals, District I.

Gail Currey

ENTERTAINMENT EXECUTIVE. Gail Currey received a Bachelor of Arts degree in liberal arts and a Masters of Fine Arts degree from the Art Institute of Chicago.

She began her career at Industrial Light & Magic (ILM) as the physical production coordinator and became involved in the growing field of computer graphics on *Terminator 2: Judgment Day.* She has served as a key member of a team that ultimately redefined the way visual effects are created. Her work on groundbreaking films such as *Jurassic Park* and *Perfect Storm* played a pivotal role in the transformation of Industrial Light & Magic into the largest, most well known and respected digital production company in the world. She served as chief operations officer at Industrial Light & Magic from 1998 to 2002 where she was responsible for the daily management of the computer graphics, animation and technology departments involved in the production of imagery for Industrial Light & Magic's feature film and commercial clients. In February 2004, Ms. Currey was appointed vice president and general manager of Lucasfilm Animation.

Nancy Jane Currie

ASTRONAUT. Nancy Jane Currie is a native of Wilmington, Delaware, but considers Troy, Ohio, to be her hometown. She is a graduate of Troy High School, Troy, Ohio, in 1977, and received a Bachelor of Arts degree in biological science from the Ohio State University, Columbus, Ohio, in 1980. She earned a Master of Science degree in safety engineering from the University of Southern California in 1985 and a doctorate in industrial engineering from the University of Houston in 1997.

Nancy Jane Currie served in the United States Army for 23 years and achieved the rank of colonel prior to her retirement in May 2005. Prior to her assignment at NASA, she attended initial rotary wing pilot training and was subsequently assigned as an instructor pilot at the U.S. Army Aviation Center. As a master Army aviator she logged over 4,000 flying hours in a variety of rotary-wing and fixed-wing aircraft. She holds an appointment as an adjunct associate professor at North Carolina State University.

Colonel Currie was assigned to NASA Johnson Space Center in September 1987 as a flight simulation engineer. Selected as an astronaut in 1990, she completed the Astronaut Candidate Training Program in 1991. A veteran of four Space Shuttle missions, she has accrued 1,000 hours in space. She flew as mission specialist 2, flight engineer, on STS-57 (1993), STS-70 (1995), STS-88 (the first International Space Station assembly mission—1988), and STS-109 (2002). During her tenure in the Astronaut Office, Currie worked as a spacecraft communicator and was the lead flight crew representative for crew safety and habitability equipment. She served as the chief of the Astronaut Office Robotics and Payloads-Habitability branches and was a consultant to NASA's Space Human Factors Engineering Project. Col. Currie also served as the technical assistant to the director, automation, robotics and simulation division and as manager, habitability and human factors office. Following the *Columbia* tragedy in 2003, she was selected to lead the Space Shuttle Program's Safety and Mission Assurance Office. After leaving NASA, she served as the senior technical advisor to the automation, robotics, and simulation division in the Johnson Space Center Engineering Directorate.

Chandra Curtis

TECHNOLOGY EXECUTIVE. Chandra Curtis is assigned as a digital avionics systems engineer for the Munitions Directorate at Eglin Air Force Base, Florida. She was selected as the 2005 Most Promising Engineer in Government "BEYA." Dr. Curtis is working on applications of reconfigurable computing for real-time processing of autonomous target acquisition algorithms and investigating its usefulness in embedded systems for autonomous vehicles.

In addition to her work in reconfigurable computing, she also advises other engineers and scientists within the lab on processing technologies in order to help determine suitable computer platforms for certain applications.

Donna Lee Dacier

MILITARY. Donna Lee Dacier received a Bachelor of Arts degree in English literature and composition from Western Maryland College and earned a Master of Science degree in instructional and performance technology from Boise State University. She has also received a Master of Science degree in national resource strategy from National Defense University.

Major General Dacier serves as the commander of the 311th Theater Signal Command at Fort Meade, Maryland. She was promoted to major general on April 28, 2005. She also serves as senior defense analyst, BCP International, Ltd. in Alexandria, Virginia.

Shana Dale

GOVERNMENT OFFICIAL. Shana Dale received a bachelor's degree with honors in management information systems from the University of Tulsa and earned a Juris Doctor degree from California Western School of Law.

Her professional career includes private law practice, serving as the assistant vice chancellor for federal relations at the University of Texas System, Federal Relation Office in Washington and as the Republican assistant legislative director and counsel on the space subcommittee. She was appointed to the Committee on Science, Space and Technology in March 1991 and served as the chief of staff and general counsel at Office of Science and Technology Policy; she cochaired the National Science and Technology Council's Committee on Homeland and National Security and supervised work of the subcommittees; she served as deputy director for homeland and national security for the Office of Science and Technology Policy. She was appointed by President George W. Bush and confirmed by the United States Senate as deputy administrator of the National Aeronautics Space Administration on November 14, 2005.

Linda Stewart Dalianis

JUDGE (FIRST). Linda Stewart Dalianis received a bachelor's degree from Northeastern University and earned her Juris Doctor from Suffolk University Law School. Her professional career includes serving twenty years on the

Superior Court bench, both as an associate justice and as chief justice. She is the first woman to hold a seat on the New Hampshire Supreme Court. She was appointed by Governor Jeanne Shaheen in 2000 as an associate justice on the Supreme Court. She now serves as the senior associate justice.

Jennifer Dangar

MEDIA EXECUTIVE. Jennifer Dangar received a Bachelor of Arts degree in ancient history from Tulane University.

Her professional career includes serving in numerous positions with C-SPAN and Viewer's Choice Cable; in her role at Turner Broadcasting, she was responsible for managing the Comcast account, as well as the affiliate marketing department and strategic marketing for Turner's 11 domestic networks.

She serves as vice president of new media distribution for Discovery Networks US, where she is charged with gaining widespread distribution for Discovery's non-linear video products, primarily within the affiliate community.

Janet Davidson

TECHNOLOGY EXECUTIVE. Janet Davidson received a bachelor's degree in physics from Lehigh University and a master's degree in electrical engineering from Georgia Tech.

Her professional career includes serving as a member of technical staff at Bell Labs. She has more than 20 years of experience in software design and development, global product strategy, marketing and product management. From 2000 to 2005, she served as president, Integrated Network Solutions, the Lucent unit that designed and delivered wireline networks for the world's largest communications service providers. In this position, she was responsible for the company's optical networking, multiservice switching, broadband access, edge access, convergence solutions and network operations software business.

Ms. Davidson serves as Lucent Technologies chief strategy officer responsible for evolving Lucent's strategy and vision for next-generation networks based on the IMS architecture. She also serves as president, Network Operations Software, the Lucent business unit that provides multivendor service quality and network management software to communications companies, governments and enterprises worldwide.

Lisa Davidson

JUDGE. Lisa Davidson graduated from Meridian High School in Meridian, Mississippi, in 1970. She received a Bachelor of Arts from the University of Michigan in 1974 and earned her Juris Doctor degree from Duke Law School in 1977.

Her professional career includes serving as an assistant public defender in Broward County from 1978 to 1980; as an assistant state attorney, Broward County, from 1980 to 1981; from 1982 to 1993, she was engaged in private law practice. In 1994, she was appointed judge, Brevard County Court in Florida; since 1998, she has served as a circuit court judge at the Florida Eighteenth Judicial Circuit in Viera, Florida.

Audrey Y. Davis

GOVERNMENT OFFICIAL. Audrey Y. Davis is a graduate of the Federal Executive Institute, the Office of Personnel Management's management development seminar, the Defense Leadership and Management Program, and the Industrial College of the Armed Forces. She is a member of the federal government's Senior Executive Service, the American Society of Military Comptrollers and Armed Forces Communications and Electronics Association. She attended Oklahoma State University and the University of Oklahoma and respectively earned Bachelor and Master of Science degrees.

Ms. Davis began her federal career as a presidential management intern with the United States Army Information Systems Engineering Command where she trained and gained experience as a computer programmer analyst. After completing her internship in 1987, she accepted a computer security specialist position with the United States Department of State where she established the department's computer security test facility serving as its program manager.

She became the

director for information and technology, Defense Finance and Accounting Service, Arlington, in January 2001. She is responsible for the oversight and direction of DFAS information technology expenditures of approximately $500 million per year. In addition, she serves as DFAS chief information officer and technical advisor to DFAS Arlington's Systems Integration Directorate.

Jo Ann Davis

ELECTED OFFICIAL. Jo Ann Davis is a native of Rowan County, North Carolina. She attended Hampton Roads Business College, Hampton Roads, Virginia. She was engaged in private business when she was elected to the Virginia General Assembly from 1997 to 2001. She was elected a United States Representative to the 107th and to the two succeeding Congresses.

Kathy L. Davis

ELECTED OFFICIAL. Kathy L. Davis received a Bachelor of Science degree in mechanical engineering from the Massachusetts Institute of Technology in 1978 and a master's degree from Harvard Business School in 1982.

Her professional career includes working at Cummins Engine Co. in Columbus, Indiana, where she managed assembly and shipping operations for Cummins' 14-liter diesel engine. In 1989, she joined the Indiana Department of Transportation as deputy commissioner; from 1995 to 1997, she served as the Indiana state budget director; in 1997 she became the secretary for the Indiana Family and Social Services Administration; in 1999 she managed the start-up of the Indiana 21st Century Research and Technology Fund. She was appointed controller for the City of Indianapolis, where she served for four years.

Ms. Davis was nominated and unanimously confirmed the 49th lieutenant governor of Indiana in October 2003 by the Indiana General Assembly. She is the first woman to hold the position.

Laura Prosser Davis

JUDGE. Laura Prosser Davis is a native of Baton Rouge, Louisiana. She received a Bachelor of Science degree in psychology and educational research from the University of Virginia in 1972 and received a Master's of Education in counseling from the University of Virginia in 1974. She earned her Juris Doctor degree from Louisiana State University Law School. She spent ten years teaching and counseling from the University of Virginia in 1974. She served as a law clerk in the 19th Judicial District Court and was engaged in private law practice. In 2000, she was elected judge to the Baton Rouge City Court.

Lisa Davis

NONPROFIT EXECUTIVE. Lisa Davis received a Bachelor of Arts degree in communication studies from the University of North Carolina at Greensboro. She earned a Master of Business Administration and public administration from Howard University in Washington, D.C.

Her professional career includes serving as national deputy press secretary for the Clinton/Gore '96 Reelection campaign; she was also press secretary for the Democratic Leadership Council and its think tank. While serving at the American Bar Association, she handled communications on the U.S. Supreme Court nomination and hearing of Justice Clarence Thomas, the Rodney King riots, and perestroika, the opening of the Soviet Union. She served as the American Association of Retired People's (AARP) director of public relations.

Ms. Davis serves as a high-level counselor to AARP's chief communications officer and the group's executive team (AARP's governing body). She is now vice president of corporate communications for the Department of Communication's Advisory Council.

Marguerite H. Davis

JUDGE. Marguerite H. Davis is a native of Washington, D.C. She received a Bachelor of Arts degree with honors from the University of South Florida in 1968.

She earned a Juris Doctor degree with honors from Florida State University in 1971.

From 1971 to 1985, she served as senior legal aid, Florida Supreme Court; from 1982 to 1984, she was executive assistant to the chief justice of the Florida Supreme Court; and in 1985, she served in private law practice. She has served as a judge, First District Court of Appeal, from 1993 to the present.

N. Jan Davis

ASTRONAUT. N. Jan Davis is a native of Cocoa Beach, Florida, but considers Huntsville, Alabama, to be her hometown. She is a graduate of Huntsville High School in 1971 and received a Bachelor of Science degree in applied biology from Georgia Institute of Technology in 1975. She earned a Bachelor of Science in mechanical engineering from Auburn University in 1977. She received both a Master of Science degree in 1983 and a doctorate in mechanical engineering from the University of Alabama in Huntsville in 1985.

After graduating from Auburn University in 1977, she joined Texaco in Bellaire, Texas, working as a petroleum engineer in tertiary oil recovery. She left there in 1979 to work for NASA's Marshall Space Flight Center as an aerospace engineer. She became an astronaut in June 1987. She is a veteran of three space flights; she has logged over 673 hours in space. She flew as a mission specialist on STS-47 in 1992 and STS-60 in 1994, and was the payload commander on STS-85 in 1997. She serves as director of Flight Projects Directorate at Marshall Space Flight Center.

Ruth A. Davis

GOVERNMENT OFFICIAL. Ruth A. Davis is a native of Phoenix, Arizona. She received a bachelor's degree in sociology magna cum laude in 1966 from Spelman College in Atlanta, Georgia. While enrolled in Spelman, she spent 15 months as a Merrill Scholar studying and traveling in Europe and the Middle East. She earned a master's degree from the School of Social Work at the University of California at Berkeley. She was a member of the 34th class of the Senior Seminar (1991–1992) which was the highest level of executive training offered by the U.S. government.

Her professional career includes joining the U.S. Foreign Service in 1969 where she was assigned as consular officer in Kinshasa, Zaire. From 1971 to 1973 she served in Nairobi, Kenya; from 1973 to 1976 she served in Tokyo, Japan; and from 1976 to 1980 she served in Naples, Italy. She returned to the United States as a Pearson Fellow working as special advisor for international affairs for the Washington, D.C., municipal government. While advising the D.C. government, she directed the city's Sister City program and its International Task Force. From 1987 to 1991, she was assigned as consul general in Barcelona, Spain. From December 1992 to November 1995, she served as the principal deputy assistant secretary for consular affairs. From June 1, 2001, to June 30, 2003, she served as director general of the foreign service and director of human resources. From July 2003 to September 2005, she served an assignment as distinguished advisor for international affairs at Howard University in Washington, D.C.

Ms. Davis serves as special adviser and chief of staff in the Africa Bureau of the Department of State.

Sarah Frances Davis

MINISTRY. Sarah Frances Davis received a Bachelor of Arts degree from the University of North Texas and a Master of Science from New York's Pace University. She earned a Master of Divinity from the Houston Graduate School of Theology and her Doctor of Ministry for Southern Methodist University's Perkins School of Theology.

Her professional career includes serving as a manager with Southwestern Bell (now retired). She was appointed pastor of the 115-year-old Bethel AME Church in San Antonio, Texas, in 1997 and served for seven years. She was the first woman in Texas to be appointed to a major African Methodist Episcopal church. Also in 1997 she became the first woman in the Connectional AME church to be appointed chair of a Board of Examiners division; she is currently the AME representative on the Churches Uniting in Christ Coordinating Council.

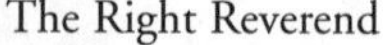

The Right Reverend

Sarah Frances Davis was elected the 126th consecrated bishop of the African Methodist Episcopal Church. Her historic election on July 6, 2004, made her only the third woman in the 218-year history of the denomination to ascend to its highest level of Episcopal service. Bishop Davis is currently assigned as the presiding prelate over the 18th Episcopal District, which is comprised of the southern African countries of Lesotho, Botswana, Swaziland, and Mozambique.

Susan A. Davis

ELECTED OFFICIAL. Susan A. Davis is a native of Cambridge, Massachusetts. She received a Bachelor of Arts degree from the University of California in Berkeley, California, in 1965 and earned her Master of Arts degree from the University of North Carolina at Chapel Hill, North Carolina, in 1968.

Her professional career includes serving as a member of the San Diego, California, Board of Education from 1983 to 1992, serving as president of the board from 1989 to 1992. She was elected a member of the California State Assembly and served from 1994 to 2001. She was elected a United States representative to the 107th and to the two succeeding Congresses.

Diann Dawson

GOVERNMENT OFFICIAL. Diann Dawson received a Bachelor of Arts degree from Bennett College in Greensboro, North Carolina, and received a masters of social work degree with a concentration in community organization and social planning from the University of North Carolina at Chapel Hill. She earned her Juris Doctor degree from the Columbus School of Law at the Catholic University of America in Washington, D.C.

Her professional career includes serving with the South Carolina Department of Social Services. Ms. Dawson serves as the director, office of regional operations in the Administration for Children and Families (ACF), U.S. Department of Health and Human Services. As a senior level director and principal advisor to the assistant secretary, she provides leadership and directions to the field/regional operations for ACF programs.

Marcela Perez de Alonso

BUSINESS EXECUTIVE. Marcela Perez de Alonso is a native of Chile. She earned an advanced degree in organizational psychology from the Catholic University in Chile. She attended the business executive program of the Columbia University Graduate School of Business and received a certificate in finance and accounting.

Her professional career includes serving as a longtime executive at Citigroup. She was head of Citigroup's North Latin America retail business operations and was in charge of deposit products for the company's international retail bank. She joined the Hewlett-Packard Company (HP) in 2004 bringing with her a deep human resources expertise and broad business experience. She serves as executive vice president of human resources for Hewlett-Packard Company. She has worldwide responsibility for all of HP's human resources activities.

Lois M. DeBerry

ELECTED OFFICIAL. Lois M. DeBerry is a native of Shelby County, Tennessee. She received a Bachelor of Arts degree from Lemoyne-Owen College and earned a real estate certification in 1981.

She has served in the Tennessee General Assembly since 1972. She is the first black female elected to the House of Representatives from the city of Memphis, the first woman chairperson of the Shelby County Democratic Caucus and the first black ever elected speaker pro tempore to the Tennessee House of Representatives. She is the founder and chairperson of Annual Legislative Retreat of Tennessee Black Caucus of State Legislators.

Susan L. Decker

TECHNOLOGY EXECUTIVE. Susan L. Decker received a bachelor's degree with a double major in computer

science and economics and a Master of Business Administration degree from Harvard Business School.

Her professional career includes 12 years as an equity research analyst, providing coverage to institutional investors on more than 30 media, publishing, and advertising stocks. She was a global and domestic head of research with Donaldson, Lufkin & Jenrette for 14 years, responsible for building and staffing a non–U.S. research product based on global sector teams. In June 2000 Ms. Decker joined Yahoo as executive vice president. She served as head of advertiser and publisher group and acting chief financial officer.

Paula Deen

ENTERTAINMENT EXECUTIVE. Paula Deen is a native of Albany, Georgia. She was a bank teller and homemaker before taking a job as a cook at a Best Western motel. She worked there for five years before opening her own restaurant.

She launched a business out of her home after her marriage failed. With only $200.00 and the help of her sons, she launched The Bag Lady. She prepared sandwiches and her sons went out and sold them. She self-published her first cookbook in 1997, titled *The Lady & Sons Savannah Country Cookbook.* She owns The Lady and Sons eatery in Savannah, Georgia. She joined the Food Network in 1999 and in October 2005 Paula's film *Elizabethtown* premiered. A special, *Paula Goes to Hollywood,* aired on the Food Network.

Anita L. DeFrantz

SPORTS EXECUTIVE. Anita L. DeFrantz is a native of Pennsylvania. She received a Bachelor of Arts with honors from Connecticut College in 1974 and earned her Juris Doctor from the University of Pennsylvania School of Law in 1977.

At the Games of the XXI Olympiad in Montreal in 1976 she was the rowing bronze medalist (eight oars with coxswain) and team captain; she was a four times finalist and silver medalist at the World Rowing Championships in 1978; she was a member of the United States team from 1975 to 1980; and was a winner of six national championships.

Her professional career includes serving as an attorney at the Juvenile Law Centre of Philadelphia from 1977 to 1979; as an administrator at Princeton University from 1979 to 1981; as counselor for the Corporation for Enterprise Development; as vice president, from 1981 to 1985, of the organizing committee of the Games of the XXIII Olympiad in Los Angeles in 1984; as staff person (1985 to 1987), then president in 1987 of the Amateur Athletic Foundation of Los Angeles. In 2006, she was serving as a member of the International Olympic Committee (IOC). She is the first American woman and first African American to serve as vice president of the IOC, the ruling body of the Olympic movement worldwide.

Mary DeGenaro

JUDGE. Mary DeGenaro received a Bachelor of Arts degree from Youngstown State University 1983 and earned her Juris Doctor degree from Cleveland-Marshall College of Law at Cleveland State University in 1986.

She was in private law practice for 14 years prior to her election in November 2000 to the Ohio Seventh District Court of Appeals.

Ellen Lee DeGeneres

ENTERTAINMENT. Ellen Lee DeGeneres is a native of New Orleans, Louisiana. She attended the University of New Orleans, where she majored in communications.

Her professional career began as an emcee and standup comedian at Clyde's Comedy Club in New Orleans. While working at Clyde's in 1981, she recorded her club performances. After traveling around the United States performing her comedy act, she was chosen in a national competition in 1982 by the cable channel Showtime as the funniest person in America. She was then invited to perform on the *Tonight Show Starring Johnny Carson* in 1986. She also appeared as a stand-up comedian on the HBO "Tenth Annual Young Comedians" special. Ms. DeGeneres began her television career on

the short-lived TV sitcom *Open House* and in 1992 *Laurie Hill.* She has also performed two HBO stand-up specials. The first was called "Ellen DeGeneres: The Beginning" in 2000 and was taped lived at the Beacon Theatre in New York City, and the second one in 2003 was called "Ellen DeGeneres." In September 2003 she launched a daytime television talk show, *The Ellen DeGeneres Show.* In August 2005, Ms. DeGeneres was selected to host the 2005 Primetime Emmy Awards ceremony and on September 7, 2006, she was chosen to host the 79th Academy Awards ceremony, which took place on February 25, 2007.

Diana DeGette

ELECTED OFFICIAL. Diana DeGette was born in Tachikawa, Japan. She graduated from South High School in Denver, Colorado. She received a Bachelor of Arts degree from Colorado College in Colorado Springs, Colorado, in 1979, and earned her Juris Doctor degree from New York University in New York, New York, in 1982. She served as a member of the Colorado State House of Representatives from 1992 to 1996; she was elected as a Democrat to the 105th and to the four succeeding Congresses since January 3, 1997.

Rosa L. DeLauro

ELECTED OFFICIAL. Rosa L. DeLauro is a native of New Haven, Connecticut, and graduated from Laurelton Hall High School in West Haven, Connecticut. She received a Bachelor of Arts degree from Marymount College in Tarrytown, New York, in 1964. She attended the London School of Economics, London, England, from 1962 to 1963 and earned a Master of Arts from Columbia University in New York in 1966.

Her professional career includes serving as an executive assistant to the mayor of New Haven, Connecticut, from 1976 to 1977. She served as campaign manager, Frank Logue for Mayor in 1978; as executive assistant to New Haven development administrator from 1977 to 1979; as campaign manager for United States Senator Christopher J. Dodd from 1979 to 1980; as administrative assistant and chief of staff for United States Senator Dodd from 1981 to 1987; as executive director, Countdown '87, 1987–1988; and executive director, EMILY'S List, 1989–1990.

Ms. DeLauro was elected in 1990 as a Democrat to the 102nd

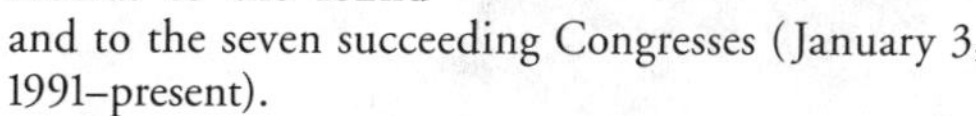

and to the seven succeeding Congresses (January 3, 1991–present).

Katherine R. Delgado

JUDGE. Katherine R. Delgado received a Bachelor of Arts in political science and history from Colorado College in Colorado Springs in 1979 and earned her Juris Doctor degree from the University of Denver College of Law in Denver, Colorado, in 1983.

Her professional career includes serving in private law practice and as a chief deputy district attorney in the Boulder County District Attorney's office. She was appointed as a judge to the Colorado 17th Judicial District in July 2002 by Governor Bill Owens.

Susan C. Del Pesco

JUDGE. Susan C. Del Pesco received a Bachelor of Arts degree from the University of California, Santa Barbara, in 1967 and earned her Juris Doctor degree (cum laude) from Widener University School of Law. She received a masters' degree in 2001 from the University of Virginia.

She was engaged in private law practice from 1975 to 1988. She was appointed judge to the Delaware First Judiciary Superior Court in 1988. She served from 1995 to 1998 on the Complex Litigation Subcommittee of the National Conference of Chief Justices.

Carolyn Webb de Macias

EDUCATION.Carolyn Webb de Macias has served as the Los Angeles–area vice president for Pacific Bell from 1985 to 1989 and as chief of staff for Los Angeles City Councilman Mark Ridley Thomas from 1991 to 1997. She served as senior associate provost at the University of Southern California, serving as facilitator for USC's Art Initiative and as the provost's liaison to the deans of four art schools and the director of the USC Fisher Gallery. She was named vice president for external relations in January 2002 and was on a partial sabbatical during 2005–2006 working with the City of Los Angeles as a senior advisor to the mayor.

Diane Denish

ELECTED OFFICIAL. Diane Denish serves as the first woman ever elected lieutenant governor in the history of New Mexico. In her position she serves as the president of the New Mexico State Senate and as acting governor when Governor Bill Richardson is out of state. Chief among her policy priorities are to help improve the lives of children in the state of New Mexico and she's also the chairperson of the Children's Cabinet, a board comprised of the directors and department heads of state agencies that work with children. She also served under Governor Toney Anaya as chair of the New Mexico Commission on the Status of Women.

Suzanne de Passe

ENTERTAINMENT EXECUTIVE. Suzanne de Passe is a native of New York City. She attended Manhattan Community College in New York in 1967.

Her professional career includes serving as talent coordinator at the Cheetah Club on Manhattan's East Side. In 1968 she met Berry Gordy, the founder and president of then Detroit-based record label Motown who hired her as his creative assistant. She was instrumental in numerous recording careers, guiding Lionel Richie to a solo career after he left the Commodores, launching Rick James and the funk era, and perhaps most importantly, shaping a group of singing brothers from Gary, Indiana, into the Jackson Five, one of the most heralded singing groups of all time. She has experience with both Motown Records and De Passe Entertainment, as well as her extensive work in the entertainment industry which has allowed her to attain extensive knowledge of management, production, and business relations and negotiations.

Ms. de Passe serves as chairman and chief executive officer of de Passe Entertainment.

Susan Y. Desjardins

MILITARY. Susan Y. Desjardins received a Bachelor of Science degree in international affairs/political science from the United States Air Force Academy in Colorado Springs, Colorado. She earned a Master of Arts degree in industrial psychology and human relations from Louisiana Tech University and a Master of Arts degree in national security and Strategic Studies from the Naval Command and Staff College. She is a graduate of the Naval War College and the Air War College. She has also completed the general manager program at Harvard Business School, Harvard University, in Cambridge, Mass.

Brigadier General Desjardins serves as the commandant of cadets at the United States Air Force Academy in Colorado Springs, Colorado. She commands the 4,000-member cadet wing and more than 300 Air Force and civilian support personnel. Her responsibilities include cadet military training and airmanship education, supervising cadet life activities and providing support to facilities and logistics.

Barbara J. Desoer

FINANCE. Barbara J. Desoer received a bachelor's degree in mathematics from Mount Holyoke College and a Master of Business Administration degree from the University of California at Berkeley.

She joined Bank of America in 1977. After a variety

of commercial lending and credit administration assignments, she served as executive assistant to two chief executive officers. She then held a number of retail banking assignments and was named group executive vice president responsible for the California Retail Banking Group in 1996. She was promoted to president of Northern California banking. She served as marketing executive from 1999 to July 2001. In addition, she is a past chair of the bank's internal diversity advisory council. She was consumer products executive for Bank of America before assuming the position of global technology and operations executive of Bank of America Corporation.

Jerri DeVard

COMMUNICATIONS. Jerri DeVard is a native of Harlem, New York. She received a bachelor's degree in economics from Spelman College and earned a Master of Business Administration from Clark Atlanta University.

Her professional career includes serving in marketing at the Pillsbury Company in Minneapolis; after 11 years at Pillsbury, DeVard was recruited by the National Football League's Minnesota Vikings to head up their private suites marketing. She served as vice president of marketing for Harrah's in New Orleans; returned to New York to serve as vice president of Revlon, marketing, for color cosmetics; and served as chief marketing officer at Citigroup, responsible for the company's e-Consumer line. She serves as senior vice president of marketing and brand management for Verizon Communications where she oversees a staff of 400 nationwide, shaping all marketing communications strategies for the telecommunication giant's consumer and small business segments since January 2003.

Ms. DeVard was appointed senior vice president—marketing and brand management in August 2005.

Londa J. Dewey

FINANCE. Londa J. Dewey is a native of Champaign, Illinois. She received her undergraduate degree in finance from the University of Illinois. Her professional career includes serving in management with the First Wisconsin Bank, initially as a personal banker, then as a branch manager and eventually as the Wisconsin division retail manager from 1982 to 1996; in 1996 she was named chairman of the Board of Firstar Bank Wisconsin and the president of Madison Market. In November 1998, she accepted the position of group manager for private banking at Firstar Bank. In her continued capacity as president of the Madison, Wisconsin, market, she actively serves her community and is proud to serve as chair of the United Way Board of Directors for 2006.

Lynn Dickerson

MEDIA EXECUTIVE. Lynn Dickerson is a native of Texas and a graduate of Texas A&M University where she earned a bachelor's degree in business administration.

She began her newspaper career in sales. In 1983, after serving as advertising director of the Lewisville, Texas, *Daily Leader*, she was appointed its publisher. That paper was bought by Harte-Hanks Communications Inc. in 1986. Six years later, Ms. Dickerson became publisher and president of Harte-Hanks Community Newspapers, a small group of daily and weekly newspapers headquartered in Dallas. In 2000, she joined McClatchy and *The Modesto Bee*, and was named publisher and president of the *Times Record News* in Wichita Falls, Texas. Ms. Dickerson was named vice president, operations, of McClatchy on March 13, 2006.

Terri A. Dickerson

GOVERNMENT OFFICIAL. Terri A. Dickerson received a Bachelor of Science degree in education from the University of Virginia in Charlottesville and a Master of Arts in government from the Johns Hopkins University in Baltimore.

She has held numerous leadership positions in the public and private sectors, including associate director for American Press Institute. She also served as executive director/chief executive officer for American Women in Radio and Television and worked with the White House Office of Public Liaison. She previously served as associate administrator for the United States

Small Business Administration's Office of Small Disadvantaged Business Certification and Eligibility. She has also served as director of evaluation, United States Commission on Civil Rights. Ms. Dickerson was appointed a member of the government's senior executive corps and she now leads the Coast Guard's Office of Civil Rights.

Betty C. Dickey

JUDGE. Betty C. Dickey received a Bachelor of Arts in English from the University of Arkansas, Fayetteville, in 1962 and earned her Juris Doctor degree from the University of Arkansas in Little Rock in 1985.

Her professional career includes serving as city Attorney for the city of Redfield; as commission attorney for Arkansas Soil and Water Conservation Commission; as assistant city attorney for the city of Pine Bluff; as prosecuting attorney, State of Arkansas, Eleventh Judicial District; as a commissioner with the Arkansas Public Service Commission; and as the chief legal counsel in the Arkansas Governor's office.

In 2004, she was appointed chief justice, Arkansas Supreme Court, and was appointed associate justice, Arkansas Supreme Court Position 5, in 2005.

Deborah M. DiCroce

EDUCATION. Deborah M. DiCroce is a native of Virginia. She received a bachelor's and master's degree in English from Old Dominion University. She earned a doctorate degree in higher education from the College of William and Mary.

Her professional career includes serving for over 30 years in higher education spanning both teaching and administrative roles. She holds adjunct faculty appointments at the University of Virginia, the College of William and Mary, and Old Dominion University. She served for nine years as president of Piedmont Virginia Community College in Charlottesville.

Dr. DiCroce began serving as president of Tidewater Community College in Norfolk, Virginia on May 15, 1998.

Victoria H. Diego-Allard

MILITARY. Victoria H. Diego-Allard enlisted in the Army in 1979 as a signal intelligence electronic warfare analyst. Upon completion of advanced individual training she attended Officers Candidate School at Fort Benning, Georgia, and was commissioned in ordnance.

Her civilian and military education includes a bachelor's degree in political science and economics at Boston University (1981) and a Jurist doctorate at Hamline University (1993). She participated in the Army's training with industry program at Honeywell/Alliant Techsystems (1987–1989); graduated from the Defense Systems Management College, Program Management Course (1998); and is a senior service college fellow at the University of Texas at Austin (2001–2002).

She has held a variety of important positions, including shop officer, 5th Maintenance Company, 66th Maintenance Battalion; commander, Heavy Maintenance Company, 122nd Maintenance Battalion, division readiness officer 3rd Armored Division; chief of contracts, Defense Contract Management Command, Twin Cities, Minnesota; proponency officer, contracts management career field, Office of the Assistant Secretary of the Army, Research Development and Acquisition (OASARDA); speechwriter and military assistant to the military deputy, Office of the Assistant Secretary of the Army, Acquisition, Logistics and Technology, United States Army Pentagon.

Janet DiFiore

ELECTED OFFICIAL. Janet DiFiore is a lifelong resident of Westchester, New York. After graduating from law school in 1981 she served as an assistant district attorney in Westchester County under administration of both Carl A. Vergari (1981–1987) and Jeanine F. Pirro (1994–1998). For the last four and one half years of her service as a prosecutor, she served as chief of narcotics for the Westchester County District Attorney's office. She also served the Westchester County District Attorney's office in the rackets and the homicide and special investigations bureaus.

Elected as a judge of the Westchester County Court in 1998 and as a justice of the New York State Supreme Court in 2002, she has presided over hundreds of cases in the county court, the family court and the New York State Supreme Court.

On February 14, 2003, she was appointed by Chief Judge Judith Kaye to serve as the supervising judge for the criminal courts in the 9th Judicial District. She served in this capacity until May 2005 when she resigned her position to run for district attorney.

On January 1, 2006, Judge Janet DiFore was sworn in as the 32nd district attorney of Westchester County.

Mary Dillon

BUSINESS EXECUTIVE. Mary Dillon is a native of Chicago, Illinois. She received a Bachelor of Science in marketing and Asian studies from the University of Illinois.

Her professional career includes serving as a marketing associate for Quaker Foods in 1984, as vice president of marketing for Gatorade, and as president of the Quaker Foods division of PepsiCo Corporation.

Ms. Dillon serves as vice president and global chief marketing officer of McDonald's Corporation. She is responsible for McDonald's global marketing strategy and overall brand development efforts, as well as the company's Balanced, Active Lifestyles initiative.

Elaine W. DiMiceli

JUDGE. Judge Elaine W. DiMiceli received a Bachelor of Arts degree and a Master's of Art degree from Loyola University. She also earned her Juris Doctor degree from Loyola University School of Law.

She served in private law practice from 1977 to 1985. She served as an assistant district attorney, 22nd District Court from 1978 to 1979, and as city attorney for the city of Slidell from 1983 to 1994. She returned to private law practice in 1994. She was appointed judge to the 22nd Judicial District Court, division "B" in Covington, Louisiana, in 1996.

Carol E. Dinkins

GOVERNMENT OFFICIAL. Carol Dinkins received a Bachelor of Science in education from the University of Texas in 1968. She earned a Juris Doctor degree from the University of Houston in 1973.

Her experience includes serving in private law practice; from 1981 to 1983 she served as assistant attorney general in charge of the environment and natural resources division of the Department of Justice; in 1984 she served as the deputy attorney general of the United States, the second-ranking official in the Department of Justice.

She was nominated by President George W. Bush and in February 2006 confirmed by the Senate to chair the newly formed Privacy and Civil Liberties Oversight Board.

Alexandra Davis DiPentima

JUDGE. Alexandra Davis DiPentima is a native of Sharon, Connecticut, and was raised in Kent, Connecticut. She received a Bachelor of Arts from Princeton University in 1975 and earned her Juris Doctor degree from the University of Connecticut School of Law in 1979. After law school she served in private law practice.

In November 1993 Governor Lowell Weicker appointed Judge DiPentima to the trial bench as a Superior Court judge. Since her appointment to the bench, she has served as presiding judge of the Hartford New Britain Housing Session; as presiding judge in Meriden; and as administrative judge of the Judicial District of Litchfield from 1998 to 2003. From 2001 to 2002 she served as president of the Connecticut Judges Association.

Althea Green Dixon

MILITARY. Althea Green Dixon is a native of Trinidad. She enlisted in the United States Army at St. Croix, United States Virgin Islands, in August 1977. She attended basic training at Fort Jackson, South Car-

olina, followed by advanced individual training at Fort Sam Houston, Texas.

She has completed numerous military courses to include all the Noncommissioned Officer Education System courses, the Battle Staff Noncommissioned Officer course, the Security Managers course, the Training Managers course, the Medical Specialist course (honor graduate); the Joint Deployment Officer course, the Ear, Nose and Throat Specialist course (distinguished honor graduate), and the United States Army Sergeant Major Academy (class 47), where she received the General Ralph E. Hanes Award for Outstanding Student Research, as well as a commendation for outstanding performance on the Army physical fitness test. She holds a Master of Science degree in business from the University of LaVerne (California).

Her leadership assignments include serving as section noncommissioned officer in charge, platoon sergeant, first sergeant, operations sergeant and command sergeant major. In August 2004, she was assigned as the command sergeant major of Dwight David Eisenhower Medical Center, and the Southeast Regional Medical Command, headquartered at Fort Gordon, Georgia.

Melba Dixon

JUDGE (FIRST). Melba Dixon graduated from Linwood Elementary School and Benton High School (valedictorian) in Yazoo County, Mississippi. She received a Bachelor of Arts degree (magna cum laude) in economics with a minor in business administration from Tougaloo College and received a Masters' of Business Administration degree from Jackson State University. She earned her Juris Doctor degree from Mississippi College of Law. She has also completed course work at the National Judicial College in Reno, Nevada.

Judge Dixon served in the area of personnel and human resource management with the Mississippi State Personnel Board and the Mississippi Library Commission for approximately ten years prior to entering the legal profession. She was a staff attorney of Central Mississippi Legal Services and served as a key advisor to the State Personnel Board and state government agencies in the area of labor and employment law and as special assistant attorney general with the Office of the Attorney General for the State of Mississippi. She currently serves as one of eight administrative law judges with the Mississippi Workers' Compensation Commission. She is the first African American female to serve in the capacity.

Sheila Dixon

ELECTED OFFICIAL. Sheila Dixon is a native of the Ashburton neighborhood of West Baltimore, Maryland. She is a graduate of the Baltimore City public school system. She received a bachelor's degree from Towson University and earned a master's degree from Johns Hopkins University.

Her professional career includes serving as an elementary school teacher and adult education instructor with the Head Start program. She worked for 17 years as an international trade specialist with the Maryland Department of Business and Economic Development. In 1986 she was elected to the Baltimore City State Central Committee representing the 40th Legislative District. In 1987, she won a seat on the Baltimore city council representing the 4th Council district, where she served the citizens of Baltimore for 12 years. She became the city council president in 1999, the first African-American woman ever elected to this position.

On January 17, 2007, Sheila Dixon became the first female ever to serve as mayor of Baltimore when Mayor Martin O'Malley was sworn in as Governor. On January 18, 2007, she took the oath as the 48th mayor of Baltimore, Maryland.

Paula J. Dorbriansky

GOVERNMENT OFFICIAL. Paula J. Dorbriansky received a Bachelor of Science in foreign service summa cum laude in international politics from Georgetown University School of Foreign Service and a Master of Arts degree and doctorate in Soviet political/military affairs from Harvard University.

Dr. Dorbriansky was nominated by President Bush on March 12, 2001, unanimously confirmed by the Senate on April 26, 2001, and sworn in as under secretary of state for global affairs on May 1, 2001. In this position, she is responsible for a broad range of foreign policy issues, including democracy, human rights, labor, counter-narcotics and law enforcement, refugee and humanitarian relief matters and environmental/scientific.

Colleen Dolan

JUDGE. Colleen Dolan received a Bachelor of Science degree in administration of justice from the University of Missouri in St. Louis and earned her Juris Doctor degree from St. Louis University Law School.

She was engaged in private law practice from 1984 until she was appointed to the bench as an associate circuit judge for Missouri Circuit Court in St. Louis County in 1994.

Elizabeth Hanford Dole

ELECTED OFFICIAL. Elizabeth Hanford Dole is a native of Salisbury, Rowan County, North Carolina. She received a Bachelor of Arts degree from Duke University in 1958, and received a Master of Arts degree from Harvard University in 1960. She earned a Juris Doctor degree from Harvard University in 1965.

Her professional career includes serving as the United States secretary of transportation from 1983 to 1987 and as the United States secretary of labor from 1989 to 1990. She was selected to serve as president of the American Red Cross from 1991 to 2000 and was an unsuccessful candidate for the Republican presidential nomination in 2000. She was elected as a United States Senator in 2002, for the term ending in January 3, 2009.

Taffi L. Dollar

MINISTRY. Taffi L. Dollar is a native of Atlanta, Georgia. She received a bachelor's degree in mental health and human services from Georgia State University.

In 1983, she was saved at a Bible study led by student Creflo Dollar, her future husband, on the campus of West Georgia College. She and Creflo Dollar founded the World Changers Ministries. She serves as co-pastor, president and chief executive officer of World Changers Church International (WCCI) and World Changers Church in New York. Ms. Dollar also serves as chief executive officer of Arrow Records, a Christian recording company. Pastor Dollar served as a guest panelist for the 2005 Vibe Music Festival in Atlanta.

Bernice B. Donald

JUDGE. Bernice B. Donald is a native of Desoto County, Mississippi. She received a Bachelor of Arts degree from Memphis State University in 1974 and earned her Juris Doctor degree from Memphis State University School of Law in 1979.

Her professional career includes serving as an adjunct professor at Shelby State Community College; in private law practice; as a staff attorney, employment law and economic development unit, Memphis Area Legal Services, Tennessee, in 1980; and as assistant public defender, Shelby County Public Defender's office, Tennessee. From 1982 to 1988, she served as a judge, General Sessions Criminal Court, State of Tennessee.

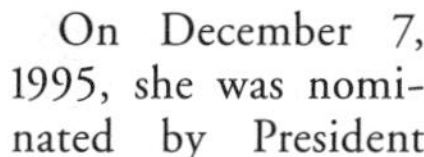

On December 7, 1995, she was nominated by President William J. Clinton to a seat vacated by Odell Horton. She was confirmed by the United States Senate on December 22, 1995, and received commission on December 26, 1995.

Mary O. Donohue

ELECTED OFFICIAL. Mary O. Donohue received a bachelor's degree from the College of New Rochelle and a Master of Science degree in education from Russell Sage College. She earned a Juris Doctor degree from Albany Law School of Union University in 1983.

Her professional career includes serving as a teacher in both elementary and junior high school in Rensselaer and Albany County School districts; as a law clerk and intern in the U.S. Attorney's office in Albany and

on the staff of Senator Joseph Bruno; and in private law practice. From 1990 to 1992 she served as an assistant Rensselaer County attorney; in 1992 she was elected as Rensselaer County's first female district attorney; and in 1996 she was elected to the State Supreme Court for the seven-county Third Judicial District.

Ms. Donohue was elected to serve as lieutenant governor of the state of New York on November 3, 1998, and re-elected on November 5, 2002. She was nominated by President George W. Bush to be United States District judge for the Northern District of New York on June 28, 2006.

Laurie Friedman Donze

MEDICINE. Laurie Friedman Donze is a native of California and received her Bachelor of Arts in psychology from the University of California at Berkeley. She earned her Master of Arts and Ph.D. in clinical psychology from Michigan State University.

Dr. Donze served as a faculty member at Johns Hopkins School of Medicine for six years before joining the Center for Scientific Review in 2003. Her scientific and clinical expertise relates primarily to the behavioral and alternative treatment of obesity. At the National Center for Complementary and Alternative Medicine she is responsible for the training and education special emphasis panel as well as other review panels as needed. She was appointed as a scientific review administrator at the National Center for Complementary and Alternative Medicine.

Hattie B. Dorsey

NONPROFIT EXECUTIVE. Hattie B. Dorsey attended Spelman College in Atlanta, Georgia, and later transferred to Clark Atlanta University where she graduated in 1964 with a B.S. degree in secretarial science. Ms. Dorsey served as president and chief executive officer at Atlanta Neighborhood Development Partnership, Inc. (ANDP), where she was a leading advocate for housing issues. One of her most important accomplishments has been the shifting of perceptions about the importance of revitalized neighborhoods and the critical need for an affordable, mixed income housing approach that includes all segments of the population.

She currently serves on committees or boards for the Washington Mutual Advisory Council, a local affiliate of International Women's Forum, and the Spelman College Corporate Roundtable. Dorsey also serves as the first vice chair for Georgia's Democratic Party. She is the former national president of the National Coalition of 100 Black Women and was the founding president of the group's metro Atlanta chapter. She also served on FannieMae Corporation's National Advisory Committee, the Enterprise Foundation Advisory Committee, the Emory University Board of Visitors, the Atlanta Women's Foundation's Board, the Central Atlanta Progress Housing Task Force and was a member of the mayor's Affordable Housing Task Force.

Dorsey participated in Leadership Atlanta and the Regional Leadership Training Institute. She has received numerous honors and awards. In 2003, she was inducted into the Atlanta Business League's Women Hall of Fame, and in 2001, she was an honoree of Women Looking Ahead's "100s List of Georgia's Post Powerful and Influential Women." She has been awarded *Business to Business* magazine's 99 Women in Business Award, the Federal Home Bank Partnership Excellence Award, the Empire Realtors Distinguished Services Award, the Georgia Black Caucus Grace Towns Hamilton Leadership Award, and the Atlanta Regional Commission's Golden Glasses Award.

Laura G. Douglas

JUDGE. Laura G. Douglas received a Bachelor of Arts degree from Hobart and William Smith College in 1979 and earned her Juris Doctor degree from the University of Pittsburgh School of Law in 1982.

Her professional career includes serving in private law practice; as a law assistant with the New York State Unified Court System; as an associate law assistant to acting justice with New York State Unified Court System; and as principal law clerk, New York State Unified Court System. In 1991 she was elected judge to the New York City Civil Court in Bronx County; in 1998 she was appointed acting justice on the Supreme Court in Bronx County; in 2000 she was elected a Supreme Court justice, Bronx County.

Mae Douglas

COMMUNICATIONS. Mae Douglas received a Bachelor of Arts degree in sociology from the University of North Carolina.

She joined Cox from Ciba-Geigy Corporation in Greensboro, North Carolina, where she was responsible for all human resources functions for the company's agricultural division. Ms. Douglas joined CableRep, Cox's advertising division, in 1995 as manager of employee relations and was promoted to director of employee relations in 1998. She was promoted to regional vice president of ad sales for CableRep in 1999. Ms. Douglas was appointed senior vice president and chief people officer for Cox Communications in 2000. She is

responsible for all of Cox's human resources functions, including talent and leadership development, organizational development, organizational development, workforce planning and recruiting, employee relations, labor relations, diversity, compensation and human resources management systems.

Joyce Draganchuk

JUDGE. Joyce Draganchuk received a Bachelor of Arts (with distinction) from the University of Michigan in 1983 and earned her Juris Doctor degree (cum laude) from Wayne State University Law School in 1986.

Her professional career includes serving as a legal intern, Senior Citizens Legal Aid Center of Detroit from 1984 to 1986; as pre-hearing attorney, the Michigan Court of Appeals, 1986–1987; as a law clerk at the Michigan Court of Appeals, 1987–1988; as an assistant prosecutor for Ingham County, 1988–2001; and as chief assistant prosecutor for Ingham County from 2001 to 2005. In November 2004 she was elected circuit court judge to the Ingham County Circuit in Lansing, Michigan.

Thelma D. Drake

ELECTED OFFICIAL. Thelma D. Drake is a native of Elyria, in Lorain County, Ohio, and graduated from Elyria High School in 1967. She was engaged in private business then was elected a member of the Virginia State House of Delegates (1996–2004). She has served as a United States representative to the 109th Congress since January 3, 2005.

Carol Enger Draper

JUDGE. Carol Enger Draper received a Bachelor of Arts degree in music education from Ithaca College in 1970 and attended graduate school at SUNY, Buffalo. She earned her Juris Doctor degree from Stetson University College of Law in 1985.

Her professional career includes serving in private law practice; in 1993, she was appointed judge for Osceola County courts.

Judy P. Draper

JUDGE. Judy P. Draper received a bachelor's degree in labor relations from the University of North Carolina at Chapel Hill and earned her Juris Doctor degree from Howard University Law School in 1980 with Law Journal honors.

Her professional career includes serving as a clerk for the United States Department of Labor, Office of the Administrative Judges in Washington, D.C.; as a prosecutor for the city of St. Louis; as an adjunct professor of pre-trial practice at Washington University School of Law; as a law clerk to Honorable Clyde S. Cahill, Federal District Court judge; and was the first female general counsel for the Missouri Department of Corrections. She served in private practice in Clayton and as a municipal judge for the cities of Northwoods and Berkeley.

Judge Draper was appointed associate circuit judge to the Missouri Circuit Court division 41 in St. Louis County on April 13, 2004, by Governor Bob Holden. She is a founding member of the Missouri Asian American Bar Association and served as president from 1999 to 2003.

Diane M. Druzinski

JUDGE. Diane M. Druzinski completed her undergraduate studies at Oakland University and received her Juris Doctor degree (magna cum laude) from the University of Detroit–Mercy School of Law.

She was engaged in private law practice prior to her election in 2002 to the Michigan Macomb County Circuit Court for a regular term beginning January 1, 2003.

Karen I. Duckett

BUSINESS EXECUTIVE. Karen I. Duckett received a Bachelor of Arts degree from Ohio University in Athens, Ohio, and received a Master of Arts degree from Occidental College/Yale University. She earned her Juris Doctor degree from Woodrow Wilson College of Law.

She is the president of Duckett and Associates, Inc., with over 30 years of design and facility planning experience, developing projects for both public and private sectors. Her planning and design experience from concept to move-in has included multimillion dollar office projects, medical facilities from hospitals to clinics, and the planning and design of law-enforcement and judicial facilities.

Sharon A. Dumas

GOVERNMENT OFFICIAL. Sharon A. Dumas received a master's degree in accounting and financial information systems from Cleveland State University.

Her professional career includes serving 14 years with LTV Steel Company, formerly Republic Steel Corporation, where she held several financial management positions; in 1988 she joined the public sector as finance director of the city of East Cleveland; she then joined the city of Cleveland as assistant director of the department of community development where she helped to manage more than 300 employees in four divisions; in 2003 she became the assistant director of finance. She was responsible for directing the Office of Budget and Management with a team of nine staff members.

Ms. Dumas serves as director of finance for the city of Cleveland, Ohio.

Bonnie J. Dunbar

ASTRONAUT. Bonnie J. Dunbar is a native of Sunnyside, Washington, and a graduate of Sunnyside High School in 1967. She received a Bachelor of Science degree and a Master of Science degree in ceramic engineering from the University of Washington in 1971 and 1975 respectively. She earned a doctorate in mechanical/biomedical engineering from the University of Houston in 1983.

Following graduation in 1971 she worked for Boeing Computer Services for two years as a systems analyst. In 1975, she was invited to participate in research at Harwell Laboratories in Oxford, England, as a visiting scientist. Following her work in England, she accepted a senior research engineer position with Rockwell International Space Division in Downey, California. She accepted a position as a payload officer/fight controller at the Lyndon B. Johnson Space Center in 1978. She served as a guidance and navigation officer/flight controller for the Skylab reentry mission in 1979 and was subsequently designated project officer/payload officer for the integration of several Space Shuttle payloads. Dr. Dunbar is a veteran of five space flights and has logged more than 1,208 hours (50 days) in space. She served as a mission specialist and was the payload commander on STS-50 in 1992 and STS-89 in 1998. She served as the deputy associate administrator for the Office of Life and Microgravity Sciences at NASA headquarters in Washington, D.C. In February 1994, she traveled to Star City, Russia, where she spent 13 months training as a back-up crew member for a 3-month flight on the Russian Space Station *Mir.* From October 1995 to November 1996, she was detailed to the NASA Johnson Space Center Mission Operations Directorate as assistant director where she was responsible for chairing the International Space Station Training Readiness Reviews and facilitating Russian/American operations and training strategies. Dr. Dunbar serves as assistant director to the NASA Johnson Space Center (JSC) with a focus on university research.

Allyson Kay Duncan

JUDGE. Allyson Kay Duncan grew up in Durham on what is now the North Carolina Central University campus. She received a Bachelor of Arts degree from Hampton University in 1972 and earned her Juris Doctor degree from Duke University School of Law in 1975.

Her professional career includes serving as an associate editor, Lawyers Co-Operative Publishing Company (1976–1977); as law clerk for the Hon. Julia Cooper Mack, District of Columbia Court of Appeals (1977–1978); as an attorney with the Equal Employment Opportunity Commission (1978–1986); and as an associate professor, North Carolina Central University School of Law (1986–1990). In 1990 she was appointed as an associate judge, North Carolina Court of Appeals, then served as a commissioner with the North Carolina Utilities Commission from 1991 to 1998, and in private law practice in Raleigh, North Carolina, from 1998 to 2003.

In 2003, President George Bush appointed her judge to the United States Court of Appeals for the Fourth Circuit in North Carolina. She became the first Carolinian since the Carter administration to serve on the 4th U.S. Circuit Court. Assuming the seat previously held by the late Sam Ervin II, she is also the first and only African-American from North Carolina and the first female from any state in the nation to serve on the 4th U.S. Circuit Court bench. She also became the 109th president of the State Bar Association. She is the first African-American to be selected.

Elaine Flowers Duncan

AEROSPACE. Elaine Flowers is a native of Montgomery, Alabama, and graduated from Jefferson Davis High School in Montgomery. She received a bachelor's degree in mathematics from Alabama State University in Montgomery and earned a Master of Science degree in urban systems engineering from Howard University in Washington, D.C.

She joined NASA in 1980 working at the Marshall Center as an operations engineer planning experiment operations for several Spacelab missions and flights of a science laboratory inside the Shuttle's payload bay. In 1988, she served at NASA headquarters in Washington, D.C., as a program manager and helped plan future operations aboard the station. She was assigned to Space Station Delivery and the Spacelab Pallet team, working at Engineering Support Room located inside the Payload Operations Center. She was named project manager for the Spacelab Pallet in the Flight Projects Directorate at NASA's Marshall Space Flight Center in Huntsville, Alabama. Her team at the Marshall Center had a special carrier that they prepared for flight on the Space Shuttle *Atlantis'* trip to the International Space Station. The Space Shuttle *Atlantis* STS-104 safely carried a new air resupply system to the International Space Station inside the Shuttle's cargo bay. Ms. Duncan's team customized the pallet to carry the special, high-pressure gas system that would repressurize the new U.S. airlock, a doorway for astronauts to use during space walks.

Linda A. Duncan

GOVERNMENT OFFICIAL. Linda A. Duncan is a native of Springfield, Massachusetts. She attended Howard University, Washington, D.C., where she earned a Bachelor of Arts degree in sociology in 1973. Following graduation she attended graduate school at Ohio State University in Columbus, Ohio, where she earned a Master of Arts degree in guidance and counseling. Her military education includes the Army Management Staff College and she attended several other professional development courses including the Community and Family Support Management, Contracting Officers Representative, and the Garrison Pre-command courses. After graduate school Ms. Duncan returned to Springfield, Massachusetts, where she began her career as a guidance counselor.

Her civil service career began with the Department of the Army in September 1977 as a guidance counselor at Pinder Barracks, Germany. In October 1980, she accepted a position as education specialist with the Department of the Navy, Navy Recruiting District, New York. In September 1984, she accepted an assignment as education specialist at the Army Education Center, New York Area Command and Fort Hamilton, Brooklyn, New York. In December 1990, she was selected as the education service officer for the New York Area Command and served until November 1995.

Ms. Duncan currently serves as civilian executive assistant, base operations, United States Army Garrison Fort Hamilton, Brooklyn, New York, the position she has held since November 1995. In addition, she serves as the base transition coordinator for Fort Totten and Bellmore Logistics Facility, sub-installations of Fort Hamilton.

Stephanie Duncan-Peters

JUDGE. Stephanie Duncan-Peters is a native of New York, New York. She is a 1970 graduate of Walt Whitman High School in Bethesda, Maryland. She received a Bachelor of Arts degree from Muhlenberg College in 1974 and earned her Juris Doctor degree from Catholic University in 1977. At Catholic University she was the chancellor of the Moot Court Board.

Following graduation from law school, she served as a law clerk at the District of Columbia Court of Appeals. She joined the staff of the Public Defender Service for the District of Columbia in 1978. She became deputy chief of felony trials in 1982 and remained with the Public Defender Service until 1985. In 1985, she became a trial attorney with the public integrity section in the criminal division of the United States Department of Justice. In 1989 she entered private law practice.

In 1992 President George H.W. Bush appointed Judge Stephanie Duncan-Peters to the Superior Court of the District of Columbia.

Wanda Dunham

LAW ENFORCEMENT. Wanda Dunham received a Bachelor of Science in criminal justice from Jacksonville State University and a Master of Arts in public administration from Columbia State University. She also successfully completed Police Command College for Law Enforcement Executives.

Chief Dunham has served for over 22 years with the Metropolitan Atlanta Transit Authority (MARTA) Police Department. She has held every rank from police officer to chief. She was the first African-American female of the department to achieve the ranks of captain, major, and assistant chief. In December 2005, she was named interim chief of MARTA police and in March 2006, she was named chief of the Metropolitan Atlanta Rapid Transit Authority Police Department, becoming the first African-American to serve in this position.

Karen-Sue Dunn

GOVERNMENT OFFICIAL. Karen-Sue Dunn is a native of Fort Dix, New Jersey. She received a Bachelor of Science degree in history from the University of Nebraska in Lincoln. She earned a Master of Arts degree in international relations and affairs at the University of Denver, Colorado, and a Master of Science degree in national resource strategy from the National Defense University at Fort Lesley J. McNair in Washington, D.C.

She began her career in 1975 at the San Antonio Air Logistics Center, Texas. She served in various managerial assignments connected with the C-5 and international logistics support. Promoted in 1984, she transferred to Headquarters United States Air Force in Washington, D.C., as a modification programmer and then moved to the office of the secretary of the Air Force for acquisition in 1988 as the senior acquisition programming and budget analyst. She later became chief of the execution and financial management branch. She served as chief of the execution team in the National Reconnaissance Office in 2000. She served as chief of the space financial team in the Directorate of Communications, managing the finances for the directorate's space communications satellite as well as ground and information security acquisition programs in the Space Program Office. She was assigned as signals intelligence systems acquisition financial management and comptroller, Office of the Under Secretary of the Air Force, National Reconnaissance Office in Chantilly, Virginia.

Debra Dupont

JUDGE. Debra Dupont received a Bachelor of Arts degree (summa cum laude) from Texas Christian University in 1990 in economics. She earned her Juris Doctor degree with honors from the University of Texas School of Law in 1994.

Her professional career includes serving as an assistant district attorney in Tarrant County, Fort Worth, Texas, for nine years and in private law practice. She was elected judge to the County Court at Law in Parker County, Texas.

Christine M. Durham

JUDGE. Christine M. Durham earned her Juris Doctor degree from Duke University. Her professional career includes serving in private law practice, as an instructor of legal medicine at Duke University Medical School and as an instructor at Brigham Young University's Law School and the University of Utah College of Law.

In 1978, she was appointed judge on the Third District Court in Utah; in February 1982, she was appointed justice to the Supreme Court of Utah. In April 2002, she became chief justice of the Utah Supreme Court.

Ysabel Duron

JOURNALISM. Ysabel Duron is a native of Salina, California. She received a Bachelor of Arts degree in journalism from San Jose State University. She is a 1990 fellow of the National Hispania Leadership Institute in Washington, D.C.

Her professional career includes serving a reporter at KTVU-TV in Oakland where she won her first Emmy award in 1974 for her reporting on the Patty Hearst kidnapping. She was honored again in 1982 while working as a reporter/anchor at KICU-TV in San Jose. Since joining KRON-4, she has garnered public acclaim with two award-winning series. "The Child I Never Held," a 1991 series about her reunion with a son she gave up for adoption, was honored by the RTNDA. The second series, 1998's "Life with Cancer," focused on her winning battle with cancer and gained her national recognition, an honorable mention for the American Women in Radio and Television's Gracie Awards, and an Excellence in Journalism award from the Northern California Society of Professional Journalists. In 1997, she was inducted into the National Academy of Television Arts and Sciences "Silver Circle" for more than 27 years of meritorious work as a journalist. In May 2000 Ms. Duron was presented with a Governor's Citation from the National Academy of Television Arts and Sciences of Northern California for her commitment to journalism.

Ann Dyke

JUDGE. Ann Dyke is a native of Cleveland, Ohio. Her early career was in the field of nursing. She became a registered nurse in 1957 after obtaining her degree from St. Vincent Charity Hospital School of Nursing. She attended John Carroll University and received a Bachelor of Science degree from St. Louis University in 1964; she earned her Juris Doctor degree from Cleveland-Marshall College of Law in 1968.

Her professional career includes serving in private law practice, as a special counsel in the Office of the Attorney General of Ohio, and on the faculty of Cleveland State University. She was elected to the Court of Common Pleas in 1980, an office she held until February 9, 1987, when she was appointed judge of the Ohio Court of Appeals, Eighth Appellate District. She served as administrative judge of the court in 1993 and 2000. She has also served as the chair of the judicial conference of the Eighth District's 11th, 12th and 13th conferences.

Elisabeth A. Earle

JUDGE. Elisabeth A. Earle is a native of Austin, Texas. She received a Bachelor of Arts degree from the University of Texas at Austin. She earned her Juris Doctor degree from St. Mary's University School of Law.

Her professional career includes serving in private law practice in London, England. Upon her return to Austin, Texas, she worked for the Texas Senate Jurisprudence Committee under Senator Gene Green and the Governor's Criminal Justice division under Governor Ann Richards.

Her legal career began as a prosecutor with the Travis County Attorney's office. In 1998, she was appointed municipal court judge for the city of Austin, and in 1999 she was named the first presiding judge of the Downtown Austin Community Court. In

March 2002, she won the democratic primary for judge of Travis County Court at Law #7 where she currently serves.

Naomi Churchill Earp

GOVERNMENT OFFICIAL. Naomi Churchill Earp is a native of Newport News, Virginia. She received a bachelor's degree from Norfolk University, Norfolk, Virginia, and a master's degree from Indiana University in Bloomington, Indiana. She earned a Juris Doctor from Catholic University's Columbus School of Law in Washington, D.C.

Her work experience includes serving with the National Institutes of Health (NIH), the Federal Deposit Insurance Corporation and the U.S. Department of Agriculture. She also served as an attorney advisor at the EEOC during the mid–1980s.

On April 28, 2003, Ms. Earp assumed the position of vice chair of the U.S. Equal Employment Opportunity Commission (EEOC). On October 26, 2005, President Bush reappointed Ms. Earp for a second term. She assumed the role of chair of the U.S. Equal Employment Opportunity Commission (EEOC) on August 31, 2006. Her current term expires on July 1, 2010.

Mary Easley

EDUCATION. Mary Easley received a bachelor's degree in politics magna cum laude from Wake Forest University and earned her Juris Doctor from Wake Forest School of Law in 1975.

Her professional career includes serving as assistant district attorney in New Hanover and Pender counties for ten years. From 1984 to 1992, she maintained her own practice in areas of civil and criminal law in Southport, North Carolina. She has also served as a clinical professor at North Carolina Central University School of Law in Durham. She is currently employed by North Carolina State University as executive in residence in the office of the provost with the rank of senior lecturer in the College of Humanities and Social Sciences. Ms. Easley is also the first lady of North Carolina and has been married to Governor Mike Easley for 27 years.

Ellen East

COMMUNICATIONS. Ellen East received a bachelor's degree in news-editorial journalism from the University of Alabama in 1983.

Her professional career began as a reporter and editor at a number of daily newspapers before she joined the Cox organization in 1987 as an assistant city editor with the *Atlanta Journal Constitution*. She joined Cox Enterprises' corporate staff as communications manager in 1990. She joined Cox Communications in 1993 as manager of public affairs. She was promoted to director of public affairs in 1995. In 1998 she assumed management of the function corporate-wide and was promoted to vice president of communications and public affairs for Cox Communications, Inc., in 1999.

Marian Wright Edelman

COMMUNITY ACTIVIST (FIRST). Marian Wright Edelman received her undergraduate degree from Spelman College and her Juris Doctor degree from Yale Law School. She began her career in the mid–60s when she became the first black woman admitted to the Mississippi Bar. She also directed the NAACP Legal Defense and Educational Fund office in Jackson, Mississippi. In 1968, she moved to Washington, D.C., as counsel for the Poor People's March that Dr. Martin Luther King, Jr., began organizing before his death. She is the founder of the Washington Research Project, a public interest law firm and the parent body of the Children's Defense Fund. For two years she directed the Center for Law and Education at Harvard University and in 1973 began the Children's Defense Fund. She has received numerous awards including the Presidential Medal of Freedom, the nation's highest civilian award, and the Robert F. Kennedy Lifetime Achievement Award in 2000.

Mari Kaye Eder

MILITARY. Mari Kaye Eder received a Bachelor of Arts degree in English from Edinboro University of

Pennsylvania. She earned a Master of Arts degree in English literature from Edinboro University of Pennsylvania and a masters of strategic studies from the United States Army War College. She is also a graduate of the United States Army Command and General Staff College.

Brigadier General Eder's professional career includes a wide variety of assignments including serving as assistant director of public affairs (DIMA), United States European Command, Stuttgart, Germany; as commander, 6th Brigade (professional development), 80th Division (institutional training), Fort Belvoir, Virginia; as the senior policy advisor in the Office of the Secretary of Defense, Reserve Forces Policy Board, Washington, D.C., from September 2003 until March 2004; and as deputy chief, Office of the Chief of Public Affairs, in Washington, D.C., since March 2004.

Sandra B. Edlitz

JUDGE. Sandra B. Edlitz received a Bachelor of Arts degree from Barnard College, Columbia University, in 1962 and received a Master's of Arts degree from Hunter College in 1969. She earned her Juris Doctor degree from Pace University School of Law in 1981.

Her professional career includes serving in private law practice; as court attorney to the supervising judge at the family court, New York County; and as a hearing examiner, New York State Unified Court System at the Family Court of the City of New York. In 1997 she was elected judge to the family court for Westchester County in White Plains, New York.

Jeanette K. Edmunds

MILITARY. Jeanette K. Edmunds received a Bachelor of Arts degree in psychology and a Master of Business Administration in logistics management. Her military education includes the Ordnance Officer Basic and Advance courses; the Command and General Staff College; the Program Manager's Course; the Defense Systems Management College and the Army War College.

Major General Edmunds' professional career included a variety of command and staff assignments including serving as the commanding general of the 13th COSCOM at Fort Hood, Texas; commanding general, U.S. Army War Reserve Support Command, Rock Island, Illinois; commander, 64th Corps Support Group at Fort Hood, Texas; commander, 306th Forward Support Battalion 6th ID (Light) at Fort Richardson, Alaska; commander of the 595th Maintenance Company in Korea; commander of the 19th Theater Support Command, headquartered in Daequ, Republic of Korea, from September 18, 2002, to October 17, 2004; and as the deputy chief of staff, G-4 (logistics) in Washington, D.C.

Ada Edwards

ELECTED OFFICIAL. Ada Edwards was elected in 2001 and again in 2003 to Houston City Council District D to represent the district she calls home. She chairs both the State of Emergency HIV/AIDS Task Force and the Flooding and Drainage Issues Committee. She is an active humanitarian and human rights activist. She is founder of the African American Advisory Panel and heads initiatives for African American women.

Genine D. Edwards

JUDGE. Genine D. Edwards received her undergraduate degree from Long Island University and earned

her Juris Doctor degree from St. John's University School of Law.

Her professional career includes serving from 1992 to 1998 with the Public Service Corporation Counsel's office and New York State Power Authority. From 1998 to 2005, she was in private law practice. She was elected judge to the New York City Civil Court on January 1, 2006.

Teresa Edwards

SPORTS (FIRST). Teresa Edwards is a native of Cairo, Georgia. She was a prep All-American at Cairo High School in Cairo, Georgia, where she led Cairo High School's girls' basketball team to the state championship her senior season in 1982. She was named the *Atlanta Journal-Constitution*'s Georgia High School Player of the Year in 1982. She finished her high school career with 1,982 points. She received a bachelor's degree from the University of Georgia. While at the University of Georgia she became one of the greatest and most exciting players ever to play basketball at the school. She was one of only three female basketball players to have her number retired (the others being Katrina McClain and Janet Harris). She played from 1982 to 1986. The University of Georgia's record was 116 wins to 17 losses during Teresa's career; the team won three Southeastern Conference Championships and reached the NCAA Final Four twice. An All-American her junior and senior years, she was an All-SEC performer her sophomore, junior, and senior years.

In 1984, she played on her first U.S. Olympic basketball team. She was the youngest member on the team, but she won her first Olympic gold medal that year. In 1986, she was selected as a member of the U.S. basketball team for the Goodwill Games where she won a gold medal in 1986 FIBA World Championship. She was named USA Basketball Player of the Year in 1987. In 1988, as a member of the U.S. Olympic basketball team she led the team in assists, steals and minutes played. She was the team's leading scorer and won her second Olympic gold medal at the 1988 Games. In 1989 she played for the Mitsubishi Electric Corporation in Nagoya, Japan. In 1990, she was selected as co-captain of the United States select basketball team, winning a gold medal in the 1990 FIBA World Championship. She was the team leader in scoring, assists, steals, and minutes played. In 1991, she was once again chosen co-captain of the United States select team, winning a bronze medal in the 1991 Pan Am games. In 1992, she was the only three-time basketball Olympian in either the men's or the women's games and she became the all-time leading scorer in United States women's Olympic history and the first woman to score more than 100 points in the Olympics; she surpassed Cheryl Miller's total of 99 points and established the new mark at 114. She also holds the record for points in a women's basketball game in the United States with 46 points. She made a record fifth Olympic basketball team, earning a fourth gold medal. Ms. Edwards was the star player and head coach for the Atlanta Glory of the American Basketball League (ABL). She also played for the Philadelphia Rage. During the 2003 WNBA draft, at the urging of Minnesota Lynx head coach Suzie McConnell Serio, the Lynx selected Edwards even though she was 38 years old. In December 2006, she was named an assistant coach of the Minnesota Lynx.

Jessica P. Einhorn

BUSINESS EXECUTIVE. Jessica P. Einhorn is a native of New York City. She received a Bachelor of Arts degree from Barnard College at Columbia University and a Master of Arts degree in international affairs from the School of Advanced International Studies (SAIS) at John Hopkins University. She earned a doctorate in politics from Princeton University.

Her professional career includes serving with the federal government in numerous positions including the United States Treasury Department and the United States International Development Cooperation Agency. She served twenty years with the World Bank (former treasurer and managing director). She also served as a consultant in the Washington office of Clark & Weinstock. Dr. Einhorn serves as dean and professor at the Paul H. Nitze School of Advanced International Studies (SAIS).

Janet Slaughter Eissenstat

GOVERNMENT OFFICIAL. Janet Slaughter Eissenstat studied international business and political science at Oklahoma State University before earning her Master's in Business Administration from the University of Oklahoma.

Her professional career includes

serving as organizational director of the Republican Party of Texas, as special assistant to the executive director of the Victory 2000 National Finance Committee and as director of public liaison for the 2001 Presidential Inaugural Committee. She served as a national spokesperson for the American Bankers Association and as vice president and managing director of Spaeth Communication.

Ms. Eissenstat was appointed by President Bush to serve as director of the President's Commission on White House Fellowships on January 3, 2005.

Maria S. Eitel

BUSINESS EXECUTIVE. Maria S. Eitel received a Bachelor of Arts degree in communications and French from McGill University in 1983 and a Master of Science degree in foreign service and international developing economies from Georgetown University in 1988.

Her professional career includes serving as the White House deputy director of media relations from 1989 to 1992 and later as special assistant to the president for media affairs; as director of public affairs for the Corporation for Public Broadcasting; as senior manager of communications and community relations at MCI Communication Corp.; and as European corporate affairs group manager for Microsoft Corp. She joined Nike Corporation in 1998 as vice president for corporate responsibility.

Ms. Eitel was named president of Nike Foundation, which focuses on the issues of globalization with particular emphasis on girls' education in the world's poorest countries.

Deborah Elam

BUSINESS EXECUTIVE. Deborah Elam is a native of New Orleans, Louisiana. She received a Bachelor of Arts degree in sociology at Louisiana State University and a masters of public administration from Southern University in Baton Rouge, LA.

Her professional career includes joining General Electric Company's (GE) Human Resources Leadership Program in 1987 during which she was given three rotational assignments at GE Global Exchange Services and GE Aircraft Engines in Evandale, Ohio. After completing the program, she was promoted to successively more challenging human resources assignments at GE Consulting Services in Atlanta and GE Capital Mortgage Corporation in Raleigh. In 1995, she was appointed senior vice president of human resources for GE Capital Insurance Services in Stamford, Connecticut. In 1997, she was appointed managing director of human resources for GE Capital Markets Services and in 2000, she served as managing director of human resources at GE Capital Commercial Finance.

Ms. Elam has served as the manager of diversity and inclusive leadership for General Electric Company since 2002.

M. Joycelyn Elders

MEDICINE. M. Jocelyn Elders was born Minnie Lee Jones in Schaal, Arkansas. She is the daughter of Curtis L. Jones and Haller Reed Jones. In college she changed her name to Minnie Joycelyn Lee (later using just Joycelyn). In 1952, she received her Bachelor of Arts degree in biology from Philander Smith College in Little Rock, Arkansas. Afterwards she worked as a nurse's aide in a Veterans Administration hospital in Milwaukee. She joined the Army in May 1953 and was commissioned a second lieutenant. She was assigned to Brooke Army Medical Center where she earned an R.P.T. degree in 1956. During her three years in the Army she was trained as a physical therapist. She then attended the University of Arkansas Medical School where she obtained her Medical Doctor degree in 1960. After completing an internship at the University of Minnesota Hospital and a residency in pediatrics at the University of Arkansas Medical Center, she earned a Master of Science degree in biochemistry in 1967. She began working as an assistant professor in pediatrics at the University of Arkansas Medical Center in 1967. She was promoted to associate professor in 1971 and professor in 1976. In 1987 she was appointed director of the Arkansas Department of Health by then–Governor Bill Clinton. In 1992 she was elected president of the Association of State and Territorial Health Officers. On September 8, 1993, President Bill Clinton appointed her Surgeon General of the Public Health Service. She became the first black surgeon general in history. The surgeon general carries the Navy rank of vice admiral as a member of the Uniformed Public Health Service.

April Phillips Elliott

JUDGE. April Phillips Elliott is a native of Arizona. She received a Bachelor of Arts degree from the University of Arizona in 1992 and earned her Juris Doctor degree from the University of Arizona Law School.

Her professional career includes serving in private law practice; in 2002, she served as a city prosecutor for the cities of Coolidge and Maricopa, Arizona. She served as a justice of the peace pro-tempore and was later appointed as a court commissioner. In November 2005, Governor Napolitano appointed her judge, Arizona Superior Court, Division VIII, in Pinal County.

Kate Ford Elliott

JUDGE. Kate Ford Elliott is a native of Pittsburgh, Pennsylvania. She received a Bachelor of Arts degree in education from Duquesne University in 1971 and received a Master of Science degree from Duquesne University in 1973. She earned her Juris Doctor degree from Duquesne University School of Law in 1978.

She was elected judge of the Superior Court of Pennsylvania in November 1989 and retained in 1999. Judge Elliott became president judge of the superior court on January 9, 2006.

Lynn Laverty Elsenhans

BUSINESS EXECUTIVE. Lynn Laverty Elsenhans received a bachelor's degree in mathematical sciences from Rice University and a Master's in Business Administration from Harvard. She joined Shell Oil Company in 1980 and served early on as an economic analyst, senior engineer and process manager. She has held assignments in oil products and chemical products business management and marketing and planning. She has served as manager of natural gas in exploration and production; manager of lubricants in oil products; general manager of business transformation; president and chief executive officer, Shell Deer Park Refining Company; and vice president, refining, for Equilon Enterprises, LLC.

Ms. Elsenhans also served as president of Shell Oil Products East, based in Singapore, and director of strategic planning, sustainable development and external affairs of Shell International Limited in London. She was selected to serve in the dual capacity as president and country chair of Shell Oil Company and president and chief executive officer of Shell Products U.S.

Elizabeth Hazlitt Emerson

JUDGE. Elizabeth Hazlitt Emerson received a Bachelor of Arts degree (magna cum laude) from Boston College and earned her Juris Doctor degree from Syracuse University College of Law (magna cum laude). Before coming to the bench she was engaged in private law practice.

She was elected justice to the supreme court at Suffolk County in 1996, and her term ends in 2009.

Flora Emerson

MILITARY. Flora Emerson is a native of Savannah, Georgia. She received a bachelor's degree from Savannah State College in 1980 and was the first female to receive a commission into the United States Marine Corps from their Naval Reserve Officer Training Corps Program. Commissioned a 2nd lieutenant she im-

mediately reported to the Basic School for training which she completed in October 1980. She went on to attend and successfully complete Maintenance Management School during November 1980. She completed Amphibious Warfare School in 1992.

Colonel Emerson has held numerous assignments of increasing authority including serving with the II Marine Expeditionary Force where she coordinated the retrograde of all personnel and equipment from Southwest Asia. She joined the Reserves in July 1993 and served as the logistics officer, Mobilization Training Unit in Pensacola, Florida. In March 1998 she returned to active duty as the action officer, Cooperative Osprey 98 at Camp Lejeune, North Carolina. From August 2000 through September 2003, she served on active duty as an assistant chief of staff, G-4 and integrated logistics coordinator at Camp Lejeune, North Carolina.

She was selected to the rank of colonel in June 2003 and was subsequently promoted in June 2004. In October 2005 Colonel Emerson reported to Marine Corps Systems Command where she serves as the assistant commander, product support.

Jo Ann Emerson

ELECTED OFFICIAL. Jo Ann Emerson is a native of Bethesda, Montgomery County, Maryland. She received a Bachelor of Arts degree from Ohio Wesleyan University in Delaware, Ohio.

She has served as deputy communications director for the National Republican Congressional Committee and as director of state relations and grassroots programs for the small-business oriented National Restaurant Association. She served as the senior vice president of public affairs for the American Insurance Association. Ms. Emerson was elected on November 5, 1996, as a Republican to the 106th and to the four succeeding Congresses since January 8, 1997.

Elma Teresa Salinas Ender

JUDGE. Elma Teresa Salinas Ender received a Bachelor of Arts degree from University of Texas in Austin, Texas, and earned her Juris Doctor degree from St. Mary's University School of Law in 1978.

Her professional career includes serving as a law clerk in the Webb County District Attorney's office, as a teacher at Laredo State University, and in private law practice. In 1983, she was appointed district judge in Texas' 341st Judicial District by Governor Mark White. She is the first Mexican-American woman in Texas history to achieve that distinction.

Kim Ennix

AEROSPACE. Kim Ennix received a Bachelor of Science degree in mechanical engineering from the University of Tennessee, in Knoxville, Tennessee, and a Master of Science degree in aerospace engineering from California Polytechnic State University, Pomona.

Her professional career began at Edwards Air Force Base in California working for the United States Air Force Rocket Propulsion Laboratory. In February 1991, she began her career with NASA at Dryden Flight Research Center located at Edwards Air Force Base. She has worked several programs during her time at Dryden. She has performed flight test studies on the acoustic effects of jet engines and looked at the F-404 engine on an F-18 aircraft. She also took acoustic measurements on other aircraft such as the F-16, F-15, SR-17 and the Space Shuttle. She was the principal investigator for the Fiber Optic Control System Integration (FOCSI) Sensors. She was the principal engineer for Linear Aerospike SR-71 Experiment (LASRE) Oxygen Sensors which were safety critical sensors for the LASRE program.

Judith C. Ensor

JUDGE. Judith C. Ensor is a native of Baltimore County, Maryland; she received her undergraduate with honors from St. Lawrence University and earned her Juris Doctor degree with honors from the University of Maryland Law School.

She was engaged in private law practice until her appointment as judge to the circuit court of Baltimore County, Maryland.

Evern Cooper Epps

BUSINESS EXECUTIVE. Evern Cooper Epps is a native of Detroit, Michigan. She received a bachelor's degree in English and journalism from Michigan State University and continued her education at Emory University and Harvard Graduate School of Business.

Her professional career includes serving as a high school teacher before joining United Parcel Service (UPS) for 33 years in strategic planning, delivery information, training and business development. She now serves as president of the UPS Foundation and vice president of corporate relations. She is responsible for the global philanthropic programs of the UPS Foundation as well as the many corporate relations and community service initiatives of UPS. She is the fourth person to head the foundation and the first female and first African American.

Mary A. Epps

MILITARY. Mary A. Epps' military career began by enlisting in the Connecticut Air National Guard in June 1976 where she received a commission as a first lieutenant on February 26, 1977. Her education includes a Bachelor of Science degree in human services from Hampshire College, Manchester; in 1994, she graduated from the Air War College, Maxwell Air Force Base in Alabama.

From February 1977 to July 1984 she was assigned as a clinical nurse with the 103rd Tactical Clinic, East Granby, Connecticut. In July 1984, she was assigned as a medical surgical nurse, 103rd Tactical Clinic, East Granby, Connecticut. From August 1989 to September 1990, she served as chief of nursing services, 103rd Tactical Clinic, East Granby, Connecticut. In September 1990, she assumed the duties of commander of the 103rd Medical Squadron, 103rd Tactical Clinic, East Granby, Connecticut. While in this assignment she was promoted to colonel on December 23, 1994. She became the first African American and the first female to achieve this rank in the history of Connecticut Air National Guard. From September 1997 to March 2001, she served as advisor to the Defense Equal Opportunity Management Institute at Patrick Air Force Base, Florida.

On March 30, 2001, she was promoted to brigadier general and was selected to serve as the assistant adjutant general-air who also serves as the commander of the Connecticut Air National Guard. She is responsible for formulating, developing, and coordinating all policies, plans and programs affecting over 1,100 members of the Connecticut Air National Guard and is tasked with ensuring their ability to respond to peacetime contingencies while maintaining readiness to accomplish their war missions.

Her military awards and decorations include the Defense Superior Service Medal; the Air Force Meritorious Service Medal (with one device); Air Force Commendation Medal; Air Force Achievement Medal; Air Force Outstanding Unit Award (with two devices); National Defense Service Medal; Air Force Reserve Medal (with two devices); Air Force Longevity Service Award (with four devices); Air Force Training Ribbon; State of Connecticut Medal of Merit; State of Connecticut Long Service Medal (with twenty-year device).

Roselyn Epps

MEDICINE. Roselyn Epps is a native of Little Rock, Arkansas. She received both her Bachelor of Science degree and Medical Doctor degree with honors and completed her pediatric residency at Howard University in Washington D.C. She earned her masters of public health degree from Johns Hopkins University and the Master of Arts degree from American University. She is certified in pediatrics and is a Fellow of the American Academy of Pediatrics.

Her professional career includes serving as a medical officer with the District of Columbia Department of Health and first acting commissioner of health for the District of Columbia. She worked for the National Cancer Institute in Bethesda, Maryland, where she developed national and international programs, and served as a scientific program administrator for several research initiatives at the National Institutes of Health.

Dr. Epps serves as a consultant and is professor emeritus and senior program advisor to the Women's Health Institute at Howard University.

Aprille Ericsson

AEROSPACE. Aprille Ericsson is a native of Brooklyn, New York. She received a Bachelor of Science degree from Massachusetts Institute of Technology and a Master of Science from Howard University in Washington, D.C. She earned a Ph.D. degree in mechanical engineering from Howard University, becoming the first black woman to receive that degree from Howard University.

She is the first black Ph.D. in engineering at NASA Goddard Space Flight Center. She has over 20 years of experience in structural dynamics, controls and instrument management of spacecraft missions. She works at NASA Guidance, Navigation & Control Center. As a NASA engineer, Dr. Ericsson has worked on many projects, including the Microwave Anisotropy Probe, the Tropical Rainfall Measurement Mission, the James Webb Space Telescope, and in the Integrated Mission Design Center. Currently she is the instrument manager for a proposed mission to bring dust from the Martian lower atmosphere back to Earth. She was featured on the NBC Nightly News series "Women to Watch" and is listed in history books honoring African-Americans in aerospace and science. She also serves as an adjunct professor at Bowie University.

Patricia G. Escher

JUDGE. Patricia G. Escher received a Bachelor of Arts degree in history from Stanford University and earned her Juris Doctor degree with highest distinction from the University of Arizona College of Law in 1976.

Her professional career includes serving private law practice from 1976 to 1983; as the vice chief attorney for Division Two of the Arizona Court of Appeals from 1983 to 1996; and as a juvenile court commissioner. In 1997, she was appointed judge to the Pima County Superior Court in Arizona.

Anna Georges Eshoo

ELECTED OFFICIAL. Anna Georges Eshoo is a native of New Britain, Hartford County, Connecticut. She received an Associate of Arts degree from Canada College in Redwood City, California, in 1975.

Her professional career includes serving as Democratic National Committeewoman from California from 1980 to 1992; as administrative assistant to the speaker pro tempore of the California state assembly from 1981 to 1982; as a member of the San Mateo County, California, Board of Supervisors 1983 to 1992 and as president in 1986; as a member, California Democratic State Central Executive Committee; and as a member of the Democratic National Commission on Presidential Nominations, 1982. She was an unsuccessful candidate for election to the 101st Congress in 1988.

Ms. Eshoo was elected as a Democrat to the 103rd and to the six succeeding Congresses (January 3, 1993–present).

Carmen E. Espinosa

JUDGE. Carmen E. Espinosa is a native of Puerto Rico and moved with her family at the age of 3 to New Britain, Connecticut, where she attended public schools. She received a Bachelor of Science degree in secondary education from Central Connecticut State College in 1971. She earned her Juris Doctor degree from George Washington University.

After law school she joined the Federal Bureau of Investigation as a special agent. In 1980, she began a career as an assistant United States attorney in the Office of the United States Attorney for the District of Connecticut. She held this position as a federal prosecutor until her appointment to the Superior Court bench.

In 1992, she became the first Hispanic sworn as a superior court judge in the state of Connecticut. She presides over criminal trials in the judicial district of New Britain. She has also served as a trial judge in the judicial district of Hartford and Waterbury.

Jane Evans

TECHNOLOGY EXECUTIVE. Jane Evans received a bachelor's degree from Vanderbilt University and served

as president of the Vanderbilt University Alumni Association as well as on its Board of Trustees.

Her professional career includes serving at age 25 as president of I. Miller Shoes; she has served in senior positions with the American Can Company, General Mills, Montgomery Securities and US West Communications.

Ms. Evans served as chief executive officer of Opnix Internet Technologies, a high-tech start-up focused on migrating mission-critical applications to the Internet.

Orinda Dale Evans

JUDGE. Orinda Dale Evans is a native of Savannah, Georgia. She received a Bachelor of Arts degree from Duke University in 1965 and earned her Juris Doctor degree from Emory University School of Law in 1968.

Her professional career includes serving as an adjunct professor of law at Emory University, 1974–1977; counsel to the Atlanta Crime Commission, Atlanta, Georgia 1970–1971; and in private law practice 1968–1979.

She was nominated by President Jimmy Carter in 1979 to a seat vacated by Albert J. Henderson. She began serving as chief judge in 1999 and is the first African-American female to serve on a federal court in Georgia.

Sue McKnight Evans

JUDGE. Sue McKnight Evans is a native of Davidson County, Tennessee, and graduated from West End High School. She received a Bachelor of Science degree with honors from the University of Tennessee. She earned her Juris Doctor degree from the Nashville School of Law in 1986.

She was serving in private law practice when, in 1996, she was elected judge to the Tennessee General Sessions Court Division IX in Davidson County, Metropolitan Nashville, Tennessee; she served as presiding judge for general sessions from 1996 to 1997. She was re-elected to Division IX in 1998. The Tennessee Supreme Court appointed her to the Court of Judiciary for a four-year term in July 1999 and a second term in 2003.

Mary Fairhurst

JUDGE. Mary Fairhurst received her undergraduate degree in political science (cum laude) from Gonzaga University in 1979 and earned her Juris Doctor degree (cum laude) from Gonzaga University School of Law in 1984.

Her professional career includes serving as a judicial clerk to the Washington Supreme Court from 1984 to 1986 and in the Washington Attorney General's office as the division chief of the revenue, bankruptcy and collection division. She also specialized in the areas of criminal justice, transportation, revenue and labor. In 2003, she was elected justice to the Washington Supreme Court.

Maria Falca-Dodson

MILITARY. Maria Falca-Dodson received a Bachelor of Science degree in nursing from College of New Jersey and a Master of Arts in administration from Central Michigan University. Her military schools include: Squadron Officer School in 1983, Nursing Services Management in 1984, Air Command and Staff College in 1991, Air War College in1994, Community Nursing Certification in 2002, and the Reserve Components National Security Course.

Brigadier General Falca-Dodson's military career includes serving in a variety of staff and command positions including medical surgical clinical nurse with the 108th Tactical Air Command Clinic, 108th Air Refueling Wing, McGuire Air Force Base in New Jersey, 1980 to 1984; assistant chief nurse, 108th Tactical Air Command Clinic, 1984 to 1993; chief nurse executive, 108th Medical Squadron, 108th Air Refueling Wing,

1993 to 1997; air transportable hospital commander, 108th Medical Squadron, 1997 to 1998; and commander, 108th Medical Group, 108th Air Refueling Wing at McGuire Air Force Base at New Jersey, 1998 to 2002.

Brigadier General Maria Falca-Dodson has served as the adjutant general — air at the New Jersey Department of Military and Veterans Affairs, Trenton, New Jersey, since 2002. She was promoted to brigadier general on February 15, 2004.

Colleen Falkowski

JUDGE. Colleen Falkowski received her undergraduate degree from Ursuline College and earned her Juris Doctor degree from Cleveland-Marshall College of Law. Her professional career includes serving as a Lake County assistant prosecuting attorney from 1979 to 1988. In 1988 she served as the staff attorney for the Lake County Department of Human Services, Child Support Enforcement Division (CSEA); she returned to the Lake County Prosecutor's office in 1997 to accept the position of supervising attorney for the office's Child Support Division.

She was elected judge in November 2002 for her term which began January 2, 2003.

Mary Fallin

ELECTED OFFICIAL. Mary Fallin is a native of Tecumseh, Oklahoma, and a graduate of Oklahoma State University. At 35, she was elected to the Oklahoma House of Representatives where she served from 1990 to 1994.

She has been making history in Oklahoma since 1994 when she was elected the state's first Republican lieutenant governor. She was re-elected in 1998 by a margin of nearly three-to-one and in 2002, voters returned her to office for a third term.

Zulima V. Farber

LAW. Zulima V. Farber received her undergraduate and graduate degrees from Montclair State University. She also studied at the University of Madrid, Spain. In 1971, she was admitted to Rutgers Law School–Newark where she became a founding member of the Association of Latin American Law Students and also served as the association's vice president.

From 1975 to 1978, she was an assistant prosecutor in Bergen County, dealing with all manner of criminal prosecutions and serving as chief of the prosecutor's grand jury section and assistant chief of the trial section. Her experience in state government includes serving as public defender and public advocate from 1992 to 1994 in the cabinet of Governor James J. Florio. She also served as assistant counsel to Governor Brendan T. Byme from 1978 to 1981. She entered private practice in 1981.

Governor Jon S. Corzine nominated her to become attorney general and she was sworn in as New Jersey's attorney general on January 30, 2006. She is the state's first Hispanic attorney general.

Margrit Marie Anne Farmer

MILITARY. Margrit Marie Anne Farmer received Bachelor of Arts degree in German from Indiana University. Her military schools attended include the Military Intelligence Officer Basic and Advanced courses, the United States Army Command and General Staff College and the United States Army War College.

Brigadier General Farmer has served in a variety of assignments of increased authority and responsibility. From October 1996 to April 1999 she served as commander, 11th Health Services/Practical Nurse Battalion, 98th Division (Institutional Training), Devens, Massachusetts; from April 1999 to May 2002 she served as commander, 2nd Simulation Exercise Group, 78th Training Support Division, in Bristol, Rhode Island; from May 2002 to February 2003 she served as chief of staff, 77th Regional Support Command, Fort Totten, New York; from February 2003 to March 2005, chief of staff, 77th Regional Readiness Command, Fort Totten, New York;

from March 2005 to February 2006 she served as deputy commander, 77th Regional Readiness Command at Fort Totten, New York. She was promoted to brigadier general on August 22, 2005.

Brigadier General Farmer serves as special projects officer in the office of the deputy chief of staff, G2, in Washington, D.C., since March 2006.

Nancy Farmer

JUDGE. Nancy Farmer received her undergraduate degree from Eastern Michigan University and earned her Juris Doctor degree from the Detroit College of Law. Her professional career includes serving in private law practice and as a member of the Workers Compensation Board. She was appointed judge to the Michigan 36th Judicial District Court in Detroit in March 1990.

Gina S. Farrisee

MILITARY. Gina S. Farrisee received a Bachelor of Arts degree in sociology from the University of Richmond and a Master of Science in national resource strategy from the National Defense University. Her military schools attended include the Adjutant General Officer Basic and Advance courses, the United States Army Command and General Staff College and Industrial College of the Armed Forces.

Brigadier General Farrisee's military career includes serving in numerous assignments of increased authority and responsibility including serving from July 1995 to July 1997 as commander, 22nd Personnel Service Battalion, Fort Lewis, Washington; from June 1998 to June 2000 as commander, United States Army Enlisted Records and Evaluations Center, Indianapolis, Indiana; from June 2000 to August 2002 as the military assistant to the assistant secretary of defense (force management policy), Office of the Secretary of Defense, Washington, D.C.; from August 2002 to August 2004 she was assigned as the adjutant general/commanding general, physical disability agency/executive director, Military Postal Service Agency, Alexandria, Virginia. She was promoted to brigadier general on August 1, 2003.

Brigadier General Farrisee serves as the commanding general of the United States Army Soldier Support Institute at Fort Jackson, South Carolina.

Barbara G. Fast

MILITARY. Barbara G. Fast received a Bachelor of Science degree in German from the University of Missouri and a Master of Science in Business Administration from Boston University. Her military schools attended include the Military Intelligence Officer Basic and Advance Course, the Armed Forces Staff College and the United States Army War College.

Major General Fast has served in numerous positions of increased authority and responsibility including serving from July 1996 to August 1998 as commander, 66th Military Intelligence Group (Provisional), United States Army Intelligence and Security Command in Munich, Germany; from August 1998 to June 2001, as associate deputy director for operations/deputy chief, Central Security Service, National Security Agency at Fort George G. Meade, Maryland; from June 2001 to June 2003, she served as director of intelligence, J-2, United States European Command, Germany; from July 2003 to July 2004 she was assigned as assistant commandant, United States Army Intelligence Center, Fort Huachuca, Arizona, with duty as C-2, Combined Joint Task Force-7, later redesignated Multi-National Force-Iraq, Operation Iraqi Freedom, Iraq. She was promoted to brigadier general on July 1, 2004.

Major General Fast has served as the commanding general/commandant of the United States Army Intelligence Center and Fort Huachuca, Arizona, since March 2005. She was promoted to major general on July 1, 2004.

Dianne Feinstein

ELECTED OFFICIAL. Dianne Feinstein is a native of San Francisco, California, attended the San Francisco public schools and graduated from the Convent of the Sacred Heart High School in 1951. She received a bachelor's degree from Stanford University in 1955.

Her professional career includes serving as a member of the California Women's Board of Terms and Parole from 1960 to 1966. She was elected and served as a member of the San Francisco Board of Supervisors from 1970 to 1978, where she served as president from 1970 to 1971, 1974 to 1975, and 1978. She was elected mayor of San Francisco, serving from 1978 to 1988, and

was selected director of the Bank of California from 1988 to 1989. She served as co-chair, San Francisco Education Fund's Permanent Fund, from 1988 to 1989. She was an unsuccessful candidate for governor of California in 1990, then was elected in a special election on November 3, 1992, as a Democrat to the United States Senate to fill the term left by a vacancy and took the oath of office on November 10, 1992; she was reelected in 1994 and in 2000.

Charlotte Ferretti

HEALTH. Charlotte Ferretti received a Bachelor of Science degree in nursing from the University of San Francisco, and received a Master's of Science from the University of California, San Francisco. She earned her doctoral in education from the University of San Francisco.

Her professional career includes serving as an RN at St. Vincent's Medical Center in New York City; as nursing case manager, Health Disparities, Workforce Diversity, Health Systems; as project director for a nurse-managed high school health center for five years in the Mission District; as project director for the Valencia Health Services; she was engaged for over 8 years working with Mission District agencies focused on health and social service access for underserved. She was selected as director for the Marian Wright Edelman Institute.

Jennifer Ferron

SPORTS EXECUTIVE. Jennifer Ferron received a Bachelor of Arts degree in communications from Boston College. She was named the vice president of marketing operations for the New England Patriots and Gillette Stadium in March 2006. She originally joined the organization as the special events and promotions manager for the New England Revolution on July 7, 1997. In her first nine seasons with the Patriots, Ferron has enjoyed six trips to the playoffs, including five as division championships, and has celebrated three Super Bowl titles.

As vice president, Ms. Ferron is responsible for the strategic direction and execution of all team advertising and collateral as well as the execution of all sponsor promotions, premium member services and client fulfillment. In addition, she coordinates and plans all special events and oversees brand awareness and recognition through the organization.

Parisa Y. Fetherson

MILITARY. Parisa Y. Fetherson entered the United States Marine Corps in 1979. Upon completion of boot camp at Marine Corps Recruit Depot, Parris Island, South Carolina, she was assigned the administration School MOS and attended the Basic Personnel Administration School and Unit Diary School at Parris Island, South Carolina.

Upon completion of MOS school, she was assigned as a unit diary clerk at Headquarters and Headquarters Squadron 28, Marine Air Control Group-28, 2nd Marine Aircraft Wing, Cherry Point, North Carolina. During her tour at Cherry Point, she was meritoriously promoted to the rank of corporal.

Sergeant Major Fetherson has served the United States Marine Corps in a numerous staff and command positions to include serving in 1989 with the 2nd Force Service Support Group, Camp Lejeune, North Carolina, where she served as an admin chief with Headquarters Service Battalion and 2nd Landing Support Battalion; in 1993, she served as the gunnery sergeant and administrative chief at Headquarters and Service Battalion at the Depot Consolidated Admin Center, Marine Corps Recruit Depot, Parris Island, South Carolina; she served with Headquarters and Service Battalion, 3rd Force Service Support Group where she was assigned to the administrative assistance team as an inspector and the officer-in-charge in Okinawa, Japan; she served as first sergeant for Headquarters and Support Company, 3rd Support Battalion, 3rd Force Service Support Group. During her tour at 3rd Support Battalion she was assigned as the first sergeant for the combat service support detachment of the Air Contingency Marine Air Ground Task Force. She once again deployed to the Marine Expeditionary Camp-Pohang, Korea, where she served as the detachment first sergeant for Combat Service Support Detachment-39. She was transferred to Headquarters and Service Battalion, Marine Corps Base Camp Lejeune, North Carolina, in 1999, where she served as the company first sergeant for Brig Company and B Company.

In 2001, she was transferred to Marine Security Guard Battalion, Quantico, Virginia, where she served as the company first sergeant for Headquarters Company. In August 2004, she was serving as sergeant major for the MCAF.

Marie T. Field

MILITARY. Marie T. Field received a Bachelor of Science degree in nursing from Southeastern Massachusetts in 1976 and a Master of Science degree in nursing from the University of Massachusetts. Her military schools attended include the Medical Service Officer Orientation in 1978, Flight Nurse Course in 1978, Air Command and Staff College in 1988, Nursing Service Management in 1994, and the Air War College in 1996.

She has held various positions in both the Air Force Reserves and the Air National Guard. Her career began in August 1978 as a nurse in the Air Force Reserves. She was assigned from February 1994 to August 1998 as chief nurse executive, 104th Medical Squadron, Barnes Air National Guard Base, Westfield, Massachusetts; from August 1998 to September 2001 as commander, 104th Medical Squadron, Barnes Air National Guard; from September 2001 to June 2005 as Air National Guard assistant in the Office of the Air Surgeon, Bolling Air Force Base, District of Columbia. She was promoted to brigadier general on June 1, 2002.

Brigadier General Field has served as the assistant adjutant general for air at the Massachusetts Joint Force Headquarters since June 2005.

Evelyn J. Fields

GOVERNMENT OFFICIAL. Evelyn J. Field is the director of the Office of the National Oceanic and Atmospheric Commissioned Corps Operations and Commissioned Corps. She was nominated for this position by President Bill Clinton on January 19, 1999, confirmed by the Senate on May 6, 1999, and subsequently promoted from captain to rear admiral, upper half. She is the first African American and first female to hold this position.

Rear Admiral Fields' career with the National Oceanic and Atmospheric Administration (NOAA) began in 1972 as a cartographer at NOAA's Atlantic Marine Center in Norfolk, Virginia. She was commissioned as an ensign and served on board the NOAA Ship *Mt. Mitchell* as junior officer. Her later ship tours included the NOAA ship *Peirce* as operations officer, NOAA Ship *Rainier* as executive officer and the NOAA ship *McArthur* as commanding officer. Admiral Fields was the first female to serve as commanding officer of a NOAA ship and a United States government oceangoing vessel.

Following her command at sea tour, she was selected as a fellow to the United States Department of Commerce Science and Technology Fellowship Program. Her following on-land assignments included tours as the administrative officer of NOAA's National Geodetic Survey and chief of coast survey's hydrographic surveys division followed by her tenure as director of the NOAA Corps' Commissioned Personnel Center. Prior to her confirmation as director of the NOAA Corps, she served as deputy assistant administrator for NOAA's National Ocean Service.

Shirley L. Fields

GOVERNMENT OFFICIAL. Shirley L. Fields serves as the first chief information officer for the Defense Information System Agency (DISA). Prior to this appointment, she served as head of DISA's defense information infrastructure hardware/software department.

She was selected and awarded the NAACP's Roy Wilkins Renown Service Award for her "unparalleled leadership in human and civil rights opportunity and human resource development" at DISA in Arlington, Virginia.

The citation cites her unwavering community support and her establishment of annual college scholarship funds through Saint Timothy's Episcopal and Cedar Hill Baptist churches that help disadvantaged minority students.

Linda D. Fienberg

BUSINESS EXECUTIVE. Linda D. Fienberg received a Bachelor of Arts with distinction in all subjects from Cornell University. She earned a Master of Arts degree with honors and earned the Armstrong Award for first place in her class from Wesleyan University and a Juris Doctor degree with exceptional and/or distinguished notoriety in all subjects from Georgetown University Law Center.

Ms. Fienberg served from 1979 and 1990 on the staff of the Securities and Exchange Commission where she held several senior staff positions including executive assistant to two chairmen and associate general coun-

sel in the General Counsel's office — first for the litigation section and then for the counseling and legislation section. She served in private law practice until June 1996 when she joined NASD. She was named president, NASD dispute resolution and executive vice president and chief hearing officer, regulatory policy and oversight.

Sherri Fike

TECHNOLOGY EXECUTIVE. Sherri Fike received a Bachelor of Science degree in computer science with a specialization in statistics from Pennsylvania State University where she graduated with highest distinction.

She began her career as a software engineer at the National Security Agency in 1980 and then worked for HRB-Systems from 1981 to 1990. She joined Ball Aerospace in 1991 as flight software lead on the ultraviolet coronagraph spectrometer program. From 1993 to 1999, she worked extensively on the Hubble Space Telescope Near Infrared Camera Multi-Object Spectrometer program as lead software engineer and on the Advanced Camera for Surveys program as command and data handing integrated product team lead. She held the position of supervisor from 1999 to 2001 in the Space Instruments Controls and Data Products Group. From 1999 to 2004, she worked as the Ball Aerospace software process improvement advisor. She coordinated the efforts of over 100 software engineers to achieve the Software Engineering Institute's Capability Maturity Model Level 2 maturity rating in 2003. She served two years as the functional manager for software quality assurance. In September 2004, was assigned the responsibility for ensuring the highest standards of quality for all Ball Aerospace processes and products.

Patricia Fili-Krushel

ENTERTAINMENT EXECUTIVE. Patricia Fili-Krushel received a Bachelor of Science degree from St. John's University and earned her Master of Business Administration degree from Fordham University.

Her professional career includes serving as controller for ABC Sports from 1975 to 1979. She joined Home Box Office (HBO) in June 1979 as director of sports and served as director of sports and specials, program budgeting, in September 1980, then was appointed director of production and programming administration. In 1988 she joined Lifetime Television as both group vice president of Hearst/ABC-Viacom Entertainment Services (HAVES) and senior vice president of programming and production of Lifetime Television; she served as president of ABC Daytime where she was responsible for leading ABC's daytime programming schedule; from July 1998 to April 2000 she served as president of the ABC television network; in April 2000 she joined WebMD Health.

Ms. Fili-Krushel serves as executive vice president of administration of Time Warner.

Julie Finley

GOVERNMENT OFFICIAL. Julie Finley is a graduate of Vassar College. Her professional career includes serving as a journalist at NBC, ABC and the *Washington Post*; and as national finance co-chairman for Bush-Cheney '04 for the District of Columbia and co-chairman of Team 100 for the Republican National Committee from 1997 through 2004. She was a founder and board member of the U.S. Committee on NATO and was chairman of the host committee for the Prague NATO summit in November 2002. She was a trustee of the National Endowment for Democracy until June 2005, and has been a trustee of the American Academy in Berlin and chairman of the Board of Directors of the Project on Transitional Democracies.

She was nominated by President George Bush to the Organization for Security and Cooperation in Europe (OSCE). She was confirmed by the U.S. Senate on August 2, 2005, and assumed her duties in Vienna on August 18, 2005.

Anne M. Finucane

FINANCE. Anne M. Finucane received an honorary Doctor of Business Administration degree from Stonehill College. Her professional career includes serving as director of creative services at WBZ-TV in Boston and as a public information officer for the city of Boston. She was chief marketing officer at FleetBoston Financial, operated her own communications consultancy and held executive positions at Hill, Holliday.

Ms. Finucane was appointed president, Northeast, for Bank of America, responsible for market leadership and setting the bank's overall brand efforts in the region. She also has oversight for the corporation's public policy group and the Bank of America Foundation, one of the largest corporate philanthropic organizations in the country.

Shelley Fischel

BUSINESS EXECUTIVE. Shelley Fischel received a Bachelor of Arts degree from Wellesley College. She earned her Juris Doctor from Columbia University School of Law and an LLM in taxation from New York University School of Law.

Her professional career includes joining HBO in December 1979 as a labor counsel. She was promoted to chief counsel, labor and special litigation in June 1982 and was named senior vice president, human resources, in November 1986. She was named senior vice president, human resources and administration, in August 1990.

Ms. Fischel was named executive vice president, human resources and administration, for Home Box Office, responsible for overseeing the development, management and administration of human resources programs and policies affecting HBO employees.

Wendy Fischer

MILITARY. Wendy Fischer graduated from Costa Mesa High School in Costa Mesa, California. She entered the United States Navy in May 1982 and completed recruit training in Orlando, Florida. She completed advanced training at the Surface Force Independent Duty Corps School, Naval School of Health Sciences, in San Diego, California, in May 1992. She is qualified as a fleet marine warfare specialist and is certified as a master training specialist.

Master Chief Fischer's military career includes serving in numerous positions to include serving as the senior medical department representative and the executive officer for Charlie Surgical Company and as an instructor at Independent Duty School. She was assigned to III Marine Expeditionary Forces, Pacific, Okinawa, Japan, as the senior IDC and adviser to the commanding general on medical issues. She deployed to Thailand in support of Cobra Gold as the protocol officer for 3rd Marine Division; during operations in East Timor she assumed the duties as the force health protection and medical planner during their periods of deployment.

Master Chief Fischer serves as the command master chief for the 1st Medical Battalion.

Anna L. Fisher

ASTRONAUT. Anna L. Fisher is a native of San Pedro, California, and a graduate of San Pedro High School in San Pedro, California, in 1967. She received a Bachelor of Science degree in chemistry and a doctorate of medicine from the University of California in Los Angeles in 1971 and 1976. She also earned a Master of Science in chemistry from the University of California in Los Angeles in 1987.

After completing her internship, she specialized in emergency medicine and worked in several hospitals in the Los Angeles area. Dr. Fisher was selected by the National Aeronautics and Space Administration (NASA) in January 1978 and completed her training in August

1979. Following the one-year basic training program her early NASA assignments (pre–STS-1 through STS-4) included the following: crew representative to support development and testing of the Remote Manipulator System (RMS); crew representative to support development and testing of payload bay door contingency EVA procedures, the extra-small Extravehicular Mobility Unit (EMU) and contingency on-orbit TPS repair hardware and procedures; verification of flight software at the Shuttle Avionics Integration Laboratory (SAIL)—in that capacity she reviewed test requirements and procedures for ascent, on-orbit and RMS software verification—and served as a crew evaluator for verification and development testing for STS 2, 3, 4. She was an on-orbit CAPCOM for the STS-9. She served as a mission specialist on STS-51A which launched from Kennedy Space Center, Florida, on November 8, 1984. In the first space salvage mission in history, the crew retrieved for return to Earth the Palapa B-2 and Westar VI satellites. STS-51A completed 127 orbits of the Earth before landing at Kennedy Space Center in Florida on November 16, 1984. With the completion of her first flight, she logged a total of 192 hours in space.

Dr. Fisher was assigned as a mission specialist on STS-61H prior to the *Challenger* accident. Following the accident she worked as the deputy of the mission development branch of the Astronaut Office and as the astronaut office representative for Flight Data File issues. She served in the Space Station Support Office where she worked part-time in space station operations. She is assigned to the Shuttle Branch and works technical assignments in that branch while awaiting an assignment as either a Space Shuttle crewmember on a space station assembly mission or as a crewmember aboard the International Space Station.

Fern A. Fisher

JUDGE. Fern A. Fisher received her Juris Doctor from Harvard Law School in 1978. Her career started in the civil court as a legal services attorney. She also served as a deputy director of Harlem Legal Services, Inc., and as an assistant attorney general of the New York State Department of Law. In 1989 she was appointed judge of the housing part of the civil court; and later in 1990 was elected to the civil court where she served as deputy supervising judge. In 1993 she was elected to the Supreme Court of the State of New York. In December 1996 she was appointed administrative judge of the civil court.

Jeanne Fites

GOVERNMENT OFFICIAL. Jeanne Fites received a bachelor's degree in psychology from Wake Forest University in 1966. She earned a master's degree in personnel and industrial psychology from George Washington University in 1969.

Her professional career includes serving as assistant director for research, Defense Manpower Data Center (1974–1976); as director for research, Office of the Assistant Secretary of Defense for Manpower and Reserve Affairs (1976–1977); and as director (1978–1985), intergovernmental affairs, Office of the Assistant Secretary of Defense (manpower, installations and logistics). In 1985 she was responsible for the research analytic program for the under secretary of defense (personnel and readiness).

Ms. Fites was appointed deputy assistant secretary of defense for requirements and resources on December 26, 1993, and deputy under secretary of defense for requirements and resources on July 7, 1994, redesignated as the deputy under secretary of defense for program integration on January 10, 1997.

Karen Flaherty

MILITARY. Karen Flaherty is a native of Winsted, Connecticut. She received a bachelor's degree from Skidmore College and a Master of Science degree from the University of Pennsylvania.

She began her career as a nurse corps officer at Quantico Naval Hospital where she served as a staff nurse, charge nurse on the surgical and orthopedic floors, and the maximum care unit. In 1977, she was transferred to the Philadelphia VA Naval Medical Center and assumed the charge nurse role for a general surgery unit and the obstetric and gynecology clinic. She resigned her regular commission and accepted a commission in the Naval Reserve in 1982 where she has held numerous assignments in leadership positions including commanding officer, executive officer, officer-in-charge, training officer, and director of nursing services. In February 1991, during *Operation Desert Shield/Storm,* she

was recalled to serve with Fleet Hospital 15, Al Jubail, Saudi Arabia; she served as commander of Naval Reserve OPNAV 093-106.

Rear Admiral Flaherty serves as the deputy chief of the Navy Nurse Corps.

Elaine Flake

MINISTRY. Elaine Flake is a Native of Memphis, Tennessee, and received a Bachelor of Arts degree in English from Fish University in Nashville, Tennessee. She earned a Master of Arts degree in English from Boston University and a Master of Divinity degree from Union Theological Seminary in New York City. She was awarded a Doctor of Ministry degree from United Theological Seminary in Dayton, Ohio.

Dr. Flake is an itinerant elder in the African Methodist Episcopal Church. She and her husband, the Reverend Floyd H. Flake, founded the Allen Christian School in 1982. This is a leading Christian educational institution which provides a competitive education and special curriculum for grades Pre-K through eight.

Dr. Flake has served as a preacher, teacher and role model at the Greater Allen A.M.E. Cathedral. She was instrumental in developing the Allen Women's Resource Center which houses women who are victims of domestic violence. She is the author of the popular book, *God in Her Midst.*

Moira Flanders

MILITARY. Moira Flanders was born in Germany and raised in California and Virginia. She received a Bachelor of Science in biology from Virginia Tech and masters in strategic studies from the Naval War College. She was commissioned after attending the Officer Candidate School.

Admiral Flanders has held numerous assignments of increased responsibility and authority to including flag secretary to the chief of naval education and training. She served as information management branch head within the Joint Staff Secretariat in Washington. She has commanded Navy Recruiting District New York and as the fleet support and human resources officer community manager. She served as deputy director, officer of program appraisal within the Office of the Secretary of the Navy. Admiral Flanders became the director of strategic planning for manpower, personnel, training and education in October 2005. She assumed command of Naval Personnel Development Command on November 15, 2006.

Rhonda Fleming-Makell

MILITARY. Rhonda Fleming-Makell is a native of the Carolinas; she was born in Morganton, North Carolina, and raised in Greenville, South Carolina. She is a 1985 graduate of South Carolina State University with a Bachelor of Science degree in psychology and a minor in special education. In addition, she completed a Master of Business Administration with a concentration in technology management from the University of Phoenix.

In June of 1984, she enlisted in the United States Coast Guard while still in college. Upon completion of Coast Guard Recruit Training at Cape May, New Jersey, she returned to school in Orangeburg, South Carolina, to complete her undergraduate degree. She is a 1986 graduate of the Coast Guard Officer Candidate School (OCS) in Yorktown, Virginia. After graduation from OCS, she was assigned to the Third Coast Guard District as the human relations counselor in New York City and became a qualified trainer and counselor in the areas of human relations and civil rights.

She was then assigned to Coast Guard Support Center New York as the assistant special services officer. Shortly after, Lieutenant Commander Fleming-Makell was stationed at Coast Guard Group New York. As a junior officer, she was assigned to the operations division, successfully qualifying as a duty officer responding to search and rescue (SAR), law enforcement, and marine safety emergencies. In 1991, she was assigned to the Coast Guard Command Center in Washington, D.C. In 1994, Lieutenant Commander Fleming-Makell was assigned as assistant operations officer at one of the busiest units in the Coast Guard, "Group Miami." As the chief of district personnel, she managed personnel support programs for all Seventh District units in an area covering the entire Caribbean basin and points between the North and South Carolina border and the easternmost portions of the Gulf of Mexico. She was then assigned to Coast Guard Headquarters, Office of Law Enforcement in Washington, D.C., for her final tour in August 2001.

Lieutenant Commander Fleming-Makell is the first African-American female Coast Guard officer to earn a 20-year retirement, nearly 30 years after women were admitted to the Coast Guard.

Paulette K. Flynn

JUDGE. Paulette K. Flynn received a Bachelor of Arts degree from College of St. Catherine in 1970 and earned her Juris Doctor degree from William Mitchell College of Law in 1974.

Her professional career includes serving as an assistant attorney in St. Paul City from 1974 to 1984; in private law practice from 1984 to 1991. Governor Arne Carlson appointed her judge on September 11, 1991, to the District Court in Ramey County, Minnesota. She has won every election since her appointment.

Kim T. Folsom

BUSINESS EXECUTIVE. Kim T. Folsom received a Bachelor of Science degree in information systems from San Diego State University and earned a Master of Business Administration from the University of Pepperdine. She also holds a teaching credential from San Diego Community College.

Her professional career includes serving as an adjunct professor of computer technology at San Diego Community College; she has held senior management positions in the area of business development, operations, and information technology at Great American Bank; Central Federal Savings; ALLTEL Communications, Inc.; Advanta Corp.; SeminarSource.com; the National Dispatch Center and the law firm of Luce, Forward, Hamilton and Scripps.

Ms. Folsom is the cofounder and co-host of the weekly business resource talk-show, *Real Business Radio Hour*, currently broadcast in San Diego on KCBQ AM 1170. She is the cofounder and principal of Momentuum Solution, Inc., a business development, research, consulting services and software firm, specializing in development strategy to grow revenues through strategic partner relationships and large customer relationships.

Delores G. Forrest

MILITARY. Delores G. Forrest is a native of Danville, Illinois. She was commissioned a second lieutenant into the United States Air Force in September 1979.

Her military and civilian education includes a Bachelor of Science in nursing from Northern Illinois University and a masters degree in human resource management and personnel administration from Troy State University; she is also a graduate of United States Air Force Flight School; Nursing Service Management; Air Command and Staff College; and Air War College.

Colonel Forrest's key military assignments include serving from June 1993 to June 1996 as nurse manager, multi service unit, 1st Medical Group, Langley Air Force Base, Virginia; from August 1996 to May 1998 as nurse manager, orthopedic — neurosurgery, Wilford Hall Medical Center, Lackland Air Force Base, Texas; from May 1998 to May 1999 as chief of health care integration, Wilford Hall Medical Center, Lackland Air Force Base, Texas; from May 1999 to July 2001 as deputy commander, 6th Medical Operations Squadron and deputy chief nurse executive, 6th Medical Group, MacDill Air Force Base, Florida; from July 2001 to July 2003 as commander of the 9th Medical Operations Squadron and chief nurse executive, 9th Medical Group, Beale Air Force Base, California. In July 2003, she was assigned as the commander, 27th Medical Group, Cannon Air Force Base, New Mexico.

Diane M. Forster

MILITARY. Diane M. Forster entered the military in May 1983 and attended Basic Combat Training at Fort Dix, New Jersey. Afterward, she attended Advanced Individual Training at Fort Eustis, Virginia, where she was awarded the military occupation specialty as a 67Y Cobra helicopter mechanic.

Her military and civilian education includes all the Noncommissioned Officer Education System courses; the First Sergeant Course; and the United States Army Sergeants Major Academy (class 51). She holds an associates degree in liberal arts from Central Texas College, a Bachelor of Science degree in psychology from University of Maryland, a Master of Science degree in

human resource management, and a masters degree in public administration with a concentration in criminology.

Her duty assignments include serving with the 503rd Attack Helicopter Battalion, 4th Aviation Brigade; HHC 3rd Armored Division; 3rd Staff and Faculty Company, USAALS; 1-227th Aviation Battalion; 1st Calvary Division, Fort Hood, Texas; HHC, United States Army Sergeants Major Academy, Fort Bliss, Texas; 1-13th Aviation Battalion, Fort Rucker, Alabama; She also served in Desert Storm. In August 2004, she was serving as the command sergeant major, 2/52nd Aviation Battalion, 17th Aviation Brigade.

Jylia Moore Foster

BUSINESS EXECUTIVE. Jylia Moore Foster is a native of Salisbury, North Carolina. She received a Bachelor of Arts in mathematics from Livingstone College and earned a Master of Business Administration from Indiana University. She is also a graduate of the Corporate Coach University.

Her professional career includes serving as a systems engineer at IBM Corp. from 1978 to 1983. In 1983, she was selected to serve as systems engineering manager at IBM. In 1996, she was promoted to vice president of operations for the Northeast at IBM. In 1997, IBM named her vice president of global channels and in 1998 as vice president and client executive for IBM. In 2000, Ms. Foster became the founder and chief executive officer of her own company, Crystal Stairs, in Hinsdale, Illinois.

Ms. Foster is the author of *Due North: Strengthen Your Leadership Assets*. She has served as international president of Zeta Phi Beta Sorority.

Nuby Fowler

GOVERNMENT OFFICIAL. Nuby Fowler is a native of Colombia, South Carolina. She received a Bachelor of Arts degree in political science and a certification in public administration from the University of Maryland, Baltimore County, and a master of administrative science degree from Johns Hopkins University.

Her professional career includes serving as the vice president for Latin American banking at Summit National Bank. She served as the director of the small business services of the Metro Atlanta and DeKalb Chambers of Commerce.

President George W. Bush appointed Ms. Fowler as regional administrator for Region IV of the U.S. Small Business Administration. As regional administrator, she has been a champion for women and minority business development.

Virginia Ann Foxx

ELECTED OFFICIAL. Virginia Ann Foxx is a native of New York. She received a Bachelor of Arts degree from the University of North Carolina at Chapel Hill, North Carolina, in 1968 and a Master of Arts from the University of North Carolina at Chapel Hill, North Carolina, in 1972. She earned an education doctor degree from the University of North Carolina at Greensboro, North Carolina.

Her professional career includes serving as a professor at Caldwell Community College in Spruce Pine, North Carolina, from 1987 to 1994; as deputy secretary for management for the North Carolina Department of Administration; as a member of the Watauga County Board of Education from 1967 to 1988; as a North Carolina State Senator from 1994 to 2004. She was elected as a Republican to the 109th Congress (January 3, 2005).

Nancy C. Francis

JUDGE. Nancy C. Francis is a native of Ann Arbor. She graduated from Ann Arbor St. Thomas High School and received her undergraduate and Juris Doctor degrees from the University of Michigan.

Her professional career includes serving in private law practice for sixteen years. She was elected judge with the Washtenaw County Probate Court, Ann Arbor, Michigan. She is the first African-American in the Washtenaw County judiciary.

Lois J. Frankel

ELECTED OFFICIAL. Lois J. Frankel is a native of New York. She graduated from Boston University and earned her Juris Doctor degree from Georgetown University Law Center. She moved to West Palm Beach in 1974 and began her law practice.

Her professional career includes serving in private law practice. In 1986 she was elected to the Florida House of Representatives where she served for fourteen years. She was elected mayor of West Palm Beach, Palm Beach County's largest and busiest city, in March 2003.

Barbara Hackman Franklin

BUSINESS EXECUTIVE. Barbara Hackman Franklin received a bachelor's degree from Penn State in 1962 and in 1964 was the first woman to receive a Master of Business Administration degree from the Harvard Business School.

Her professional career includes serving as staff assistant to President Richard M. Nixon in 1971; as commissioner and vice chairman of the newly established Consumer Product Safety Commission in 1973; as a senior fellow of the Wharton School of Business and director of the Wharton Government and Business Program at the University of Pennsylvania; as a member of the President's Advisory Committee for Trade Policy Negotiations; as the 29th U.S. Secretary of Commerce in 1992–1993, where she was the highest ranking woman in the Bush Administration; and as a U.S. Delegate to the 44th Session of the United Nations General Assembly. She has also served as a director of the Dow Chemical Company; Aetna, Inc.; Milacron, Inc.; MedImmune, Inc.; and Watson Wyatt & Company.

Ms. Franklin serves as president and chief executive officer of Barbara Franklin Enterprises.

Shirley Clarke Franklin

ELECTED OFFICIAL. Shirley Clarke Franklin received a Bachelor of Arts degree in sociology from Howard University and earned her Master of Arts degree in sociology from the University of Pennsylvania. She has received honorary degrees from Howard University, the Atlanta College of Art and Cambridge College.

Prior to moving to Atlanta in 1972, she was a contract compliance officer with the United States Department of Labor and a member of the faculty of Talladega College in Alabama. She has served in Atlanta as the commissioner of cultural affairs for Mayor Maynard Jackson. In that position she developed innovative programs such as the First Atlanta Free Jazz Festival and the Arts Project at the Atlanta Hartsfield–Jackson International Airport. She was subsequently named chief administrative officer under Mayor Jackson. After successfully managing Andrew Young's campaign for mayor of Atlanta, she was appointed the city's first female chief administrative officer in 1982. Franklin held this important position during the eight years of Young's administration. Upon being elected as mayor of Atlanta for a third term, Maynard Jackson reorganized city government and appointed Franklin as his executive officer for operations, with responsibility over the operation departments and offices. She served as senior vice president for external relations for the Atlanta Committee for the Olympic Games. She also served as CEO of Shirley Clarke Franklin & Associates.

In 2001, the people of Atlanta elected Shirley Franklin, a first-time candidate for public office, to serve as the 58th mayor of the city of Atlanta. She is the first female mayor of Atlanta and the first African-American woman to serve as mayor of a major southern city.

Elizabeth Frasier

EDUCATION. Elizabeth Frasier is a native of Yanceyville, North Carolina. She received a bachelor's degree from Fayetteville State College (now Fayetteville State University) in 1945 and earned her master's degree from North Carolina College (now Central University) in 1956.

Ms. Frasier began

her professional career in 1945 as a teacher in North Carolina. She has also served as the director of field placement for the North Carolina Teaching Fellows program at the School of Education at the University of North Carolina at Chapel Hill. She is the first black female principal at Frank Porter Graham Elementary School in Chapel Hill. She is also the first black director of the North Carolina Kindergarten Institute at East Carolina University and director of Project Head Start in Durham. In 1997 she spearheaded an effort to develop a child development center at her church, the White Rock Baptist Church Child Development Center, which opened in 1998 and was accredited in 2002 by the National Association for the Education of Young Children. She published a book entitled *Wow! What a Wonderful World* in 1990.

Sharee Freeman

GOVERNMENT OFFICIAL. Sharee Freeman received a bachelor's degree from Saint Lawrence University and a Juris Doctor degree from Georgetown University Law Center.

Her professional career includes serving as full committee counsel for the United States House Committee on the Judiciary and committee liaison to the Subcommittee on the Courts. Before joining the House Judiciary Committee, she served in the Office of the Solicitor in the Department of Interior Bureau of Indian Affairs from 1984 to 1997.

Karen Freeman-Wilson

JUDGE. Karen Freeman-Wilson is a native of Gary, Indiana. She received a bachelor's degree with honors from Harvard University and earned her Juris Doctor from Harvard Law School.

Between 1989 and 1992, she was the director of the Indiana Civil Rights Commission. She was a drug court judge for the city of Gary, a public defender, the chief legal officer for the State of Indiana. She also served as the director of the Indiana Office of Drug Control Policy and was appointed the attorney general of the State of Indiana in 2000. She ran for mayor of Gary in the 2003 primary. She also runs her own law practice. Judge Freeman-Wilson serves as chief executive officer of the National Association of Drug Court Professionals and executive director of the National Drug Court Institute and heads the Indiana Governor's Commission for Drug-Free America and the Council on Impaired and Dangerous Driving.

Judith L. French

JUDGE. Judith L. French received a Bachelor of Arts degree from the Ohio State University in 1984 and received a Masters' of Arts and a Juris Doctor degree from the Ohio State University in 1988.

Her professional career includes serving in private law practice; as the deputy directive for legal affairs, Ohio Environmental Protection Agency (1993–1997); as chief counsel and assistant attorney general, Office of Attorney General Betty D. Montgomery (1997–2002); and as chief legal counsel to Governor Bob Taft (2002–2004). In October 2004 she was appointed judge to the Ohio's Tenth District Court of Appeals.

Margaret O'Mara Frossard

JUDGE. Margaret O'Mara Frossard is a native of Chicago, Illinois. She received her Bachelor of Art degree with honors in political science from Northwestern University in 1973 and her J.D. degree from IIT/Chicago-Kent College of Law in 1976 where she was a member of the Law Review and the National Moot Court Team.

Judge Frossard was an assistant state's attorney in Cook County from 1976 to 1988, where she was chief of the felony trial division. Her judicial experience includes serving as an associate judge of the Circuit Court of Cook County (1994–97); and judge of the Appellate Court, First District, since 1997.

Cynthia A. Fry

JUDGE. Cynthia A. Fry received her Juris Doctor degree from the University of New Mexico School of Law in 1981. She was engaged in private law practice. In 2006, she was serving as a judge on the New Mexico Court of Appeals in Santa Fe, New Mexico.

Ping Fu

TECHNOLOGY EXECUTIVE. Ping Fu received both a Bachelor of Science degree in computer science and a Master of Science degree in computer science from the University of Illinois at Urbana-Champaign. She earned a Master of Arts in Chinese literature from Suzhou University and a doctorate degree in Chinese literature from Nanjing University.

Her professional career includes serving as an adjunct professor at Duke University. She has served as director of visualization at the National Center for Supercomputing Applications (NCSA) where she initiated and managed the NCSA Mosaic software project that led to Netscape and Internet Explorer. She has more than 20 years of software industry experience in database, networking, geometry processing and computer graphics.

Ms. Fu is chairman, president and chief executive officer of Geomagic. She cofounded Geomagic and has led its growth from start-up to worldwide leader in the digital shape sampling and processing industry.

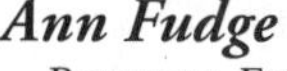

Ann Fudge

BUSINESS EXECUTIVE. Ann Fudge received a Bachelor of Arts degree from Simmons College in 1973 and earned a Master of Business Administration from Harvard University in 1977.

Her professional career includes serving with General Mills and at General Foods where she served in a number of positions including president of Kraft General Foods' Maxwell House Coffee Company and president of Kraft's beverages, desserts and Post divisions. She serves as chairman and chief executive officer of Young & Rubicam Brands, a global marketing communications network in New York City.

Nancy A. Fuerst

JUDGE. Nancy A. Fuerst is a native of Cleveland, Ohio, and graduated from Beaumont School. She received a Bachelor of Arts degree from Central State University. She earned her Juris Doctor degree from Cleveland-Marshall College of Law.

Her professional career includes serving as clerk at the court of appeals; as a law clerk (federal magistrate) at the United States District Court; and in private law practice from 1989 to 1996. In 1997, she was appointed judge to the Cuyahoga County Common Pleas Court in Cleveland, Ohio.

Kathryn Fuller

BUSINESS EXECUTIVE. Kathryn Fuller received a Bachelor of Arts degree from Brown University and did graduate studies in marine, estuarine and environmental science at the University of Maryland. She earned a Juris Doctor degree from the University of Texas Law School.

Her professional career includes serving with the Department of Justice where she worked first in the Office of Legal Counsel and then the Land and Natural Resources division. She became chief of the division's Wildlife and Marine Resources section in 1981 with responsibility for supervising litigation involving the trade in animal and plant resources. She was selected to serve as president and chief executive officer of the World Wildlife Fund–US. She also chairs the Board of Trustees of the Ford Foundation.

Martha Fuller

SPORTS EXECUTIVE. Martha Fuller received a bachelor's degree summa cum laude from Drake University. She is also a certified public accountant.

She began her career working for Arthur Andersen from 1984 to 1995 before moving on to become the director of finance for the city of St. Paul from 1995 to 1997. In 1997, she was appointed the chief finance officer of the National Hockey League's Minnesota Wild, becoming the first female to hold that position in the league's history. At the Wild, she was responsible for negotiation of the Xcel Energy Center lease with the city of Saint Paul, related loan agreements with the state of Minnesota, and various contracts relating to construction of the Xcel Energy Center.

Ms. Fuller came to Seattle in 2004 following two years as director of planning and economic development for the city of St. Paul, overseeing the city's housing and economic development portfolio. She joined the National Football League's Seattle Seahawks as its chief financial officer. In 2006, she was named senior vice president, responsible for the financial oversight of First & Goal Inc. and the Seahawks, including budgeting, cash flow management, reporting to and transactions with the Washington State Public Stadium Authority and risk management.

Carol Fulp

BUSINESS EXECUTIVE. Carol Fulp received a bachelor's degree from the University of the State of New York.

Her professional career includes serving as manager of employee relations at the Gillette Company and as community services/human resources director for WCVB-TV, ABC-TV's Boston affiliate. She was appointed by Mayor Menino as a co-chair of Boston 2004, the organization formed to bring the Democratic National Convention to Boston.

Ms. Fulp serves as vice president of community relations at John Hancock Financial Services.

Gay Hart Gaines

GOVERNMENT OFFICIAL. Gay Hart Gaines received a bachelor's degree from Sweet Briar College. She chaired the National Review Institute from 1991 to 1993. An interior designer by training, she has been active in a wide range of charitable, civic, and arts organizations. She serves as a member of the American Enterprise Institute, the Heritage Foundation, and the Madison Council of the Library of Congress. She was elected regent of the Board of Directors of Mount Vernon, where she previously represented the state of Florida as vice regent. She has served as a trustee of the Palm Beach County Republican Party, and a board member and president of the Palm Beach Republican Club.

Mrs. Gaines was named to the Corporation for Public Broadcasting board as a recess appointment by President Bush in December 2003, and was confirmed by the Senate in November 2004 to a term ending in 2010.

Linda Gambatesa

GOVERNMENT OFFICIAL. Linda Gambatesa received a bachelor's degree from George Mason University. She has served as director of administration for the American Automobile Manufacturers Association; as special assistant to the secretary and deputy chief of staff at the United States Department of Transportation; as the confidential assistant to the assistant secretary for trade development at the United States

Department of Commerce; special assistant to the chief of staff during the presidency of George H.W. Bush; as special assistant to the deputy assistant in the White Office of Intergovernmental Affairs during the Reagan Administration.

She was appointed deputy assistant to the president for management, administration and Oval Office operations.

Marilda Lara Gandara

BUSINESS EXECUTIVE. Marilda Lara Gandara is a native of Cuba and now lives in Hartford, Connecticut. She has a Bachelor of Arts degree from St. Peter's College in Jersey City, New Jersey, and earned a Juris Doctor degree from the University of Connecticut Law School in Hartford.

She joined Aetna in 1978 as an attorney specializing in real estate, workout and environmental law. During the 1990s, she was managing director and vice president in Aetna's real estate investments area. She was appointed president of the Aetna Foundation, an independent charitable organization funded solely by Aetna Inc.

Pamela Gann

EDUCATION. Pamela Gann is a native of Monroe, North Carolina. She received a bachelor's degree in mathematics from the University of North Carolina at Chapel Hill and earned her Juris Doctor from Duke University School of Law in 1973 where she was articles editor of the Duke Law Journal and was elected to the Order of the Coif.

Her professional career includes serving in private law practice. She served for 11 years as dean of the Duke University School of Law, where she developed an international reputation as an expert in federal income taxation, international taxation, international trade and international business transactions. She was named the 4th president of Claremont McKenna College on July 1, 1999.

Jeanne Garcia

JUDGE. Jeanne Garcia received a bachelor's degree from Northern Arizona University in 1982 and earned her Juris Doctor degree from Arizona State University in 1990. She was engaged in private law practice from 1990 to 1993. From 1993 to 2005, she served as an assistant attorney general, Arizona Attorney General's office. On April 4, 2005, she was appointed judge to the Superior Court of Arizona, Maricopa County, in Phoenix, Arizona.

Juliet V. Garcia

EDUCATION (FIRST). Juliet V. Garcia received a Bachelor of Arts degree in speech and English and a Master of Arts degree in speech and English from the University of Houston. She earned her Ph.D. degree in communication and linguistics from the University of Texas at Austin. Her postdoctoral studies include work at the Institute for Educational Management and the JFK School of Government at Harvard, Massachusetts Institute of Technology and the London School of Business as a member of the Society for International Business Fellows program.

Dr. Garcia was named president of the University of Texas at Brownsville (UTB) in 1992 after serving as the president of Texas Southmost College (TSC) for six years. While at Texas Southmost College she was recognized as the first Mexican-American woman in the nation to become president of a college or university. She has also served as chair of the American Council on Education, the nation's foremost educational policy organization representing organization representing members of 1,800 colleges and universities. She also served on the National Advisory Council on Institutional Quality and Integrity and as a commissioner on the White House Initiative on Educational Excellence for Hispanic Americans.

Mildred Garcia

EDUCATION. Mildred Garcia received an Associate of Science degree from New York City Community College of City University of New York, and received a Bachelor of Science degree from New York University; she earned both her master's and doctorate degrees from Teachers College, at Columbia University.

She served as vice provost for academic personnel and tenured professor in the social and behavioral sciences department at Arizona State University West and as an associate director of the Hispanic Research Center, Arizona State University, Tempe, Arizona. She now serves as president of Berkeley College.

Sylvia R. Garcia

ELECTED OFFICIAL. Sylvia R. Garcia is a native of the South Texas farming community of Palo Blanco. She attended Texas Woman's University on a scholarship, graduating with a degree in social work, and received her Juris Doctor degree from Thurgood Marshall School of Law at Texas Southern University.

Her professional career includes serving as controller for the city of Houston and before that, as the appointed director and presiding judge of the Houston Municipal Court System. In 2002, she was elected commissioner, Harris County Precinct Two in Houston, Texas. On January 2, 2003, she was sworn in as commissioner of Precinct Two.

Janice Gardner

GOVERNMENT OFFICIAL. Janice Gardner was born in Japan and grew up in Ohio. She received a bachelor's degree in history from Wake Forest University and earned a master's degree in international relations from American University.

Her professional career includes serving from 1990 to 1992 as an economic officer in the United States Embassy in Tokyo. She served from 1993 to 1995 as chief of the Persian Gulf branch in the Office of Leadership Analysis. From 1995 to 1996, she served on the National Security Council and as a liaison officer to the White House. From 1996 to 1999, she served as chief of the East Asia group in Foreign Broadcast Information Service, where she managed a headquarters component and four overseas bureaus. In 1996, she worked in the office of the vice president as a special advisor for international affairs. From 1999 to 2002, she served as the deputy director of the Foreign Broadcast Information Service. In May 2004, she assumed the position of deputy assistant secretary for intelligence and analysis. Ms. Gardner was sworn in as the first assistant secretary for intelligence and analysis in September 2005.

Giana Garel

ENTERTAINMENT. Giana Garel is a native of Cleveland, Ohio, and grew up in Atlanta, Georgia. She is a writer, filmmaker, entrepreneur, consultant, and musician. She began her endeavors into entertainment and writing by the age of ten. She had written a three-act musical at age fourteen and by age seventeen was working as a writer for cable TV sketch comedy shows. After moving to California in 1987, Ms. Garel cultivated skills as a writer and script doctor, developing spec screenplays for production companies and some major artists over the years. Between 1989 and 1994 she started her film production company Meridian Pics/GG Films. She also acted as co-executive director of Westside Stories, Inc. an Atlanta-based production company producing music videos directed by Keith Ward. The team worked during those years under an umbrella formed by Garel & Ward called Noir Cinema.

In 1995, Ms. Garel relocated to Los Angeles, California, and co-founded A-List Consultants, Inc., an entertainment consulting firm that worked with industry publicists to create cross-over campaigns for artists looking to connect with film, TV, publishing and fashion. Currently, she is producer and co-host of the national talk radio show "On the Real" with rapper Chuck D as well as an active writer and international columnist. She is currently writing a nonfiction book of essays entitled *The Sinister Plot Behind My Self Destruction* and is a dual resident of New York and Atlanta.

Rita B. Garman

JUDGE. Rita B. Garman is a native of Aurora, Illinois. She was valedictorian of Oswego High School in 1961. She received her Bachelor of Science degree in economics with highest honors from the University of Illinois in 1965. She earned her Juris Doctor degree with distinction from the University of Iowa College of Law in 1968.

She served as an assistant state's attorney in Vermilion County (1969–1973); was engaged in private practice in 1973; was an associate circuit judge for 12 years; served as a circuit judge in the Fifth Judicial Circuit (1986–1995), where she was presiding circuit judge (1987–1995). She was assigned to the Appellate Court, Fourth District, in July 1995 and was elected to that position in November 1996; she was appointed to the Illinois Supreme Court on February 1, 2001, and elected to that court on November 5, 2002.

Sandy Garrett

EDUCATION. Sandy Garrett is a native of Muskogee, Oklahoma, and graduated from Stilwell High School. She received a bachelor's degree and master's degree from Northeastern State University and pursued postgraduate studies at the University of Oklahoma and the John F. Kennedy School of Government at Harvard University.

Her professional career includes serving as a classroom teacher and gifted programs coordinator in Muskogee County Schools. She joined the State Department of Education as gifted and talented programs coordinator then became executive director of education which included rural education, technology, satellite instruction, media applications and library resources.

In 1988, she was named cabinet secretary of education by the Oklahoma governor. In November 2002, she was elected state superintendent of public instruction and became the first and only Oklahoma woman elected to a constitutional statewide office for a fourth consecutive term.

Toba Garrett

CHEF. Toba Garrett is a master chef/instructor at the Institute of Culinary Education in New York City. She has studied in the United States, Canada, England, and France.

She has been featured on *Emeril Live*, *Home Matters*, *Our Home*, *Wake-up America*, and other nationally syndicated television programs. She is one of the nation's top cake designers and is a renowned educator in the field of cake decorating and design. She has been designing cakes and teaching for over 30 years. Her work has appeared in almost every major magazine publication in the United States and several publications abroad. She has authored three books, the third released in September 2006.

Tracy L. Garrett

MILITARY. Tracy L. Garrett is a former Navy Reserve Officer Training Candidate (NROTC) student and received a Bachelor of Arts degree in English from the University of Washington in 1978. She is a graduate of the Reserve Amphibious Warfare Course, the Reserve Command and Staff Course, Reserve Intelligence Officers' Course and the Advanced Logistics Officers' Course. In 1998, she graduated from the Naval War College in Newport, Rhode Island, receiving a master's degree in national security and strategic studies.

Brigadier General Garrett was first commissioned a second lieutenant in the Marine Corps in June 1978. She has held numerous military assignments of increasing responsibility and authority, to include serving as commander of the 1st Force Service Support Group (FSSG). She served in Iraq from September 2004 to March 2005.

Marguerite C. Garrison

MILITARY. Marguerite C. Garrison is a native of Buffalo, New York. She received a Bachelor of Science from Saint Bonaventure University. She is a graduate of the FBI National Academy, the United States Army Command and General Staff College and the Industrial College of the Armed Forces.

Colonel Garrison has served as the Army's criminal investigation command inspector general from 2002 to 2003. She was then assigned to the Office of the Assistant Secretary of Defense (special operations/low-intensity conflict) as the deputy director for antiterrorism policy. She serves as the garrison commander for Fort McPherson and Fort Gillem in the Atlanta metropolitan area.

Robin S. Garson

JUDGE. Robin S. Garson received her undergraduate degree from City University of New York, Brooklyn College, and earned her Juris Doctor from Brooklyn Law School.

Her professional career includes serving as editor, *Social Action & The Law*; as the co-developer of the Research Coordinator Kings County Jury Project; as project coordinator and housing specialist; as a certified mediator; as principal drafter, Brooklyn's local rules for the administration of Part 137 of the Rules of the Chief Administrator; and in private law practice.

She was elected judge to the New York City Civil Court in King County and her first term began January 1, 2003.

Kathern L. Gaskins

GOVERNMENT OFFICIAL. Kathern L. Gaskins received a Bachelor of Arts degree in liberal arts from the University of the Pacific, Stockton, California. She earned a Master of Arts degree in English from California State University at Sacramento. She is also a graduate of the Air War College at the Air University, Maxwell Air Force Base in Alabama (1983); Senior Officials in National Security Program from the John F. Kennedy School of Government at Harvard University in Cambridge, Massachusetts (1990); and the Defense Systems Management College, Fort Belvoir, Virginia (1992).

Her professional career includes assignments at the Sacramento Air Logistics Center at McClellan Air Force Base where she served in packaging design, labor relations, depot industrial operations and weapon system management. She has served as the deputy for resource management with the directorate of maintenance; deputy system program director for the A-10 and A-7 aircraft weapon systems; and as associate director of aircraft management. She also held the dual-hatted position at the center of deputy to the Detachment 25 commander and deputy for space with the Space and Command, Control, Communication and Intelligence Systems Directorate. She serves as the director of systems acquisition, Space and Missile Systems Center at Los Angeles Air Force Base in California.

Alice P. Gast

EDUCATION. Alice P. Gast received a Bachelor of Science in chemical engineering from the University of Southern California. She earned her Ph.D. in chemical engineering from Princeton University. She spent a postdoctoral year on a NATO fellowship at the Ecole Superieure de Physique et de Chimie Industrielles in Paris.

Her professional career includes serving 16 years as a professor of chemical engineering at Stanford University and at the Stanford Synchrotron Radiation Laboratory. In her research she studies surface and interfacial phenomena, in particular the behavior of complex fluids. Some of her areas of research include colloidal aggregation and ordering, protein lipid interactions and enzymes reactions at surfaces. In 1997, she co-authored the sixth edition of *Physical Chemistry of Surfaces.* She served as the Robert T. Haslam professor of chemical engineering and the vice president for research and associate provost at Massachusetts Institute of Technology.

Dr. Gast was appointed the 13th president of Lehigh University on August 1, 2006.

Marilyn Hughes Gaston

MEDICINE. Marilyn Hughes Gaston received her Medical Doctor degree from the University of Pennsylvania School of Medicine in 1960. Of the six women in her class, she was the only African American. Upon graduation, she would go on to achieve a number of "firsts" in a world in which African-American women physicians were virtually nonexistent at that time.

Dr. Gaston completed her residency in pediatrics in her hometown of Cincinnati and went on to become an associate professor of pediatrics at the University of Cincinnati College of Medicine and direct a center aimed at eradicating sickle cell disease. She would continue her work in this area at the National Institutes of Health where changes she instigated in the management of the disease resulted in significant decreases in morbidity and mortality in young children. Following her desire to provide quality health care to the uninsured, she also helped found a health center in Cincinnati in an impoverished, underserved African-American community.

In 1990, Dr. Gaston's scientific credentials, combined with her work in disadvantaged communities, led to her appointment as the director of the Bureau of Primary Care within the Health Resources and Services Administration, a federal entity with a budget of $5 billion and a mission to increase access to quality preventive and primary health care for approximately 12 million underserved individuals. She is the first African-American woman to direct a public health service bureau. She served as Assistant Surgeon General of the United States, Department of Health and Human Services. She was the second African-American woman to achieve the position of assistant surgeon general and rank of rear admiral in the U.S. Public Health Service.

She serves as the co-director of the Gaston & Porter Health Improvement Center.

Melinda Gates

NONPROFIT EXECUTIVE. Melinda Gates is a native of Dallas, Texas. She received a bachelor's degree in economics and computer science at Duke University in Durham, North Carolina, and earned a Master of Business Administration from the Duke University Fuqua School of Business in 1987.

She began working for Microsoft in 1987, where she would meet her future husband. She served as general manager of information products. She married Bill Gates on January 1, 1994.

The couple started the Bill and Melinda Gates Foundation in 2000 with $106 million. Her responsibilities at the Bill and Melinda Gates Foundation involve identifying strategies to pursue, promoting the foundation's issues, and reviewing the results achieved. As the wife of the richest man in the world, she has worked to solve some of the world's many health and educational problems. The foundation aims to improve health conditions worldwide, eliminate poverty in some of the world's poorest regions, promote education and provide technology to libraries.

Rosa Gatti

MEDIA EXECUTIVE. Rosa Gatti received a Bachelor of Arts degree from Villanova in 1972. She enjoyed a distinguished career as the first female sports information director at a NCAA major college, her alma mater, Villanova University, in 1974 and later at Brown University.

Ms. Gatti is an ESPN and cable television pioneer who joined the company in its first year of operation in July 1980 as director of communications and with her staff built the communications department. A year later she became a vice president and in July 1988 she was promoted to senior vice president, communications. She has also overseen human resources and diversity initiatives for the company. She was named senior vice president for corporate communications and outreach at ESPN.

Helene D. Gayle

MEDICINE. Helene D. Gayle is a native of Buffalo, New York. She received a bachelor's degree with honors from Barnard College in New York City and earned her Medical Doctor degree from the University of Pennsylvania School of Medicine. She earned a master of public health from the Johns Hopkins University School of Hygiene and Public Health. She pursued an internship and residency in pediatrics at the Children's Hospital National Medical Center in Washington, D.C.

In 1984, she began her career at the Centers for Disease Control (CDC) as an epidemic intelligence service officer in the epidemiology branch then entered the preventive medicine residency program at the CDC in 1985. In 1987, she was serving as a medical epidemiologist in the CDC's AIDS Program. She has also served as the AIDS coordinator and chief of the HIV/AIDS division for the U.S. Agency for International Development and from 1995 to 2001, she served as director of the CDC's National Center for HIV, STD, and TB Prevention and collaborated with public and private partners at the community, state, national and international levels.

Dr. Gayle was named director of the Bill and Melinda Gates Foundation's HIV/AIDS and Tuberculosis program, where she is responsible for research, policy, public awareness, and program issues on HIV/AIDS infection among women, children, and adolescents in developing countries.

Kathleen R. Gearin

JUDGE. Kathleen R. Gearin received a Bachelor of Arts degree with honors from the College of St. Catherine in 1970; and earned her Juris Doctor degree from William Mitchell College of Law in 1975.

Her professional career includes serving as a teacher at Cretin-Derham Hall High School (1967–1971); as a law clerk at Ramsey County District Court (1973–1974); and as the assistant attorney for Ramsey County (1975–1987). She was elected judge to the Minnesota State District Court in Ramsey County in 1986 and in 2006 she was serving as assistant chief judge.

Judy Genshaft

EDUCATION. Judy Genshaft is a native of Ohio. She received a bachelor's degree in social work and psychology from the University of Wisconsin–Madison. She earned a master's degree in school psychology and a doctorate in counseling psychology, both from Kent State University. A national leader in the field of school psychology, she is the author and co-author of 69 journal articles and three books.

Her professional career includes serving as vice president for academic affairs at the University at Albany where she also served as dean of the College of Education. She was named president, chief executive officer and corporate secretary of the University of South Florida.

Hulane George

JUDGE. Hulane George serves as a judge in Baldwin County, Georgia. In 1994, Governor Miller appointed her judge to the Georgia Ocmulgee Judicial Circuit in Baldwin County, Milledgeville, Georgia. She is the first female Superior Court judge in the Ocmulgee Judicial Circuit's history.

Kathryn A. George

JUDGE. Kathryn A. George is a native of Macomb County, Michigan. After graduating from Harper Hospital School of Nursing as a registered nurse in 1973, she received a Bachelor of Science degree in nursing from Oakland University. She earned her Juris Doctor degree in 1988.

Her professional career includes serving as a nurse in critical care and emergency room nursing, working as the nurse manager of the U.S. Embassy in Kuwait and teaching at Oakland County Community College School of Nursing. She was appointed by the governor to the State of Michigan Worker's Compensation Appeals Board and by the State of Michigan Board of Law Examiners to grade bar exams for attorneys. She was engaged in private law practice from 1991 until her election.

She has served as a member on the Sterling Heights City Council as both councilwoman and mayor pro tem from 1999 to 2002. In 2002, she was elected judge of the Michigan Macomb County Probate Court.

Patricia Gerard

ELECTED OFFICIAL. Patricia Gerard is a native of New Jersey. She received a Bachelor of Arts degree in psychology from the University of South Florida and earned a Master of Arts in rehabilitation counseling from the University of South Florida.

Her professional career includes serving in the mental health field working with the chronically mentally ill; from 1984 to 1986, she served as victim advocate for the Largo Police Department; in 1986, she became director of the Spouse Abuse Shelter of Religious Community Services; in 1992, she served as executive director of Helpline and is currently vice president of Pinelias. From 1996 to 2000, she served on the Largo Public Library Advisory Board; in 2000, she was elected to the city commission, city of Largo, Florida. In 2006, she was serving as mayor of the city of Largo, Florida.

Julie Louise Gerberding

MEDICINE. Julie Louise Gerberding received a Bachelor of Arts degree magna cum laude in chemistry and biology and earned her Medical Doctor degree at Case Western Reserve University in Cleveland, Ohio. She completed her internship and residency in internal medicine at University of California in San Francisco (UCSF) where she served as chief medical resident before completing her fellowship in clinical pharmacology and infectious diseases at UCSF. She earned a masters of public health degree from the University of California, Berkeley, in 1990.

Her professional career includes serving as an associate professor of medicine (infectious diseases) at UCSF and as an associate clinical professor of medicine (infectious diseases) at Emory University. She joined the Center for Disease Control and Prevention (CDC) in 1998 as director of the division of health quality promotion, National Center for Infectious Diseases.

Dr. Gerberding serves as the director of the Centers for Disease Control and Prevention (CDC) and the administrator of the Agency for Toxic Substances and Disease Registry.

Sylvia Gercke

GOVERNMENT OFFICIAL. Sylvia Gercke received a Bachelor of Arts degree as well as a secondary education teaching credential from San Francisco State University. She has a Masters in Business Administration from Golden Gate University and was a scholarship student at the American Conservatory Theater in San Francisco. She is a certified fraud examiner.

Her professional career includes serving 14 years as a fraud examiner in forensic auditing of large and small enterprises for federal and state agencies. She has extensive background in stage, film television, radio, public speaking, TV production and journalism. She created, wrote, produced and hosted three public affairs television shows for KRON TV.

Ms. Gercke serves as the regional communications director for Region X of the U.S. Small Business Administration.

Julia Smith Gibbons

JUDGE. Julia Smith Gibbons is a native of Pulaski, Tennessee. She received a Bachelor of Arts degree magna cum laude from Vanderbilt University and earned her Juris Doctor degree from the University of Virginia in 1975. After law school she served as law clerk for the Hon. William E. Miller, U.S. Court of Appeals for the Sixth Circuit from 1975 to 1976. She served in private law practice from 1976 to 1979.

In 1981, she was appointed judge, Tennessee Circuit Court in Memphis, Tennessee. In 1983, she was appointed judge, U.S. District Court, Western District of Tennessee, and she served as chief judge of the U.S. District Court, Western District of Tennessee, from 1994 to 2000.

In 2002, Judge Gibbons was appointed judge, U.S. Court of Appeals for the Sixth Circuit.

Patricia Gilbreath

Elected Official. Patricia Gilbreath received a Bachelor of Science degree in business administration from California Polytechnic University and earned a masters of business taxation, University of Southern California. Her professional career includes serving as a certified public accountant. In November 1993, she was elected mayor pro-tem of Redlands, California.

Shelley Ilene Gilman

Judge. Shelley Ilene Gilman received her undergraduate degree from the University of Illinois and received her Juris Doctor degree from the University of Denver College of Law in 1978.

Her professional career includes serving several county trial offices and in the appellate division of the Colorado State Public Defender and before serving in private law practice in Denver. She was appointed judge to the Denver District Court bench in February 1998.

Marie Gilmore

Elected Official. Marie Gilmore was born in the West Indies on the tiny island of Dominica. Her family moved to New York when she was still an infant and by the time she was in second grade had relocated to Santa Barbara, California. She received a bachelor's degree in human biology from Stanford University and earned her Juris Doctor from the University of California in Berkeley.

She was elected on September 4, 2003, to the Alameda City Council, making her the first black woman to hold this title. After Al DeWitt, the first black person elected to city council, died on July 3 at the age of 70 from stomach cancer, his wife supported the vote for Gilmore to take her husband's seat.

Vanessa Gilmore

Judge. Vanessa Gilmore is a native of St. Albans, New York. She received a Bachelor of Science degree from Hampton University in 1977 and earned her Juris Doctor degree from the University of Houston Law Center in 1981. She served in private law practice until 1994. She also served as an adjunct professor at the University of Houston College of Law in 1984.

On March 22, 1994, she was nominated by President William J. Clinton to judge on the United States District Court, Southern District of Texas. She was confirmed by the United States Senate on June 8, 1994, and received her commission the following day.

Natalie M. Givans

Business Executive. Natalie M. Givans received a Bachelor of Science degree in electrical engineering from the Massachusetts Institute of Technology and a Master of Science in electrical engineering from Johns Hopkins University.

She serves as Herndon-based vice president of Booz Allen Hamilton's information and mission assurance and resilience work. She oversees more than 300 information security and assurance professionals focused on the East Coast defense and intelligence community who provide security policy and planning, certification and accreditation, risk management, and the full life cycle of system security architecture, engineering and integration services to critical communications and command and control system.

Linda M. Godwin

Astronaut. Linda M. Godwin is a native of Cape Girardeau, Missouri. Her hometown is Jackson, Missouri, and she is a 1970 graduate of Jackson High School. She received a Bachelor of Science in mathematics and physics from Southeast Missouri State in 1974 and a Master of Science degree in 1976. She earned a doctorate degree in physics from the University of Missouri in 1980.

Her professional career began in 1980 when she joined NASA and became an astronaut in July 1986. In 1991, she served as a mission specialist on STS-37

Atlantis; was the payload commander on *Endeavour* STS-59 in 1994; flew on *Atlantis* STS-76 in 1996, a Mir docking mission; and served on *Endeavour* STS-108/International Space Station Flight UF-1 in 2001.

She has logged over 38 days in space including 10 EVA hours in two spacewalks. She has also logged over 917 hours in space and 606 orbits around the earth.

Dr. Godwin serves as the assistant to the director for Exploration Flight Crew Operations Directorate at the Johnson Space Center.

Mary Goff

ELECTED OFFICIAL. Mary Goff was appointed to the St. Joseph City Commission in 1986 because she was active in the community and cared deeply about the future of her hometown. She was elected mayor of the city of St. Joseph, Michigan, becoming the first woman to be elected mayor of the five-member commission that governs St. Joseph.

Frances A. Gonzalez

GOVERNMENT OFFICIAL. Frances A. Gonzalez received a Bachelor of Arts degree in political science from Pan American University and earned a Master of Arts in urban studies from Trinity University. She is also a graduate of the Harvard University, John F. Kennedy School of Government Program for senior executives in state and local government.

In November 2003, she began serving as assistant city manager for the city of San Antonio, Texas. In this position, she coordinated the city's Better Jobs efforts which are designed to link education, economic development and workforce development programs and initiatives. She also has served as director of the city's nationally recognized Neighborhood Action Department.

Lizbeth Gonzalez

JUDGE. Lizbeth Gonzalez received her undergraduate degree from State University of New York at Stony Brook where, as an exchange student, she attended the University of Puerto Rico. She earned her Juris Doctor from New York University School of Law.

Her professional career includes serving an assistant corporation counsel, New York City Law Department; as assistant attorney general, New York State; in private law practice; as an administrative law judge, Environmental Control Board; as administrative law judge, Taxi and Limousine Commission; as court attorney for Bronx Housing Court; Housing Court judge. In 2005, she was elected judge to the New York Civil Court in the Bronx.

Sara M. Gonzalez

ELECTED OFFICIAL. Sara M. Gonzalez was raised and educated in Sunset Park of New York City. She is a graduate of Fort Hamilton High School, Staten Island College and also attended Columbia Graduate School of Business Management.

Her experience includes serving as a civic activist and community leader for over three decades; serving as the first Latina chairperson of Community Board 7 in Brooklyn; and as the executive director of Hispanic Young People's Alternatives.

In November 2002, she was elected to the New York City Council in a special election to represent the 38th Council District. She was re-elected in November 2003.

Linda Gooden

TECHNOLOGY EXECUTIVE. Linda Gooden received a bachelor degree in computer technology from

Youngstown State University and completed post-baccalaureate studies at San Diego State University. She was awarded an honorary Doctor of Public Service degree in 2005 from the University of Maryland's University College.

Ms. Gooden serves as president of Lockheed Martin Information Technology (LMIT) and an officer of Lockheed Martin Corporation. LMIT is an operating company within the corporation's information and technology services business area. Under her guidance, the company provides software development and maintenance, enterprise-wide IT infrastructure and managed services.

Amanda Goodson

AEROSPACE. Amanda Goodson is a native of Decatur, Georgia, and a graduate of Decatur High School. She received a Bachelor of Science degree in electrical engineering from Tuskegee University in Tuskegee, Alabama. She earned a master's degree in management from the Florida Institute of Technology in Melbourne and a Doctor of Ministry from United Theological Seminary in New Brighton, Minnesota. She has also completed NASA's Senior Executive Service Center Development Program.

She began her NASA career in 1983 as an intern in Marshall's Safety and Mission Assurance Office. In 1989, she served as senior resident engineer at Martin Marietta in Denver for Marshall's Safety and Mission Assurance Office. She returned to Marshall in 1991 as chief of the product evaluation branch of the Quality Assurance Office, part of Marshall's safety office. In 1993, she again took a senior resident engineer position, this time with the Shuttle Main Engine project in Canoga Park, California. She later served as chief of the Payloads Quality Assurance Office in Canoga Park. She now serves as director of safety and mission assurance, overseeing safety and quality activities for all Marshall Center programs.

Diane Schafer Goodstein

JUDGE. Diane Schafer Goodstein is a native of Dillon, South Carolina. She received a bachelor's degree from the University of North Carolina at Chapel Hill in 1978 and earned her Juris Doctor degree from the University of North Carolina School of Law in 1981.

She served as the county attorney for Dorchester County from 1986 to 1988 then was engaged in private law practice until 1998. She was elected by the South Carolina General Assembly to the position of resident circuit judge for the First Judicial Circuit in May 1998. She has since been appointed to the Circuit Court Judges Advisory Committee and is a member of the Commission on Judicial Conduct.

Debra Gore-Mann

SPORTS. Debra Gore-Mann received a bachelor's degree in industrial engineering from Stanford University in 1982 and earned a Master of Business Administration with an emphasis on capital markets and finance from Stanford University in 1987. She played basketball at Stanford from 1978 to 1982 and led the Cardinals' inaugural NCAA Tournament berth during her senior campaign.

She has served as a basketball broadcaster on various professional games for ESPN, PrimeTicket, BET Sports and Fox Sports Net. Ms. Gore-Mann worked in corporate development and project finance with Bechtel Enterprises, Inc. and other private corporations. She has served as the senior associate athletic director and senior women's administrator since 1999 and played in the Stanford Athletics program that has won an unprecedented 12 consecutive Sports Academy Director's Cups. During her tenure in Palo Alto the Stanford Cardinals captured 14 division national championships. In July 2006, Ms. Gore-Mann was named athletics director for the University of San Francisco (USF) effective August 1, 2006. She became the first female director of athletics at USF and just the third black female athletic director in the United States.

Maureen Gottfried

JUDGE. Maureen Gottfried is a native of Washington, D.C. She received a Bachelor of Arts degree in English from Trinity College in 1983 and earned her Juris Doctor from the University of Georgia in 1986. Her professional career includes serving as chief assistant solicitor from 1986 to 1993. She then served as solicitor for Columbus, Georgia. She has been serving as a state court judge in Columbus, Georgia, since 2000.

Victoria A. Graffeo

JUDGE. Victoria A. Graffeo is a native of Rockville Centre, New York. She received her undergraduate degree from the State University College at Oneonta in 1974 and earned her Juris Doctor degree from Albany Law School of Union University in 1977.

She was engaged in private law practice from 1978 to 1982 and entered government service in 1982 as assistant counsel to the New York State Division of Alcoholism and Alcohol Abuse. She served as counsel to State Legislature Assembly Minority Leader Pro Tempore Kemp Hannon in 1984 and as chief counsel to Assembly Minority Leader Clarence D. Rappleyea, Jr., from 1989 to 1994.

On January 1, 1995, she was appointed solicitor general for State of New York Attorney General Dennis C. Vacco and served in that capacity until she was appointed by Governor George E. Pataki and confirmed by the State Senate to fill a vacancy in the State Supreme Court, Third Judicial District, in September 1996. She was elected to a full term in November 1996 as justice of the state supreme court and in March 1998 she was named associate justice of the appellate division, Third Department. Her appointment to the Court of Appeals by Governor George E. Pataki was confirmed by the State Senate on November 29, 2000.

Jennifer M. Granholm

ELECTED OFFICIAL. Jennifer M. Granholm is a native of Vancouver, British Columbia. She is an honors graduate of both the University of California at Berkeley and Harvard Law School. She began her career in public service as a clerk for U.S. Judge Damon Keith on the 6th Circuit Court of Appeals. In 1994, she was appointed Wayne County corporation counsel.

She was elected Michigan's first female attorney general in 1998, and on November 6, 2002, she was elected the 47th governor of the state of Michigan. Jennifer M. Granholm is the first female governor of the state of Michigan.

Beverly G. Grant

JUDGE. Beverly G. Grant received a Bachelor of Arts degree in political science from the University of Washington in 1973 and earned her Juris Doctor from the University of Washington in 1976.

Her professional career includes serving as a law clerk for a federal judge before serving in private law practice. She was elected judge on April 21, 2003, to the Washington Pierce County Superior Court, Department 18.

Susan Grant

MEDIA EXECUTIVE. Susan Grant received a Bachelor of Arts degree from Vassar College. She worked eight years with TBS serving in various capacities throughout the organization. A CNN original, she was the first director of public relations in 1980, helping to launch the global news network and later assuming the position of CNN marketing manager. In 1981, she moved into sales as a regional manager for Turner Cable Network Sales for the Southeast region. Ms. Grant served as executive vice president responsible for all sales and marketing activities. She was later promoted to national accounts manager and was ultimately promoted to director of regional sales for Turner Cable Network Sales, a position she held until 1985. She was promoted to president of CNN Newsource Sales and Turner Learning. She has also served as president of Turner Program Services responsible for the domestic syndication sales and marketing for the company's television programming.

She is executive vice president of CNN News Services, a business unit consisting of CNN Business Operations, CNN.com, CNN Content Sales/Business Development sales, CNN Radio and Turner Learning.

Ms. Grant oversees all distribution, sales and affiliate relations, marketing, business affairs and public relations for these groups.

Barbara Kydd Graves

BUSINESS EXECUTIVE. Barbara Kydd Graves received her Bachelor's and Master's degrees in education from the University of New York at Brooklyn. Before joining Earl G. Graves, Ltd., Mrs. Graves taught at the elementary school level in the New York City school sytem. She is also a former member of the Board of the Brooklyn College Foundation.

Mrs. Graves served as vice president and general manager of Earl G. Graves, Ltd., and as the liaison between senior management and the chief administrative officer. Most recently, she has assisted the chairman and publisher on special projects.

Shauna Graves-Robertson

JUDGE. Shauna Graves-Robertson is a native of Salt Lake City, Utah. She graduated from West High School and received a Bachelor of Science degree in criminal justice from Arizona State University in 1980. She received a master's degree in public administration in 1987 and earned her Juris Doctor degree from the University of Utah in 1990.

Prior to taking the bench she worked for the Salt Lake Legal Defenders Association. She was appointed judge to the Salt Lake County Justice Court by the Salt Lake County Commission in January 1999. She is currently serving as presiding judge in Salt Lake County.

Karla Gray

JUDGE. Karla Gray is a native of Escanaba, Michigan. She received a Bachelor of Arts degree and a Master's of Art degree in African history from Western Michigan University in Kalamazoo, Michigan. She earned a Juris Doctor degree from Hastings College of the Law in San Francisco in 1976.

Her professional career includes serving as a law clerk for Senior United States District Court Judge W. D. Murray until 1977 and in private law practice. In 1991, she was appointed justice to the Montana Supreme Court and was elected to her seat in 1992. She ran successfully for chief justice in 2000.

Melvia B. Green

JUDGE. Melvia B. Green received her Bachelor of Science degree from Northwestern University in 1975. She earned a Juris Doctor degree from the University of Miami School of Law in 1978.

Her experience includes serving as a staff attorney with Florida Power Corporation from 1978 to 1980; as an assistant United States attorney, Department of Justice, Southern District of Florida, (1980–1983); in private law practice from 1983 to 1987. In 1987, she was appointed judge on the Dade County Court; in 1989, she was appointed judge, Circuit Court, 11th Judicial Circuit; and in 1994, she was appointed judge, Third District Court of Appeal, State of Florida.

Peggy Green

MEDIA EXECUTIVE. Peggy Green received a Bachelor of Arts degree from the University of Michigan and a masters in French from Columbia University.

She began her career as a spot television buyer at Dancer Fitzgerald Sample. Ms. Green was promoted to executive vice president of Program Syndication Services, a subsidiary formed to produce and syndicate television programs. In that role she was responsible for developing short form programs. She spearheaded distribution on behalf of several clients such as "Campaign Buttons" for Toyota and "Tax Tips" for Beneficial Finance.

Ms. Green was promoted to president of broadcast at Zenith Media. She supervises the annual purchase of over two billion dollars worth of broadcast media time (network television, local broadcast, cable, syndication, national radio). Ms. Green served as a governor of the International Radio & Television Foundation and represents Zenith Media on the National Television and Radio Committee of the 4A's.

Phyllis J. Green

MILITARY. Phyllis J. Green is a native of Gary, Indiana. She earned bachelors and masters degrees from Ball State University and Louisiana Tech University respectively. During her 22 years of military service she was assigned in Greece, Guam, Egypt, West Coast, Southwest and the East Coast.

Now retired from the United States Air Force, she serves as senior aerospace science instructor at Westfield High School's JROTC program.

Deborah S. Greene

JUDGE. Deborah S. Greene is a graduate of the University of Georgia and earned her Juris Doctor from the University of Georgia School of Law. Her professional career includes serving as the first female prosecutor for the State Court of Fulton County in 1976 and in private law practice.

In 1990, Mayor Maynard Jackson appointed her judge to the Atlanta Municipal Court. In April 2004, she was appointed chief judge for the Atlanta Municipal Court.

Ellen Pfeiffer Greene

MILITARY. Ellen Pfeiffer Greene received a Bachelor of Arts degree in sociology from Loyola University and a Master of Business Administration degree from the University of New Orleans. She received a master's degree in strategic studies from the United States Army War College. Her military schools attended include the Adjutant General Officer Basic Course, Transportation Officer Advanced Course, United States Army Command and General Staff College and the United States Army War College.

She has held numerous assignments of increasing responsibilities including serving as commander, Headquarters and Headquarters Detachment, 1192nd United States Army Transportations Terminal Brigade, New Orleans, Louisiana; as commander, 1192nd United States Army Transportation Terminal Brigade, New Orleans, Louisiana; as commander, 1190th Deployment Support Brigade, in Baton Rouge, Louisiana, from November 2001 to January 2003; as chief of staff, 90th Regional Support Command, North Little Rock, Arkansas, from June 2003 to July 2003; as chief of staff, 90th Regional Readiness Command, North Little Rock, Arkansas, from July 2003 to October 2005.

Brigadier General Greene was assigned as the deputy commander, 377th Theater Support Command in New Orleans, Louisiana. She was promoted to brigadier general on March 21, 2006.

Lillian J. Greene

JUDGE. Lillian J. Greene graduated from the Rayen School, Youngstown, Ohio. She received her undergraduate degree from Western Reserve University and earned her Juris Doctor degree from Case Western Reserve University.

Her professional career includes serving in private law practice; as a referee, Common Pleas Court, Probate division, from 1980 to 1987. Since 1987, she has served as a judge to the Cuyahoga County Common Pleas Court in Cleveland, Ohio.

Lillian Greene-Chamberlain

SPORTS. Lillian Greene-Chamberlain is a native of Silver Springs, Maryland; she received a bachelor's degree in exercise and sports science from Colorado State University. She earned her masters degree and Ph.D. in educational administration and supervision from Fordham University.

A runner, she was the first United States national champion in the 800m before an Olympic event, the first African-American woman to represent the United States in the 400m and 800m in international competition, a gold medalist in the exhibition 400m at the 1959 Pan American Games, a world and national record setter in women's middle-distance track events and three-time member of the All America Track & Field Team. She is the first woman and American to serve as director of the Physical Education & Sports Program for the United Nations Educational, Scientific and Cultural Organization, headquartered in Paris, a position she held for ten years (1979–1989).

Dr. Greene-Chamberlain was the first woman and American to be invited to deliver the Prince Philip Fellows Lecture in the House of Lords in London in 1982.

She has played an integral role in the expansion of the Special Olympics in the United States and served as the first director of the Mega-Cities Program for Special Olympics International. She was appointed to serve on the President's Council on Physical Fitness and Sports.

Pamela T. Greenwood

JUDGE. Pamela T. Greenwood received her Juris Doctor degree from the University of Utah College of Law in 1972. Her professional career includes serving in private law practice and as counsel for the Utah State Bar from 1977 to 1980. She is a past president of the Utah State Bar. In January 1987, she was appointed judge to the Utah Court of Appeals by Governor Norman H. Bangerter.

Chris Gregoire

ELECTED OFFICIAL. Chris Gregoire was raised in Auburn, Washington. After graduating from Auburn High School, she went on to the University of Washington where she graduated with a teaching certificate and Bachelor of Arts degree in speech and sociology.

Prior to serving as governor, she served three terms as attorney general. She was the first woman to be elected attorney general in the state of Washington. She was elected the 22nd governor in the state of Washington.

Patricia W. Griffin

GOVERNMENT OFFICIAL. Patricia W. Griffin received a Bachelor of Arts degree (cum laude) from Duke University and earned her Juris Doctor degree from the Washington and Lee School of Law. Her professional career includes serving in private law practice in Sussex County; in the administrative office of the United States Courts; and as assistant dean at the University of North Carolina School of Law and Washington and Lee School of Law. In 1993, she was appointed chief magistrate of the Justice of the Peace Court; in February 2005, she was appointed state court administrator for the Delaware First State Judiciary.

Carolyn Griner

AEROSPACE. Carolyn Griner received a bachelor's degree in astronautical engineering from Florida State University in Tallahassee and completed graduate work in industrial and systems engineering at the University of Alabama in Huntsville.

Ms. Griner joined the space agency in 1964 as a co-op student and progressed to positions of increasing responsibilities within several key program areas including the Space Station Utilization Division at NASA Headquarters and the Spacelab 3 mission. She served as director of the Marshall Center Mission Operations Laboratory and managed the Marshall Payload Projects Office and served as acting director of the Marshall Center for nine months in 1998. She served as deputy director of NASA's Marshall Space Flight Center in Huntsville, Alabama.

Emanuella Groves

JUDGE. Emanuella Groves is a native of Canton, Ohio. She graduated from Canton McKinley High School in 1975 and received a bachelor's degree in business management from Kent State University. She earned her Juris Doctor degree from Case Western Reserve University.

Her professional career includes serving as an assistant police prosecutor. In 1983, she served as a staff attorney at Cuyahoga Metropolitan Housing Authority and by 1988 she was serving as assistant deputy director of administrative services; in 1989, she served in private law practice. She was elected judge to the Cleveland Municipal Court on November 6, 2001.

Rose Grymes

AEROSPACE. Rose Grymes received a Bachelor of Science degree in bacteriology from the University of Cal-

ifornia at Davis and a Ph.D. in cancer biology/ medical microbiology from Stanford University where she completed her postdoctoral work in the School of Medicine.

She began her career at NASA as a cell biologist with the life sciences division at NASA Ames Research Center. After three years as a principal investigator in her own laboratory, with students, technicians, and visiting colleagues, she switched her emphasis to education and public communication as NASA's life sciences outreach program manager. She was promoted to deputy director of the NASA Astrobiology Institute.

Lani Guinier

EDUCATION (FIRST). Lani Guinier received a bachelor's degree from Radcliffe College of Harvard University and earned a Juris Doctor degree from Yale Law School.

During the 1980s she was head of the voting rights project at the NAACP Legal Defense Fund and had served in the civil rights division during the Carter Administration as special assistant to then assistant Attorney General Drew S. Days. She was nominated by President Bill Clinton in 1993 to head the civil rights division of the Department of Justice, only to have her name withdrawn without a confirmation hearing. In 1998, Ms. Guinier became the first black woman to be appointed to a tenured professorship at Harvard Law School.

She served as a member of the faculty of the University of Pennsylvania Law School.

Diane Gulyas

BUSINESS EXECUTIVE. Diane Gulyas is a native of Chicago, Illinois. She received a Bachelor of Science degree in chemical engineering from the University of Notre Dame and completed the Advanced Management Program at Wharton in 1994.

She joined DuPont in 1978 and spent her first 10 years in a variety of sales, marketing, technical and systems development positions, primarily in the DuPont polymers business. For the next four years, she was European business manager based in Geneva for engineering polymers and plant superintendent at the Mechelen, Belgium, site. She served as executive assistant to the chairman of the board from 1993 to 1994. In 1994, she was assigned as global business director for nylon fibers new business development and global Zytel engineering polymers. In 1997, she was selected to serve as vice president and general manager for DuPont advanced fiber business at the Spruance Plant in Richmond, Virginia. In April 2004, she was named chief marketing and sales officer and in April 2006 named group vice president for DuPont Performance Materials.

Noma D. Gurich

JUDGE. Noma D. Gurich is a native of South Bend, Indiana. She graduated magna cum laude from Indiana State University and received her Juris Doctor degree from the University of Oklahoma College of Law.

After law school she served in private law practice in Oklahoma City, Oklahoma. She began her judicial career on the Oklahoma Workers' Compensation Court by governor appointment, where she served as presiding judge for four years. She won a county-wide election for district judge in November of 1998 and was re-elected without opposition in 2002. She served as the presiding administrative judge for the Seventh Judicial District, Oklahoma County, from January 1, 2003, to December 2004.

Pamela C. Gutierrez

JUDGE. Pamela C. Gutierrez received a Bachelor of Science degree in business management and received a masters' degree in criminal justice. She has worked in a variety of administrative and criminal justice–related areas. Prior to her tenure on the bench she was engaged in private law practice and served in the Judge Advocate General's office (JAG) while serving in the United States Air Force at Williams Air Force Base.

In 1999, she was appointed by then Arizona Supreme Court Justice Thomas Zlaket to serve three years as a mentor judge of newly appointed limited jurisdiction judges.

Beverly L. Hall

EDUCATION. Beverly L. Hall is a native of Jamaica, West Indies. She immigrated to the United States upon completion of her high school education. She received a Bachelor of Arts degree in English and a Master of Science degree in guidance counseling from Brooklyn College of the City University of New York. She earned her doctor of education degree from Fordham University in 1990.

Her professional career includes serving as principal of a junior high school in Brooklyn, New York; as superintendent, Community School District 27 in Queens, New York; and as deputy chancellor for instruction, New York City Public Schools. She was appointed state district superintendent of the Newark Public Schools.

Dr. Hall was appointed the 15th superintendent of the Atlanta Public Schools on July 1, 1999.

Diana R. Hall

JUDGE. Diana R. Hall is an Ohio native and graduated cum laude from California State University in Northridge in 1972. She earned her Juris Doctor degree from the University of La Verne College of Law with scholastic honors.

Prior to her appointment to the bench, she served as a deputy district attorney for thirteen years. She was appointed judge to the municipal court in Santa Maria Division by Governor Deukmejian on December 20, 1990. In August 1998, she was elevated to Superior Court judge to the Santa Barbara County Superior Court, California.

Ethel H. Hall

EDUCATION. Ethel H. Hall received a bachelor's degree (cum laude) from Alabama A&M University, and received master's degrees from the University of Chicago and Atlanta University. She earned a doctorate degree from the University of Alabama.

Her professional career includes serving as a teacher in Hale and Jefferson counties' school systems; as executive director, Neighborhood Youth Corps and Early Childhood School Transition Programs, Jefferson County Committee for Economic Opportunity; as associate professor, University of Montevallo; and as associate professor, University of Alabama. She was first elected to the Alabama State Board of Education in 1987 and has served District 4 ever since. She now serves as the vice president of the board.

Lisa Gersh Hall

ENTERTAINMENT EXECUTIVE. Lisa Gersh Hall received a Bachelor of Arts degree in political science and economics from the State University of New York Binghamton in 1980 and earned a Juris Doctor degree from Rutgers Law School in 1983 where she was an editor of the *Computer and Technology Law Journal.*

Her professional career includes serving the New York law firm Friedman Kaplan & Seiler LLP as a founding partner from 1986 to 1998. During this time the firm grew from six lawyers to over 40 serving a wide range of corporate clients in complex corporate transactions and commercial litigation.

Ms. Hall serves as president, chief operating officer and co-founder of Oxygen Network, the only women-owned and -operated network. She is responsible for the day-to-day operations of the company. She was the principal engineer of Oxygen's foundation partnerships including Carsey-Werner and Harpo, as well as the company's financing and major MSO agreements.

Shelvin Louise Marie Hall

JUDGE. Shelvin Louise Marie Hall is a graduate of Hampton University in Hampton, Virginia, and Boston University School of Law in Boston, Massa-

chusetts. She worked in private practice for six years in Houston, Texas, and in 1980 she went to Washington, D.C., to serve as legislative director to the late U.S. Congressman Mickey Leland. She served as senior attorney with the Illinois Department of Human Rights in 1982 and became general counsel for the agency in 1984.

She was appointed a circuit court judge of Cook County in 1991 and was elected to the court in 1992. Judge Hall was assigned to the Appellate Court in 1999 and elected to the court in 2000. She is serving as appellate judge for the First District, 3rd Division for the State of Illinois.

Judith Haller

JUDGE. Judith Haller is a native of Los Angeles, California. She is a summa cum laude and Phi Beta Kappa graduate of UCLA and received her Juris Doctor degree from California Western School of Law. She also holds a master's degree in history from San Diego State University.

Her professional career includes serving as a deputy district attorney with the San Diego County District Attorney's office for three years and in private law practice. On November 22, 1989, Governor George Deukmejian appointed her judge to the San Diego County Superior Court. In 1994, Governor Deukmejian appointed her an associate justice to the California Court of Appeal, 4th District, and Division One.

Cheryl Halpem

MEDIA. Cheryl Halpem received a bachelor's degree from Barnard College of Columbia University and a Master of Business Administration with a concentration in finance from New York University.

Mrs. Halpem was confirmed as a member of the board for International Broadcasting and as a director of Radio Free Europe/Radio Liberty in 1990. From 1995 through 2002, she served on the Broadcasting Board of Governors overseeing Voice of America, Radio and TV Marti, WorldNet, Radio Free Asia and Radio Free Iraq. While serving on the Broadcasting Board of Governors she helped create Radio Sawa, America's Arabic radio service to the Middle East. In August 2002, she was appointed by President George W. Bush to serve as a director of the Corporation for Public Broadcasting. In September 2005, she was elected to be chairman of the Corporation for Public Broadcasting.

Rebecca S. Halstead

MILITARY. Rebecca S. Halstead is a native of Willseyville, New York. She was commissioned in the Ordnance Corps upon graduation from the United States Military Academy, West Point, New York, in 1981. She earned a master's degree in military art and science from the Command and General Staff College and a master's degree in national resource strategy from the National Defense University.

Her military education includes completion of the Ordinance Officers' Basic and Advanced courses at Aberdeen Proving Ground, Maryland, and Redstone Arsenal in Huntsville, Alabama; the United States Army Command and General Staff College, Fort Leavenworth, Kansas; and the Industrial College of the Armed Forces, Fort McNair, Washington, D.C.

Brigadier General Halstead has served in a wide variety of command assignments including commander, 325th Forward Support Battalion, 25th Infantry Division (Light), Schofield Barracks, Hawaii; commander, 10th Mountain Division Support Command, 10th Mountain Division (Light Infantry), Fort Drum, New York; executive assistant to the combatant commander, United States Southern Command, Miami, Florida; and deputy commanding general for the 21st Theater Support Command, USAREUR, Kaiserslautem, Germany.

Joyce Hamilton

JUDGE. Joyce Hamilton received a Bachelor of Science degree (magna cum laude) in economics and business administration from the University of North Carolina at Greensboro in 1972. She earned her Juris

Doctor degree the University of North Carolina Chapel Hill School of Law in 1975.

Her professional career includes serving as an assistant district attorney in Wake County where she progressed through the positions of executive director, NCATL; as a staff attorney, North Carolina Court of Appeals; and in private law practice. In September 1986, she was appointed judge to the District Court in Wake County; she became chief District Court judge in December 2000.

Phyllis Jean Hamilton

JUDGE. Phyllis Jean Hamilton is a native of Jacksonville, Illinois. She received a Bachelor of Arts degree from Stanford University in 1974 and earned her Juris Doctor degree from Santa Clara University School of Law in 1976.

Her experience includes serving as a deputy public defender, Office of the Public Defender, California from 1976 to 1980; as manager, EEO Programs, Farinon Electric Corporation, 1980; as an administrative judge, U.S. Merit Systems Protection Board, San Francisco Regional Office, California (1980–1985); she served as a court commissioner, Municipal Court, Oakland-Piedmont-Emeryville Judicial District, 1985–1991. She was appointed as a U.S. magistrate judge, U.S. District Court for the Northern District of California from 1991 to 2000.

Judge Hamilton was nominated by President William J. Clinton on February 9, 2000, confirmed by the Senate on May 24, 2000, and received commission on May 25, 2000.

Lauren Hammond

ELECTED OFFICIAL. Lauren Hammond is a graduate of C.K. McClatchy High School in Sacramento, California, and earned a bachelor's degree after attending Sacramento City College and California State University.

After working 22 years for the state senate's coordinator for the Americans with Disabilities Act, Ms. Hammond chose to concentrate full time on her council duties. She was elected to the Sacramento City Council on March 4, 1997. She is a long-time community leader and neighborhood activist and has lived in Sacramento for 35 years.

Karen Handel

ELECTED OFFICIAL (FIRST). Karen Handel is a native of Washington, D.C., and grew up in Upper Marlboro, Maryland. She has served as Georgia's Governor Sonny Perdue's deputy chief of staff. In 2002, she was elected the first woman chairman and chief executive of Fulton County, Georgia. Fulton County is the state's largest and most populous county. In 2006, she was elected Georgia Secretary of State.

Karla J. Hansen

JUDGE. Karla J. Hansen received a bachelor's degree in nuclear medicine technology from the University of Wisconsin–LaCrosse and earned her Juris Doctor from the University of Utah. She served as a deputy district attorney in El Paso County from 1986 to 1994; she served in private law practice from 1994 to 1998.

In 1998, she was appointed as a municipal judge for Colorado Springs. In 2001, Judge Hansen was appointed as a county court judge for the 4th District, Colorado State Judicial.

Marka Hansen

BUSINESS EXECUTIVE. Marka Hansen received a Bachelor of Arts degree in liberal studies from Loyola Marymount University in Los Angeles, California.

Ms. Hansen joined the Gap, Inc., in 1987 as mer-

chandise manager for Banana Republic's women's division. She spent six years with the brand in various positions including vice president of men's merchandising. In 1993, she joined Gap's International Division as vice president of merchandising, leading expansion in Europe and Japan. She was promoted to senior vice president in 1995. After seven years, she served as head of Gap Inc.'s human resources organization before taking on the role of executive vice president of Gap Adult Merchandising in March 2002. She now serves as president of Gap brand where she leads all aspects of the business in North America including Gap, GapKids, babyGap, GapMaternity and gapbody.

Jane F. Harman

ELECTED OFFICIAL. Jane F. Harman is a native of New York, New York, and a graduate of University High School in Los Angeles, California. She received a Bachelor of Arts degree from Smith College in Northampton, Massachusetts, and earned her Juris Doctor degree from Harvard University School of Law in Cambridge, Massachusetts, in 1969.

Her professional career includes serving as a member of the staff of United States Senator John V. Tunney of California from 1972 to 1973; as an adjunct professor at Georgetown University Law School Center in Washington, D.C., from 1974 to 1975; as deputy secretary to the Cabinet, the White House, from 1977 to 1978; and as special counsel at the Department of Defense in 1979. She was elected United States Representative to the 103rd and to the two succeeding Congresses (January 3, 1993–January 3, 1999); was not a candidate for reelection to 106th Congress in 1998 but was an unsuccessful candidate for nomination as governor of California; she was elected as a United States Representative to the 107th and to the two succeeding Congresses (January 3, 2001–present).

Ruth Ann Harnisch

JOURNALISM. Ruth Ann Harnisch is a native of Buffalo, New York. She spent 30 years in media work, including Emmy-nominated television reporting and anchoring at the CBS-TV affiliate in Nashville, Tennessee, a daily talk-radio program on WLAC-AM and 17 years as a columnist for the *Nashville Banner*.

Ms. Harnisch serves as president of the Harnisch Family Foundation which has given grants to hundreds of not-for-profit organizations since its founding in 1998. She serves as chair emerita of the Board of Directors of More Than Money.

Jane V. Harper

JUDGE. Jane V. Harper has been a Charlotte, North Carolina, resident since 1970. She is a 1980 honors graduate of University of North Carolina, School of Law. Her professional career includes serving as a lawyer for Legal Aid from 1980 to 1984; in private law practice from 1984 to 1990; as a family law specialist; and as a judge for the District Court in the 26th Judicial District since 1990. She has served as judge in family court since 1992.

Nicki (Virginia) Harrington

EDUCATION. Nicki (Virginia) Harrington received a bachelor's degree in nursing from the University of Michigan. She earned two master's degrees, one from the University of San Francisco in education and another from California State University in Dominguez Hills in nursing education. She earned her doctorate degree in educational leadership from the University of San Diego.

Her professional career includes serving for ten years (1983 to 1993) as an instructor and administrator in the Health Occupations Department at College of the Redwoods in Eureka, California. She is also a published author of a college textbook and is currently in the process of completing a second textbook. She served as president and chief executive officer of Blue Mountain Community College. Dr. Harrington serves as superintendent and president of Yuba Community College District.

Gayle Elizabeth Harris

MINISTRY. Gayle Elizabeth Harris is a graduate of the Church Divinity School of the Pacific. She served as an adjunct professor at Colgate Rochester Seminary. She was ordained a deacon in 1981 and ordained a priest in Newark, New Jersey, diocese in 1982. She was priest-in-charge of Holy Communion Church in Washington, D.C.

Bishop Harris served as rector of St. Luke and St. Simon Cyrene Episcopal Church in Rochester, New York. In June 2002, she was elected the seventh Bishop Suffragan of the Diocese of Massachusetts. Her election was particularly notable because it was the first time in which a black woman was called in immediate succession after the retirement of another black woman. She replaced retiring Bishop Barbara C. Harris, Massachusetts' first female Bishop.

Gene T. Harris

EDUCATION. Gene T. Harris received a Bachelor of Arts in English from the University of Notre Dame and a masters of education in educational administration from the Ohio State University. She earned a Ph.D. in educational administration from the Ohio State University in 1999.

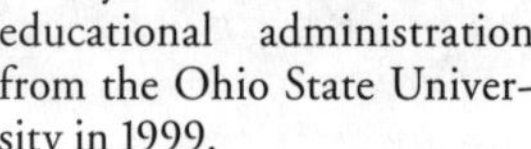

Her professional career includes serving as a teacher in Columbus Public Schools from 1980 to 1995. She moved from the classroom to principal, supervisor of principals and deputy superintendent. After developing new teacher education and licensure standards as assistant superintendent for the Ohio Department of Education, she returned to Columbus Public Schools becoming deputy superintendent in 2000.

Dr. Harris was appointed the 19th superintendent of the Columbus Public Schools in 2001.

Kamala D. Harris

ELECTED OFFICIAL. Kamala D. Harris was born in Oakland, California, and raised in Berkeley, California. She received a bachelor's degree from Howard University in Washington, D.C., and earned a Juris Doctor degree from the University of California, Hastings College of the Law in 1990.

Her professional career includes serving as deputy district attorney in Alameda County, California, from 1990 to 1998. She served as managing attorney of the Career Criminal Unit in the San Francisco District Attorney's office. In 2000, City Attorney Louise Renne recruited her to join the city attorney's office where she was chief of the community and neighborhood division. Ms. Harris was elected district attorney of San Francisco in December 2003 after a run-off election. She is the first woman to be elected as district attorney in San Francisco and the first female Indo-African-American to serve as top prosecutor in the state's history. Her mother is a prominent Indian-American breast cancer specialist who emigrated to the United States in 1960.

Katherine Harris

ELECTED OFFICIAL. Katherine Harris is a native of Key West, Monroe County, Florida. She attended the University of Madrid in Madrid, Spain, in 1978 and received a Bachelor of Arts degree from Agnes Scott College in Decatur, Georgia, in 1979. She earned a master of public administration from Harvard University in Cambridge, Massachusetts, in 1966.

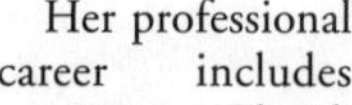

Her professional career includes serving as a Florida State Senator from 1994 to 1998 and as the Florida Secretary of State from 1999 to 2002. She was elected as a Republican to the 108th Congress and to the succeeding Congress.

Mamie Harris

MINISTRY. Mamie Harris is a native of Griffin, Georgia. She received a bachelor's degree from Beulah Heights University in Atlanta, Georgia.

She is the founder and senior pastor of the New Generation Christian Fellowship Church in Griffin, Georgia. She has traveled worldwide to Brazil, Europe,

Ghana, Guatemala, Kenya, Mexico, Morocco, South Africa, and Trinidad, ministering at revivals, retreats, conferences and empowering leaders. She has been recognized, co-hosted and appeared on national and international television and radio programs such as TBN's "Praise the Lord," Atlanta Live TV-57, the "Dr. Bobby Hurd Show," and "Bobby Jones Gospel."

Marcelite J. Harris

MILITARY. Marcelite J. Harris is a native of Houston, Texas. She graduated from Kashmere Gardens Junior-Senior High School in 1960. She earned a Bachelor of Arts degree in speech and drama from Spelman College in 1964 and a Bachelor of Science degree in business management from the University of Maryland, Asian Division, in 1989. The general completed Squadron Officer School in 1975, Air War College in 1983, Harvard University's Senior Officers National Security Course in 1989, and the CAPSTONE General and Flag Officer Course in 1990.

In September 1965 she entered the United States Air Force through officer training school, Lackland Air Force Base in Texas. Upon graduation in December 1965, she was assigned to the 60th Military Airlift Wing, Travis Air Force Base, California, as assistant director for administration. In January 1967 she became administrative officer for the 388th Tactical Missile Squadron, Bitburg Air Base, West Germany, and in May 1969 was reassigned as maintenance analysis officer, 388th Tactical Fighter Wing, Bitburg.

She completed her tour of duty in West Germany and upon graduation in May 1971 from the Aircraft Maintenance Officer Course at Chanute Air Force Base, Illinois, became the Air Force's first woman to be an aircraft maintenance officer. Three months later she became maintenance supervisor, 49th Tactical Fighter Squadron, Korat Royal Thai Air Force Base, Thailand. On return to the United States, she was assigned as job control officer, 916th Air Refueling Squadron, Travis Air Force Base, California; in September 1973 she became the maintenance supervisor. In September 1975 General Harris was assigned as a personnel staff officer, headquarters, United States Air Force, Washington, D.C., where she served as a White House aide to President Jimmy Carter.

In May 1978 she became Commander of Cadet Squadron 39, United States Air Force Academy, Colorado Springs, Colorado, an assignment that made her one of the first two women to be Air Officers Commanding. The general returned to maintenance when she became maintenance control officer, the 384th Air Refueling Wing, McConnell Air Force Base, Kansas, in July 1980. In July 1981 she became Strategic Air Command's first woman maintenance squadron commander when she assumed command of the 384th Avionics Maintenance Squadron at McConnell. Eight months later, she assumed Command of McConnell's 384th Field Maintenance Squadron.

In November 1982 she was assigned to the Pacific Air Forces Logistic Support Center, Kadena Air Base in Japan. She became the Air Force's first woman deputy commander for Maintenance at Keesler Air Force Base, Mississippi, in March 1986 and the first woman wing commander in Air Training Command's 3300th Technical Training Wing, Keesler Technical Training Center in December 1988. In September 1990, she was selected Vice Commander of Oklahoma City Air Logistics Center at Tinker Air Force Base.

On May 1, 1991, she was promoted to Brigadier General, becoming the first black female general in the United States Air Force. From July 1993 to August 1994, she served as the director of technical training at Headquarters Air Education and Training Command, Randolph Air Force Base, Texas. From September 1994 to February 1997, she was the director of maintenance at Headquarters United States Air Force in Washington, D.C. She organized, trained, equipped a work force of more than 125,000 technicians and managers and maintains the $260 billion plus Global Reach–Global Power aerospace weapons system inventory. She was promoted to Major General on May 25, 1995, and retired on February 22, 1997.

Skila Harris

GOVERNMENT OFFICIAL. Skila Harris is a native of the Tennessee Valley. She received a bachelor's degree in political science from Western Kentucky University. She earned a master's degree in legislative affairs from George Washington University.

Her professional career includes working for private engineering and management consulting firms that specialize in energy. She has held positions with the United States Synthetic Fuels Corporation and the United States Department of Energy under both the Carter and Clinton administrations. She served from 1989 to 1992 as vice president for development and compliance at Steiner-Liff Iron and Metal Company in Nashville, Tennessee. From 1993 to 1997, she served as special assistant to vice president Al Gore and chief of staff to Tipper Gore.

Ms. Harris was appointed the 25th member of the Tennessee Valley Authority (TVA) Board of Directors and TVA's first woman director. She was appointed by President Bill Clinton and confirmed by the United States Senate in November 1999. Her nine-year term expires May 18, 2008.

Stayce D. Harris

MILITARY. Stayce D. Harris is a native of Los Angeles, California, and is the daughter of a career enlisted man. In 1977, she graduated from 71st High School in Fayetteville, North Carolina. She was then accepted into the University of Southern California on an engineering ROTC scholarship which later she changed to a pilot training scholarship.

However, in her college senior year she did not pass the physical requirements to be an Air Force pilot because of slightly poor eyesight. As a result, she graduated with an industrial systems engineering degree. She spent her first year and a half in the Air Force as chief of industrial engineering and then as the squadron section commander of civil engineering at Hill Air Force Base, Utah.

Determined to correct her vision to 20/20, she began doing eye exercises which enabled her to reapply for pilot training. She attended pilot training in Arizona and within three years qualified as an aircraft commander on the C-141B Starlifter cargo aircraft.

In August 1990, she separated from active duty and became an airline pilot for United Airlines. She flew a Boeing 747-400 aircraft each week from Los Angeles to Tokyo or Los Angeles to Sydney.

From April 1991 to February 1995, she was an air operations officer and C-141 pilot in the 445th Airlift Wing at March Air Reserve Base, California. She was a mobility force planner for the Air Force deputy Chief of Staff for plans and operations in the Pentagon from February 1995 to January 1997. For the next three years, she served as an individual mobilization augmentee to the deputy Assistant Secretary of the Air Force at the Pentagon.

In February 2000, Colonel Harris returned to March Air Reserve Base first as deputy commander of the 452nd Operations Group and then as commander of the 729th Airlift Squadron. From May 2002 to May 2005, she was vice commander of the 507th Air Reserve Wing at Tinker Air Force Base where she began flying KC-135 Stratotankers.

As commander of the 459th ARW and a first officer with United Airlines, Colonel Harris served as a traditional reservist and flies an abbreviated schedule with United out of Los Angeles while living in the national capital region.

She has more than 2,500 hours flying military aircraft and 8,000 hours flying for United Airlines and often makes herself available to participate with the Tuskegee Airmen.

Vera F. Harris

MILITARY. Vera F. Harris is a native of Dallas, Texas. She enlisted into the United States Army Women Corps in November 1975. She attended Basic Combat Training and Advanced Individual Training at Fort Jackson, South Carolina.

Her military education includes all the Noncommissioned Officer Education System Courses and the United States Army Sergeants Major Academy. She is one of only a few enlisted soldiers who are certified by the International Food Service Executive Association as a food service executive and as a professional food manager. She holds an associate degree from Pikes Peak College in Colorado, a bachelor's degree from Trinity Southern University in Texas, and a bachelor of science degree from Excelsior College in New York.

She has held a wide variety of leadership positions and assignments including serving as dining facility manager; food operations sergeant; supply and logistics noncommissioned officer in charge; first sergeant; two assignments as brigade food advisor culminating with the most prestigious of all in the food service area, the department of Army Philip A. Connelly senior noncommissioned officer in charge program manager. In October 2004, she was serving as the command sergeant major for the Regimental Support Squadron, 2nd Armored Cavalry Regiment at Fort Pork, Louisiana.

Patricia de Stacy Harrison

MEDIA EXECUTIVE. Patricia de Stacy Harrison is a native of Brooklyn, New York. She received a bachelor's degree from American University and a honorary doctorate from the American University of Rome in 2002. In 2000, she was a visiting fellow at the Institute for Public Service of the Annenberg Policy Center, University of Pennsylvania. In 1992, she was a visiting fellow at the John F. Kennedy School of Government at Harvard University.

Dr. Harrison was appointed by President Bush in 1990 to the President's Export Council, United States Department of Commerce. In 1992, she was appointed to serve on the United States Trade Representative's Service Policy Advisory Council. In 1997, she was elected co-chairman of the Republican National Committee and served until January 2001. She was appointed acting under secretary for public diplomacy and public affairs at the State Department. In October 2, 2001, she was appointed assistant secretary of state for educational and cultural affairs. While at the State Department, she directed the historic resumption of the Fulbright Program in Afghanistan and Iraq. Dr. Harrison was awarded the Secretary's Distinguished Service Award by Secretary of State Condoleezza Rice for excellence in leadership in these positions.

On June 23, 2005, Dr. Harrison was named president and chief executive officer of the Corporation for Public Affairs.

Cynthia Harriss

BUSINESS EXECUTIVE. Cynthia Harriss received a bachelor's degree from St. Louis University. Her professional career includes serving 19 years with Paul Harris Stores, a specialty apparel retailer for women and as president of the Disneyland Resort division of the Walt Disney Company. She also served as senior vice president of Stores for the Disney Store.

Ms. Harriss joined Gap Inc. in February 2004 as president of Gap Inc. Outlet, and is responsible for nearly 250 outlet stores across the United States. She serves as president of Gap Brand, where she leads all aspects of the business in North America, including Gap, Gapkids, BabyGap, GapMaternity and Gapbody. Assuming this role in May 2005, she oversees the brand's more than 1,300 North America stores.

Cathy J. Hart

BUSINESS EXECUTIVE. Cathy J. Hart received a Bachelor of Science degree in journalism from Ohio University at Athens and completed the Public Utilities Executive Course at the University of Idaho and Leadership Denver.

Her professional career includes serving as a communications professional for more than 20 years. She has held public relations positions at American Electric Power; Desbrow & Associates, and Old Ben Coal Co.; she also served as city editor of the *Lancaster Eagle-Gazette* in Lancaster, Ohio; as corporate secretary for New Century Energies; and as chief compliance officer for Xcel Energy.

Ms. Hart serves as vice president and corporate secretary of Xcel Energy and its various subsidiaries and serves as a liaison between management and the board of directors.

Clare Hart

BUSINESS EXECUTIVE. Clare Hart received a Bachelor of Science degree in finance and computer systems management from Drexel University in Philadelphia, Pennsylvania, and a master of business administration degree from Rider University, Lawrenceville, New Jersey.

Her professional career includes serving as vice president and director of Factiva Global Sales where she managed about a third of Factiva's workforce. In 2000, Ms. Hart was appointed president and chief executive officer at Factiva. She drives the strategic vision and direction for the award-winning and innovative content, technology and services company.

Deborah L. Hart

MILITARY. Deborah L. Hart received a Bachelor of Science degree in biology from the University of Pittsburgh and earned a doctor of dental medicine from the University Pittsburgh. She is a graduate of the Squadron Officer School, the Air Command and Staff College, and the Air War College.

Colonel Hart has held a wide variety of command and staff position to include serving as acting base dental surgeon, assistant base dental surgeon, Geilenkirchen NATO Air Base in Germany from November 1989 to October 1990; individual mobilization augmentee at Pease Air Force Base, New Hampshire; she served as chief dental services, 106th Clinic, Air National Guard Base, Westhampton Beach, New York; as chief of dental service, 910th Medical Squadron, Air Reserve Base, Youngtown, Ohio. She now serves as the mobilization assistant to the assistant surgeon general for dental services at Bolling Air Force Base in Washington, D.C.

Melissa A. Hart

ELECTED OFFICIAL. Melissa A. Hart is a native of Pittsburgh, Pennsylvania and a graduate of North Allegheny High School, North Allegheny, in Pennsylvania. She received a Bachelor of Arts degree from Washington and Jefferson College in Washington, Pennsylvania, in 1984 and earned her Juris Doctor degree from the University of Pittsburgh, Pennsylvania, in 1987.

She was engaged in private law practice, then served as a member of the Pennsylvania State Senate from 1991 to 2000; she was elected a United States Representative to the 107th and to the two succeeding Congresses.

Carol C. Harter

EDUCATION. Carol C. Harter is a native of New York, New York. She received from the State University of New York at Binghamton a Bachelor of Arts degree in English with honors in 1964, a master of arts in 1967 and a Ph.D. in English and American literature in 1970.

Her professional career includes serving for 19 years at Ohio University where she was a faculty member, ombudsman and served in two vice presidential roles; and as president of the State University of New York (SUNY) at Geneseo for six years.

Dr. Harter serves as the seventh president of the University of Nevada, Las Vegas (UNLV), a post she has held for more than 10 years.

Maureen A. Hartford

EDUCATION. Maureen A. Hartford is a native of Charlotte, North Carolina. She received a Bachelor of Arts in French and history and a Master of Arts in college teaching from the University of North Carolina in Chapel Hill. She earned her doctorate in higher education administration from the University of Arkansas.

Her professional career includes serving as a senior administrator at Washington State University, Case Western Reserve, the University of Arkansas and the University of Maine. She has served as vice president for student affairs at the University of Michigan.

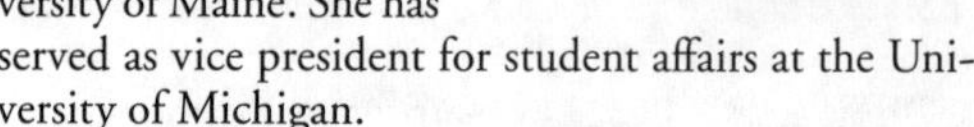

Dr. Hartford was appointed president of Meredith College on February 26, 1999, and officially assumed the duties of the position the following July 1. She is the first female president of Meredith, the largest private college for women in the Southeast.

Tammy Harthcock

JUDGE. Tammy Harthcock received her Bachelor of Arts degree from Belhaven College, graduating magna cum laude. She earned her Juris Doctor degree from Mississippi College School of Law. She earned the American Jurisprudence award in Civil Procedure during law school. She was on the Moot Court National Competition team, and the Dean's Student Advisory Committee.

Her professional career includes serving as a senior attorney with the Mississippi Secretary of State's office. She was appointed special assistant United States attorney in order to prosecute federal criminal securities fraud cases.

In March 1997, she was appointed an administrative judge with the Mississippi Worker's Compensation Commission.

Keiko Harvey

BUSINESS EXECUTIVE. Keiko Harvey is a native of Japan and came to the United States when she was 17 years old. She received a bachelor's degree from Rutgers School of Engineering.

Her professional career includes serving in 1972 as an interoffice facilities engineer at Bell Atlantic's New Jersey Bell Division; she has served as vice president, network engineering and planning as well as senior vice president and chief executive officer of Verizon Global Networks Inc. In June 2003, she was appointed to serve as senior vice president, fiber to the premises, for Verizon's Network for the overall coordination of the design, deployment, systems planning, operations processes and product development for Verizon's high-speed fiber network to the premises of consumer and general business customers.

Ms. Harvey was appointed senior vice president, Video Network Services in December 2004. She is responsible for video operations, engineering and planning and video services such as content management, subscriber management and performance assurance.

Glenda Hatchett

JUDGE. Glenda Hatchett is a native of Atlanta, Georgia. She received a Bachelor of Arts in political science from Mount Holyoke College and earned her Juris Doctor degree from Emory University School of Law in Atlanta, Georgia.

Her professional career includes serving as a law clerk to United States District Court Judge Horace T. Ward. During the 1980s, she was senior attorney and served as national and international spokesperson for Delta Air Lines in Atlanta. On October 1, 1990, she was appointed as a juvenile court judge for Fulton County, Georgia. On March 1, 1991, she was appointed chief presiding judge and department head of juvenile court of Fulton County where she is noted as the first woman and African American to serve in this position. Since 2000, she has starred in the television show, *Judge Hatchett*. On December 14, 2006, she also played Judge Warren on an episode of *The Young and the Restless.*

Carol Hawkins

EDUCATION. Carol Hawkins earned both her bachelor's and master's degree in English from the University of Florida.

Her professional career includes teaching English composition at the high school and community college levels. In 1978, she began her 19-year tenure at Polk Community College in Winter Haven. She worked her way from adjunct to full-time instructor to director and finally dean. She serves as Seminole Community College vice president of institution effectiveness, planning and information services.

Carol Hooks Hawkins

AUTHOR. Carol Hooks Hawkins is a native of Birmingham, Alabama. She graduated from Carol W. Hayes High School and in 1970 received a Bachelor of Science degree in business from Stillman College in Tuscaloosa, Alabama. She attended John Marshall Law School, Atlanta, Georgia, from 1972 to 1974. She holds a master cosmetology license and a Georgia state insurance license for property, casualty, life, accident and sickness.

Her professional career includes serving as general manager at Charles Styles Realty Company in Atlanta, Georgia; as a managing associate with Wyatt and Zagoria, P.A., Attorneys; as an executive associate at F. A. Johnson & Associates Developer, Atlanta, Georgia; as in-house production administrator for projects from early feasibility studies to completion with J. W. Robin-

son & Associates, Architects; as managing associate with Duckett Design Group, Architect/Interior Designer. Ms. Hawkins served as co-owner and operator of the Wiz Hair Salon from 1988 to 1999.

She later utilized her business management and sales skills, serving as senior staff agent for State Farm Insurance Company — Thomas Walker's Agency in Union City , Georgia, and Aaron Frazier's Agency in Brookhaven, Georgia. Since 2001, she has served as senior sales staff agent with State Farm Insurance Company — Anita Price Agency in Fayetteville, Georgia.

Ms. Hawkins is the author of this book.

Carla G. Hawley-Bowland

MILITARY. Carla G. Hawley-Bowland received a Bachelor of Science degree in biochemistry from Colorado State University and a Medical Doctor degree in general medicine from Creighton University. She earned a Master of Science degree in strategic studies from the United States Army War College. Her military schools attended include the Army Medical Department Officer Basic and Advanced Courses, the United States Army Command and General Staff College and the United States Army War College.

She has held numerous assignments of increasing responsibility including serving as deputy commander for clinical services at Womack Army Medical Center, Fort Bragg, North Carolina, with additional duty as OB/GYN consultant to the Army surgeon general; from 1998 to July 2000, she served as hospital commander, United States Army Medical Department Activity, Fort Leonard Wood, Missouri; from July 2000 to July 2002, she served as the hospital commander, William Beaumont Army Medical Center, Fort Bliss, Texas; from July 2002 to July 2004, she served as deputy director, Health Policy and Services Division/Chief, Clinical Services Division/Chief, Consultants Branch, United States Army Medical Command at Fort Sam Houston, Texas; from July 2004 to September 2006, she served as the commanding general, European Regional Medical Command/Lead Agent, TRICARE Europe/Command Surgeon, United States Army Europe and Seventh Army, Germany. She was promoted to Brigadier General on September 1, 2004.

Major General Hawley-Bowland was assigned as the commanding general of the Tripler Army Medical Center/Pacific Regional Medical Command/United States Army Pacific Surgeon/Lead Agent, TRICARE Pacific in Honolulu, Hawaii. She was promoted to Major General on September 29, 2006.

Dorothy Hayden-Watkins

BUSINESS EXECUTIVE. Dorothy Hayden-Watkins received a Bachelor of Arts degree in social science and English from University of Northern Colorado. She earned a master's in education and administration and a doctorate in community and human resources from the University of Nebraska at Lincoln.

Her professional career included serving as an educator and administrator in the Denver Public Schools where she assisted with implementation of court ordered school desegregation efforts, and serving the Lincoln Nebraska Public School System where she administered the district's multi-cultural education program for administrators and teachers. From 1981 to 1989 she served as the director of the Colorado Civil Rights Commission. She served as the senior vice president for diversity for the Hilton Hotels Corporation in Beverly Hills, California.

Dr. Hayden-Watkins is the principal of Hayden-Watkins & Associates, an executive consulting firm providing technical advice and services in strategic planning, implementation and evaluation of diversity and equal opportunity programs. She was named assistant administrator for equal opportunity programs in December 2002.

Lou V. Hayes

MILITARY. Lou V. Hayes entered the United States Army in September 1978. She completed Basic Training and Advanced Individual Training at Fort Jackson, South Carolina.

Her military and civilian education includes all the Noncommissioned Officer Education System Courses, Unit Deployment Course, Master Fitness Course, Battle Staff Course, the Inspector General Course, First

Sergeant Administrative Course, the United States Air Force Senior Noncommissioned Officer Course, and the United States Army Sergeants Major Academy (Class 51). She holds an associate and bachelor of arts from the University of Tampa and a master of arts in management from Webster University.

She has served in every leadership position from squad leader to command sergeant major. She was assigned to Headquarters and Headquarters Company at Fort Huachuca, Arizona; at Headquarters Defense Communication Agency (DCA) in Washington, D.C.; Readiness Command, MacDill Air Force Base in Florida; 501st Military Intelligence Group, Camp Humphries, Korea; Headquarters, Allied Powers in Belgium, Europe; Delta Company, Special Forces Diving School in Key West Florida; the Joint Staff (J8), Washington, D.C.; Headquarters United States Central Command, MacDill Air Force Base; Alpha Company, 120th Adjutant General Battalion, Fort Jackson, South Carolina; Forces Command Inspector General Sergeant Major, Fort McPherson, Georgia. In January 2005 she was serving as the command sergeant major, Unites States Army, NATO, Allied Forces North Battalion.

Maxine Hayes

MEDICINE. Maxine Hayes received a Bachelor of Science degree in biology (with honors) from Spelman College in Atlanta, Georgia. She was a Merrill Fellow at the University of Vienna, Austria, and attended the State University of New York School of Medicine in Buffalo. Her post-graduate training was in pediatrics at Vanderbilt University Hospital in Nashville, Tennessee, and at the Children's Hospital Medical Center in Boston, Massachusetts. She earned a master of public health degree at Harvard University. While at Harvard, she also worked as a consultant to Project COPE, a program sponsored by the University of Massachusetts at Worcester to offer pediatric health care information to mothers of infants born in prison.

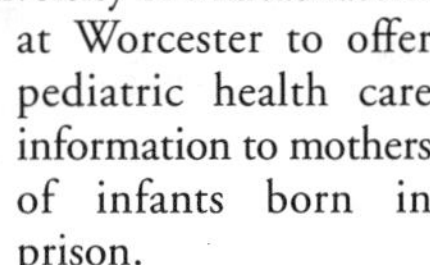

Her professional career includes serving in 1977 as a teacher at the Department of Pediatrics of the University of Mississippi Medical Center. In 1978, she served on the Center for Disease Control's Advisory Committee for Immunization Practices; in 1985, she joined the faculty of the University of Washington School of Medicine and she became medical director of the Odessa Brown Children's Clinic which serves a predominantly low-income population in central Seattle. She was also appointed to the Physician's Task Force on Hunger in America alongside many prominent physicians, health experts, academic, and religious leaders. Since 1988, she has served in the Washington State Department of Health and was appointed state health officer.

Joanne Hayes-White

GOVERNMENT OFFICIAL. Joanne Hayes-White received a bachelor's degree in business from the University of Santa Clara. In 1990, she began her career as a firefighter with the San Francisco Fire Department. Prior to 1988 women were not allowed to join the fire department. She was promoted to lieutenant in 1993 and to captain in 1996. After her promotion to captain, she served as a battalion chief with oversight of the department's dispatch and communication systems. She later unified dispatch communication in 1998 under the Emergency Communication Department which brought Fire, EMS and Police dispatch communications under one roof. She was promoted to assistant chief in 1998 and assigned as director of training.

In January 2004, she was appointed fire chief for the City of San Francisco Fire Department. She became the first female to serve as fire chief of the 1,500 member department in San Francisco history.

Karen Haynes

EDUCATION. Karen Haynes received a Bachelor of Arts from Goucher College and a master's of social work from McGill University in Montreal, Canada. She earned a Ph.D. from the University of Texas.

Dr. Haynes has served ten

years as dean and professor of the Graduate School of Social Work at the main campus of the University of Houston. She served nine years as president of the University of Houston at Victoria. In 2004, she was named president of Cal State San Marcos in North County San Diego.

JoAnn W. Haysbert

EDUCATION. JoAnn W. Haysbert is a native of Kingstree, South Carolina. She received a bachelor's degree in psychology from Johnson C. Smith University. She earned a master's and doctorate in administration and supervision in higher education from Auburn University. She also studied at California State University in San Jose and Harvard University's Graduate School of Education.

Dr. Haysbert has served more than thirty years as an academician and higher education administrator. She served for 25 years at Hampton University in Hampton, Virginia. While there, she served in several key positions, including acting president, provost, assistant provost, professor and coordinator of graduate programs in education, dean of freshman studies, assistant vice president for academic affairs, director of summer sessions, and director of the assessment and learning support center. She came to Hampton after serving at Virginia State University, Auburn University and Alexander City State Junior College.

Dr. Haysbert was appointed fifteenth president of Langston University in August 2005 by the Board of Regents for Oklahoma State University and the A&M Colleges. This appointment distinguishes her as the first African-American female president of an institution of higher education in the state of Oklahoma.

Jessica Heacock

MEDIA EXECUTIVE. Jessica Heacock holds a Bachelor of Arts degree in political science and a master of business administration.

Her professional career includes serving with U.S. West, Inc., where she worked primarily in the wireless division; as director in marketing at Cox Communications Corporate in Atlanta, Georgia; as vice president, programming and marketing with Newscorporations/ASkyB which merged briefly with Exhostar; and as vice president, affiliate marketing at VH1 in 1997. In October 2001 she was appointed group vice president, consumer and affiliate marketing at VH1.

Ms. Heacock serves as senior vice president, MTV Networks Affiliate Marketing.

Wanda Keyes Heard

JUDGE. Wanda Keyes Heard is a native of Long Branch, New Jersey. She received a Bachelor of Arts from the University of Maryland, Baltimore County, in 1979 and earned her Juris Doctor degree from the University of Maryland School of Law in 1982.

Her professional career includes serving as an assistant state's attorney, Baltimore City, 1983–1985; as division chief, sex offense unit, Office of State's Attorney, Baltimore City, 1988–1990; as assistant attorney general, 1986–1987; as an assistant federal public defender, 1987–1988; as an assistant United States attorney, St. Croix Division, U.S. Virgin Islands, 1991–1994; as the chief of the criminal division, 1994; as executive assistant U.S. attorney, 1994–1997; and as special assistant to director in the office of the U.S. Attorney, Middle District of Florida, 1997–1998. On February 3, 1999, she was appointed judge, Baltimore City Circuit Court, Maryland's 8th Judicial Circuit in Baltimore.

Kaye G. Hearn

JUDGE. Kaye G. Hearn received her Bachelor of Arts degree (magna cum laude) from Bethany College in 1972 and her Juris Doctor degree (cum laude) from the University of South Carolina School of Law in 1977. She received an L.L.M. degree from the University of Virginia's Graduate Program for Judges in May 1998.

Her experience includes serving as a law clerk to the Honorable J.B. Ness, Associate Justice of the South Carolina Supreme Court from 1977 to 1979. She served as a bar examiner from 1984 until 1986. From 1986 until her election to the Court of Appeals, she served as family court judge for the 15th Judicial District comprising of Horry and Georgetown Counties. She was the chief administrative judge in the 15th Circuit from 1987 until her election to the Court of Appeals.

On March 21, 1995, she was elected to the South Carolina Court of Appeals. On June 21, 1999, she was elected chief judge of the Carolina Court of Appeals.

Pamela G. Heffernan

JUDGE. Pamela G. Heffernan received a Bachelor of Arts degree in sociology in 1974 from St. Cloud State University in Minnesota. She received a master's of arts degree in sociology from Washington State University and earned her Juris Doctor degree from the University of Utah College of Law in 1981.

She served in private law practice until her appointment to the bench. In 1989, Governor Norman H. Bangerter appointed her judge in July 1996 to the Second Circuit Court in Utah.

Christie Hefner

MEDIA EXECUTIVE. Christie Hefner received a Bachelor of Arts degree in English and American literature summa cum laude from Brandeis University in 1974.

She is a director of the Magazine Publishers Association and the Business Committee for the arts and is on the Board of Governors of the Museum of Television & Radio Media Center. She is a member of the Chicago Council on Foreign Relations and the National Cable & Telecommunications Association's Diversity Committee.

Ms. Hefner serves as chairman and chief executive officer of Playboy Enterprises, overseeing policy, management and strategy in all areas of the New York Stock Exchange–traded international media and entertainment company.

Ellen M. Heller

JUDGE. Ellen M. Heller received a Bachelor of Science degree with honors from the Johns Hopkins University and earned her Juris Doctor degree cum laude from the University of Maryland School of Law.

Prior to her appointment to the bench, she served as an assistant attorney general of Maryland and was deputy chief of the Educational Affairs Division. She was an adjunct professor at the University of Maryland School of Law from 1984 to 1993.

Judge Heller was appointed as a judge of the Circuit Court for Baltimore City in December 1986. She became the judge in charge of the civil docket in 1993 and served in that position until she was appointed the circuit administrative judge overseeing the entire court in 1999. Although she retired in December 2003, she continues to sit part time as a trial judge.

Mary Jane Hellyar

BUSINESS EXECUTIVE. Mary Jane Hellyar received a Bachelor of Arts in chemistry and mathematics from the College of St. Catherine in St. Paul, Minnesota. She earned a Master of Science degree and Ph.D. degree in chemical engineering from Massachusetts Institute of Technology (MIT). She also received a master of business administration in the management of technology from the Sloan School at Massachusetts Institute of Technology.

She joined Eastman Kodak Company in 1982 as a research scientist in the Kodak Research Laboratories. In 1992, she was named director of the chemicals development division. Following a one-year program at the Sloan School, she joined consumer imaging in the strategic planning function in 1994. In 1995, she became director of the color product platform, responsible for development and commercialization of color negative films, papers and chemicals. In 1999 Ms. Hellyar was named general manager, consumer film business, consumer imaging and was elected a corporate vice president. Subsequently, her responsibilities were expanded and in 2003 she added responsibilities for professional films. In November 2004, Ms. Hellyar was named president, display and components croup. In January 2005, the board of directors elected her a senior vice president. She became president, film & photofinishing systems group while also continuing responsibility for Kodak's Display business. In January 2007 her business was renamed the Film Products Group. At the same time she assumed the added responsibility of president, entertainment imaging.

Linda S. Hemminger

MILITARY. Linda S. Hemminger is a native of Pierre, South Dakota. She received a bachelor's degree in nursing from Augustana College in Sioux Falls, South Dakota, and a masters degree in nursing from the University of Nebraska Medical Center, Omaha. She also received an associate of arts degree in health care administration, Des Moines Area Community College in Ankeny, Iowa.

Major General Hemminger entered the Air Force in October 1975 by direct commission. In June 1978, she made a direct transfer from active duty to the Air Force Reserve. She has served as unit commander, chief nurse, staff development officer, flight nurse, family practice nurse practitioner, intensive care nurse and obstetrical clinical nurse. Her most recent assignment was as mobilization assistant to the assistant surgeon general for nursing services and the assistant surgeon general for health care operations, Headquarters, Air Force, Office of the Surgeon General, Bolling Air Force Base in Washington, D.C. She serves as deputy joint staff surgeon and director, Joint Reserve Medical Readiness Operations and Affairs, the Joint Staff, Logistics Directorate, J4, Health Service Support Division at the Pentagon in Washington, D.C. She was promoted to Major General on February 16, 2006.

Mary Jane Henderson

JUDGE. Mary Jane Henderson earned an undergraduate degree from the University of Alabama and earned her Juris Doctor degree from Samford University. Her professional career includes serving in private law practice.

In 1990, she was elected judge, Division 78, Volusia County Court, New Smyrna Beach, Florida.

Naomi Henderson

BUSINESS EXECUTIVE. Naomi Henderson is a native of California. She received her undergraduate degree (magna cum laude) in broadcast journalism from San Francisco State University. She serves as the chief executive officer for Big River Coffee Company in California. She is a second-generation member of the corporation and started in production while in junior high school; she literally learned the business from the bottom up.

Sylvia Sieve Hendon

JUDGE. Sylvia Sieve Hendon earned her Juris Doctor degree from the Salmon P. Chase College of Law in June 1975. After three years of private practice she was appointed as referee in the Hamilton County Juvenile Court serving from 1979 to 1983, the last year she served as chief referee. She was elected to the Hamilton County Municipal Court bench in November 1983 where she served for ten years, serving her last two years as administrative and presiding judge.

In January 1993, she was appointed to the Juvenile Court bench serving as presiding judge from 1998 to November 2004. She was elected to the Ohio's First District Court of Appeal in November 2004.

Jane E. Henney

GOVERNMENT OFFICIAL. Jane E. Henney received a bachelor's degree from Manchester College and earned her medical doctor degree from Indiana University School of Medicine. She completed her medical internship at St. Vincent's Hospital and her residency at Georgia Baptist Hospital. She was a fellow in Medical Oncology at M.D. Anderson Hospital and Tumor Institute and completed graduate medical work at the Cancer Therapy Evaluation Program at National Cancer Institute (NCI). She has also completed management training at the John F. Kennedy School of Government at Harvard University.

Her professional career includes holding various positions at the National Cancer Institute (NCI) of the National Institutes of Health. From 1980 to 1985, she served as deputy director of the National Cancer Institute. From 1985 to 1992, she served as acting director of the University of Kansas Mid America Cancer Center. From 1992 to 1994, she served as the deputy commissioner for operations Food and Drug Administration (FDA). From 1994 to 1998, she served as the first vice president of the University of New Mexico Health Sciences.

Dr. Henney was appointed commissioner of the Food and Drug Administration (FDA) in November 1998.

Kim Henry

FIRST LADY (STATE). Kim Henry is married to Oklahoma's Governor Brad Henry. She received a Bachelor of Science degree in secondary education from the University of Oklahoma in 1986. She spent most of her teaching career at her alma mater, Shawnee High School, where she taught Oklahoma history, economics, government and American history. Oklahoma's First Lady Kim Henry has devoted much of her life to education from her 10 years teaching in the classroom to raising three children.

Larissa Herda

BUSINESS EXECUTIVE. Larissa Herda received a bachelor's degree from the University of Colorado. She was selected to serve with Time Warner Telecom Inc. as senior vice president of sales and marketing on March 1, 1997.

Ms. Herda took the helm of Time Warner Telecom Inc., as president and chief executive officer on June 22, 1998. She was elected chairman of the Time Warner Telecom Inc. Board of Directors effective June 7, 2001, and currently holds the titles of chairman, president and chief executive officer.

Alexis M. Herman

GOVERNMENT OFFICIAL. Alexis M. Herman is a native of Mobile, Alabama. She received a Bachelor of Arts degree from Xavier University in New Orleans.

Ms. Herman has served as the national director of the Minority Women Employment Program. In 1977, President Jimmy Carter appointed her director of the Women's Bureau of the United States Department of Labor where she served until 1981. She was the founder and president of A.M. Herman & Associates in Washington, D.C. In 1988, she served as a member of the executive committee and as deputy convention manager. In 1991, she was appointed deputy chair of the Democratic National Committee as well as chief executive officer of the Democratic National Convention. On May 1, 1997, Ms. Herman was sworn in as America's 23rd Secretary of the United States Department of Labor, the first black American ever to serve in that position. She serves as chair and chief executive officer of New Ventures, Inc.

Mindy Herman

MEDIA EXECUTIVE. Mindy Herman received a Bachelor of Science in economics from the University of Pennsylvania's Wharton School. She earned a Juris Doctor degree and a Master of Business Administra-

tion in finance from the University of California of Los Angeles.

Her professional career includes serving in 1993 as senior vice president, business affairs, at FX Networks. She played a key role in the launch of Fox's first cable network and as president and chief executive officer of Demand LLC (formerly Viewer's Choice).

Ms. Herman serves as president and chief executive officer of E! Networks, the world's largest producer and distributor of entertainment news and lifestyle related programming.

Carol Herrera

ELECTED OFFICIAL (FIRST). Carol Herrera is a native of Albuquerque, New Mexico. She received an associate's degree from Mount San Antonio Community College. In November 1995, she was elected to the Diamond Bar City Council. After serving her first term as mayor pro-tem in 1997, the city council selected her to serve as mayor in 1998. She was the first Latina mayor in the city's history. In November 1999, she was elected to a second council term. She was elected to serve a second term as mayor for 2003 and subsequently a second term as mayor pro-tem in 2004.

Mary Herrera

ELECTED OFFICIAL. Mary Herrera is a native of Albuquerque, New Mexico. She received a Bachelor of Arts degree and a Master of Arts degree in business administration from the College of Santa Fe, a certificate in program administration for senior executives from the John F. Kennedy School of Government at Harvard University, and certificates in labor, employment and benefits law from the Institute for Applied Management.

Her professional career includes serving as assistant comptroller of Bernalillo County government in 1989. From 1996 to 2000, she served as director of human resources, Bernalillo County, then she was elected county clerk for Bernalillo County and took office in January 2001.

Ms. Herrera was elected Secretary of State for the State of New Mexico in November 2006 with 54 percent of the vote.

Stephanie Herseth

ELECTED OFFICIAL. Stephanie Herseth is a native of Houghton, South Dakota, and a graduate of Groton High School in Groton, South Dakota. She received a Bachelor of Arts degree from Georgetown University in Washington, D.C., in 1993 and earned her Juris Doctor from Georgetown University Law School in Washington, D.C., in 1997.

She was engaged in private law practice, and was an unsuccessful candidate for election to the 108th Congress in 2002.

Ms. Herseth was then elected as a Democrat to that Congress by special election to fill a vacancy caused by the resignation of United States Representative William Janklow. She was reelected to the succeeding Congress (June 1, 2005, to present).

Deborah A. P. Hersman

GOVERNMENT OFFICIAL. Deborah A. P. Hersman received Bachelor of Arts degrees in political science and international studies from Virginia Tech in Blacksburg, Virginia, in 1992 and a Master of Science degree in conflict analysis and resolution from George Mason University in Fairfax, Virginia, in 1999.

Her professional career includes serving as staff director and senior legislative aide to Congressman Bob Wise of West Virginia from 1992 to 1999; from 1999 to 2004, she served as a senior professional staff member of the U.S. Senate Committee on Commerce, Science and Transportation.

Ms. Hersman was sworn in as the 35th member of the National Transportation Safety Board on June 21, 2004.

Juanita Hicks

ELECTED OFFICIAL. Juanita Hicks is a graduate of Spencer High School in Columbus, Georgia. She attended Bennett College in Greensboro, North Carolina, and earned a Master of Science degree in urban administration from Georgia State University.

Her professional career includes serving from 1973 to 1976 as a program analyst and as an insurance manager

in 1976 coordinating property and casualty insurance programs for Fulton County. In 1980 she left the finance department to become the chief of the Delinquent Tax Office. She was elected clerk of Fulton County Superior Court in Atlanta, Georgia, on August 9, 1988, and took office on January 1, 1989.

Eve J. Higginbotham

EDUCATION. Eve J. Higginbotham received a Bachelor of Science degree and a Master of Science degree in chemical engineering, both from the Massachusetts Institute of Technology (MIT). She earned her medical degree from Harvard Medical School and completed her fellowship training in the subspecialty of glaucoma at the Massachusetts Eye and Ear Infirmary in Boston. She is a board-certified ophthalmologist.

Her professional career includes serving from 1985 to 1990 on the faculty at the University of Maryland; as chief of the Glaucoma Clinic at the University of Illinois; from 1990 to 1994, and as an associate professor with tenure at the University of Michigan where she also served as assistant dean for faculty affairs. She is the past president of the Maryland Society of Eye Physicians and Surgeons from 2000 to 2001 and recently completed her term as the 100th president of the Baltimore City Medical Society in 2004. She also served as the president of the Alumni Council of Harvard Medical School in 2004.

Dr. Higginbotham has served as dean and senior vice president for academic affairs at the Morehouse School of Medicine since April 24, 2006.

Joan E. Higginbotham

ASTRONAUT. Joan E. Higginbotham was born in Chicago, Illinois. She graduated from Whitney M. Young Magnet High School in Chicago, Illinois, in 1982, earned a Bachelor of Science degree in electrical engineering from Southern Illinois University at Carbondale in 1987, a masters of management from Florida Institute of Technology in 1992, and a masters in space systems from Florida Institute of Technology in 1996.

She began her career in 1987 at the Kennedy Space Center (KSC), Florida, as a payload electrical engineer in the Electrical and Telecommunications Systems Division. Within six months she became the lead for the Orbiter Experiments (OEX) on OV-102, the Space Shuttle *Columbia*. She later worked on the shuttle payload bay reconfiguration for all shuttle missions and conducted electrical compatibility tests for all payloads flown aboard the shuttle. She was also tasked by KSC management to undertake several special assignments where she served as the executive staff assistant to the director of shuttle flow in support of a simulation model tool and worked on an interactive display detailing the space shuttle processing procedures at Spaceport USA (Kennedy Space Center's Visitors Center). She then served as backup orbiter project engineer for OV-104, Space Shuttle *Atlantis* where she participated in the integration of the orbiter docking station (ODS) into the space shuttle used during Shuttle/Mir docking missions. Two years later, she was promoted to lead orbiter project engineer for OV-102, Space Shuttle *Columbia*. In this position, she held the technical lead government engineering position in the firing room where she supported and managed launches during her 9-year tenure at Kennedy Space Center.

She was selected as an astronaut candidate by NASA in April 1996 and reported to the Johnson Space Center in August 1996. Since that time, she had been assigned technical duties in the payloads and habitability branch, the Shuttle Avionics & Integration Laboratory (SAIL) and the Kennedy Space Center (KSC) Operations (Ops) Support Branch where she tested various modules of the International Space Station for operability, compatibility, and functionality prior to launch. She has also worked in the Astronaut Office CAPCOM (Capsule Communicator) Branch in support of numerous space station and space shuttle missions. In January 2005, she was assigned to the Robotics Branch and was the lead for the International Space Station Systems Crew Interface Section. She was assigned to crew of STS-117.

Kathryn O'Leary Higgins

GOVERNMENT OFFICIAL. Kathryn O'Leary Higgins received a Bachelor of Science degree from the University of Nebraska.

She began her career in 1969 as a manpower specialist with the Employment and Training Administration at the U.S. Department of Labor. From January 1981 to January 1986, she served as the senior legislative associate and minority staff director with the U.S. Senate Labor and Human Resources Committee. In January

1986, she was selected to serve as chief of staff to Congressman Sander Levin. In January 1993, she was named chief of staff to the Secretary of Labor. In February 1995 she moved to the White House to serve as assistant to the President and secretary to the Cabinet. From July 1997 to May 1999, she served as deputy secretary of the U.S. Department of Labor. In May 1999, she was employed as president and chief executive officer of TATC Consulting and was vice president for public policy at the National Trust for Historic Preservation. On January 3, 2006, Ms. Higgins was sworn in as the 36th member of the National Transportation Safety Board.

Chris A. Hill

BUSINESS EXECUTIVE. Chris A. Hill received a Bachelor of Arts (summa cum laude) from the Ohio State University in 1983 and earned a Juris Doctor (with honors) from the Ohio State University College of Law. She also completed the Nextel Strategic Business Leadership Certificate Program at the Georgetown University McDonough School of Business in 2004.

Her professional career includes serving in private law practice and as counsel for Honda of America Manufacturing, Inc. She currently serves as vice president, corporate governance and ethics, and corporate secretary at Sprint Nextel Corporation.

Valarie A. Hill

JUDGE. Valarie A. Hill received her undergraduate degree from the Ohio State University and earned her Juris Doctor degree from the University of Akron School of Law where she received the Black Law Student Association Highest GPA Award.

Her professional career includes serving as a deputy first assistant, senior assistant and assistant state public defender in the Milwaukee Trial Office where she was a member of the management team. From 1998 until her election to the bench, she served as a Milwaukee County judicial court commissioner. She was elected judge in April 2004 to Branch 1 of the Milwaukee Municipal Court

Priscilla Hill-Ardoin

COMMUNICATIONS. Priscilla Hill-Ardoin is a native of Houston, Texas. She received a Bachelor of Arts degree in theatre art from Drury College and Master's of Business Administration from Washington University. She also earned a Juris Doctor degree from St. Louis University. She holds an honorary doctorate of law from Harris-Stowe State College.

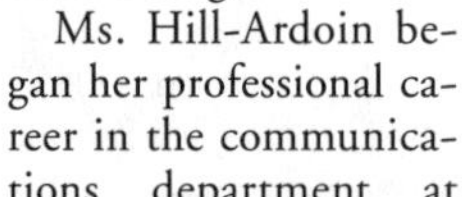

Ms. Hill-Ardoin began her professional career in the communications department at Prairie View A&M University, in Prairie View, Texas. She joined Missouri's Southwestern Bell Company Communications Inc. (SBC) and represented the company in an executive exchange program where she served on the International Operations Subcommittee of the Foreign Affairs Committee of the U.S. House of Representatives handling international telecommunications issues. In October 1997, she was named president of Missouri's Southwestern Bell.

Ruth H. Hilliard

JUDGE. Ruth H. Hilliard received her undergraduate degree from Connecticut College for Women in 1971 and earned her Juris Doctor degree from Case Western Reserve University in Cleveland, Ohio, in 1977.

Her professional career includes serving in private law practice until she was appointed a commissioner to the Arizona Superior Court in Maricopa County in 1985. She has served as judge, Arizona Superior Court in Maricopa County in Phoenix, Arizona.

Leticia Hinojosa

JUDGE. Leticia Hinojosa received a bachelor's degree (magna cum laude) from the University of Texas and earned her Juris Doctor degree from the University of Texas Law School.

Her professional career includes serving in private

law practice. In 1999, Governor Ann Richards appointed her judge to the 139 District Court in the state of Texas. She becomes the first woman to serve as judge in her county. In 2006, she was serving as the presiding judge at the 139th District Court.

Kathryn P. Hire

ASTRONAUT. Kathryn P. Hire is a native of Mobile, Alabama, and a graduate of Murphy High School in Mobile, Alabama, in 1977. She received a Bachelor of Science degree in engineering resources management from the United States Naval Academy in 1981 and earned a Master of Science degree in space technology from Florida Institute of Technology in 1991.

She was commissioned as a Naval officer in May 1981; she earned her Naval Flight Officer Wings in October 1982. For three years she conducted worldwide oceanographic research aboard specially configured P-3 Orion aircraft while serving with Oceanographic Development Squadron Eight (VXN-8), based at Naval Air Station Patuxent River in Maryland. She served as an instructor for student naval flight officers at the Naval Air Training Unit at Mather Air Force Base in California. In 1989, she joined the Naval Reserve at Jacksonville, Florida.

Captain Hire began work at the Kennedy Space Center in May 1989, first as an Orbiter Processing Facility 3 activation engineer and later as a space shuttle orbiter mechanical systems engineer for Lockheed Space Operations Company. In 1991, she certified as a Space Shuttle Test Project Engineer (TPE) and headed the checkout of the Extravehicular Mobility Units (spacesuits) and Russian Orbiter Docking System. In 1994, she was assigned supervisor of space shuttle orbiter mechanisms and launch pad swing arms. She was selected by the National Aeronautics and Space Administration (NASA) for astronaut training in December 1994. She reported to the Johnson Space Center in March 1995. After a year of training, she worked in mission control as a spacecraft communicator. Captain Hire flew as Mission Specialist-2 on STS-90 Neurolab from April 17 — May 3, 1998, and logged over 381 hours in space during the 16-day Spacelab flight. She served as the astronaut office lead for Shuttle Avionics Integration Laboratory, Shuttle Payloads and Flight Crew Equipment. Hire is assigned to the Astronaut Office Shuttle Branch and serves on the Astronaut Support Personnel team traveling to Florida in support of operations conducted at the Kennedy Space Center.

Sharon Latchaw Hirsh

EDUCATION. Sharon Latchaw Hirsh is a native of Mt. Lebanon, Pennsylvania, a suburb of Pittsburgh. She received a Bachelor of Arts in history of art and studio art from Rosemont College in 1966. She earned a master's degree in history of art in 1971 and a doctoral degree in 1974, both from the University of Pittsburgh.

Her professional career includes serving as a member of the faculty of Dickinson College; as a visiting curator at the Montreal Museum of Fine Arts and at the Schweizerisch Institute fur Kunstwissenschaft in Zurich; in 1998, she was visiting senior fellow at the Center for Advanced Studies in the Visual Arts; she was a visiting scholar at the Art Institute of Chicago.

Dr. Hirsh was appointed as the acting president of Rosemont College on December 12, 2005. On March 4, 2006, she was appointed the thirteenth president of Rosemont Community College. Her inauguration was held on September 30, 2006.

Jeanne D. Hitchcock

ELECTED OFFICIAL. Jeanne D. Hitchcock is a graduate of Morgan State University. She received her Juris Doctor degree from the University of Maryland School of Law in 1977. Upon graduation, she received the Regional Heber Smith Fellowship three-year assignment to the Legal Aid Bureau of Maryland as a litigator. She has served as an assistant professor of law at the University of Maryland Law School and associate professor of business law for both the graduate and undergraduate schools of Morgan State.

Her legal career includes serving in private law practice. From 1980 to 1988, she served as assistant attorney general for the State of Maryland as defense counsel in the civil litigation department; in 1989, she served as director of urban market development for 7-Eleven in Dallas, Texas; she joined the NAACP in 1996 as an executive-on-loan from the Southland Corporation, owner and operator of 7-Eleven stores worldwide. She serves as deputy mayor for the City of Baltimore, Maryland. As deputy mayor, she is Baltimore City's chief lobbyist in the Maryland State Legislature and in the United States Congress.

M. Jean Hoag

JUDGE. M. Jean Hoag received a bachelor's degree in secondary education from Minnesota State University in 1969 and earned her Juris Doctor degree (cum laude) from William Mitchell College of Law in 1982.

Her professional career includes serving as an assistant county attorney for Hennepin County Attorney's office in Minnesota; as an assistant attorney general, Arizona Attorney General's office; as a deputy county attorney, Maricopa County Attorney's office. Since 1996, she has served as a judge, Superior Court of Arizona for Maricopa County.

Mellody Hobson

MEDIA EXECUTIVE. Mellody Hobson is a native of Chicago, Illinois. She graduated from St. Ignatius College Preparatory in 1987 and received a Bachelor of Arts degree from Princeton University, Woodrow Wilson School of International Relations and Public Policy.

During college, Ms. Hobson interned at Ariel Capital Management as well as the investment firm, T. Rowe Price Associates. Upon graduation, she accepted a position with Ariel overseeing client service and taking part in strategic planning. By 2000, she had worked her way up to president of Ariel Capital Management, LLC, one of the largest black-owned money management and mutual fund companies in the country which today has more than $16 billion in assets under her management. In the fall of 2006, Ms. Hobson was elected chairman of the Ariel Mutual Funds Board of Trustees.

She has become a nationally recognized voice on financial literacy and investor education. She has been educating viewers on important financial decisions as ABC's *Good Morning America*'s financial contributor since 2000. She is also a spokesperson for the annual Ariel/Schwab Black Investor Survey.

Susan Hockfield

EDUCATION (FIRST). Susan Hockfield received a Bachelor of Arts in biology from the University of Rochester and a Ph.D. from the Georgetown University School of Medicine while carrying out her dissertation research in neuroscience at the National Institute of Health (NIH). She was a National Institute of Health postdoctoral fellow at the University of California at San Francisco in 1979–1980.

She joined the scientific staff at the Cold Spring Harbor Laboratory in New York. From 1985 to 2004 she was on the faculty of Yale University where she also served as a professor and as the dean of the Graduate School of Arts and Sciences and then as provost. In December 2004, she was named the 16th president of Massachusetts Institute of Technology (MIT). She is the first female to serve as MIT's president in its history.

Adele E. Hodges

MILITARY. Adele E. Hodges received a bachelor's degree from Southern Connecticut State College in June of 1977 and enlisted into the United States Marine Corps in June of 1978.

In February 1979, she transferred to the 1st Force Service Support Group and in December 1979, while assigned to 1st Medical Battalion, 1st Force Service Support Group, she was accepted into the Enlisted Commissioning Program and was commissioned in December 1980 following her graduation from Officer Candidate School in Quantico, Virginia. She completed the Command and General Staff College in June 1997. In July 2002 she attended the United States Naval War College.

Colonel Hodges has held numerous assignments of increasing authority to include serving as the commander of the 1st Maintenance Battalion and as the executive officer for the Brigade Service Support Group One during their preparations and deployment for Operation Natural Fire 2000 in Kenya. She served as chief of staff G-4 at the Joint Headquarters North transformed into the NATO Joint Warfare Center in Stavanger, Norway. During the summer of 2005 she was selected to command Marine Corps Base Camp Lejeune and she transferred to Camp Lejeune in December 2005.

On January 23, 2006, she became the first female colonel to command Marine Corps Base Camp Lejeune, replacing Major General Robert. C. Dickerson.

She is the highest ranking black female in the Marine Corps.

Beverly Wade Hogan

EDUCATION. Beverly Wade Hogan received a Bachelor of Art degree in psychology from Tougaloo College and a master's degree in public policy and administration from Jackson State University. She earned her doctorate degree in organizational management and leadership from Fielding Graduate Institute.

Her professional career includes serving for 10 years as the commissioner for the Mississippi Workers Compensation Commission; four years as the executive director of the Governor's Office of Federal State Programs; nine years as the executive director of the Mental Health Association in Hinds County and the State of Mississippi, respectively. She is the founding director of the Owens Health and Wellness Center and executive assistant to the president; she served as vice president for institutional advancement at Tougaloo College; she served as interim president of Tougaloo College.

Dr. Hogan serves as president of Tougaloo College in Tougaloo, Mississippi.

Karen A. Holbrook

EDUCATION. Karen A. Holbrook received a Bachelor of Science degree and a Master of Science degree in zoology from the University of Wisconsin–Madison. She earned a Ph.D. in biological structure from the University of Washington School of Medicine in 1972 and then pursued further training in dermatology.

Her professional career includes serving as a biology teacher at Ripon College; as a professor of biological structure and medicine at the University of Washington School of Medicine; as vice president for research and dean of the graduate school at the University of Florida; as Senior vice president for academic affairs and provost at the University of Georgia.

Dr. Holbrook was appointed the 13th president of the Ohio State University and she took office on October 1, 2002.

Evelyn Hollis

MILITARY. Evelyn Hollis enlisted in the Army on July 16, 1979. She attended Basic Combat Training at Fort Leonard Wood, Missouri, and Advanced Individual Training at Fort Jackson, South Carolina. Her military and civilian education includes all the Noncommissioned Officers Leadership Courses, the Air Defense Artillery Intelligence Assistant Operator Course, the Army Recruiting Course, the First Sergeant Course, and the Sergeants Major Academy. She holds a Master of Arts degree in human resources development and management.

Command Sergeant Major Hollis' assignments include serving as the S-3 Sergeant Major, 108th Air Defense Artillery Brigade. In April 2004, she became the first female command sergeant major of a combat arms unit when she assumed command of the 1st Battalion, 1st Air Defense Artillery Command. The change of command ceremony was held at the Fort Bliss Air Defense Artillery Museum on April 26, 2004.

Cathy M. Holt

JUDGE. Cathy M. Holt received a Bachelor of Arts degree with highest distinction from the University of Arizona in 1982 and earned her Juris Doctor degree (Order of the Coif) from the University of Arizona in 1985.

From 1986 to 1999, she was engaged in private law practice; since 1999 she has served as judge for the Superior Court of Arizona in Maricopa County.

Karen E. Holt

GOVERNMENT OFFICIAL. Karen E. Holt received a Bachelor of Science degree in zoology from the University of Illinois (Urbana-Champaign). She earned a Juris Doctor degree cum laude from the Brandeis School of Law at the University of Louisville and a Ph.D. in political science from the University of Tennessee.

Her professional career includes serving with the

United States Department of Justice in Washington, D.C., where she worked in both the civil and civil rights division. She then went on to work in the general counsel's office of the University of Tennessee, where she also taught American government and administrative law in the Department of Political Science. She served as a professor at the University of Virginia where she taught a course on higher education and the law at the Curry School of Education. She also directed the Office of Equal Opportunity Programs at the University of Virginia. On August 15, 2003, Dr. Holt joined Project Pericles as its first executive director.

Anne Holton

FIRST LADY (STATE). Anne Holton is a native of Roanoke, Virginia. She received a bachelor degree from Princeton University's Woodrow Wilson School of Public and International Affairs in 1980 and earned a Juris Doctor degree from Harvard Law School in 1983 where she met her husband Governor Tim Kaine.

Her professional career includes serving as law clerk to the Honorable Robert R. Merhige Jr. in the United States District Court in Richmond from 1984 to 1985; in 1985, she joined the Central Virginia Legal Aid Society as an attorney in the city of Richmond, Virginia; she served as a substitute judge for the district courts in Richmond and in 1998, she was appointed to a judgeship in the Juvenile and Domestic Relations District Court for the City of Richmond.

The First Lady resigned her judgeship following Kaine's election to focus on their three children and her duties as First Lady of Virginia. Her father, Linwood Holton, served as Virginia's governor from 1970 to 1974 while she was a teenager.

Judith A. Holtz

JUDGE. Judith A. Holtz received a Bachelor of Arts degree from the University of Michigan in 1966 and earned her Juris Doctor degree from Wayne State University Law School in 1969. Her professional career includes serving in private law practice from 1970 to 1988. In 1992, she became a magistrate of the Michigan 52nd District Court, 1st Division.

Lucy Hood

ENTERTAINMENT EXECUTIVE. Lucy Hood is a graduate of Columbia University's Graduate School of Business and Yale University. Her professional career includes overseeing a number of new media industry firsts, including the successful ATTWS–Fox partnership for *American Idol* that introduced text messaging widely in the United States. Winning a listing in the Guinness Book of World Records, the program generated over 40 million SMS messages.

Ms. Hood and her team invented the program format of video "mobisodes," short-form 3G mobile content which rolled out on wireless carriers worldwide in 2005. She was named president, Fox Mobile Entertainment and senior vice president, content and marketing, for News Corporation, one of the world's largest media companies. She oversees wireless strategy, content and marketing for Fox Entertainment worldwide, structuring partnerships with Vodafone, Cingular, Sprint, T-Mobile, Verizon and Nokia. Ms. Hood guides Fox's creative, digital and marketing councils and has built international alliances for divisions including 20th Century–Fox Film and Fox Television.

Ingrid Van Den Hoogen

TECHNOLOGY EXECUTIVE. Ingrid Van Den Hoogen received a Bachelor of Arts degree in mathematics and computer from San Jose State University. Her professional career includes serving as director of strategic marketing for Java business development; as director of marketing and business development for Project Juxtapose; as vice president, Java technology and software

strategic marketing, leading strategic software marketing, messaging and competitive analysis as well as Java technology brand marketing and programs. She serves as vice president, brand experience and community marketing, Sun Microsystems, Inc.

Tamara T. Hooks

BUSINESS EXECUTIVE. Tamara T. Hooks is a native of Atlanta, Georgia, and a former resident of Inglewood, California. She is a graduate of Westchester High School and attended Howard University in Washington, D.C., where she majored in business. After receiving an MBA in management from Howard University, she spent four years of her career in sales and merchandising with Nike, Inc., while based in Los Angeles and Dallas. At Nike, she earned the coveted Merchandiser of the Year award for outstanding performance. A transition from fashion to beauty led her to an assistant product manager position at Mary Kay, Inc. During her four years with the cosmetics giant, she developed some of the company's best-selling products. Her contributions in idea generation and product development were integral in the success of yearly product launches and marketing promotions. She then utilized her skills as brand manager for the highly successful California Tan Sunless, Los Angeles.

Ms. Hooks relocated to St. Petersburg, Florida, where she is one of the newest hosts of America's Store (AS), an affiliate station of the Home Shopping Network (HSN). She also hosts NFL Gear on the Home Shopping Network.

Darlene Hooley

ELECTED OFFICIAL. Darlene Hooley is a native of Williston, North Dakota, and grew up in Salem, Oregon. She received a Bachelor of Science degree in education from Oregon State University.

Her professional career includes serving as a former reading, music and physical education teacher. After serving on the Park District Board, she was elected to the West Linn city council where she served for four years. In 1980 she was elected to the Oregon state legislature and in 1987 she was elected as a Clackamas County commissioner. Ms. Hooley was elected a United States representative from Oregon as a Democrat to the 105th and to the five succeeding Congresses (January 3, 1997, to present).

Michele J. Hooper

BUSINESS EXECUTIVE. Michele J. Hooper received a Bachelor of Science degree in economics from the University of Pennsylvania and earned a Master of Business Administration from the University of Chicago.

Her professional career includes serving as president and chief executive officer of Stadlander Drug Company, Inc. She served as president and chief executive officer of Voyager Expanded Learning. Ms. Hooper serves as the managing partner and founder of the Directors' Council in Chicago, Illinois, an organization that helps companies around the globe bring increased independence, effectiveness and diversity to corporate boards.

Vanessa Hopkins

JUDGE. Vanessa A. Hopkins received a Bachelor of Science in marketing from Chicago State University and received a Master of Business Administration from Roosevelt University in Chicago. She earned her Juris Doctor degree from Northern Illinois University College of Law in 1993.

Her professional career includes serving in private law practice from 1994 to 1996. In 1996, she was elected judge, Illinois Circuit Court of Cook County, civil jury division, in Chicago, Illinois.

Deborah Parham Hopson

MEDICINE. Deborah Parham Hopson received a Bachelor of Science degree in nursing from the University of Cincinnati. She earned a Master of Science degree in public health and a Doctor of Philosophy in

public health from the University of North Carolina at Chapel Hill.

Her professional career includes her clinical practice in neonatal intensive care nursing in Columbus, Ohio, and Washington, D.C. She has served in various positions in the federal Department of Health and Human Services and worked at the National Academy of Sciences, Institute of Medicine. She served as the director of the Division of Community Base Programs in the HIV/AIDS Bureau (HAB). Dr. Hopson served as acting associate administrator of HAB between January 2002 and her permanent appointment and had been the bureau's deputy associate administrator since November 2000. She was appointed associate administrator for HIV/AIDS in the United States Department of Health and Human Services' Health Resources and Services Administration (HRSA) on July 29, 2002.

Michele Hoskins

BUSINESS EXECUTIVE. Michele Hoskins received a bachelor's degree from Johnson & Wales University. She is the president and chief executive officer of Michele Foods. The company's products can currently be found in over 4,000 food stores nationwide. Some of the larger food companies that sell Michele brand syrup are Stop & Shop, Super Wal-Mart, Albertson's Kroger, Publix, Super Target, Cub Foods, H.E. Butt Grocery, Jewel Foods, and Dominick's Finer Foods. Michele Foods has branched out into relates products such as providing condiments for Church's Chicken.

Michele D. Hotten

JUDGE. Michele D. Hotten received a Bachelor of Arts degree from the University of South Florida in 1975 and earned her Juris Doctor from Howard University School of Law in 1979.

Her professional career includes serving as an assistant state's attorney (1985–1989), in private law practice (1989–1994), and as an associate judge for the District Court of Maryland, Prince George's County (1994–1995). In 1995, she was appointed an associate judge at the Prince George's County Circuit Court.

Michelle J. Howard

MILITARY. Michelle J. Howard is a graduate of Gateway High School in Aurora, Colorado, in 1978. She attended the United States Naval Academy, graduating in 1982. She was a distinguished graduate from Department Head School in September 1990. She graduated from the United States Army's Command and General Staff College in June 1998. She completed a masters in military arts and sciences with a focus in history.

Her key military assignments include serving onboard USS *Mount Hood* (AE 29) as chief engineer in 1990. She was deployed to the Persian Gulf for operations Desert Shield and Desert Storm. She assumed duties as first lieutenant onboard the USS *Flint* (AE 32) in July 1992. In December 1993, she rotated to the bureau of personnel as the Navy's liaison to the Defense Advisory Committee on Women in the Military Services. She was also the action officer for the assignment of women in the Navy policy. In January 1996, she became the executive officer of USS *Tortuga* (LSD 46). She was the first woman in the Navy to be assigned duties as XC of a combatant. During her tour, the ship deployed to the Adriatic Sea in support of Operation Joint Endeavor, a peacekeeping effort in the former Republic of Yugoslavia. Sixty days after returning from the Mediterranean deployment, *Tortuga* departed on a West African training cruise, where the ship's sailors, with embarked Marines and United States Coast Guard detachment, operated with the naval services of seven African nations.

When she assumed command of USS *Rushmore* (LSD 47) on 12 March 1999, she became the first African American woman to command a ship in the United States Navy. *Rushmore* is the Navy's only amphibious "smart ship." The smart ship concept integrates and evaluates commercial off-the-shelf technologies for future fleet application. In December 1999, *Rushmore* became the first smart ship to complete a six-month deployment. In November 2000, she was assigned to J-3, Global Operations and Readiness on the Joint Staff in the Pentagon. In February 2003, she became the executive assistant to the joint staff director of operations. In May 2004, she assumed duties as commander, Amphibious Squadron Seven.

Michelle Howard-Vital

EDUCATION. Michelle Howard-Vital is a native of Chicago, Illinois. She received a bachelor's degree in

English language and literature and a master's degree from the University of Chicago. She earned a doctorate in public policy analysis from the University of Illinois at Chicago.

Her professional career includes serving as associate vice president for academic programs and dean of the University College at Edinboro University in Pennsylvania; as dean of continuing education and nontraditional programs at Chicago State University; as vice chancellor for public service and continuing studies, associate provost and vice president for academic affairs at the University of North Carolina at Wilmington for nearly a decade.

Dr. Howard-Vital was appointed interim chancellor of Winston-Salem State University on July 17, 2006.

Caroline Hoxby

EDUCATION. Caroline Hoxby received a Bachelor of Arts degree in economics from Harvard University. She earned a master's degree from Oxford University and a doctorate degree from M.I.T.

Dr. Hoxby is a professor of economics at Harvard University and is one of the county's leading experts on the economics of public education. In recent years she has become the foremost expert in the country on the benefits to students of school choice and competition in education. She has testified before Congress, state legislatures and courts on school finance equalization, tax policy of education initiatives and charter school legislation. She is faculty research fellow with the National Bureau of Economic Research, and a senior advisor to the Brookings Institution.

Dawn Hudson

BUSINESS EXECUTIVE. Dawn Hudson received a Bachelor of Science degree in English and economics from Dartmouth College in Hanover, New Hampshire.

Her professional career includes serving as a partner at TLK in Chicago and a brand manager for Bristol Myers in the early 1980s. She first joined PepsiCo in 1996 as executive vice president of sales and marketing for Frito-Lay. In 1999, she launched Pepsi's popular "Joy of Cola" campaign and guided Pepsi into its largest summer promotion ever, a tie-in with "Star Wars, Episode I — The Phantom Menace." In June 2002, she was selected to serve as president of Pepsi-Cola North America.

Dianne Atkinson Hudson

ENTERTAINMENT EXECUTIVE. Dianne Atkinson Hudson received a Bachelor of Arts degree in broadcast journalism from Ohio University.

She began her career in 1976 as a broadcast news writer for the Associated Press. Since 1986, she has been affiliated with Harpo Studios in Chicago, Illinois, and has served as vice president of Harpo Productions and president of the Oprah Winfrey Foundation and Oprah's Angel Network. She conceptualized and implemented this viewer-driver public charity which has raised more than $12 million to date. For nine seasons, between 1994 and 2003, she was executive producer of the number-one-rated, award-winning *Oprah Winfrey Show,* preceded by ten seasons as producer. She has received nine Emmy Awards and is also credited with establishing Oprah's book club.

Natalie E. Hudson

JUDGE. Natalie E. Hudson graduated from Arizona State University in Tempe, Arizona, and received her Juris Doctor from the University of Minnesota Law School. She served as a staff attorney with Southern Minnesota Regional Legal Service, Inc., from 1982 to 1986, where she practiced housing law. She served in private law practice until 1988; as an assistant dean of student affairs at Hamline University School of Law from 1989 to 1992; and as a St. Paul city attorney from 1992 to 1994. She was employed with the Office of the Minnesota Attorney General from 1994 until her appointment to the Court of Appeal on May 2, 2002.

Sheryl Huggins

MEDIA EXECUTIVE. Sheryl Huggins received a Bachelor of Arts in history from University of Pennsylvania (1988) and earned her Master of Science in journalism from Columbia University's Graduate School of Journalism (1991) where she received the Cowan Award for excellence in the study of publishing.

Her professional career includes serving as president and publisher of Shade Communications in New York; as special projects manager in *Fortune* magazine's conference division; as senior vice president of interactive information services at Urban Box Office Network (1999–2000).

Since 2001, Ms. Huggins has served as the editor-in-chief of NiaOnline, director of information services for Nia Enterprises and an editor of *The Nia Guide For Black Women* series.

Catherine Liggins Hughes

MEDIA EXECUTIVE. Catherine Liggins Hughes is a native of Omaha, Nebraska. She attended Creighton University. While attending Creighton University she became involved with a troubled black radio station in Omaha both as a volunteer staffer and as a small investor. It was her first exposure to the inner workings of radio. She moved to Washington, D.C., in 1971 and became a lecturer in the newly established School of Communications at Howard University.

Her professional career includes serving in 1973 as general sales manager at WHUR-FM (Howard University Radio). In 1975, she became the first woman vice president and general manager of a station in the nation's capital and created the format known as the "Quiet Storm"— the most listened to nighttime format in urban radio heard on over 400 stations nationally. Ms. Hughes purchased her first station in 1980, WOL-AM in Washington, D.C. She is the founder and chairperson of Radio One, Inc., the largest African-American owned and operated broadcast-company in the nation. Radio One is the first African-American company in radio history to dominate several major markets simultaneously. In 1995, Radio One purchased WKYS in Washington, D.C., for $40 million, the largest transaction between two black companies in the history of America.

In May of 1999, Cathy Hughes and her son Alfred Liggins (president and CEO) took their company public. Ms. Hughes made history again by becoming the first African-American woman with a company on the stock exchange. Radio One's market cap is currently in excess of $2 billion. In 2000, *Black Enterprise* named Radio One "Company of the Year," *Fortune* rated it one of the "100 Best Companies to Work For" and Radio One was inducted into the Maryland Business Hall of Fame.

Karen P. Hughes

GOVERNMENT OFFICIAL. Karen P. Hughes received both a Bachelor of Arts degree (summa cum laude) in English, and a Bachelor of Fine Arts degree in journalism from Southern Methodist University.

Her professional career includes serving as the executive director of the Republican Party of Texas; as a television news reporter in Dallas/Fort Worth; as director of communications for Governor George W. Bush for six years in Texas and during his 2000 presidential campaign; as communications consultant for his 2004 reelection campaign. On June 29, 2005, she was nominated by President George W. Bush to serve as under secretary of state for public diplomacy and public affairs. She was confirmed by the United States Senate on July 29, 2005, and sworn in on September 9, 2005.

Marvalene Hughes

EDUCATION. Marvalene Hughes received a Bachelor of Science degree in English and history and a Master of Science degree in administrative counseling, both from Tuskegee University. She earned her doctorate degree in counseling and administration from Florida

State University. She has also studied at New York University, Columbia University, Harvard University and at Oxford University in England.

Her professional career includes serving as senior-level administrator and professor at San Diego State University; as associate vice president at Arizona State University; as vice president and professor at the University of Toledo; as vice president and professor at the University of Minnesota; and as president of California State University at Stanislaus for eleven years.

Dr. Hughes was appointed the ninth president of Dillard University in New Orleans on July 1, 2005. She is the first woman to lead Dillard University. Her leadership has been most profound as she guides the university through transformation towards new heights following the effects of the nation's most devastating natural and human disaster precipitated by Hurricane Katrina.

Teresa P. Hughes

ELECTED OFFICIAL. Teresa P. Hughes is a native of New York, New York. She received a Bachelor of Arts degree in physiology and public health from Hunter College. She earned her Master of Arts degree in education administration from New York University and a doctorate in education administration from Claremont Graduate School.

Her professional career includes serving as a member of the California Assembly, representing the 47th assembly district, which includes South Central Los Angeles, beginning in 1975. After serving 17 years in the California Assembly, she was elected to the California State Senate in 1992. She represented the 25th Senate district and was past chair of the Legislative Black Caucus. She was a delegate to the Democratic National Convention from California in 2000. She is the founder of Aware Women and she is on the Board of Directors for the local coalition of One Hundred Black Women. Ms. Hughes was appointed to the California Medical Assistance Commission for a four-year term which was effective January 1, 2001.

Lorraine T. Hunt

ELECTED OFFICIAL. Lorraine T. Hunt moved to Henderson, Nevada, in 1943 with her parents from Niagara Falls, New York. She graduated from Las Vegas High School. She began her musical studies at age of nine and attended Westlake College of Music in Los Angeles, California.

Her professional career began her musical career at 19 when she started performing in Las Vegas, Reno and Lake Tahoe. She was later elected to the Clark County Commission in Clark County, Nevada; in November 1998, she was elected lieutenant governor for the state of Nevada. She took office in January of 1999. As the lieutenant governor, she is president of the Nevada State Senate and serves as chair of the Nevada Commission on Economic Development and vice chairman of the Nevada Department of Transportation Board of Directors. She is the first woman to chair the Las Vegas Convention and Visitors Authority.

Ms. Hunt is also the owner of the Bootlegger Bistro, a nightclub long popular with Las Vegas locals and showroom performers. A singer, she performs at the restaurant.

Mattie Hunter

ELECTED OFFICIAL. Mattie Hunter is a native of Chicago, Illinois. She received a bachelor's degree in government from Monmouth College and earned her master's degree in sociology from Jackson State University. She is also a certified alcohol and drug counselor and prevention specialist.

Her professional career includes serving from 1982 to 2000 in numerous capacities with Human Resources Development Institute, Inc., and as the managing director of the Center for Health and Human Services located in Johannesburg, South Africa, from 1994 to 1996. She has participated, coordinated and presented lectures at numerous health and human services conferences in Zimbabwe, Nigeria, and Zambia. Those conferences include Human Resources Development Institute/South African Department of Health Workshop and the U.S. Department Alcohol and Drug Abuse Demand Reduction Workshop.

Ms. Hunter serves as a state senator for the 3rd district of the state of Illinois. She also serves as the director for the Chicago Housing Authority, Service Connector Program.

Iris J. Hurd

MILITARY. Iris J. Hurd is a native of Montgomery, Alabama. She holds a Bachelor of Science degree in microbiology from the University of Alabama and a Master of Science degree in public administration and health science from Golden Gate University in California.

She served as chief information operation officer and congressional relations analyst at the United States Army Forces Command, Fort McPherson, Georgia. On October 5, 2004, she assumed command of Army Reserve Officer Training Corps (ROTC) "Tiger" Battalion at Tuskegee University. She will serve as the commander/professor of military science at Tuskegee University, becoming the first female to serve in this position at Tuskegee.

Sandra Hutchens

GOVERNMENT OFFICIAL. Sandra Hutchens received a bachelor's degree in public administration from the University of La Verne in 1988. She is also a 1992 graduate of the FBI National Academy and has served as an instructor for the supervisory ethics course taught at the department's training bureau. She began her career in 1976 as a deputy sheriff after graduating from the training academy; worked at assignment, including Sybil Brand Institute, Lynwood Station and the Metropolitan Bureau; served as a watch commander and as the operations lieutenant; was promoted to captain in July 1999 and assumed command of Norwalk Station; was promoted to commander in February 2001 and was first assigned to Field Operations Region III and then as the sheriff's executive assistant; was promoted to division chief, Office of Homeland Security in April of 2003.

Susan F. Hutchinson

JUDGE. Susan F. Hutchinson received her Bachelor of Arts degree in political science from Quincy University in 1971 and her J.D. degree from DePaul University School of Law in 1977. She served as an assistant state's attorney in McHenry County from 1977 to 1981 and as a judge in the 19th Judicial Circuit from 1981 to 1994.

She was elected to the Second District Appellate Court in 1994 and was still serving as an appellate judge for the Second District for the State of Illinois.

Kathyrn Ann Bailey Hutchison

ELECTED OFFICIAL. Kathyrn Ann Bailey Hutchison is a native of Galveston, Texas, and attended the public schools in La Marque, Texas. She received a bachelor's degree from the University of Texas at Austin and earned her Juris Doctor degree from the University of Texas School of Law in 1967.

Her professional career includes serving as a television reporter; as a member of the Texas House of Representatives (1972–1976); as vice-chair of the National Transportation Safety Board (1976–1978); as a bank executive and general counsel; and in private business. She was elected Texas state treasurer (1990–1993) and served as temporary co-chair of the Republican National Convention in 1992. She was elected a United States senator on June 5, 1993, and took the oath of office on June 14, 1993. She was reelected in 1994 and again in 2000 for the term ending January 3, 2007.

Ellen Segal Huvelle

JUDGE. Ellen Segal Huvelle received a Bachelor of Arts degree from Wellesley College in 1970. She earned a Masters in city planning from Yale University in 1972 and a Juris Doctor from Boston College Law School in 1975.

Following law school, she served as law clerk to Chief Justice Edward F. Hennessey of the Massachusetts Supreme Judicial Court. From 1976 until 1984, she was in private law practice. She was appointed associate judge of the District of Columbia Superior Court in September 1990 and served in the civil, criminal and family divisions until her appointment to the federal bench.

She was appointed to the United States District Court in October 1999.

Gwen Ifill

JOURNALISM. Gwen Ifill is a native of New York City and received a bachelor's degree from Simmons College in Boston, Massachusetts. She has also received 15 honorary degrees.

She has served as a journalist for the *Boston Herald*, the *Baltimore Sun*, the *Washington Post*, and the *New York Times*. She joined NBC News from the *New York Times* where she covered the White House and politics. Ms. Ifill became moderator of the PBS program *Washington Week in Review* in October 1999 and is also senior correspondent for the *NewsHour with Jim Lehrer*. On October 5, 2004, she moderated the vice presidential debate between Dick Cheney and John Edwards.

Karin J. Immergut

GOVERNMENT OFFICIAL. Karin J. Immergut is a native of Brooklyn, New York. She received her undergraduate degree from Amherst College in 1982 and earned her Juris Doctor degree from Boalt Hall School of Law at the University of California, Berkeley.

Her professional career includes serving in private law practice, as a deputy district attorney in Portland, Oregon, and as an assistant United States attorney in Oregon. She was sworn in as interim United States attorney on October 3, 2003, and the United States Senate confirmed her nomination on that same date. President George W. Bush signed her commission to serve as the United States Attorney for the District of Oregon on October 4, 2003, and she was sworn in as the United States Attorney on October 8, 2003.

Pam H. Inman

BUSINESS EXECUTIVE. Pam H. Inman is a native of Tennessee. She received a bachelor's degree in journalism and communications and was a graduate of the Institute for Organizational Management at the University of Notre Dame.

She worked in Tennessee Governor Lamar Alexander's press office in 1979 and has worked with the state's tourism department as well as overseeing marketing and advertising for Tennessee's parks and resorts. She served as chief executive officer of the Tennessee Hotel & Lodging Association and the Greater Nashville Hotel & Lodging Association.

Ms. Inman serves as the executive vice president and chief operating officer for the American Hotel & Lodging Association.

Pam Iorio

ELECTED OFFICIAL. Pam Iorio attended Hillsborough County public schools and received a Bachelor of Science degree in political science from American University in Washington, D.C. She earned a master's degree in history from the University of South Florida in Tampa, Florida, in 2001.

At the age of 26, she was the youngest person ever elected to the Hillsborough County Commission and served from 1985 to 1992; her fellow commissioners elected her chairman. She was elected three times to the office of supervisor of elections for Hillsborough County (1993–2003). In 2000, she was elected president of the Florida State Association of Supervisors of Elections. On April 1, 2003, she was sworn into office as the mayor of the nation's 55th largest city, Tampa, Florida.

Joan K. Irion

JUDGE. Joan K. Irion received her undergraduate degree with high honors from the University of California at Davis in 1974. Two years later she earned her master's degree in the field of public administration with highest honors from San Diego State University. In 1979, she earned her Juris Doctor from the University of California at Davis.

After graduating from law school she entered private

law practice. She was appointed justice to the California Court of Appeals Fourth District, Division One, in September 2003.

Teresa Isaac

ELECTED OFFICIAL. Mayor Teresa Isaac is an honors graduate of Bryan Station High School and received a bachelor's degree (magna cum laude) from Transylvania University. She earned her Juris Doctor degree from the University of Kentucky Law School.

Her professional career includes serving as prosecutor in the Fayette County attorney's office and as associate professor in the Eastern Kentucky University Department of Government. In 1989, she was elected to the Urban County Council at-large seat where she served for nine years as vice mayor. She was elected mayor of Lexington, Kentucky.

Arlene Isaacs-Lowe

FINANCE. Arlene Isaacs-Lowe received a bachelor's degree of business administration in accounting from Howard University and earned a Master of Business Administration degree from Fordham University.

Ms. Isaacs-Lowe serves as vice president in Moody's Investors Service's Financial Institutions Group where she is the lead analyst responsible for overseeing the credit and financial strength analysis for a portfolio of mortgage insures, financial guarantors and asset managers.

Marsha S. Ivins

ASTRONAUT. Marsha S. Ivins is a native of Baltimore, Maryland. She is a graduate Nether Providence High School in Wallingford, Pennsylvania, in 1969. She received a Bachelor of Science degree in aerospace engineering from the University of Colorado in 1973.

She holds a multi-engine airline transport pilot license with a Gulfstream-1 type rating, single engine airplane, land, sea, and glider commercial licenses, and airplane, instrument, and glider flight instructor ratings. She has logged over 6,300 hours in civilian and NASA aircraft.

Her professional career includes serving at the Lyndon B. Johnson Space Center since July 1974 and until 1980 was assigned as an engineer working on orbiter displays and controls and man machine engineering. Her major assignment in 1978 was to participate in development of the Orbiter Head-Up Display (HUD). In 1980, she was assigned as a flight engineer on the Shuttle Training Aircraft (Aircraft Operations) and a co-pilot in the NASA administrative aircraft (Gulfstream-1). She was selected in the NASA Astronaut Class of 1984 as a mission specialist. She is a veteran of five space flights — STS-32 in 1990, STS-46 in 1992, STS-62 in 1994, STS-81 in 1997, and STS-98 in 2001— and has logged over 1,318 hours in space.

Ms. Ivins is currently assigned to the Astronaut Office, Space Station/Shuttle Branches for crew equipment, habitability and stowage and the Advance Projects Branch at the Johnson Space Center.

Pam B. Jackman-Brown

JUDGE. Pam B. Jackman-Brown received her undergraduate degree from John Jay College of Criminal Justice and earned her Juris Doctor degree from the City University of New York Law School at Queens College.

Her professional career includes serving as a mediator for Children's Aid Society; as a small claims arbitrator; as a trial attorney, the Legal Aid Society, criminal division; and as a law assistant. Since June 1998, she has served as judge for the New York City Civil Court, Housing Part.

Carol E. Jackson

JUDGE. Carol E. Jackson is a native of St. Louis, Missouri. She received a Bachelor of Arts degree from Wellesley College in 1973. She earned a Juris Doctor degree from the University of Michigan Law School in 1976.

Upon graduating from law school, she served in private law practice fro 1976 to 1986. She received an appointment as a United States magistrate judge and served in that capacity until her appointment to the district court in 1992.

She was nominated by George H. W. Bush on April 1, 1992, confirmed by the Senate on August 12, 1992, and received commission on August 17, 1992. She was the first female to receive an appointment to the federal bench in the Eastern District of Missouri. She has served as chief judge of the U.S. District Court, Eastern District of Missouri, since 2002. She is also the first United States magistrate judge to be appointed to the United States District Court and the first African American woman to serve as chief judge of that court.

Edna Jackson

ELECTED OFFICIAL. Edna Jackson is a native of Savannah, Georgia. She worked for Savannah State University for 30 years before being elected to the city council. She has been serving on the Savannah City Council as the at-large alderman for Post 1; she also serves as the mayor pro-tem.

Kathryn J. "Kate" Jackson

BUSINESS EXECUTIVE. Kathryn J. "Kate" Jackson received a Bachelor of Science in physics from Grove City College and a Master of Science in industrial engineering management from the University of Pittsburgh. She earned a Master of Science degree and doctorate in engineering and policy from Carnegie Mellon University.

Her career includes serving as a fellow at the National Academy of Engineering in Washington, D.C. She previously held positions with Westinghouse Electric Corporation and Alcoa Industries as a design engineer, as a project/marketing engineer, and technology forecaster. She serves on advisory boards of the Sloan Foundation/Carnegie Mellon Electricity Industry Center and the Carnegie Mellon University School of Engineering and is on the Board of Directors of the Electric Power Research Institute. She is a member of the president's National Science and Technology Council and served as presidential appointee to the National Recreation Lakes Study Commission.

Dr. Jackson serves as the executive vice president of River System Operation & Environment and the environmental executive at the Tennessee Valley Authority (TVA). She is responsible for the operation of TVA's integrated river management system.

Lorna Graves Jackson

AEROSPACE. Lorna Graves Jackson is a native of Boston, Massachusetts, and graduated from Columbia High School in Decatur, Georgia. She received an Associate of Arts degree at the Oxford College of Emory University in Oxford, Georgia. She earned a Bachelor of Science degree in electrical engineering from Georgia Institute of Technology in Atlanta.

She joined the NASA Marshall Center in 1986 as an engineer. She is the avionics lead engineer for vehicle integrated performance analysis activities on NASA's Space Launch Initiative. She has worked on many of the Marshall's top programs providing power subsystem design, engineering development, testing and documentation for the Hubble Space Telescope and the Chandra X-ray Observatory. Ms. Jackson also has played a key role as an avionics lead subsystem engineer for systems studies on the Space Launch Initiative.

Patricia A. Jackson

MILITARY. Patricia A. Jackson began her naval career by enlisting in the United States Navy in 1974. After receiving her Bachelor of Science degree in health care administration in 1981, she was commissioned through Officer Candidate School in Newport, Rhode Island. Her education include a Master of Arts degree in national security and strategic studies from the Naval War College; a Master of Arts degree in personnel management from Central Michigan University; a Ph.D. in humanities (international relations) from Salve Regina University. She completed the Armed Forces Staff College, and in 1997, she completed the six-month-long Italian Language Course at the Defense Language Institute.

Her military assignments include serving as the director of the United States Naval Academy, Family Service Center; as an instructor at the United States Naval Academy; as military liaison officer she was assigned to the United

States Atlantic Command serving at the United States embassy in Haiti; as commanding officer, personnel unit, at Treasure Island, California; as the commanding officer, United States Naval Support Activity in Gaeta, Italy. In November 1999, she reported to the Office of the Secretary of Defense, International Security Office of the Secretary of Defense, International Security Affairs as country director for East Africa; in June 2003, she was assigned as the commander of Naval Station Ingleside.

Sherry R. Jackson

MILITARY. Sherry R. Jackson entered the active military service in January 1982 as a petroleum supply specialist, private first class, at Fort Dix, New Jersey. Upon completion of basic combat training and advanced individual training at Fort Lee, Virginia, and Airborne School at Fort Benning, Georgia, she was assigned to the 229th Supply and Service Company in Augsburg, Germany, where she served for 18 months.

Her education includes a bachelor's degree in physical education from Southern University in Baton Rouge, Louisiana; all the Noncommissioned Officer Education System Courses; the Airborne School; the Defense Equal Opportunity Management Course; and the United States Army Sergeants Major Academy.

She has served in various command, staff and leadership positions to include serving as a section sergeant with a petroleum, oil, and lubricants platoon with the 226th Field Service Company in Ludwigsburg, Germany; as a petroleum oil platoon sergeant, later a headquarters platoon sergeant and support operations non-commissioned officer in charge; as a platoon sergeant with the 705th Main Support Battalion, 5th Infantry Division, at Fort Polk, Louisiana; as the Warrior Brigade's equal opportunity advisor; as noncommissioned officer-in-charge of the Defense Fuel Office–Korea; as support operations non-commissioned officer-in-charge at the 142nd Corps Support Battalion. While at Fort Polk, she served twice as the command sergeant major of the 142nd Corps Support Battalion and first sergeant of the 229th Field Service Company. She was assigned as sergeant major for petroleum and water departments, then the command sergeant major for the 240th Quartermaster Battalion at Fort Lee, Virginia. In April 2005, she was serving as command sergeant major for the 505th Quartermaster Battalion in Japan.

Sheila Jackson-Lee

ELECTED OFFICIAL. Sheila Jackson-Lee is a native of Queens, New York, and a graduate of Jamaica High School. She received a Bachelor of Arts degree from Yale University in New Haven, Connecticut, and earned her Juris Doctor degree from the University of Virginia Law School in Charlottesville, Virginia, in 1975.

Her professional career includes serving in private law practice; as staff counsel to the United States House Select Committee on Assassinations from 1977 to 1978; as a member of the Houston, Texas, City Council from 1990 to 1994; as a Houston, Texas, municipal court judge from 1987 to 1990. She was elected as a Democrat to the 104th and to the five succeeding Congresses since January 3, 1995.

Nina Jacobson

ENTERTAINMENT EXECUTIVE. Nina Jacobson received a bachelor's degree from Brown University. Her professional career includes serving as a documentary researcher for Arnold Shapiro Productions. In 1987, she joined the Disney Sunday Movie as a story analyst. In 1988, she moved to Silver Pictures as director of development. She went on to head development at MacDonald/Parkes Productions before leaving to join Universal.

Ms. Jacobson worked at Universal as senior vice president of production where she was involved with the development and making of *Twelve Monkeys, Dazed and Confused* and *Dragon: The Bruce Lee Story*. She then moved to DreamWorks SKG as senior film executive where she developed *What Lies Beneath* and originated the idea for DreamWorks' first animated feature *Antz*.

Ms. Jacobson was named president of the Buena Vista Motion Pictures Group, responsible for developing scripts and overseeing film production for Walt Disney Pictures, Touchstone Pictures and Hollywood Pictures. She has been with the studio since February 1998 where she supervised production of *The Sixth Sense* and

Remember the Titans as well as *Pearl Harbor* and *The Princess Diaries.*

Barbara Jaffe

JUDGE. Barbara Jaffe received a Bachelor of Arts degree from Syracuse University in 1974 and received a Master of Arts degree from Syracuse University in 1981. She earned her Juris Doctor degree from Brooklyn Law School in 1984.

Her professional career includes serving as an associate appellate counsel, criminal appeals bureau, the Legal Aid Society, from 1984 to 1986; as court attorney to Hon. Jay Gold, Supreme Court of the State of New York, from 1986 to 1993; as the principal court attorney to Hon. Marcy Kahn, Supreme Court of the State of New York, from 1993 to 2002. She was elected judge, New York City Civil Court Small Claims Part.

Barbara James

HEALTH. Barbara James received a Masters of Public Health in population planning and maternal and child health from the University of Michigan School of Public Health.

Her professional career includes serving 14 years as the minority program health specialist at the National Heart, Lung and Blood Institute, National Institutes of Health; she served as the associate director of health education and development at the Howard University Center for Sickle Cell Disease; served as a research assistant at Wayne Miner Neighborhood Health Center; as project director and associate project director of numerous federally-funded research projects.

In September 2000, Ms. James joined the Office on Women's Health, Division of Program Management as a program analyst and director of the National Community Centers of Excellence in Women's Health program.

Gloria Schumpert James

BUSINESS EXECUTIVE. Gloria Schumpert James is a native of Columbia, South Carolina. She was educated in Richland County public schools and graduated from C.A. Johnson High School. She received a Bachelor of Science degree from Virginia State College in Petersburg, Virginia.

After college she returned to South Carolina to join the family business. Her father, Frederick Benjamin Schumpert, established F.B. Schumpert Lumber Co. in 1939 in Columbia, South Carolina. She serves as the company's president and CEO. The company primarily manufactured and sold framing lumber to the home building industry throughout the eastern seaboard. Now it also sells wood shipping components to industries and the government. These components include pallets, skids, boxes, crates and specified cut lumber.

Kay Coles James

GOVERNMENT OFFICIAL. Kay Coles James is a native of Richmond, Virginia. She received a bachelor's degree from Hampton University and has received numerous honorary degrees.

Her professional career includes serving as chair of the National Gambling Impact Study Commission and as Virginia's secretary of health and human resources, a position to which she was appointed by former Virginia Governor George Allen in January 1994. She served as dean of the School of Government at Regent University's Robertson School of Government in Virginia Beach, Virginia, from 1996 to 1999. She was appointed to serve as the director of the Federal Office of Personnel Management. As director, she ran an agency charged with the personnel administration of 1.8 million federal workers. In 2005, she became the director of heritage distinguished fellow and director of the Citizenship Project.

Judith Jamison

PERFORMING ARTS. Judith Jamison is a native of Philadelphia, Pennsylvania. After attending Fisk University as a psychology major she transferred to the Philadelphia Dance Academy, now the University of the Arts. She received honorary doctorates from Harvard, Yale, Manhattanville College, the University of the Arts, New York University, the University of Pennsylvania, Colgate University and Juilliard.

She became a member of the Alvin Ailey American Dance Theater in 1965 and toured the United States, Europe, Asia, South America and Africa. From the Ailey Company she went on to star in the hit Broadway

musical *Sophisticated Ladies.* In 1984 she choreographed her first work, *Divining,* for the Alvin Ailey American Dance Theater. She then went on to create new works for Maurice Bejart, Dancers Unlimited of Dallas, the Washington Ballet, Jennifer Muller/The Works, Alvin Ailey Repertory Ensemble, and Ballet Nuevo Mundo de Caracas. She choreographed her first opera, Boito's *Mefistofele,* for the Opera Company of Philadelphia in January 1989 and her PBS special, *Judith Jamison: The Dancemaker*, was aired nationally in the spring of the same year. After the death of Alvin Ailey in 1989, Ms. Jamison became the director of his company.

Valerie Jarrett

GOVERNMENT OFFICIAL. Valerie Jarrett is a native of Chicago, Illinois. She attended the University of Chicago's Laboratory Schools before receiving a Bachelor of Arts degree in psychology from Stanford University and earned a Juris Doctor degree from the University of Michigan Law School.

Her professional career includes serving eight years in Chicago government posts, first as deputy corporation counsel for finance and development, then as deputy chief of staff for Mayor Richard Daley in 1991. She served as commissioner of the Department of Planning and Development from 1992 to 1995. From 1995 to 2003, Ms. Jarrett served as chair of the Chicago Transit Board, the body that oversees the business of the Chicago Transit Authority. She also serves as chair of the board of the Chicago Stock Exchange, vice chair of the executive council of Metropolis 2020 and as chair of the University of Chicago Medical Center board. She is co-chair of President-elect Barack Obama's transition team and serves as one of his senior advisors.

Deadra L. Jefferson

JUDGE. Deadra L. Jefferson was born in Charleston, South Carolina. She earned a Bachelor of Arts degree in both politics and English in 1985 from Converse College, Spartanburg, South Carolina. She received her Juris Doctor degree from the University of South Carolina School of Law in Columbia in 1989.

Judge Jefferson was elected by the South Carolina General Assembly to the position of resident family court judge for the Ninth Judicial Circuit on February 14, 1996. She served in that position from 1996 to 2001. She was elected by the South Carolina General Assembly to the position of resident circuit judge for the Ninth Judicial Circuit on May 30, 2001. She has served continuously in this position.

Mae C. Jemison

ASTRONAUT. Mae C. Jemison was born in Decatur, Alabama, but considers Chicago, Illinois, to be her hometown. She graduated from Morgan Park High school in Chicago, Illinois, in 1973; received a Bachelor of Science degree in chemical engineering (and fulfilled the requirements for a Bachelor of Arts in African and Afro-American Studies) from Stanford University in 1977 and a doctorate degree in medicine from Cornell University in 1981.

She has a background in both engineering and medical research. She has worked in the areas of computer programming, printed wiring board materials, nuclear magnetic resonance spectroscopy, computer magnetic disc production and reproductive biology.

She completed her internship at Los Angeles County/USC Medical Center in July 1982 and worked as a general practitioner with INA/Ross Loos Medical Group in Los Angeles until December 1982.

From January 1983 through June 1985, she was the area Peace Corps medical officer for Sierra Leone and Liberia in West Africa. Her task of managing the health care delivery system for U.S. Peace Corps and U.S. embassy personnel included provision of medical care, supervision of the pharmacy and laboratory, medical administrative issues and supervision of medical staff. She developed curriculum and taught volunteer personal health training, wrote manuals for self-care, developed and implemented guidelines for public health/safety issues for volunteer job placement and training sites. She developed and participated in research projects on Hepatitis B vaccine, schistosomiasis and rabies in conjunction with the National Institute of Health and the Center for Disease Control.

Dr. Jemison was selected for the astronaut program in June 1987. Her technical assignments since then have included launch support activities at the Kennedy Space Center in Florida; verification of Shuttle computer software in the Shuttle Avionics Integration Laboratory

(SAIL); Science Support Group activities. She was the science mission specialist on STS-47 Spacelab-J (September 12–20, 1992). STS-47 was a cooperative mission between the United States and Japan. The eight-day mission was accomplished in 127 orbits of the Earth and included 44 Japanese and U.S. life science and materials processing experiments. She was a co-investigator on the bone cell research experiment flown on the mission. The *Endeavour* and her crew launched from and returned to the Kennedy Space Center in Florida. In completing her first space flight, she logged 190 hours, 30 minutes, 23 seconds in space. She left NASA in March 1993.

Loretta Sweet Jemmott

MEDICINE. Loretta Sweet Jemmott received a Bachelor of Science in nursing from Hampton University. She received both her Master of Science in psychiatric mental health nursing and her Ph.D. in education from the University of Pennsylvania.

Her professional career includes serving as professor and co-director for its School of Nursing Center for Health Disparities Research; as assistant provost for minority and gender equity; and serves secondary appointments in the university's School of Medicine and Graduate School of Education. She was recently appointed the van Ameringen Chair in Psychiatric Mental Health Nursing at the University of Pennsylvania's School of Nursing.

Dr. Jemmott has served as principal or co-principal investigator on a number of research projects that test culturally sensitive strategies to reduce HIV risk-associated sexual behaviors among African American and Latino populations.

Jo Ann C. Jenkins

GOVERNMENT OFFICIAL. Jo Ann C. Jenkins received a bachelor's degree from Spring Hill College, Mobile, Alabama.

Her professional career includes serving with the Department of Housing and Urban Development from 1981 until 1985. In 1985, she served as special assistant for minority affairs to Secretary of Transportation Elizabeth Dole. In 1988, she was a partner in a management consulting firm in Chantilly, Virginia. From 1990 to 1993 she was director of the Office of Advocacy at the Department of Agriculture. She served for 19 months as a consultant to the Office of Diversity at the Federal National Mortgage Association. She was appointed chief operating officer for the Library of Congress effective January 1, 2007. As chief operating officer, she will continue to lead efforts to finalize the library's strategic plan for 2008–2013.

Sebeth Jenkins

EDUCATION. Sebeth Jenkins was appointed to the President's Board of Advisors on Historically Black Colleges and Universities by President William Clinton.

Dr. Jenkins was appointed president of Jarvis Christian College in Hawkins, Texas. Her stature has been recognized by her appointment to a number of prestigious organizations, commissions and boards. She has served as a board member of the Independent College and Association of Black Women in Higher Education and the Christian Church Foundation Board.

Joyce R. Jenkins-Harden

MILITARY. Joyce R. Jenkins-Harden received a Bachelor of Science degree in computer science and was a distinguished ROTC graduate from Kansas State University, in Manhattan, Kansas, in 1981. She earned a Master of Science degree in computer science, Arizona State University, in Tempe, Arizona, in 1986. Her military education includes Squadron Officer School, Maxwell Air Base, Alabama, in 1987; Advanced Comm-Computer Systems Officer Training, Paschall Award, Webb Award, distinguished graduate, Top Academic Graduate, Keesler Air Force Base, Mississippi, in 1990; Air Command and Staff College, distinguished graduate, Maxwell Air Force Base, in 1994; Armed Forces

Staff College, Norfolk, Virginia, in 1994; Industrial College of the Armed Forces, Fort Lesley J. McNair, Washington, D.C., in 2000.

Colonel Jenkins-Harden was commissioned upon graduation from the Air Force Reserve Officer Training Corps program in 1981, and has been assigned to numerous staff positions. Her most recent assignment was as commander of the 721st Mission Support Group, and installation commander of Cheyenne Mountain Air Force Station, Colorado. She led a more than 550-person group composed of two squadrons, a civil engineer division, and test control division, providing and operating secure, survivable systems and facilities for North American Aerospace Defense Command, United States Northern Command, and Air Force Space Command crews to perform their air defense, space surveillance, and missile warning missions. She directed all support operations, maintenance, and testing for Cheyenne Mountain's integrated tactical warning and attack assessment systems, and actively participates in ongoing system upgrades.

Toni Jennings

ELECTED OFFICIAL. Toni Jennings is a native of Orlando, Florida. She received a bachelor's degree from Wesleyan College.

Her professional career includes serving as a public school teacher at Killarney Elementary in Orange County. She served two terms as a Florida state representative and was elected as a Florida state senator in 1980 and was re-elected to represent central Florida for 20 consecutive years. She served as Florida's only two term state Senate president from 1996 to 2000; after 24 years of public service, she also successfully ran Jack Jennings & Sons, a family-owned construction business. After 20 years of leading the company as president she stepped down to become lieutenant governor.

Toni Jennings serves as the 16th lieutenant governor of Florida, the nation's fourth most populous state. She is the first woman to hold the office.

Joori Jeon

BUSINESS EXECUTIVE. Joori Jeon is a native of Korea. She received a bachelor's degree from Old Dominion University in Norfolk, Virginia.

Her professional career includes serving in several management positions at the Personal Communications Industry Association, Inova Health System and Arthur Anderson LLP. Ms. Jeon serves as the vice president and chief financial officer for the American Hotel & Lodging Association. As senior financial executive of the largest trade association representing the U.S. lodging industry she oversees the association's $20 million operating budget.

Tamara E. Jernigan

AEROSPACE. Tamara E. Jernigan is a native of Chattanooga, Tennessee, and graduated from Santa Fe High School in Santa Fe Springs, California, in 1977. She received both a Bachelor of Science degree in physics (with honors) in 1981 and a Master of Science degree in engineering science from Stanford University in 1983. She earned a Doctor in space physics and astronomy from Rice University in 1988.

Her professional career began as a research scientist in the Theoretical Studies Branch at NASA Ames Research Center from June 1981 until July 1985. She was selected as an astronaut candidate by NASA in June 1985; she became an astronaut in July 1986. Her assignments since then have included software verification in the Shuttle Avionics Integration Laboratory (SAIL); operations coordination on secondary payloads; spacecraft communicator (CAPCOM) in Mission Control for STS-30, STS-28, STS-34, STS-33, and STS-32; lead astronaut for flight software development; chief of the Astronaut Office Mission Development Branch; and deputy chief of Astronaut Office. She was payload commander on STS-67, served as mission specialist on STS-80 and STS-96, and served as lead astronaut for Space Station external maintenance.

Marie C. Johns

BUSINESS EXECUTIVE. Marie C. Johns is a native of Indianapolis, Indiana. She received a Bachelor of Science degree and a master of public administration from the Indiana University. She has also completed graduate management studies at Harvard

University's John F. Kennedy School of Government and the Darden Graduate School of Business Administration at the University of Virginia.

Her professional career includes serving as a fiscal analyst in the Indiana Legislative Services Agency. From there, she was hired as the staff supervisor for Bell Atlantic Network Services in Arlington, Virginia. She then became director, Federal Commerce Commission at the Bell Atlantic Corporation, C & P Telephone Company and Bell Atlantic. In April 1998, she was named president and chief executive officer of Atlantic Bell and then served as president of Verizon in Washington, D.C.

Ms. Johns provided leadership in the formation of the Washington, D.C., Technology Council and the Georgia Avenue Business Resource Center. She was appointed by the Washington, D.C., mayor to the National Capital Revitalization Corporation.

Abigail Johnson

FINANCE. Abigail Johnson received her undergraduate degree from Harvard University and began her career at Fidelity in 1988 as an analyst, eventually managing several Fidelity funds including Fidelity OTC, Dividend Growth and Trend funds.

Since 1997, she has served as an associate director and senior vice president of the Equity Division of FMR. She oversees all of Fidelity's fund managers, traders and analysts, including Robert Stansky, manager of Fidelity Magellan, the nation's largest stock mutual fund.

Arlene Johnson

JUDGE. Arlene Johnson is a native of St. Paul, Minnesota. She received a Bachelor of Arts degree in English from the University of Oklahoma, and earned her Juris Doctor degree from the University of Oklahoma School of Law.

Her professional career includes serving in private law practice; as judicial law clerk to the Court of Criminal Appeals; Oklahoma County assistant district attorney; as assistant Oklahoma attorney general; and as assistant United States attorney for the Western District of Oklahoma for 21 years. On February 18, 2005, she was appointed judge to the Oklahoma Court of Criminal Appeals, District 4.

Barbara Gilleran Johnson

JUDGE. Barbara Gilleran Johnson received her law degree from the IIT/Chicago-Kent College of Law and was admitted to practice in Illinois in 1978. She served as an assistant attorney general where she was chief of the Crime Victims Compensation Division; and as assistant state's attorney of Lake County where she was chief of the Juvenile Division.

She was an attorney in private practice before receiving an appointment in 1987 as an associate judge. She appointed a circuit judge in 1996 and was elected to that position in 1998. She was elected to the Appellate Court in 2002 and serves as an appellate judge for the Second District, State of Illinois.

Beverly Johnson

ELECTED OFFICIAL. Beverly Johnson is a native of Alameda, California, and a graduate of Alameda High School. She received a Bachelor of Arts degree in music from Cal State University–Hayward and earned her Juris Doctor degree from the University of Pacific Law School in 1988.

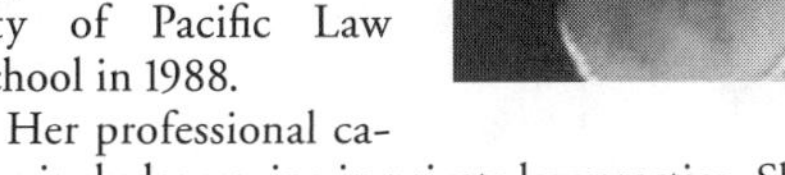

Her professional career includes serving in private law practice. She serves the mayor of Alameda, California. The city is built on an island in San Francisco Bay; Alameda has a population of 76,000.

Carol D. Johnson

ELECTED OFFICIAL. Carol D. Johnson is a native of Washington, D.C., and a graduate of Woodrow Wilson High School in Washington, D.C. She received a Bachelor of Arts degree in biblical studies. Carol D. Johnson currently serves as mayor for the city of District Heights and is employed with the Prince George's county council serving as the special events coordinator. The mayoral office is a three-year term. She was elected as mayor on May 5, 2003 and served as commissioner, ward 2, from May 2000 until May 2003.

Christyl Johnson

AEROSPACE. Christyl Johnson received a bachelor's degree in physics from Lincoln University and earned a master's degree in electrical engineering from Pennsylvania State University.

Her professional career includes serving at Langley Research Center in Hampton, Virginia, in 1985 in the remote sensing technology branch where she assisted in designing and building laser systems for advanced active remote sensors. In 1991, she became the program manager and lead engineer of the Diode-Pumped CrL-liSAF Technology Development Program. In this role she established several initiatives, one of which was an industry and laboratory collaboration to build an efficient Differential Absorption Lidar for remote sensing of water vapor. She then served as the subsystem manager for the diode seeding subsystem of the Lidar Atmospheric Sensing Experiment (LASE) flight project for which she successfully conducted the subsystem planning and scheduling, the coordination of the systems engineering, hardware/software procurement, design and fabrication activities and integration and environmental testing activities. In 1997, Johnson became assistant head of the Electro-Optics and Controls Branch where she was responsible for directing a group of 29 employees in the design, development, and application of state-of-the-art and advanced electro-optic systems and subsystems for atmospheric, aeronautic and space flight research missions. She served as the deputy chief engineer for program integration and operations at the Office of the Administrator. She serves as the assistant associate administrator in the Office of the Administrator at NASA. In this role, she assists the associate administrator in the oversight of the agency's technical mission areas and field center operations.

Eddie Bernice Johnson

ELECTED OFFICIAL. Eddie Bernice Johnson is a native of Waco, Texas, and a graduate of A.J. Moore High School in Waco, Texas, in 1952. She received a nursing certificate from St. Mary's College at the University of Notre Dame, Indiana, in 1955. She received a Bachelor of Science degree from Texas Christian University in Fort Worth, Texas, in 1967 and earned her masters of public administration from Southern Methodist University in Dallas, Texas, in 1976.

Her professional career includes serving as chief psychiatric nurse and psychotherapist at Veterans Administration Hospital in Dallas, Texas; as a Texas state representative (1972–1977); as an administrator, United States Department of Health, Education and Welfare (1977–1981); in private business; as a Texas state senator (1987–1993). She was elected a United States representative to the 103rd and to the seven succeeding Congresses and has served since January 3, 1993.

Glorious Johnson

ELECTED OFFICIAL. Glorious Johnson is a native of Jacksonville and has always called it home. She received a bachelor's degree in music as a concert pianist from Jacksonville University. She received her first master's degree in school administration and supervision from Nova University and earned a second master's in educational administration/organizational leadership from Teachers College, Columbia University.

Her professional career includes serving as the master admissions representative at Florida Metropolitan University at Jacksonville campus. She served as the lead faculty teaching business administration courses at Jones College where she later became the admissions representative for the West campus. She was elected to the city of Jacksonville City Council at large.

Karen A. Johnson

GOVERNMENT OFFICIAL. Karen A. Johnson received a bachelor's degree in communications from Appalachian State University in North Carolina. She was a fellow at the University of Pennsylvania's Annenberg School for Communications.

Her professional career includes serving as a staff assistant for Congressman Duncan Hunter; as vice president of social marketing and

public affairs at Porter Novelli where she provided strategic public affairs and communications counsel for a variety of not-for-profit and foundation clients.

Ms. Johnson was nominated by President George W. Bush on January 21, 2003, for the post of assistant secretary for legislation and congressional affairs. She was confirmed by the United States Senate on May 23, 2003, and was sworn in on June 2, 2003.

Katherine E. Johnson

GOVERNMENT OFFICIAL. Katherine E. Johnson received a Bachelor of Arts degree magna cum laude from Northeastern University and earned a Master of Arts degree from the Fletcher School of Law and Diplomacy.

She has held numerous assignments in the Office of the Secretary of Defense to include serving as director, Central Asia, the Caucasus and Eurasian regional programs. She served as director for counter-proliferation policy and as co-chair to NATO's Senior Defense Group on Proliferation Steering Committee. She was assigned as principal director, Western Hemisphere Affairs, Office of the Secretary of Defense. Ms. Johnson was selected to serve as director of international affairs and foreign policy advisor to the commandant of the Coast Guard in February 2005.

Melissa Johnson

HEALTH. Melissa Johnson is a native of Newport Beach, California. She received a Bachelor of Science degree in kinesiology from the University of California at Los Angeles and earned a Master of Science degree in health/fitness management from American University in Washington, D.C.

Her professional career includes serving from 1992 to 1997 as director of operations for National Fitness Leaders Association (NFLA), a national not-for-profit organization formerly based in Washington, D.C. She was appointed executive director of the California Governor's Council on Physical Fitness and Sports from 1997 to 2002. Ms. Johnson was appointed by President George W. Bush as executive director of the President's Council on Physical Fitness and Sports.

Nancy L. Johnson

ELECTED OFFICIAL. Nancy L. Johnson is a native of Chicago, Illinois, and graduated from elementary and secondary classes of the University of Chicago Laboratory School. She received a Bachelor of Arts degree from Radcliffe College in Cambridge, Massachusetts, in 1957 and then attended the University of London Courtauld Institute from 1957 to 1958.

Her professional career includes serving as a teacher, member of the Connecticut State Senate from 1977 to 1982, and as a delegate to the Republican National Convention in 1980.

Ms. Johnson was elected as a Republican to the 98th and to the eleven succeeding Congresses from January 3, 1983, to present. She serves as chair of the Committee on Standards of Official Conduct.

Norma Holloway Johnson

JUDGE. Norma Holloway Johnson is a native of Louisiana. She received her undergraduate degree from the University of the District of Columbia and earned her Juris Doctor degree from Georgetown University Law Center in 1962.

Her professional career includes serving as a trial attorney with the civil division of the United States Department of Justice and as an assistant corporation counsel at the Office of the Corporation Counsel in Washington, D.C. In 1970, she was appointed associate judge of the Superior Court of the District of Columbia; in 1980, she was appointed as a United States district judge in the District of Columbia. She was appointed chief judge of the United States District Court for the District of Columbia on July 21, 1997.

Odessa Johnson

EDUCATION. Odessa Johnson received a Bachelor of Arts degree from Tennessee State University and

her Master of Arts degree from Columbia University.

Her professional career includes serving over 25 years as an instructor, counselor and director of community education. She served as assistant dean of education at Modesto Junior College; she serves as dean emeritus of community education at Modesto Junior College and a member of the Modesto City Schools Board of Education.

Ms. Johnson was appointed regent on May 4, 1999, to fill the remainder of a twelve-year term which expired on March 1, 2000, by Governor Davis. On March 1, 2000, Governor Davis reappointed her to a term expiring March 1, 2012.

Sheila Crump Johnson

BUSINESS EXECUTIVE. Sheila Crump Johnson received a Bachelor of Arts in music from the University of Illinois. She has received an honorary doctorate degree from Morrisville State College. She has taught music and authored a textbook.

Her professional career includes serving as co-founder and executive vice president for corporate affairs of Black Entertainment Television (BET). She was the creator of BET URBAN NATION H.I.P.H.O.P.—focusing on Hope, Integrity, Power and Helping Our People. She joined Lincoln Holdings as a partner in 2005 and serves as president, managing partner and governor of the Women's National Basketball Association's Washington Mystics. She is owner-partner in the Washington Capitals and Washington Wizards. She is the first woman of color to owner-partner in three professional sports franchises. She is the founder of Crump-Johnson Foundation.

Ms. Johnson is the chief executive officer of Salamander Hospitality. Market Salamander in Middleburg, Virginia, one of the first components in the portfolio of Salamander Hospitality, is a working chefs' market. Future additions include Market Salamander in Palm Beach, Florida, and the luxurious Salamander Resort & Spa in Middleburg, Virginia.

Shelia R. Johnson

JUDGE. Shelia R. Johnson is a native of Detroit, Michigan. She is a graduate of Dartmouth College and the University of Michigan Law School where she was the first African-American to be elected president of the Law School Senate and to deliver the commencement address to her graduating class.

After law school, she served as a law clerk for Judge Benjamin F. Gibson, United States District Court in the Western District of Michigan. She served for 18 years in private law practice in Southfield. She further served as a legal analyst on the radio talk show program, "Speaking of Sports," where she addressed legal issues concerning athletes in professional sports.

Judge Johnson was elected to a seat as judge in the 46th District Court in November 2002, becoming the first African American to serve in that capacity.

Suzanne Nora Johnson

FINANCE. Suzanne Nora Johnson received a Bachelor of Arts degree in economics, philosophy/religion and political science magna cum laude from the University of Southern California. She earned a Juris Doctor degree from Harvard Law School.

Her professional career includes serving as a law clerk to the Honorable Francis Murnaghan of the United States Court of Appeal. She served in private law practice in New York. In 1992, she was named a partner at Goldman Sachs. From 1994 to 2002, she served as head of the global healthcare business in the investment banking division. In February 2002, she was selected to head the global investment research division. In April 2004, she was named chairman of the global market institute. She was named vice chairman of Goldman Sachs in November 2004.

Vickki Johnson

MILITARY. Vickki Johnson enlisted in the United States Army in 1983 upon completion of high school. She has been assigned to the 440th Signal Battalion, Darmstadt, Germany; the 35th Signal Brigade, Fort Bragg, North Carolina; the 122nd Signal Battalion, Camp Casey, South Korea; and the 19th Theater Support Command, Taegu, South Korea.

Her military education includes the Primary Leadership Development course; the Basic Noncommissioned Officer Course; the United States Army Airborne School; Adjutant General Officer Basic and Advanced Courses and the Combined Arms Senior Staff School. She holds a Master of Science degree in health services administration from Central Michigan University and is pursuing a doctorate in public health.

Upon her return to the United States, she was commissioned in the Adjutant General Corps as a Distinguished Military Graduate of Officer Candidate School in 1992. After completing the Adjutant General Officer Basic Course, she returned to Fort Bragg and was assigned to XVIII Airborne Corps where she served as chief, reassignments division, executive officer and battalion personnel officer, 18th Personnel Services Battalion. Upon completion of the Adjutant General Officer Advanced Course, she was assigned to V Corps, Heidelberg, Germany, as chief, enlisted management branch, and commander, Headquarters And Headquarters Company, 1st Personnel Command.

Upon returning from Germany, she was assigned to the national capital region to serve in several positions including operations officer at headquarters, United States Army Materiel Command; distribution/assignment officer; chief, officer promotions; and chief, officer evaluation policy; United States Army Human Resources Command.

Wilma Robena Johnson

MINISTRY. Wilma Robena Johnson received a Bachelor of Arts degree in business administration, a Master of Arts degree in pastoral ministry and a Doctor of Ministry degree from the Ecumenical Theological Seminary in Detroit, Michigan.

Her ministry journey began in September of 1974. She was licensed by the the Rev. Russell Fox, Sr., pastor of Mt. Olive Baptist Church in East Orange, New Jersey, and the late Dr. E.A. Freeman at First Baptist Church in Kansas City, Kansas. In 1992, she was ordained by the Rev. Dr. Charles Gilchrist Adams for full-time ministry. She serves as the assistant to the pastor in Christian nurture for almost nine years.

For thirty years, Dr. Johnson has continued to teach, conduct workshops and preach. Speaking engagements, revivals, retreats, conferences and seminars have taken her throughout the United States.

Gloria Johnson-Goins

BUSINESS EXECUTIVE. Gloria Johnson-Goins is a native of Miami, Florida. She received a Bachelor of Arts degree from Stanford University and earned a Juris Doctor degree from the University of Pennsylvania School of Law. She also earned a Master of Business Administration from Mercer University.

Her professional career includes serving as an attorney with BellSouth Cellular Corp., law department. From 2000 to 2002, she served as the vice president of Cingular Wireless. She was selected to serve as vice president of diversity and inclusion for Home Depot with responsibility for creating and implementing company-wide diversity initiatives for the world's second largest retailer.

Nicole Johnson-Reece

BUSINESS EXECUTIVE. Nicole Johnson-Reece received a Bachelor of Science degree in economics from Rutgers University in New Brunswick, New Jersey.

She served as international marketing manager for AT&T's sub–Sahara Africa and Caribbean regions as well as other marketing and management positions from 1989 to 1997. She served for the next two years as staff director for ethnic and premium marketing and sales for the African-American market for Bell Atlantic. In 1999, she joined the Cendant Hotel Group as director of multicultural marketing and sales. Ms. Johnson-Reece was named vice president for diversity and community involvement. She joined ARAMARK, which is based in Philadelphia, as vice president of diversity.

Carol A. Jones

MILITARY. Carol A. Jones is a native of Pennsylvania. After completing secondary education in Pittsburgh, she moved to New York, New York, enrolled and com-

pleted a diploma program in nursing from Harlem Hospital School of Nursing. She earned a Bachelor of Science in nursing from Tuskegee University, Alabama; a Masters degree in community health nursing from Emory University in Atlanta, Georgia; and a Masters degree in nursing education from Columbia Teachers' College, New York. She is a Wharton Fellow, recently completing the program for nurse executives at the University of Pennsylvania.

Colonel Jones is a graduate of the Industrial College of the Armed Forces (ICAF), National Defense University. Other professional military education includes Command and General Staff College; Officer Advanced and Basic Courses; Combat Casualty Care Course; Principles of Advanced Nursing Practice; Personnel Management for Executives; and the Federal Interagency Institute for Health Care Executives.

She served in several key positions to include National Defense University nurse consultant at Fort McNair, D.C.; chief nursing administration, WRAMC in Washington, D.C.; nursing consultant and chief nurse 18th Medical Command, Yongsan, Korea; chief, medical/surgical/psychiatric nursing section, 97th General Hospital, Frankfurt, Germany; chief nurse, Joint Task Force Bravo, Honduras, Central America; and deputy director, practical nurse course, William Beaumont Army Medical Center in El Paso, Texas.

In September 2004, she was serving as chief nurse, North Atlantic Regional Medical Command (NARMC) and chief nurse, Walter Reed Army Medical Center (WRAMC) in Washington, D.C.

Edith Hollan Jones

JUDGE. Edith Hollan Jones is a native of Philadelphia, Pennsylvania. She received a Bachelor of Arts degree from Cornell University in 1971, and earned her Juris Doctor degree from the University of Texas School of Law in 1974.

Her career began in private law practice in Houston, Texas (1974–1985). She was nominated by Ronald Reagan on February 27, 1985, confirmed by the Senate on April 3, 1985 and received commission on April 4, 1985, as a judge on the U.S. Court of Appeals for the Fifth Circuit. Since 2006, she has served as chief judge for the U.S. Court of Appeals for the Fifth Circuit.

Elaine Hollan Jones

BUSINESS EXECUTIVE. Elaine Hollan Jones is a native of Norfolk, Virginia. She received a bachelor's degree in political science with honors from Howard University and earned her Juris Doctor degree from the University of Virginia School of Law, becoming the first African American woman to graduate from that school.

Her professional career includes serving with the Peace Corps where she was one of the first African Americans to serve in Turkey. She became the first African American to serve on the Board of Governors of the American Bar Association. While serving with the NAACP Legal Defense Fund, she became the one of the first African American women to defend death row inmates. In 1993, she was appointed the first woman to head the NAACP's Legal Defense Fund.

Ms. Jones has served as president and director-counsel for the NAACP Legal Defense Fund.

Michele S. Jones

MILITARY. Michele S. Jones is a native of Baltimore, Maryland. Command Sergeant Major Jones has an Associate of Arts degree in general studies and a Bachelor of Science degree (cum laude) in business administration from Fayetteville State University. She is currently completing her Master of Arts in management/international relations. Her military education include: the Battle Staff Operations Course; First Sergeant's Course; Instructor Training Course; Civil Affairs Operation Course; Master Fitness Course; Retention NCO Basic and Advanced Courses; and the Sergeants Major Academy.

CSM Jones entered the Army in 1982. She attended basic training at Fort Jackson, South Carolina, and advanced individual training at Fort Benjamin Harrison, Indiana. She has held every key NCO position including squad leader, platoon sergeant, first sergeant and command sergeant.

She was the first woman to serve as class president at the United States Sergeants Major Academy (Class 48). Her overseas assignments include Hanau and Rhineberg, Germany; Honduras; and Panama. She was called to active duty for operations Desert Shield and Desert Storm, Restore Hope, Provide Comfort, Joint Endeavor, and Noble Eagle. Her most recent assignment was that of command sergeant major of the 78th Division (training support), Edison, New Jersey.

On August 28, 2002, she was selected as the ninth command sergeant major of the Army Reserve. She is the first woman in the Army's history to serve as a top command sergeant major for the Army Reserves. She took office on October 28, 2002.

Patricia Jones

ELECTED OFFICIAL. Patricia Jones is a native of Opelika, Alabama. She received a Bachelor of Science in English/library science and earned a master's degree in secondary education and English from Alabama State University in Montgomery, Alabama. She is certified in municipal government.

Her professional career includes serving as an English teacher in the Tallapoosa County school system for 24 years. She joined the staff of the Alabama Education Association (AEA) where she serves as the UniServ director. She was the first woman appointed in 1992 by the mayor of Opelika to be on the Board of Commissioners of the Housing Authority and the first woman elected vice chair of that board. She continued to make history in 1995 when she was elected a city council member for Ward 1 in the city of Opelika, becoming the first African American female to do so. She was also elected to serve as the first African American female president pro tem of the city council. She has served three terms on the city council.

Stephanie Tubbs Jones

ELECTED OFFICIAL. Stephanie Tubbs Jones is a native of Cleveland, Ohio, and graduated from Collinwood High School in Cleveland, Ohio. She received a Bachelor of Arts degree in 1971 and a Juris Doctor degree from Case Western Reserve University at Cleveland, Ohio, in 1974.

She was elected judge to the Cleveland, Ohio, Municipal Court in 1981; has served as a judge to the Court of Common Pleas of Cuyahoga County, Ohio, 1983–1991; and has served as prosecutor, Cuyahoga County, Ohio, 1991–1998; she was elected a United States representative to the 106th and to the three succeeding Congresses (January 3, 1999–present).

Wilmer Jones-Ham

ELECTED OFFICIAL (FIRST). Wilmer Jones-Ham is a graduate of the Saginaw, Michigan, public school system. She received an Associate Arts degree from Delta College and received a bachelor's degree in elementary education and a Masters' degree in supervision and administration from Saginaw Valley State University.

In 1994, she was elected to the Saginaw city council and on November 12, 2001, she was elected as the city of Saginaw's first female mayor.

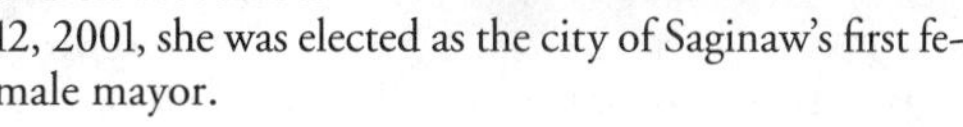

Karen Jordan

JOURNALISM. Karen Jordan is a native of Nashville, Tennessee. She received a Bachelor of Arts degree in English from Spelman College in Atlanta, Georgia. She earned a master's degree in broadcast journalism from Northwestern University's Medill School of Journalism in 1995.

Her professional career includes serving as a general assignment reporter for WIFR-TV in Rockford, Illinois (1995–1997); as a weekend anchor and general assignment reporter for WKEF-TV in Dayton (1997–1999); as a main anchor and reporter at WRGT-TV in Dayton, Ohio; and as weekend anchor and general assignment reporter at WPHL-TV in Philadelphia, Pennsylvania. She joined Chicago's ABC 7 News in July 2003 as co-anchor for ABC 7's weekend news.

Annette Joseph

MILITARY. Annette Joseph is a native of Dallas, Texas, where she graduated from high school in May 1978 and began her career in the United States Army on June 5, 1978. Her military and civilian education includes all the Noncommissioned Officers Leadership Courses; Distinguished Honor Graduate of Class 03-83 of the III Corps Noncommissioned Officer Academy; Battle Staff Course; First Sergeants Course and the United States Army Sergeants Major Academy. She holds an associate degree in general studies from Central Texas College; a Bachelor of Science degree in management/human resources from Park College and a Master of Science degree in human resource management from the University of Central Texas.

Command Sergeant Major Joseph's assignments include motor transport operator; unit clerk; assistant personnel staff NCO; battalion personnel staff NCO; brigade personnel staff NCO; group personnel staff NCO; United States Army Pacific liaison NCO; senior analyst; first sergeant for Headquarters and Headquarters Detachment; 546th Personnel Service Battalion; first sergeant for 21st Replacement Company; battalion command sergeant major for 203rd Personnel Services Battalion, Fort Wainwright, Alaska. In August 2004, she was serving as the command sergeant major for 3rd Personnel Group at Fort Hood, Texas.

Phyllis R. Joseph

MILITARY. Phyllis R. Joseph is a native of West Palm Beach, Florida. She entered the United States Army in February of 1980. She attended basic combat training at Fort Leonard Wood, Missouri, and advanced individual training at Fort Sam Houston, Texas, as a combat medic.

Command Sergeant Major Joseph holds a Bachelor of Science degree from Benedict College, Columbia, South Carolina. Her military education includes all the Noncommissioned Officer Education System Courses; Medical NCO Course (91B); Emergency Medical Technician Course; Small Group Leaders Course; Instructor Development Course; Mobilization Officer Course; Movement Course (Ground and Air); Air Operation Movement Course; Master Fitness Course; Battle Staff Course; First Sergeants Course; the United States Army Sergeants Major Academy Class 52 and the Command Sergeants Major Course.

She has served in a variety of positions of increased responsibility including command sergeant major, troop command, BAMC; chief operations NCO, VII Corps NCO Academy, Augsburg, Germany; noncommissioned officer in charge of resource management, Southwest Asia; chief of operations for the NCO Academy (PLDC and BNCOC), Fort Carson, Colorado; senior medical operation NCO, Readiness Group 5th United States Army, Salt Lake City, Utah; first sergeant, Echo Company, 232nd Medical Battalion, Fort Sam Houston, Texas; plans and operations NCO, V CORPS Surgeon's Office, Heidelberg, Germany; sergeant major for the command surgeon of the combined coalition component land forces, 3rd United States Army, Kuwait; she deployed in support of Desert Shield/Desert Storm, Operation Enduring Freedom; and Operation Iraqi Freedom. In January 2005, she was serving as command sergeant major, Moncrief Army Community Hospital at Fort Jackson, South Carolina.

Donna Richardson Joyner

HEALTH. Donna Richardson Joyner of Dallas, Texas, began teaching other instructors and eventually competed nationally and internationally in aerobics competitions. In 1992 she was hired to co-host the ESPN Fitness Pros Show and co-starred in her first commercial fitness tape, *Platinum Buns of Steel.* She developed her own fitness video, *Sweating in the Spirit,* and health books to help spread her message. In addition to speaking at various conferences and meetings, Ms. Joyner can be seen on TV One on the *Donna Richardson: Mind, Body, & Spirit* show and on her *Sweating in the Spirit* TV show on the Word Network.

Mrs. Joyner was appointed to the President's Council on Physical Fitness and Sports.

Pamela J. Joyner

FINANCE. Pamela J. Joyner received a Bachelor of Arts degree and an honorary Master of Arts degree from Dartmouth College. She earned a Master of Business Administration degree from Harvard University.

Her professional career includes serving as a partner at Bowman Capital Management, LLC, and working for a number of years in the marketing and client service group at Capital Guardian Trust Company. Her other investment experience includes positions at Fidelity Management Trust Company, Kidder Peabody and Merrill Lynch.

Ms. Joyner serves as the managing partner and founder of Avid Partners, LLC, which serves as an investment management firm in the diversification, product positioning and global distribution of their investment programs.

Andrea Jung

BUSINESS EXECUTIVE. Andrea Jung, the child of Chinese immigrants, received a bachelor's degree (magna cum laude) from Princeton University. She first went to work for Bloomingdale's and I. Magnin department stores and rose to the post of senior vice president. She worked as general merchandising manager at I. Magnin's San Francisco headquarters. She joined Neiman-Marcus as executive vice president in charge of women's apparel, cosmetics, and accessories. In November 1999, she was appointed president and chief executive officer of Avon Products, Inc.

Jan R. Jurden

JUDGE. Jan R. Jurden received a Bachelor of Arts degree (summa cum laude) from Muhlenberg College in 1985 and earned her Juris Doctor degree from the Dickinson School of Law at the Pennsylvania State University in 1988.

She was engaged in private law practice from 1988 to 2001. In May 2001, she was appointed judge to the Superior Court of Delaware, First State Judiciary.

Cheryl C. Kagan

ELECTED OFFICIAL. Cheryl C. Kagan is a native of Washington, D.C. She attended Winston Churchill High School in Potomac, Maryland. She received a Bachelor of Arts in political science from Vassar College and has attended graduate studies at the University of Maryland in College Park.

Ms. Kagan has served as a member of the Maryland House of Delegates since January 11, 1995. She has served as vice-chair, House Democratic Research Group; as vice-chair, Transportation Committee Montgomery County Delegation; and as House vice-chair, Joint Audit Committee.

Elena Kagan

EDUCATION. Elena Kagan received a bachelor's degree summa cum laude from Princeton University. She attended Worcester College, Oxford, as Princeton's Daniel M. Sachs Graduating Fellow and received and a master's degree in 1983. She received her Juris Doctor degree magna cum laude from Harvard Law School where she was supervising editor of the *Harvard Law Review*.

Her professional career includes serving as a law clerk for Judge Abner Mikva of the United States Court of Appeals for the D.C. Circuit from 1986 to 1987. The next year she clerked for Justice Thurgood Marshall of the United States Supreme Court. She served in private law practice. From 1995 to 1999, she served in the White House, first as associate counsel to the president and then as deputy assistant to the president for domestic policy and deputy director of the domestic policy council. She came to Harvard Law School as a visiting professor in 1999 and became professor of law in 2001. On July 1, 2003, she was selected to serve as the dean of Harvard Law School. In February 2007, she was named president of Harvard University, becoming the first woman president of Harvard.

Charlene Kammerer

MINISTRY. Charlene Kammerer is a native of Orlando, Florida. She received a Bachelor of Arts degree in religion and philosophy in 1970 and a Master of Christian Education from Evanston, Illinois. She earned a Master of Divinity degree from Garrett-Evangelical Theological Seminary in Evanston, Illinois, and a Doctorate of Ministry degree from United Theological Seminary in Dayton, Ohio, in 1991. She was ordained deacon in 1975 and elder in 1977.

Her professional career includes serving as a clinical unit manager at the Work Release Center of the Mecklenburg County Sheriff's Department, working with inmates who receive addiction counseling as part of their sentencing; as director of the General Commission on the Status and Role of Women and as a director of the General Board of Global Ministries, United Methodist Church; as chairperson of the United Methodist Committee on Relief from 1992 to 1996; as a campus minister at Duke University; and as a district superintendent of the Tallahassee District, Florida Conference.

Dr. Kammerer was elected to the Episcopacy at the Southeastern Jurisdictional Conference (SEJ) at Lake Junaluska, North Carolina, in July 1996, where she was assigned to the Charlotte area. At the Southeastern Jurisdictional Conference meeting in July 2000, Bishop Kammerer was reassigned to the Western North Carolina Conference. In 2004, she was assigned to the Virginia Conference.

Carol Ronning Kapsner

JUDGE. Carol Ronning Kapsner is a native of Bismarck, North Dakota. She received a Bachelor of Arts degree in English from the College of St. Catherine in St. Paul, Minnesota, studied 17th century English literature at Oxford University, and received a Master of Arts degree in English literature from Indiana University. She earned her Juris Doctor degree from the University of Colorado School of Law in Boulder, Colorado, in 1977.

After law school she served in private law practice. On October 6, 1998, Governor Edward T. Schafer appointed her a justice on the North Dakota Supreme Court to fill the vacancy created by the retirement of Justice Herbert L. Meschke. In November 2000, she was elected to a full 10-year term.

Diane Karpinski

JUDGE. Diane Karpinski graduated from Notre Dame Academy in 1953 and received a Bachelor of Arts degree from the Ohio State University in 1962. She also received a Masters' of Arts degree from the Ohio State University in 1964 and earned her Juris Doctor degree from Cleveland-Marshall College of Law in 1981. She attended doctoral studies at Harvard University Summer School and the University of Chicago.

Her professional career includes serving as assistant investment officer and then director of personnel in the office of treasurer of Ohio; as a member of the faculty at the Ohio State University; as a member of the faculty, Department of English at Cleveland State University; and as an assistant attorney general in Ohio. Judge Karpinski serves as a member of the Ohio Court of Appeals in Cleveland, Ohio.

Nancy Landon Kassebaum

ELECTED OFFICIAL. Nancy Landon Kassebaum is a native of Topeka, Kansas. She received a bachelor's degree from the University of Kansas in 1954 and earned her master's degree from the University of Michigan in 1956.

Her professional career includes serving as a radio station executive in Wichita, Kansas. She was elected a United States senator on November 7, 1978, for a six-year term commencing January 3, 1979; she was reelected in 1984 and 1990 and served until January 1997. She served as chair of the Committee on Labor and Human Resources (104th Congress).

Karen L. Katen

BUSINESS EXECUTIVE. Karen L. Katen is a native of Missouri. She received a Bachelor of Arts degree in political science and a Master of Business Administration from the University of Chicago.

After receiving her business degree, she joined Pfizer Inc., over thirty years ago. In 1983, she was named vice president of marketing and later vice president and general manager. Ms. Katen became executive vice president of Pfizer Pharmaceuticals Group in 1993 and president of Pfizer U.S. Pharmaceuticals and Pfizer Global Pharmaceuticals in 1995. In 2005, she was named president of Pfizer Human Health and vice chairman of Pfizer, Inc.

Vera Katz

ELECTED OFFICIAL. Vera Katz was born in Dusseldorf, Germany, and moved to the United States as a child. She received a Bachelor of Arts degree in 1955 and earned a Master of Arts degree in 1957 from Brooklyn College in New York. She holds honorary doctorate degrees from Lewis & Clark College and Portland State University.

Her professional career includes working on Robert F. Kennedy's presidential campaign; she was elected to the Oregon House of Representatives in 1972. In 1985, she became the first woman Speaker of the Oregon House of Representatives and later became the only person in state history to hold the post for three consecutive terms; she was elected mayor of Portland, Oregon, in 1992. She served as Portland's mayor from January 1993 to January 2005.

Yvonne Kauger

JUDGE. Yvonne Kauger is a fourth generation Oklahoman from Colony, Oklahoma. She was appointed to the Oklahoma Supreme Court on March 11, 1984, by Governor George Nigh. She chaired the building committee for the Oklahoma Judicial Center. She served as chief justice of the Oklahoma Supreme Court from January 1997 to December 1998. She has served as presiding judge for the Court on the Judiciary and the Law School and Bench and Bar committees of the Oklahoma Bar Association. She founded the Gallery of the Plains Indian in Colony and co-founded Re Earth.

Elizabeth Kautz

ELECTED OFFICIAL. Elizabeth Kautz serves as the mayor of the city of Burnsville, Minnesota. She was elected mayor in 1994 and was re-elected in 1996, 1998, 2000 and 2004. She represents Burnsville on the Metro Mayors Association, the Minnesota Valley Transit Authority, and the Municipal Legislative Commission She is the co-chair of the Minnesota Regional Council of Mayors and is on the U.S. Conference of Mayors Advisory Board of Directors.

Judith S. Kaye

JUDGE (FIRST). Judith S. Kaye is a native of Monticellor, New York. She received a Bachelor of Arts degree from Barnard College 1958 and earned her Juris Doctor degree from New York University School of Law (cum laude) in 1962. Her professional career includes serving in private law practice.

She was appointed by Governor Mario M. Cuomo on February 22, 1993, as a justice on the New York Supreme Court. She was confirmed by the State Senate on March 17, and sworn in on March 23, 1993. She is the first woman to occupy the state judiciary's highest office. She became the first woman to serve on New York state's highest court when Governor Cuomo appointed her associate judge of the Court of Appeals on September 12, 1983. In 2006, she was serving as chief justice of the New York State Supreme Court, that state's first female chief justice.

Amalya L. Kearse

JUDGE. Amalya L. Kearse is a native of Vauxhall, New Jersey. She received a Bachelor of Arts degree from

Wellesley College in 1959 and earned her Juris Doctor degree from the University of Michigan Law School in 1962.

Her professional career includes serving in private law practice (1962–1979) and as an adjunct lecturer at the New York University Law School (1968–1969). On May 3, 1979, she was nominated by President Jimmy Carter to judge on the United States Court of Appeals for the Second Circuit. She was confirmed by the Senate on June 19, 1979, and received commission on June 21, 1979. She assumed senior status on June 11, 2002.

Lynda Keever

MEDIA EXECUTIVE. Lynda Keever received a Bachelor of Arts in government at Florida State University in 1969. She serves as chair and publisher of *Florida Trend* magazine in St. Petersburg, Florida. At *Florida Trend*, she has been the prime mover in the creation of new annual magazines such as *Business Florida*, the official publication for recruiting new business to the state; *Florida Small Business*; and *TopRank Florida*, the only statewide ranking of companies in 60 industries.

Patricia A. Keit

MILITARY. Patricia A. Keit, a Georgia native, entered the United States Army in July 1976. She graduated from basic combat training at Fort Jackson, South Carolina, and advanced individual training as a radio operator at Fort Monmouth, New Jersey.

Her military education includes all the Noncommissioned Officer Education System Courses; Communications Security Custodian Course (honor graduate); the Instructor Training Course; Systems Approach to Training; Small Group Leadership Course; the First Sergeant Course; the Command Sergeant Major's Designee Course; and the United States Army Sergeants Major Academy (class 50). She earned an associate's degree in applied science from Georgia Military College, Milledgeville, Georgia.

Her key military assignments include serving as instructor, Regimental Noncommissioned Officer's Academy at Fort Gordon, Georgia; nodal platoon sergeant, 304th Signal Battalion, Camp Colbern, Republic of Korea; operations sergeant, 15th Regimental Signal Brigade, Fort Gordon, Georgia; first sergeant of Alpha and Bravo Company, 551st Signal Battalion at Fort Gordon, Georgia; first sergeant of Alpha Company, 307th Signal Battalion, Camp Carroll, ROK; first sergeant of Headquarters and Alpha Company, 369th Signal Battalion, Fort Gordon, Georgia; special projects sergeant major, United States Army Sergeant's Major Academy, Fort Bliss, Texas; command sergeant major, 551st Signal Battalion, Fort Gordon, Georgia; command sergeant major, 41st Signal Battalion at Yongsan Garrison, Republic of Korea. In August 2004, she was serving as the command sergeant major, Area IV Support Activity in Korea.

Marcia V. Keizs

EDUCATION. Marcia V. Keizs is a native of Kingston, Jamaica, and has lived and worked in New York City since graduating from high school in Kingston. She received a bachelor's degree from the University of Manitoba in Winnipeg in 1967 and a Master of Arts from Teachers College, Columbia University, in 1971. She earned her Doctorate of Education from Teachers College at Columbia University in 1984 and a certificate in educational management from the Harvard Graduate School of Education in 1995.

Her professional career includes serving as a professor of English at Queensborough Community College/City University of New York (CUNY) and as assistant director in the external education degree program for the homebound student. From 1984 to 1988, she worked at LaGuardia College/City University of New York where she achieved the title of assistant dean for external affairs, labor relations and personnel; from 1988 to 1994, Dr. Keizs was vice president and dean of student services at Queensborough Community College with a one-year stint as acting vice chancellor for student affairs of CUNY. She served at Borough of Manhattan Community College from September 1994 to August 1995 and at York College from January 5, 1996, to August 1996. She served as the vice president of academic affairs at Bronx Community College/City University of New York from October 1, 1997, to February 13, 2005.

Dr. Keizs was appointed the 6th president of York College, City University of New York on February 13, 2005.

Marilyn J. Kelly

JUDGE. Marilyn J. Kelly is a native of Detroit, Michigan. She received a Bachelor of Arts degree from Eastern Michigan University in 1960. She received a master's degree in French language and literature from Middlebury College in Vermont, completing her graduate studies at La Sorbonne, the University of Paris. She earned her Juris Doctor degree with honors from Wayne State University Law School in 1971. From 1962 to 1967, she taught French at Grosse Pointe public schools, at Albion College, and Eastern Michigan University; from 1969 to 1988, she held several clerkships and served in private law practice. In 1988, she was elected judge to the Michigan Court of Appeals for a six-year term and was re-elected to the Court of Appeals in 1994. She was elected to the Michigan Supreme Court for an eight-year term in 1996.

Sue Kelly

ELECTED OFFICIAL. Sue Kelly is a native of Lima, Ohio, and graduated from Lima Central High School. She received a Bachelor of Arts degree from Denison University in Granville, Ohio, in 1958 and earned a Master of Arts degree from Sarah Lawrence College in Bronxville, New York, in 1985.

Her professional career includes serving as a biomedical researcher at Boston City Hospital, in Boston, Massachusetts; as a teacher at New England Institute for Medical Research; on the staff of United Senator Hamilton Fish of New York; as an adjunct professor at Sarah Lawrence College; as a certified New York ombudsman for nursing homes. She was elected as a Republican to the 104th and 105th Congresses beginning January 3, 1995. She represents the 19th Congressional District of New York, which includes all of Putnam County and portions of Dutchess, Orange, Rockland and Westchester counties. The district is home to the United States Military Academy at West Point, two veteran's hospitals — Castle Point and Montrose — and the Delaware and Hudson rivers.

Suedeen G. Kelly

GOVERNMENT OFFICIAL. Suedeen G. Kelly received a Bachelor of Arts degree with distinction in chemistry and earned a Juris Doctor degree from Cornell Law School.

Her professional career includes serving as a professor of law at the University of New Mexico School of Law. She also served in private law practice in Albuquerque, New Mexico. In 2000, she served as counsel to the California independent system operator. Ms. Kelly was nominated by President George W. Bush and confirmed by the U.S. Senate to serve as a commissioner at the Federal Energy Regulatory Commission.

Susan Kelly

EDUCATION. Susan Kelly received a bachelor's degree in psychology and English literature from the University of Tasmania and a master's degree in education from the University of Canberra. She earned a Ph.D. in psychology from the University of Melbourne.

Her professional career includes serving from 1979 to 1988 as a tenured faculty at Swinburne University of Technology. She served from 1994 to 1998 as general manager at Australia's largest single provider of adult and continuing education, the Council of Adult Education. In 1998, she was recruited from Melbourne, Australia, to become dean of the School of Continuing Education, associate provost for outreach and e-learning and a tenured full professor at the University of Wisconsin–Milwaukee. On May 1, 2006, Dr. Kelly was appointed as the eighth president of Charles R. Drew University of Medicine and Science.

Kathryn Kemp

LAW ENFORCEMENT (FIRST). Kathryn Kemp received a bachelor's degree and a master's degree in business from the University of La Verne.

Her professional career includes serving as a member of the 1981 task force that created Ventura County Jail division's operations manual and served as a lieutenant in charge of the main jail. From 1993 to 2000, she served as chief of police for Thousand Oaks, the department's largest contract city. From April 2000 to April 2005 she managed the sheriff's human resources unit. In April 2005, she was promoted to chief deputy of the Ventura County Sheriff's Department. The appointment made Chief Deputy Kemp the first woman to serve in this position and the highest-ranking female officer in the history of the Ventura County Sheriff's Department.

Joyce L. Kennard

JUDGE. Joyce L. Kennard received an Associate in Arts degree in 1970 and a Bachelor of Arts (magna cum laude) degree in German from University of Southern California in 1971. In 1974, she graduated from the University of Southern California's Gould School of Law and at the same time received a master of public administration degree from University of Southern California School of public administration.

Her experience includes serving as associate justice on the State Court of Appeal in Los Angeles (Division Five) from April 1988 to April 1989; judge of the Los Angeles County Superior Court from February 1987 to March 1988; associate justice pro tempore on State Court of Appeal in Los Angeles (Division Three) from September 1987 to November 1987; judge on Los Angeles County Municipal in Los Angeles from 1979 to 1986; deputy attorney general in Los Angeles from 1975 to 1979.

Joyce L. Kennard was appointed to the California Supreme Court in April 1989. Since May 1996, she has served as chair of California Judicial Council's Appellate Advisory Committee, appointed by the chief justice of California, and chair of the Judicial Council.

Lydia H. Kennard

AVIATION. Lydia H. Kennard received a Bachelor of Arts degree from Stanford University and a master's degree from Massachusetts Institute of Technology. She earned a Juris Doctor degree from Harvard University.

Her professional career includes serving as president of KDG Development Construction Consulting, a Los Angeles–based firm. She joined Los Angeles World Airports (LAWA) in 1994 as deputy executive director for design and construction. In that capacity, she managed an annual capital improvement budget of over $600 million and oversaw the activities relating to planning, design, engineering, construction, real estate and facilities at Los Angeles World Airports.

Ms. Kennard was appointed executive director of the Los Angeles World Airports in March 2000 after acting as interim executive director since August 1999. She is the highest-ranking woman general manager in the history of the city of Los Angels. She is also one of the highest ranking women in aviation management in the world running the second largest system of airports. LAWA airports include Los Angeles International, Ontario International, Van Nuys and Palmdale Regional.

Claudia Kennedy

MILITARY (FIRST). Claudia J. Kennedy received a Bachelor of Arts degree in philosophy from Southwestern at Memphis. She is a graduate of the United States Army's Command and General Staff College and the United States Army's War College.

She entered the United States Army on June 2, 1969, as a second lieutenant. Her military career included serving as the commander of an intelligence battalion; in a recruiting battalion; commander of an intelligence brigade; as director of intelligence, forces command, at Fort McPherson, Georgia. She was promoted to major general on November 1, 1996, and was selected to serve as deputy commander, United States Army Intelligence Center and Fort Huachuca/Assist Commandant United States Army Intelligence School at Fort Huachuca. She was promoted to lieutenant general on May 21, 1997, becoming the first woman to achieve the rank of three-star general in the United States Army. She was selected to serve as deputy chief of staff for intelligence, United States Army.

Cornelia G. Kennedy

JUDGE. Cornelia G. Kennedy is a native of Detroit, Michigan. She received a Bachelor of Arts degree from the University of Michigan in 1945 and earned her Juris Doctor degree from the University of Michigan in 1947.

She has served as law clerk for the chief judge of United States Court of Appeals for the Washington, D.C., circuit; and in private law practice from 1948 to 1966. In 1967, she was appointed judge, Third Judicial Circuit of Michigan; in 1970, she was appointed judge, United States District Court for the Eastern District of Michigan; in 1977, she served as chief judge, United States District Court for the Eastern District of Michigan; in 1979 she was appointed judge, U.S. Court of Appeals for the Sixth Circuit; in 1999, she became the senior judge for the United States Court of Appeals for the Sixth Circuit.

Yvonne Kennedy

EDUCATION (FIRST). Yvonne Kennedy attended Bishop State Community College and received an Associate in Arts degree. She received a Bachelor of Science degree from Alabama State University and a Master of Arts degree from Morgan State University in Baltimore, Maryland. She earned her Ph.D. from the University of Alabama and has received an honorary doctorate from Lane College in Jackson, Tennessee.

Dr. Kennedy is the first black woman east of the Mississippi River to head a state college. She has served as president of Bishop State Community College since 1981. She was elected in 1982 to the Alabama House of Representatives where she represents District 97 and serves on the House Ways and Means Committee and is chair of the Education Committee. She was twice elected the national president of the Delta Sigma Theta sorority. She is the chairperson of the Board of Trustees of the Southeast Alabama Conference of the CME Church. She is a member of the Board of Trustees of Miles College.

Kristie Anne Kenney

GOVERNMENT OFFICIAL. Kristie Anne Kenney received a bachelor's degree in political science from Clemson University and a master's degree in Latin American studies from Tulane University. She is a graduate of the National War College.

Her professional career includes serving as director of the State Department Operations Center, a detail to the White House in the National Security Council staff and political-military officer in the Office of NATO Affairs. She served as executive secretary of the State Department, the first woman to hold that key position. She served as senior advisor to the assistant secretary for international narcotics and law enforcement from 2001 to 2002. On September 6, 2002, she was sworn in as ambassador to Ecuador and presented her credentials to President Gustavo Noboa on September 25, 2002.

Shirley Strum Kenny

EDUCATION. Shirley Strum Kenny received a bachelor's degree in English and journalism from the University of Texas and a Master of Arts from the University of Minnesota. She earned a Ph.D. from the University of Chicago. She has also received honorary doctorate degrees from the university of Rochester; Chonnam National, Dongguk and Ajou universities in Korea.

Her professional career includes serving from 1985 to 1994

as president of Queens College. In 1994, Dr. Kenny was appointed the first woman and first humanist to serve as president of Stony Brook University. She is the fourth president of Stony Brook University.

Kathleen Ann Keough

JUDGE. Kathleen Ann Keough is a native of the Cleveland, Ohio, area. She received a Bachelor of Arts degree in English and history from Youngstown State University and her Juris Doctor degree from the Cleveland Marshall College of Law.

Her professional career includes serving as a Cuyahoga County public defender for a total of ten years. She was elected to the Cleveland Municipal Court in 1995 and re-elected in 1999.

Gladys Kessler

JUDGE. Gladys Kessler received a Bachelor of Arts degree from Cornell University and an LL.B. degree from Harvard Law School. Following graduation, she was employed by the National Labor Relations Board; served as legislative assistant to a U.S. senator and a U.S. congressman; worked for the New York City Board of Education; and served in private law practice. In June 1977, she was appointed associate judge of the Superior Court of the District of Columbia; from 1981 to 1985, she served as presiding judge of the family division.

Judge Kessler was appointed to the United States District Court for the District of Columbia in July 1994.

Joan F. Kessler

JUDGE. Joan F. Kessler received a Bachelor of Arts from the University of Kansas in 1966 and earned her Juris Doctor (cum laude) from Marquette University School of Law in 1968.

Her professional career includes serving law clerk at the U.S. District Court of Eastern District of Wisconsin (1968–1969); in private law practice (1969–1978); as the United States attorney, Eastern District of Wisconsin (1978–1981); and in private law practice (1981–2004). In 2004, she was appointed judge on the Wisconsin Court of Appeals, District I.

Mary Ellen Kicza

GOVERNMENT OFFICIAL. Mary Ellen Kicza received a bachelor's degree in electrical and electronics engineering from California State University and a Master's in Business Administration from the Florida Institute of Technology.

In 1982, Ms. Kicza joined NASA's Kennedy Space Center where she served as a lead engineer participating in the preparation of Atlas Centaur and Shuttle Centaur launch vehicles in support of NASA, DoD and NOAA satellites. Since that time, she has served as a program manager, as deputy director of the Solar System Exploration Division, assistant associate administrator for space science, associate center director for Goddard Space Flight Center and associate administrator for biological/physical research. In these roles, Ms. Kicza led and managed large, complex ground-based and space flight programs, many of which are international in scope in support of U.S. space and earth science programs. As the associate center director at Goddard, she managed a diverse scientific and engineering community of approximately 3,100 civil servants and 6,000 contractors. She currently serves as the assistant administrator for satellite and information service at National Oceanic and Atmospheric Administration (NOAA).

Mary J. Kight

MILITARY. Mary J. Kight received an Associates of Arts degree from Monterey Peninsula Junior College in 1970 and a Bachelor of Arts degree from California State University in Chico, California, in 1973. She earned a Master of Science degree from Gonzaga University in Spokane, Washington. She graduated from Squadron Officers School in 1976, Command and Staff College in 1992, Air War

College in 1999, and received a Masters of Science degree from the Air University at Maxwell AFB, Alabama, in 2000.

Her professional career includes enlisting into the United States Air Force and received her commission in 1974. She had a successful career as a personnel officer at Fairchild Air Force Base at Spokane, Washington, followed by an assignment with the Department of the Army. She ended her initial active duty career at Headquarters Strategic Air Command (SAC) at Omaha, Nebraska. While continuing her military affiliation, she was assigned as the wing executive officer upon joining the Nebraska Air National Guard in 1981. She later returned to her home state of California in 1984 when she joined the California Air National Guard in Fresno. She served as the avionics maintenance officer from 1984 to 1987, field maintenance officer from 1987 to 1990 and aircraft maintenance officer from 1991 to 1994. She served as the first aircraft generation squadron commander for the 144th Fighter Wing from 1994 through 1998. Brigadier General Kight was the 144th Mission Support Group commander in Fresno, California, and also served as the 201st Mission Support Squadron, detachment commander for all members on Title 10. She was promoted to colonel on July 10, 2001. In 2004, she was assigned as the assistant adjutant general, air, for the California Air National Guard. She serves as a military assistant and advisor to the adjutant general for Army and Air National Guard matters in the state of California. She was promoted to brigadier general on April 3, 2006.

Carolyn Cheeks Kilpatrick

ELECTED OFFICIAL. Carolyn Cheeks Kilpatrick is a native of Detroit, Michigan and graduated from the High School of Commerce, Detroit, Michigan. She attended Ferris State University in Big Rapids, Michigan, 1968–1970, and received a Bachelor of Science degree from Western Michigan University, Kalamazoo, Michigan, in 1972. She earned her Masters of Science degree from the University of Michigan, Ann Arbor, in 1977.

Her professional career includes serving as a teacher. She was elected a member of the Michigan State House of Representatives from 1979 until 1996; she was elected a United States representative to the 105th Congress and to the four succeeding Congresses (January 3, 1997–present).

Donna Mercado Kim

ELECTED OFFICIAL. Donna Mercado Kim is a native of Hawaii. She graduated from Farrington High School in Hawaii. She attended the University of Hawaii from 1970 to 1972 and received a Bachelor of Arts from Washington State University in 1974.

Her professional career includes serving as a recreation director; as a small business executive director; as a communications sales representative; as a hotel catering sales representative; as a member of the Board of Directors, Bank of America Hawaii; as a trained facilitator at the Pacific Institute; and as a public relations director at KUMU Radio. She served 15 years as a member of the Honolulu City Council from 1985 to 2000.

Ms. Kim has served as a state senator for the state of Hawaii since 2000.

Jennifer Kim

ELECTED OFFICIAL. Jennifer Kim she received a Bachelor of Arts degree in political science (magna cum laude) from Texas A&M in 1993. She earned a master's degree in public affairs from Woodrow Wilson School in 1998.

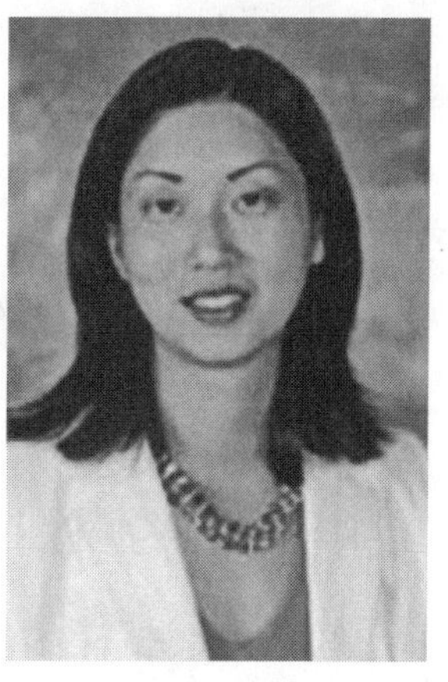

Her professional career includes serving on the Social Equity Commission, on the Census 2000 Complete Count Committee, and on the Commission on Immigrant Affairs. From 1998 to 2000, she worked for the U.S. Department of Commerce's Economic Development Administration as an economic development specialist and as a member of the executive management team. She serves as member of the Austin City Council in Texas.

Marjorie L. Kimbrough

EDUCATION. Marjorie L. Kimbrough earned a master's degree in Christian education from Interdenominational Theological Center in Atlanta. She has written several programming language textbooks and was named Georgia Author of the Year in the area of nonfiction.

Her professional career includes serving over 28 years in data processing in corporate America. She has served as a minister's wife and as an instructor in religion and philosophy at Clark Atlanta University.

Barbara L. King

MINISTRY. Barbara King is a native of Houston, Texas. She received a bachelor's degree from Texas Southern University in 1955 and a master's degree from Atlanta University in 1957. She holds honorary doctorate degrees from the University of Metaphysics in Portland, Oregon; the Christian Church of Universal Philosophy in Seattle, Washington; and Bethune-Cookman College in Daytona Beach, Florida.

Reverend King is the founder of the Hillside Chapel and Truth Center, Inc., in Atlanta, Georgia. She is also the founder and president of the Barbara King School of Ministry, which opened in 1971.

Carolyn Dineen King

JUDGE. Carolyn Dineen King is a native of Syracuse, New York. She received a Bachelor of Arts degree from Smith College in 1959 and earned her Juris Doctor degree from Yale Law School in 1962. She served in private law practice from 1962 to 1979.

On April 30, 1979, she was nominated by President Jimmy Carter to fill a seat as judge, U.S. Court of Appeals for the Fifth Circuit and was confirmed by the U.S. Senate on July12, 1979. She served as chief judge from 1999 to 2006.

Gayle King

ENTERTAINMENT. Gayle King is a native of Chevy Chase, Maryland, and grew up in Bethesda, Maryland. She received a degree in psychology from the University of Maryland and currently lives in Greenwich, Connecticut.

She started her career as a production assistant at WJZ-TV in Baltimore and later WTOP-TV in Washington, D.C., where she trained as a reporter. King moved to Kansas City, Missouri, where she was a reporter and weekend anchor at WDAF-TV. In 1981, she was hired as a news anchor for WFSB in Hartford, Connecticut, where she worked for 18 years. In 1991, King briefly co-hosted an NBC daytime talk show with Robin Wagner called *Cover to Cover*. In 1997 she was offered her own syndicated talk show, *The Gayle King Show*, which ran for one year. King joined *O, The Oprah Magazine* in 1999 and is currently editor-at-large. She has also worked as a special correspondent for *The Oprah Winfrey Show* and *Good Morning America*. In September 2006, King began to co-host "Oprah & Friends" on XM Satellite Radio.

Gwendolyn King

BUSINESS EXECUTIVE. Gwendolyn King received a Bachelor of Arts degree in French and education from Howard University, and earned a master's degree in public administration from George Washington University. She has received honorary doctorates of humane letters and public service from the University of New Haven and the University of Maryland Baltimore County, respectively.

Her professional career includes serving as the 11th commissioner of Social Security. She has served as a senior vice president of corporate and public affairs for PECO Energy Company (formerly Philadelphia Electric Company). Ms. King serves as president of Podium Prose, a Washington, D.C.–based speakers bureau and speechwriting service.

Karen King

Business Executive. Karen King began her career at McDonald's in 1975 as a restaurant crew employee in Lawrenceville, Georgia. She has served in a variety of leadership positions throughout her McDonald's career to include serving as licensing manager, operations manager, field service manager and director of operations. In 1998, she was promoted to regional manager/vice president for McDonald's Raleigh region. In 2002, she was named general manager/vice president for McDonald's Florida region.

Ms. King was appointed president of McDonald's East Division in March 2005, and is responsible for more than 5,000 restaurants.

Reatha Clark King

Business Executive. Reatha Clark King is a native of Pavo, Georgia. She received a Bachelor of Science degree from Clark College (now Clark Atlanta University) and a degree in finance from Columbia University. She earned a Master of Science degree and Ph.D. degree in thermochemistry from the University of Chicago. She has been awarded fourteen honorary degrees.

Her professional career includes serving as a research chemist at the Natural Bureau of Standards in Washington, D.C.; as an associate dean for natural sciences and math at New York City College; and as president of Metropolitan State University in St. Paul, Minnesota. From 1988 to 2002, she served as president and executive director of General Mills Foundation and vice president of General Mills, Inc.; in 2002, she was elected chairman of the Board of Trustees for General Mills Foundation.

Dr. King serves on the boards of Exxon Mobil Corporation, Minnesota Mutual, H.B. Fuller Co., Wells Fargo, the Clark Atlanta University, and the International Trachoma Initiative.

Teresa V. King

Military. Teresa V. King was born in Fernandina Beach, Florida. She entered the United States Army in August 1974 as a clerk typist completing three years of active duty before leaving the Army in 1977. After a brief departure, she returned to active duty as a motor transport operator in 1978.

Her military education includes all the Non-Commissioned Officer Education System Courses, Drill Sergeant School, the First Sergeant School, and the United States Army Sergeants Major Academy (class 49).

Her key military assignments include serving as a drill sergeant, in Charlie, Delta and Alpha companies at Fort Dix, New Jersey; as a PLDC instructor, 64th Support Battalion in Wiesbaden, Germany; as a squad leader, 15th Supply and Transport Battalion; drill sergeant leader at the Drill Sergeant School at Fort Knox, Kentucky; as a transportation coordinator, 227th Maintenance Battalion, Yongson, Korea; as a platoon sergeant, Bravo Company, 724th Main Support Battalion at Fort Stewart, Georgia; as first sergeant, 24th Forward Support Battalion, Fort Stewart, Georgia; as an active duty advisor, the National Guard, 1454th Transportation Battalion, Concord, North Carolina; as the non-commissioned officer in charge of the division transportation office, 2nd Infantry Division, Camp Red Cloud, Korea; as both first sergeant and command sergeant major at Fort Story, Virginia; as command sergeant major, Advanced Individual Training Battalion, 58th Transportation Battalion, Fort Leonard Wood, Missouri; from May 2001 to June 2003, as the brigade command sergeant major, 1st Transportation Movement Control Agency, in Kaiserslautern, Germany. In July 2005, she was serving as the command sergeant major, Installation Management Agency–European Region in Heidelberg, Germany.

Patricia Kirk-McAlpine

Government Official. Patricia Kirk-McAlpine began her federal service as a member of the three-year United States Army Career Intern Program. Following graduation from the intern program, she was immediately assigned as lead negotiator with the United States Army Missile Commands Hawk Missile System Program Office. As an Air Force civilian, her first assignment with the Air Force Plant Representative Office at Northrop Corp. was followed by a position as negotiator for the Space and Missile Systems organizations Advanced Ballistic Reentry System. Shortly thereafter, she became a contracting officer for the secretary of the Air Force Office of Special Projects. In January 2005, she was serving as director of contracting, Space and Mis-

sile Systems Center, Air Force Space Command, Los Angeles Air Force Base, California.

Her education includes a Bachelor of Arts degree from Stillman College, Tuscaloosa, Alabama; Master of Business Administration degree from Alabama A&M University; Executive Development Course, University of Southern California; Defense Systems Management Course, Fort Belvoir, Virginia; Senior Executive Fellows Program, Harvard University, Cambridge, Massachusetts; Leadership for a Democratic Society, Federal Executive Institute; National Security Leadership Course, Johns Hopkins University; and Defense Systems Management College, Fort Belvoir, Virginia.

Cynthia N. Kirkland

MILITARY. Cynthia N. Kirkland received an Associate of Arts degree in liberal studies from Truckee Meadows Community College in Reno, Nevada, and a Bachelor of Science degree in business administration from the University of Nevada in Reno. She is a graduate of the Air Command and Staff College and the Air War College.

Brigadier General Kirkland's military assignments include serving from March 2002 to December 2002 as deputy commander of the Nevada Air National Guard headquarters in Carson City, Nevada. From December 2002 to November 2003, she served as chief of staff for the Nevada Air National Guard Headquarters in Carson City, Nevada. From November 2003 to June 2005, she was assigned as chief, Standing Joint Force Headquarters in Carson City. In June 2005, she was appointed by the governor of Nevada to serve as the state of Nevada adjutant general. She is the military chief of staff to the governor and is responsible for both the federal and state missions of the Nevada National Guard. General Kirkland now commands more than 3,000 members of the Nevada Air and Army National Guard including the Nevada Air National Guard's 152nd Airlift Wing and 152nd Intelligence Squadron and the Nevada Army Guard's units.

Elizabeth Kiss

EDUCATION. Elizabeth Kiss received a bachelor's degree from Davidson College and earned a doctorate degree in philosophy from Oxford University in England. A former Rhodes Scholar, she has held fellowships at the Harvard Program in Ethics and the Professions, the National Humanities Center and at Melbourne University's Centre on Applied Philosophy and Public Ethics.

Her professional career includes serving as a professor at Princeton University for eight years; as a professor at Randolph-Macon College; as a professor at Deep Springs College; as an associate professor of the practice of political science and philosophy at Duke University; as the former Nannerl O. Keohane director of the Kenan Institute for Ethics.

Dr. Kiss was appointed president of Agnes Scott College in Decatur, Georgia.

Marilyn S. Kite

JUDGE. Marilyn S. Kite received a Bachelor of Arts degree with honors from the University of Wyoming in 1970 and earned her Juris Doctor degree from the University of Wyoming Law School in 1974.

Her professional career includes serving as an assistant attorney general for the state of Wyoming from 1974 to 1979. She was engaged in private practice until her appointment to the bench. She was appointed judge to the Wyoming State Court by Governor Jim Gerringer and was sworn into office on June 2, 2000.

Helen Klanderud

ELECTED OFFICIAL. Helen Klanderud is a native of Denver, Colorado. She received a Bachelor of Arts degree from St. Mary's College, Notre Dame, in Indiana, a Master's in Social Work from the University of Nebraska in Lincoln, Nebraska, and a Juris Doctor degree from the University of Nebraska. Her professional career includes serving from 1971 to 1976 as director of

Touchstone Mental Health Clinic in Aspen; as a social worker for the Aspen Public Schools from 1971 to 1973; and as a Pitkin County commissioner from 1981 to 1987. In 2006, she was serving as mayor of the city of Aspen, Colorado.

Amy Jean Klobuchar

ELECTED OFFICIAL. Amy Jean Klobuchar is a native of Plymouth, Minnesota. She received a bachelor's degree in political science magna cum laude from Yale University and her Juris Doctor from the University of Chicago Law School.

Her professional career includes private law practice. In 1998, she was elected Hennepin County attorney in Minnesota and was re-elected in 2002 with no opposition. In November 2006, Ms. Klobuchar was elected United States senator from Minnesota.

Liz Kniss

ELECTED OFFICIAL. Liz Kniss received a Bachelor of Science degree in nursing from Simmons College in Boston and earned a master's in public administration in public and health care policy from California State University. She has also completed graduate work in health policy and economics at the University of California, Berkeley.

Her professional career includes serving as a registered nurse in hospital care and as a public health nurse for San Mateo County. She served as a school nurse for Cupertino Union School District and as a marketing and communications manager at Sun Microsystems, Inc. In 1985, she was elected to Palo Alto Unified School Board (California). In 1989, she was elected to the Palo Alto City Council where she was re-elected twice and served as mayor in 1994 and 2000. In November 2000, she was elected to represent Santa Clara County's Fifth District on the Board of Supervisors. Ms. Kniss was elected by her colleagues to serve as chair of the Board of Supervisors during 2005. In 2006, she served as chair of the Health Committee as well as chair of the Legislative Committee and vice-chair of Finance and Government.

Catherine Baker Knoll

ELECTED OFFICIAL. Catherine Baker Knoll is a native of McKees Rocks, Pennsylvania. She attended Duquesne University.

Her professional career includes working at the Pennsylvania Department of Transportation. In 1988, she was elected state treasurer of Pennsylvania; in 2002, she was elected lieutenant governor of Pennsylvania. She was sworn in as lieutenant governor on January 23, 2003, becoming the first woman to serve as lieutenant governor in the state's history.

Laurette Koellner

BUSINESS EXECUTIVE. Laurette Koellner is a native of Brooklyn, New York. She received a bachelor's degree in business management from the University of Central Florida and earned a Masters of Business Administration degree from Stetson University. She holds a certified professional contracts manager designation from the National Contracts Management Association.

She began her career in the aerospace industry in 1978 when she joined McDonnell Douglas as an analyst. She was promoted several times over the next eight years and in 1986 McDonnell Douglas appointed her to manage contracts and pricing for its Missile Systems Company. In 1994, she was named director of human resources for McDonnell Douglas. She continued to hold numerous positions of increasing responsibility at McDonnell Douglas and later Boeing, following the merger of the two companies in 1997. In 1999, she was named Boeing's vice president and corporate controller where she was responsible for financial and cost accounting, cost policy, company wide estimating, common business systems, insurance and risk management. She has served as president of Shared Services Group, which is the business unit that employs almost 18,000

in every major location where Boeing operates. In 2002, she was named the executive vice president and chief people and administration officer of the Boeing Company. She led people and labor strategy, people services, diversity, the Boeing Leadership Center, corporate administration, corporate services, corporate contributions and community relations for the global enterprise.

Colleen Kollar-Kotelly

JUDGE. Colleen Kollar-Kotelly received a Bachelor of Arts degree from the Catholic University of America in 1965 and earned her Juris Doctor degree from Columbus School of Law in 1968.

She served as law clerk to Judge Catherine B. Kelly of the District of Columbia Court of Appeals. From 1969 to 1972, she was an attorney in the criminal division of the U.S. Department of Justice and then served as the chief legal counsel to Saint Elizabeth's Hospital until 1984. She was appointed associate judge of the D.C. Superior Court in October 1984 and served as deputy presiding judge of the criminal division from 1995 until her appointment to the federal bench.

Judge Kollar-Kotelly was appointed to the United States District Court in May 1997. In May 2002, Chief Justice Rehnquist appointed Judge Kollar-Kotelly to serve as presiding judge of the United States Foreign Intelligence Surveillance Court, a seven-year appointment.

Kay Koplovtz

ENTERTAINMENT EXECUTIVE. Kay Koplovtz is a native of Milwaukee, Wisconsin. She received a Bachelor of Science degree from the University of Wisconsin and a master's degree in communications from Michigan State University. She holds honorary doctorate degrees from Emerson College and St. John's University.

She is the founder of USA Networks, television's first advertiser-support basic cable network and was the first female network president in television history. She served as chairman and chief executive officer from USA's premiere in 1977 as an all sports service; she stepped down in 1998. During her tenure, she built USA into the #1 ranking in primetime viewership among cable networks for 13 consecutive years at the helm. Under her direction, USA launched the SCI-FI channel in 1992 which has become one of the industry's top ranked networks in viewership according to Nielson and is distributed to over 140 million households worldwide. In 1994, she launched USA Networks International which now operates in countries around the world. The company was sold in 1998 for $4.5 billion and became a publicly listed company.

Ms. Koplovtz serves as the principal of Koplovtz & Company, LLC, which provides advisory services to entertainment companies, sports organizations, advertisers and distributors and advises companies on growth strategies.

Julia A. Kraus

MILITARY. Julia A. Kraus received a Bachelor of Arts degree in sociology from Olivet College and a master of strategic studies from the United States Army War College. She is a graduate of the Military Intelligence School Basic and Advanced courses, the United States Army Command and General Staff College, and the United States Army War College. She received her commission into the United States Army as a second lieutenant on June 24, 1977.

She has served in numerous positions of increased authority and responsibility to include serving from June 1998 to May 2001 as commander, United States Army Reserve Military Intelligence Group Europe, 7th Army Reserve Command, Heidelberg, Germany; from June 2001 to March 2004 as commander, 5115th Garrison Support Command, Fort Meade, Maryland; from March 2004 to July 2004 as deputy commander, (IMA), United States Army Intelligence and Security Command, Fort Belvoir, Virginia; from August 2004 to March 2005, she served as deputy commander, United States Army Intelligence and Security Command, Fort Belvoir, Virginia. She was promoted to brigadier general on October 22, 2004.

From March 2005 to March 2006, she served as assistant deputy chief of staff, G2, Headquarters, Department of the Army, Pentagon, Washington, D.C.; from April 2006 to July 2006 as deputy commander, United States Army Intelligence and Security Command at Fort Belvoir, Virginia.

Brigadier General Kraus serves as the deputy commander (IMA) United States Army Intelligence and Security Command at Fort Belvoir, Virginia.

Sallie L. Krawcheck

FINANCE EXECUTIVE. Sallie L. Krawcheck is a native of Charleston, South Carolina. She received a Bachelor of Arts with honors from the University of North Carolina at Chapel Hill and a master's degree in business from Columbia University.

Her professional career includes serving as a financial analyst at Salomon Brothers; as an associate in the corporate finance department of Donaldson, Lufkin & Jenrette; as a senior equity research analyst responsible for the coverage of life insurance and securities brokerage companies from 1994 to 1999; as the director of research at Bernstein & Company; as executive vice president of Bernstein's parent company, Alliance Capital Management from 1999 to 2001; chairman and chief executive officer of Stanford C. Bernstein & Company.

Ms. Krawcheck has served as chief financial officer and head of strategy for Citigroup Inc. since October 2002.

Judith L. Kreeger

JUDGE. Judith L. Kreeger received a Bachelor of Arts from Randolph Macon Women's College in 1962 and earned her Juris Doctor degree from the University of Miami in 1966. Her professional career includes serving as a law clerk to the chief judge of the United States District Court from 1966 to 1969. She was engaged in private law practice from 1969 to 1992. In 1993, she was appointed judge to Florida Circuit Court. She has served as the presiding judge, Dade County Grand Jury, since 1997.

Beth Krom

ELECTED OFFICIAL. Beth Krom received a Bachelor of Science degree in education from the University of Texas at Austin in 1981. She began her career as a teacher of the visually impaired. In 1997, she established her own home based creative services business, All Things Creative, providing freelance creative services to private and corporate clients.

She was first elected to the Irvine City Council in November 2000 and again in 2002. On November 2, 2004, she was elected as mayor of the city of Irvine, California.

Kate B. Kronmiller

AEROSPACE. Kate B. Kronmiller received a Bachelor of Science degree in biology with a minor in ocean engineering from the University of Pennsylvania and American University. She earned a master's degree in science, technology and public policy at George Washington University.

She joined Rockwell in 1985 as representative for Rocketdyne Propulsion and Power and its diverse, space-related programs, including the Space Shuttle Main Engine, International Space Station, Expendable Launch Vehicle, Peacekeeper and Directed Energy programs. In total, Kronmiller has more than 26 years of experience in the aerospace community. She has served as vice president of Space Services Inc., the first commercial expendable launch vehicle company, located in Houston, Texas. She began in government service as committee professional staff in Congress, and then directed legislative affairs for satellite programs at the National Oceanic and Atmospheric Administration. She serves as vice president of government relations for United Space Alliance in Washington, D.C.

Liz Krueger

ELECTED OFFICIAL. Liz Krueger received a bachelor degree in social policy and human development from Northwestern University and earned a masters degree from the University of Chicago's Harris Graduate School of Public Policy.

Her professional career includes serving as

an associate director of the Community Food Resource Center for 15 years where she was responsible for directing their efforts to expand access to government programs in New York City. She was elected to the New York State Senate in a special election in February 2002 and is the ranking Democratic member of the Senate Standing Committee on Housing, Construction and Community Development.

Mary Ann Krusa-Dossin

MILITARY. Mary Ann Krusa-Dossin holds a Bachelor of Arts degree in psychology and sociology from Texas Christian University in 1974 and a Master of Science degree in human relations from Golden Gate University in 1981. She earned a Master of Science degree in national resource strategy from the Industrial College of the Armed Forces, National Defense University. She is a graduate of the Basic School at Quantico and Military Police Officers Basic Course at Fort McClellan in 1976. She is a graduate of the Marine Corps Command and Staff College, Quantico, in 1987. She was commissioned a second lieutenant in August 1975 through Officer Candidate School.

Her military career includes serving in numerous assignments of increased authority and responsibility to include serving as the provost marshal at Marine Corps Air Station Yuma; in 1991, she assumed command of the Headquarters and Headquarters Squadron at Marine Corps Air Station Yuma; in August 1992, she became the executive officer of Headquarters and Service Battalion at Marine Corps Base Camp Smedley D. Butler, Okinawa; served as deputy camp commander at Camp Foster and Camp Lester; in July 1996, she transferred to the Pentagon to serve as an action officer with the Joint Staff, J-7, Operational Plans and Interoperability Directorate; in July 1998, she assumed command of Security Battalion, Marine Corps Base Camp Pendleton; she then served as the assistant chief of staff, Marine Corps Community Services, Marine Corps Base Camp Pendleton from July 2000 to June 2002; she transferred to the Pentagon in July 2002 to serve as the deputy director, Marine Corps public affairs; in June 2003, she assumed the duties of director, Marine Corps public affairs.

Major General Krusa-Dossin serves as the commanding general, Marine Corps Base, Camp S.D. Butler.

Ellen J. Kullman

BUSINESS EXECUTIVE. Ellen J. Kullman received a Bachelor of Science degree in mechanical engineering from Tufts University and earned a Master of Business Administration from Northwestern University.

Her professional career includes working for General Electric in various business development, marketing and sales positions. She began her career at DuPont in 1988 as marketing manager in the medical imaging business. In 1994, she joined White Pigment & Mineral Products as global business director and was named vice president and general manager in 1995. She assumed leadership of two high-growth business, DuPont Safety Resources in 1998 and Bio-Based Material in 1999.

Ms. Kullman was named group vice president and general manager in 2000 with the addition of corporate new business development and intellectual assets licensing. In 2001, she assumed responsibility for DuPont Flooring Systems and DuPont Surfaces. She was named group vice president for DuPont safety and protection in February 2002 and assumed her current position in June 2006, as executive vice president at DuPont.

Mary Lacy

ELECTED OFFICIAL. Mary Lacy received her Juris Doctor degree with honors from the University of Iowa Law School in 1978. She was engaged in private law practice and has served with the Boulder Colorado District Attorney's office since 1983. In 2006, she was serving as the district attorney for Boulder, Colorado.

Maureen E. Lally-Green

JUDGE. Maureen E. Lally-Green is a native of Sharpsville, Pennsylvania. She received her Bachelor of Science degree in secondary education, mathematics from Duquesne University in 1971. She earned her Juris Doctor degree from Duquesne University in 1974.

From 1983 to 1998, she served as a professor of law at Duquesne University; she served as a consultant to justices of the Pennsylvania Supreme Court (1985–1987; 1988–1998); she served as counsel to Commodity Futures Trading Commission in Washington,

D.C. (1975–78); and from 1974 to 1975 she served in private law practice.

In 1998, Pennsylvania Governor Tom Ridge appointed her judge to the Superior Court. She was confirmed by the State Senate and in 1999 was elected for a term of ten years.

Terri Lynn Land

ELECTED OFFICIAL. Terri Lynn Land is a graduate of Grandville High School and received a Bachelor of Arts degree in political science from Hope College in Holland, Michigan. Land is a longtime Republican activist: she has served as precinct delegate, county party executive director, and county chair and state committeewoman. She was first involved during her high school years when she served as a "scatter blitzer" for the Gerald R. Ford Presidential Campaign. She served as Kent County Clerk from 1992 to 2000 at a time of tremendous change and growth in Michigan's 4th largest county.

She was elected to office as Michigan's 41st secretary of state in November 2002. With more than 1.7 million votes, she carried more votes than any other candidate on the year's ballot, securing her place as Michigan's top-elected Republican official.

Maxine Cohen Lando

JUDGE. Maxine Cohen Lando received a Bachelor of Arts degree from the University of Michigan (Ann Arbor) in 1971 and earned her Juris Doctor degree from the University of Miami in 1974.

Her professional career includes serving as an assistant public defender from 1974 to 1985. She was engaged in private law practice from 1985 to 1991. In 1991, she was appointed a judge to a Florida county court. In 1995, she was appointed judge to the Florida Circuit Court.

Mary L. Landrieu

ELECTED OFFICIAL. Mary L. Landrieu is a native of Arlington, Virginia, and a graduate of Ursuline Academy in New Orleans. She received a bachelor's degree from Louisiana State University in Baton Rouge in 1977.

Her professional career includes serving as a member of the Louisiana House of Representatives from 1980 to 1988 and as Louisiana state treasurer from 1988 to 1996. She was elected a United States senator in 1996 and reelected in 2002 for the term ending January 3, 2009.

Bensonetta Tipton Lane

JUDGE. Bensonetta Tipton Lane is a native of Washington, D.C., and grew up in Bridgeport, Connecticut, where she was an honors-curriculum high school graduate. She received a Bachelor of Arts degree in political science from New York University in 1972 and received a Master's of Education degree from the University of Massachusetts at Amherst in 1973. She earned her Juris Doctor degree from the University of Virginia in 1976. She is currently pursuing a Masters of Judicial Studies from the University of Nevada.

While in college, she would cut several weeks of classes and head South to help with voter education in Huntsville, Alabama, and Albany, Georgia. She met a veteran activist in Albany who became a source of personal inspiration and a significant influence on her eventual career choice, the legendary civil rights attorney C. B. King.

Her professional career includes serving with the Teacher Corps Intern, a program where she taught adult education at a prison in Providence, Rhode Island, from 1973 to 1974; as a law clerk for the Honorable Romae T. Powell, Fulton County Juvenile Court; as a law clerk for Atlanta Legal Aid Society; and in private law practice from 1976 to 1992. In 1986, she was appointed judge, *pro hac vice* to the City Court of Atlanta; from 1992 to 1993, she served as an administrative law judge at the Georgia Department of Medical Assistance; from 1992 to 1995, she served as judge at the City Court of Atlanta; since 1995, she has served as judge, Fulton County Superior Court, in Atlanta, Georgia. She has received numerous awards to include Lawyer of the Year from the National Conference of Black Lawyers and the R. E. Thomas Civil Rights Award from the Gate City Bar Association.

Karen Lansing

JUDGE. Karen Lansing is a native of Kendrick, Idaho, where she graduated from Orofino High School in 1968. She received a Bachelor of Arts degree in political science from the University of Idaho in 1972. She earned her Juris Doctor degree from the University of Washington in 1978. She was employed by the Idaho Personnel Commission as a personnel analyst from 1972 to 1973 and served as a planner in the Idaho State Planning Agency from 1973 to 1975. She served as an assistant city attorney for the city of Boise, Idaho, in 1978 and 1979. She served in private law practice in 1979.

In June 1993, she was appointed judge to the Idaho State Court of Appeals.

Sherry Lansing

ENTERTAINMENT EXECUTIVE. Sherry Lansing is a native of Chicago, Illinois. She received a Bachelor of Science degree from Northwestern University. Her professional career includes serving as a teacher with the Los Angeles Unified School District from 1966 to 1969. She also worked as an actor, model and script reader. From 1973 to 1975, she served as a story editor and later as chief editor at MGM. In 1977, she was appointed vice president for creative affairs and served from 1977 to 1980 as senior vice president of production at Columbia Pictures. From 1980 to 1982, she was president of 20th Century–Fox Productions, becoming the first woman president of a major U.S. film studio. Ms. Lansing served as producer with Jaffe-Lansing Productions.

In 1990, she was appointed president of Paramount Communications and in 1992 named chairman of Paramount Motion Pictures Group.

Theresa C. Lantz

GOVERNMENT OFFICIAL. Theresa C. Lantz received an associate's degree in law enforcement, a bachelor's degree in criminal justice and a master's in criminal justice.

Her professional career includes serving an adjunct instructor at Tunxis Community College. She began her career in corrections as a front line correctional officer in the Washington, D.C., prison system in 1976. During that assignment she became the first woman correction officer in that department to work inside the maximum-security men's housing unit; she began her tenure with the Connecticut Department of Correction in July of 1989 as the director of training and staff development.

Ms. Lantz was appointed as the sixth commissioner of the Connecticut Department of Correction on March 11, 2003.

Judith Ann Lanzinger

JUDGE. Judith Ann Lanzinger received her undergraduate degree with a dual major in education and English (magna cum laude) from the University of Toledo and also earned a masters of judicial studies degree from the National Judicial College and University of Nevada, Reno. She earned her Juris Doctor degree from the University of Toledo College of Law.

Her professional career includes serving an elementary school teacher. She was elected to the Toledo Municipal Court in 1985, then served on the Lucas County Common Pleas Court from 1989 to 2003 and on the 6th District Court of Appeals from 2003 to 2005. She has judged at every level of the Ohio court system during the last 20 years. In 2004, she was elected to the Supreme Court of Ohio and took her seat on that court in January 2005.

Alicia L. Latimore

JUDGE. Alicia L. Latimore received a Bachelor of Science degree in psychology from Duke University in 1985 and earned her Juris Doctor degree from the University of Florida. She was engaged in private law practice. In 2006, she was selected judge to the Florida Circuit for Orange County Criminal Division.

Constance H. Lau

BUSINESS EXECUTIVE. Constance H. Lau received a Bachelor of Science degree from Yale College. She earned a Juris Doctor degree from the University of California's Hastings College of Law and a Master of Business Administration from Stanford University's Graduate School of Business.

Her professional career includes serving in real estate, corporate and banking law in San Francisco before returning to Hawaii as assistant counsel for Hawaiian Electric Company, Inc. By 1987, she was both treasurer at Hawaiian Electric Company and assistant treasurer of Hawaiian Electric Industries, Inc. Then April 1989 she was elevated to treasurer of Hawaiian Electric, Inc., and later added additional responsibilities as financial vice president and treasurer of Hawaiian Electric Industries, Inc. In 1999, Ms. Lau was named senior executive vice president, chief operating officer, chairman, president and chief executive officer of American Savings Bank, Hawaii's third largest financial institution. She was later named chairman, president and chief executive officer of Hawaiian Electric Industries, Inc.

Peggy A. Lautenschlager

ELECTED OFFICIAL. Peggy A. Lautenschlager is a graduate of Oklahoma State University. Her prior experience include serving in private practice; as a member of the adjunct faculties of the University of Wisconsin Law School, University of Wisconsin–Oshkosh, and Ripon College; as interim circuit court commissioner of Winnebago County; from July 1985 to December 1988, as the district attorney for Winnebago County; and in the Wisconsin Assembly from 1989 to 1993 representing the Fond du Lac area. In 1996, she was appointed by Janet Reno to serve on the 15-member Attorney General's Advisory Committee; until April 2001, she served as United States attorney for the Western District of Wisconsin. She was the chief federal law enforcement officer for the state's westernmost 44 counties.

Peggy A. Lautenschlager was elected attorney general of Wisconsin in 2002, the first woman ever to hold that position. She leads the Department of Justice and its major divisions and offices.

Janelle A. Lawless

JUDGE. Janelle A. Lawless received a Bachelor of Science degree in political science from Central Michigan University and earned her Juris Doctor degree from Thomas Cooley Law School in 1981. She was engaged in private law practice from 1981 to 1990. She served in the Ingham County Probate Court as administrator, register, and attorney referee from 1990 to 2002. On January 1, 2003, she was elected Circuit Court judge and serves as chief circuit judge pro-tempore in Ingham County, Lansing, Michigan.

Brenda L. Lawrence

ELECTED OFFICIAL. Brenda L. Lawrence is a longtime resident of the city of Southfield. A product of the Michigan public school system, Mayor Lawrence is an alumna of Pershing High School

and received her Bachelor of Arts in public administration from Central Michigan University.

She was elected mayor of the city of Southfield in November 2001. She is the first African-American and first woman mayor of Southfield, a city with a resident population of 78,300, a city budget of $118 million and 833 city employees.

Deirdre M. Lawrence

MEDICINE. Deirdre M. Lawrence received a bachelor's degree from Spelman College, and her Ph.D. in toxicology from Massachusetts Institute of Technology. She earned a master's of public health from Harvard University. She was the first National Institute of Health scientist to be awarded the Mansfield Fellowship.

The Mike Mansfield Fellowship, an intensive two-year program established by Congress in 1994, enables a select group of federal employees to develop an in-depth understanding of Japan and its government. She was selected for the fellowship program by a bi-national committee. She spent 10 months of full-time Japanese language and area studies training in the Washington, D.C., area, followed by one year in Japan working in a ministry or agency of its government. During her time in Japan, she worked to gain an understanding of Japan's procedures for developing, implementing and evaluating its national health policies, especially cancer control policies.

Dr. Lawrence serves as an epidemiologist in the risk factor monitoring and methods branch, division of cancer control and population science, at the National Cancer Institute.

Gwendolyn H. Lawrence

BUSINESS EXECUTIVE. Gwendolyn H. Lawrence is a native of Spartanburg, South Carolina, and graduated valedictorian at Carver High School in 1967. She was one of five females and one of two black females to receive a bachelor's degree in economics from Wofford College, a predominately all-male institution.

With her planning and budgeting skills, she became certified in Christian financial concepts through the late Dr. Larry Burkett's Money Matters ministry. With her certification in hand, she presently holds workshops, does personal counseling and teaches about personal budgeting and other financial matters. As part of a missionary trip to Fiji, Ms. Lawrence taught a budgeting course at the University of South Pacific in Fiji Islands. In addition to her teaching assignment, she, among others, was honored to have dinner at the Government House with President Ratu Josefa Iloilo, president of Fiji.

Employed by Dana Corporation for 28 years as a marketing, communications and planning coordinator, Ms. Lawrence travels around the world planning and coordinating trade shows for the company.

Honors that Ms. Lawrence has achieved include the President's Award for CHIPS process from Dana Corporation, Leadership Award from Clark's Chapel Baptist Church, and Woman of the Year Award from W.H.E.E.L., Leadership Award from Girl Scouts of America. Ms. Lawrence served as director of the children's ministry at her church for ten years and was also the first black and first black female owner of a video store in Statesville, North Carolina.

Kelli Richardson Lawson

ENTERTAINMENT EXECUTIVE. Kelli Richardson Lawson is a native of Cleveland, Ohio. She received a bachelor's degree in economics from Howard University and completed post-graduate work at the Center for Creative Leadership.

Ms. Lawson joined BET in 1996 after working in brand management at Procter & Gamble for seven years. She has served as vice president and publisher of BET Books after BET acquired the Arabesque Books line from Kensington Publishing in June 1998. In July 1999, she was named executive vice president, corporate marketing at BET.

Barbara Lawton

ELECTED OFFICIAL (FIRST). Barbara Lawton is a native of southeastern Wisconsin and lived in Green Bay. She received a bachelor's degree from Lawrence University and earned a master's degree in Spanish from the University of Wisconsin at Madison.

Barbara Lawton is the current lieutenant governor of Wisconsin. She became the first woman elected to the position in 2002 as the running mate of Democratic Governor Jim Doyle. Lawton was re-elected on November 7, 2006.

As lieutenant governor, Lawton has taken on many

issues, most related to economic development and fiscal responsibility. She is seen as a leading advocate for women in the workplace; in 2003 she launched an economic development initiative called "Wisconsin Women–Prosperity" and later convened the Lt. Governor's Task Force on Women and Depression. Lawton has also championed such issues as clean energy policy and stem cell research. In 2007, Lawton authored and passed the landmark Energy Independence and Climate Protection Resolution at the National Lieutenant Governors Association. Lawton has been called "the boldest and most active lieutenant governor in state history."

Geraldine Laybourne

ENTERTAINMENT EXECUTIVE. Geraldine Laybourne is a native of Martinsville, New Jersey. She received a Bachelor of Arts in art history from Vassar College and a Master of Science in elementary education from the University of Pennsylvania. She earned Film Muse Award from the University of Missouri at Kansas City.

Her professional career includes serving with Nickelodeon in the 1980s; in 1985, her team launched Nick at Nite. She served as vice chairman, MTV Networks, and as president of Disney/ABC Cable networks from 1996 to 1998 where she was responsible for overseeing current cable programming for the Walt Disney Company and its ABC subsidiary.

Ms. Laybourne is the founder, chairman and chief executive officer of Oxygen Media which was founded in 1998 and is currently available in over 50 million cable homes.

Rochelle B. Lazarus

BUSINESS EXECUTIVE. Rochelle B. Lazarus received a bachelor's degree from Smith College and earned a Master of Business Administration degree from Columbia University.

Her professional career includes joining Ogilvy & Mather Worldwide, a multinational advertising agency in 1971, becoming president of its U.S. direct marketing business in 1989. She then became president of Ogilvy & Mather New York and president of Ogilvy & Mather North America before becoming president and chief operating officer of the worldwide agency in 1995, chief executive officer in 1996 and chairman in 1997. She also served as a director of Merck, New York Presbyterian Hospital, American Museum of Natural History and the World Wildlife Fund and is a member of the Board of Overseers of Columbia Business School. She serves as a director on the General Electric Company's Board of Directors.

Ms. Lazarus serves as chairman and chief executive officer, Ogilvy & Mather Worldwide Advertising, New York, New York.

Jeanette Leahey

ELECTED OFFICIAL. Jeanette Leahey received her undergraduate degree in health sciences and earned a master's degree in education from Western Michigan University. She serves as the Berrien County 6th District commissioner in St. Joseph, Michigan. She serves as vice-chairman of the board and sits on the administration committee.

Margaret Leclaire

GOVERNMENT OFFICIAL. Margaret Leclaire received a Bachelor of Science degree from Cornell University and earned a Master of Business Administration degree from Wright State University. She is also a graduate of the Institute for Women Executives at the University of Alabama; the Program Managers Course at the De-

fense Systems Management College; Program for Senior Executive Fellows from the John F. Kennedy School of Government at Harvard University; Leadership for a Democratic Society, Federal Executive Institute; the National Security Leadership Course at Johns Hopkins and Syracuse Universities.

Her professional career includes serving in a wide variety of management positions since she entered federal civil service in 1975 as a management intern with the San Antonio Air Logistics Center; she has served as the director of systems management at Aeronautical Systems Center in Wright-Paterson Air Force Base, Ohio; as the deputy director for plans and programs, United States Transportation Command at Scott Air Force Base, Illinois; as deputy director for strategy and policy for the United States Transportation Command at Scott Air Force Base in Illinois.

Alison Renee Lee

JUDGE. Alison Renee Lee is a native of Washington, D.C. She received a Bachelor of Arts degree from Vassar College and earned her Juris Doctor degree from Tulane University School of Law in New Orleans, Louisiana, in 1982.

Her professional career includes serving in private law practice. In 1989, she was employed at the South Carolina Legislative Council. She then served as one of the first administrative law judges elected by the general assembly to the administrative law judge division. She was elected in February 1994 to a one year term and took office on March 1, 1994. In February 1999, she was elected by the general assembly to the position of circuit court judge, at large.

Barbara Lee

ELECTED OFFICIAL. Barbara Lee is a native of El Paso, Texas, and graduated from San Fernando High School, San Fernando, California. She received a Bachelor of Arts degree from Mills College in Oakland,

California, in 1973 and earned her masters of social works from the University of California at Berkeley, California, in 1975.

Her professional career includes serving as a staff member for United States Representative Ron Dellums of California. She served as a member of the California State Assembly from 1991 to 1997 and was elected as a member of the California State Senate from 1997 to 1998.

Ms. Lee was elected as a Democrat to the 105th Congress in a special election to fill the vacancy created by the resignation of United States Representative Ron Dellums and was reelected to the four succeeding Congresses (April 7, 1998–present).

Esther Lee

BUSINESS EXECUTIVE. Esther Lee received a bachelor's degree from Cornell University. Her professional career includes serving as senior vice president at J. Walter Thompson Co. She moved in 1993 to Independent Deutsch, where she was closely involved in new business and strategy as vice president and director of agency development and client service. Ms. Lee left Deutsch in 1997 with creative director Greg DiNoto in order to open New York agency DiNoto Lee. She spent five years with the boutique. She was appointed chief creative officer of North America for the Coca-Cola Company. Ms. Lee oversees media, creative and agencies for all brands of the world's largest soft-drink concern and was involved at every shoot for Coke's "Real" campaign from the time she joined Coke in September 2002.

Sharon Gail Lee

JUDGE. Sharon Gail Lee is a native of Knoxville, Tennessee. She attended Vanderbilt University. She received a Bachelor of Science degree in business administration from the University of Tennessee and a degree in accounting from the College of Business. She earned her Juris Doctor degree from the University of Tennessee College of Law in 1978.

Her professional career includes serv-

ing in private law practice in Madisonville, Tennessee from 1978 to 2004. She has served as county attorney for Monroe County, as Madisonville city judge, and as city attorney for Vonore and Madisonville. On June 4, 2004, she was appointed judge by Governor Phil Bredesen to the Tennessee Court of Appeals, Eastern Section in Knoxville, Tennessee.

Sherry A. Lee

JUDGE. Sherry A. Lee received a bachelor's degree from Albion College and earned her Masters of Business Administration from Baker College.

Her professional career includes serving as city assessor for the city of Birmingham; as the chief assessor on the Board of Assessors for the City of Detroit. She was appointed assessor member judge to the State of Michigan Tax Tribunal in 2004.

Ellen Leesfield

JUDGE. Ellen Leesfield received a Bachelor of Arts degree with honors from the University of Florida in 1972 and earned her Juris Doctor degree from Nova/Shepard Broad School of Law in 1979. In 1993, she was appointed a judge to the Florida Circuit Court.

Susan M. Leeson

JUDGE. Susan M. Leeson received a Bachelor of Arts degree in political science (magna cum laude) from Willamette University in 1968 and received a Master of Arts degree in Government from Claremont Graduate School in 1970. She earned a Ph.D. in government, (with distinction) from Claremont Graduate School in 1971 and her Juris Doctor degree (cum laude) from Willamette University in 1981.

Her professional career includes serving as a law clerk at the United States Court of Appeals for the Ninth Circuit from 1982 to 1983; as a judicial fellow, United States Supreme Court from 1983 to 1984; as a visiting professor of law, University of Bridgeport, 1985; as an associate professor of law, Willamette University from 1984 to 1992. In 1993, she was appointed judge to the Oregon Court of Appeals; in February 1998, Governor John Kitzhaber appointed her an associate justice to the Oregon Supreme Court.

Nancy J. Lescavage

MILITARY. Nancy J. Lescavage is a native of Port Carbon, Pennsylvania. She received a diploma in nursing is from Saint Joseph Hospital School of Nursing in Reading, Pennsylvania. She received a bachelor's degree in nursing from the University of Maryland and master's degree in nursing from the University of Pennsylvania School of Nursing. She earned a certificate in management from the Wharton School of Business and is a licensed nurse in the state of Pennsylvania.

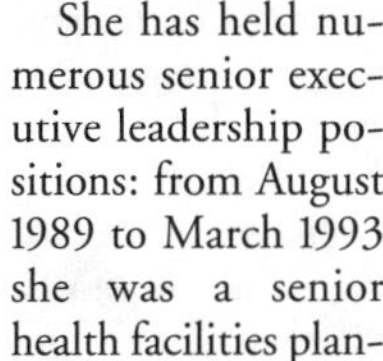

She has held numerous senior executive leadership positions: from August 1989 to March 1993 she was a senior health facilities planner for the Assistant Secretary of Defense (Health Affairs); from March 1993 to January 1995, she served as a congressional fellow in the office of United States Senator Daniel K. Inouye (Hawaii); from 1995 to 1997, as commanding officer, Fleet Hospital Five; from 1997 to 1999, as commanding officer, Naval Hospital, Corpus Christi, Texas; from 1999 to 2001, as deputy assistant chief for health care operations, Bureau of Medicine and Surgery; serving as assistant chief, health care operations, Bureau of Medicine and Surgery from 2001 to 2002; as the 20th director of the Navy Nurse Corps; as the commander, Naval Medical Education and Training Command, Bethesda, Maryland.

Rear Admiral Lescavage serves as the regional director of the TRICARE Regional Office in West San Diego, California.

Cheryl Levick

SPORTS. Cheryl Levick is a native of St. Louis, Missouri. She received a bachelor's degree from the University of Missouri and earned a master's degree in athletic administration from Indiana University.

Her professional career includes serving in 1976 as an assistant coach for both gymnastics and synchronized swimming. She served as an assistant commissioner of the Pac-10 Conference, as assistant director of commu-

nications and women's programs at the NCAA, and as the women's gymnastics coach and associate athletic director at Slippery Rock University. She spent 12 years as the senior associate athletic director and senior women's administrator at Stanford University. During Ms. Levick's tenure at Stanford, the Cardinals won 44 national championships and six straight Sears Cup titles. She was selected to serve as the first female athletic director at both Santa Clara University and within the West Coast Conference. In June 2004, she was named director of athletics at Saint Louis University in St. Louis, Missouri.

Cynthia Lewis

BUSINESS EXECUTIVE. Cynthia Lewis received a Bachelor of Science degree in psychology from Cedar Crest College.

Her professional career includes serving as cosmetics and fragrance manager at Town & Country. She was the founding publisher of *SHOP Etc.*, a fashion, home and beauty shopping magazine from Hearst Magazines. She also served as executive fashion director of *Elle*; as vice president of *Marie Claire* magazine, a joint venture between the Hearst Corporation and Marie Claire Album; as publisher of *Marie Claire* magazine; as vice president of *Harper's Bazaar*; and as publisher of *Harper's Bazaar*.

Ms. Lewis serves as vice president and publisher at the Hearst Corporation.

Daree M. Lewis

EDUCATION. Daree M. Lewis received a bachelor's degree from Queens College in sociology, concentrating on the impact of education of different groups.

Her professional career includes serving as the vice president of education at Junior Achievement for New York, a franchise of the world's largest and fastest growing economic education organization; she services the programmatic arm of the business. She has served on the Board of Directors of the Pomonok Neighborhood Center for the past five years. She left her post at Junior Achievement to serve as a National Urban Fellow.

Leslie A. Lewis

JUDGE. Leslie A. Lewis earned her Juris Doctor degree from the University of Utah College of Law in 1974. Her professional career includes serving in private law practice; she worked at Salt Lake City Attorney's office from 1978 to 1989. In January 1991, Governor Norman H. Bangerter appointed her judge to the Utah State Third District Court. She has since served twice as the presiding judge of the Third District Court and is a former chair and past member of the Board of District Court Judges.

Shirley A. R. Lewis

EDUCATION. Shirley A. R. Lewis received a Bachelor of Arts in Spanish and speech and master of social work degrees from the University of California at Berkeley. She earned a Ph.D. in education from Stanford University and she holds a certificate in African studies from the Universities of Ghana and London. She received an honorary doctorate degree from Bethune Cookman College.

Her professional career includes serving as a junior and senior high school teacher in California, New York and Ohio; as a researcher and teacher trainer on nationally based research projects concerning teacher effectiveness and academic achievement of African American studies; as a professor in a number of colleges and universities including George Peabody College of Vanderbilt University and Meharry Medical College. She was the first associate dean of academic affairs in the School of Medicine at Meharry Medical College. From 1986 to 1994, she served as assistant general secretary of the Black College Fund of the General Board of

Higher Education and Ministry of the United Methodist Church in Nashville, Tennessee.

Dr. Lewis was appointed the first woman president of Paine College.

Kay A. Lias

JUDGE. Kay A. Lias received a Bachelor of Arts degree from the University of Delaware in 1963 and earned her Juris Doctor degree (cum laude) from Capital University Law School in 1977.

A former secondary education teacher, she taught middle school English at I.S. 88 in Harlem, New York City (1965–1968). She was a professional actress from 1963 to 1973. She was admitted to the law practice in 1977. Engaged in private practice until 1981, she was appointed a domestic relations magistrate in 1987 and in 1988 was the first woman ever elected as judge of the Franklin County Common Pleas Court, Division of Domestic Relations. Judge Lias previously served nine years as administrative judge.

Maya Lin

ARTIST. Maya Lin grew up in Athens, Ohio, where her parents were on the faculty of Ohio University. Both immigrated to the United States from China. She received her undergraduate degree from Yale University in Connecticut.

In October 1980, an organization called the Vietnam Veterans Memorial Fund announced it would sponsor a nationwide competition to design a memorial honoring those who had served in Vietnam War. Nearly 1,500 aspiring artists submitted proposals. A panel of distinguished judges, including architects, sculptors and landscape architects chose the final design. The designer was a senior architecture student at Yale named Maya Lin, a total unknown in the art world. She was only 21 years of age at the time. Her memorial design is the most-visited monument in the country. Lin has worked on numerous other public and private projects since then.

Blanche Lambert Lincoln

ELECTED OFFICIAL. Blanche Lambert Lincoln is a native of Helena, Phillips County, Arkansas. She received a Bachelor of Arts degree from Randolph-Macon Woman's College in 1982.

Her professional career includes serving a member of the staff of Representative William V. Alexander, Jr., from 1982 to 1984. She was elected a United States Representative to the 103rd and 104th Congresses and served from January 3, 1993, to January 3, 1997; she was elected as a United States senator in 1998 and was re-elected in 2004 for term ending January 3, 2011.

Virginia L. Linder

JUDGE. Virginia L. Linder received a Bachelor of Arts degree in political science (with highest honors) from Southern Oregon State College in Ashland, Oregon. She earned her Juris Doctor degree (with honors) from Willamette University College of Law in Salem, Oregon, in 1980.

Her professional career includes serving as an assistant attorney general, appellate division, Oregon Department of Justice (1980–1983); as attorney-in-charge, education section of the general counsel division, Oregon Department of Justice (1983–1984); as an assistant solicitor general, appellate division, Oregon Department of Justice (1984–1986); as the solicitor general, appellate division, Oregon Department of Justice (1986–1987). In October 1997, she was appointed to the Oregon Court of Appeals by Governor John A. Kitzhaber. She has been twice elected to that position in uncontested races.

Linda Lingle

ELECTED OFFICIAL. Linda Lingle is a native of St. Louis, Missouri, and at the age of 12, she and her family moved to Southern California where she attended public schools. She relocated to Hawaii in 1975 after

graduating cum laude with a journalism degree from California State University at Northridge.

In 1976, she founded and began serving as publisher of the *Moloka'i Free Press*, a community newspaper serving the 6,000 residents of the Island of Moloka'i. In 1980, she was elected to the Maui County Council. She served five two-year terms on the council. In 1990, she was elected mayor of Maui County and was re-elected in 1994. She served the maximum two consecutive four-year terms. She was the youngest, the first woman and the only non–Maui born person ever elected to the office. In 1998, Ms. Lingle campaigned for governor, lost by just one percent of the vote and was later named the most respected woman in Hawaii.

In 2002, she was elected the sixth elected governor of Hawaii. She became the first woman, the first person of Jewish faith, and the first person not born in Hawaii to serve as governor. She is the first Republican to serve as governor in over 40 years.

Joanna Lipper

ENTERTAINMENT. Joanna Lipper received a Bachelor of Arts degree from Harvard University and earned a Master of Science degree from the Anna Freud Centre and University College London.

She is an award-winning author and documentary filmmaker. She runs Sea Wall Entertainment, a New York City–based company dedicated to the development and production of feature films. One of her films, *Growing Up Fast*, addresses the subject of teen parenthood. This film was featured on *The Jane Pauley Show* (NBC).

Janet Littlejohn

JUDGE. Janet Littlejohn graduated from Baylor University with degrees in mathematics and political science. She earned her Juris Doctor degree from South Texas College of Law in 1979. She worked as a briefing attorney for Justice Fred Klingeman in the Texas Fourth Court of Appeals; she served in private law practice for 14 years before her election to the bench.

In 1994, she was elected judge, to the 150th District Court of Bexar County, in San Antonio, Texas.

Ann M. Livermore

TECHNOLOGY EXECUTIVE. Ann M. Livermore was born in Greensboro, North Carolina. She holds a bachelors' degree in economics from the University of North Carolina at Chapel Hill and a Master's in Business Administration from Stanford University.

She serves as executive vice president for Technology Solutions Group, Hewlett-Packard Company. Technology Solutions Group encompasses enterprise storage and systems, software, services and sales. The products and services from this organization serve enterprise and public sector customers.

Anne H. Lloyd

BUSINESS EXECUTIVE. Anne H. Lloyd received a Bachelor of Science degree in business administration from the University of North Carolina at Chapel Hill. She is a certified public accountant.

She served with Ernst & Young, LLP, an international public accounting firm and joined Martin Marietta Materials Company in 1998 as vice president and controller. She was promoted to chief accounting officer in 1999.

Ms. Lloyd was appointed senior vice president, chief financial officer and treasurer for Martin Marietta Materials. She has served as the chief financial officer since June 2005 and was elected treasurer in March 2006.

Deborah A. Loewer

MILITARY. Deborah A. Loewer is a native of Springfield, Ohio. She received a bachelor's degree in theoretical mathematics and computer science from Wright State University in Dayton, Ohio, and earned a doctorate in international law from the University of

Kiel, Germany. She is a graduate of Officer Candidate School and was commissioned an ensign on December 17, 1976; she is a graduate of the Surface Warfare Officer Basic Course in 1979; a graduate of the Defense Language Institute in Monterey, California; the Goethe Institute in Stuttgart, Germany; she attended Surface Warfare Officer Department Head School, graduating first in her class.

Her professional career includes commanding USS *Yellowstone* (AD-41) in July 1987 and served as engineer and executive officer. In February 1990, she reported to USS *Monongahela* (AE-34). She served as the military assistant to the deputy secretary of defense from August 1995 until January 1997; and as the military assistant to the secretary of defense from January 1997 to July 1998. From December 1998 to July 2000, she commanded USS *Camden* (AOE-1); in September 2000, she returned to Washington for duty as the military assistant to the secretary of defense; in May 2001, she assumed duties as director, White House Situation Room and director, System and Technical Planning Staff; from July 2003 to January 2005 she served as vice commander, Military Sealift Command.

Rear Admiral Loewer was assigned as the commander, Mine Warfare Command on January 13, 2005.

Zoe Lofgren

ELECTED OFFICIAL. Zoe Lofgren is a native of San Mateo, California. She received a Bachelor of Arts degree from Stanford University, Stanford, California, in 1970. She earned her Juris Doctor from Santa Clara University School of Law in Santa Clara, California.

Her professional career includes serving in private law practice; as a member of the faculty of Santa Clara University School of Law from 1978 to 1980; as a member of the staff for United States Representative Don Edwards of California; and as executive director, Community Housing Developers. She was elected as a United States representative to the 104th and five succeeding Congresses (January 3, 1995–present).

Eugenia L. Loggins

ELECTED OFFICIAL. Eugenia L. Loggins is a native of Opp, Alabama. She received a Bachelor of Science in business administration with high honors from Auburn University and earned her Juris Doctor degree from the Cumberland School of Law at Sanford University.

Her professional career includes private law practice. She served as a municipal court judge in the city of Opp, Alabama.

Ms. Loggins has served as the district attorney for the 22nd Judicial Circuit of the state of Alabama for the past 20 years. She was one of the first women elected to this position in the state.

Irene Duhart Long

AEROSPACE. Irene Duhart Long is a native of Cleveland, Ohio, and graduated from East High School in Cleveland. She received a Bachelor of Arts degree in premedicine and biology and earned her Medical Doctor degree from the St. Louis University School of Medicine in 1977. After two years of a general surgery residency at the Cleveland Clinic and the Mount Sinai Hospital of Cleveland, she completed a three-year residency in aerospace medicine through Wright State University School of Medicine in Dayton, Ohio, and received a Master of Science in aerospace medicine.

From July 1981 to July 1982 Dr. Long served at the NASA John F. Kennedy Space Center during her aerospace medicine residency, including rotations at the Ames Research Center. In July 1982 she served as chief,

medical and environmental health office, biomedical operations and research office, at NASA's John F. Kennedy Space Center in Florida. Her medical and environmental health office is responsible for assuring a comprehensive occupational medicine and environmental health program, directed toward maintaining the health of the Kennedy Space Center workforce. Her responsibilities include the provision and planning of emergency medical services in support of STS launch and landing activities, as well as day-to-day shuttle-related activities. Additional responsibilities include coordinating human life sciences flight experiment requirements and the operational management of the Baseline Data Collection Facility used for pre- and postflight physiological data collection. Her research-related activities include medical screening and monitoring of research laboratory subjects and participation in research protocol development and implementation.

Dr. Long serves as American aerospace physician administrator, the first female chief medical officer of NASA's Kennedy Space Center.

Vanessa Griffin Long

MINISTRY. Vanessa Griffin Long a native of Columbus, Georgia. She received a Bachelor of Science degree from Morris Brown College in Atlanta, Georgia.

She served ten years with the United States Department of Education. She is the wife of Bishop Eddie L. Long and first lady of New Birth Missionary Baptist Church in Lithonia, Georgia. She came to New Birth in 1990 upon her marriage to the bishop.

In October 2004, she was elevated to a new level; Bishop Long declared her as a New Birth elder, pronouncing blessings upon her anointed ministry of healing. She serves as host of the annual Heart to Heart women's conference and ministers to women from around the globe.

Tami Longaberger

BUSINESS EXECUTIVE. Tami Longaberger received a Bachelor of Science degree in business administration from the Ohio State University. After graduation from college she joined the family business in 1984.

She was named president of the Longaberger Company in 1994 and chief executive officer in 1998. A respected leader and active participant in international, national and statewide affairs, Ms. Longaberger was appointed in May 2005 by President George W. Bush as chair of the National Women's Business Council, a bi-partisan federal advisory council created to advise and recommend policy to the president, Congress and the U.S. Small Business Administration on economic issues important to women business owners.

Maria Lopez

ENTERTAINMENT (FIRST). Maria Lopez was born in Havana, Cuba, and fled to the United States as a child with her parents to escape the Cuban revolution. She received a bachelor's degree from Smith College and earned a Juris Doctor degree from Boston University Law School.

Her professional career includes serving in private law practice as a civil rights attorney for nearly ten years before becoming a judge. In 1988, Massachusetts Governor Michael Dukakis appointed her to be a district court judge and in February 1993, Governor William F. Weld appointed her to be a Massachusetts Superior Court judge. She is the first female Hispanic judge ever appointed a judge to the Massachusetts court. After resigning from the bench she launched a half-hour syndicated courtroom series, *Judge Maria Lopez*. She is the first Hispanic judge to appear on national television.

Shirlene Lopez

BUSINESS EXECUTIVE. Shirlene Lopez attended California State University at Long Beach. She began her career at Del Taco at the age of 14 mopping floors and wiping tables. Within four years she was a restaurant general manager and by age 20 she was a training manager and part of the new store opening team.

In 1989, she became human resources manager for the company and later she handled special projects including store remodeling, corporate office relocation and other brand-wide initiatives. In 2002, she became executive vice president, operations services, where she oversaw all operations, training and human resources. Since the acquisition of Del Taco by Sagittarius Brands, she served as overall brand leader for the chain.

Ms. Lopez was named president of Del Taco in 2006. Del Taco's leadership team will report directly to Lopez including facilities, legal, franchise operations, store operations, human resources, purchasing/quality control, training and marketing.

Adena Williams Loston

GOVERNMENT OFFICIAL. Adena Williams Loston received a Bachelor of Science degree from Alcom State University. She earned her master's degree and Doctor

of Philosophy degree from Bowling Green State University. She also attended the Institute for Educational Management at Harvard University, the Oxford Roundtable at Oxford University and the Wharton School of Business.

Dr. Loston served as president of San Jacinto College South in Houston for five years. She served as the second president of the College and was the first African American president in the district. She possesses more than thirty years of higher education experience. She began her career with NASA in September 2002 as the administrator's senior education advisor. On October 28, 2002, she assumed the role of associate administrator for education. She serves as chief education officer at NASA headquarters in Washington, D.C.

Deneise Turner Lott

JUDGE. Deneise Turner Lott received a Bachelor of Arts degree in English cum laude from the University of Mississippi and earned her Juris Doctor from the University of Mississippi School of Law.

She has served in private law practice. From 1985 to 1988, she served as a senior staff attorney with the Worker's Compensation Commission. In November 1988, she was appointed an administrative judge with the Mississippi Worker's Compensation Commission.

Martha A. Lott

JUDGE. Martha A. Lott received a Bachelor of Arts degree in psychology from the University of Florida in 1974 and earned her Juris Doctor degree from the University of Florida in 1981.

She served as a judge on the County Court in Gainesville, Florida, from 1991 to 1997. In 1997, she was appointed judge to the Florida Circuit Court in Gainesville, Florida.

Gail T. Lovelace

GOVERNMENT OFFICIAL. Gail T. Lovelace holds degrees from the University of Maryland and the University of Louisville. She has served as the United States General Services Administration's Director (GSA) and deputy director of human resources.

She was named the federal government's first chief people officer (CPO) on September 11, 1998. In 2003, she was also appointed to be GSA's chief human capital officer (CHCO) in accordance with the CHCO Act of 2002.

Lovelace is responsible for agency-wide human capital management and has three closely interrelated programs. She leads the agency-wide development and implementation of GSA's Human Capital Strategic Plan, provides a full range of human resources advice and services to all GSA organizations, and provides human resources information technology support to a number of other federal agencies, boards and commissions in addition to providing the same support within GSA. Chief People Officer programs are carried out in central office and nine regional locations.

Valoria H. Loveland

GOVERNMENT OFFICIAL. Valoria H. Loveland is a graduate of Columbia Basin College. She has served as a state senator representing the 16th legislative district from 1993 to 2001. She has served as Franklin County treasurer.

She was appointed by Governor Locke in June 2002 to serve as the director of the Washington State Department of Agriculture.

Melendy Lovett

BUSINESS EXECUTIVE. Melendy Lovett received a bachelor's degree in management and management in-

formation systems from Texas A&M and a master's degree in accounting from the University of Texas–Dallas. She is also a certified public accountant.

Her professional career includes serving as a senior manager with consulting firm Coopers & Lybrand; she served as vice president in for Texas Instrument Worldwide compensation and benefits programs in human resources.

Ms. Lovett serves as senior vice president of Texas Instruments and president of the company's Worldwide Educational & Productivity Solutions business.

Challis M. Lowe

BUSINESS EXECUTIVE. Challis M. Lowe received a Master of Business Administration from the J. L. Kellogg School of Management at Northwestern University. She served as chair of the Board of Trustees of Florida A&M University.

Her professional career includes serving from 1993 to 1997 as executive vice president at Heller International; as executive vice president at Sanwa Business Credit Corporation and at Continental Illinois Corporation; from 1997 to 1998 she held executive positions as executive vice president, human resources and administrative services, at Beneficial Management Corporation; from 1998 to 1999 she served as a consultant to the merger of Beneficial Management Corp. with Household Finance; in May 2000 she served as executive vice president of human resources at Ryder System Inc.; in November 2000 she served as executive vice president for corporate communications and public affairs at Ryder System Inc.

Ms. Lowe has served as executive vice president of human resources at Dollar General since September 1, 2005.

Melissa Lowe

PERFORMING ARTS. Melissa Lowe graduated from Professional Children's School in New York City. Her professional career includes serving with the Pittsburgh Ballet Theatre as a soloist; as a soloist with the Houston Ballet and principal dancer with Pacific Northwest Ballet in Seattle; as a principal dancer with Pacific Northwest Ballet in Seattle; from 1984 to 1987 she served as an assistant professor of ballet at Indiana University; as director of the pre-college ballet program; in 2002 she produced her fourth dance instructional video.

Ms. Lowe serves as professor at the University of Arizona where she teaches in the ballet area of the BFA curriculum. One of her current areas of research has led to the development of a movement therapy program for breast cancer patients and survivors.

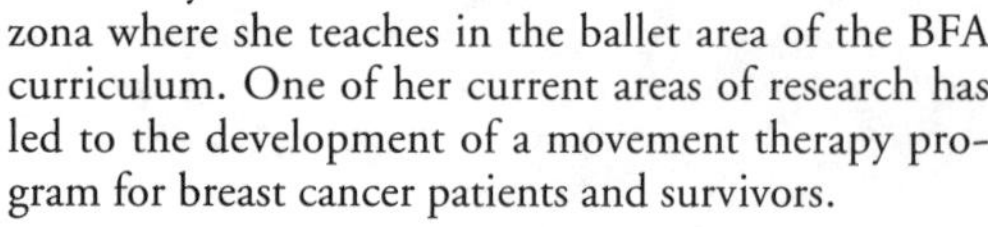

Nita M. Lowey

ELECTED OFFICIAL. Nita M. Lowey is a native of New York City and a graduate of Bronx High School of Science. She received a Bachelor of Science degree from Mount Holyoke College in South Hadley, Massachusetts in 1959.

Her professional career includes serving as an assistant to the New York secretary of state for economic development and neighborhood preservation and deputy director, New York state division of economic opportunity from 1975 to 1985. She served as a New York assistant secretary of state from 1985 to 1987. She was elected a United States representative to the 101st and the eight succeeding Congresses (January 3, 1989–present).

Marian M. Lucia

BUSINESS EXECUTIVE. Marian M. Lucia is a native of Pittsburgh, Pennsylvania. She received a Bachelor of Science degree in computer science from Pennsylvania State University and a Master's of Science in business administrative for Morris University.

Her professional career includes serving as principal managing director of technology at Bear Stearns and Company, Inc., and as vice president of technology with Merrill Lynch. Her earlier background included technology management positions at Texas Commerce Bank in Houston and Bank of Oklahoma in Tulsa.

She serves as executive vice president and chief information officer at the Federal Home Loan Bank, "The Bank" in Atlanta.

Shannon W. Lucid

AEROSPACE. Shannon W. Lucid is a native of Bethany, Oklahoma, where she graduated from Bethany High School. She received a Bachelor of Science degree in chemistry from the University of Oklahoma in 1963. She received her Master of Science and Doctor of Philosophy degrees in biochemistry from the University of Oklahoma in 1970 and 1973.

She was selected by NASA in January 1978 and became an astronaut in August 1979. She has been assigned to the Shuttle Avionics Integration Laboratory (SAIL); to the Flight Software Laboratory in Downey, California; to the Astronaut Office Interface at the Kennedy Space Center, Florida, participating in payload testing, Shuttle testing and launch countdowns; as spacecraft communicator in the Johnson Space Center Mission Control Center during numerous Space Shuttle missions; as chief of mission support; and chief of astronaut appearances. She has logged 5,354 hours (223 days) in space; she served as a mission specialist on STS-51G (June 17–24, 1985), as board engineer 2 on Russia's Space Station Mir (launching March 22, 1996, aboard STS-76 and returning September 26, 1996, aboard STS-79). She holds the record for the most flight hours in orbit by any woman in the world. From February 2002 until September 2003, Dr. Lucid served as NASA's chief scientist stationed at NASA headquarters in Washington, D.C. She has resumed duties as the Johnson Space Center in Houston.

Barbara M. G. Lynn

JUDGE. Barbara M. G. Lynn is a native of Binghamton, New York, and was raised in North Miami Beach, Florida. She received a Bachelor of Arts degree from the University of Virginia in 1973 and earned her Juris Doctor degree from Southern Methodist University in 1976. She was engaged in private law practice in Dallas, Texas, from 1976 to 1999.

On March 25, 1999, President William J. Clinton nominated her a seat vacated on the United States District Court. She was confirmed by the Senate on November 17, 1999, as judge to the United States District Court for the Northern District of Texas and received her commission on November 22, 1999.

Cathy Lyons

TECHNOLOGY EXECUTIVE. Cathy Lyons received a Bachelor of Science degree in business administration and marketing from the University of Colorado.

Her professional career includes serving as general manager of Hewlett Packard's laser jet solutions group European operation in Bergamo, Italy; she served as vice president and general manager of the supplies business at Hewlett Packard; she served as senior vice president of business and imaging printing at HP.

Ms. Lyons serves as executive vice president and chief marketing officer of HP and is responsible for the company's comprehensive global marketing strategy.

Chung-Pei Ma

EDUCATION. Chung-Pei Ma received a Bachelor of Science degree from Massachusetts Institute of Technology and a Ph.D. from Massachusetts Institute of Technology. She was also a postdoctoral fellow in theoretical astrophysics at Caltech in 1993.

Her professional career includes serving as an assistant professor of physics and astronomy at the University of Pennsylvania in 1996; as associate professor of physics and astronomy at the University of Pennsylvania in 2001; she moved to the department of astronomy at University of California–Berkeley in 2002.

Dr. Ma's central theme of her recent research is working to understand the formation and evolution of galaxies and large scale structures. Working with the aid of large supercomputers, she and collaborators have performed numerical simulations of the clustering of dark matter in various cosmological models of structure formation from the early universe until the present day. She has received numerous awards, including the Lindback Award for Distinguished Teaching. Ma is an avid violin player.

Cynthia MacKinnon

JUDGE. Cynthia MacKinnon received Bachelor of Arts and Master of Arts degrees from Emory University. She earned her Juris Doctor degree from Holland College of Law from the University of Florida.

Her judicial career includes serving as judge, Florida Circuit Court of Orange County Criminal Court; in 1999 as judge for Orange County Juvenile Court; from 2000 to 2001, as administrative judge, Orange County Juvenile Court; from 2002 to 2003, as judge, Orange County Domestic Court. Since 2004, she has served as judge, Florida Circuit Court, Orange County Civil Court.

Teresa S. Madden

BUSINESS EXECUTIVE. Teresa S. Madden received a Bachelor of Science degree in accounting from Colorado State University and earned a Master of Business Administration from Regis University.

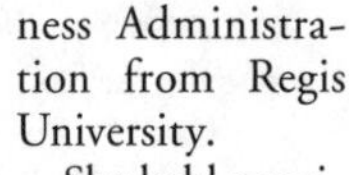

She held a variety of positions with Public Service Company of Colorado, served as corporate controller of New Century Energies; and most recently was vice president of finance for Xcel Energy customer and field operations.

Yvonne T. Maddox

HEALTH. Yvonne T. Maddox received a Bachelor of Science in biology from Virginia Union University in Richmond, Virginia, and earned her doctorate in physiology from Georgetown University. She is a graduate of the Senior Managers in Government Program of the Kennedy School of Government at Harvard University.

Her professional career includes serving as the acting deputy director of the National Institutes of Health (NIH) from January 2000 to June 2002. Since 1995, Dr. Maddox has served as deputy director, National Institute of Child Health and Human Development at the National Institutes of Health.

Lisa Madigan

ELECTED OFFICIAL. Lisa Madigan received her bachelor's degree from Georgetown University and her J.D. degree from Loyola University Law School. Before her election as attorney general, Madigan served in the Illinois Senate and worked as a litigator for a Chicago law firm. Prior to becoming an attorney, she worked as a teacher and community advocate, developing after-school programs to help kids stay away from drugs and gangs. She also traveled to South Africa during apartheid to work as a volunteer high school teacher.

Lisa Madigan was elected the 41st attorney general of Illinois on November 5, 2002. She is the first woman to hold this position.

Paula Madison

MEDIA EXECUTIVE. Paula Madison is a native of Harlem, New York, and a graduate of Vassar College. Her career in television news began at WFAA-TV in Dallas. It carried her to other stations in Tulsa and Houston before she moved to WNBC as assistant news director in 1989. Earlier, she was a reporter, investigative journalist and assistant city editor for newspapers in upstate New York and Texas.

Ms. Madison joined NBC4 from WNBC, NBC's

New York station where she was vice president and news director. Under her direction, WNBC became the No. 1 television station in New York. She was named regional general manager for the three NBC/Telemundo television stations in Los Angeles (KNBC, KVEA AND KWHY) when NBC purchased the Telemundo network in 2002. She also serves as president of the 30,000 Alumnae/i Association of Vassar College and serves on the Vassar College Board of Trustees.

Patricia A. Madrid

GOVERNMENT OFFICIAL. Patricia A. Madrid received a Bachelor of Arts degree from the University of New Mexico and earned her J.D. degree from the University of New Mexico in 1973. Her experience includes serving in private practice. From 1978 to 1984, she served as a district court judge in New Mexico and was the first woman elected to the District Court bench in New Mexico; she also served as chief presiding judge, Second Judicial District.

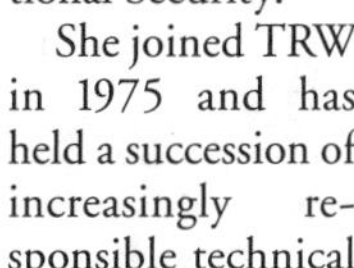

In 1998, she became New Mexico's 29th attorney general, New Mexico's first woman attorney general. In 2002, she was re-elected to a second term.

Barbara A. Madsen

JUDGE. Barbara A. Madsen is a native of Renton, Washington. She received her undergraduate degree from the University of Washington in 1974 and earned her Juris Doctor degree from Gonzaga University School of Law in 1977.

Her professional career includes serving as a public defender in King and Snohomish counties, Washington; as a staff attorney at the Seattle city attorney's office and as a special prosecutor. In that role, she was responsible for developing the child abuse component of the Family Violence Project for the city attorney's office. She was appointed judge to the Seattle Municipal Court bench in 1988. In 1992, she was elected justice, becoming only the third woman to be elected to a seat on the bench of the Washington State Supreme Court since the formation of the court in 1889. She was re-elected in 1998 and re-elected for a third term on September 14, 2004.

Joanne M. Maguire

TECHNOLOGY EXECUTIVE. Joanne M. Maguire received a bachelor's degree in electrical engineering from Michigan State University and a Master's degree in engineering from the University of California at Los Angeles (UCLA). She is a graduate of the executive program in management at UCLA's Anderson School of Management and completed the Harvard Program for Senior Executives in National and International Security.

She joined TRW in 1975 and has held a succession of increasingly responsible technical and management positions participating broadly in space system design and development activities. She served as program manager for the defense support program, directing spacecraft production and satellite integration, test, launch and deployment. She served as vice president and general manager of Space & Electronics' Space & Laser Programs Division, managing contracts for civil space systems as well as laser systems. She served as deputy and vice president of business development for TRW Space & Electronics, now Northrop Grumman Space Technology. Ms. Maguire joined Lockheed Martin in July 2003 and was appointed vice president and deputy of Space Systems Company. In July 2006, she was named executive vice president of Lockheed Martin Space Systems Company.

Patricia Mahan

ELECTED OFFICIAL. Patricia Mahan received a Bachelor of Arts degree from San Jose Sate University and

earned her Juris Doctor degree from Santa Clara University. She was engaged in private law practice. From 1994 to 2002 she served as a city councilmember for the city of Santa Clara, California; from 2002 to 2006 she served as mayor of Santa Clara, California.

Nicole Malachowski

MILITARY (FIRST). Nicole Malachowski graduated from Western High School in Las Vegas in 1992. She received a Bachelor of Science degree in management from the United States Air Force Academy in 1996. She received her pilot training at Columbus Air Force Base, Mississippi, and F-15E training at Seymour Johnson Air Force Base, North Carolina.

Major Malachowski has served as an F-15 pilot with the RAF Lakenheath, England, and at Seymour Johnson Air Force Base in North Carolina. She served as an Army liaison officer at Camp Red Cloud in South Korea. She served as an F-15E instructor pilot and flight commander with the 494th Fighter Squadron at RAF Lakenheath, United Kingdom. She served a four-month deployment in support of Operation Iraqi Freedom. She is a senior pilot with more than 1,400 flying hours, including more than 1,000 hours in the F-15E.

In 2006, she became the first woman ever selected to fly as part of the Air Force Air Demonstration Squadron, "Thunderbirds." Her first public performance was in March 2006, becoming the first female to do so in the squadron's 52-year history.

Beverly Malazzo

JUDGE. Beverly Malazzo received a Bachelor of Science from Texas A&M University in 1976 and received a Master of Education from Texas A&M University in 1983. She earned her Juris Doctor from South Texas College of Law in 1992.

Her professional career includes serving as an assistant district attorney in the Harris County District Attorney's office and as chief judge for the 313th Juvenile District Court. In 2001, she was appointed associate judge of the Harris County Juvenile District Court in Houston, Texas.

Lydia G. Mallett

BUSINESS EXECUTIVE. Lydia G. Mallett received a Bachelor of Arts degree in psychology, a master's degree in labor/industrial relations, and a Ph.D. in social psychology from Michigan State University.

Her professional career includes being selected to serve as the director of human resources for the snacks unlimited division and the consumer insights function at General Mills. She was selected to serve as chief diversity officer for General Mills.

Carolyn Bosher Maloney

ELECTED OFFICIAL. Carolyn Bosher Maloney is a native of Greensboro, North Carolina. She received a Bachelor of Arts degree from Greensboro College in Greensboro, North Carolina, in 1968.

Her professional career includes serving as a community affairs coordinator in New York City's Board of Education welfare education program from 1972 to 1975; as special assistant for New York City's Board of Education center for career and occupational education from 1975 to 1976; as a legislative aide to the New York State Assembly Committee on Housing in 1977; as senior

program analyst for the New York State Assembly Committee on Cities from 1977 to 1979; as executive director, advisory council, office of the New York State Senate minority leader from 1979 to 1982; as director of special projects in the office of the New York State Senate minority leader from 1980 to 1982; as a member of the New York, New York, City Council from 1982 to 1992. She was elected a United States Representative to the 103rd and to the six succeeding Congresses since January 3, 1993.

Frances Maloy

BUSINESS EXECUTIVE. Frances Maloy received a Bachelor of Arts degree in history from St. Lawrence University in 1980 and earned an M.L.S. from State University of New York at Albany in 1982. Her professional career includes serving as an assistant reference librarian at Hamilton College 1982–1983; as director of public services, Hamilton College, 1983–1992; as head of the circulation department at Emory University, 1992–2001; and as division leader, access services at Emory University. In 2004, she was elected to serve as president of the American Library Association.

Blanche M. Manning

JUDGE. Blanche M. Manning is a native of Chicago, Illinois. She received a bachelor's of education degree from Chicago Teachers College in 1961 and received a Masters' of Arts degree from Roosevelt University in 1972. She earned her Juris Doctor degree from John Marshall Law School in 1967 and received an LL.M. degree from University of Virginia School of Law in 1992.

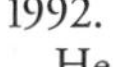

Her professional career includes serving as an assistant state attorney, Cook County State Attorney's office, Illinois, 1968–1973; as supervisory trial attorney, U.S. Equal Opportunity Commission, Chicago, 1973–1977; and as a general attorney at United Airlines 1977–1978. From 1979 to 1986 she served as an associate judge, Circuit Court, Cook County, Illinois. She was elevated to circuit judge, Illinois Circuit Court in Cook County, 1986–1987; in 1987 she became the first woman justice on the Illinois Appellate Court, First Judicial District. On May 5, 1994, she was nominated a District Court jurist for the Northern District of Illinois by President William J. Clinton to a vacant seat, was confirmed by the Senate on August 9, 1994, and received commission on August 10, 1994.

Mary Manross

ELECTED OFFICIAL. Mary Manross holds a bachelor's degree in political science and a teaching credential. She served two terms as a city councilwoman from 1992 to 2000 before her election as mayor of the city of Scottsdale, Arizona, in June 2000.

Sylvia A. Manzanares

JUDGE. Sylvia A. Manzanares was born and raised in Trinidad, Colorado. She received her undergraduate degree from the University of Colorado at Boulder and earned her Juris Doctor degree from the University of Colorado Law School at Boulder in 1977.

Her professional career includes serving as an assistant attorney general for the state of Colorado; as an administrative law judge; a small claims magistrate; and as a Colorado Springs Municipal Court judge. She was also engaged in private law practice.

In August 1995, she was appointed judge to the Colorado 4th Judicial District in El Paso County.

Barbara Manzi

BUSINESS EXECUTIVE. Barbara Manzi is a native of Massachusetts. She earned an associate degree in business marketing and business management.

In 1982, she left retail and used the sales experience and her mathematical ability to get a job with aerospace supplier Northern Alloys of Amityville, New York. In 1995, she started her own company in Florida. Her company, Manzi Metals, distributes aluminum, stainless steel, titanium, brass and other alloys to aero-

space and commercial industries throughout the United States and Canada. The company also supplies raw metals in all shapes and forms. Her customers include Lockheed Martin, Raytheon, Gulfstream Aerospace, Boeing, and General Motors, as well as shipyards, and federal and local government facilities. Ms. Manzi is the first and only black female metal supplier in the United States.

Mary Muehlen Maring

JUDGE. Mary Muehlen Maring is a native of Devils Lake, North Dakota. She received a Bachelor of Arts degree in political science and German from Moorhead State University in 1972. She earned her Juris Doctor degree from the University of North Dakota School of Law.

She began her professional career as a law clerk for the Honorable Bruce C. Stone, Hennepin County District Court, Minneapolis, Minnesota, from 1975 to 1976; she entered the private practice of law and spent 20 years practicing law in North Dakota and Minnesota.

On March 1, 1996, she was appointed by Governor Edward T. Schafer to the North Dakota Supreme Court to fill the vacancy created by Justice Levine's retirement. On November 5, 1996, she was elected to complete that term. In 1998, she was re-elected to a ten-year term.

Andrea R. Marks

MILITARY. Andrea R. Marks was born in Kingston, Jamaica. She moved to the United States from London, England, in 1980. In October 1981 she enlisted into the United States Army.

Her civilian and military education includes a Bachelor of Science degree from Regents College; a masters degree in public administration from Troy State University; she is a distinguished graduate of the United States Army Sergeants Major Academy; the Command Sergeant Major Course; the Garrison Command Sergeant Major Course; First Sergeant Course; Battle Staff Course; Army Force Management School; the Defense Equal Opportunity School; all the Noncommissioned Officer Education System Courses; Drill Sergeant School; Airborne School; Master Fitness Trainer Course and the Personnel Administrative Specialist Course.

She has served in a variety of assignments both in the continental United States and overseas. She completed basic training at Fort Dix, New Jersey, and advanced individual training at Fort Jackson, South Carolina. Her assignments include Fort McClellan, Alabama; Bremerhaven, Germany; Fort McPherson, Georgia; Fort Benjamin Harrison, Indiana; K-16 Airbase, Korea; Staff Action Control Office, deputy chief of staff for operations and plans, Pentagon; Office of the Chief of Staff, Army, Pentagon; Fort Meade, Maryland; Eighth United States Army, Korea; Joint Action Control Office, deputy chief of staff for operations and plans, Pentagon; Fort Bliss, Texas; and the Defense Threat Reduction Agency, Fort Belvoir, Virginia. She served as the command sergeant major for the Headquarters Command Battalion, Fort George G. Meade, in Maryland. In January 2005, she was serving as the command sergeant major for the 1st Personnel Command in Germany.

Elaine F. Marshall

ELECTED OFFICIAL (FIRST). Elaine F. Marshall earned a Juris Doctor degree from Campbell University. Her professional career includes operating her own business; teaching in North Carolina's public schools and community colleges systems; and serving as a North Carolina state senator. In 1996, she was elected secretary of state for North Carolina and became the first woman ever elected to a statewide executive branch office in North Carolina.

Helen M. Marshall

Elected Official. Helen M. Marshall is a native of New York and is a graduate of the city's public school system. She received a Bachelor of Arts degree in education from Queens College, New York.

Her professional career includes serving as an early childhood teacher and as the first director of the Langston Public Library, a post she held for five years. In 1975, she became a Democratic National Committee committeewoman; beginning in 1982, she served five terms in the New York State Assembly. She was elected as a member of the New York City Council, where she served as chair of the city council's higher education committee. She represented the 21st District for ten years. She was the first minority and woman elected from the district.

Ms. Marshall was elected overwhelmingly as Queens Borough president in November 2001 with 68 percent of the vote and re-elected in November 2005. She is the 18th borough president of Queens, the first African American and the second woman to assume the post in a borough with a population of more than 2.2 million people.

Susan G. Marshall

Government Official. Susan G. Marshall received a bachelor's degree in political science from Pennsylvania State University in 1987. Prior to 1986, she attended University of Exeter in Exeter, England, concentrating on political studies.

Ms. Marshall has served in the private sector in the Information Technology Association of America (ITAA), and Aerospace Industries Association of America, Inc. She has worked for the Senate Committee on Governmental Affairs and the House Committee on Government Reform and Oversight. In 2001, President George W. Bush appointed her to the General Services Administration.

Leslie Baranco Martin

Elected Official. Leslie Martin received an undergraduate degree in industrial engineering from the University of California at Berkeley and earned her Juris Doctor from University of California Hastings College of the Law.

She served as the deputy district attorney for San Joaquin County, California, for seven years. In 2001, she was elected to the Stockton, California, City Council.

Miriam B. Martin-Clark

Judge. Miriam B. Martin-Clark is a native of Detroit, Michigan, and graduated from Central High School. She received her undergraduate degree from Howard University in Washington, D.C. She earned her Juris Doctor degree from Wayne State University.

Her professional career includes serving in private law practice for six years. In 1997, she was appointed judge to the Michigan's 36th Judicial District Court in Detroit.

Carmen M. Martinez

Government Official. Carmen M. Martinez holds a Master of Arts degree in medieval history and a Master of Science degree in national security and strategic resources. She speaks Portuguese, Spanish, and Thai.

Her professional career includes serving with the United States Department of State as a consular officer in Caracas, Venezuela (1983 to 1985), and in Bangkok, Thailand (1986 to 1989). From 1989 to 1993, she served as the chief of the consular section in Quito, Ecuador. She was the principal officer at the United States Consulate in Barranquilla,

Colombia (1993–1994). From 1997 to 1999, she was assigned as deputy chief of mission in Maputo, Mozambique, and as principal officer at the United States Consulate General in Sao Paulo, Brazil (1999–2002). From 2002 to 2005, she served as chief of mission in Rangoon, Burma.

Ms. Martinez was sworn in as ambassador to the Republic of Zambia on November 28, 2005, and presented her credentials to President Levy Mwanawasa of the Republic of Zambia on December 12, 2005.

Laura A. Martinez

MILITARY. Laura A. Martinez joined the United States Navy under the delayed entry program. She reported to boot camp at Recruit Training Center, Orlando, Florida, on April 16, 1979. She attended Hospital Corps "A" School at Great Lakes, Illinois.

She is qualified as an enlisted fleet marine warfare specialist. She is a graduate of the Navy Senior Enlisted Academy and the Air Force Senior Non-Commissioned Academy.

In February 1981, she was assigned to Naval Hospital, Guam, in the Staff Medical Record Section, Manpower Department and Officer in Charge, Inpatient Medical Records Department. She was selected Naval Hospital Guam's "Sailor of the Year."

In March 1984, she transferred to Naval Hospital, Jacksonville, Florida, for duty as the administrative assistant to the director, Branch Medical Clinics. She was subsequently reassigned as the command's career counselor. She was selected as Naval Hospital, Jacksonville, "Sailor of the Year" and Jacksonville, Florida's Military "Woman of the Year." Her next assignment started her sea duty with the Fleet Marine Force.

In March 1988, she attended Field Medical Service School, Camp Johnson. Reporting to 2nd Force Service Support Group, Headquarters and Service Battalion, she was assigned to the Navy Personnel Office as the group education service officer and career counselor. After her promotion to chief petty officer, she was reassigned to Medical Logistics Company, 2nd Supply Battalion serving as leading chief petty officer of the Battalion Medical Administration Team (BMAT) and administrative chief.

In November 1991, she was selected to fill a hot fill billet on the staff of the Surgeon General, Bureau of Medicine and Surgery (BUMED) in Washington, D.C. She served as the administrative assistant to the chief of staff for the bureau and administrative chief for the officers and enlisted staff assigned. In September 1993, she requested termination of shore duty for overseas sea duty for rotational purposes to Naval Hospital, Okinawa, Japan. Her assignments during this tour included medical board coordinator and assistant head, patient administration department. During this tour she was promoted to senior chief petty officer.

In January 1996, Senior Chief Martinez was transferred to 3rd Medical Battalion, 3rd Force Service Support Group. During this tour of duty, she served as the executive officer, Bravo Surgical Company where she deployed to Korea for Ulchi Focus Lens and Thailand for Operation Cobra Gold. She was promoted to master chief petty officer. In July 2000, she returned to the Naval Hospital, Okinawa, Japan, as the command master chief.

In August 2002, Chief Martinez reported as the command master chief, 2nd Force Service Support. She deployed to Southwest Asia as command master chief of the Marine Logistics Command, Kuwait.

Shirley A. Martinez

GOVERNMENT OFFICIAL. Shirley A. Martinez received a Bachelor of Arts degree (magna cum laude) from University of the Incarnate Word, San Antonio, Texas. She began her federal career with the Air Force in 1975 as a clerk-stenographer at Lackland Air Force Base, Texas. She acquired experience in staffing, classification and equal employment opportunity at three Air Force bases in San Antonio, Texas. In 1983, she transferred to Air Force Systems Command at Andrews Air Force Base, Maryland, and managed the special emphasis programs until 1986. In 1990, she was promoted to GM-15 and was responsible for oversight of the department's programs in outreach and partnership, small and disadvantaged business utilization and the office of construction management. In 1992, she was selected as the associate director of affirmative action and special emphasis programs with the U.S. Environmental Protection Agency in Washington, D.C.

From 1999 to 2001, she served as chief of discrimination complaints, San Antonio ALC, Kelly Air Force Base, in Texas; in September 2001 she was selected to serve as deputy assistant secretary for equal opportunity, Office of the Assistant Secretary of the Air Force for Manpower and Reserve Affairs in Washington, D.C.

Wendy Martinson

MILITARY. Wendy Martinson is a native of Red Wing, Minnesota. She received her undergraduate degree from Mankato State University in 1978 and completed Officer Candidate School at Fort Benning, Georgia. She is a graduate of the Army Command and General Staff College; the Industrial College of the Armed Forces, National Defense University at Fort Leslie J. McNair, Washington, D.C., where she earned a Masters degree in national resource strategy. She also holds a Masters of Science in health care professions from Southwest Texas State University, San Marcos, Texas.

She has held a wide variety of important command and staff positions which include chief, congressional liaison office for the Army Surgeon General, Falls Church, Virginia; as a brigade commander, Brooke Army Medical Center at Fort Sam Houston, Texas; she served as chief of the strength management branch, U.S. Army Medical Command at Fort Sam Houston, Texas; as chief, health services branch, Enlisted Personnel Management Directorate, Human Resources Command, Alexandria, Virginia; she now serves as the garrison commander at Fort Sam Houston, Texas.

Sylvia Mathews

BUSINESS EXECUTIVE. Sylvia Mathews received a Bachelor of Arts degree in government, cum laude, from Harvard University and a Bachelor of Arts in philosophy, politics and economics with honors from Oxford University where she was a Rhodes Scholar.

Her professional career includes serving as an associate for McKinsey & Co.; she managed President-elect Clinton's economic transition team from 1992 to 1993; from 1993 to 1995, she served as staff director for the National Economic Council; from 1995 to 1997, she served as chief of staff for Treasury Secretary Robert E. Rubin; she also served in the Bill Clinton administration as deputy director of the Office of Management and Budget.

Ms. Mathews joined the Bill & Melinda Gates Foundation in 2001 as chief operating officer and executive director. She directs the foundation's grants making for global libraries and special projects overseeing foundation-wide strategic issues for existing and new opportunities, legal affairs, advocacy and evaluation.

Dennise Mathieu

GOVERNMENT OFFICIAL. Dennise Mathieu is a native of New Jersey. She received a bachelor's degree in Spanish and Latin American studies from Antioch College and earned her Juris Doctor degree from Rutgers University School of Law. She also attended the Johns Hopkins School of Advanced International Studies.

Her professional career includes serving with the United States State Department in key positions at United States missions in Geneva, Jeddah, Paris, Port of Spain and Santo Domingo. From 1995 to 1997, she served as deputy director of Pacific Island affairs. From 1997 to 1999, she served at the Department of State as deputy office director of West African affairs. She served as the deputy chief of mission in Accra where she oversaw all aspects of embassy operations.

Dennise Mathieu was sworn in as United States ambassador to Niger on October 30, 2002.

Doris Okada Matsui

ELECTED OFFICIAL. Doris Okada Matsui is a native of Arizona. She received a Bachelor of Arts degree from the University of California in Berkeley, California. Her professional career includes serving on the staff at the White House in Washington, D.C., from 1992 to 1998; and as a private advocate. She was elected a United States representative to the 109th Congress by special election on March 8, 2005, to fill the vacancy caused by the death of her husband, United States Representative Robert Matsui.

Candace Matthews

BUSINESS EXECUTIVE. Candace Matthews is a native of New Brighton, Pennsylvania. She received a Bache-

lor of Science degree in metallurgical science, engineering and administrative and management science from Carnegie-Mellon University in Pittsburgh, Pennsylvania. She earned a Masters of Business Administration from the Stanford Graduate School of Business.

Her professional career includes holding senior marketing positions at General Mills, Cover Girl Cosmetics, Bausch & Lomb and CIBA Vision Corporation. She has served as the managing director of non-cola brands and vice president of new products and package innovation for the Coca-Cola Company.

From Coca-Cola, she joined L'Oreal USA, which acquired Soft Sheen Products Inc. in 1998 and Carson Products in 1999. The two companies merged in August 2000 to become Soft Sheen/Carson, L'Oreal's worldwide headquarters for hair-care products for people of African descent. Ms. Matthews took the helm as president of Soft Sheen/Carson on November 5, 2001, and, realizing the significant growth opportunities in the ethnic hair-care market made her top priorities for the company innovation and technology.

Carolyn C. Matthews

JUDGE. Carolyn C. Matthews is a native of Columbia, South Carolina. She received a Bachelor of Arts degree from Furman University in 1972 and earned her Juris Doctor degree the University of South Carolina School of Law in 1978.

Her professional career includes serving as a staff attorney at the South Carolina Supreme Court from 1978 to 1981; as a law clerk to Supreme Court Justice George T. Gregory, Jr., from 1981 to 1982; as an assistant attorney general for the state of South Carolina from 1982 to 1988; in private law practice from 1988 to 1998. On June 2, 1999, she was elected an administrative law judge in South Carolina and has served continuously since.

Rebecca Dirden Mattingly

GOVERNMENT OFFICIAL. Rebecca Dirden Mattingly received a Bachelor of Arts degree in journalism from West Virginia University. Her professional career includes serving as Florida's film commissioner in the governor's Office of Film and Entertainment. Through her leadership and partnership with the industry the state realized more than $2 billion in total revenue generated by Florida's film industry.

On March 5, 2003, she was appointed secretary of the Florida Lottery by Governor Jeb Bush. She is the first African-American to serve in this post. On August 29, 2003, she announced the new provider of online gaming system and services. GTECH Corporation was selected to design, construct and operate the on-line gaming system that runs the lottery's computerized games.

Mabel Johnson Mayfield

JUDGE. Mabel Johnson Mayfield received a Bachelor of Science degree in economics from the Krannert School of Manageme University in West Lafayette, Indiana. She earned her Juris Doctor degree from Valparaiso University School of Law.

She served seven years as a juvenile court attorney referee and served in private law practice. In 2000, she was appointed judge to the Berrien County Probate Court in Michigan.

Anita Laster Mays

JUDGE. Anita Laster Mays is a native of Cleveland, Ohio. She graduated from James Ford Rhodes High in 1982 and received a bachelor's degree from the Ohio State University in accounting and management information systems. She earned her Juris Doctor degree from Cleveland-Marshall College of Law.

Her professional career includes serving as an assistant Cleveland prosecutor. In 1996, she joined the Clerk of Courts office as director of operations for the criminal division. In November 2003, she was elected judge on the Cleveland Municipal Court.

Nora McAniff

MEDIA EXECUTIVE. Nora McAniff received a Bachelor of Arts degree in marketing from Baruch College.

She joined Time Inc. in 1982 as a marketing information manager at *People*. In 1990, she was promoted to the newly-created position of New York advertising director before becoming publisher. She was appointed president of *People* in November 1998 after serving as publisher of the magazine since September 1993 and taking on the additional role of publisher of *Teen People* during its development and launch in 1998. In 2001, she was named president of the *People* Magazine Group. Ms. McAniff was named executive vice president of Time Inc. in August 2002.

Veronica Simmons McBeth

JUDGE. Veronica Simmons McBeth is a native of San Diego, California. She received a Bachelor of Arts degree from California State University in Los Angeles in 1972. She earned her Juris Doctor degree from UCLA School of Law in 1975.

She worked for the Los Angeles City Attorney's office where she served as a trial attorney and assistant supervising attorney for the Van Nuys branch. From 1977 to 1978 she was special counsel to the city attorney. She served as president of the Black Women Lawyers Association in Los Angeles. She was appointed judge to the Los Angeles Municipal Court on June 23, 1981, by Governor Edmund G. Brown, Jr. She was re-elected in November 1986 and again in November 1992. From 1994 to 1995 she served as the supervising judge of the central criminal bench of the court. She served as assistant presiding judge from 1996 to 1997. She was elected as presiding judge in November 1997.

In 1997, Judge McBeth was unanimously elected at the Las Vegas, Nevada, meeting of National Consortium of Task Force and Commissions on Racial and Ethnic Bias in the Courts as moderator-elect to take office as moderator in 1999.

Anita McBride

GOVERNMENT OFFICIAL. Anita McBride received a bachelor's degree in international studies from the University of Connecticut and studied at the University of Florence in Italy.

Her professional career includes serving from 1987 to 1992 in the Reagan and Bush administrations as director of White House personnel; she served as special assistant to the president for White House management where she oversaw six operational units in direct support of the president, First Lady and White House staff; she served at the State Department as a senior advisor in the State Department's Bureau of International Organizations.

Ms. McBride was selected to serve in the President George W. Bush administration as deputy assistant to the president and chief of staff to the First Lady. She oversees the day to day activities of Mrs. Bush's office. Mrs. Bush's offices include social, projects/policy, press, correspondence, scheduling, speechwriting and advance.

Margaret Stanton McBride

JUDGE. Margaret Stanton McBride is a native of Evanston, Illinois, and received her Bachelor of Art degree from Newton College of the Sacred Heart in Newton, Massachusetts, and earned her J.D. degree from DePaul University College of Law.

She served as an attorney in private practice from 1976 to 1977 and as a Cook County assistant state's attorney from 1977 to 1987. Judge McBride was appointed to the Circuit Court in

1987 and elected a circuit judge in 1990 where she served in the First Municipal District, Criminal, Law and Chancery Divisions. When elected to the Appellate Court in 1998 she was the presiding judge of the Third Municipal District. She now serves as an appellate judge for the First District, 2nd Division, for the state of Illinois.

Jewell Jackson McCabe

BUSINESS EXECUTIVE. Jewell Jackson McCabe is president of Jewell Jackson McCabe Associates, Inc., a management consulting firm specializing in strategic communications. She is the founder and chair of the National Coalition of 100 Black Women (NCBW). She was appointed by President William Clinton to the United States Holocaust Memorial Council; she serves on the council's Education and Community Outreach Committee and Committee on Conscience. New York Governor Mario M. Cuomo appointed her to the New York State Council on Fiscal and Economic Priorities and New York State Job Training Partnership Council. Her mayoral appointments include membership on the New York City Commission on the Status of Women.

Dawn L. McCall

MEDIA EXECUTIVE. Dawn L. McCall received a bachelor's degree in journalism from the University of Georgia. Her professional career includes serving as a regional vice president and senior director of Discovery's Western Region. She has served as senior vice president and general manager of Discovery Networks in Latin America and Iberia. Based in Miami, she directed all regional operations for Discovery Channel, Discovery Kids, People & Arts and Animal Planet. She also spearheaded the launch of the Discovery Television Center, Discovery's first wholly owned production facility.

Ms. McCall serves as president of Discovery Networks International where she is responsible for the strategic development and global operations of one of the most flexible and efficient network infrastructures in the media industry.

Renetta McCann

BUSINESS EXECUTIVE. Renetta McCann received a Bachelor of Science degree in speech from Northwestern University. Her professional career began with what was then part of Leo Burnett Agency in 1978. She was named a vice president of Starcom North America in 1988 and in early 1989 she became a media director. She was elected a senior vice president in 1995 and has served as chief executive of Starcom North America since 1999.

Carolyn McCarthy

ELECTED OFFICIAL. Carolyn McCarthy is a native of Brooklyn, New York. She graduated from Mineola High School in Garden City Park, New York. She is a graduate of Glen Cove Nursing School in Glen Cove, New York.

Her professional service includes serving as a Licensed Practical Nurse in Intense Care Unit (ICU) at Glen Gove Hospital in Glen Gove, New York. She was elected to the United States House of Representatives in 1996. She began serving as a Democrat to the 105th and to the five succeeding Congresses (January 3, 1997–present). She represents New York's 4th congressional district.

Alison McCarty

JUDGE. Alison McCarty graduated from Wheaton College in Wheaton, Illinois, in 1984 and Wake Forest University School of Law in North Carolina in 1987. From 1987 to 1989, she served as a staff attorney for the Ninth District Court of Appeals. From 1989 to 1999, she served as an assistant Summit County prosecutor handling felony criminal cases. She was appointed judge to the Akron Municipal Court in May 1999.

Susan Rasinski McCaw

GOVERNMENT OFFICIAL. Susan Rasinski McCaw is a native of Orange County, California. She received a Bachelor of Arts in economics from Stanford University and earned a Masters of Business Administration from Harvard Business School.

Her professional career includes serving as a business analyst for McKinsey & Company, an international management consulting firm in New York and Hong Kong.

She served as an associate in Robertson Stephens' Venture Capital Group and was a principal at Robertson Stephens' & Company, a San Francisco–based investment bank where she was responsible for financing emerging growth companies in the technology industry.

Mrs. McCaw was sworn in as ambassador to Austria by Justice Sandra Day O'Connor of the U.S. Supreme Court on November 30, 2005. United States Secretary of State Condoleezza Rice presided over the ceremony. Mrs. McCaw officially assumed her post as ambassador after presenting her diplomatic credentials to Austrian Federal President Heinz Fischer on January 9, 2006.

Pamela McClain

LAW ENFORCEMENT. Commander Pamela McClain received a bachelor's degree from the University of Michigan at Ann Arbor and earned her Juris Doctor degree from the University of Detroit Mercy School of Law. In 2000, she graduated from the Eastern Michigan University School of Staff and Command.

Her professional career with Wayne County Sheriff Department includes serving civil process, felony warrants, Friend of the Court enforcement, special projects in the jails division, support services and internal affairs. She was also assigned to the Wayne Macomb Auto Theft Multi-Jurisdictional Task Force.

Commander McClain serves as the executive commander of the Court Services Division for Wayne County, Michigan. She is responsible for uniformed courtroom security in the Frank Murphy Hall of Justice, Civil Division, Friend of the Court, Juvenile Court and the Juvenile Detention facilities.

Shelia K. McCleve

JUDGE. Shelia K. McCleve received her Juris Doctor degree from J. Reuben Clark College of Law at Brigham Young University in 1976. Before her appointment to the bench, she served as a deputy Salt Lake county attorney; an assistant Salt Lake City prosecutor; and an administrative law judge for the Utah Public Service Commission. She also worked as a senior research attorney for Justice Richard C. Howe at the Utah Supreme Court.

In March 1984, Governor Scott M. Matherson appointed her judge in the Third Circuit Court. In July 1996, she was appointed to the Third District Court serving Salt Lake, Summit, and Tooele counties.

Ellyn A. McColgan

FINANCE. Ellyn A. McColgan received a Bachelor of Arts degree in psychology from Montclair State College in New Jersey and earned a Master of Business Administration from Harvard Business School.

Since joining Fidelity Investments in 1990, she has held senior management positions with each of Fidelity's three major distribution businesses. During her tenure with Fidelity, McColgan has managed fund accounting and custody operations, the 401(k) client services division, the 403(d) business for not-for-profit institutions and the intermediary business that distributed Fidelity funds through banks, broker-dealers and insurance firms. She was named president of Fidelity Brokerage Company in 2002 and is responsible for management of both the retail and institutional

brokerage businesses. As of June 2003, Fidelity Brokerage Company managed more than $750 billion in total assets. Ms. McColgan is a vice chair of the Board of Trustees of Babson College and a vice chair of the board of directors of the Securities Industry Association.

Judith McConnell

JUDGE. Judith McConnell received a Bachelor of Arts degree from the University of California at Berkeley and earned her Juris Doctor degree from the University of California, Boalt Hall School of Law.

Her professional career includes serving as a trial attorney in the California Department of Transportation Legal Division in 1969 and in private law practice. In 1997, she was elected to the American Law Institute. She was appointed to the California Court of Appeals, 4th District, Division One, in August 2001 and took office upon her confirmation October 3, 2001. On September 25, 2003, she was confirmed as presiding justice of the court. On September 29, 2003, she was appointed by the chief justice as administrative presiding justice of the Fourth Appellate District. She served for 23 years as a trial judge in San Diego (21 years on the Superior Court and 2 years on the Municipal Court).

Mary McDade

JUDGE. Mary McDade is a native of Columbia, South Carolina, and was raised in Ann Arbor, Michigan. She graduated with a Bachelor of Arts degree in sociology from the University of Michigan in 1961. She earned her J.D. degree from the University of Illinois College of Law.

She was elected to the Peoria Board of Education, serving as president from 1972 to 1973; she also served as a member of the Peoria Public Library Board. She served as a member of the Board of Trustees of Eureka College, serving as president in 1982 and 1982. In 1981, she enrolled in the University of Illinois College of Law.

She served as a law clerk for U.S. District Judge Michael Mihm from 1984 to 1986. She was an attorney in private practice in 1986. Judge McDade is the first African American woman elected to the Appellate Court outside Cook County. She now serves as an appellate judge for the Third District, State of Illinois.

Marie V. McDemmond

EDUCATION. Marie V. McDemmond is a native of New Orleans, Louisiana. She received a bachelor's degree from Xavier University and a Master's degree from the University of New Orleans. She earned a doctorate from the University of Massachusetts at Amherst.

Her professional career includes serving as the director of Higher Education Opportunity Program (HEOP) at the College of New Rochelle in New Rochelle, New York; as assistant professor of education at the University of New Orleans; as an associate in higher education for the New York State Board of Regents; as the acting deputy director for administration and business officer at the Bronx Psychiatric Center; as the director of finance for the 15 community colleges in Massachusetts; as assistant vice president of finance at Emory University in Atlanta, Georgia; as associate vice chancellor for administration and finance and budget director at the University of Massachusetts at Amherst; as vice president for budget and finance at Atlanta University; as vice president for finance for Florida Atlantic University and its seven campuses. She is the first African American woman to serve as chief operating officer for finance in Florida; she teaches in Wellesley and Bryn Mawr Colleges' Project HERS and she has published articles in professional journals.

Dr. McDemmond was appointed president of Norfolk State University (NSU) in July 1997. She is the first African American woman president of Norfolk State University and the first African-American woman to serve as president of a four-year university in Virginia.

Gabrielle Kirk McDonald

JUDGE (FIRST). Gabrielle Kirk McDonald is a native of St. Paul, Minnesota. She attended Boston University (1959–1961) and Hunter College (1961–1963); she entered Howard University School of Law without an undergraduate degree and graduated first in the class of 1966.

Her professional career included serving as a staff attorney for the NAACP Legal Defense and Education Fund; she was engaged in private law practice from

1969 to 1979; in 1979, she was nominated judge by President Jimmy Carter to serve on the United States District Court for the Southern District of Texas. She was the first African American to be appointed in Texas and just the third African-American female federal judge in the United States. She resigned from her for-life appointment as a federal judge to return to private practice and teaching of law; she taught at Thurgood Marshall School of Law at Texas Southern University, at the University of Texas School of Law in Austin and St. Mary's School of Law in San Antonio. In 1993, she agreed to stand as the United States candidate for a judgeship on the International Criminal Tribunal for the former Yugoslavia. She received the highest number of votes, becoming the sole American on the court and one of only two women. Judge McDonald presided over the first full war crimes trial of the tribunal, the first one conducted since Nuremberg after World War II.

In May 1997, Judge McDonald was re-elected for a second term on the tribunal and in November of that year was nominated and endorsed by the judges on the court as its president and presiding judge for the next two years.

Ysleta W. McDonald

JUDGE. Ysleta W. McDonald received a Bachelor of Arts degree in English from the University of Florida in 1980 and a Juris Doctor degree from the University of Florida.

Her professional career includes serving as judge at the Alachua County Juvenile Delinquency and Dependency Juvenile Drug Court; as judge for the Alachua County Dependency Drug Court Family. Since January 2006, she has served as the administrative judge of Alachua County Family Court in Gainesville, Florida.

Linda M. McGee

JUDGE. Linda M. McGee is a native of Marion, North Carolina. She graduated from Marion High School in 1967 and received a Bachelor of Arts degree from the University of North Carolina at Chapel Hill in 1971. She earned her Juris Doctor degree from the University of North Carolina at Chapel Hill School of Law in 1973.

Her professional career includes serving as the first executive director of the North Carolina Academy of Trial Lawyers from 1973 to 1978 and in private law practice for over 17 years.

In 1995, Governor James B. Hunt, Jr., appointed her judge on the Court of Appeals for North Carolina. She was elected to an eight-year term in 1996 and re-elected in 2004.

Peg McGetrick

FINANCE. Peg McGetrick received a Bachelor of Science in business management and a Bachelor of Arts in psychology from Providence College. She earned a Master of Science in finance from Fairfield University.

Ms. McGetrick's career includes serving with Commonfund, a nonprofit endowment management group, and establishing The Common Fund for International Investments. She joined GMO in 1984 during the early stages of international equity investing. She served as a partner at Grantham, Mayo, Van Otterloo and Company where she headed the International Active Equity Division.

Ms. McGetrick is co-founder and managing partner of Liberty Square Asset Management. Liberty Square was founded in 1998 and manages non–U.S. equities in a long-short equity hedge fund and specialized long strategies for foundations, endowments and other institutions and individuals.

Anna-Maria Rivas McGowan

AEROSPACE. Anna-Maria Rivas McGowan is a native of the West Indian Island nation of Trinidad and Tobago, but grew up outside Washington, D.C. She received a Bachelor of Science degree in aeronautical and astronautical engineering from Purdue University.

Ms. McGowan started working at National Aeronautics and Space Administration (NASA)–Langley Research Center in Hampton, Virginia. She serves as project manager for the morphing project at Langley.

The $12 million project involves more than ninety researchers from twenty NASA branches and a number of university researchers. NASA celebrates the Future of Flight at Space Day each year and Ms. McGowan was a national spokesperson and NASA representative for the 2003 event.

Judy McGrath

ENTERTAINMENT EXECUTIVE. Judy McGrath received a Bachelor of Arts degree in English from Cedar Crest College in Allentown, Pennsylvania.

Ms. McGrath has held a succession of positions at MTV Networks since the launch of MTV. She served as MTV Networks Group president responsible for MTV, MTV2, VH1, CMT: County Music Television, and Comedy Central. She was appointed chairman and chief executive officer of MTV Networks, a position she has held since July 2004. She currently oversees the management and operation of MTV Network's 122 channels which reach more than 480 million households worldwide in 171 countries and in 28 languages. The company's portfolio of channels includes MTV, MTV2, VH1, VH1 Classic, Nickelodeon, Nick at Nite, Comedy Central, CMT, TV Land, Spike TV, mtvU, the 13 Digital Suite networks and Logo. Ms. McGrath manages all of the company's digital music services as well as MTV and Nickelodeon Films, MTV Networks International, and all of the company's consumer product and digital businesses.

Sandra McGruder-Jackson

MEDICINE. Sandra McGruder-Jackson is a native of Pittsburgh, Pennsylvania. She received a bachelor's degree (magna cum laude) from Lincoln University in Oxford, Pennsylvania. She is the first female graduate to receive the Lincoln University Outstanding Alumna award. She received her Medical Doctor degree from the Medical College of Pennsylvania and completed her residency in internal medicine.

Dr. McGruder-Jackson serves as president of the Keynote State Medical Society which is the Pennsylvania Society of the National Medical Association. She serves as the chair of Region II of the National Medical Association which includes Pennsylvania, Virginia, West Virginia, Maryland, Delaware and the District of Columbia.

She has been practicing general internal medicine in Philadelphia for more than twenty years.

Judith A. McHale

ENTERTAINMENT EXECUTIVE. Judith A. McHale received a bachelor's degree in politics from the University of Nottingham in England and earned her Juris Doctor from Fordham Law School.

Her professional career includes serving in private law practice in New York. In 1995 she was appointed president and chief operating officer for Discovery Communications. Under her leadership, Discovery Communications has grown from its core property, the Discovery Channel, first launched in 1985, to become the leading global real-world media and entertainment company. Discovery Communications now operates in 170 countries and territories reaching 1.4 billion total subscribers.

Ms. McHale serves as the president and chief executive officer of Discovery Communications.

Carolyn B. McHugh

JUDGE. Carolyn B. McHugh received her Juris Doctor degree from the University of Utah College of Law in 1982. Her professional career includes serving as law clerk at the United States District Court for the District of Utah; in private law practice; and as past president of Women Lawyers of Utah. In August 2005, she was appointed judge to the Utah Court of Appeals.

Jeanine McIntosh

MILITARY (FIRST). Jeanine McIntosh attended Vaz Preparatory School in Kingston, Jamaica, before migrating to South Florida where she attended Killian High School in Miami, Florida. She received a bachelor's degree from the Florida International University in 2001. She took flying lessons at North Perry Airport in Pembroke Pines near Miami, Florida. She graduated from the Coast Guard's Officer Candidate School and the Coast Guard Aviation training at Naval Air Station Corpus Christi, Texas, in January 2005. She earned her wings on June 24, 2005, and was assigned to fly HC-130 Hercules aircraft out of Air Station Barbers Point, Hawaii.

Prior to joining the Coast Guard, she served as a flight instructor at Opa-Locka Airport in North Miami. Lieutenant McIntosh is the first black female aviator in the 215-year history of the United States Coast Guard.

Vashti Murphy McKenzie

MINISTRY (FIRST). Vashti Murphy McKenzie received a bachelor's degree from the University of Maryland in College Park, Maryland, and received a Masters of Divinity degree from Howard University School of Divinity in Washington, D.C. She earned her Doctor of Ministry degree from the United Theological Seminary in Dayton, Ohio.

She has served as a pastor of more than three congregations from the rural setting to the inner-city. She served ten years as the pastor of historic 103-year-old Payne Memorial AME Church in Baltimore, Maryland. She made history on July 11, 2000, when she was elected the 117th bishop of the African Methodist Episcopal Church, making her the first woman to achieve that highest rank. She presides over the 18th Episcopal District of the AME church. Her district includes Lesotho, Mozambique, Botswana, and Swaziland in Southeast Africa.

Cynthia Ann McKinney

ELECTED OFFICIAL. Cynthia Ann McKinney is a native of Atlanta, Georgia, and a graduate of St. Joseph High School. She received a Bachelor of Arts degree from the University of Southern California in Los Angeles in 1978. She attended Fletcher School of Law and Diplomacy in Medford, Massachusetts and was a diplomatic fellow at Spelman College in Atlanta, Georgia.

Her professional career includes serving on the faculties of Clark Atlanta University and Agnes Scott College. She was elected as a Georgia state representative and served from 1988 to 1992. She was elected a United States representative to the 103rd and to the four succeeding Congresses (January 3, 1993–January 3, 2003). She was an unsuccessful candidate for nomination to the 108th Congress in 2002; she was elected a United States representative to the 109th Congress (January 3, 2005–January 3, 2007).

Cheryl Mayberry McKissack

BUSINESS EXECUTIVE. Cheryl Mayberry McKissack received a Bachelor of Science in political science from Seattle University and Master's in management from the Kellogg School of Management at Northwestern University.

Her professional career includes serving 15 years with IBM in various sales and marketing management positions; as vice president of sales/Americas for 3Com Corporation (formerly U.S. Robotics), where she established and managed its Network Systems Division; and as senior vice president and general manager of worldwide sales and marketing for Open Port technology since November 1997.

Ms. McKissack is founder, president and chief executive officer of Nia Enterprises, LLC, which publishes NiaOnline. She is also an editor of *The Nia Guide For Black Women* series.

Rhine McLin

ELECTED OFFICIAL. Rhine McLin is a native of Dayton, Ohio. She received a Bachelor of Arts in sociology and secondary education from Parsons College in Iowa and earned a Master of Education in guidance counseling from Xavier University in Cincinnati. She earned an associate degree in mortuary science from Cincinnati College of Mortuary Science. She is a licensed funeral director and embalmer for McLin Funeral Home in Dayton.

Her professional career includes serving six years in the Ohio House of Representatives from 1988 to 1994, and was then elected state senator for the 5th Ohio Senate District serving Montgomery and Miami counties. When elected in 1994, she became the first African-American woman to serve in the Ohio Senate. In 1998, she was elected by her peers to serve in leadership as the minority whip. Two years later, she was elected again to serve in the Senate leadership as minority leader.

Ms. McLin became the first female mayor of Dayton when she was elected to the City Commission for the term beginning January 7, 2002. She is Dayton's 67th mayor and the third African-American mayor in the city's history. She was re-elected mayor in November 2005.

Cathy McMorris

ELECTED OFFICIAL. Cathy McMorris is a native of Salem, Oregon. She received a Bachelor of Arts degree from Pensacola Christian College in Pensacola, Florida, in 1990 and a Masters of Business Administration from the University of Washington in Seattle, Washington, in 2002.

Her career includes serving as a fruit orchard worker. She served as a Washington state representative from 1994 to 2004 and was elected a United States representative to the 109th Congress, entering that office in January 3, 2005.

Claudia A. McMurray

GOVERNMENT OFFICIAL. Claudia A. McMurray received a Bachelor of Arts degree with honors in government from Smith College and earned her Juris Doctor from Georgetown University where she served as an associate editor of the law review *The Tax Lawyer*.

Her professional career includes serving in private law practice. From 1991 to 1995, she held the position of Republican counsel to the Senate Environment and Public Works Committee. Until 1996, she served as a senior policy advisor and counsel to three senators, all of whom served as chairmen of major committees. From 1998 to 2000, she served as a vice president at Van Scoyoc Associates, Inc. (VSA), a leading government relations firm in Washington, D.C. From 2001 to 2003, she served as associate deputy administrator and chief of staff to the deputy administrator of the U.S. Environmental Protection Agency. From 2003 to 2006, she served as deputy assistant secretary of state for environment.

Ms. McMurray was sworn as assistant secretary for oceans, environment and science on February 21, 2006.

Colleen McNally

JUDGE. Colleen McNally received a bachelor's degree in 1983 from the University of California in San Diego and earned her Juris Doctor degree from the University of Arizona in 1986.

Her professional career includes serving as a deputy county attorney, Maricopa County Attorney's office; as an assistant attorney general, Arizona Attorney General's office; as a deputy county public defender, Maricopa County Public Defender's office; from 1997 to 2001 she served as a commissioner at the Superior Court in Maricopa County; in 2001 she was appointed judge to the Superior Court of Arizona in Maricopa County.

Violet C. McNeirney

MILITARY. Violet C. McNeirney is a native of New York and enlisted into the United States Army in December 1982. She completed Basic Combat Training and Advance Individual Training at Fort Jackson, South Carolina.

Her military education includes Leadership Team Awareness Course; (DEOMI 04V); First Sergeant Course; all the Non-Commissioned Officer Education System Courses; Publications Managers Course; Equal Opportunity Representative Course; Combat Lifesavers Course; Instructor Training Course; Cadre Training Course; Airborne School; the United States Army Sergeants Major Academy (class 53); the Command Sergeants Major Course; Garrison Command Sergeant Major Course.

Her military assignments include battalion administrative NCO at Fort Bragg, North Carolina; administrative supervisor, G-1, VII Corps, in Germany; secretary of the general staff, administrative non-commissioned officer in charge, VII Corps, in Germany; administrative non-commissioned officer in charge to the commanding general, VII Corps, during this assignment, she deployed to Southwest Asia in support of operations Desert Shield/Desert Storm and Operation Provide Comfort; she was assigned as the executive administrative assistant to the commanding general, Training and Doctrine Command at Fort Monroe, Virginia; as senior drill sergeant, 1st Battalion, 26th Infantry Regiment (BCT); operations non-commissioned officer in charge, S3, 1/34th Infantry Regiment at Fort Jackson, South Carolina; as protocol non-commissioned officer-in-charge, United States Forces Korea (USFK) and Eighth United States Army (EUSA) in Korea. She was selected to serve as first sergeant, Headquarters and Headquarters Company, 43rd AG Battalion; as first sergeant, Fitness Training Company at Fort Leonard Wood in Missouri; as sergeant major, SGS/SACO, Headquarters Military District of Washington (MDW), Washington, D.C.; as the command sergeant major, Headquarters Command Battalion at Fort Myer, Virginia.

Jill K. McNulty

JUDGE. Jill K. McNulty is a native of Peoria, Illinois, and received her Bachelor of Art and J.D. degrees from Northwestern University. She served as a professor at IIT/Chicago-Kent College of Law from 1972 to 1981; as an associate circuit judge from 1979 to 1982; and as a circuit judge from 1982 to 1990. She now serves as an appellate judge for the First District, 1st Division of Illinois.

Linda K. McTague

MILITARY. Linda K. McTague received a Bachelor of Arts degree in liberal arts from Florida International University in Miami and a Master of Science degree in adult education from Florida International University in Miami. Her military schools include Squadron Officer School at Maxwell Air Force Base in Alabama in 1986; the Air Command and Staff College (Joint) in 1992; and the Air War College in 1996.

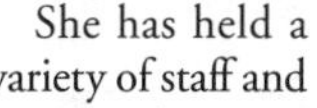

She has held a variety of staff and command positions including from November 2001 to November 2003 as Air National Guard advisor to director of operations, Headquarters Air Education and Training Command, Randolph Air Force Base in Texas.

Brigadier General McTague has served as the commander, 113th Wing, at Andrews Air Force Base in Maryland since December 2003. She was promoted to brigadier general on May 22, 2006.

Heather McTeer-Hudson

ELECTED OFFICIAL (FIRST). Heather McTeer-Hudson is a native of Greenville, Mississippi. She graduated from T. L. Weston High School and received a Bachelor of Arts degree from Spelman College. She earned her Juris Doctor from Tulane University Law School in New Orleans.

In 2003, she was elected mayor of Greenville, Mississippi, becoming the first female and African-American mayor of the largest municipality in the Delta. At 28, she is also the youngest person elected mayor of Greenville.

Jacque McVay

JUDGE. Jacque McVay is a native of Arizona. She received her undergraduate degree from Arizona State University and earned her Juris Doctor degree from the National Judicial College in Reno, Nevada. She has served as the justice of the peace for the Northeast Phoenix Justice Court precinct since early 1989 after first being elected in the fall of 1988.

Shirlyon J. McWhorter

JUDGE. Shirlyon J. McWhorter received a Bachelor of Arts degree (honors, summa cum laude) from Bethune-Cookman College in 1981. She earned her Juris Doctor degree from the University of Florida in 1991.

Her professional career includes serving as a trial attorney in the Office of the State Attorney from 1991 to 1997; as an assistant general counsel for the Dade County Police Benevolent Association (1997–2000); and in private law practice. In 2003, she was appointed judge to the County Court Criminal Division in Miami.

Carrie P. Meek

ELECTED OFFICIAL. Carrie P. Meek is a native of Tallahassee, Leon County, Florida. She received a Bachelor of Science degree from Florida A&M University, Tallahassee, in 1946 and a Masters of Science degree from the University of Michigan in 1948.

Her professional career includes teaching at several colleges and universities, including Bethune-Cookman College where she served as the physical education director for ten years and as a board member of Health System–Health Planning Council from 1972 to 1975. In 1979, she was elected to the Florida legislature; she was the first African-American woman elected to the Florida State Senate where she served from 1983 to 1993. In 1992 Meek, at 66 years of age, was elected to the United States Congress. She became one of three African-Americans since Reconstruction to win election to Congress from the state of Florida. She went to Washington in January 1993 as the U.S. Representative of Florida's 17th Congressional District which runs through northern Dade County. She served in Congress until January 2003 and was not a candidate for reelection to the 108th Congress.

Judith Meierhenry

JUDGE. Judith Meierhenry received a Bachelor of Science degree in 1966 and a Master's of Arts degree from the University of South Dakota in 1968. She earned her Juris Doctor degree from the University of South Dakota in 1977.

Her professional career includes serving in private law practice; in 1979 she was appointed to the South Dakota Economic Opportunity Office; she was next appointed as Secretary of Labor in 1980; and appointed Secretary of Education and Cultural Affairs in 1983; then she returned to private law practice. She was appointed as a Second Circuit Court judge and in 1997 was named as presiding judge of the Second Judicial Circuit.

Justice Meierhenry was appointed to the Supreme Court by Governor Janklow in November 2002. She is the first woman to be appointed to the Supreme Court in South Dakota.

Gail O. Mellow

EDUCATION. Gail O. Mellow received an Associate of Arts degree from Jamestown Community College

and a Bachelor of Arts degree from the State University of New York in Albany. She earned a Master of Arts degree and doctorate from George Washington University.

Her professional career includes serving in various capacities at community colleges in Maryland, Connecticut, New York and New Jersey; as an adjunct faculty, tenured faculty, academic dean, provost and president. In addition, she was the director of the Women's Center at the University of Connecticut and the director of the Project on Women and Technology.

Dr. Mellow was appointed president of LaGuardia Community College in Queens, New York.

Joan Orie Melvin

JUDGE. Joan Orie Melvin is a native of Pittsburgh, Pennsylvania. She received a Bachelor of Arts degree in economics from the University of Notre Dame and earned her Juris Doctor degree from Duquesne University School of Law in 1981.

Her professional career includes serving in private law practice from 1981 to 1985; in 1985, she was appointed a magistrate for the City of Pittsburgh Municipal Courts; she next served as chief magistrate in 1987 for the City of Pittsburgh Municipal Courts. In 1990, she was appointed judge to the Pennsylvania Allegheny County Court of Common Pleas and later was elected to a full term in 1991. In 1997, she was elected judge to the Allegheny County Superior Court.

Astrid E. Merget

EDUCATION. Astrid E. Merget received a bachelor's degree magna cum laude from Mount Holyoke College. She earned her MPA and Ph.D. from the Maxwell School at Syracuse University.

Her professional career includes serving as an instructor at Barnard College of Columbia University in New York and as a special assistant to the assistant secretary for policy development and research at the U.S. Department of Housing and Urban Development during the first year of President Carter's Administration. She served for 11 years as the chair of the Department of Public Administration at the George Washington University in Washington, D.C.; she spent eight years at the Ohio State University, where she directed the School of Public Policy and Management and spent a year as the acting dean of the College of Business; in 1994, Dr. Merget took leave from academic life to serve in Washington D.C. as senior adviser to the secretary of the U.S. Department of Health and Human Services; she served as chair of the Department of Public Administration and associate dean at the Maxwell School of Citizenship and Public Affairs at Syracuse University.

Dr. Merget serves as the third dean of the university-wide School of Public and Environmental Affairs (SPEA) at Indiana University.

Kathryn Davis Messerich

JUDGE. Kathryn Davis Messerich received a Bachelor of Science degree in nursing (magna cum laude) from Northern Michigan University in 1979 and received a Masters of Science in maternal-child nursing from the University of Minnesota in 1984. She earned her Juris Doctor degree from William Mitchell College of Law in 1987.

Her professional career includes serving as a registered nurse from 1979 to 1987 and in private law practice from 1987 to 2004. On March 9, 2004, she was appointed judge to the Minnesota Judicial District for Dakota County by Governor Tim Pawlenty.

Dorothy M. Metcalf-Lindenburger

ASTRONAUT. Dorothy M. Metcalf-Lindenburger is a native of Colorado Springs, Colorado, but considers Fort Collins, Colorado, her hometown where she graduated from Fort Collins High School. She received a Bachelor of Arts degree in geology cum laude from Whitman College in Washington and earned her teaching certification from Central Washington University, Washington, in 1999.

She has served as a teacher of earth science and astronomy at Hudson's Bay High School in Vancouver, Washington. She also served as a coach for cross-country at the high school level and a coach for the Science Olympiad. She was selected by NASA in May 2004 and in February 2006 she completed Astronaut Candidate Training that included scientific and technical briefings, intensive instruction in Shuttle and International Space Station systems, physiological training, T-38 flight training and water and wilderness survival training. Completion of this initial training qualifies her for various technical assignments within the Astronaut Office and future flight assignment as an educator mission specialist.

Leslie May Metzen

JUDGE. Leslie May Metzen received a Bachelor of Science degree from the University of Minnesota in 1970 and earned her Juris Doctor degree from William Mitchell College of Law in 1979.

Her professional career includes serving as director of development at Derham Hall High School from 1975 to 1976 and in private law practice from 1980 to 1986. In May 1986 she was appointed judge to the Minnesota District Court in Dakota County. She has won every re-election bid for her seat.

Helen M. Meyer

JUDGE. Helen M. Meyer received a bachelor's degree in social work at the University of Minnesota and earned her Juris Doctor degree from William Mitchell College of Law.

Her professional career includes serving twenty years in private law practice. In June 2002, Governor Jesse Ventura appointed her an associate justice on the Minnesota Supreme Court. She took the oath of her office on August 5, 2002.

Ann Meyers-Drysdale

SPORTS. Ann Meyers-Drysdale is a graduate of Sonora (CA) High School in 1974. While in high school she was basketball MVP in 1972, 1973 and 1974. She was named the St. Anthony's High School Tournament MVP in 1972; Athlete of the Year in 1974; an All-American 1971–1974; School Athlete of the Year; and a member of the United States National Team in 1974. She is the first high school player to make the women's national team. She earned a silver medal as part of the first women's U.S. Olympic basketball team in 1976. She received a bachelor's degree from the University of California at Las Angeles where she was a four-time All American in women's basketball from 1974 to 1978 and led the UCLA's Bruins to the 1978 AIAW Championship. She also played volleyball at UCLA and was a member of the 1975 NCAA championship track and field team.

She was the first woman ever to sign a free agent contract with an NBA team when she signed with the Indiana Pacers in 1979; is the first four-time Kodak All-American, male or female; and was the first woman to serve as a broadcaster of an NBA team. She served as a part-time color commentator for the Indiana Pacers in 1979; she also has served as a commentator for the SportsChannel, Prime Ticket, SportsTime and SportsVision covering various events. Since 1983, she has served as an ESPN analyst; from 1985 to 1996 she served as an analyst on Prime's coverage of NCAA basketball; from 1991 to 1995 she served as a commentator for CBS coverage of the NCAA men's and women's basketball championship; in 1984 she was a commentator for ABC's summer Olympics; in 1986 the WTBS's Goodwill Games; from 2000 to 2004 she has served as a commentator at the summer Olympics on NBC.

Ms. Meyers-Drysdale is the first woman inducted into the National Basketball Hall of Fame and to have her uniform on display inside Dr. Naismith's shrine; she was also inducted into the UCLA Sports Hall of Fame, the Women's Sports Hall of Fame and the National High School Hall of Fame. She and her husband, the Late Los Angeles Dodger pitcher and Baseball Hall of Famer Don Drysdale, make up the first husband-wife team in any hall of fame.

Jeanette A. Michael

GOVERNMENT OFFICIAL. Jeanette A. Michael received a Bachelor of Arts degree in political science from Manhattanville College and a Juris Doctor degree from George Washington University. She is a certified public manager.

Her professional career includes serving as a deputy director in the Washington, D.C., Department of Human Services, as a supervisory attorney in the city's Office of the Corporation Counsel, and as chief of staff to D.C.'s former mayor, Marion Barry, Jr.

Ms. Michael was appointed executive director for the Washington, D.C., Lottery & Charitable Games Control Board.

Kathryn Michael

JUDGE. Kathryn Michael graduated from the University of Akron in 1982 and earned her Juris Doctor degree from the University of Akron School of Law in 1986. She was engaged in private law practice and as a part-time magistrate judge. She was elected as a municipal court judge in November 2005.

Harriet R. Michel

NONPROFIT EXECUTIVE. Harriet R. Michel is a native of Pittsburgh, Pennsylvania. She received a Bachelor of Arts degree from Juniata College in Huntingdon, Pennsylvania and an honorary degree of Doctor of Humane Letters from Baruch College in New York.

Her professional career includes serving as executive director of the New York Foundation from 1972 to 1977. She was the first black woman to head a major foundation. She is a founding member of the Association of Black Foundation Executives and has been a board member of the Council on Foundations. From 1977 to 1979, she served as the director of the U.S. Department of Labor's Office of Community Youth Employment Programs/CETA in Washington, D.C. From 1983 to 1988, she served as president and chief executive officer of the New York Urban League. She was the first woman to head the New York Urban League.

Ms. Michel serves as the president of the National Minority Supplier Development Council, a private non-profit organization that expands business opportunities of minority-owned companies.

Harriet Miers

GOVERNMENT OFFICIAL. Harriet Miers received both a bachelor's degree and her Juris Doctor degree from Southern Methodist University.

Her professional career includes being engaged in private law practice and serving as a member-at-large on the Dallas City Council. In 1985, she became the first woman president of the Dallas Bar Association; in 1992, she became the first woman president of the Texas State Bar; from 1995 to 2000 she was chair of the Texas Lottery Commission. She was also assistant to the president, staff secretary and deputy chief of staff in the White House.

Ms. Miers was appointed counsel to President George W. Bush at the White House in Washington, D.C.

Barbara Ann Mikulski

ELECTED OFFICIAL. Barbara Ann Mikulski is a native of Baltimore, Maryland. She received a bachelor's de-

gree from Mount St. Agnes College in 1958 and received a Master's degree from the University of Maryland School of Social Work in 1965.

Her professional career includes serving as a social worker in Baltimore, Maryland; as a college professor; as a member of the Baltimore City Council from 1971 to 1976; she was elected a United States Representative to the 95th Congress and was reelected to the four succeeding Congresses and served from January 3, 1977, to January 3, 1987; she was elected to the United States Senate in 1986 and reelected in 1992, 1998 and 2004 for the term ending January 3, 2011.

Dianne Bitonte Miladore

MEDICINE. Dianne Bitonte Miladore received a Bachelor of Science degree summa cum laude from Youngstown State University and earned her Medical Doctor degree from Northeastern Ohio Universities College of Medicine. She completed residencies in emergency medicine at Akron General Medical Center and St. Vincent's Medical Center in Toledo where she was the physician in charge of the Life Flight helicopter during her final year of residency.

Dr. Miladore served as an emergency room attending physician at the Medical College of Ohio at Toledo and at St. Elizabeth Health Center and the Beeghly Urgent Care Center. She has been very active at NEOUCOM, where she has served as a clinical faculty member and a member of the Admissions Committee, the Academic Review Committee and the Clinical Competency Assessment Medical Advisory Board.

Susan Miles

JUDGE. Susan Miles's career as a judge began in January 1997. She has sat on the Minnesota State District Court located in Washington County Government Center in Stillwater, Minnesota. She also serves as the lead judge for the Washington County Children Justice Initiative.

Vicki Miles-LaGrange

JUDGE. Vicki Miles-LaGrange is a native of Oklahoma City, Oklahoma. She attended the University of Ghana in Legon, Ghana, West Africa, and received a Bachelor of Arts degree with honors from Vassar College in Poughkeepsie, New York, in 1974. She earned her Juris Doctor degree from Howard University School of Law in Washington, D.C., in 1977 and also graduated from the National College of District Attorneys in Houston, Texas, in 1984.

Her professional career includes serving in private law practice; as an assistant district attorney of Oklahoma County; as an attorney with the Office of Enforcement Operations, United States Department of Justice, Criminal Division, in Washington, D.C., from 1982 to 1983; as law clerk to United States District Judge Woodrow Seals in Houston, Texas; as an aide to the speaker of the U.S. House of Representatives in Washington, D.C.; as a news reporter for KWTV, Channel 9, in Oklahoma City; as an Oklahoma State Senator (District 48). In 1993 she gave up her elective post as an Oklahoma State Senator when she was confirmed as United States attorney for the Western District of Oklahoma, becoming the first black female to serve as U.S. attorney in Oklahoma. On September 22, 1994, President William J. Clinton nominated Vicki Miles-LaGrange as a judge to the United States District Court in the Western District of Oklahoma. She was confirmed by the U.S. Senate on October 7, 1994, and received commission on November 28, 1994.

Donna Robinson Milhouse

JUDGE. Donna Robinson Milhouse is a native of Detroit, Michigan. She received a Bachelor of Arts degree in business administration from Eastern Michigan University and earned her Juris

Doctor degree from Wayne State University Law School in 1984. She began her career in private law practice for 15 years. In 2000, she was appointed judge to the Michigan 36th District Court in Detroit, Michigan.

Maria Milin

JUDGE. Maria Milin received a Bachelor of Arts degree from St. John's University in 1983 and earned her Juris Doctor degree from Brooklyn Law School in 1986. Her professional career includes serving as a law assistant, trial part; as associate court attorney, trial part; and as the principal court attorney, trial part, all for the New York State Unified Court System.

Chief Administrative Judge Jonathan Lippman appointed her judge to the New York City Civil Court Housing Part in 1998.

B. Pennie Millender

JUDGE. B. Pennie Millender received her undergraduate education from Olivet College and Southern University in Baton Rouge, Louisiana, receiving a Bachelor of Arts degree in psychology from the latter in 1974. She received a Master's of Art degree in vocational rehabilitation counseling from Wayne State University. She earned her Juris Doctor degree from Detroit College of Law.

Her professional career includes serving as an attorney for the National Labor Relations Board, Region 7, from 1987 to 1990. In 2004, she was appointed judge to the Michigan's 36th Judicial District Court in Detroit.

Candice Miller

ELECTED OFFICIAL (FIRST). Candice Miller is a native of Macomb County, Michigan, where she graduated from Lakeshore High School. She attended both Macomb Community College and Northwood University. She worked in the marina business on the Clinton River that her family owned for several years before she became involved in public service.

In 1979, she was elected to the Harrison Township Board of Trustees; in 1980 she was elected Harrison Township supervisor, becoming the youngest supervisor in the township's history and the first woman ever elected to the post; in 1992 she was elected Macomb County treasurer; in 1994 she was elected secretary of state for the state of Michigan. She is the first woman to ever be elected in a partisan statewide office in her own right and the first Republican to serve as secretary of state in over 40 years.

Cheryl Miller

SPORTS (FIRST). Cheryl Miller is a native of Riverside, California, and graduated from Polytechnic High School. She played basketball while in school and became the first player male or female named a Parade All-American four straight years and was named Street and Smith's High School Player of the Year in 1981 and 1982. She received a bachelor's degree from the University of Southern California (USC). She led USC to consecutive national titles in 1983 and 1984. She was the first player to "elevate" the women's game with her leaping ability. In 1986, *Sports Illustrated* named Ms. Miller the best player male or female in college basketball. She was a member of the NCAA All-Tournament team three times and was named NCAA Tournament MVP in 1983 and 1984.

She led the United States Olympic team to a gold medal in 1984 and gold medals at the 1983 Pan American and 1986 Goodwill Games. In 1986, she became the first female ever nominated for the prestigious Sullivan Award and in March of that year, USC retired her jersey, making her the first Trojan athlete so honored. Her basketball career continues as a stu-

dio host, reporter and analyst for TNT and TBS covering the NBA. She has also served as head coach and general manager of the WNBA Phoenix Mercury. In November 1996, she became the first female analyst to work on a nationally televised NBA game. She has worked as a broadcaster for NBA studio as an analyst. She has also worked as an actor with guest starting roles in several television series.

Cylenthia LaToye Miller

JUDGE. Cylenthia LaToye Miller received a Bachelor of Arts degree in sociology from Wayne State University in 1988. She earned her Juris Doctor degree (cum laude) from Michigan State University—Detroit College of Law in 1996.

Her professional career includes serving as a crisis line counselor and supervisor at the Wayne County Crisis Line; in private law practice; as the assistant general counsel to Kwame M. Kilpatrick, mayor of the city of Detroit and as director of the Detroit Workforce Development Department. On April 10, 2006, Governor Jennifer Granholm appointed her judge to the Michigan's 36th Judicial District Court in Detroit.

Laura Miller

ELECTED OFFICIAL. Laura Miller is a native of Baltimore, Maryland, and is a graduate of the University of Wisconsin–Madison. Before being elected to the Dallas City Council in 1998 she was an award-winning journalist for 18 years. She worked as an investigative reporter for the *Dallas Observer*, the *Dallas Times Herald*, the *New York Daily News* and *The Dallas Morning News Herald*. In February 2002, she was elected mayor of the city of Dallas, Texas, after serving three-and-a-half years as a member of Dallas City Council.

M. Yvette Miller

JUDGE. M. Yvette Miller is a native of Georgia. In 1977, she earned her Bachelor of Arts degree (cum laude) from Mercer University in Macon, Georgia, and in 1980 she graduated from that university's Walter F. George School of Law. In 1988, she earned an LL.M. in litigation from Emory University School of Law in Atlanta, Georgia. In 2004, she received a Master of Law in judicial process from the University of Virginia School of Law in Charlottesville, Virginia.

She has made history many times in the course of her distinguished career. Her experience includes serving as a law clerk in Fulton State Court, as a senior associate counsel at MARTA, and in private practice. She made history in 1992 when Governor Zel Miller appointed her as the first African-American, the first woman, and the youngest person ever to serve as director/judge of the appellate division on the State Board of Workers' Compensation. Prior to this appointment, Judge Miller had been appointed by Governor Zel Miller to the State Court of Fulton County and was re-elected without opposition in 1998.

In 1999, Governor Roy Barnes appointed her as the first African American woman and the 65th judge to serve on the Georgia Court of Appeals. In November of 2000, she was elected statewide to the Court of Appeals without opposition.

Peggy Miller

EDUCATION. Peggy Miller received a bachelor's degree in English from Transylvania University and a Master's degree in English and secondary education from Northwestern University. She earned her doctorate in secondary education from Indiana University. She holds honorary degrees from Transylvania University and Chungnam National University in Korea.

Her professional career includes serving from 1983 to 1992 as chancellor at Indiana University Northwest and from 1992 to 1996 as president of the University of Akron. She was a senior fellow and acting vice president for academic and international programs at the American Association of State Colleges and Universities in Washington, D.C.

Dr. Miller was appointed the 18th president of South Dakota State University on January 1, 1998.

Lindsey Miller-Lerman

JUDGE. Lindsey Miller-Lerman received a Bachelor of Arts degree from Wellesley College, Massachusetts, in 1968 and earned her Juris Doctor degree from Columbia University School of Law in New York in 1973.

Her professional career includes serving in private law practice, serving as a judge on the Nebraska State Court of Appeals from 1992 to 1998, and as chief judge for the Court of Appeals from 1996 to 1998. On September 1, 1998, she assumed a position of justice on the Nebraska Supreme Court.

Pamela K. Milligan

MILITARY. Pamela K. Milligan received a Bachelor of Arts in psychology from Ohio State University in Columbus, Ohio; earned a Master of Arts in public administration from Ohio State University; and earned a Doctor of Philosophy in organization and management from Capella University in Minnesota. Her military schools include Squadron Officers School, Air Command and Staff College, and Canadian Joint Forces Command and Staff College in Toronto, Canada. She graduated from the Air War College.

Colonel Pamela Milligan serves as the commander of the 624th Regional Support Group, headquartered at Hickam Air Force Base in Hawaii. Her prior assignments included serving as chief of training, 940th Air Refueling Wing, Beale Air Force Base, in California; as commander, 940th Mission Support Squadron, Beale AFB in California; as chief, tanker operations branch at Headquarters, 4th Air Force, March Air Reserve Base in California; as vice commander, 376 Expeditionary Air Wing, Manas Air Base, Kyrgyzstan; as commander, 624th Regional Support Group. Presently, She is mobilization assistant to the director of operations, J3, United States Pacific Command, Hickam AFB, Hawaii.

Cathy E. Minehan

FINANCE. Cathy E. Minehan is a native of Jersey City, New Jersey. She received a Bachelor of Arts degree in political science from the University of Rochester in 1968 and she earned a Masters of Business Administration degree from New York University in 1977.

She began her career with the Federal Reserve System in 1968 holding various staff positions at the Federal Reserve Bank of New York including bank examiner, analyst, and supervisory positions in public information and accounting control. She was named operations analysis officer in 1975 and served as manager of the management information department from 1976 to 1978. In 1978, she served as visiting assistant secretary to the Board of Governors of the Federal Reserve System. Upon returning to the New York Reserve Bank in 1979, she was named assistant vice president with responsibilities in data processing and subsequently, as a senior aide to the president. In 1982, she was named vice president and over the next five years served in the accounting, check processing, funds and securities and accounts group. She was named first vice president of the Federal Reserve Bank of Boston in 1991 and she held that position until she was named president in July 1994.

Jenny Ming

BUSINESS EXECUTIVE. Jenny Ming received a bachelor's degree from San Jose State University. After graduating, she took a job in 1986 with Gap, Inc., the San Francisco–based clothing manufacturer. She served as a member of the Gap, Inc. executive team that launched the Old Navy division in 1994. She was the executive vice president of merchandising and was selected to serve as president of Old Navy. She has turned Old Navy into a multi-billion dollar brand of its own and under her leadership it became the world's fastest-growing retail brand.

Ruth Ann Minner

ELECTED OFFICIAL. Ruth Ann Minner is a native of Slaughter Neck in Sussex County, Delaware. She left school at age 16 to help on her family's farm, later marrying Frank Ingram. Widowed suddenly at 32 with three sons to raise, she worked two jobs while going to school, earning her G.E.D. She built a family towing business with her second husband, Roger Minner, who died of lung cancer in 1991. She was elected to four terms in the Delaware House of Representatives beginning in 1974, to three terms in the state Senate beginning in 1982 and to two terms as lieutenant governor in 1992 and 1996.

She was elected governor of Delaware in 2001. Governor Minner has worked to get things done in Delaware by improving schools, preserving and protecting the environment, improving health care and fighting cancer as well as creating and keeping jobs.

Helena O. Mishoe

GOVERNMENT OFFICIAL. Captain Helena O. Mishoe received her Ph.D. in microbiology from Georgetown University School of Medicine in Washington, D.C., and earned her Masters of Public Health degree in 2002 from the Unformed Services University School of Medicine.

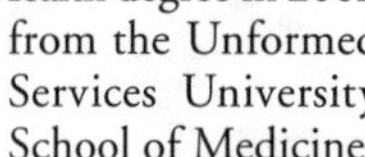

In 1981, she joined the National Institute of Health intramural research teams and moved up the research ranks as staff fellow, senior staff fellow and expert in molecular biology and gene expression research areas. She joined the extramural program in the Commissioned Corps officer; she has served several offices in the department including the Office of the Surgeon General.

Captain Mishoe has served as the first director of the Office of Minority Health Affairs (OMHA) in the office of the director of the National Heart, Lung, and Blood Institute. In August 2005, she was appointed the chief professional officer for the scientist category, responsible for providing leadership and coordination of public health service scientist professional affairs for the Office of the Surgeon General and the department.

Andrea Mitchell

JOURNALISM. Andrea Mitchell is a native of New York. She received a Bachelor of Arts degree in English literature from the University of Pennsylvania. Her professional career began in 1967 as a broadcast journalist for KYW Radio and KYW-TV in Philadelphia. She served as a correspondent for WDVM-TV (then WTOP), the CBS affiliate in Washington, D.C. She joined NBC News in 1978 as a general correspondent based in Washington, D.C. In 1979 she was named NBC News energy correspondent. In that capacity, she reported on the energy crisis and the Three Mile Island nuclear incident. She covered the White House for NBC News from 1981 to 1988, during both of Ronald Reagan's terms as president. From 1988 to 1992, she served as chief congressional correspondent and in 1992 she assumed the position of chief White House correspondent. In November 1994, she was named chief foreign affairs correspondent for NBC News and reports on *NBC Nightly News*, the *Today Show*, on CNBC and MSNBC.

Eithel P. Mitchell

MILITARY. Eithel P. Mitchell entered the Air Force in 1973, while attending medical school at the Medical College of Virginia, Richmond and began her military career by receiving a commission through the health professions scholarship program. She graduated in 1974 in the accelerated graduation program and entered active duty in 1978 after completion of her residency in internal medicine at Meharry Medical College, Nashville, Tennessee. She completed a fellowship in medical oncology at Georgetown University. She is board-certified in internal medicine and medical oncology and is a flight surgeon. Prior to assuming her current position, she served as the state air surgeon of Missouri and director of diversity at Headquarters Missouri Air National Guard.

Her education includes a Bachelor of Science degree in biochemistry from Tennessee State University in Nashville in 1969. She earned a Doctor of Medicine degree from Medical College of Virginia in Richmond, Virginia, in 1974. She also completed the Air War College in 1995.

In February 1987, she served as a physician, later as commander with the 131st Medical Squadron, Lambert–St. Louis International Airport, Missouri. From October 1995 to December 2000, she served as the state air surgeon, Headquarters Missouri Air National Guard in Jefferson City, Missouri. In December 2000, she was selected as the Air National Guard assistant to the command surgeon at the United States Transportation Command and Headquarters Air Mobility Command at Scott Air Force Base, Illinois. In this assignment she serves as the senior medical Air National advisor to the command surgeon and is the medical liaison between the active Air Force and the Air National Guard.

Her awards and decorations include the Meritorious Service Medal (with one oak leaf cluster); the Air Force Commendation Medal; Air Force Achievement Medal; Air Force Outstanding Unit Award (with one oak leaf cluster); Air Force Organizational Excellence Award; National Defense Service Medal; Humanitarian Service Medal; Air Force Longevity Service Award (with four oak leaf clusters); Armed Forces Reserve Medal (with hourglass device); Small arms Expert Marksmanship Ribbons; Air Force Training Ribbon; Missouri National Guard Conspicuous Service Medal; Missouri National Guard Commendation Ribbon; Missouri National Guard Long Service Ribbon for 10 years; Missouri National Guard Recruiting and Retention Ribbon.

Hala Moddelmog

BUSINESS EXECUTIVE. Hala Moddelmog received a bachelor's degree in English from Georgia Southern University.

Ms. Moddelmog has served as president of Church's Chicken since 1996 when she became the first female president of a "quick service restaurant" chain (better known as fast food restaurants). During her leadership of Church's Chicken more than 19 percent of Church's Chicken franchises have become owned by female franchisees. This is due in large part to the company's attempts to network female investors and would-be female franchisees together to evade the biased appearance that some "quick service restaurants" presents toward female entrepreneurs.

Gloria Molina

ELECTED OFFICIAL (FIRST). Gloria Molina's political career begin during the 1970s Chicano movement as a women's health advocate. She served in the Carter White House and the San Francisco Department of Health and Human Services. She was elected to the California State Assembly in 1982 and the Los Angeles City Council in 1987. On February 19, 1991, she became the first Latina-American ever elected to the Los Angeles County Board of Supervisors. She served as one of four vice chairs of the Democratic National Committee through 2004.

Susan Molinari

ELECTED OFFICIAL. Susan Molinari is a native of Staten Island, New York, and a graduate of St. Joseph Hill Academy in 1976. She received Bachelor of Arts degree from State University of New York, Albany, in 1980 and a Master of Arts in 1982.

Her professional career includes serving as a research analyst for the New York State Senate Finance Committee; as a finance assistant for the National Republican Governors Association; as a ethnic community liaison for the Republican National Committee from 1983 to 1984; as a member of the New York City Council from 1986 to 1990. She was elected a United States Representative to the 101st Congress by special election to fill the vacancy caused by the resignation of United States Representative Guy V. Molinari and was re-elected to the four succeeding Congresses, serving until her resignation on August 2, 1997. She served from March 20, 1990, to August 2, 1997.

Patricia N. Moller

GOVERNMENT OFFICIAL. Patricia N. Moller is a native of Arkansas. She received a bachelor's degree from the University of Tampa. Her professional career includes serving as an investment banker and tax shelter specialist with Smith Barney; serving as a Foreign Service officer in April 1987; serving in Consulate General Madras, India, from 1989 to 1991. From 1991 to 1996, she worked in Washington at the Department of State, first as a watch officer, then as staff aide to the assistant secretary for intelligence and research, and finally for two years as Vietnam desk officer during the interesting days of bilateral negotiations to reestablish diplomatic relations between the two countries; from 2000 to 2002 she served as deputy chief of mission in Yerevan, Armenia. Her posting to Georgia began in August 2002 when she traveled to Tbilisi to begin three years as deputy chief of mission to Ambassador Richard Miles. On March 4, 2006, she was sworn in as ambassador extraordinary and plenipotentiary of the United States to the Republic of Burundi.

Susan Oki Mollway

JUDGE. Susan Oki Mollway is a native of Honolulu, Hawaii. She received both a Bachelor of Arts degree and a Masters of Arts degree from the University of Hawaii. She earned her Juris Doctor degree from Harvard Law School in 1981.

After law school, she served in private law practice in Honolulu, Hawaii, from 1981 to 1998. She was nominated by President William J. Clinton on January 7, 1997, to judge on the United States Court for the District of Hawaii. She was confirmed by the U.S. Senate on June 22, 1998, and received her commission on June 23, 1998.

Carol Molnau

ELECTED OFFICIAL. Carol Molnau is a native of Carver County and attended public schools in Waconia, Minnesota. She received a bachelor's degree from the University of Minnesota.

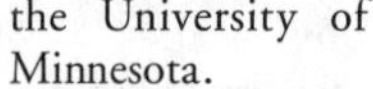

She has been a farm owner/operator since 1971. She spent time in Russia assisting post–Soviet farmers to improve their agricultural practices. She was elected to the Chaska City Council where she served one term. In 1992, she was elected as a member of the Minnesota House of Representatives where she served five terms. In 2002, she was elected lieutenant governor for the state of Minnesota. She is entrusted with more responsibility than any lieutenant governor in modern times; she serves Minnesota both as the state's number two executive and also as commissioner of the Minnesota Department of Transportation.

Stephanie J. Monroe

GOVERNMENT OFFICIAL. Stephanie J. Monroe is a native of Baltimore, Maryland. She received a bachelor's degree in government and politics from the University of Maryland in College Park. She earned a Juris Doctor degree from the University of Baltimore.

Her professional career includes serving from 1998 to 2001 as the chief counsel and minority staff director of the former Senate Labor and Human Resources Subcommittee on Children, Family, Drugs and Alcoholism. From 2001 to 2005, she was the chief counsel for the United States Senate Committee on Health, Education, Labor and Pension.

Ms. Monroe was nominated as assistant secretary for civil rights on June 23, 2005, and she was confirmed by the United States Senate on December 17, 2005. As assistant secretary, Monroe is Secretary Spelling's primary adviser on civil rights and is responsible for enforcing U.S. civil rights laws as they pertain to education, ensuring the nation's schools, colleges and universities receiving federal funding do not engage in discriminatory conduct related to race, sex, disability or age.

Nancy Monsarrat

BUSINESS EXECUTIVE. Nancy Monsarrat received a bachelor's degree from the University of Portland. Her professional career includes serving as vice president of Elgin Syferd advertising and serving at Cole & Weber Advertising and KING-AM.

Ms. Monsarrat has served 15 years at Nike. She move south to Oregon and Nike headquarters to work as a senior director for the sneaker and apparel giant before taking over as Nike's Asia Pacific advertising director in 1999 working out of Nike's Beaverton, Oregon, headquarters.

Carla Moore

JUDGE. Carla Moore received a Bachelor of Arts degree in German from the University of Akron and earned her Juris Doctor degree from Ohio State University College of Law.

She served as an assistant U.S. attorney as a deputy chief of the civil division in 1984 and as chief of appellate litigation. She left the U.S. Attorney's office in 1988 for a private law practice.

Judge Moore was appointed to the bench in 1989 by Governor Richard Celeste. She retained the seat in the November 1989 election. She became the first African-American woman elected to a judicial seat in Summit County.

Frankie J. Moore

JUDGE. Frankie J. Moore received a Bachelor of Arts degree from Nebraska Wesleyan University in 1980 and earned her Juris Doctor degree from the University of Nebraska College of Law in 1983. She served in private law practice from 1983 to 2000. She was appointed judge for the Nebraska Commission of Industrial Relation from 1989 to 2000.

On January 28, 2000, she was appointed a judge on the Nebraska Court of Appeals.

Gwendolynne (Gwen) S. Moore

ELECTED OFFICIAL. Gwendolynne (Gwen) S. Moore is a native of Racine, Wisconsin. She received a Bachelor of Arts degree in political science from Marquette University in Milwaukee, Wisconsin.

She served as a housing officer with the Wisconsin Housing and Development Authority. In 1988 she was elected a member of the Wisconsin State Assembly. In 1992, she was elected a Wisconsin State Senator (1993–2003). In 2004, she was elected a United States Representative from Wisconsin as a Democrat to the 109th Congress and to the succeeding Congresses.

Kimberly Ann Moore

JUDGE. Kimberly Ann Moore is a native of Baltimore, Maryland. She received a Bachelor of Science in electrical engineering from Massachusetts Institute of Technology in 1990 and a Masters of Science from Massachusetts Institute of Technology in 1991. She earned her Juris Doctor degree from the Georgetown University Law Center in 1994.

Her professional career includes serving as an electrical engineer at the Naval Surface Warfare Center; as a law clerk to the chief judge of the United States Court of Appeals for the Federal Circuit; in private law practice; as a professor at the University of Maryland School of Law; as a professor at Chicago-Kent College of Law; as the associate director of the Chicago-Kent Intellectual Property Law Program; as a professor at the George Mason University School of Law, first as an associate professor from 2000 to 2004 and then as a professor of law from 2004 to 2006. She was appointed a judge to the United States Court of Appeals for the Federal Circuit. She was nominated to the Federal Circuit by President George W. Bush on May 18, 2006, to fill a seat vacancy. The United States Senate confirmed her nomination on September 5, 2006.

Lois Jean Moore

MEDICINE. Lois Jean Moore received a nursing diploma from Prairie View A&M's School of Nursing in 1957 and a Bachelor of

Science degree in nursing from Texas Woman's University in Houston in 1970. She earned a Master of Education from Texas Southern University in 1974. She received an honorary Doctor of Humane Letters degree from Our Lady of the Lake University in San Antonio, Texas.

Her professional career includes serving as president and chief executive officer at the Harris County Hospital District where in four decades she rose from nurse to chief executive officer. She served as the interim dean of Prairie View A&M's School of Nursing. She serves as the University of Texas Harris County Psychiatric Center's chief administrator.

Madeleine Moore

BUSINESS EXECUTIVE. Madeleine Moore received a bachelor's degree from New York University and a Master's degree from Columbia University. She earned a doctorate degree from City University of New York.

Her professional career includes serving as president emeritus of the New York Coalition of One Hundred Black Women; she is a founder of the 21st Century Women's Leadership Center; she serves as chairman of Public New York and the founder of Moore Creative, marketing firms which have launched identity campaigns for several major New York hospitals and provide concepts and training tools to such organizations as the Association of Junior Leagues International and the National Urban League.

Ms. Moore was appointed state president of AARP New York.

Thelma Wyatt Cummings Moore

JUDGE. Thelma Wyatt Cummings Moore is a native of Texas where her desire to seek justice and equality has been catalyzed by her many life experiences. The Ku Klux Klan burned her family's home and later burned crosses in their yard. Her father, Dr. J. O. Wyatt, ran for election to the school board following the *Brown v. Board of Education* decision won by Thurgood Marshall. In 1974, her brother J. O. Wyatt II was elected one of the two first black Fulton County commissioners, and he was the first black to serve as vice chairman of the Board of Commissioners. It was this brother who urged her to attend Emory Law School with him.

She received a bachelor's degree from the University of California at Los Angeles and completed a graduate fellowship in psychodynamics at the Illinois Institute of Technology. She earned her Juris Doctor degree (with distinction) from Emory University.

Early in her legal career, she served as a trial attorney with the Equal Employment Opportunity Commission under the leadership of the Honorable Donald L. Hollowell. She served as general counsel to the Institute for Entrepreneurship and Management under the leadership of Judge Horace T. Ward. The Honorable Maynard H. Jackson appointed her to the bench as judge to the Atlanta Municipal Court and the City Court of Atlanta. She became the first woman to serve full-time on the Atlanta Court. She was the first African-American woman to serve on the State Courts of Georgia. Judge Moore was the first woman to serve as chief judge of the Superior Court of Fulton County, Georgia's busiest trial court of general jurisdiction and the first African-American woman to serve as chief administrative judge of any judicial circuit in Georgia. She has been re-elected to the bench six times.

Judge Moore is the architect of the Fulton County Family Court and the Family Law Information Center innovative projects and the first of their kind in Georgia providing access to justice for all. Judge Moore received the United States Chief Justice Award for Judicial Excellence at a reception and dinner in her sole honor in the Great Hall of the Supreme Court of the United States.

Constance A. Morella

GOVERNMENT OFFICIAL. Constance A. Morella is a native of Somerville, Bristol County, Massachusetts. She received a Bachelor of Arts degree from Boston University in Boston in 1954 and a Master of Arts degree from American University in Washington, D.C., in 1967.

Her professional career includes serving as a professor at Montgomery College from 1970 to 1986; as a member of the Montgomery County, Maryland, Commission for Women from 1971 to 1975; as a member of the Maryland State House of Delegates from 1979 to 1986. She was elected a United States Representative to the 100th and to the seven succeeding Congresses

(January 3, 1987 to January 3, 2003). She has served as a United States ambassador to the Organization for Economic Corporation and Development from 2003 to the present.

Barbara R. Morgan

ASTRONAUT. Barbara R. Morgan is a native of Fresno, California, and a graduate of Hoover High School in Fresno. She received a Bachelor of Arts degree in human biology, with distinction, from Stanford University in 1973 and received her teaching credential from the College of Notre Dame in Belmont, California, in 1974.

Her teaching career includes teaching on the Flathead Indian Reservation at Arlee Elementary School in Arlee, Montana; at McCall-Donnelly Elementary School in McCall, Idaho, from 1975 to 1978; English and Science at Colegio Americano deQuito in Quito, Ecuador; at McCall Donnelly Elementary School from 1979 to 1998.

Ms. Morgan was selected by the National Aeronautics and Space Administration (NASA) as the backup candidate for the NASA Teacher in Space Program on July 19, 1985. From September 1985 to January 1986, Morgan trained with Christa McAuliffe and the Challenger crew at NASA's Johnson Space Center in Houston, Texas. Following the Challenger accident, she assumed the duties of Teacher in Space designee. From March 1986 to July 1986, she worked with NASA, speaking to educational organizations throughout the country. In the fall of 1986, Morgan returned to Idaho to resume her teaching career. She was selected by NASA in January 1998 as the first educator astronaut. Morgan reported to the Johnson Space Center in August 1998. Following the completion of two years of training and evaluation, she was assigned technical duties in the Astronaut Office Space Station Operations Branch. Most recently she served in the Astronaut Office CAPCOM Branch, working in Mission Control as prime communicator with on-orbit crews. Morgan is assigned to the crew of STS-118, an assembly mission to the International Space Station. The mission will launch in 2007.

Betty L. G. Morgan

MILITARY. Betty L. G. Morgan is a native of Savannah, Georgia, and graduated from Sol C. Johnson High School in 1968. She enlisted into the Georgia Air National Guard in March 1978 and after recruit training was assigned to the 165th Airlift Wing in Savannah, Georgia.

Her military education includes Personnel Technical School, Combat Aircrew Training, Personnel Intelligence Course, Senior Noncommissioned Officer Academy, Noncommissioned Officer Academy Instructors Course, Chief Executive Course, and in 2002, the Human Relations Course. Her civilian education includes a Bachelor of Arts in elementary education from Savannah State University in 1972; she earned a Master of Education in elementary and middle school concentrating in reading from Armstrong and Savannah State University.

In January 2003, was selected as the first African American and first female to serve in the top enlisted position as the command chief master sergeant for the Georgia Air National Guard. In this position, Morgan is a member of the senior staff of the Georgia Air National Guard and represents the issues and concerns of the 2,500-member enlisted force.

Prior to her selection to this top enlisted position, she was the human resources advisor for the Georgia Air National Guard assigned to state headquarters in Atlanta. A thirty-five year veteran of the Georgia Air National Guard, she was also the first African American female selected as wing command chief for Savannah's 165th Airlift Wing. She competed against twelve other senior enlisted officers for the command position.

She has been employed for 24 years with the Savannah–Chatham County Public School System. She is a sixth grade language arts teacher at John W. Hubert Middle School where she was twice selected Teacher of the Year including the year 2002. She was recently named WTOC-TV "Top Teacher" for 2002. She has also been named the New Future's Initiative Teacher of the Year on two occasions. In 1988, she was selected for Who's Who Among American's Best Teachers and is the recipient of the prestigious Woman of Achievement Award 2000 for the Port City's Business and Professional Women's Organization, Inc.

Elizabeth M. Morris

MILITARY. Elizabeth M. Morris is a native of Glenside, Pennsylvania. She received a Bachelor of Science degree in nursing from the University of Delaware in 1973. She earned a Master of Science degree in nursing from the University of Florida in 1985 and completed the post–Master's Pediatric Nurse Practitioner Program at the Catholic University of America in Washington, D.C., in 1999. She was a participant in the Navy Nurse Corps Collegiate Candidate Program. Following Officer Indoctrination School in Newport, R.I., she entered active duty at Naval Hospital Charleston.

Her naval career includes serving in a variety of clinical staff and nursing faculty positions to include serving as assistant to director, Navy Nurse Corps for Reserve matters. Completing this four-year headquarters assignment, she was affiliated with the Naval Reserve BUMED 106 Unit from 1996 through 1997; served as commanding officer of Navy Reserve NNMC Bethesda 106th from January 1998 to September 1999; from October 2000 to September 2002, she served as deputy director, Navy Nurse Corps, Reserve component. She was promoted to rear admiral (lower half).

She was appointed as a member of the secretary of the Navy's National Naval Reserve Policy Boards from 2002 to 2004 and chaired the Quality of Service Committee; she served as special assistant to deputy chief, Reserve affairs at the Bureau of Medicine and Surgery (BUMED) through December 2004. She was promoted to rear admiral (upper half) on October 1, 2004.

Rear Admiral Morris was assigned as deputy chief for Reserve affairs at the Bureau of Medicine and Surgery on January 1, 2005. This position transitioned to associate chief, human capital for Navy medicine in May 2005 at BUMED.

Denise Morrison

BUSINESS EXECUTIVE. Denise Morrison received a Bachelor of Science degree in economics and psychology (magna cum laude) from Boston College in 1975.

Her professional career includes serving in the sales organization at Procter & Gamble in Boston, Massachusetts. She joined Pepsi-Cola in trade and sales development. She spent most of the 1980s at Nestle USA where she held senior sales and marketing positions, including business director for confections marketing, national sales manager frozen/chilled and vice president sales and marketing for Nestle Ice Cream Company; she served as executive vice president and general manager of Kraft Foods' Snacks and Confections divisions; she joined Campbell Soup Company in April 2003 as president–global sales and chief customer officer.

Ms. Morrison was appointed president of Campbell USA in June 2005.

Lorraine H. Morton

ELECTED OFFICIAL. Lorraine H. Morton is a native of Winston-Salem, North Carolina, and has been a resident of Evanston since 1953. She received a Bachelor of Science from Winston-Salem State University and earned a Master's of Arts in education from Northwestern University. She has also received an honorary doctorate for public service from Kendall College.

She was elected mayor in 1993 and reelected in 1997 and 2001. She has served on Evanston's City Council as the Fifth Ward alderman for nine years. She began her career as an educator at Foster School and continued as a middle school teacher at Nichols and Chute and principal of Haven Middle School.

Lesia Bates Moss

FINANCE. Lesia Bates Moss received a Bachelor of Arts degree in American government from the University of Virginia and a Master of Science in real estate investment analysis and finance from New York University.

Her professional career includes serving as an assistant manager in the retail division of Chemical Banking Corporation; as the manager, New York City Housing Authority; as director, New York City Department of General Services; as director, New York State Insurance Department Liquidation Bureau; in various real estate–related positions to include serving as an associate with Glaves and Associates, Inc.; as the United States senior analyst for Japanese real estate. In April 1997 she joined the Moody's Investors Service where she served as a senior vice president in the Real Estate Finance Group.

Ms. Moss joined Fannie Mae in October 2005 to serve as vice president for single-family counterparty management.

Virginia Wilson Mounger

JUDGE. Virginia Wilson Mounger received a Bachelor of Arts degree from Mississippi State University in 1975 and completed graduate studies at the University College, Oxford University at Oxford, England. She earned her Juris Doctor from the University of Mississippi Law Center in 1979 where she served on the Moot Court Board. She was a Dean's List Scholar and recipient of an American Jurisprudence Award.

Her professional career includes serving in private law practice and as the city of Jackson public defender. She also worked for Southern Natural Gas and its exploration division, SONAT, Inc.

In 1994, she was appointed an administrative judge with the Mississippi Workers' Compensation Commission.

Judith Davidson Moyers

BUSINESS EXECUTIVE. Judith Davidson Moyers is a native of Dallas, Texas. She received a bachelor's degree from the University of Texas. She has had a keen interest in education which began with her teaching experience in Scotland in the 1950s. She has served as a U.S. commissioner to UNESCO, as a member of a White House Commission on Children and as a member of the National Governor's Association Task Force on Education and Economic Development.

Her professional career includes serving as a director of mutual funds for Capital Research Group, Paine Webber and on the board of Columbia Residential Realty, Inc.; she served as director of the Research Foundation of New York and of the Rockefeller Institute of Government; she was also a founder of the Day Care Council of Nassau County; she now serves as president of Public Affairs Television, Inc. (PAT), an independent production company in which she collaborates with her husband, journalist Bill Moyers.

Rosa Mroz

JUDGE. Rosa Mroz received a bachelor's degree in accounting (cum laude) from Arizona State University in 1986 and earned her Juris Doctor degree (cum laude) from Arizona State University in 1993.

From 1991 to 1992, she served as a law clerk at the Arizona Supreme Court; from 1993 to 1994, she served as a law clerk at the Arizona Court of Appeals; from 1994 to 1995, she was engaged in private law practice; from 1995 to 1999, she served as a deputy county attorney, Maricopa County Attorney's office; from 2000 to 2004, she served as an assistant attorney general, Arizona Attorney General's office; since 2004, she has served as judge on Superior Court of Arizona Maricopa County in Phoenix, Arizona.

Anne Marie Mulcahy

BUSINESS EXECUTIVE. Anne Marie Mulcahy received a Bachelor of Arts degree in English and journalism from Marymount College.

She began her Xerox career as a field sales representative in 1976 and assumed an increasingly responsible sales and senior management positions. From 1992 to 1995, she served as vice president for human resources; then as vice president and staff officer for customer operations covering South and Central America, Europe, Asia and China; she became chief staff officer in 1997 and corporate senior vice president in 1998; she served as president of Xerox's general markets operations; from May 2000 to July 2001, she served as president and chief operating officer of Xerox.

Ms. Mulcahy serves as chairman of the board and chief executive officer of Xerox Corporation in Stamford, Connecticut. She was named CEO of Xerox on August 1, 2001, and chairman on January 1, 2002.

Arlene J. Mulder

ELECTED OFFICIAL. Arlene J. Mulder is a native of California. She received a Bachelor of Arts degree in biology and physical education from San Francisco State University and is a graduate of the Kennedy School of Government at Harvard University.

Her professional career includes serving an appointment in 1979 to fill a vacancy on the Arlington Heights Park District Board of Commissioners; in 1981, she was elected to the park board and served as commissioner and president through 1991; she served as a village trustee before being elected to her first four year term as mayor in 1993.

Lisa Munyon

JUDGE. Lisa Munyon received a Bachelor of Science degree in finance from the University of Florida in 1982 and earned a Juris Doctor degree from the University of Florida. She was engaged in private law practice prior to her appointment. From 2003 to 2005, she served as a circuit judge at the Florida Circuit Court in Orange County Criminal Court. From 2003 to 2005, she served as circuit judge, Orange County Criminal Court. In 2006, she served as Orange County Criminal associate administrative judge and is currently administrative circuit judge, Criminal and Drug Court.

Linda A. Murakata

MILITARY. Linda A. Murakata is a native of Manhattan, grew up in Long Branch, New Jersey, and graduated from Monmouth Regional High School in Shrewsbury, New Jersey.

In August 1972, she joined the Air Force and completed her basic training at Lackland Air Force Base in Texas. She completed ground radio operator schooling at Keesler Air Force Base in Mississippi.

In 1978, after serving four years in the Air Force, she attended college full time. In 1979, she joined the United States Coast Guard. In 1981, she earned a bachelor's degree in biology and a minor in chemistry from Montclair University, New Jersey. She started medical school in 1981 and graduated in 1985 with a degree in medicine from the University of Medicine and Dentistry at the New Jersey Medical School in Newark, New Jersey.

She finished four years of anatomical and clinical pathology and a year of internal medicine in 1990. She was commissioned into the United States Navy and held three staff positions in three different departments at the Institute of Pathology in Washington, D.C.: officer in charge of the POW registry in the Department of Environmental and Toxicological Pathology; and an associate editor for the institute's Center for Scientific Publications. She serves as a medical doctor and Navy commander at the Armed Forces Walter Reed Army Medical Center in Washington.

Lisa Murkowski

ELECTED OFFICIAL. Lisa Murkowski is a native of Ketchikan, Alaska, and attended public schools in Fairbanks, Alaska. She attended Willamette University in Salem, Oregon, in 1975–1977 and received a Bachelor of Arts degree in economics from Georgetown University in 1980. She earned her Juris Doctor degree from Willamette College of Law in 1985.

Her professional career includes serving as an attorney at the Anchorage District Court from 1987 to 1989; in private law practice from 1989 to 1996; as a member of the Alaska State House of Representatives from 1999 to 2002. She was appointed to the United States Senate on December 20, 2002, to fill the vacancy caused by the resignation of her father, Frank H. Murkowski; she was elected to the United States Senate in 2004 for the term ending January 3, 2011.

Frances Murphy

JOURNALISM. Frances Murphy received a Bachelor of Science degree in education from Coppin State College. She is a graduate of the University of Wisconsin School of Journalism and earned a Master's of Science degree in education from the Johns Hopkins University. She also studied at the University of Southampton, England.

Her career includes serving as a teacher at Howard University (journalism) from 1984 to 1991, and as a lecturer at Buffalo State in journalism sequence from 1975 to 1984. Ms. Murphy has taught at Morgan State University. She has been chairman of the board and is publisher emeritus and editorial page editor of the *Afro-American Newspaper*.

Dana Elizabeth Murray

JUDGE. Dana Elizabeth Murray served as a deputy district attorney for Colorado's 18th Judicial District. She served as a county court magistrate from July 1989 to October 1992. She has served as a judge to Colorado's 18th Judicial District for Arapahoe County since 1992.

Patty Murray

ELECTED OFFICIAL. Patty Murray is a native of Seattle, Washington. She received a bachelor's degree from Washington State University in 1972. Her professional career includes serving from 1984 to 1987 as an instructor at Shoreline Community College in Shoreline, Washington; as a citizen lobbyist for environmental and educational issues from 1983 to 1988; as a member of the board of directors, Shoreline School District, from 1985 to 1989; as a Washington state senator from 1988 to 1992 and as Democratic whip 1990–1992. She was elected as a United States senator in 1992 and was reelected in 1998 and 2004 for the term ending January 3, 2011.

Marilyn N. Musgrave

ELECTED OFFICIAL. Marilyn N. Musgrave is a native of Greeley, Colorado. She received a Bachelor of Arts degree from Colorado State University in 1972. She has been engaged in private business; served as a teacher; served as a member of the Fort Morgan, Colorado, School Board from 1990 to 1994; she was elected a member of the Colorado State House of Representatives from 1994 to 1998; she served as a member of the Colorado State Senate from 1998 to 2002. She was elected a United States representative to the 108th and to the succeeding Congress since January 3, 2003.

Sue E. Myerscough

JUDGE. Sue E. Myerscough is a native of Springfield. She received her Bachelor of Arts degree with honors from Southern Illinois University in 1973 and her J.D. degree from Southern Illinois University in 1980 where she was an editor for the *Law Review*.

She served as a law clerk for Judge Harold A. Baker, U.S. District Court in Danville, Illinois. She was an attorney in private practice until she received an appointment as associate judge in 1987. She served until her election to the Circuit Court in 1990; she later became the presiding judge of Sangamon County in 1994; and in 1996, she became chief judge of the Illinois Seventh Judicial Circuit.

Judge Myerscough was elected to the Fourth District Appellate Court in 1998.

Sue Myrick

ELECTED OFFICIAL. Sue Myrick is a native of Tiffin, Ohio. She attended Heidelberg College from 1959 to 1960 and received an honorary Doctorate of Humane Letters from Heidelberg College in 1995.

Her professional career includes serving as the president/CEO of Myrick Advertising from 1971 to 1992 and Myrick Enterprises from 1992 to 1994; as a member of the Charlotte, North Carolina, City Council from 1983 to 1985; and as mayor of Charlotte from 1987 to 1991. She has served as a United States representative since 1995.

Grace F. Napolitano

ELECTED OFFICIAL. Grace F. Napolitano is a native of Brownsville, Texas, and a graduate of Brownsville High School. She attended Cerritos College in Norwalk, California, and Texas Southmost College in Brownsville, Texas.

Her professional career includes serving on the Norwalk, California, City Council in 1986; as mayor of Norwalk, California, from 1989 to 1990; as a member of the California state legislature from 1992 to 1998. She was elected a United States representative to the 106th and to the three succeeding Congresses since January 3, 1999.

Janet Napolitano

ELECTED OFFICIAL. Janet Napolitano is a native of New York City and was raised in Albuquerque, New Mexico. She is a distinguished alumna of Santa Clara University and the University of Virginia Law School. She has lived in Arizona since 1983 when she moved to Phoenix to practice law.

Prior to her election as governor of Arizona, she served one term as Arizona attorney general and four years as U.S. attorney for the District of Arizona. In January 2003, Janet Napolitano became governor of the state of Arizona.

Denise Lynn Nappier

ELECTED OFFICIAL. Denise Lynn Nappier is a native of Hartford, Connecticut. She received a Bachelor of Arts degree from Virginia State University and a master's degree from the University of Cincinnati.

Her professional career includes serving as Hartford City treasurer for nearly ten years. Ms. Nappier is the first African-American woman elected to serve as a state treasurer in the United States and the first African-American woman ever elected to a statewide office. She was elected treasurer in 1998 and re-elected in 2002. Nappier is also the only woman to be elected state treasurer in Connecticut history.

Nicole Nason

GOVERNMENT OFFICIAL. Nicole Nason received a bachelor's degree from American University and earned her Juris Doctor degree from Case Western University Law School. Her professional career includes serving with the United States Customs Service as assistant commissioner of the Office of Congressional Affairs. She served as counsel for the House Judiciary Committee under Chairman Henry Hyde of Illinois and as counsel and communications director for Intelligence Committee Chairman Porter Goss of Florida. She served as government affairs counsel for the Metropolitan Life Insurance Company. In July 2003, she named the assistant secretary for governmental affairs for the Department of Transportation.

Ms. Nason was appointed administrator of the National Highway Traffic Safety Administration.

Diana S. Natalicio

EDUCATION. Diana S. Natalicio received a bachelor's degree from St. Louis University and a Master's degree in Portuguese and a Ph.D. in linguistics from the University of Texas at Austin. She has received honorary doctorates from Smith College and the Universidad Autonoma de Nuevo Leon. She was also inducted into the Texas Hall of Fame in 1999.

She has served at the University of Texas at El Paso since 1971 as faculty member, department chairman,

dean and vice president for academic affairs. In 1988, she was named president of the University of Texas at El Paso.

In 1999, Dr. Natalicio was appointed by President Bill Clinton to serve as a member of the National Science Board as a member of the Advisory Commission on Educational Excellence for Hispanic Americas. She was appointed by President George W. Bush to serve as a member on the NASA Advisory Committee.

Dianne Neal

BUSINESS EXECUTIVE. Dianne Neal received a Bachelor of Science from Michigan State. Her professional career includes holding multiple executive merchandising positions within the Target Corporation across various hard-line and apparel divisions; she served as president of the Mervyn's for three years; she joined the Gap Inc. in 2004 as senior vice president of merchandising for Gap Inc. Outlet.

Ms. Neal was named president of Gap Inc. Outlet. In this role, she oversees all aspects of the division, supporting about 300 Gap Outlet, Gap Outlet Kids and Baby, Old Navy Outlet and Banana Republic factory stores across the United States.

Carrie Lee Nero

MILITARY. Carrie Nero received a Bachelor of Science degree in social and behavioral science from the University of South Florida. She earned a Master of Arts degree in guidance and counseling and a Masters of Science degree in nursing from the University of South Florida. She has also earned an EdD in higher education from Nova University. Her military education includes the Army Medical Department Officer Advanced Course, the United States Army Command and General Staff College, and the United States War College.

She received a direct commission to first lieutenant on March 11, 1975. Her first military assignments included an assignment as a medical surgical nurse, later head nurse, operating room with the 349th Combat Support Hospital in St. Petersburg, Florida. From December 1986 to January 1991, she was assigned as the chief of nursing services at the 349th Combat Support Hospital St. Petersburg, Florida. In January 1991, she served as casualty assistance officer at the 3388th United States Army Reserve Forces School in Tampa, Florida. From July 1991 to August 1992, she was assigned as staff nurse advisor and chief of the drug abuse prevention program at the 349th Combat Support Hospital in St. Petersburg, Florida. In August 1992, she was selected to serve as Army Medical Department advisor, Task Force, Future Army School-2-1, Operation Division Office, Chief Army Reserves in Washington, D.C. From February 1993 to January 1995, she was assigned as chief drug team and chief nursing service at the 349th Combat Support Hospital in St. Petersburg, Florida. From February 1995 to January 1996, she was assigned as chief drug team and chief nursing service at the 73rd Field Hospital in St. Petersburg, Florida. From February 1996 to May 2001, she was assigned as chief nursing service at 345th Combat Support Hospital in Jacksonville, Florida. In May 2001, she was selected to serve as the chief nurse for the 3rd Medical Command in Decatur, Georgia.

Beverley Nettles-Nickerson

JUDGE. Beverley Nettles-Nickerson received a Bachelor of Arts degree in political science from Michigan State University in 1979 and received a Masters' of Arts degree in political science in 1980. She earned her Juris Doctor degree from Thomas M. Cooley Law School in 1983. She served as a district court judge in Ingham County. On January 1, 2003, she was elected a circuit court judge in Ingham County, Lansing, Michigan.

Andrea Fischer Newman

BUSINESS EXECUTIVE. Andrea Fischer Newman received a Bachelor of Arts degree from the University of Michigan in 1979 and a Juris Doctor degree from the George Washington University National Law Center

in 1983.

Her professional career includes serving as a vice president of the Detroit Economic Club; as a member on the Board of Directors of the American Council of Young Political Leaders; as a member of the Michigan Thanksgiving Day Parade Foundation; as a member of the Congressional Economic Leadership Institute. She served as vice chair of the George W. Bush for President campaign and co-chair of the Bush for President Finance Committee in Michigan in the 2000 presidential election. She was elected to the Board of Regents in 1994 and re-elected in 2002.

Ms. Newman serves as vice president of government affairs at Northwest Airlines, with responsibility for the company's international, federal, state and local government affairs.

Constance Berry Newman

GOVERNMENT OFFICIAL. Constance Berry Newman received a bachelor's degree in political science from Bates College in Maine and a law degree from the University of Minnesota School of Law. She has received Doctor of Law degrees from Bates College, Amherst College and Central State University.

Ms. Newman has a long career of public service which includes serving from 1989 to 1992 as director of the United States Office of Personnel Management. From 1992 to 2000 she was under secretary of the Smithsonian Institution. She served as assistant administrator for Africa of the United States Agency for International Development (USAID). Ms. Newman was sworn in as assistant secretary of state for African affairs on June 24, 2004.

J. Bonnie Newman

EDUCATION. J. Bonnie Newman received a Bachelor of Arts degree in sociology from St. Joseph's College and a Master of Education degree in higher education administration from the Pennsylvania State University. She received honorary degrees from Rivier College, Notre Dame College, Keene State College, St. Joseph's and New Hampshire College.

She served from 1969 to 1972 at the University of New Hampshire as assistant dean of students and in 1972 she was named dean of students. She served as chief of staff for New Hampshire Congressman Judd Gregg. She was nominated by President Ronald Reagan to serve as assistant secretary of commerce for economic development and the United States Senate confirmed her appointment in February 1984. From 1989 to 1991 she served as assistant to the president for management and administration where she oversaw all administrative operations for the White House and executive office of the president during the transition and administration of George H.W. Bush. From 1998 to 1999 she served at the University of New Hampshire as interim dean of the Whittemore School of Business and Economics. From 2000 to 2005 she served as the executive dean at Harvard University's Kennedy School of Government. She was named interim president of the University of New Hampshire on June 19, 2006.

Sandra Schultz Newman

JUDGE (FIRST). Sandra Schultz Newman received a Bachelor of Science degree from Drexel University and received a Master's of Arts degree from Temple University. She earned her Juris Doctor degree from Villanova Law School in 1972.

Her professional career includes serving as assistant district attorney in Montgomery County; from 1974 to 1993 she served in private law practice. She was elected judge for Commonwealth Court of Pennsylvania and in 1995 she was elected justice of the Supreme Court of Pennsylvania. She is the first woman to be elected to Pennsylvania's highest court.

Kim Ng

SPORTS EXECUTIVE. Kim Ng is a native of Ridgewood, New Jersey. She received a bachelor's degree in public policy from the University of Chicago where she played softball for four years.

She began her career in baseball with the Chicago

White Sox serving as special projects analyst from 1991 to 1994 and was then promoted to assistant director of baseball operations in 1995. In those positions, she assisted in analyzing player tendencies, signing free agents, tracking major league player movement, arbitration, negotiating contracts and budgeting. In 1999, she served as director of waivers and records for the American League. She approved all player transactions and contracts and assisted American League general managers to interpret and apply the major league rules and the basic agreement. From 1998 to 2001 she served as assistant general manager for the New York Yankees. She was the youngest assistant general manager in major league baseball. In her four seasons with the Yankees, New York advanced to the World Series four times and won three World Championships. In 2004, she assumed the interim position of director of player development and was responsible for overseeing the Dodgers' minor league department.

Ms. Ng enters her fifth season as vice president and assistant general manager of the Los Angeles Dodgers. She is one of only two female executives in major league baseball to hold such a position in baseball operations and was the first woman to interview for a general manager's position in major league history when she did so with the Dodgers in 2005.

Pamela M. Nicholson

BUSINESS EXECUTIVE. Pamela M. Nicholson received a Bachelor of Arts degree from the University of Missouri.

Her professional career began in 1981 at Enterprise Rent-A-Car as a management trainee in St. Louis. Some of her subsequent assignments include serving as Corporate vice president at Enterprise's worldwide headquarters in 1994; in 1997, she was promoted to the top job with Enterprise's New York Group where she directed the rental car, fleet service and car sales operations for the company's second largest operating group; in 1999, she was promoted back to St. Louis as senior vice president, North American operations; in 2003, she was promoted to executive vice president for North American Operations.

Ms. Nicholson serves as executive vice president and chief operating officer of Enterprise Rent-A-Car.

Karen S. Nobumoto

ELECTED OFFICIAL. Karen S. Nobumoto is a native of Cleveland, Ohio. She received a bachelor's degree from the University of Harford in West Harford, Connecticut, in 1973 and earned a Juris Doctor degree from Southwestern University School of Law in 1989.

She serves as a deputy district attorney in Los Angeles. In addition to her bar activities which began as a student member of the bar's Ethnic Minority Relations Committee, she was president of the John M. Langston Bar Association in 1997 and served on Governor Davis' Diversity Task Force. She was selected by KFWB radio as a Los Angeles County Unsung Hero.

Ms. Nobumoto was elected the first minority woman president of the State Bar of California. She is also the first government lawyer and only the second woman ever to lead the 175,000-member bar. She served as the 76th president of the California bar, the largest in the country.

Indra K. Nooyi

BUSINESS EXECUTIVE. Indra K. Nooyi is a native of India. She received a Bachelor of Science from Madras Christian College and earned a Master of Business Administration from the Indian Institute of Management in Calcutta. She also received a Master of public and private management from Yale University in 1980.

Her professional career includes working her way from product management at Johnson & Johnson to vice president and director of corporate strategy and planning for Motorola to senior vice president of strategy for Asea Brown Boveri. She joined PepsiCo and serves as the chief financial officer, engineering the $14 billion PepsiCo merger with Quaker Oats and PepsiCo's purchase of Tropicana juices.

Laureen K. Van Norman

JUDGE. Laureen K. Van Norman received a Bachelor of Arts degree in social work from the University of Nebraska in Lincoln. She earned her Juris Doctor degree from the University of Nebraska College of Law.

Before her appointment, she served as legal counsel to the Nebraska Department of Labor. On July 6, 1993, she was appointed judge in Lincoln, Nebraska.

Anne Meagher Northup

ELECTED OFFICIAL. Anne Meagher Northup is a native of Louisville, Kentucky, and graduated from Sacred Heart Academy in Louisville, Kentucky, in 1966. She received a Bachelor of Arts degree from Saint Mary's College in 1970.

Her professional career includes serving as a Kentucky state representative from 1987 to 1996; she was elected a United States representative to the 105th and to the four succeeding Congresses (January 3, 1997, to present).

Eleanor Holmes Norton

ELECTED OFFICIAL. Eleanor Holmes Norton is a native of Washington, D.C., and attended public schools. She received a Bachelor of Arts degree from Antioch College of Antioch University in Yellow Springs, Ohio, in 1960 and earned her Master of Arts from Yale University in New Haven, Connecticut, in 1963. She also earned an LL.B. from Yale University Law School in 1964.

Her professional career includes serving private law practice; as a law clerk to United States District Judge A. Leon Higginbotham, 3rd Circuit, 1964–1965; as an assistant legal director, American Civil Liberties Union, 1965–1970; and as an adjunct assistant professor, New York University Law School from 1970 to 1971. She was selected to serve as the executive assistant to the mayor of New York City, 1971–1974; served as chair, New York City Commission on Human Rights, 1970–1977; served as the chair, United States Equal Employment Opportunity Commission, 1977–1981; served as a senior fellow, Urban Institute, 1981–1982; and served as a professor at Georgetown University Law Center from 1982 to 1990. She was elected as a delegate to the United States 102nd and to the seven succeeding Congresses (January 3, 1991, to present).

Deborah Norville

MEDIA. Deborah Norville is a native of Dalton, Georgia. She received a bachelor's degree in journalism from the University of Georgia in Athens, Georgia.

Her professional career includes serving as a news reporter and an anchor for local television stations, first at WAGA-TV in Atlanta and then at WMAQ-TV in Chicago. At the age of 28, she was named anchor of *NBC News at Sunrise*, the network's early morning newscast and then co-host of NBC's *Today Show*. After leaving NBC, Norville hosted the Deborah Norville radio program on ABC's Talk Radio network and later joined CBS News as a reporter and anchor.

Ms. Norville is an author and lecturer who has been a member of the board of directors for the Greater New York Council of Girl Scouts since 1989.

Georgia Nugent

EDUCATION. Georgia Nugent received a Bachelor of Arts degree cum laude from Princeton University and earned a doctorate degree from Cornell University.

She was the first female graduate of Princeton to hold a full-time faculty appointment at the university. She served as Princeton's associate provost and as dean of Princeton University's Harold W. McGraw Jr. Center for Teaching and Learning. Dr. Nugent was selected by the Kenyon College Board of Trustees to serve as Kenyon College's eighteenth president.

Victoria Nuland

GOVERNMENT OFFICIAL. Victoria Nuland received a Bachelor of Arts degree from Brown University. She

has served in numerous assignments with the United States Department of State. From 1993 to 1996, she was chief of staff to the deputy secretary of state where she worked on the nuclear disarmament of Ukraine, Kazakhstan and Belarus, Bosnia and Kosovo policy and the United States intervention in Haiti. In 1997, she was assigned as deputy director for former Soviet Union affairs at the Department of State. In July 2000, she was appointed United States deputy permanent representative to NATO in Brussels, Belgium. She served as principal deputy national security advisor to Vice President Cheney from July 2003 to May 2005.

Ms. Nuland was appointed by President Bush to serve as the 18th United States permanent representative to the North Atlantic Treaty Organization (NATO) on July 13, 2005.

Annetta W. Nunn

LAW ENFORCEMENT. Annetta W. Nunn is a native of Birmingham, Alabama. She received a bachelor's degree with honors from the University of Alabama in Tuscaloosa, Alabama. She is a graduate of the FBI National Academy in 1997.

She joined the Birmingham Police Department in 1980 and served in various divisions including detention, patrol, detective bureau and administration. On March 24, 2000, she was promoted to deputy chief and commanded the field operations bureau. She was the first African-American woman to hold this rank in the department. On February 11, 2003, she was appointed chief of the police and assumed office on March 7, 2003. She is the first woman to serve as chief of police in the history of Birmingham, Alabama.

Michelle Obama

COMMUNITY ACTIVIST. Michelle Obama was born on Chicago's South Side and graduated from Whitney M. Young Magnet High School in Chicago's West Loop. She attended Princeton University where in 1985 she graduated with a B.A. in sociology and a minor in African American studies. She continued her education at Harvard Law School, earning her degree in 1988.

For three years after law school, Michelle worked as an associate in the area of marketing and intellectual property at a Chicago law firm, Sidley and Austin, where she met Barack Obama. She left the corporate law world in 1991 to pursue a career in public service, serving as an assistant to the mayor and then as the assistant commissioner of planning and development for the city of Chicago. In 1993, she became the founding executive director of Public Allies — Chicago, a leadership training program that received AmeriCorps National Service funding and helped young adults develop skills for future careers in the public sector. She began her involvement with the University of Chicago in 1996, where as associate dean of student services, she developed the university's first community service program. Michelle also served as executive director of community and external affairs until 2005, when she was appointed vice president of community and external affairs at the University of Chicago Medical Center. She also fostered the University of Chicago's relationship with the surrounding community and developed the diversity program, making them both integral parts of the Medical Center's mission. She will become First Lady in January 2009.

Jeanette O'Banner-Owens

JUDGE. Jeanette O'Banner-Owens received her undergraduate degree from Wayne State University and earned her Juris Doctor from Wayne State Law School. She served in private law practice. On May 24, 1988, she was appointed judge to Michigan's 36th District Court in Detroit, Michigan.

Sheila M. O'Brien

JUDGE. Sheila M. O'Brien graduated from the University of Notre Dame with a Bachelor of Art degree in 1977 and a J.D. degree in 1980. She served as an assistant public defender and was an attorney in private practice. She taught law at St. Louis University and served as an associate judge from 1985 until her election to the Appellate Court in 1994. In 1995, the University

of Notre Dame awarded her its first "Women of Achievement" Award.

She serves as appellate judge for the First District, 4th Division, State of Illinois.

Ellen Ochoa

ASTRONAUT. Ellen Ochoa is a native of La Mesa, California, and a graduate of Grossmont High School, La Mesa, California, in 1975. She received a Bachelor of Science degree in physics from San Diego State University in 1980 and a Masters of Science degree in electrical engineering from Stanford University in 1981. She also earned her doctorate in electrical engineering from Stanford University in 1985.

She is a co-inventor on three patents for an optical inspection system, an optical object recognition method and a method for noise removal in images. As chief of the Intelligent Systems Technology Branch at Ames she supervised 35 engineers and scientists in the research and development of computational systems for aerospace missions.

Dr. Ochoa was selected by the National Aeronautics and Space Administration (NASA) in January 1990 and she became an astronaut in July 1991. Her technical assignments in the Astronaut Office includes serving as the crew representative for flight software, computer hardware and robotics, assistant for space station to the chief of the Astronaut Office, lead spacecraft communicator (CAPCOM) in Mission Control and acting deputy chief of the Astronaut Office. She serves as deputy director of flight crew operations, helping to manage and direct the Astronaut Office and Aircraft Operations. A veteran of four space flights, Dr. Ochoa has logged over 978 hours in space. She was a mission specialist on STS-56 (1993), was the Payload Commander on STS-66 (1994) and was a mission specialist and flight engineer on STS-96 (1999) and STS-110 (2002).

Karen L. O'Connor

JUDGE. Karen L. O'Connor received a bachelor degree from Illinois State University in 1979 and earned her Juris Doctor degree from John Marshall Law School in 1984.

Her professional career includes private law practice from 1984 to 1986 and serving as deputy county attorney for Maricopa County attorney's office in Arizona from 1986 to 1999. Since 2000, she has served as judge of Superior Court of Arizona for Maricopa County in Phoenix, Arizona.

Maureen O'Connor

JUDGE. Maureen O'Connor is a native of Washington, D.C., and was raised in Strongsville, Ohio, and Parma, Ohio. She received a Bachelor of Arts from Seton Hill College in 1973 and earned a Juris Doctor degree from Cleveland-Marshall College of Law in 1980.

Her professional career includes serving in private law practice from 1981 to 1985. In 1985, she was appointed magistrate to the Ohio Summit County Probate Court; in 1993, she was appointed judge to the Ohio Summit County Court of Common Pleas and elected by her peers to serve as administrative judge; in 1995, she served as prosecuting attorney for Summit County; in November 2002, she was elected justice to the Supreme Court of Ohio.

Carmen Hooker Odom

GOVERNMENT OFFICIAL. Carmen Hooker Odom received a bachelor's degree in sociology and political science from Springfield College and a Master's degree in regional planning from the University of Massachusetts at Amherst.

Prior to moving to North Carolina, she served as a member of the Massachusetts House of Representatives for nearly 11 years. In January 2001, she was appointed secretary of the North Carolina Department of Health and Human Services.

E. Jeannette Ogden

JUDGE. E. Jeannette Ogden is a graduate of Buffalo public schools and received a Bachelor of Science degree in criminal justice from Buffalo State College. She earned her Juris Doctor degree from the University at Buffalo School of Law.

Her career includes serving in private law practice and as a prosecutor in the Erie County District Attorney's office and a former assistant county attorney.

In June of 1995, she was appointed judge, Buffalo City Court and in November 1995 she was elected to serve a ten-year term on the city court.

Julie Hions O'Kane

JUDGE. Julie Hions O'Kane received her undergraduate degree from Florida Atlantic University in 1987 and she earned her Juris Doctor degree from Stetson University College of Law in 1991.

Her professional career includes serving in private law practice. She was appointed judge by Governor Jeb Bush to the 9th Judicial Circuit Court which serves Orange and Osceola counties.

Hazel O'Leary

EDUCATION. Hazel O'Leary is a native of Newport News, Virginia. She received a Bachelor of Arts from Fisk University in Nashville in 1959 and received a Juris Doctor degree from Rutgers University Law School in Newark, New Jersey, in 1966.

Her professional career includes serving in private law practice in Washington, D.C.; she served in Washington, D.C., during both the Ford and Carter administrations; she served as an assistant prosecutor for Essex County; she was appointed first vice president and later president of Northern States Power Company in Minnesota. In 1993, President William (Bill) Clinton appointed her secretary of energy, making her the first African American to hold that post. She served as president of the international energy-consulting firm O'Leary & Associates, Inc., that she founded in 1997 to focus on issues of corporate change, leadership and arms control; from 2001 to 2002 she served as president and chief operation officer at Blaylock & Partners, L.P., a top-ranked African American investment-banking firm in New York.

Ms. O'Leary was appointed the 14th president of Fisk University on July 13, 2004.

Jody Olsen

GOVERNMENT OFFICIAL. Jody Olsen received a bachelor's degree in sociology with a teaching certification from the University of Utah and a master's degree in social work from the University of Maryland. She earned a doctorate degree from the University of Maryland's College of Education.

Her professional career at the Peace Corps began in the agency's earliest years when she served as a volunteer in Tunisia from 1966 to 1968. In 1979, she was country director for the Peace Corps' mission in Togo. In 1981, she served as regional director for the Peace Corps, managing operations in 17 countries throughout North Africa, Near East, Asia, and the Pacific. From 1989 to 1992, she was the chief of staff for the Peace Corps. During this time the agency expanded into 25 new countries. From 1992 to 1997, she served as executive director for the Council for International Exchange of Scholars (CIES). She was the senior vice president at the Academy for Educational Development (AEDI).

Dr. Olsen was nominated by President George W. Bush and confirmed by the United States Senate in 2002 to serve as the deputy director of the Peace Corps.

Kathie Olsen

AEROSPACE. Kathie Olsen received a Bachelor of Science degree with honors in both biology and psychology from Chatham College in Pittsburgh, Pennsylvania. She earned her Ph.D. from the Department of Psychobiology at the University of California at Irving.

After spending one year as a postdoctoral fellow in the Department of Neuroscience at Children's Hospital of Harvard Medical School in Boston, she moved to

the State University of New York at Stony Brook where she was a research scientist at Long Island Research Institute and as assistant professor in the Department of Psychiatry and Behavioral Science at the medical school until 1988. From February 1996 to November 1997, she served as a Brookings Institute legislative fellow and then as a National Science Foundation detailee in the office of Senator Conrad Burns of Montana. Her research on the neural and genetic mechanisms underlying the development and expression of behavior was supported by grants from the National Institutes of Health. Prior to joining NASA on May 24, 1999, she served as the senior staff associate for the science and technology centers in the National Science Foundation's (NSF) Office of Integrative Activities. She was named NASA's chief scientist and serves as the most senior ranking woman at NASA. In her position as chief scientist she serves as the administrator's senior scientific advisory and principal interface with the national and international scientific community.

Denise M. O'Malley

JUDGE. Denise M. O'Malley is a native of Chicago, Illinois, and received her Bachelor of Art degree from Mundelein College in 1954. She earned her Master's of Art degree from the University of Chicago in 1971 and her J.D. degree from the John Marshall Law School in 1981.

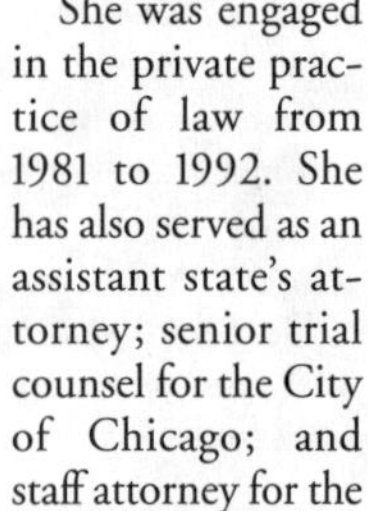

She was engaged in the private practice of law from 1981 to 1992. She has also served as an assistant state's attorney; senior trial counsel for the City of Chicago; and staff attorney for the Chicago Transportation Authority.

Judge O'Malley served as a judge in the Circuit Court from 1992 to 2002 and was elected to the Appellate Court in 2002. She serves as an appellate judge for the First District, 1st Division, State Appellate Court in Illinois.

Elaine M. O'Neal

JUDGE. Elaine M. O'Neal is a lifelong resident of Durham, North Carolina. She received a mathematics degree from North Carolina Central University in 1984 and worked as a staff specialist at the Duke University Medical Center. She earned her Juris Doctor degree from North Carolina University in 1991 and started a private law practice. In 1994, the citizens of Durham County, North Carolina, elected her judge in the 14th Judicial District, where she currently serves as the chief district court judge.

Harriet O'Neill

JUDGE. Harriet O'Neill graduated in 1982 from the University of South Carolina School of Law. Her professional career includes serving in private law practice. In 1992, she was elected to the Texas 152nd District Court in Houston, Texas; in 1995, Governor George W. Bush appointed her to the 14th Court of Appeals and she won election to that seat in 1996. In 1998, she was elected justice to the Texas Supreme Court and was re-elected to a second term in 2004.

Donna Orender

SPORTS EXECUTIVE. Donna Orender received a bachelor's degree from Queens College in New York and she did graduate studies in social work at Adelphi University.

She was an All-American basketball player at Queens College of New York and played professionally for the New York Stars, New Jersey Gems and the Chicago Hustle of the Women's Basketball League (WBL) where she was an All-Star. She entered the business of sports and spent 17 years with the PGA Tour serving most recently as senior vice president of strategic development in the Office of the Commissioner. Her television production career began at ANC Sports and continued at Sports Channel. She also owned her own production company, Primo Donna Productions. In February 2005, Ms. Orender was named president of the Women's National Basketball Association.

Suze (Susan) Orman

FINANCE. Suze Orman is a native of Chicago, Illinois. She received a Bachelor of Arts degree in social work from the University of Illinois at Urbana–Champaign. In 1973, she moved to Berkeley, California, where she became a waitress at a local bakery until 1980. From 1980 to 1983, she was trained by and worked as an account executive at Merrill Lynch and from 1983 to 1987 she was vice president of investments for Prudential Bache Securities. In 1987, she founded her own business, the Suze Orman Financial Group, which she directed from 1987 to 1997. She has authored two books and coproduced her television show, *The Suze Orman Show*.

Darleen Ortega

JUDGE. Darleen Ortega is a native of Montebello, California, and spent her early childhood in Los Angeles, moving to Banks, Oregon, with her family when she was 10. She graduated with honors from Banks High School in 1980. She received a Bachelor of Arts degree (summa cum laude) from George Fox College (now University) in Newberg, Oregon, and earned her Juris Doctor degree from the University of Michigan Law School in Ann Arbor, Michigan (magna cum laude, 1989).

She served in private law practice first in Detroit, Michigan (1989–1992); and then in Portland, Oregon (1992–2003). In 2003, she was appointed judge on the Oregon Court of Appeals.

Maria D. Ortiz

JUDGE. Maria D. Ortiz received a Bachelor of Arts and Bachelor of Science degrees from the University of Miami in 1985 and earned her Juris Doctor degree from Nova University Center for the Study of Law in 1989.

Her professional career includes serving as an assistant city attorney for the city of Miami; as a judge of compensation claims for the state of Florida from 1997 to 2003. In 2004, she was appointed judge for the County Court Criminal Division in Miami.

Susan Owens

JUDGE. Susan Owens is a native of Kinston, North Carolina. She received her undergraduate degree from Duke University in 1971 and earned her Juris Doctor degree from the University of North Carolina Law School at Chapel Hill in 1975.

She served as a chief judge of the Lower Elwha S'Klallam Tribe for more than six years and as the Quileute Tribe's chief judge for five years in the state of Washington. She served nineteen years as a Washington State District Court judge in Washington's Western Clallam County. On November 7, 2000, she was elected the seventh woman to serve on the Washington State Supreme Court.

Betty S. Pace

MEDICINE. Betty S. Pace received a Bachelor of Science degree in mathematics from Marquette University and her Medical Doctor degree from the Medical College of Wisconsin. She was a pediatrics intern/resident at Children's Hospital of Wisconsin; she completed her hematology/oncology fellow-

ship at the University of Colorado Health Sciences Center and postdoctorate training in medical genetics at the University of Washington.

Dr. Pace, as a molecular hematologist, has been principal or co-principal investigator of more than 30 research projects that link genetic characteristics to blood disease in infants, children and adults with sickle cell disease. The results of these studies have been published in national medical journals such as the *Journal of Biological Chemistry, Experimental Hematology, Gene Therapy,* and *Cellular & Molecular Biology.*

Dr. Pace serves as a researcher and director of the University of Texas at Dallas Sickle Cell Disease Research Center and is also a professor in the Department of Molecular and Cellular Biology at the University of Texas at Dallas.

Sandra L. Pack

GOVERNMENT OFFICIAL. Sandra L. Pack received a Bachelor of Arts degree in business summa cum laude from Notre Dame College of Maryland. She is a Certified Public Accountant.

Her professional career includes serving as the treasury director for both Bush for President, Inc., and Bush-Cheney 2000, Inc.; as deputy treasury director for Bob Dole for President, Inc.; and as treasury directory for Phil Gramm for President, Inc.; as the principal advisor to the secretary of the Army for all comptroller and financial management activities and operations.

Ms. Pack was appointed assistant secretary (for management) and chief financial officer of the Treasury Department by President George W. Bush on August 11, 2005, where she serves as the principal policy adviser to the secretary of the treasury and deputy secretary of the treasury on the management of the annual planning and budget process and on matters involving the internal management of the department and its bureaus.

Sarah Heath Palin

ELECTED OFFICIAL. Sarah Heath Palin was born in Idaho and moved to Alaska with her family in 1964. She graduated from Wasilla High School in 1982 and received a Bachelor of Science degree in communications/journalism from the University of Idaho in 1987.

Palin started her professional career as a newscaster before making her way into local politics on the Wasilla City Council in 1992, where she served two terms. She was then elected mayor of the town and served two terms as mayor/manager. During her tenure, she reduced property tax levels while increasing services and made Wasilla a business-friendly environment, drawing in new industry. She has served as chair of the Alaska Conservation Commission, which regulates Alaska's most valuable non-renewable resources: oil and gas. She was elected to serve as president of the Alaska Conference of Mayors.

On December 4, 2006, Sarah Palin made history when she took office as the 11th governor of Alaska, becoming the first woman to hold the office. During her first legislative session, Governor Palin's administration passed two major pieces of legislation — an overhaul of the state's ethics laws and a competitive process to construct a gas pipeline. Governor Palin is chair of the Interstate Oil and Gas Compact Commission, a multistate government agency that promotes the conservation and efficient recovery of domestic oil and natural gas resources while protecting health, safety and the environment. She was recently named chair of the National Governors Association (NGA) Natural Resources Committee, which is charged with pursuing legislation to ensure state needs are considered as federal policy is formulated in the areas of agriculture, energy, environmental protection and natural resource management. Prior to being named to this position, she served as co-chair of this committee.

In August 2008, Republican presidential candidate John McCain chose Palin to be his vice presidential running mate. She is the first woman in history selected and nominated by the Republican Party as its vice presidential candidate.

Vicki R. Palmer

BUSINESS EXECUTIVE. Vicki R. Palmer is a native of Memphis, Tennessee, and a graduate of South Side High School in 1971. During her years at South Side High School, she was both a cheerleader and a valedictorian. She received a Bachelor of Arts degree and a Masters of Business Administration, both from the University of Memphis.

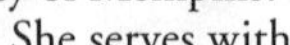

She serves with

Coca-Cola Enterprises, Inc., as senior vice president, treasurer, and as special assistant to the chief executive officer at Coca-Cola Enterprises, Inc.

Violet Palmer

SPORTS. Violet Palmer is a native of Compton, California. She attended college at Cal Poly Pomona where she played point guard on the 1985 and 1986 NCAA Division II women's championship teams.

After years of refereeing at various levels, including NBA pre-season and exhibition games, Ms. Palmer was offered an opportunity to officiate the NCAA Division I men's tournament in 1996. She accepted, but the offer was later retracted when NCAA members balked at the idea of having a female referee male players. In 1997, however, Ms. Palmer and Dee Kantner were signed by the NBA to together become the first female referees in any major U.S. professional sport. On October 31, 1997, Ms. Palmer made history when she and Kantner officiated the NBA season opener between the Vancouver Grizzlies and the Dallas Mavericks in British Columbia, Canada. In 2001, she established "Violet Palmer's Official Camp" to train youths in the art of refereeing. She was one of three NBA referees who officiated the brawl on December 19, 2006, game between the Denver Nuggets and the New York Knicks.

Sue Panzer

ENTERTAINMENT EXECUTIVE. Sue Panzer received a Bachelor of Arts degree in education from the University of Richmond and earned a Master of Business Administration degree from the College of William and Mary in Williamsburg, Virginia. She has served on the board of directors of the MBA Alumni Association for the graduate business school.

Her professional career includes serving as the assistant general manager for TeleCable's Lexington, Kentucky, system and the Richardson/Plano, Texas, systems; she worked at Showtime Networks for eleven and a half years, beginning as the regional sales manager, followed by positions as regional operations manager, director of field operations, regional director, area general manager and finally as the vice president, area general manager in the Northeast Region; she served as vice president, distribution and field marketing for the Eastern region responsible for the distribution efforts in twenty-five states.

Ms. Panzer serves as vice president, national distribution, for Lifetime Television. She joined Lifetime in 1999 and is responsible for managing the team increasing the distribution of Lifetime, Lifetime Movie Network and Lifetime Real Women among cable operators and other distributors across the country.

Barbara J. Pariente

JUDGE. Barbara J. Pariente is a native of New York City. She attended public schools in New York and New Jersey. She graduated with highest honors from Boston University majoring in communication. She then attended George Washington University Law School where she graduated fifth in her class in 1973.

She moved to Fort Lauderdale, Florida, in 1973 for a two year judicial clerkship with United States District Court Judge Norman C. Roettger, Jr., of the Southern District of Florida. After her judicial clerkship, she settled in West Palm Beach and served in private law practice.

In September 1993, she was appointed to the Fourth District Court of Appeal where she served until her appointment as the 77th justice of the Florida Supreme Court on December 10, 1997.

Jennifer J. Parker

BUSINESS EXECUTIVE. Jennifer J. Parker received her undergraduate degree from Johnson C. Smith University in 1981. She moved from Charlotte, North Carolina, to Buffalo, New York, to attend SUNY at Buffalo Law School. After receiving a Juris Doctor degree in 1984, her professional career began in private law practice.

She is the president and co-founder of the Black Capital Network LLC. The company provides public relations, strategic planning and technology services to support business advancement and development.

Jill N. Parrish

JUDGE. Jill N. Parrish earned her Juris Doctor degree from the Yale Law School in 1985. She has served as law clerk at the United States District Court for the District of Utah. She served in private law practice, before serving as an assistant United States attorney in the civil division of the United States Attorney's office for the District of Utah.

In January 2003, she was appointed judge on the Utah Supreme Court by Governor Michael O. Leavitt.

Patricia G. Parrish

JUDGE. Patricia Parrish received a Bachelor of Arts degree in political science from Oklahoma State University and earned her Juris Doctor degree from the University of Oklahoma.

Her professional career includes serving in private law practice. In February 2003, she was sworn in as a special judge to the Oklahoma Judicial District Court in Oklahoma County.

Angela M. Pasula

JUDGE. Angela M. Pasula graduated from New Buffalo High School in 1974. She received a bachelors degree from Western Michigan University in 1977 and earned her Juris Doctor degree from Valparaiso University School of Law in 1980.

Her professional career includes serving as an assistant prosecuting attorney for the Kalamazoo County Prosecutor's office from 1980 to 1982; as an assistant prosecuting attorney for Berrien County from 1982 to 1989; as chief assistant prosecuting attorney from 1989 to 1996; and as a prosecuting attorney from 1996 to 1999. She was appointed judge to the Michigan District Court in Berrien County, Michigan, in 1999.

Libby Pataki

FIRST LADY (STATE). Libby Pataki attended the American College in Paris and received a Bachelor of Arts in political science with a minor in French from Clark University in Worcester, Massachusetts.

Her professional career includes serving at Warner Communications and at Paine Weber where her responsibilities included overseas trading operations.

As first lady of New York, she serves as an advocate for victims of domestic violence and has traveled across the state visiting shelters and speaking out against domestic violence. She has been the annual keynote speaker at the New York Coalition Against Domestic Violence and Sexual Assault.

She is married to New York Governor George E. Pataki.

Sally Pederson

ELECTED OFFICIAL. Sally Pederson is a native of Vinton, Iowa, and a graduate of Iowa State University. She is a former executive at Meredith Corporation in Des Moines, Iowa, where she was the senior food editor for *Better Homes and Gardens*.

She was elected lieutenant governor in 1998 and reelected to a second four-year term in 2002. In March 2003, she hosted Iowa's first statewide summit on disability housing.

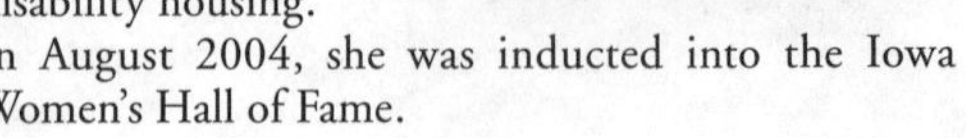

In August 2004, she was inducted into the Iowa Women's Hall of Fame.

Nancy Pelosi

ELECTED OFFICIAL. Nancy Pelosi received a Bachelor of Arts degree from Trinity College in 1962. Her political career includes serving as chair of the California State Democratic Party from 1981 to 1983 and as finance chairman for the Democratic Senatorial Campaign Committee from 1985 to 1986. She was elected as a Democrat to the 100th Congress by special election to fill the vacancy caused by the death of United States Representative Sala Burton. She was reelected to the ten succeeding Congresses (June 2, 1987–present). She served as the minority whip (107th Congress) and minority leader (108th and 109th Congresses). On January 4, 2007, she was elected Speaker of the United States House of Representatives. She is the first woman in history to serve in this role.

Beverly Eaves Perdue

ELECTED OFFICIAL. Beverly Eaves Perdue is a native of Grundy, Virginia. She received a bachelor's degree from the University of Kentucky. She earned a Master's degree in education and a Ph.D. from the University of Florida at Gainesville, Florida.

Her professional career includes serving in the North Carolina House of Representatives from 1986 to 1990 and in the North Carolina Senate from 1990 to 2000. In 2000, she defeated Republican Betsy Cochrane for the lieutenant governor's seat, becoming North Carolina's first female lieutenant governor. She was elected to a second term in 2004. She has also served as a teacher in health care with Geriatric Health Care Consultant.

Mary Perdue

FIRST LADY (STATE). Mary Perdue is a native of New Orleans, Louisiana. She received a bachelor's degree from the University of Georgia.

Her professional career included serving as a speech therapist in the public schools, serving children from pre-kindergarten to high school. In 1998, she and her husband served as foster parents for eight newborns awaiting adoption. In August 2003, she launched her "Our Children" campaign to raise awareness about the need for foster care programs in Georgia and to encourage individuals, corporations and faith-based organizations to take an active role in addressing the needs of their community.

Mary Perdue is married to Georgia Governor Sonny Perdue.

Anna M. Perez

MEDIA EXECUTIVE. Anna M. Perez received a bachelor's degree from Hunter College and is a fellow of the Institute of Politics at the John F. Kennedy School of Government at Harvard University.

Her professional career includes serving as a manager of communications, National Safety Council; as head of the office of media, communication and speech writing at the National Safety Council; as vice president of California government relations at the Walt Disney Co.; as head of media relations at Creative Artists Agency, Inc., a Los Angeles literary and talent agency. From 1989 to 1993, she served as press secretary to First Lady Barbara Bush. She also served as a staff member of U.S. Congressman John Miller and U.S. Senator Slade Gorton. In 2001, she was appointed deputy assistant to the president and counselor for communication to National Security Advisor Condoleezza Rice. She has also served as chief communications executive at NBC in New York.

Ms. Perez has served as executive vice president, communications, at NBC in New York since May 2004.

Lucille C. Norville Perez

MEDICINE. Lucille C. Norville Perez received her Medical Doctor degree from the New York Medical College in 1979.

Dr. Perez is the 102nd

president of the National Medical Association. She also is a pediatrician who specializes in HIV disease and AIDS. She serves as the associate director of the government's Center for Substance Abuse Prevention and directs the HIV

Prevention Initiative in Rockville, Maryland. She educates other physicians and the general public in treating and preventing AIDS.

Tanya Perrin-Johnson

Business Executive. Tanya Perrin-Johnson received a Bachelor of Science degree from Syracuse University and earned her Master's of Science degree from Canisius College. She started her career as a fourth-grade teacher at St. Columba School. She then worked as a counselor for Transitional Services, an independent living program for individuals diagnosed with mental illness. She served with the employment and training division within the Clarkson Center (formerly Allentown Youth Services).

In 1998, she was appointed the chief executive officer of the YWCA of Western New York, Buffalo's oldest and largest organization for women.

Anita Perry

First Lady (State). Anita Perry received a bachelor's degree in nursing from West Texas State University, now known as West Texas A&M University, and a master's degree in nursing from the University of Texas Health Science Center at San Antonio.

Her career includes serving 17 years in the health care profession including nursing in the areas of surgery, pediatrics, intensive care and administration. She is currently the outreach and development coordinator for the Texas Association Against Sexual Assault where she draws on her nursing experience with sexual assault victims.

As Texas' first lady, she continues to pursue her dedication to improving the health of Texans. She often cites her own nursing experiences when promoting health care issues and actively encourages Texans to consider careers in nursing. She serves as an advocate on a variety of issues including family violence prevention, immunizations education, and breast cancer and heart disease awareness. Her husband Texas Governor Rick Perry often refers to her not only as the first lady, but also as the "first nurse" of Texas.

Cynthia Perry

Government Official. Cynthia Perry received a bachelor's degree from Indiana State University and earned a doctorate in education from the University of Massachusetts.

Her professional career includes serving as chief of education and human resources in the Africa Bureau of U.S.A.I.D. from 1982 to 1986; as ambassador to Sierra Leone from 1986 to 1989; as ambassador to Burundi from 1990 to 1993; and as honorary consul general of Senegal. In 1996, she was appointed the director of international investment advisory services for FCA Corp. in Houston, Texas.

Dr. Perry serves as United States executive director of the African Development Bank, Department of the Treasury.

June Carter Perry

Government Official. June Carter Perry received a Bachelor of Arts degree from Loyola University in Chicago and earned a Master of Arts degree from the University of Chicago.

Ms. Perry has held numerous assignments with the State Department of the United States to include serving as director of public affairs at the national volunteer agency, ACTION including Peace Corps. She served as senior advisor in the Africa Bureau, special assistant to the deputy secretary, chief of internal political affairs and narcotics coordinator at Embassy Paris and deputy director/acting director, Office of Policy and Plans, Political Military Affairs Bureau. She also served in Zambia and Zimbabwe. She served as director of the Office of Social and Humanitarian Affairs in the International Organizations (IO) Bureau with responsibility for policy matters within the United Nations Commission on Human Rights, the Economic and Social Council and the Commission on the Status of Women.

On July 29, 2004, June Carter Perry was sworn in as ambassador to the Kingdom of Lesotho.

Regina S. Peruggi

EDUCATION. Regina S. Peruggi is a native of New York. She received a Bachelor of Arts degree in sociology from the College of New Rochelle and a Master of Business Administration degree from New York University and her doctorate of education degree from Columbia University's Teachers College.

Her professional career includes serving as a drug abuse counselor in New York City. She taught at the elementary, college and graduate levels and has coordinated continuing education programs for psychiatrists, social workers and other mental health professionals in Washington, D.C. In 1974, she joined the faculty of the University of New York at York College; in 1984, she moved to the office of academic affairs of the City University of New York; and in 1986, she became the university's associate dean for adult and continuing education for the 20 colleges of the City University.

Dr. Peruggi was appointed president of Kingsborough Community College of the City University of New York.

Mary E. Peters

GOVERNMENT OFFICIAL. Mary E. Peters is a native of Arizona. She received a bachelor's degree from the University of Phoenix and attended Harvard University's John F. Kennedy School of Government Program for State and Local Government Executives.

She served from 1985 to 2001 with the Arizona Department of Transportation (ADOT). In 2001, the president asked her to lead the Federal Highway Administration (FHWA). Ms. Peters was nominated by President George W. Bush on September 5, 2006, and confirmed by the United States Senate as the 15th Secretary of Transportation on September 30, 2006. She is responsible for maintaining a safe, reliable and efficient transportation system while leading an agency with almost 60,000 employees and a $62 billion budget that oversees air, maritime and surface transportation missions.

Sandra N. Peuler

JUDGE. Sandra N. Peuler received her Juris Doctor from the University of Baltimore Law School in 1977. From 1978 to 1980 she served in private law practice. In 1980 she served as deputy Salt Lake County attorney. In 1982 she served as court commissioner in the Third District Court until her appointment.

In May 1994, Governor Michael O. Leavitt appointed her judge to the Third District Court.

Colette A. M. Phillips

COMMUNICATIONS. Colette A. M. Phillips is a native of Antigua. She received a Bachelor of Science degree in communications from Emerson College in Boston, Massachusetts, and a master's degree in business communications from Emerson College.

Her professional career includes serving as press secretary and publications manager for the prime minister of Antigua; she has also been a correspondent, host and producer on Antigua television and radio.

Ms. Phillips is the president and chief executive officer of Colette Phillips Communications, Inc. (CPC).

Lynn Pickard

JUDGE. Lynn Pickard received a Bachelor of Arts degree from New York University in 1970 and she earned her Juris Doctor degree from Northeastern University School of Law in 1974. Her professional career includes serving as a law clerk at the

New Mexico Court of Appeals and in private law practice. In 1981, she returned to the Court of Appeals as chief staff attorney. In 1991, she was appointed judge to the New Mexico Court of Appeals in Santa Fe, New Mexico.

Alma Pinckney

MILITARY. Alma Pinckney entered the United States Army on November 17, 1981, and completed both basic combat training and advanced individual training at Fort Jackson, South Carolina. Her military education includes all the Noncommissioned Officer Education System Courses, the First Sergeants Course, the Command Sergeants Major Course, and the United States Army Sergeants Major Academy. She holds a Bachelor of Arts in political science from the University of Mississippi and is pursing her master's degree in human resource development.

Her first duty assignment was with the 1st Infantry Division at Fort Riley, Kentucky. She has served in a myriad of duty positions including squad leader; platoon sergeant; personnel sergeant, SIDPERS-3; writer/developer and 75 series chief; first sergeant, Headquarters and Headquarters Detachment, 55th Personnel Services Battalion; sergeant major for the Directorate of Human Resource and Adjutant General Division at Fort Jackson, South Carolina. In October 2004, she was serving as the command sergeant major, Regional Command South, Allied Forces Southern Europe, in Naples, Italy.

Belinda Pinckney

MILITARY. Belinda Pinckney was commissioned into the United States Army on February 22, 1979, as a second lieutenant. She holds a Bachelor of Science degree in business administration from the University of Maryland; a master's of public accounting/finance from Golden Gate University; a Master of Science degree in national resources strategy from National Defense University. Her military education includes the finance officer basic and advanced courses, United States Army Command and General Staff College, and Industrial College of the Armed Forces.

She has served in numerous key military positions to include serving as chief, Commercial Operations Division, later commander, Headquarters and Headquarters Company, 266th Theater Finance Command, United States Army Europe and Seventh Army, Germany; program budget officer in the office of the Chief of Staff Army, Washington, D.C.; in June 1995, she served as military assistant to the secretary of the Army (financial management and comptroller) in Washington, D.C.; in September 1996, she served as commander, Training Support Battalion, later director, Financial Management and Operation Department, United States Army Soldier Support Institute, United States Training Center, Fort Jackson, South Carolina; in June 2000, she was assigned as commander, 266th Finance Command, United States Army Europe and Seventh Army, Germany.

She was selected the first African American woman to be inducted in the Officer Candidate School's Hall of Fame in 2003. She began her military career as an enlisted soldier, a private, and after two years in the Army at the rank of specialist, she was accepted into Officer Candidate School at Fort Benning, Georgia, and was promoted to lieutenant.

She is assigned as a Congressional appropriations liaison officer for the undersecretary of defense comptroller, plans and systems office, Defense Pentagon, Washington, D.C. In September 2004, the secretary of defense nominated her for promotion to the rank of brigadier general.

Diccia T. Pineda-Kirwan

JUDGE. Diccia T. Pineda-Kirwan received her Juris Doctor degree from the City University of New York Queens School of Law. Her professional career includes serving as a court attorney, senior court attorney and principal court attorney for the New York State Unified

Court System in Queens County. In 2003, she was elected judge to the Civil Court of the City of New York, Queens County, New York Unified Court System in Jamaica, New York.

Vivian Pinn

MEDICINE. Vivian Pinn is a native of Lynchburg, Virginia. She received a bachelor's degree from Wellesley College. She graduated from the University of Virginia School of Medicine in 1967 where she was the only woman and minority in her class.

Dr. Pinn has taught pathology at Harvard Medical School and Tufts University. She moved to Washington, D.C., in 1982, and became the first African-American woman to chair the pathology department at Howard University. In 1991, she was named the first director of the Office of Research on Women's Health. By 2002, she had assumed responsibility for chronic fatigue syndrome program within the office of the director. Dr. Pinn serves as head of the Office of Research on Women's Health at the National Institutes of Health. She has also served as president of the National Medical Association.

Tracey L. Pinson

GOVERNMENT OFFICIAL. Tracey L. Pinson was born in Washington, D.C. She received a Bachelor of Science degree in political science from Howard University. She also received a law degree from Georgetown University Law Center. She is a member in good standing of the Maryland Bar Association and the National Contract Management Association.

She participated in the Lyndon Baines Johnson Internship with the United States House of Representatives. She worked in the Congressional office of Representative Augustus Hawkins and was responsible for constituent affairs and legislative analysis. From November 1982 to June 1986, she served as counsel to the Committee on Small Business, United States House of Representatives, and special counsel to the late Representative Joseph P. Addabbo. From 1986 to 1995, she served as assistant to the director, Office of Small and Disadvantaged Business Utilization, Office of the Secretary of Defense. During this time she served as the program manager of the DOD Small Disadvantaged Business Program and the HBCU/MI Program. She also developed the implementation strategy for the DOD Mentor-Protégé Program resulting in over 250 participants with a budget allocation as high as $120 million.

She became the director for small and disadvantaged business utilization, Office of the Secretary of the Army in May 1995. Ms Pinson advises the secretary of the Army and the Army staff on all small-business procurement issues and is responsible for the implementation of the federal acquisition programs designed to assist small businesses, including small disadvantaged businesses and women-owned businesses. She is responsible for the management of the historically black colleges and universities and minority institutions program, and develops policies and initiatives to enhance their participation in Army funded programs.

Shirley Robinson Pippins

EDUCATION. Shirley Robinson Pippins is a native of East Chicago, Indiana. She earned a bachelor's degree from the University of Illinois. She earned master's degrees from the University of Illinois and New York's Manhattanville College. She received a doctorate degree from Columbia University.

Dr. Pippins has served as dean of community services, adult and continuing education and vice president of Westchester Community College in Valhalla, New York. She served as the fifth president of Thomas Nelson Community College at Hampton in the Virginia Peninsula. She was selected to serve as president of Suffolk County Community College in New York.

Charlotte D. Placide

EDUCATION. Charlotte D. Placide received a Bachelor of Science in accounting from Southern University and a Master of Science degree in professional accountancy from Southern University.

Her professional career includes serving at Eastman Kodak in Rochester, New York, in the comptroller's division for approximately nine years. She began her career with the East Baton Rouge Parish School System in the finance department as an accountant, chief accountant and ad-

ministrative director of finance and purchasing. In July 2004, the school board appointed Ms. Placide as acting superintendent of the East Baton Rouge Parish School System. In July 2004, she was selected to serve as interim superintendent and in November 2006 she was unanimously selected by the school board to serve as superintendent of East Baton Rouge Parish School System.

Beverly Plummer

JUDGE. Beverly Plummer received a Bachelor of Arts (magna cum laude) from the University of South Florida in 1984. She earned her Juris Doctor degree from Stetson University College of Law in 1988.

Prior to her appointment she served in private law practice. In January 1999, she was appointed magistrate for the Sixth Judicial Circuit of Florida and has been in this position since, primarily presiding over family law, juvenile dependency and probate cases.

Gale S. Pollock

MILITARY. Gale S. Pollock received a Bachelor of Science degree in nursing from the University of Maryland and a Master of Business Administration from Boston University. She earned a master's degree in health services administration and a master's degree in national security and strategic studies from the National Defense University. She also earned a doctorate degree in public service from the University of Maryland.

Her military schools attended include the Army Medical Department Officer Basic and Advanced Courses, the United States Army Command and General Staff College, and the Air War College and Industrial College of the Armed Forces.

She has held a variety of command assignments including serving as the surgeon general's initiatives group officer, Office of the Surgeon General, Falls Church, Virginia; from June 1999 to June 2001, as commander, United States Army Medical Department Activity at Fort Drum, New York; from June 2001 to July 2003, as commander, Fort McClellan and Fort Benning United States Army Medical Department Activities at Fort Benning, Georgia; from July 2003 to July 2004, as special assistant to the commanding general, United States Army Medical Command/the Surgeon General, United States Army, Falls Church, Virginia; from August 2004 to October 2006, she served as the commanding general, Tripler Army Medical Center, Pacific Regional Medical Command, United States Army Pacific surgeon; lead agent, TRICARE Pacific; chief, United States Army Nurse Corps, Honolulu, Hawaii. She was promoted to major general on October 1, 2004.

Major General Pollock serves as the deputy surgeon general United States Army and chief, United States Army Nurse Corps, Falls Church, Virginia, since October 2006.

Anne Ponder

EDUCATION. Anne Ponder is a native of Asheville, North Carolina. She received a bachelor's degree in English, master's degree in English and her doctorate degree in English all from the University of North Carolina at Chapel Hill.

Her professional career began at Elon College in North Carolina in 1977 where she was the first woman and first pre-tenure professor to receive the Daniels-Danieley Award for Excellence in Teaching. During her nine years at Elon, she taught English and communications, founded the college's honors program and rose through the academic ranks to tenured associate professor.

In 1986 she joined Guilford College in North Carolina where she was an associate professor of English and interdisciplinary studies and served as associate academic dean. She was recruited to Kenyon College in Ohio in 1989. There she served as professor of English and drama, academic dean and vice president for information technology before being named to the presidency at Colby-Sawyer College. She served as president of the North Carolina Honors Association and the National Collegiate Honors Council and has served on the Advisory Council of the Appalachian College Association.

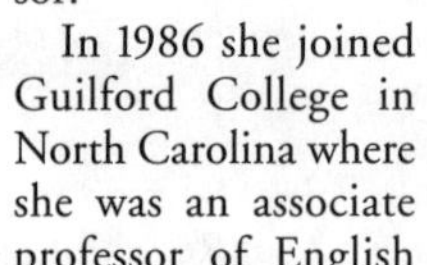

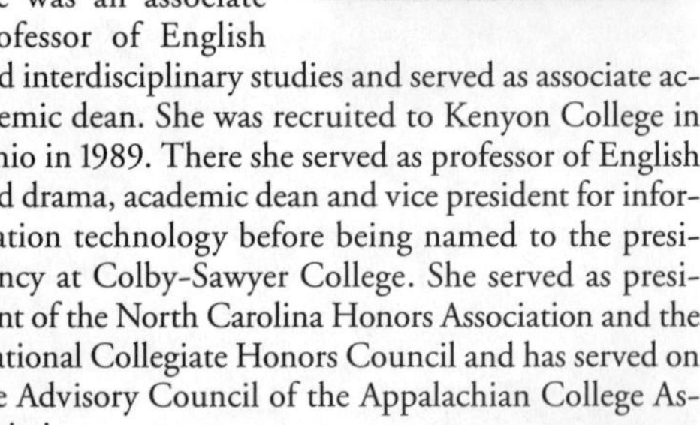

Dr. Ponder was elected the sixth chancellor of the University of North Carolina Asheville in May 2005 and took office the following October 1.

Suzan S. Ponder

JUDGE. Suzan S. Ponder received a Bachelor of Arts degree from Louisiana State University and earned her Juris Doctor from Southern University Law School.

Her professional career includes serving as an assistant district attorney for East Baton Rouge Parish from 1983 to 1988; she was engaged in private law practice until 1993. In 1993, she was appointed judge for Division E of the Baton Rouge City Court where she still serves.

Christine Poon

BUSINESS EXECUTIVE. Christine Poon received a Bachelor of Science degree in biology from Northwestern University. She earned a Master of Science degree in biology/biochemistry from St. Louis University and a Masters of Business Administration in finance from Boston University.

She spent 15 years working for Bristol-Myers Squibb, serving in 1994 as vice president and general manager of Squibb Diagnostics before in 1997 being named president of international medicines. In 2000, she joined Johnson & Johnson. She serves as vice chairman of Johnson & Johnson Company and is a member of the board of directors.

Gayle K. Porter

MEDICINE. Gayle K. Porter is a licensed clinical psychologist. She is currently a principal research analyst and a senior mental health advisor for the Technical Assistance Partnership (TAP) of the American Institutes for Research.

Until May 2000, Dr. Porter was the director of the school-based program of Johns Hopkins University/Hospital. She was on the faculties of Johns Hopkins Child and Adolescent Psychiatry Department and Howard University. Before joining the staff at Johns Hopkins she directed two outpatient mental health clinics for children and families for the Washington, D.C., area. She was the first director of two outpatient mental health centers for the Washington, D.C., Commission on Mental Health Services. She developed and was the first full-time director of what has become a nationally known school-based mental health program for Johns Hopkins University/Hospital in Baltimore. It was the first school-based program in Baltimore in which psychiatrists and psychiatric residents provided services to children and their families in the schools. Governor Parris Glendening and Lieutenant Governor Kathleen Kennedy designated her program the model school-based program for Maryland.

Dr. Porter is an internationally known expert and lecturer in the area of mental health, particularly as it relates to African-Americans, children and women. She has also contributed articles to the mental health care literature and was first author on a chapter for the *Handbook of Child and Adolescents Systems of Care*. She has co-written several articles, a book chapter and recently co-authored *Prime Time: The African American's Woman's Complete Guide to Midlife Health and Wellness*.

Lisa J. Porter

GOVERNMENT OFFICIAL. Lisa J. Porter received a bachelor's degree in nuclear engineering from the Massachusetts Institute of Technology in Cambridge, Massachusetts, and earned a doctorate in applied physics from Stanford University, California.

Her professional career includes serving as a scientist in the advanced technology office of the Defense Advanced Research Projects Agency (DARPA) in Arlington, Virginia where she was program manager for projects that focused on applications of advanced computational fluid dynamics, including the design of quieter and more efficient helicopter rotor blades and research on friction drag reduction for naval platforms. Dr. Porter is NASA's associate administrator for the Aeronautics Research Mission Directorate, leads the agency's aeronautics research efforts and is co-lead in the development of a national aeronautics policy in cooperation with other government agencies. She most recently served as the NASA administrator's senior adviser for aeronautics.

Dorothy L. Powell

EDUCATION. Dorothy L. Powell received a Bachelor of Science in nursing from Hampton University and a

Master of Science in maternal-infant nursing from Catholic University of America. She earned a doctorate in higher education administration from the College of William and Mary.

Her professional career includes serving 25 years as a teacher and administrator at Thomas Nelson Community College, Norfolk State University, George Mason University and Hampton University. In July 2002 she was promoted to the rank of full professor. She serves as associate dean for nursing in the College of Pharmacy, Nursing and Allied Health Sciences at Howard University, Washington, D.C.

Dr. Powell has served on the National Advisory Councils on Nursing Research. She is a member of the board of directors of the American Association of Colleges of Nursing and has extensive local and regional affiliations related to nursing education and primary care access. She is a fellow of the American Academy of Nursing.

Shirley Powell

ENTERTAINMENT EXECUTIVE. Shirley Powell received a Bachelor of Arts degree in journalism at Temple University.

Her professional career includes serving in Orlando at an affiliate agency of Manning, Selvage and Lee Public Relations. She served at Nickelodeon Studios in Orlando, overseeing the studio's grand opening and subsequent press and special events; she served as vice president of media relations for the Disney Channel and Toon Disney, responsible for developing and leading all public relations and publicity strategies for the Disney/ABC networks. In 1992, she joined Turner Broadcasting's Cartoon Network in Atlanta where she led publicity for the launch of the network and spent five years helping position and establish its global brand. She also served as senior vice president of media relations for NBC Entertainment, NBC Studios and NBC Enterprises in Burbank, California. In 2001, she returned to Turner Entertainment Networks to serve as vice president of network communications.

Ms. Powell serves as senior vice president of corporate communications for Turner Broadcasting System, Inc. (TBS).

Janie Mae Powell-Mims

MILITARY. Janie Mae Powell-Mims earned a Bachelor of Science in business administration from Mississippi Valley State University in Itta Bena, Mississippi, in 1990. She received a Master of Arts degree in business administration from Webster University in Corpus Christi, Texas, in 1992. Her professional military education includes the Command and General Staff College at Fort Leavenworth, Kansas, graduating in 2003; and the Joint Forces Staff College in Norfolk, Virginia, graduating also in 2003.

She entered the United States Navy in November 1990 through Officer Candidate School in Newport, Rhode Island. Her first duty assignment took her to Naval Air Station Corpus Christi, Texas, where she served as public affairs officer/administrative officer from December 1990 through December 1993. In January 1994, she became the administrative, military standards, training support and administration schools officer at the Naval Technical Training Center in Meridian, Mississippi. She served in that position until January 1998 when she became officer-in-charge, Naval Air Facility, Misawa, Japan, until January 2000. She then moved on to Pensacola, Florida, where she served as aviation machinist mate schools and statistical officer, Naval Air Technical Training Center, from January 2000 through June 2002. In November 2004 she was serving as the commander of the Amarillo Military Entrance Processing Station in Amarillo, Texas.

A. Kathryn Power

HEALTH. A. Kathryn Power received a Bachelor of Arts degree in education from St. Joseph's College in Maryland and earned a Master's degree in education from Western Maryland College. She is a graduate of the Toll Fellowship program of the Council of State Legislators and completed the pro-

gram in executive and leadership government administration from the Harvard Kennedy School of Government.

Her professional career includes teaching at both elementary and secondary levels, counseling, leadership and advocacy in rape crisis and domestic violence agencies and computer systems analysis for the Department of Defense. She served from 1985 to 1990 as executive director of the Rhode Island Council of Community Mental Health Centers and for over 10 years as the director of the Rhode Island Department of Mental Health, Retardation and Hospitals, a cabinet position reporting to the governor.

Ms. Power serves as director of the Substance Abuse and Mental Health Services Administration's (SAMHSA) Center for Mental Health Services.

Karen H. Pozza

JUDGE. Karen H. Pozza received a Bachelor of Arts degree in finance and economics from Baylor University in 1986 and earned her Juris Doctor degree from St. Mary's University School of Law in 1991.

She serves on the boards of Community Justice Foundation, Child Guidance Center, Alternative Dispute Resolution Center, and the Bexar County Juvenile Board. She is also president of the San Antonio Bar Association where she is co-founder and co-chair of the community justice program.

She has served in private law practice. In January 2001, she was appointed as judge of the 407th District Court in San Antonio, Texas.

Loretta A. Preska

JUDGE. Loretta A. Preska is a native of Albany, New York. She received a Bachelor of Arts from the College of St. Rose in 1970 and received a Masters' of Law from New York University in 1978. She earned her Juris Doctor degree from Fordham University School of Law in 1973.

She was engaged in private law practice in New York City from 1973 to 1992. On March 31, 1992, she was nominated by President George H. W. Bush as judge to the United States District Court in the Southern District of New York. On August 11, 1992, she was confirmed by the United States Senate and received her commission on August 12, 1992.

Vivian Mathews Presley

EDUCATION. Vivian Mathews Presley is a native of Clay County (West Point) Mississippi and attended the public schools of West Point, Mississippi. She received her bachelor's degree in education, Master's degree in education and doctorate degree in education from Mississippi State University.

Her professional career includes serving for over 25 years in several capacities including counselor, vice president for institutional advancement and executive vice president.

Dr. Presley was appointed president of Coahoma Community College in 1992. She became the first woman president of Coahoma Community College and she is the first and only woman president of a publicly supported community college in Mississippi.

Yvonne J. Prettyman-Beck

MILITARY. Yvonne J. Prettyman-Beck was commissioned upon graduation from New Mexico Military Institute in 1979 and is a 1981 graduate of Angelo State University, San Angelo, Texas. She holds a Bachelor of Science degree in biology; she earned a Masters of Science degree in management science and a Masters of Science degree in national security and strategic. Her military education includes the Engineer Basic and Advanced Courses, the Combined Arms School, Services Staff School, the Command and General Staff College, and the National War College.

Her assignments include serving as commander, 84th Engineer Combat Battalion (Heavy), Schofield Barracks, in Hawaii; at Headquarters, Department of the Army Secretary for Joint Affairs at the Pentagon in Washington, D.C.; as secretary of the general staff and facilities engineer, 13th Corps Support Command and Battalion operations officer, 62nd Engineer Combat Battalion (Heavy) at Fort Hood, Texas; executive officer, Office Distribution Division, United States Army Personnel Command, Alexandria, Virginia; plans and operations officer, Defense Nuclear Agency, Alexandria, Virginia; company commander and battalion adjutant, 249th Engineer Combat Battalion (Heavy), and brigade intelligence officer, 18th Engineer Brigade, Karlsruhe, Germany; executive officer and platoon leader, HHC, 30th Engineer Topographic Battalion, Fort Belvoir, Virginia; and test officer, training & doctrine combined arms test activity, Fort Hood, Texas. Her most recent assignment is as operations officer in the Joint Operations Directorate, the Joint Staff, the Pentagon in Washington, D.C.

Since August 4, 2003, she has served as the commander of the Norfolk District Engineer Corps where she oversees the corps' water resources development and the operation of navigable waterways for four river basins in the Commonwealth of Virginia. She is also responsible for the corps' military design and construction projects for Army, Army Reserve and Air Force installations throughout Virginia.

Anita Price

BUSINESS EXECUTIVE. Anita Price is a native of Kansas City, Missouri. She received a Bachelor of Science degree in business management from Jackson State University.

Ms. Price joined State Farm Insurance in June 1980. She completed Insurance Institute of America General Insurance education series in 1984 and earned her Chartered Life Underwriter designation in 1991. She has served as a systems analyst in Bloomington. From 1991 to 1993 she was an assistant manager of agency resources and later served as the manager of an agency resources department. In 1993 she was promoted to agency staff assistant at corporate headquarters. In 1995, she was selected to serve as an agency field specialist in the newly created Metro West Agency Field Office. In March 2000 she was selected the first black State Farm agent in Fayette County, Georgia. Fayette County is one of the richest counties in the state of Georgia. She has been acknowledged as a Legion of Honor qualifier, a Bronze Tablet qualifier and as an Ambassador Traveler. In 2007, she was still the only black female State Farm agent in Fayetteville, Georgia.

Tiffany Provence

JUDGE. Tiffany Provence is a native of Montgomery, Alabama, and was raised in Summerville, South Carolina. She received a Bachelor of Science degree in telecommunications from the University of Florida and earned her Juris Doctor from the University of South Carolina in 1998.

After law school she was selected to fill the un-expired probate court term of Judge William Wylie in July 1998. She was re-elected to her first full term in office in January 2001.

Marla Provencio

BUSINESS EXECUTIVE. Marla Provencio is a native of California. She received a Bachelor of Arts in English from the University of California at Los Angeles.

She started her career in on-air promotion at ABC in 1979 as production coordinator. Over the years she has held various positions, including producer, senior producer and executive director of daytime and children's promotion. Most recently she served as vice president overseeing all on-air creative for drama and long-form programming.

Ms. Provencio was named senior vice president, marketing, for ABC Entertainment in June 2003. In this position she help oversee marketing, advertising and promotion for ABC's primetime and late-night lineup while also establishing the on-air tone and brand of the network.

Deborah D. Pryce

ELECTED OFFICIAL. Deborah D. Pryce is a native of Warren, Ohio. She

received a Bachelor of Arts degree from Ohio State University in Columbus, Ohio, in 1973 and earned her Juris Doctor degree from Capital University in Columbus, Ohio, in 1976.

She was engaged in private law practice; served as an administrative law judge, Ohio State Department of Insurance, from 1976 to 1978; served as the first assistant city prosecutor, senior assistant city attorney, the assistant city manager, Columbus City Attorney's office, Ohio, from 1978 to 1985; served as judge, Franklin County, Ohio, Municipal Court, 1989, 1990 and 1992. She was elected a United States Representative to the 103rd and to the six succeeding Congresses since January 3, 1993.

Marilyn A. Quagliotti

MILITARY. Marilyn A. Quagliotti received a Bachelor of Science degree in physical education from Louisiana State University. Her military education includes the Signal Officer Basic and Advanced courses, the United States Army Command and General Staff College and the National War College.

Her military career began in August 1975 when she was commissioned as a second lieutenant in the United States Army. She has held numerous command and staff assignments including serving from June 1995 to May 1997 as commander, 106th Signal Brigade, United States Army South at Fort Clayton, Panama; from June 1997 to July 1998 as deputy director for command, control, communication and computers (C4) command operations, J-6, The Joint Staff, Washington, D.C.; from June 1998 to June 2000 as vice director for command, control, communications and computer systems, J-6, the Joint Staff, Washington, D.C.; as the commanding general, 5th Signal Command, and deputy chief of staff G-6, United States Army Europe; in March 2003, she was assigned as the deputy director for operations (D-3), Defense Information Systems Agency, Arlington, Virginia; since November 2003 she has served as vice director, Defense Information Systems Agency, Arlington, Virginia. She was promoted to major general on February 1, 2003.

Joan Renee Queen

MILITARY. Joan Renee Queen is a native of Baltimore, Maryland. She graduated from the Institute of Notre Dame, Baltimore, Maryland, and received a Bachelor of Arts degree in health, science and policy concentrating in health care administration from the University of Maryland Baltimore County. She earned a master's degree in health science from the Johns Hopkins University School of Hygiene and Public Health in health care administration and planning. She also completed the Fleet Hospital Operations Indoctrination and Orientation Course and four Fleet Hospital Operation Field Training courses.

Captain Queen received a direct commission into the Medical Service Corps, United States Naval Reserve, in September 1983 at the rank of lieutenant junior grade and then attended Officer Indoctrination School in Newport, Rhode Island, in October 1983. In November 1983 she reported to her first duty assignment at the Naval Hospital, at Portsmouth, Virginia, in the patient administration department. She was promoted to the rank of lieutenant in September 1984. She was the assistant head of the patient administration department prior to detaching from the hospital.

During her career she has held numerous leadership and management position including serving in June 1995 with the Bureau of Medicine and Surgery as the administrative officer to the deputy surgeon general. She also served as the assistant to the chief of staff. In June 1998, she reported to the Naval Hospital at Camp Lejeune in North Carolina as the director for administration and the executive officer of the fleet hospital. She was selected for promotion to captain in May 2001 and promoted June 4, 2002. In June 2002 she reported to the United States Naval Hospital, in Naples, Italy, as the executive officer. In May 2004 she reported to the National Naval Medical Center, in Bethesda, Maryland as the director for administration. In July 2006 she reported to the Naval Health Clinic at Quantico, Virginia, as the commanding officer.

Peggy A. Quince

JUDGE. Peggy A. Quince is a native of Norfolk, Virginia. She received a Bachelor of Science in zoology from Howard University in 1970; she earned her Juris Doctor degree from the Catholic University of America in 1975. Her experience includes serving in private law practice. She moved to Florida in 1978 and in February 1980 worked with the attorney general's office as an assistant attorney general.

In 1993, Justice Quince became the first African-American female to be appointed to one of the district courts of appeal with her appointment by Governor

Lawton Chiles to the Second District Court of Appeal to a term effective January 4, 1994. She was retained in office by the electorate in November 1996. On December 8, 1998, she was appointed by the late Governor Lawton Chiles and Governor-elect Jeb Bush to the Florida Supreme Court.

Jennifer J. Raab

EDUCATION. Jennifer J. Raab is a native of New York and a graduate of Hunter College High School in New York. She received a Bachelor of Arts degree with distinction from the College of Arts and Sciences at Cornell University and a master's degree in public affairs from the Woodrow Wilson School of Public and International Affairs at Princeton University. She received her Juris Doctor degree cum laude from Harvard Law School.

Her professional career includes serving in 1979 as special projects manager for the South Bronx Development Organization. She was named director of public affairs for the New York City Planning Commission. Mayor Michael Bloomberg appointed her to the Charter Revision Commission where she and 12 commission members reviewed the entire New York Charter. She has also been engaged in private law practice.

Ms. Raab was appointed the 13th president of Hunter College, the largest college in the City University of New York (CUNY) system. The college also oversees the Hunter College campus schools which serve gifted and talented students, Kindergarten through grade 12.

Anne-Imelda Radice

GOVERNMENT OFFICIAL. Anne-Imelda Radice is a graduate of Wheaton College in Norton, Massachusetts. She earned a Master of Arts degree from the Villa Schifanoia School of Fine Arts in Florence, Italy and a doctorate degree from the University of North Carolina at Chapel Hill. She also holds a Master of Business Administration from American University.

Her professional career includes serving as curator and architectural historian for the architect of the Capitol and an assistant curator at the National Gallery of Art. From 1983 to 1989, she served as the first director of the National Museum of Women in the Arts. From 1989 to 1991 she served as chief of the creative arts division of the United States Information Agency. In the early 1990s she served as the acting chairman and senior deputy chairman of the National Endowment for the Arts. Dr. Radice was selected to serve as chief of staff to the secretary of the United States Department of Education. She was most recently acting assistant chairman for programs at the National Endowment for the Humanities.

Dr. Radice was nominated by President Bush and confirmed by the United States Senate to serve as the director of the Institute of Museum and Library Services. The institute, an independent United States government agency, is the primary source of federal support for the nation's 122,000 libraries and 17,500 museums.

Patti Radle

ELECTED OFFICIAL. Patti Radle received a Bachelor of Arts degree in theology from Marquette University. She holds a teacher certification and second major in English from Our Lady of the Lake University.

Her professional career includes serving as a teacher in the San Antonio Independent School District at J.T. Brackeridge and on the founding board of San Antonio Cultural Arts. She established and is directing a cooperative home school at inner city development for the purpose of one-on-one attention to neighborhood students and increased involvement from parents. She was elected councilwoman to the San Antonio, Texas, City Council.

Marguerita Ragsdale

GOVERNMENT OFFICIAL. Marguerita Ragsdale is a native of Richmond, Virginia, and grew up on a farm in Dinwiddie County, Virginia. She received a Bachelor of Arts degree from the American University in Washington, D.C. She earned a Master of Arts degree

and a doctorate degree from the University of Virginia. She also received a Juris Doctor degree from Columbia University in New York.

Her diplomatic career began at the American embassy in Kuwait in 1984, where she served as junior consular and general services officer. From 1986 to 1988, she served as political officer at the United States embassy in Mogadishu, Somalia, then returned to Washington to serve as watch officer in the Department of State operations center and then as desk officer for the United Arab Emirates and Oman (1989–1991). In 1992, she was appointed political/economic officer and, later, deputy chief of mission at the United States embassy in Doha, Qatar. In 1995, she worked directly with the under secretary of state for management as a management analyst and was subsequently selected to participate in the Department's prestigious senior seminar executive development program. Afterwards, she served as deputy director of the Office of Arabian Peninsula Affairs where she supervised desk officers for the Arabian Peninsula states of Saudi Arabia, Kuwait, Oman, the United Arab Emirates, Qatar, Bahrain and Yemen. In 1999, the Bureau of African Affairs selected Ms. Ragsdale to head its political section at the United States embassy in Pretoria. In 2002, she took on the portfolio of deputy chief of mission at the United States embassy in Khartoum. In 2003, President George Bush nominated Ms. Ragsdale to be United States ambassador to the Republic of Djibouti and she was confirmed by the United States Senate.

Shirley C. Raines

EDUCATION. Shirley C. Raines is a native of Bells, Tennessee. She received a Bachelor of Science degree from the University of Tennessee at Martin. She earned her Master of Science degree and her doctorate in education, both from the University of Tennessee in Knoxville. She also completed the management development program from the Harvard Graduate School of Education.

Her professional career includes serving as vice chancellor for academic services at the University of Memphis and as dean of the College of Education at the University of Kentucky. She is the author of 14 books and numerous journal articles, and as a faculty member was widely regarded as an expert in teacher education and early childhood education. She has served as chair of the board of directors of C-USA and as the 2006 chair of the Memphis Regional Chamber.

Dr. Raines became the 11th president of the University of Memphis on July 1, 2001. She is the first woman to hold the presidency of the university which was founded in 1912.

Judith A. Ramaley

EDUCATION. Judith A. Ramaley received a bachelor's degree in zoology from Swarthmore College in 1963 and earned her doctor in anatomy from the University of California in Los Angeles in 1966.

Her professional career includes serving a presidential professorship in biomedical science at the University of Maine and as a fellow of the Margaret Chase Smith Center of Public Policy. She served as president and professor of biology at the University of Vermont from July 1, 1997, to June 30, 2001. From 2001 to 2002, she was assistant director of education and human resources directorate at the National Science Foundation. She also completed a residency as a visiting senior scientist at the National Academy of Sciences from January to June 2005. On July 18, 2005, she was appointed president of Winona State University by the Minnesota State Colleges and Universities Board of Trustees. She is the first woman and the 14th president of Winona State University.

Pamela M. Ramble

MILITARY. Pamela M. Ramble is a native of Monterrey, California. Her military career began February 1981. Her military education includes the completion of all the Noncommissioned Officer Education System courses, Instructor Trainer Course, Small Group Instructor Training, Battle Staff, First

Sergeants Course, and the United States Army Sergeants Major Academy. Her civilian education includes a bachelor's degree in business. She is currently pursuing her master's degree in applied arts in organization development through the University of Incarnate Word.

Her assignments include three tours at 267th Finance Battalion, Fort Richardson, Alaska; deployed in support of Desert Storm; ARCENT Kuwait; 201st Finance Support Unit, Frankfurt, Germany; Readiness Group, Fort Jackson, South Carolina; Headquarters and Headquarters Company, Fort Sam Houston, Texas. In September 2004, she was serving as the command sergeant major of the 106th Finance Battalion, Wurzburg, Germany.

Margaret D. Rappaport

ELECTED OFFICIAL. Margaret D. Rappaport graduated from the University of Maryland and taught school in Anne Arundel and Howard counties. She was elected clerk of the circuit court for Howard County, MD, in 1990. Prior to becoming clerk, she served as judge of the Orphans' Court for Howard County from 1986 to 1989.

Sheila A. Rappaport

JUDGE. Sheila A. Rappaport received her undergraduate degree from the University of Colorado at Denver and earned her Juris Doctor degree from the University of Denver. In 2006, she was serving as a district judge to the Colorado 2nd Judicial District in Denver.

Sandra Ray

EDUCATION. Sandra Ray received a Bachelor of Science degree in education from the University of Alabama. She has served as a former elected member and past president of the Tuscaloosa County Board of Education and is a past local and district PTA president. She served as director of Alabama Association of School Boards. She has served as member, past director, and vice president of the chamber of commerce of West Alabama. In 1995, she was elected to the Alabama State Board of Education and has been reelected in every election.

Susan P. Read

JUDGE. Susan P. Read is a native of Gallipolis, Ohio. She received a Bachelor of Arts degree (summa cum laude) from Ohio Wesleyan University, Delaware, Ohio, in 1969 and earned her Juris Doctor degree as a Floyd R. Mechem Prize scholar from the University of Chicago Law School in Chicago, Illinois, in 1972.

Her professional career includes serving with United States Atomic Energy Commission as a legal intern from 1972 to 1973; as an assistant counsel at the State University of New York from 1974 to 1977; from 1977 to 1988, she worked for General Electric and served as the chief environmental counsel nationwide from 1980 to 1985; from 1988 to 1994, she was engaged in private law practice; from 1995 to 1997, she served as deputy counsel to Governor George E. Pataki. She was appointed to the State of New York Court of Claims on April 30, 1998, for an unexpired term. On June 2, 1999, she was appointed to a full term, designated presiding judge of the New York State Court of Claims. On January 6, 2003, she received an interim appointment as associate judge of the New York Court of Appeals and on January 22, 2003, she was confirmed as associate judge of the New York Court of Appeals.

Nancy A. Readon

BUSINESS EXECUTIVE. Nancy A. Readon received a Bachelor of Science degree in psychology (with honors) from Union College in Schenectady, New York, and earned her Master of Science degree in social psychology from Syracuse University.

Her professional career includes serving as executive vice president of human resources for Comcast Cable Communications, Inc., where she planned and led the integration of AT&T Broadband; she was partner and executive vice president, human resources and corpo-

rate affairs for Borden Capital Management Partners; she served as a member of the board of directors of Borden Foods, Wise Products Inc. and Elmer's Products, Inc. In August 2004, she was appointed senior vice president and chief human resources and communications officer for Campbell Soup Company.

Dana Redd

ELECTED OFFICIAL. Dana Redd is a native of Camden, New Jersey. She received a bachelor's degree in political science and business from Rutgers University in Camden, New Jersey.

She has devoted herself to public service by serving as the director of operations for Camden County's Department of Buildings and Operations. She was elected to the Camden City Council in 2001 and serves as board liaison to the Department of Administration and co-chairs the Law Department and Department of Health & Human Services. She has also served on the board of directors for the Camden Council of Girl Scouts and Literacy Volunteers of America.

Sharon H. Redpath

MILITARY. Sharon H. Redpath received a Bachelor of Arts degree in economics from the University of Washington and was commissioned from the Navy Reserve Officer Training Corps (NROTC) program in 1976.

She has held numerous positions of increased authority and responsibility to include serving from December 1998 to September 2000 as the deputy director, Joint Total Asset Visibility (JTAV) Office, Defense Logistics Agency; from October 2000 to September 2002, she served as commander of Navy Reserve Supply Systems Command Headquarters; from October 2002 to September 2004, she served as commanding officer of Navy Supply Support Battalion Two, headquartered in West Hartford, Connecticut; she was promoted to rear admiral and assigned as assistant director, plans and policy, N41R, OPNAV and subsequently as served as deputy commander, Naval Inventory Control Point in Mechanicsburg, Pennsylvania.

Rear Admiral Redpath serves as vice commander, Navy Expeditionary Combat Command and commander, Navy Expeditionary Logistics Support Group.

Susan D. Reed

ELECTED OFFICIAL. Susan D. Reed is a native of San Antonio, Texas, and graduated from Alamo Heights High School. She received her undergraduate degree from the University of Texas at Austin in economics and earned her Juris Doctor degree from the University of Texas School of Law in 1974.

She began her legal career as an assistant district attorney for Bexar County in November 1974, serving in that position for eight years; she was chief prosecutor in the 144th and 187th district courts. She has served as judge of the 144th District Court for 12 years. Her civil law experience stems from four years in private practice.

In November of 1998 she became the first woman to be elected district attorney of Bexar County.

Trudie Kibbe Reed

EDUCATION. Trudie Kibbe Reed received a Bachelor of Arts degree in sociology and a Master of Science in social work from the University of Texas at Austin. She earned a Master of Arts degree and a doctorate degree from Columbia University in adult and higher education.

Her professional career includes serving 18 years as a senior-level administrator with the United Methodist Church. At the age of 28, she became the youngest

elected general secretary (CEO) of a national program agency of the United Methodist Church; from 1994 to 1998 she served as dean of the Leadership Institute and a tenured professor at Columbia College of South Carolina where she founded and edited a refereed journal; she has taught in the doctoral program at United Theological Seminary in Dayton, Ohio, and in the Master's Conflict Resolution program at Antioch University in Ohio.

Dr. Reed was appointed the fifth president and the first woman to serve in this capacity in the 100 years since the college's founder, Dr. Mary McLeod Bethune. Dr. Reed assumed the presidency of Bethune-Cookman College on August 16, 2004.

Wendy Reed

BUSINESS EXECUTIVE. Wendy Reed received a bachelor's degree in computer-based management with a minor in communications from Clarkson University in 1984. She started her career in information technology at Accenture (formerly Andersen Consulting), where she was responsible for implementing solutions for the healthcare, banking and manufacturing industries.

Prior to founding InfoMentis in 1996, Ms. Reed worked for MSA (formerly Dun & Bradstreet Software), ViaSoft and Clarus where she held positions in sales, marketing and sales management. She is the founder and CEO of InfoMentis. Under Ms. Reed's direction, the company continues to experience tremendous growth and leadership in the skills training and consulting marketplace.

Joan Reede

MEDICINE. Joan Reede received a Bachelor of Science degree in biochemistry from Brown University in Providence, Rhode Island, in 1977 and earned her Medical Doctor degree from Mount Sinai School of Medicine in New York in 1980. She received a Master of Science in public health from Harvard School of Public Health in Boston in 1990 and a Master of Science in health policy and management from Harvard School of Public Health in 1992.

Her professional career includes serving as medical director for the Commonwealth of Massachusetts Department of Youth Services, Boston, and as a pediatrician with the Boston public schools from 1983 to 1986; she served as the medical director, Mattapan Community Health Center in Boston from 1987 to 1989; shortly after arriving at Harvard in 1990, she created the Biomedical Science Careers Program which encourages students from the middle-school level and above to take an interest in science. Younger participants learn about research laboratories and science careers; high school and college students receive help with everything from course work to medical-school applications.

Dr. Reede is the first African American woman ever named as a dean at the world-renowned institution. She manages a staff of about 20 and oversees all diversity activities at Harvard for students, trainees, faculty and staff. Dr. Reede recently was named winner of the Herbert W. Nickens Award.

Martha Rees

BUSINESS EXECUTIVE. Martha Rees received a Bachelor of Science degree in civil engineering from Purdue University and earned a Juris Doctor degree from Georgetown University Law Center. She was admitted to the District of Columbia Bar in 1984.

She joined DuPont in 1973 as a research engineer at the experimental station in Wilmington, Delaware, and then transitioned to a career in DuPont Legal. Her experience in DuPont Legal includes assignments as a commercial attorney representing the pharmaceuticals and agricultural products business, as a corporate and securities lawyer, and as a federal lobbyist. She was named associate general counsel in 1998 and was appointed vice president with functional responsibility for the commercial, environment/real estate, corporate/securities, and mergers and acquisitions legal practices for DuPont. She also serves as chief anti-trust counsel and chief environmental counsel.

Andrea D. Reese

MILITARY. Andrea D. Reese was born in San Juan, Trinidad, West Indies. She entered the Air Force in November 1977 receiving basic military training at Lackland Air Force Base in Texas.

Her military and civil education includes Inventory Management Specialist School at Lowry Air Force Base, Colorado; Noncommissioned Orientation Course, Clark Air Base, Philippines; United States Air Force Supervisory Development Course, Clark Air Base, Philippines; Noncommissioned Officer Academy, Keesler Air Force Base, Mississippi; United States Air Force Senior Noncommissioned Officer Academy, Maxwell Air Force Base, Gunter Annex, Alabama; associate of applied sciences in logistics management, Community College of the Air Force; she holds a Bachelor of Science degree in business technology, Peru State College, Peru, Nebraska.

Her key military assignments include serving from September 1979 to September 1983 as funds management specialist, Clark Air Base, Philippines; from November 1983 to August 1987, noncommissioned officer-in-charge requirements (NCOIC) stock control and NCOIC procedures element, Moody Air Force Base, Georgia; from September 1987 to September 1990, noncommissioned officer in charge stock control, 43rd Supply Squadron, Anderson Air Base, Guam; from October 1990 to May 1997, supply procedures superintendent, Directorate of Logistics, Headquarters Strategic Air Command; resource manager, United States Strategic Air Command, Command Section; superintendent materiel management flight; and chief, materiel storage and distribution flight, 55th Supply Squadron, Offutt Air Force Base, Nebraska; from June 1997 to June 2000, chief, management and systems flight, 31st Supply Squadron, Aviano Air Base, Italy; from June 2000 to May 2004, chief, Supply Systems Management Branch, Maxwell Air Force Base, Gunter Annex, Alabama. In January 2005, she was serving as chief master sergeant, superintendent for the Headquarters Standard Systems Group. She is responsible for advising the executive director on matters affecting the 750 enlisted members, 250 officers and 600 civilian personnel.

Desma Reid-Coleman

BUSINESS EXECUTIVE. Desma Reid-Coleman holds a master's degree in business management from Central Michigan University. In 1994, she left the corporate life at Modern Engineering as the manager of human resources to found Quality Professional Services which includes seven businesses, including Fashion ense Upscale Resale for the entire family; Lady Valet Concierge and Valet Parking Services for business events, private parties, residential and commercial.

Carolyn Reid-Wallace

EDUCATION. Carolyn Reid-Wallace received a bachelor's degree in speech and drama from Fisk University in Nashville, Tennessee, and received a master's degree from Adelphi University in New York. She earned her Ph.D. from George Washington University in Washington, D.C.

Her professional career includes serving as a professor of humanities at Talladega College in Alabama; Howard University in Washington, D.C.; Grinnell College in Iowa; and Bowie State College in Maryland. She served as dean of Bowie College and as vice chancellor of City University of New York. In November 1991, President George Bush appointed her as the assistant secretary of education for the United States Department of Education; after leaving the Department of Education, she served as vice president for education and senior vice president for programming at Corporation for Public Broadcasting. She was selected to serve as the 13th president of Fisk University.

Debbie Reif

BUSINESS EXECUTIVE. Debbie Reif is a native of Connecticut. She received a bachelor's degree from the University of Bridgeport and earned a Masters of Business Administration from the University of Connecticut.

She served as a financial analyst at General Electric Capital from 1982 to 1985 before moving into the risk management area. She served six years as the company's chief risk officer. She was at commercial equipment finance from 1985 to 1989. She served as senior risk officer for telecom and equipment and as vice president of global asset management and telecom. She served for two years as chief executive officer of the Financial Guaranty Insurance Company (FGIC), a part of GE's insurance portfolio. In 2004, she was selected

to serve as NBC Universal's executive vice president for financial structuring. In December 2005, she was named president and chief executive officer at General Electric's Equipment Services Business.

M. Jodi Rell

ELECTED OFFICIAL. M. Jodi Rell is a native of Norfolk, Virginia. She received her undergraduate degree after attending Old Dominion University and Western Connecticut State University. She received honorary doctor of law degrees from the University of Hartford in 2001 and the University of New Haven in 2004.

Her professional career includes serving as a state representative for the 107th District for ten years in Connecticut's General Assembly where she held various leadership posts including assistant House minority leader and deputy House minority leader; she served as Connecticut's lieutenant governor for over nine years. On July 1, 2004, she was sworn-in as Connecticut's 87th governor.

Marjorie O. Rendell

FIRST LADY (STATE). Marjorie O. Rendell received a bachelor's degree cum laude from the University of Pennsylvania and earned a Juris Doctor degree from the Villanova University School of Law.

Her professional career includes serving in private law practice for over 20 years. She was appointed a judge to the United States District Court for the Eastern District of Pennsylvania in March 1994. She was appointed a judge to the United States Court of Appeals for the Third Circuit in November 1997. She serves as the chair of the United States Judicial Conference Committee on the Administration of the Bankruptcy System and also serves on several Third Circuit committees.

Judge Rendell became the 43rd First Lady of Pennsylvania when her husband, Governor Edward G. Rendell, was sworn in as governor of Pennsylvania on January 21, 2003.

Arlene Render

GOVERNMENT OFFICIAL. Arlene Render is a native of Virginia. She is a career member of the Senior Foreign Service, class of minister-counselor and is the new U.S. ambassador to the Republic of Cote d'lvoire where her foreign service career began as vice consul 31 years earlier. She directed the Office of Southern African Affairs in the Bureau of African Affairs and served as United States ambassador to Zambia from 1996 to 1999. She directed the Office of Central African Affairs from 1993 to 1996. She was United States ambassador to Gambia from 1990 to 1993 and deputy chief of mission in the United States embassy in Accra from 1986 to 1989. Since joining the foreign service in 1970, she has also served in Kingston, Brazzaville, Genoa and Tehran. She speaks French and Italian.

Ada Pozo Revilla

JUDGE. Ada Pozo Revilla received Bachelor of Arts and Bachelor of Science degrees from the Florida International University in 1994. She earned her Juris Doctor degree from the University of Miami in 1997.

Her professional career includes serving as an assistant public defender and in private law practice. In 2005, she was appointed judge to the County Court Criminal Division in Miami.

Penny Brown Reynolds

JUDGE. Penny Brown Reynolds received a bachelor's degree and her Juris Doctor degree from Georgia State University.

Her professional career includes serving as an assistant attorney general for the state of Georgia. She made history when she was selected to serve as executive counsel to former Georgia Governor Roy Barnes, making her the first African American in Georgia history to hold that position. Ms. Reynolds was appointed judge to the State Court of Fulton County (Atlanta), Georgia, by Governor Roy Barnes. She has served as co-chair of the Governor's Commission of Sentencing. She also serves as first lady of Midway Missionary Baptist Church in College Park, Georgia. She is a student at the Interdenominational Theological Center at the Morehouse School of Religion with a goal of becoming a licensed minister.

Shonda Rhimes

ENTERTAINMENT. Shonda Rhimes received a Bachelor of Arts degree in English literature from Dartmouth College and earned a Master of Fine Arts from the University of Southern California School of Cinema-Television.

In the mid-to-late 1990s she wrote and sold her first screenplay, *Human Seeking Same.* In 2002, she wrote a script for a television series that followed the lives of a group of war correspondents. Some of the other films she has written include *Princess Diaries 2: Royal Engagement, Crossroads,* and *Introducing Dorothy Dandridge* which won Halle Berry both an Emmy and a Golden Globe.

Ms. Rhimes is the creator of the ABC's hit television show *Grey's Anatomy*, which is about the romantic entanglements and complicated lives of surgeons and their overworked interns at a Seattle hospital. While in high school she worked for two years as a candy striper. She's the only black woman with a dramatic show on television. Her show's mixture of medicine, drama and sex has proved a winning formula that more than 25 million viewers tuned in each week to watch. Since its debut in 2005, it's been one of television's top-rated series, and the network signed Ms. Rhimes to a two-year, $10 million deal. The show won a Golden Globe in January 2007.

Anne Rhoades

BUSINESS EXECUTIVE. Anne Rhoades received a bachelor's degree in business from the College of Santa Fe and a Masters of Business Administration from the University of New Mexico.

Her professional career includes serving as vice president of the people department for Southwest Airlines, as executive vice president of team services for Promus Hotel Corporation, and as the executive vice president for JetBlue Airways where she currently remains as a board member.

Ms. Rhoades serves as president of People Ink, her human resources consulting company.

Brenda T. Rhoades

JUDGE. Brenda T. Rhoades was born in Seoul, Korea, and became a naturalized citizen in 1974. She graduated magna cum laude from Arizona State University, College of Law, in 1989. She has served in private law practice in Anchorage, Alaska; Miami, Florida; and in Dallas, Texas.

The United States Court of Appeals for the Fifth Circuit selected Brenda T. Rhoades for appointment as a United States bankruptcy judge for the Eastern District of Texas at Plano. On August 31, 2003, she became the first Asian American on the bankruptcy bench in the Fifth Circuit.

Condoleezza Rice

GOVERNMENT OFFICIAL. Condoleezza Rice is a native of Birmingham, Alabama. She started learning French, music, figure skating and ballet at age three. At age 15, she began classes with a goal of becoming a concert pianist. In 1967, she moved to Denver, Colorado, with her family, where her father accepted an administrative position at the University of Denver. She attended St. Mary's Academy High School, a small all-girls Catholic high school. After studying piano at the Aspen Music Festival and School, she enrolled at the University of Denver, where her father served as an assistant dean and taught "The Black Experience in America." She graduated from St. Mary's Academy in 1970. In 1974, at age 19, she received a Bachelor of Arts degree in political science cum laude from the University of Denver. In 1975, she earned her master's degree in political science from the University of Notre Dame and her doctorate degree in political science from the Graduate School of International Studies at Denver in 1981. In addition to English, she speaks fluent Russian, and with varying degrees of fluency, German, French, and Spanish. She holds honorary doctorate degrees from Morehouse College, the University of Alabama, the University of Notre Dame, the National Defense University, Mississippi College

School of Law, the University of Louisville, Michigan State University, and Boston College.

Her professional career includes serving as a professor at Stanford University in 1981. From 1989 to 1991 she was an adviser on Soviet and Eastern European affairs on President George H. W. Bush's National Security Council; from 1993 to 1999, she served as Stanford University's provost. She served as George W. Bush's foreign policy adviser, during the 2000 presidential campaign; in 2001, President Bush appointed her to serve as national security adviser, becoming the first woman and second African American (after Colin Powell) to hold that post.

On January 26, 2005, Dr. Rice was appointed secretary of state, the first African American female to hold this post.

Judith C. Rice

GOVERNMENT OFFICIAL. Judith C. Rice is a native of Waterbury, Connecticut. She received a Bachelor of Arts degree in communication (cum laude) from Loyola University and earned her Juris Doctor degree from John Marshall Law School in 1988.

Her professional career includes serving from 1982 to 1989 as an assistant to assistant state's attorney in Cook County State's Attorney's office. She began her city career in 1989 as an assistant corporation counsel; she served as managing deputy director, then director, of the Department of Revenue; she was appointed commissioner of the Chicago Department of Water from 1996 to 1999; she headed the Chicago Department of Transportation from 1999 to 2000. In November 2000, she was appointed city treasurer of the city of Chicago by Mayor Richard M. Daley. On February 25, 2005, she was elected city treasurer.

Linda Johnson Rice

BUSINESS EXECUTIVE. Linda Johnson Rice is a native of Chicago, Illinois. She received a bachelor's degree in journalism from the University of Southern California and earned a Master of Business Administration from Northwestern University's Kellogg Graduate School of Management in 1987.

After her graduation in 1987, she was named president and chief operating officer of Johnson Publishing, a job she held until being promoted in 2002 to her current position as president and chief executive officer.

Andra V. Richardson

JUDGE. Andra V. Richardson received her Juris Doctor degree from Wayne State University Law School in 1987. Her professional career includes serving as an assistant prosecutor for Oakland County, in private law practice, and as an adjunct professor at Eastern Michigan University. In 1990, she was appointed a magistrate judge of the California 52nd District Court, Division One.

Barbara Richardson

FIRST LADY (STATE). Barbara Richardson is a native of Concord, Massachusetts. She received an Associate of Arts degree from Colby Junior College and a Bachelor of Arts degree magna cum laude from Wheaton College in Massachusetts.

The first lady and her husband, New Mexico Governor Bill Richardson, lived in Washington, D.C., during his tenure as U.S. Congressman and as secretary of energy under the Clinton administration, and in New York City while the governor served as the United States ambassador to the United Nations.

Ms. Richardson served as 2003 chair for Read Across America in New Mexico and for the past four years as statewide chair of Big Brothers/Big Sisters First Lady's Bowl for Kids Sake. Because of her interest in the issue of domestic violence, she was instrumental in the formation of the governor's Domestic Violence Advisory Board, serving as its chairman in the establishment of the Office of Domestic Violence Czar.

Sandra V. Richardson

MILITARY. Sandra V. Richardson is a native of Beatrice, Alabama, and was commissioned a second lieutenant in the Finance Corps in 1978.

Her military and civilian education includes the Finance Officer Basic and Advanced courses; Joint Professional Military Education Course; Professional Military Comptroller School; United States Army Command and General Staff College; the Army War College. She earned a Bachelor of Science degree in accountancy from Tuskegee University and a Master of Accounting from the University of Alabama.

Colonel Richardson has held a variety of command and staff positions to include commander, 176th Finance Battalion, Yongsan, Korea; commander, 45th

Finance Support Unit, and deputy finance and accounting officer, Kaiserslautern, Germany; training/executive officer and chief, Military Pay Branch, United States Army Military Police School and Training Center, Fort McClellan, Alabama; and central accounting officer, Second Infantry Division, Camp Casey, Korea.

Key staff positions held include serving as military assistant for the assistant secretary of the Army (financial management and comptroller); chief, financial management, Office of the Comptroller and the Joint Staff, and program/budget officer, officer of the assistant secretary of the Army (financial management and comptroller), Washington, D.C.; staff finance officer and assistant executive officer, United States Finance and Accounting Center, Indianapolis, Indiana. In September 2004, she was assigned as the senior military assistant to the director, Defense Finance and Accounting Service.

Velma L. Richardson

MILITARY. Velma L. Richardson is a native of South Carolina. She received a Bachelor of Science degree in mathematics from Livingstone College in Salisbury, North Carolina, in May 1973. Upon graduation from college, she received a direct commission as a second lieutenant in the United States Army Reserve. She earned a Master of Arts degree in human resources management from Pepperdine University. Her military education includes graduating from the Air Defense Artillery Officer Basic Course, Signal Officer Advanced Course, United States Army Command and General Staff College, and the United States Army War College.

In August 1973, she entered active duty at Fort McClellan, Alabama, as a member of the Women's Army Corps. Following her initial orientation, she attended the Air Defense Officer Basic Course and the Communications-Electronics Staff Officer Course. She was assigned as the signal officer for 1st Battalion, 55th Air Defense Artillery at Fort Bliss, Texas. An assignment to Korea ensued, where she served as platoon leader and company commander in the 51st Signal Battalion. After attending the Signal Officer Advanced Course, she was assigned in November 1978 as an organizational effectiveness staff officer at Fort Gordon, Georgia. From June 1984 to November 1986, she was assigned as a personnel assignment officer at the United States Army Military Personnel Center, Alexandria, Virginia. In December 1986, she was assigned as a plans officer with the 35th Signal Brigade, XVIII Airborne Corps at Fort Bragg, North Carolina. In May 1987, she served as the executive officer with the 426th Signal Battalion, 35th Signal Brigade at XVIII Airborne Corps, Fort Bragg, North Carolina. From June 1988, she served as a company grade management officer, G-1 (personnel), XVIII Airborne Corps, Fort Bragg, North Carolina.

Following a 19-month tour of duty in Europe as the United States Army signal center liaison officer for mobile subscriber equipment, she assumed command in September 1991 of the 426th Signal Battalion, later reflagged the 51st Signal Battalion at Fort Bragg, North Carolina. In July 1994, she was assigned as a staff analyst in the office of the assistant secretary of defense for command, control, communications and intelligence. She was promoted to colonel on June 1, 1996.

In June 1996, she assumed command of the 1108th United States Army Signal Brigade at Fort Ritchie, Maryland. On July 7, 1998, she was assigned as the deputy commander of the United States Signal Center and Fort Gordon at Fort Gordon, Georgia. She was the first woman to hold either title at Fort Gordon and was responsible for overseeing the communications training of nearly 20,000 service members and foreign students each year. On February 1, 2000, she was promoted to brigadier general.

In September 2000, she was assigned as the deputy commanding general for the Army and Air Force Exchange Service in Dallas, Texas. In July 2002, she was selected to serve as deputy commanding general for the network enterprise technology command at the 9th United States Army Signal Command at Arlington, Virginia.

Sharon Ivey Richie

MILITARY. Sharon Ivey Richie is a native of Philadelphia, Pennsylvania. She is the second eldest of seven children raised in a Philadelphia government-housing project. She earned her Bachelor of Science degree in nursing at Wagner College, New York, in 1971. Subsequently she received a Master of Science degree in psychiatric nursing as a clinical nurse specialist from the University of Texas, San Antonio. She was a doctoral student at the George Washington University, majoring in organizational behavior and spirituality in organizations. Her military education includes graduation from the United States Army War College, as well as completion of Command and General Staff College; the Field Combat Nursing Course at Fort Sam Houston, Texas; Combat Psychiatry, Baumholder, Germany; AMEDD Officer's Advanced Course, Fort Sam Hous-

ton, Texas; United States Navy Alcoholism Orientation Course, Long Beach, California; Clinical Head Nurse Course, Fort Sam Houston, Texas; Psychiatric Mental Health Clinician Course, Walter Reed Army Medical Center, Washington, DC; AMEDD Officer's Basic Course, Fort Houston, Texas.

From November 1971 to July 1972, she was a staff nurse in the orthopedic ward and later in medical intensive care unit at Walter Reed Army Medical Center in Washington, D.C. From December 1972 to July 1974 she was the assistant head nurse, behavior modification ward at Walter Reed Army Medical Center, Washington, D.C. From August 1974 to August 1975, she was the assistant head nurse in the psychiatric ward at Brooke Army Medical Center at Fort Sam Houston, Texas. From August 1976 to September 1977, she was assigned as hospital psychiatric nurse consultant and head nurse of the 2nd General Hospital in Landstuhl, Germany. From October 1977 to June 1979, she served as a psychiatric clinical nurse specialist at the alcoholism treatment facility in Stuttgart, Germany. From January 1980 to August 1980, she served as a nursing consultant and clinical liaison officer for the United States Surgeon General Drug and Alcohol Abuse at the Pentagon, Washington, D.C. From September 1982 to September 1983, she served as a White House fellow in the Office of Intergovernmental Affairs at the White House in Washington, D.C.

From October 1983 to February 1984, she was the assistant chief nurse for evenings/nights, Letterman Army Medical Center, Presidio of San Francisco, California. In January 1984, she was profis chief nurse at the 8th Evacuation Hospital, Fort Ord, California. In February 1984, she was assigned as chief of ambulatory nursing service at Letterman Army Medical Center, Presidio of San Francisco, California. From August 1985 to May 1986, she was assigned as director of quality assurance, Department of Nursing, Letterman Army Medical Center in San Francisco, California. From May 1986 to June 1987, she served as both chief and assistant chief of the Department of Nursing, at Kimbrough Army Community Hospital at Fort Meade, Maryland. In June 1988, she was assigned as chief of clinical nursing service at Walter Reed Army Medical Center in Washington, D.C. In May 1990, she was assigned chief of the Department of Nursing at Letterman Army Medical Center at Presidio of San Francisco, California. In October 1991, she was assigned director, health services directorate, United States Army Recruiting Command, Fort Knox, Ky. In August 1993, she was selected as the new chief nurse Southeast health service support area/DOD Region III and chief, Department of Nursing, Dwight D. Eisenhower Army Medical Center, Fort Gordon, Georgia.

Lisa A. Rickard

BUSINESS EXECUTIVE. Lisa A. Rickard received a bachelor's degree from Lafayette College in Easton, Pennsylvania, and earned a Juris Doctor from American University in Washington, D.C., where she was executive editor of the *Law Review*.

Ms. Rickard has spent 25 years as a public policy advocate, most recently as vice president, federal and state government affairs, for the Dow Chemical Company. Previously, she was senior vice president, federal and state government relations for Ryder System, Inc. She has served as president of the United States Chamber Institute for Legal Reform since March 2003.

Roslyn Ridgeway

ENTERTAINMENT EXECUTIVE. Roslyn Ridgeway received a bachelor's degree from Clark Atlanta University. She is founder of the National Council of Women in Entertainment and as president of the Business and Professional Women/USA, the nation's leading advocacy organization for working women on work/life balance and workplace equity issues.

Ms. Ridgeway is president and chief executive officer of entertainment production company De Roz Productions Inc.

Sandra R. Riley

GOVERNMENT OFFICIAL. Sandra R. Riley received a Bachelor of Science degree in business administration and a graduate degree in organizational communication from George Mason University. Her professional career includes serving as an employee relations specialist in the Directorate of Personnel and Employment Service in Washington; in October 1986, she became the deputy director for the Studies and Analysis Office; in September 1995, she became the director of policy and

plans/safety, Security and Support Services in Washington; she served as deputy administrative assistant to the Secretary of the Army; On November 4, 2004, she was appointed to the position of administrative assistant (AA) to the Secretary of the Army.

Ruth Ellen Riley

SPORTS (FIRST). Ruth Ellen Riley is a native of Ransom, Kansas, and grew up in Macy, Indiana. She received a bachelor's degree in psychology, making the dean's list every semester at Notre Dame. She played basketball at Notre Dame with a college career of 2,072 points and school records for rebounds (1,007), blocked shots (370), and field goal percentage (.632).

Her Notre Dame team won the NCAA women's championship in 2001 and her Detroit Shock team won the WNBA championship in 2003 and 2006. She was the Most Valuable Player in the 2001 and 2003 championship series, becoming the first person to win the MVP awards in both the NCAA and WNBA championships. She has also played on teams that won the NWBL championship and the gold medal at the Olympic Games. She played for the Shock in the 2004, 2005, and 2006 season. In 2005 she was selected for the Eastern conference team in the WNBA All-Star Game. In 2006, she was the starting center when the Shock on its second WNBA championship defeating the Sacramento Monarchs. In February 2007, she was traded to the San Antonio Silver Stars in exchange for Katie Feenstra.

Mary E. Rittling

EDUCATION. Mary E. Rittling received a Bachelor of Science degree in nursing from D'Youville College in Buffalo, New York, and a Master of Science degree in nursing from Binghamton University in Binghamton, New York. She also earned a Master of Science degree and a doctorate of education in higher and adult education from Columbia University in New York.

She held several positions in education at State University of New York, College of Technology at Delhi, including that of vice president of academic affairs and interim president. She has served as president of Potomac State College and regional vice president of West Virginia University.

Dr. Rittling was appointed as the third president of Davidson County Community College.

Aurea L. Rivera

GOVERNMENT OFFICIAL. Aurea L. Rivera is a native of Mayaguez, Puerto Rico. She received a Bachelor of Science degree in electrical engineering (cum laude), University of Puerto Rico, Mayaguez, in 1980; received a Master of Science degree in systems engineering at Wright State University in Dayton, Ohio; and earned a Master of Science degree in electrical engineering from the University of Dayton, Ohio. She is a graduate of the career broadening program, foreign technology division at Wright-Patterson Air Force Base, Ohio; the senior development program, foreign technology division, Wright-Patterson Air Force Base, Ohio; and the national security management course, Syracuse University, New York.

Her professional career includes serving for 14 years as a radar analyst, assigned as a senior intelligence analyst for the center's technology division where she was selected as the division chief in 1998. She served as the U.S. Air Force representative to the Scientific and Technical Intelligence Committee from 1998 through 2001 and served as the alternate U.S. Air Force representative to the Weapons and Space Systems Intelligence Committee from 1996 to 2001. She was selected to serve as associate chief scientist of data exploitation, National Air and Space Intelligence Center, Wright-Patterson Air Force Base in Ohio.

Fanny Rivera

Government Official. Fanny Rivera received a Master's degree in mathematics from the University of Miami. She is a graduate of the Federal Agency's Senior Executive Service candidate development program.

She began her federal service in 1973 with the Office of Personnel Management in New York. Eleven years later, she joined Federal Aviation Administration's Eastern region human resource management division, later heading up that region's civil rights office. She was named deputy regional administrator for the Western-Pacific region where she shared in the responsibility for the general management of a region with a population of approximately 5,700 employees. She currently serves as the assistant administrator for civil rights for the Federal Aviation Administration (FAA). She is the principal advisor to the administrator on agency civil rights, equal employment opportunity, managing diversity and affirmative action matters.

Gloria A. Rivera

Judge. Gloria A. Rivera is a native of Southern California. She graduated from the University of Colorado at Denver in 1983 and received her Juris Doctor degree in 1988 from the University of Denver College of Law.

Prior to her appointment, she was a Denver deputy district attorney for approximately ten years. She was appointed to the Denver Court bench on March 22, 1999, by Governor Bill Owens.

Margaret Rivera

Military. Margaret Rivera is a native of Brooklyn, New York. She received a Bachelor of Science degree in biology and earned a Masters of Science degree in anatomy from the University of Puerto Rico where she was commissioned a second lieutenant through the Reserve Officer Training Program.

Colonel Rivera has held numerous key assignments in the Army Medical Service Corps to include serving as deputy commander for administration and chief of staff at William Beaumont Army Medical Center and the Southwest Regional Medical Command at Fort Bliss, Texas. She has served as commander of Munson Army Health Center at Fort Leavenworth, Kansas, and as the director of the Advanced Medical Test Support Center located at Fort Gordon, Georgia.

Sonya L. Rivera

Military. Sonya L. Rivera is a native of Queens, New York, and graduated from high school in Brooklyn, New York. She enlisted into the United States Navy in January 1985 and attended recruit training in Orlando, Florida, followed by Radioman "A" School at Service School Command, San Diego, California.

Her key military assignments include serving at Naval Telecommunications Center in Mayport, Florida; NAVCOMMDET Guantanamo Bay, Cuba, as leading petty officer; NAVCOMTELESTA, Jacksonville, Florida as leading petty officer; USS *John Hancock* (DD 981) as division leading chief; onboard USS *John F. Kennedy* (CV 67) as division leading chief; onboard USS *Barry* (DDG 52) as division leading chief. In October 2004, she was serving as the senior enlisted advisor, commander, Carrier Strike Group Twelve.

Lynn Nancy Rivers

Elected Official. Lynn Nancy Rivers is a native of Au Gres, Arenac County, Michigan, and a graduate of Au Gres-Sims High School, Arenac, Michigan. She received a Bachelor of

Arts degree from the University of Michigan in 1987 and earned her Juris Doctor degree from Wayne State University in Detroit, Michigan, in 1992.

Her professional career includes serving as a trustee of Ann Arbor, Michigan, Board of Education from 1984 to 1992 and as a member of the Michigan State House of Representatives from 1993 to 1994. She was elected as a Democrat to the 104th and to the three succeeding Congresses from January 3, 1995, to January 3, 2003.

Elizabeth H. Roberts

ELECTED OFFICIAL. Elizabeth H. Roberts is a native of Virginia and a graduate of Langley High School, McLean, Virginia. She received a Bachelor of Arts degree from Brown University in 1978 and a Master of Business Administration from Boston University in 1984.

Ms. Roberts was elected a Rhode Island state senator for District 28 in 1996.

Robin Roberts

MEDIA. Robin Roberts received a Bachelor of Arts degree in communications cum laude from Southeastern Louisiana University. She was also a standout performer on the women's basketball team, ending her career as the school's third all-time leading scorer (1,446 points) and rebounder (1,034). She is one of the only three Lady Lions to score 1,000 career points and grab 1,000 career rebounds. During her senior season, she averaged a career-high 15.2 points per game.

Ms. Roberts began her broadcasting career while in college at WHMD/WFPR radio in Hammond, Louisiana (1980–1983), where she was the sports director. She also served as a special assignment sports reporter for KSLU-FM in 1982. She has worked at WDAM-TV in Hattiesburg, Mississippi, at WLOX-TV in Biloxi, Mississippi, and WSMV-TV in Nashville, Tennessee. In 1988, she worked as a sports reporter and anchor at WAGA-TV in Atlanta, Georgia. She was also a morning personality on WVEE-FM in Atlanta. From 1990 to 2005, she served as a contributor to ESPN, where she was one of the network's most versatile commentators, whose assignments have included hosting *SportsCenter* and contributing to *NFL PrimeTime* from 1990 to 1994. Ms. Roberts has contributed to *Good Morning America* since June 1995. In March 2003, she traveled to the Persian Gulf region to report from Kuwait on the impending war with Iraq. In March 2004, she returned to the war zone reporting on the one-year anniversary of the war. In May 2005, she was named third anchor of ABC News' *Good Morning America.*

Victoria A. Roberts

JUDGE. Victoria A. Roberts is a native of Detroit, Michigan. She received a Bachelor of Science from the University of Michigan in1973 and earned her Juris Doctor degree from Northeastern University School of Law in 1977.

Her career experience includes serving as a research attorney, Michigan Court of Appeals 1977–1979; as a legal research and writing teaching fellow at Detroit College of Law, Michigan State; in private law practice in Michigan; as an assistant U.S. Attorney, Eastern District of Michigan; general counsel, Mayor-elect Dennis Archer Transition Team.

Judge Roberts was nominated by William J. Clinton on July 31, 1997, to a seat vacated by George LaPlata, was confirmed by the U.S. Senate on June 26, 1998 and received commission on June 29, 1998, as a judge, U.S. District Court, Eastern District of Michigan.

Vicki Robertson

JUDGE. Vicki Robertson is a native of Ponca City, Oklahoma, and graduated from high school in Houston, Texas. She received a Bachelor of Science degree in mathematics and a minor in economics from the University of Oklahoma. In 1978, she received her Juris Doctor degree from the Oklahoma City University School of Law. She began her career in private law practice.

On April 1, 1996, she was sworn in as a special judge for Oklahoma County. On April 16, 1999, she was appointed judge in the District Court, Oklahoma County, Oklahoma. In 2002, she was unopposed for election and in 2006, she was serving as vice presiding judge.

Audrey Robinson

GOVERNMENT OFFICIAL. Audrey Robinson is a native of Montgomery, Alabama. She received a bachelor's degree in chemistry from Oakwood College in Huntsville. She earned a master's degree in management from the Florida Institute of Technology in Huntsville and a Juris Doctor from Emory University School of Law in Atlanta, Georgia.

She first worked with NASA as a high school apprentice in 1981. In 1986, she joined the NASA Marshall Center full-time as a materials engineer in the Professional Intern Program. She was assigned to the Office of Chief Counsel at NASA's Kennedy Space Center in Florida. She returned to the Marshall Center in 1996. She now serves as the director of the Office of Equal Opportunity at NASA's Marshall Space Flight Center in Huntsville, Alabama.

Deborah A. Robinson

JUDGE. Deborah A. Robinson is a graduate of Morgan State University and Emory University School of Law. She served as a law clerk for Chief Judge H. Carl Moultrie of the Superior Court of the District of Columbia from 1978 to 1979. Following her clerkship, she joined the United States Attorney's office for the District of Columbia, where she served for eight years prior to her appointment.

She was sworn in as United States magistrate on July 18, 1988.

Kathleen Robinson

LAW ENFORCEMENT. Kathleen Robinson received a bachelor's degree from the University of Arizona in 1981 and earned her Master's degree in educational leadership from Northern Arizona University in 1999. She is a graduate of the FBI National Academy.

Her professional career began in January 1984 at the Tucson Police Department. Her police assignments include serving as a patrol officer in the Operations Division South, as a field training officer, as a physical training instructor, as a sergeant, as a field supervisor, and as an investigator assigned to the Office of Professional Standards (Internal Affairs). From 1990 to 1994, she served as the administrative supervisor for Tucson Police Department Hostage Negotiation Unit; in 1994, she was promoted to lieutenant and served in Operations Division Midtown and Operations Divisions South; she was next assigned to special investigation which includes the operations unit, intelligence unit, the gang interdiction unit, and the tactical gang unit; in 1998, she was promoted to captain, assigned as commander of the Operations Division West; on January 16, 2000, she assumed her current rank of assistant chief, assigned as the commander of the Investigative Services Bureau.

Nikki Rocco

ENTERTAINMENT EXECUTIVE. Nikki Rocco joined the Universal Pictures sales department in New York in 1967. She was promoted to assistant to the general sales manager in 1981 and was named vice president of distribution in 1984. In 1990, she was named senior vice president of distribution and marketing.

Ms. Rocco was named president of Universal Pictures' distribution in February 1996, becoming the first woman to head a major studio distribution operation in Hollywood's history. In addition to overseeing the studio's relations with theater owners, she is responsible for all distribution functions and strategic planning, including sales, branch operations, print control and national accounting.

Rene A. Roche

JUDGE. Rene A. Roche received a Bachelor of Arts degree from Auburn University in 1980 and earned her

Juris Doctor from University of Florida in 1984. Her professional career includes serving as a judge in Orange County Traffic Court (1995–1997); as a Florida Circuit judge, Osceola County Juvenile Dependency & Delinquency (1997–1999); as circuit judge for the Orange County Juvenile Dependency (2000–2003); in 2003, she served as circuit judge for Florida's Orange County Civil Court. In 2004, she was assigned circuit judge, Orange County Civil Court.

Sharon Percy Rockefeller

MEDIA EXECUTIVE. Sharon Percy Rockefeller received a bachelor's degree from Stanford University. She has served the public broadcasting community for more than 27 years as a leading policymaker. She has been president and chief executive officer of WETA, Washington, D.C.'s flagship public television and radio station since 1989. Before assuming the top post at WETA, she was a member of WETA's Board of Trustees for seven years and a member of the board of directors of the Corporation for Public Broadcasting for 12 years, including four years as chairman. In 2000, Ms. Rockefeller was elected to the PBS board of directors for her fourth term.

Judith Rodin

EDUCATION. Judith Rodin is a graduate of the Philadelphia school system. She received a bachelor degree from the University of Pennsylvania and earned her doctorate from Columbia University in 1970.

Her professional career includes serving as an assistant professor of psychology at New York University; as an associate professor at Yale University, later professor of psychology, then professor of medicine and psychiatry. In 1992, she was appointed Yale's provost; she served two years as chair of the Department of Psychology and one year as dean of the Graduate School of Arts and Science. She returned to the University of Pennsylvania after 22 years on the faculty of Yale University, serving two years there as provost; she served on President Clinton's Committee of Advisors on Science and Technology and co-chaired the transition team of Philadelphia Mayor John F. Street; she also served from 1994 to 1995 on a presidential panel to review security at the White House. In 1994, Dr. Rodin was appointed president of the University of Pennsylvania. She became the first woman to be named to the presidency of an Ivy League institution (1994–2004).

Dr. Rodin has served as a member of the Comcast board of directors since November 2002. She serves as president of the Rockefeller Foundation. She also served on the board of directors of Aetna, Inc., AMR Corporation and Citigroup and also serves as a trustee of 43 of the mutual funds managed by the BlackRock Funds.

Jennifer Rodriguez

SPORTS. Jennifer Rodriguez is a native of Miami, Florida. She holds five U.S. speed-skating records. She is the first Cuban American woman to compete in the Olympic Winter Games and to win an Olympic medal. She is the first American woman to earn a spot on the Olympic Team in all five ice speed-skating events in 2002, and won two bronze medals in Salt Lake City. She has won over 33 World Cup medals and 14 individual international medals.

Julia I. Rodriguez

JUDGE. Julia I. Rodriguez received her undergraduate degree from City University of New York in Hunter College and earned her Juris Doctor degree from Fordham University School of Law.

Her professional career includes serving as a staff attorney for the Legal Aid Society; in private law practice; as court attorney to civil court; as the principal law clerk to a Supreme Court justice; as judge of the housing court, New York City Civil Court. She was elected judge to the New York City Civil Court in the Bronx. Her first term began on January 1, 2004.

Rose E. Rodriguez

GOVERNMENT OFFICIAL. Rose E. Rodriguez received a Bachelor of Science degree in business administration and finance from Fordham University. She earned a Master's degree in political management from the Graduate School of Political Management at Baruch College and a Juris Doctor from Fordham University School of Law and was the recipient of the Philip D. Reed Scholarship. She served as a Stein Public Interest Law Scholar and on the Urban Law Journal.

Ms. Rodriguez served in 1993 as Governor Mario M. Cuomo's special advisor and executive director of the governor's Office for Hispanic Affairs. She served as Governor Cuomo's deputy campaign manager in his 1994 re-election campaign and as the state-wide Hispanic community field coordinator for the Clinton-Gore 1992 campaign. She previously served as an appointee of President William Jefferson Clinton assigned to the United States Department of Housing and Urban Development (HUD) as special assistant to Secretary Andrew Cuomo. She served as deputy director for the Office of Policy within the Department of Community Planning and Development. Ms. Rodriguez was appointed senior advisor to Senator Hillary Rodham Clinton. As senior advisor to the Senator she manages the Office of Constituent Affairs, and advises the senator on matters pertaining to the Hispanic community.

Wanda Yancey Rodwell

BUSINESS EXECUTIVE. Wanda Yancey Rodwell received a bachelor's degree from Spelman College in Atlanta, Georgia.

Ms. Rodwell served as vice president of public affairs for the Grady Health System in Atlanta, Georgia. She serves as a member of the Development Authority of Dekalb County, Georgia. She also served as chair of the Calvin A. Rowell Foundation. She was selected to serve as general manager of corporate communications for Delta Air Lines in Atlanta, Georgia.

Lesa B. Roe

AEROSPACE. Lesa B. Roe received a bachelor's degree in electrical engineering from the University of Florida at Gainesville and a master's degree in electrical engineering from the University of Central Florida in Orlando.

Her professional career includes performing satellite communications analysis for Hughes Space and Communications in El Segundo, California. She began her National Aeronautics and Space Administration (NASA) career at Kennedy Space Center, Florida, in 1987 as a radio frequency communications engineer in the Space Shuttle Engineering Directorate. She also managed the International Space Station Payloads Office at Johnson Space Center in Houston. She served as Langley associate director for business management from August 2003. She was then named the Langley deputy director in June 2004 until being named director in October 2005.

Ms. Roe serves as director of NASA's Langley Research Center in Hampton, Virginia. NASA Langley, founded in 1917, is the nation's first civilian aeronautical research facility and NASA's original field center. Ms. Roe is the senior management official of the laboratory employing approximately 2,100 civil service personnel. She is responsible for the center's aeronautical and space research programs, as well as facilities, personnel and administration.

Chase T. Rogers

JUDGE. Chase T. Rogers is a native of Connecticut. She received a Bachelor of Arts degree from Stanford University in 1979 and earned her Juris Doctor degree from Boston University School of Law in 1983. After law school she served in private law practice.

In January of 1998, she was appointed judge for the Superior Court. Her assignments as a Superior Court judge included serving as the presiding judge for juvenile matters in Bridgeport and being assigned to the Regional Child Protection Session in Middletown. Between 2001 and 2005, she was assigned to the complex litigation docket in Stamford and from 2005 to 2006, she served as the presiding judge for civil matters in the Stamford-Norwalk district.

In February of 2006, Judge Rogers was nominated by Governor M. Jodi Rell for the Appellate Court and on March 15, 2006, she was sworn in as an Appellate Court judge.

Patience Drake Roggensack

JUDGE. Patience Drake Roggensack is a native of Joliet, Illinois. She received her bachelor's degree from Drake University in 1962 and earned her Juris Doctor degree from the University of Wisconsin Law School in 1980.

Her professional career includes serving in private law practice from1980 to 1996. She was elected to the Wisconsin Court of Appeals in 1996. In 2003, she was elected justice on the Wisconsin Supreme Court.

Ann E. Rondeau

MILITARY. Ann E. Rondeau is a native of San Antonio, Texas, but grew up in Beacon, New York. She received a bachelor's degree in history from Eisenhower College in 1973 where she was selected as "most distinguished graduate." She earned her commission in 1974 through Officer Candidate School.

She held numerous positions in a variety of assignments of increasing authority and responsibility to include serving in the Office the Secretary of Defense as assistant for policy analysis; serving in the Office of African Affairs; as a special assistant to the Attorney General for National Security Affairs as a White House Fellow; as Chief of Naval Operations (CNO) Executive Panel as assistant for political-military analysis; military assistant to the principal deputy under secretary of defense for policy; as the deputy chief of staff for shore installations for commander in chief, U.S. Pacific Fleet Staff; as the commander of Naval Training Center Great Lakes and subsequently as the first commander of Naval Service Training Command which was established June 30, 2003. She assumed command of naval personnel development command in November 2004.

Vice Admiral Rondeau has served as director, Navy staff, in Washington, D.C., since August 2005.

Ellen Roper

JUDGE. Ellen Roper received her undergraduate degree from Brandeis University and earned her Juris Doctor degree from the University of Missouri–Columbia, School of Law. Her professional career includes serving as an assistant attorney general for the state of Missouri; as deputy director of the Missouri Commission on Human Rights; and executive director of the Missouri Commission on Human Rights. She was first appointed to the court in 1976 and has been elected since 1982. With the Court Reorganization Act of 1978, she became the first woman to serve as a circuit judge in the state of Missouri. She serves as a circuit judge at the Missouri Division III, Circuit Court.

Ileana Ros-Lehtinen

ELECTED OFFICIAL. Ileana Ros-Lehtinen was born in Havana, Cuba. She received a an Associate of Arts from Miami-Dade Community College, Miami, Florida, and a Bachelor of Arts degree from Florida International University in Miami, Florida. She received

a Masters of Science degree from Florida International University in Miami, Florida, in 1987 and earned a Doctor of Education from the University of Miami in 2004.

Her professional career includes founding of the Easter Academy, serving as a member of the Florida state house of representatives from 1982 to 1986, and serving as a Florida state senator from 1986 to 1989. She was elected to the 101st Congress by special election to fill a vacancy and since August 29, 1989, has served as a United States representative. She has been re-elected to the eight succeeding Congresses.

Marilyn Brown Rosenbaum

JUDGE. Marilyn Brown Rosenbaum received a Bachelor of Arts degree from the University of Illinois, Champaign-Urbana, Illinois, in 1966 and earned her Juris Doctor degree from Georgetown University Law Center in Washington, D.C., in 1969.

Her professional career includes serving in private law practice from 1970 to 1972; as an estate and gift tax attorney, Internal Revenue Service, United States Department of the Treasury, from 1973 to 1977; and in private law practice from 1977 to 1979. In 1979, she accepted a position as hearing examiner, Minneapolis Civil Rights Commission; in 1984, she returned to private law practice. In 1992, she was appointed judge to the Minnesota District Court and was elected in 1994 and 2000.

Barbara Ross-Lee

MEDICINE. Barbara Ross-Lee is a native of Detroit, Michigan. She received a Bachelor of Science degree in biology and chemistry from Wayne State University in 1965. She joined the National Teacher Corps, a federal program in which she could earn a degree while teaching simultaneously in the Detroit public school system. After completing the program in 1969, she attended Michigan State University College of Osteopathic Medicine where she received her Medical Doctor degree. She also holds an honorary Doctor of Science degree from New York College of Osteopathic Medicine.

Her professional career includes serving as the first osteopathic physician to participate in the prestigious Robert Wood Johnson Health Policy Fellowship where she served as legislative assistant for health to Senator Bill Bradley. She served on the board of directors for the Association of Academic Health Centers, the National Fund for Medical Education and the National Health Service Corps Association of Clinicians for the Underserved.

Dr. Ross-Lee is one of only seven women deans of medical schools in the United States and the first African American woman to hold that title. She served as dean of the College of Osteopathic Medicine of Ohio University until 2001. She serves as vice president for health sciences and medical affairs at the New York Institute of Technology (NYIT) and dean of the NYIT New York College of Osteopathic Medicine.

Leslie B. Rothenberg

JUDGE. Leslie B. Rothenberg began her legal career in 1986 as a prosecutor in the Miami-Dade State Attorney's office, and after a year she was promoted to the felony division; in 1992, she was elected to the circuit court bench serving for eleven years in the criminal, civil and the appellate divisions; in October 2003, after eleven years on the circuit court, she stepped down from the bench and was engaged in private law practice. In January 2005 she was appointed judge to the Florida Third District Court of Appeals.

Barbara Jacobs Rothstein

JUDGE. Barbara Jacobs Rothstein is a native of Brooklyn, New York. She received a Bachelor of Arts degree from Cornell University in 1960 and earned her Juris Doctor degree from Harvard Law School in 1966.

Her professional career includes serving in private law practice and as an assistant attorney general and chief trial attorney. She served in the Washington State Attorney General's office from 1968 to 1977; she also served as an adjunct professor at the University of

Washington Law School from 1975 to 1977. She served as judge at the Superior Court of Washington in King County, Washington, from 1977 to 1980.

On December 3, 1979, President Jimmy Carter nominated her to be judge, United States District Court, Western District of Washington. She was confirmed by the U.S. Senate on February 20, 1980, and received commission that day. She served as chief judge from 1987 to 1994. In 2003, she was appointed the ninth director of the Federal Judicial Center for Northern District of California.

Gina L. Routen

GOVERNMENT OFFICIAL. Gina L. Routen was educated in the Cleveland public schools and graduated from Collinwood High School with a focus on business. She received a bachelor's degree in business administration from Baldwin-Wallace College and earned her master's degree in Labor relations and human resources from Cleveland State University.

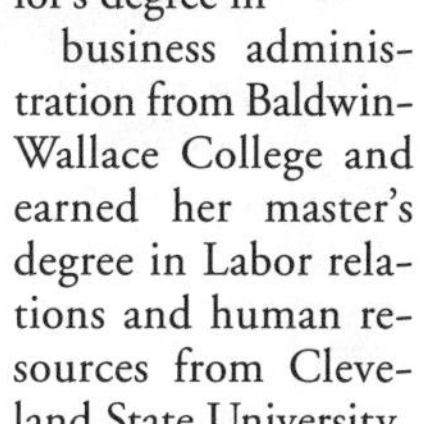

Her career began as a human resources generalist for one of Cleveland's leading manufacturing companies. She also worked for Case Western Reserve University. In July 2003, she was appointed director of personnel and human resources for the city of Cleveland, Ohio.

Loriene Roy

EDUCATION. Loriene Roy was born in Cloquet and raised in Carlton, Minnesota. She studied at the College of St. Benedict, Oregon Institute of Technology, the University of Arizona and the University of Illinois at Urbana–Champaign. She earned a Master of Library Science degree from the University of Arizona.

Her professional career includes serving as a medical radiological technologist working in hospitals in Oregon and Arizona. She worked as a reference librarian at the Yuma (Arizona) City-County Public Library. She joined the faculty at the University of Texas at Austin in January 1987. She was elected president of the American Library Association on June 28, 2006. She was inaugurated as the 2007–2008 president of the American Library Association at the 2007 American Library Association Annual Conference in Washington, D.C.

Dianna R. Roybal

JUDGE. Dianna R. Roybal graduated from Colorado State University in Fort Collins, Colorado, in 1981 with a Bachelor of Science degree in psychology. She earned her Juris Doctor degree from the University of Colorado School of Law in Boulder, Colorado, in 1995. She was engaged in private law practice, and she served as a deputy district attorney for the Adams County District Attorney's office. She served as a magistrate for the Colorado Seventeenth Judicial District. She was appointed as an Adams County Court judge by Governor Bill Owens in 2003.

C. Lorene Royster

JUDGE. C. Lorene Royster is a native of Mississippi. She received a Bachelor of Science degree from Oakwood College Academy in Huntsville, Alabama. She received a Master's of Science degree from Wayne State University and earned her Juris Doctor degree from Wayne State University Law School.

Her professional career includes serving in private law practice. She was later selected to serve as a magistrate judge in Detroit, Michigan. In 1990, she was appointed judge of the Michigan 36th District Court. She was first elected in 1994 to the same position. In 2006, she was still serving in that position.

Kay E. Royster

EDUCATION. Kay E. Royster received a Master of Education Administration from the University of Illinois in 1979 and earned a Doctor of Educational Administration from the University of Rochester in 1990. She served as deputy chief executive officer in Detroit, Michigan, from 2000 to 2002. Since 2002, she has served as the superintendent of Peoria, Illinois, schools.

Virginia P. Ruesterholz

COMMUNICATIONS. Virginia P. Ruesterholz received a Bachelor of Science degree in chemical engineering from Stevens Institute of Technology in 1983 and a Master of Science degree in telecommunications management from Brooklyn Polytechnic Institute in 1991.

Her professional career includes serving as a manager with New York Telephone in 1984; in 1993, she served as vice president and general manager for service delivery and field operations supporting consumer and business customers at New York Telephone. After the Bell Atlantic/NYNEX merger, she was named vice president, complex installation and maintenance for network services and, later vice president, operations assurance. After the Bell Atlantic/GTE merger, she was named senior vice president of wholesale markets; she served as president of Verizon Partner Solutions, responsible for Verizon's wholesale business including marketing, sale, provisioning and maintenance.

Ms. Ruesterholz serves as president of Verizon Telecom, responsible for sales, customer service, operations and IT for the consumer, general business and domestic wholesale markets.

Patricia F. Russo

BUSINESS EXECUTIVE. Patricia F. Russo received a bachelor's degree from Georgetown and completed the advanced management program at Harvard University in 1989. She has received an honorary doctorate of engineering from Stevens Institute of Technology, as well as an honorary doctorate in entrepreneurial studies from Columbia College in South Carolina.

Her professional career includes serving eight years in sales and marketing at IBM. She also served as president and chief operating officer at Eastman Kodak Company. In 1981, she joined AT&T and in 1996 she helped launch Lucent Technologies. She has spent more than 20 years of her career managing some of Lucent's and AT&T's largest divisions and most critical corporate functions. She was appointed chief executive officer in January 2002

Ms. Russo serves as chairman and chief executive officer of Lucent Technologies. She was appointed by President George W. Bush as vice chair of the National Security Telecommunications Advisory Committee, a position she held from April 2003 to May 2006. She currently is a member of the Network Reliability Interoperability Council.

Mary Jean Ryan

GOVERNMENT OFFICIAL. Mary Jean Ryan is a Bachelor of Arts from Georgetown University and a Master of public administration from the University of Southern California. She is a 1988 graduate of the Seattle Chamber/United Way Leadership Tomorrow program.

Her professional career includes serving from 1986 to 1992 as the director of the Evergreen Community Development Association and serving in Washington, D.C., in the Clinton administration as the associate deputy administrator for economic development for the U.S. Small Business Administration. In 1992, Mayor Norm Rice hired her to create Seattle's Economic Development Office; she serves on the Board of the Seattle Jobs Initiative and on the Seattle School District's Community Advisory Committee for Investing in Educational Excellence.

Ms. Ryan was appointed to the Washington State Board of Education in January 2006. She also serves as director of the city of Seattle's Office of Policy and Management.

Miriam P. Rykken

JUDGE. Miriam P. Rykken graduated from Concordia College at Moorhead, Minnesota, in 1976 and earned her Juris Doctor degree from the University of Minnesota Law School in 1987.

She served in private law practice for twelve years before her appointment to the Minnesota Workers' Compensation Court of Appeals in June 1999.

Mary Ann Saar

GOVERNMENT OFFICIAL. Mary Ann Saar received a bachelor's degree in criminology/sociology and earned a Juris Doctor from the University of Maryland. She is also a graduate of the IBM's Executive Management Training Program and Harvard University's Program for Senior Executives in State and Local Government.

Her professional career includes serving in law enforcement, corrections, and legal experience to her role as secretary. Her service includes serving as a probation officer and adoption custody investigator in Baltimore City; as associate commissioner of juvenile services for the Maine Department of Corrections; as Baltimore City deputy state's attorney; from 1991 to 1995, she served as secretary of the Maryland Department of Juvenile Services; as state director for the office of Senator Barbara Mikulski.

Ms. Saar was appointed secretary of the Department of Public Safety and Correctional Services for the state of Maryland in January 2003.

Shirley Strickland Safford

JUDGE. Shirley Strickland Safford graduated from Montclair High School in New Jersey. She received a Bachelor of Arts degree from Central State University and earned her Juris Doctor degree from Cleveland-Marshall College of Law. After she was admitted to the Ohio State Bar, she engaged in the practice of law with the Legal Aid Society of Cleveland Defender's office. In 1987, she was elected judge to the Cleveland Municipal Court. In 1994, she was elevated to judge to the Cuyahoga County Common Pleas Court.

Dail St. Claire

FINANCE. Dail St. Claire received a Bachelor of Arts degree from the University of California, San Diego, and a Master of Arts degree in public policy from the University of Chicago.

Her professional career includes serving as senior investment officer for the New York City comptroller's office for four years; as principal, Utendahl Capital Management, L.P., for seven years; as first vice president for Amalgamated Bank where she launched its settlement fund/cash management business.

Ms. St. Claire was appointed president and co-portfolio manager of the Williams Capital Liquid Assets Fund and managing director of Williams Capital Management, LLC.

Lucille S. (Lucie) Salhany

ENTERTAINMENT EXECUTIVE. Lucille S. (Lucie) Salhany began her television career as program director at WKBF-TV in Cleveland in 1967. She has also served as program manager for WLVI-TV in Boston in 1975; as vice president of television and cable programming at Taft Broadcasting Co. from 1979 to 1985; as president at Paramount Domestic Television, Paramount Pictures, from 1985 to 1991; and as chair, Twentieth Television (a division of FOX Broadcasting Company), 1991.

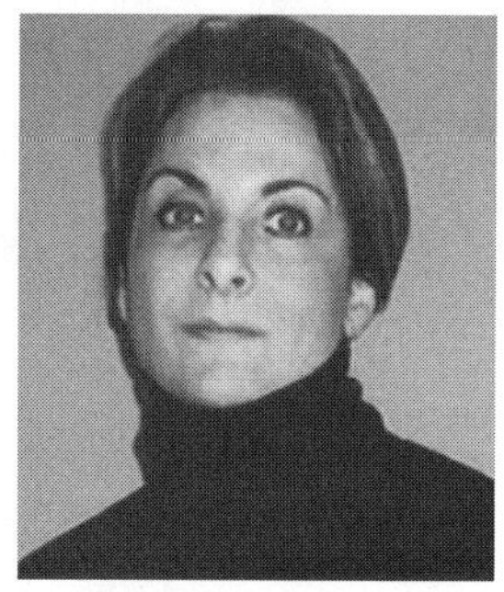

Ms. Salhany became the first woman to manage an American broadcast television network when she was appointed as chair, FOX Broadcasting Company in January 1993. She was named president and chief executive officer at United Paramount Network in 1994. In the history of American television broadcasting there had been no previous female who had shattered the "glass ceiling" barrier to the senior executive suite.

Angela Salinas

MILITARY. Angela Salinas is the first Hispanic woman to be selected for promotion to the rank of brigadier general in the United States Marine Corps. She received a Bachelor of Arts degree in history from Dominican College of San Rafael, California. She earned a master's degree from the Naval War College. She is a graduate of the Amphibious Warfare School, the Naval War College's Command and Staff College and the United States Army War College.

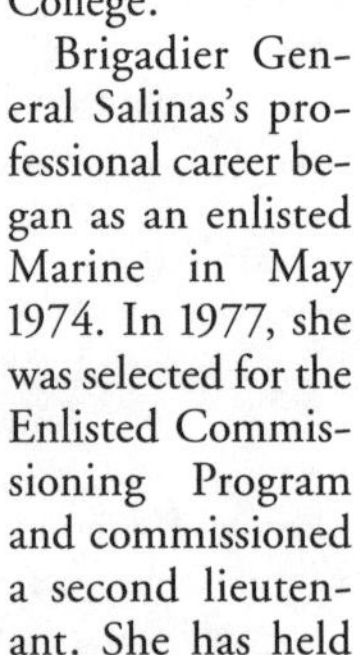

Brigadier General Salinas's professional career began as an enlisted Marine in May 1974. In 1977, she was selected for the Enlisted Commissioning Program and commissioned a second lieutenant. She has held numerous positions of increasing authority to include in 1986 assuming command of Headquarters and Service Company, 1st Maintenance Battalion. In 1988, she was transferred to serve as the executive officer, Recruiting Station Charleston, West Virginia. In 1989, she assumed command of the recruiting station. In 1992, she served as a combat service support ground monitor, Manpower Management and Officer Assignments, Navy Annex, Washington, D.C. In 1993, she became deputy special assistant for general/flag officer matters, Office of the Director, Joint Staff, at the Pentagon. In 1996, she assumed command of the 4th Recruit Training Battalion, Parris Island. In 1999, she served as the assistant chief of staff, G-5, for III Marine Expeditionary Force, Okinawa, Japan. In 2001, Colonel Salinas assumed command of the 12th Marine Corps District. In 2004, she was selected to serve as chief of staff, Marine Corps Recruiting Command, Quantico, Virginia.

Jeneene Sams

AEROSPACE. Jeneene Sams is a native of Birmingham, Alabama, and a graduate of John Carroll Catholic High School in Birmingham. She received a bachelor's degree in mathematics and a minor in computer science from the University of Alabama at Birmingham and earned a master's degree in management from the Florida Institute of Technology, attending classes at its Huntsville campus.

She joined the NASA Marshall Center in 1986 as a materials engineer in the Materials Processes and Manufacturing Department. She helped develop a materials and processes database. Today, this database is still used by NASA materials engineers who design spacecraft and even by engineers who design other Earth-based products. In 1994, NASA selected her to participate in the Program Control Development Program. She now serves as a market segment manager within NASA's Space Product Development Program.

Linda T. Sanchez

ELECTED OFFICIAL. Linda T. Sanchez is a native of Orange County, California. She received a Bachelor of Arts degree from the University of California at Berkeley, California, and earned her Juris Doctor from the University of California at Los Angeles, California, in 1995.

She was engaged in private law practice. In 2002, she was elected as a Democrat to the 108th and to the succeeding Congress serving from January 3, 2003, to the present.

Loretta Sanchez

ELECTED OFFICIAL. Loretta Sanchez is a native of Lynwood, California, and a graduate of Katella High School in Anaheim, California. She received a Bachelor of Arts degree from Chapman University in Orange, California, in 1982 and earned her Masters of Business Administration from American University in Washington, D.C., in 1984.

Her professional career includes serving as a financial analyst from 1984 to 1996. She was elected a United States Representative to the 105th Congress and to the four succeeding Congresses since January 3, 1997.

Annette M. Sandberg

GOVERNMENT OFFICIAL. Annette M. Sandberg received a Master of Business Administration (magna cum laude) from City University in Bellevue, Washington, and earned her Juris Doctor from the University of Puget Sound School of Law in 1993. In 1996, she was selected to attend an executive institute at Harvard University's John F. Kennedy School of Government. She was also chosen to attend the FBI's National Executive Institute in 1998.

She was engaged in private law practice and as chief of the Washington State Patrol for six years. She was the first woman in the country to lead a state police agency. She served 17 years in a variety of law enforcement, supervisory and administrative posts with the Washington State Patrol prior to her appointment. In November 2002, she was appointed deputy administrator of the Federal Motor Carrier Safety Administration and served as acting administrator. On August 1, 2003, following her confirmation by the United States Senate, she was appointed administrator of the Federal Motor Carrier Safety Administration.

Robin Renee Sanders

GOVERNMENT OFFICIAL. Robin Renee Sanders was born on Langley Air Force Base in Hampton, Virginia. She received a Bachelor of Arts in communications from Hampton University. She earned a Master of Science degree in communications and journalism from Ohio University and a Master of Arts degree in international relations and Africa studies.

Ms. Sanders has worked as a political affairs officer abroad for the Department of State for 13 years, most notably serving in Senegal, Namibia, Sudan, Portugal and the Dominican Republic. She has also been assigned to special missions to Angola and the Democratic Republic of the Congo. She has served twice as the director for Africa at the National Security Council at the White House (under former Presidents Bush 1988–1989, and Clinton 1997–1999), as the special assistant for Latin America, Africa and international crime for the undersecretary for political affairs at the Department of State in Washington, D.C., and as chief of staff and senior foreign policy for members of the House International Relations Committee. She served as director for public diplomacy for Africa for the State Department. She was appointed ambassador, Republic of the Congo on December 9, 2002.

Linda S. Sanford

TECHNOLOGY EXECUTIVE. Linda S. Sanford received a Bachelor of Science degree from St. John's University and earned her Master of Science in operations research from Rensselaer Institute. Her professional career includes heading IBM Global Industries, the organization that manages relationships with IBM's largest customers worldwide and is responsible for generation almost 70 percent of IBM's revenue. She served as senior vice president and group executive, IBM Storage Systems Group where she helped take IBM from fifth place in storage market share to second in two years.

Ms. Sanford was named senior vice president, enterprise on demand transformation & information technology. She leads the strategy for IBM's internal transformation to the industry's premier on demand business. In this role, she is responsible for working across IBM to transform core business processes and to create an IT infrastructure to support those processes.

Gloria Santona

BUSINESS EXECUTIVE. Gloria Santona received a Bachelor of Science degree from Michigan State University in 1971 and a Juris Doctor cum laude from the University of Michigan Law School.

Her professional career includes joining

the McDonald's Corporation legal department in 1971. Since then she has held positions of increasing responsibility in the company's legal department, serving as corporate general counsel since 2001.

Paulette Sapp-Peterson

JUDGE. Paulette Sapp-Peterson received a Bachelor of Arts degree from Douglass College and earned her Juris Doctor from Rutgers School of Law in Camden, New Jersey. She began her professional career as a deputy attorney general and then served as a special assistant to the adjutant general for the New Jersey Department of Military and Veterans' Affairs. In 1980, she joined the New Jersey Air National Guard where she served as a staff judge advocate for the 170th Air Refueling Group and later the 108th Air Refueling Wing until her retirement in 1994.

She served as a municipal court judge in 1981 and served in that capacity until her appointment to Superior Court by Governor Thomas H. Kean in 1989. She has served in the family, criminal, and civil divisions of Superior Court in the Mercer Vicinage. In 2001, she was appointed presiding judge of the civil division. She served a temporary assignment to the appellate division in the fall of 2005.

Patti B. Saris

JUDGE. Patti B. Saris is a native of Boston, Massachusetts. She received a Bachelor of Arts degree from Radcliffe College in 1973 and earned her Juris Doctor degree from Harvard Law School in 1976.

Her professional career includes serving as a law clerk at the Supreme Judicial Court of Massachusetts from 1976 to 1977; she was engaged in private law practice 1977 to 1979; she served as a staff counsel to the United States Judiciary Committee from 1979 to 1981; as an assistant U.S. Attorney in the District of Massachusetts from 1982 to 1986; as chief, civil division, U.S. Attorney's office in Massachusetts, 1984 to 1986; as an associate justice, Trial Court of Massachusetts, Superior Court Department from 1989 to 1993. On October 27, 1993, she was nominated by President William J. Clinton to be a judge to the United States District Court in the District of Massachusetts. She was confirmed by the United States Senate on November 20, 1993, and received her commission on November 24, 1993.

Ellen R. Sauerbrey

GOVERNMENT OFFICIAL. Ellen R. Sauerbrey is a native of Baltimore, Maryland, and graduated from Towson Senior High School. She received a bachelor's degree (summa cum laude) from Western Maryland College. She is a Republican National committeewoman, former minority leader of the Maryland House of Delegates, and former Republican nominee for governor. She represented her northern Baltimore County district in the House of Delegates from 1978 to 1994. In 1994 and 1998, she was the Republican nominee for governor. She was the first recipient of the prestigious National Federation of Republican Women's Margaret Chase Smith Award.

President George Bush appointed her to represent the United States at the March-April 2001 session of the United Nation Commission of Human Rights and to the U.S. Delegations 2002 and 2003 Substantive Sessions of the Economic and Social Council and the United Nations General Assembly. On January 1, 2006, she began service as the assistant secretary, Bureau of Population, Refugees and Migration.

Mary L. Saunders

MILITARY. Mary L. Saunders is a native of Nacogdoches, Texas, and grew up in Houston. She began her military career through the Officer Training School at Lackland Air Force Base, Texas. Her education includes receiving a Bachelor of Science degree in social work in 1970 from Texas Woman's University, Denton; and she earned her Master of Arts degree in guidance and counseling in 1978 from Rider College, Lawrenceville, New Jersey. Her military education includes Squadron Officer School (1973), Maxwell Air Force Base, Ala-

bama; in 1993 she graduated from the Air War College at Maxwell Air Force Base and in 1997 she completed the National Security Leadership Course, Johns Hopkins University, Baltimore, Maryland.

She was commissioned a second lieutenant and entered active duty in 1971. She has held various assignments in transportation and logistics plans in the squadron, wing, numbered air force, headquarters and joint arenas. In August 1971, she was assigned as protocol officer, 437th Aerial Port Squadron, Charleston Air Force Base in South Carolina. From November 1971 to February 1973, she was assigned as traffic duty officer, 610th Military Airlift Support Squadron, Yokota Air Base in Japan. From November 1973 to July 1975, she was assigned as air terminal operations officer, then in July 1975, she was assigned as assistant airfreight officer with the 610th Military Airlift Support Squadron, Yokota Air Base, Japan. In January 1976, she returned to the United States to serve as deputy commander and later commander, Military Air Traffic Coordinating Office, Military Traffic Management Command, McGuire Air Force Base, New Jersey. From July 1979 to April 1982, transportation staff officer, Headquarters 10th Air Force, Bergstrom Air Force Base, Texas; in April 1982, chief of transportation, 6168th Combat Support Squadron, Teagu Air Base, South Korea; from May 1983 to November 1984, as deputy director for transportation, 5th Air Force, Yokota Air Base, Japan, and promoted to major on March 1, 1983.

In November 1984, she was selected commander, 475th Transportation Squadron, Yokota Air Base, Japan; in July 1986, transportation staff officer, Joint Deployment Agency, MacDill Air Force Base, Florida; she was promoted to lieutenant colonel October 1, 1987; from September 1988 to October 1990, transportation staff officer, J5, United States Transportation Command, Scott Air Force Base, Illinois; from October 1990 to August 1992, she served as chief, Contingency Plans Division, J5, United States Southern Command, Quarry Heights, Panama; she was promoted to colonel November 1, 1992.

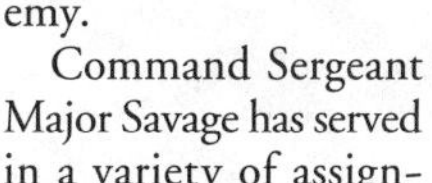

From July 1993 to August 1996, she was assigned as chief for logistics plans at Headquarters Air Force Reserve, Robins Air Force Base, in Georgia. In August 1996, she was selected as the director of transportation, office of the deputy chief of staff, Installations and Logistics, Headquarters United States Air Force, in Washington, D.C. Mary L. Saunders was promoted to brigadier general on August 1, 1997, making her the only black female general on active duty in the Air Force at that time. As director of transportation, she is responsible for developing policies, plans and programs to move passengers, personal property and cargo, by all modes, commercial and military. The guidance she provides pertains to approximately 32,000 active-duty and Reserve personnel, their training and the entire 115,000-vehicle fleet valued at $3.8 billion. She supports overall readiness through coordination with other services, the Joint Staff, the Department of Defense, and other government agencies.

From August 1998 to September 2001, she served as the commander of the Defense Supply Center Columbus, at the Defense Logistics Agency in Columbus, Ohio. She was promoted to major general on May 24, 2001. In September 2001, she was selected as director of supply in the office of deputy chief of staff for installations and logistics, at Headquarters United States Air Force in Washington, D.C. In late 2002, she was selected to serve as the vice director for the Defense Logistics Agency at Fort Belvoir, Virginia.

Janice R. Savage

MILITARY. Janice R. Savage is a native of New Orleans. She is a graduate from Xavier University Preparatory High School in New Orleans in 1982 and received a Bachelor of Science degree in accounting from Southern University in New Orleans in May 1988. Her military education includes the First Sergeants Course and the United States Army Sergeants Major Academy.

Command Sergeant Major Savage has served in a variety of assignments to include serving as the command sergeant major of the 377th Theater Support Command Special Troops Battalion in New Orleans, a position she has held since May 2006.

Diane Sawyer

JOURNALISM. Diane Sawyer is a native of Glasgow, Kentucky, and was raised in Louisville, Kentucky. She received a Bachelor of Arts degree from Wellesley College in 1967 and completed a semester of law school before deciding on a career in broadcasting.

Her professional career began in broadcasting in 1967 in Louisville, Kentucky, where she was a reporter for WLKY-TV until 1970; prior to joining CBS News, she held several positions in the Nixon administration. She was part of the Nixon-Ford transition team from 1974 to 1975. She also assisted former President Nixon in the writing of his memoirs in 1974 and 1975. She was a floor correspondent for the 1980 Democratic Conven-

tion, for the 1984 Republican and Democratic National Conventions, and was podium correspondent for the 1988 Democratic and Republican National Convention; prior to joining ABC News, she spent nine years at CBS News; she was a co-anchor for *60 Minutes*, co-anchored the *CBS Morning News* and was CBS News' State Department correspondent; she joined ABC News in February 1989 as co-anchor of *Prime Time Live* and was also one of the anchors of ABC News' *Turning Point* which premiered in March 1994; she joined ABC News' *Good Morning America* as co-anchor in February 1998 and *20/20*'s co-anchor in September 1998.

Velma Scantlebury

MEDICINE. Velma Scantlebury received a bachelor's degree in biology from Long Island University's Brooklyn Campus, in New York. She earned her Doctor of Medicine from Columbia University College of Physician and Surgeons followed by the completion of both an internship and residency in general surgery at Harlem Hospital Center in New York City.

Dr. Scantlebury began her work at the University of Pittsburgh in 1986 as a clinical fellow in transplant surgery under the direction of liver transplant pioneer Thomas E. Starzl, M.D., Ph.D. She served as an assistant professor in 1989 and then as an associate professor at the University of Pittsburgh. In 2002, Dr. Scantlebury was appointed professor of surgery and director of the University of South Alabama's Gulf Coast Regional Transplant Center. She is a transplant surgeon, professor of surgery, assistant dean for community education, director of the division of transplantation, and director of the University of South Alabama Regional Transplant Center. Dr. Scantlebury is the first African-American female transplant surgeon, and the only African-American woman transplant surgeon in the United States.

Lynn Scarlett

GOVERNMENT OFFICIAL. Lynn Scarlett received a bachelor's degree and master's degree from the University of California at Santa Barbara.

Her professional career includes serving in a variety of positions, the most recent being president of the Reason Foundation. She served as assistant secretary of the U. S. Department of Interior for Policy, Management & Budget. Ms. Scarlett also served as deputy secretary of the U. S. Department of the Interior.

Yvonne Scarlett-Golden

ELECTED OFFICIAL. Yvonne Scarlett-Golden is a native of Daytona Beach, Florida, and a graduate of Campbell Senior High School. She received a bachelor's degree with honors from Bethune-Cookman College. She has attended Boston University for graduate work and received an honorary law degree from Bethune Cookman-College.

Her professional career includes serving more than 38 years as an educator in the Florida School System and in the San Francisco Unified School District. She taught elementary, middle, high school, and junior and senior college levels. She served as counselor and as principal of Alamo Park High School. She was elected mayor of Daytona Beach, Florida.

Saliann Scarpulla

JUDGE. Saliann Scarpulla received her undergraduate degree from Boston University and earned her Juris Doctor degree from Brooklyn Law School. Her professional career includes serving as a court attorney to Justice Alvin F. Klein, Supreme Court, New York; in private law practice; as court attorney for Justice Eileen Bransten, Supreme Court of New York. She was elected judge, New York City Civil Court for New York County.

Diane Schafer

JUDGE. Diane Schafer was born in Dillon, South Carolina. She holds a bachelors' degree from the University of North Carolina at Chapel Hill. She went on to obtain her Juris Doctorate degree from the University of North Carolina School of Law in 1981.

She served as the county attorney for Dorchester County from 1986 to 1988. She was elected by the South Carolina General Assembly to the position of resident circuit judge for the First Judicial Circuit in May 1998. She has since been appointed to the Circuit Court Judges Advisory Committee and is a member of the Commission on Judicial Conduct.

Janice D. Schakowsky

ELECTED OFFICIAL. Janice D. Schakowsky is a native of Chicago, Illinois, and graduate of Sullivan High School in Chicago, Illinois. She received a Bachelor of Science degree from the University of Illinois in 1965.

Her professional career includes serving as director of the Illinois State Council of Senior Citizens from 1985 to 1990; she served as a member of the Illinois State General Assembly from 1990 to 1998; she was elected as a United States Representative to the 106th and to the three succeeding Congresses since January 3, 1999.

Jean Schmidt

ELECTED OFFICIAL. Jean Schmidt is a native of Ohio. She received two Bachelor of Arts degrees; one in political science in 1974 and a second in secondary education for social studies in 1986 from the University of Cincinnati in Cincinnati, Ohio.

Her professional career includes working in her father's bank, the Midwestern Savings Association, as a branch manager from 1971 to 1978. She served as a fitness instructor from 1984 to 1986 and then served as a schoolteacher for four years. She was elected as a Miami Township trustee in 1989. She was elected to the Ohio State House of Representatives (2000–2004). In 2004, she was elected a United States Senator from Ohio as a Republican to the 109th Congress by special election to fill a vacancy. She was re-elected to the succeeding Congress (August 2, 2005).

Alison Scholly

BUSINESS EXECUTIVE. Alison Scholly is a native of Chicago, Illinois. She received a bachelor's degree in anthropology and communications from Vanderbilt University and a master's degree in journalism from Medill School at Northwestern University.

She joined the Tribune Company in 1994 to work on eWorld, an online service for Macintosh users. She joined the *Chicago Tribune* in 1998, serving as editor of Metromix and executive producer of Chicago Tribune Interactive. She also served as editor of Digital City Chicago, as well as one of the principal programming liaisons to this America Online and Tribune Company joint venture. On January 26, 2007, *Chicago Tribune* named Ms. Scholly vice president of the company.

Katharine Jefferts Schori

MINISTRY (FIRST). Katharine Jefferts Schori is a native of Pensacola, Florida. She received a Bachelor of Science in biology from Stanford University and a Master of Science in oceanography from Oregon State University. She earned a Ph.D. from Oregon State University and a Master of Divinity from Church Divinity

School of the Pacific. She also earned a Doctor of Divinity from Church Divinity School of the Pacific.

She is the author of numerous books including *When Conflict and Hope Abound*, and *Building Bridges/Widening Circles*. She is an active, instrument-rated pilot with more than 500 hours logged. She served as a visiting assistant professor at Oregon State University's Department of Oceanography and as an oceanographer with the National Marine Fisheries service in Seattle. She was ordained deacon and priest in 1994, and served as assistant rector at the Episcopal Church of the School of Theology, and priest-in-charge, El Buen Samaritano, Corvallis. She was consecrated the ninth bishop of Nevada on February 24, 2001. She serves a diocese of some 6,000 members in 35 congregations. Bishop Jefferts is the first woman selected as a nominee for presiding bishop.

Mary B. Schroeder

JUDGE. Mary B. Schroeder received a Bachelor of Arts degree in history from St. Louis University. She earned her Juris Doctor from St. Mary's University in San Antonio, Texas.

Her professional career includes serving as a circuit attorney for the city of St. Louis from 1980 to 1982. She was engaged in private law practice from 1983 until 1999. On May 11, 1999, she was appointed associate circuit judge in St. Louis County, Missouri.

Debbie Wasserman Schultz

ELECTED OFFICIAL. Debbie Wasserman Schultz is a native of Queens County, New York. She received a Bachelor of Arts degree from the University of Florida in Gainesville, Florida, in 1988 and earned a Master of Arts degree from the University of Florida in 1990.

Her professional career includes serving as an aide to United States Representative Peter Deutsch from 1989 to 1992; as a member of the Florida State House of Representatives from 1992 to 2000; as a Florida State Senator from 2000 to 2004; since January 3, 2005, she has served as United States Representative to the 109th Congress.

Deborah Schumacher

JUDGE. Deborah Schumacher received a Bachelor of Arts degree with honors (College Scholar) from Valparaiso University in 1977, and received a Master of Arts degree in United States history from the University of Chicago in 1978. She earned her Juris Doctor degree from the University of Notre Dame in 1983.

She was engaged in private law practice from 1983 to 1997. She served as a part-time court master, Family Division at the Second Judicial District Court from 1992 to 1997. In 1997, she was appointed judge, District Court, Department 5, Second Judicial District Court for the State of Nevada, Washoe County.

Allyson Y. Schwartz

ELECTED OFFICIAL. Allyson Y. Schwartz is a native of Queens, New York, and graduated from the Calhoun School, New York. She received a Bachelor of Arts degree from Simmons College in Boston, Massachusetts, in 1970 and earned a master's degree in social work from Bryn Mawr College, Bryn Mawr, Pennsylvania, in 1972.

Her professional career includes serving as a health care administrator and as a member of the Pennsylvania State Senate from 1991 to 2004.

Ms. Schwartz was elected in 2004 as a Democrat to the 109th Congress (January 3, 2005, to present).

Karen Sclafani

BUSINESS EXECUTIVE. Karen Sclafani received a Bachelor of Arts degree from LeMoyne College in Syracuse, New York, and earned her Juris Doctor degree

from New York University School of Law.

Her professional career includes serving in private law practice in New York. She was appointed general counsel of Avis Rent a Car in 1998 after serving eight years as deputy general counsel and nine years in various capacities within Avis' legal department. She was appointed executive vice president and general counsel for Avis Budget Group, the parent company of Avis Rent a Car, Budget Rent a Car and Budget Truck Rental. She is responsible for the general legal affairs of the company and oversees all contracts, acquisitions, litigation and governmental affairs.

Beverly Scott

GOVERNMENT OFFICIAL. Beverly Scott received a Bachelor of Arts degree in political science magna cum laude from Fisk University and earned a doctorate in political science with specialization in public administration from Howard University.

Dr. Scott began her public transportation career in 1977 in the State of Texas Southern University, as one of four national recipients of a Carnegie Foundation fellowship. In 1979, with the creation of the Houston Metropolitan Transit Authority, she was the regional transit authority's first director of affirmative action. In addition to her professional transportation positions, she has served as assistant professor of government and public affairs at Tennessee State University and also taught graduate courses at Howard University (Washington, D.C.). She served as assistance executive director, administration, at New Jersey Transit Corporation (10,000 employees; fourth largest transit system in the United States); as the executive director, National Forum for Black Public Administrators, a nonprofit association of more than 3,000 members; as deputy general manager for administration of the Washington Metropolitan Area Transit Authority (WMATA); and in October 2002, she was selected to serve as the general manager and chief executive officer for the Sacramento Regional Transit District.

In August 2007, she was named general manager of Metropolitan Atlanta Rapid Transit Authority (MARTA).

N. H. Scott

GOVERNMENT OFFICIAL. N. H. Scott received a Bachelor of Arts degree in sociology from Longwood University in 1972. She was the first black graduate of Longwood University. She has nearly 30 years of experience in corrections.

She began her corrections career in 1973 as a probation officer in the Sixteenth District Juvenile and Domestic Relations Court in Charlottesville. She rose to become the director of court services for the Sixteenth District before being promoted to employment manager senior in 1988 and coming to Department of Corrections Headquarters in Richmond, Virginia. She now serves as the deputy director of administration. She assumed the position on November 10, 2002.

Susan Scott

BUSINESS EXECUTIVE. Susan Scott received a bachelor's degree in education from the University of North Carolina at Chapel Hill.

Her professional career includes serving as a sales executive at Summit Cable Services; as director of business development for Turner Entertainment Networks International where she managed strategic planning across networks, licensing and merchandising, home video and publishing, launched TNT and Cartoon Network in Europe, developed and launched TNT and Cartoon Network Asia; as vice president of business development at Fox News; as vice president of sales at FeedRoom.com; as senior vice president of distribution for the pay-per-view movie service, IN DEMAND LLC, in New York; as senior vice president of distribution for the Weather Channel; she has served as past chair and national chair of Women in Cable & Telecommunications. Ms. Scott serves as a partner in CarterBaldwin.

Alice Seagren

GOVERNMENT OFFICIAL. Alice Seagren received a Bachelor of Science degree in business from Southeast Missouri State University. She was elected to the Minnesota House of Representatives in 1992. She served six terms in the House before Governor Tim Pawlenty appointed her Commissioner of the Minnesota Department of Education in July 2004.

Leah Ward Sears

JUDGE. Leah Ward Sears was born in Heidelberg, Federal Republic of Germany, where her father was serving in the U.S. Military. She is a 1976 graduate of Cornell University, receiving a Bachelor of Arts degree; a 1980 graduate of Emory University School of Law earning her Juris Doctor degree; and a 1995 graduate of the University of Virginia School of Law (LL.M degree).

Her experience includes serving as judge in the Atlanta city courts; she was the first African-American woman to serve as superior court judge in Georgia. When appointed by the governor of Georgia in February 1992, she was the first woman and the youngest person ever to serve on Georgia's Supreme Court. She is the first woman to win a contested state-wide election in Georgia, winning re-election to the Supreme Court.

She is the first woman to serve as chief justice of the Georgia Supreme Court.

Kathleen Sebelius

ELECTED OFFICIAL. Kathleen Sebelius is a native of Cincinnati, Ohio. She received her Bachelor of Arts degree from Trinity College in 1970 and a MPA degree from the University of Kansas in 1977. She served four terms in the Kansas House of Representatives and two terms as the state's insurance commissioner.

Governor Sebelius is the first daughter of a governor (John Gilligan, Ohio, 1971–75) in U.S. history to be elected to that same position. She was sworn in as the 44th governor of Kansas in January 2003.

Cathy H. Serrette

JUDGE. Cathy H. Serrette received a Bachelor of Science (summa cum laude) from the University of Pittsburgh in 1975 and received a Masters' of Law from American University in 1991. She earned her Juris Doctor degree from George Washington University in 1980.

Her professional career includes serving in private law practice from 1981 to 1984; as a legislative assistant at the United States House of Representatives, Washington, D.C., 1985–1986; in 1986 she returned to private law practice. In 2003, she was appointed associate judge, Maryland 7th Judicial Circuit, Prince George County.

Mary Pat Seurkamp

EDUCATION. Mary Pat Seurkamp received a Bachelor of Arts degree in psychology from Webster University in 1968; a Master's of Art from Washington University in 1969; and earned her Ph.D. in higher education from the State University of New York at Buffalo in 1990.

Her career includes serving at St. John Fisher College in Rochester, New York, for 21 years. During that time, she held the positions of vice president for institutional planning and research, vice president for academic services and planning and vice president for academic affairs.

In July 1987, Dr. Seurkamp was named the first permanent lay president of College of Notre Dame of Maryland.

Donna E. Shalala

EDUCATION. Donna E. Shalala is a native of Cleveland, Ohio. She received a Bachelor of Arts degree in history from Western College for Women and earned her Ph.D. degree from the Maxwell School of Citizenship and Public Affairs at Syracuse University.

From 1962 to 1964, she served as a volunteer for the U.S. Peace Corps in Iran. She was an associate professor and director of the program in politics and education at Teachers College, Columbia University, from 1972 to 1979. She served as director and treasurer of the Municipal Assistance Corporation for the city of New York. She also served as president of Hunter College of the City University of New York (1980 to 1987); and chancellor of the University of Wisconsin–Madison (1987–1993). President Bill Clinton appointed her to serve as secretary of Health and Human Services in 1993 where she served until 2001. She is currently serving as president of the University of Miami in Florida.

Mary Joe Shanks

MILITARY. Mary Joe Shanks enlisted in the United States Army as a private first class in 1977. In 1980, she was commissioned through the Officer Candidate School Program as a second lieutenant in the Ordnance Corps and joined the 124th Maintenance Battalion, 2nd Armored Division at Fort Hood, Texas.

She holds a Bachelor of Science degree in business administration and masters degrees in both education and public administration.

Her assignments include: serving as commander, 201st Materiel Management Cent, Livorno, Italy; executive officer, 16th Ordnance Battalion, 61st Ordnance Brigade, Aberdeen Proving Ground, Maryland; special assistance to the secretary for defense for reform, OSD; and in 2003, headquarters commandant, United States European Command, Patch Barracks, Germany.

Judith R. Shapiro

EDUCATION. Judith Shapiro received a bachelor's degree magna cum laude from Brandeis University and earned a Ph.D. in anthropology from Columbia University.

Her professional career includes serving at Bryn Mawr College where she was chair of the Department of Anthropology and served as provost and the chief academic officer for eight years beginning in 1986. In 1994, she was selected to serve as the 10th president of Barnard College.

Rajamalliga N. Sharma

MEDICINE. Rajamalliga N. Sharma is a native of Wilmington, North Carolina, and completed high school in Auburn, North Carolina. She received a bachelor's degree in music performance with honors from Davidson College in North Carolina. She earned her Medical Doctor degree from the University of Alabama and completed her residency training in obstetrics and gynecology at Parkland Memorial Hospital in Dallas, Texas.

Her professional career includes serving in several state and national positions in organized medicine and speaking at national meetings on the impact of managed care on residence training. She was the only resident physician on a standing national committee that approved residency training guidelines. It was during her service on this Graduate Medical Education Advisory Committee that she first became interested in resolving physician labor disputes.

Dr. Sharma returned to her hometown and served in private medical practice. She earned a master's degree in conflict resolution from Columbia College in South Carolina. She has worked for hospitals in training and mediation and has published several articles on dispute resolution in medicine.

Lisa Webb Sharpe

GOVERNMENT OFFICIAL. Lisa Webb Sharpe was born the third of four children in Seville, Spain, where her father was serving in the U.S. military. She was raised in Detroit, Michigan, and reared in an environment that fostered public service, integrity, and performance.

She holds a bachelor of business administration degree in personnel and industrial relations from Eastern Michigan University and a Master of Business Administration degree in international business from Wayne State University.

Her experience includes serving as the director of housing services for the Traverse Group, an environmental engineering firm. She served as the governor's cabinet secretary and policy director, working closely with all 19 state departments on operational and policy issues.

Governor Jennifer M. Ganholm appointed Lisa Webb Sharpe to serve as director of the Department of Management and Budget, a department of 850 employees, beginning August 1, 2005.

Cheryl Shavers

BUSINESS EXECUTIVE. Cheryl Shavers received a Bachelor of Science degree in chemistry in 1976 and earned a doctorate in 1981 in solid-state chemistry from Arizona State University. She holds an honorary master's degree in business management from California Polytechnic State University in 1997.

Her professional career includes serving as a product engineer at Motorola; a process development engineer and patent agent at Hewlett-Packard; as a senior manager of corporate business development for Intel Corporation; as under secretary for technology at the U.S. Department of Commerce.

Dr. Shavers serves as chairman and chief executive officer of Global Smarts in Santa Clara, California, a company she founded in June 2001.

Nina Shaw

LAW. Nina Shaw received a bachelor's degree from Barnard College and earned her Juris Doctor degree from Columbia Law School in 1979.

Her professional career includes being engaged in private law practice. She is a founding partner in the entertainment law firm of Del, Shaw, Moonves, Tanaka, Finkelstein & Lezcano. Her practice is in the television, motion picture and live stage area.

Carol Shea-Porter

ELECTED OFFICIAL. Carol Shea-Porter is a native of New York City. She graduated from Oyster River High School in Durham, New Hampshire. She received a Bachelor of Arts degree and a master of public administration from the University of New Hampshire, Durham.

Ms. Shea-Porter worked as a social worker and professor. She was elected a United States Representative as a Democrat to the 110th Congress.

Barbara L. Shelton

GOVERNMENT OFFICIAL. Barbara L. Shelton received a Bachelor of Science degree in industrial engineering from the University of Pittsburgh and earned a Master of Business Administration from Columbia University.

She gained thirteen years of private industry experience in her field of information technology with PPG Industries in Pittsburgh and with Philip Morris, Inc. in Richmond, Virginia, and New York City. She served as deputy secretary for administration in Pennsylvania's Department of Labor and Industry from January 2000 through December 2001; she has served as deputy secretary for procurement in the state's Department of General Services from March 1996 through December 1999. On February 11, 2005, she was appointed acting commissioner for the Federal Technology Service at the General Services Administration.

Diane Sherman

EDUCATION. Diane Sherman, Ph.D., NCAC-II, is an organizational consultant and national trainer. Her doctorate degree is in the specialization of industrial/organizational psychology. She has worked in the social services profession since 1975. Her firm specializes in three areas: executive coaching, organizational consulting and continuing education.

Dr. Sherman's career started in the United States Army where she proudly served her country for 15 years as a behavioral science specialist. She entered the private sector in 1991 and she founded ACTS Consulting International, Inc. Since 1991, she has consulted with hundreds of companies — private and non-profit — throughout the United States and internationally in Germany and Panama. Her newest venture is in Costa Rica where she provides consultation, coaching, and training at Villas Congas, a luxury vacation retreat.

ACTS Consulting covers a spectrum of services including: national (CARF) accreditation — preparation, readiness, and maintenance; local contact monitoring; state and federal regulatory compliance; organizational management strategies: analysis, development, and strategic planning. It is Diane's goal to design programs firmly established upon evidence based research and implement strategies and interventions that will improve performance and enhance optimal organizational competence.

She has trained at national conferences including NAADAC — The Association of Addiction Professionals, National Association of Drug Court Professionals, and CARF. Regional and state-sponsored events include Southeast School of Addiction Studies, South Carolina Behavioral Health Services Association, Tennessee Advanced School on Addiction, Georgia Department of Human Resources, Georgia Council on Substance Abuse, and Georgia Addiction Counselors Association, and Georgia Department of Juvenile Justice.

Dr. Sherman teaches online through Brown University in affiliation with the Northeast Addiction Transfer and Technology Center, the Institute for Addiction and Criminal Justice Studies.

Susan Sheskey

TECHNOLOGY EXECUTIVE. Susan Sheskey received a bachelor's degree from Miami University in Oxford, Ohio.

Her professional career includes serving 20 years with Ameritech's corporate and services functions and at Ohio Bell. She joined Dell in 1993. She served as Dell's vice president of information technology for the Americas region.

Ms. Sheskey was appointed vice president and chief information officer for Dell in August 2005. Her responsibilities span Dell's global information systems and technology infrastructure.

Maria Shriver

FIRST LADY (STATE). Maria Shriver is a native of Chicago, Illinois, and is the niece of the late U.S. President John F. Kennedy. She received a Bachelor of Arts degree in American studies from Georgetown University in June 1977.

The first lady of California was introduced to Austrian bodybuilder, actor and current governor of California, Arnold Schwarzenegger, by Tom Brokaw at a charity tennis tournament being held at Eunice Kennedy's (her mother) home. She married Schwarzenegger on April 26, 1986.

Her professional career includes serving as a broadcast journalist with KYW-TV in Philadelphia, Pennsylvania and as an anchor on *Dateline NBC* from 1989 to 2004. In August 2003, she took an unpaid leave of absence from NBC News when her husband became a candidate in the 2003 California recall. Upon her husband's inauguration as the 38th governor of California on November 17, 2003, she became the first lady of California. She then returned to reporting, making two more appearances for *Dateline NBC*.

Ms. Shriver has embraced her role as first lady with a can-do attitude. She has launched California's first state-wide disaster preparedness campaign, "Be Smart, Be Responsible, Be Prepared. Get Ready!"

Mary Evans Sias

EDUCATION. Mary Evans Sias is a native of Jackson, Mississippi. She received a bachelor's degree in sociology summa cum laude from Tougaloo College in 1972. She earned her Master of Science degree in 1974 and a doctorate degree in sociology from the University of Wisconsin–Madison in 1980. She also received a Mas-

ter of Business Administration degree in management from Abilene Christian College at Dallas.

Her professional career includes serving 13 years as chief executive officer of the YWCA of Metropolitan Dallas; she has served as an associate provost, associate professor, and assistant professor at the University of Texas at Dallas; she has also served eight years as senior vice president for student affairs and external relations at the University of Texas at Dallas.

Dr. Sias was named president of Kentucky State University.

Bernice D. Siegal

JUDGE. Bernice D. Siegal received a Bachelor of Arts degree from Queens College and a masters' of public administration from New York University. She earned her Juris Doctor degree from New York Law School.

She was engaged in private law practice and as a legislative aide and counsel to the New York City Council. On January 1, 2002, she was elected judge, New York City Civil Court, Queen County, New York Unified Court Systems.

Leslie E. Silverman

GOVERNMENT OFFICIAL. Leslie E. Silverman is a native of Needham, Massachusetts. She received a bachelor's degree from the University of Vermont and a Juris Doctor degree from the American University, Washington College of Law, in Washington, D.C.

Her professional career includes serving for five years as labor counsel to the Senate Health, Education, Labor and Pensions Committee; from 1990 to 1997, she was an associate specializing in employment law and litigation in private law practice in Washington, D.C.

Ms. Silverman became vice chair of the U.S. Equal Employment Commission on September 8, 2006, after serving as a commissioner since March 7, 2002. She was first nominated by the U.S. Senate on March 1, 2002. Ms. Silverman was nominated to a full term in July 2003 and unanimously confirmed by the Senate in October 2003. Her current term expires on July 1, 2008.

Bettye Hill Simmons

MILITARY. Bettye Hill Simmons is a native of San Antonio, Texas. She received a Bachelor of Science degree in nursing from Incarnate Word College. She earned a Master of Science degree in nursing, medical surgery from University of Texas School of Nursing. Her military schooling includes the United States Army Medical Officer Basic and Advanced Courses; the United States Army Command and General Staff College; United States Army War College. She was commissioned a second lieutenant on November 9, 1970. From September 1971 to November 1971 she was a student at the United States Army Medical Field Service School, Brooke Army Medical Center at Fort Sam Houston, Texas. She was promoted to first lieutenant on May 23, 1971. In November 1980, she was a student at the Army Medical Officer Advanced Course, Academy of Health Sciences, Fort Sam Houston, Texas. From June 1981 to June 1982, she was assigned as the director of Patient Care Specialist Course, at Fitzsimmons Army Medical Center, Aurora, Colorado. From July 1982 to June 1983, she was a student at the United States Army Command and General Staff College, Fort Leavenworth, Kansas. From June 1983 to June 1991, she was assigned first as the assistant inspector general for the United States Army Health Services Command, next as chief of the Officer Instructional Branch, later deputy chief of the Nursing Science Division, Academy of Health Sciences, at Fort Sam Houston, Texas. She was promoted to lieutenant colonel on Septemberl, 1986. From 1991 to March 1994, she was assigned as the chief of the Department of Nursing at the United States Army Medical Department Activity, Fort Polk, Louisiana. She was

promoted to colonel on November 1, 1992. From March 1994 to December 1995, she was assigned chief nurse of the United States Army Medical Command at Fort Sam Houston, Texas. In January 1996, she was selected deputy commandant of the United States Army Medical Department Center and School, Fort Sam Houston, Texas. She was promoted to brigadier general on December 1, 1996. In April 1999, she was assigned as the commanding general, United States Army Center for Health Promotion and Preventive Medicine at Aberdeen Proving Ground, in Maryland. She retired in January 2000.

Renee V. H. Simons

BUSINESS EXECUTIVE. Renee V. H. Simons received a Bachelor of Arts degree in urban affairs from New York City's Hunter College in 1971. She earned a Master of Science degree in education planning from the Graduate School of Education at Fordham University in New York in 1975, and a Master of Business Administration degree in marketing/general management from the Columbia Graduate School of Business in 1978.

Her professional career includes serving with the Seven-Up Company, a former Philip Morris subsidiary, and in 1983 as brand manager for Seven-Up and Diet Seven-Up. From 1985 to 1998, she worked for Philip Morris USA and Philip Morris Management Corp. in various positions including director of media, director of consumer marketing services, director of sales promotions, group director for Virginia Slims, Parliament and Cartier, and brand manager for Benson & Hedges. She was appointed vice president of corporate marketing and communications at the Chase Manhattan Bank in May 1998.

Ms. Simons now serves as senior vice president of marketing and communications supporting JPMorgan Chase's ETech organization, a central infrastructure service provider.

Arlene Singer

JUDGE. Arlene Singer received a Bachelor of Arts degree from the University of Toledo in 1972, and earned her Juris Doctor degree from the University of Toledo College of Law in 1976.

Her professional career includes serving in private law practice; as an assistant Lucas County prosecutor; as a state legislator in the 117th Ohio General Assembly. In 2002, she was elected judge to the Ohio Sixth District Court of Appeals.

Michele Sison

GOVERNMENT OFFICIAL. Michele Sison is a native of Arlington, Virginia. She received a Bachelor of Arts degree from Wellesley College and also studied in the London School of Economics.

She served at U.S. missions in Port-au-Prince, Haiti (1982–1984); Lome, Togo (1984–1988); Cotonou, Benin (1988–1991); Douala, Cameroon (1991–1993); as consul general at the U.S. Consulate General in Chennai, India (1996–1999); and as deputy chief of mission and charge d' affaires at the U.S. Embassy in Islamabad, Pakistan.

She was confirmed by the U.S. Senate as ambassador to the United Arab Emirates on May 6, 2004, and sworn in by Secretary of State Powell on July 12, 2004. Prior to her appointment to the UAE, she served as principal deputy assistant secretary in the Bureau of South Asian Affairs, charged with providing broad policy oversight of U.S. relations with Pakistan, Afghanistan, Bangladesh, India, Nepal, and Sri Lanka.

Suzanne Sitherwood

BUSINESS EXECUTIVE. Suzanne Sitherwood received a Bachelor of Science degree in industrial engineering technology from Southern College of Technology and earned a Master of Business Administration from Brenau University.

Her professional career includes serving with Atlanta Gas Light (AGL) for more than 27 years. She has held a variety of positions including vice president of engineering and construction, chief engineer, director of competition planning, director of rates and regulatory affairs and director of residential markets. In June 2002, she was appointed vice president of gas operations and capacity planning. Ms. Sitherwood was named senior vice president, Southern operations in November 2004. Primary among her responsibilities is executive oversight of three utilities, Atlanta Gas Light, Florida City Gas and Chattanooga Gas.

Rebecca Skillman

ELECTED OFFICIAL. Rebecca Skillman is a native of Bedford, Lawrence County, Indiana. Her professional career began in 1977 when she was elected to the office of Lawrence County recorder. Eight years later she was elected as county clerk. She held county offices for 15 years, during that time she served as president of the Association of Indiana Counties. In 1992, she was elected to the Indiana State Senate. Rising quickly through the leadership, she became majority caucus chair, the first woman in history to serve in the Senate Republican leadership. She served three terms in the Indiana State Senate.

Lt. Governor Skillman assumed the post of lieutenant governor for the state of Indiana in 2005. She also oversees the first ever Indiana State Department of Agriculture and Office of Community and Rural Affairs.

Patricia A. Skinner

EDUCATION. Patricia A. Skinner received a bachelor's degree from Lake Michigan College, a master's degree and Specialist of Arts degree from Western Michigan University. She received her doctorate in higher education administration from Ohio State.

Her professional career includes serving as an instructor of business office administration and management at colleges and universities in Michigan, Massachusetts and Ohio. She served as vice president of academic and student affairs at Clark State Community College in Springfield, Ohio.

Dr. Skinner became president of Gaston College in August 1994.

Louise McIntosh Slaughter

ELECTED OFFICIAL. Louise McIntosh Slaughter is a native of Harlan County, Kentucky. She received a Bachelor of Science degree from the University of Kentucky in Lexington in 1951 and earned a Masters of Science from the University of Kentucky.

Her professional career includes: serving as a member of the Monroe County, New York, Legislature from 1976 to 1979; as the regional coordinator for New York Department of State from 1979 to 1979; as coordinator, Regional Office of New York Lieutenant Governor from 1979 to 1982; as a member of the New York State Assembly from 1982 to 1986; she was elected as a United States Representative to the 100th and to the nine succeeding Congresses since January 3, 1987.

Marva Smalls

BUSINESS EXECUTIVE. Marva Smalls received a bachelor's degree and a Master of Business Administration both from the University of South Carolina. She holds an honorary doctorate of humanities from Frances Marion University and Coker College.

Her professional career includes serving as staff director of South Carolina's Private Industry Council for Governor Richard Riley and later as chief of staff for Congressman Robin Tallon for 10 years. In 1993, she joined Nickelodeon in the public sector.

Ms. Smalls serves as executive vice president of global inclusion strategy, as executive vice president of public affairs and chief of staff of Nickelodeon/MTVN Kids & Family Group. As chief of staff, she is the principal administrative officer for the Nickelodeon Networks and their ancillary businesses, coordinating and directing financial resources, employees and facilities for the New York, Los Angeles and international offices.

Adrienne M. Smith

GOVERNMENT OFFICIAL. Adrienne Smith received a Bachelor of Science degree in biology pre-med from Norfolk State University and a Master of Science degree from Hampton University in nutritional science. She holds a Doctor of Philosophy degree in women's health from the Department of Public and Community Health at the University

of Maryland in College Park, and is a Certified Health Education Specialist.

She has worked as a public health nutritionist with the Virginia Department of Health focusing on breastfeeding promotion and prenatal nutrition among minority and underserved women. Additionally, she worked with the District of Columbia Department of Health in the State Center for Health Statistics. She worked in the Office on Women's Health (OWH), United States Department of Health and Human Services, as a public health advisor in the division of policy and program development; in this capacity she coordinates the minority women's health programs/activities and facilitates OWH's Minority Women's Health Panel of Experts.

Alma Wheeler Smith

ELECTED OFFICIAL. Alma Wheeler Smith received a Bachelor of Arts degree in journalism from the University of Michigan and took advanced degree work in journalism and business administration.

Her professional career includes serving as a senior producer at the University of Michigan Television Center and on the staff of Senator Lana Pollack in 1986. She served eight years on the South Lyon Community School Board (three as President), a two-year term on the Michigan Washtenaw County Commission, and eight years in the Michigan State Senate where as Democratic vice-chair of the Appropriations Committee she was the first woman to hold a leadership position on the committee. Elected in November 2004, she represents Michigan's 54th District.

In 2001, Ms. Smith became the first black candidate for governor in the state of Michigan.

Jane E. Smith

EDUCATION. Jane E. Smith received a Bachelor of Arts in sociology from Spelman College in Atlanta and a master's in sociology from Emory University in Atlanta, Georgia. She earned a doctorate of education in social policy analysis from Harvard University.

Her professional career includes joining Spelman College where she served as an assistant to the president. From 1981 to 1990, she was the managing director of INROADS/Atlanta and INROADS/Detroit; in 1991, Mrs. Coretta Scott King invited her to serve as director of development at the Martin Luther King Center for Nonviolent Social Change; from 1994 to 1998, she directed the Atlanta Project, a community development initiative at the Carter Center. She reported directly to former President Jimmy Carter. From 1998 to 2001, she served as president and chief executive officer of the National Council of Negro Women.

Dr. Smith serves as the chief executive officer of the Executive Leadership Center, Spelman College.

Melody D. Smith

MILITARY. Melody D. Smith is a native of Jacksonville, Florida, and graduated from the United States Military Academy at West Point in 1989 with a Bachelor of Science degree in mathematics, and was commissioned in the United States Army Corps of Engineers.

Colonel Smith attended the Officer Basic Course at Fort Belvoir, Virginia. She is a graduate of the Command and General Staff College; the Combined Armed Staff Service School; the Mapping, Charting, and Geodesy Officer's Course; the Engineer Officer's Advanced Course; and the Engineer Officer's Basic Course.

While serving with the 34th Engineer Combat Battalion (Heavy) at Fort Riley, Kansas, as a vertical construction platoon leader, she deployed her platoon to Bolivia to conduct humanitarian civil-action projects and also served in Saudi Arabia and Kuwait for Operation Desert Storm as Bravo Company's executive officer.

In January 2005, she was serving as the deputy commander, United States Army Corps of Engineers, Rock Island District.

Mittie Smith

MILITARY. Mittie Smith is a native of Pittsview, Alabama, and graduated from Chavala High School as Salutatorian with a scholarship in academics. She joined the United States Army in November 1981 and completed Basic Combat Training and Advanced Individual Training at Fort Jackson, South Carolina.

Command Sergeant Major Smith's military education includes all the Noncommissioned Officers Education System Courses; Instructors Training Course (Honor Graduate); NBC Course (Distinguished Honor Graduate); Drill Sergeant School (Distinguished Honor

Graduate and Leadership Award); Master Fitness Trainers Course; First Sergeant Course (Commandant's List); Senior Enlisted Equal Opportunity Course; the United States Army Sergeants Major Academy; and the Garrison Command Sergeant Major Course. She holds a Bachelor of Science degree in business and management from the University of Maryland, and she also earned a masters degree in computer resources and information management from Webster University in St. Louis, Missouri.

She has held numerous leadership positions including squad leader; personnel management; primary leadership development course instructor; drill sergeant; platoon sergeant, operations sergeant chief/adjutant of the Personnel and Administration Division; PAC supervisor; chief, Administrative Service Division; detachment sergeant; first sergeant; garrison command sergeant major. In August, she was serving as the commandant at the Noncommissioned Officers Academy, 3rd Infantry Division, Fort Stewart, Georgia.

Teresa Guerra Snelson

JUDGE. Teresa Guerra Snelson received a Bachelor of Arts degree from the University of Houston and earned her Juris Doctor degree from the University of Houston Law Center in 1991.

Her professional career includes serving as an assistant attorney general in Austin, Texas and as senior assistant general counsel, Texas Department of Public Safety, 1996–1997. She was engaged in private law practice from 1997 to 2004. In 2004, she was appointed associate judge, Texas District Court, in Dallas, Texas.

Stacey Snider

ENTERTAINMENT EXECUTIVE. Stacey Snider is a native of Philadelphia, Pennsylvania. She received a Bachelor of Arts degree from the University of Pennsylvania in 1982 and earned her Juris Doctor degree from the University of California at Los Angeles (UCLA) in 1985.

Her professional career includes working in the mail room at the Triad Agency and soon became an assistant at Simpson-Bruckheimer Productions; from 1986 to 1990, she served as director of development and ultimately as executive vice president at Guber-Peters Entertainment Company; from 1992 to 1996, she became president of TriStar Pictures and was in charge of such films as *Sleepless in Seattle*, *Philadelphia*, *Jumanji* and *Legends of the Fall*; from 1996 to 1998, she was co-president of production; in 1998, president of production; in 1998 as president of Universal Pictures.

Ms. Snider was named chairman and chief executive officer of Universal Pictures in 1999.

Olympia Jean Snowe

ELECTED OFFICIAL. Olympia Jean Snowe is a native of Augusta, Maine. She attended St. Basil's Academy in Garrison, New York, in 1962, and graduated from Edward Little High School, Auburn Maine, in 1965. She received a Bachelor of Arts degree from the University of Maine, Orono, in 1969.

Her professional career includes engagement in private business. She served as the district office manager for Representative William S. Cohen; with the Auburn Board of Voter Registration from 1971 to 1973; as a Maine State Representative from 1973 to 1976; as a Maine State Senator from 1976 to 1978. She was elected as a United States Representative to the 96th and to the seven succeeding Congresses (January 3, 1979–January 3, 1995). She was elected to the United States Senate in 1994; she was re-elected in 2000 for the term ending January 3, 2007.

Susan Sobbott

FINANCE. Susan Sobbott is a native of New Jersey. She received a bachelor's degree from Georgetown University and earned her Masters of Business Administration from the Darden School of Business at the University of Virginia.

She served fifteen years with American Express in sales and

marketing positions in the establishment services group where she built relationships with merchants to accept the American Express card, and was an internal strategic consultant within the corporation's strategic planning group. From 2000 to 2003, Susan was a senior vice president and general manager for consumer cards. Her experience spanned to managing American Express co-brand credit card portfolios and loyalty programs such as the company's award-winning Membership Rewards programs. She was appointed president of OPEN from American Express, the team dedicated exclusively to the success of small business owners and their companies.

Annette L. Sobel

MILITARY. Annette L. Sobel received a Bachelor of Science in chemistry/biochemistry/computer science from Cook College of Rutgers University in New Brunswick, New Jersey, in 1979. She earned a Doctor of Medicine from Case Western Reserve University in Cleveland, Ohio, in 1983. She was a graduate of the Army Command and General Staff College in 1989. She earned a Master of Science in human factors and aerospace medicine from Wright State University, Dayton, Ohio.

Her professional career includes serving from January 1986 to September 1988 as director of undergraduate medical education , family medicine faculty at the United States Army Medical Department Activity, Fort Bragg, North Carolina; from April 1988 to August 1989 as commander of the Medical Holding Company, United States Army Medical Guard, Springfield, Ohio; from June 1994 to September 1995, as commander, 178th Medical Squadron, Ohio Air National Guard, Springfield, Ohio; from September 1995 to September 1998 as commander, 150th Medical Squadron at New Mexico Air National Guard, Kirtland Air Force Base in New Mexico; from September 1998 to January 2000, she served as state air surgeon at Headquarters New Mexico Air National Guard, Kirtland Air Force Base, New Mexico; from January 2000 to June 2003, she was assigned as National Guard assistant for weapons of mass destruction and civil support to the chief, National Guard Bureau at Arlington, Virginia. She was promoted to brigadier general on March 24, 2002.

Brigadier General Sobel serves as director of intelligence, National Guard Bureau and is a standing member of the Defense Intelligence Agency's Advisory Board.

Hilda Solis

ELECTED OFFICIAL. Solis Hilda is a native of Los Angeles, California. She received a Bachelor of Arts degree from California Polytechnic University, Pomona, California, in 1979 and earned her Master of Arts degree from the University of Southern California, Los Angeles.

Her professional career includes serving at the White House Office of Hispanic Affairs; as an analyst in the Office of Management and Budget; as a member of the Rio Hondo, California, Community College Board of Trustees from 1985 to 1992. She was elected a member of the California State Assembly from 1992 to 1994; she was elected a Senator for the California State Senate from 1994 to 2001; in 2000, she was elected a United States Representative to the 107th and to the two succeeding Congresses, serving since January 3, 2001.

Bonnie Soodik

BUSINESS EXECUTIVE. Bonnie Soodik is a native of New Jersey. She received a Bachelor of Arts degree in psychology from George Washington University in 1972 and a Master of Science degree in administration from California State University in 1980. In 1987, she graduated from the Advanced Management Institute of Claremont Graduate School.

She began her career in 1977 with the McDonnell Douglas Automation Company, where she led the development and implementation of major engineering and business systems used throughout the corporation. In 1985, she joined Douglas Aircraft as program manager, Information Resource Management. She was promoted in 1989 to vice president at McDonnell Douglas Space Systems Company and was responsible for the quality thrust and most support functions. She later served as vice president, deputy general manager of operations–West. In 1995, she became vice president of quality at Doug-

las Aircraft. She was assigned to the C-17 program in April 1997 as vice president of production assurance and services. She later became regional vice president/general manager of Boeing Share Services Group. Ms. Soodik is the senior vice president of the office of internal governance.

Sonia Sotomayor

JUDGE. Sonia Sotomayor is a native of the Bronx, New York. She received a Bachelor of Arts degree from Princeton University in 1976 and earned her Juris Doctor degree from Yale Law School in 1979.

Her professional career includes serving as an assistant district attorney, New York County District Attorney's Office, from 1979 to 1984; she was engaged in private law practice from 1984 to 1992. On November 27, 1991, she was nominated judge by President George H. W. Bush to the United States District Court for Southern District of New York. She was confirmed by the United States Senate on August 11, 1992, and received her commission on August 12, 1992. On June 25, 1997, she was nominated judge by President William J. Clinton to the United States Court of Appeals for the Second Circuit. She was confirmed by the United States Senate on October 2, 1998, and received her commission on October 7, 1998.

Lea N. Soupata

BUSINESS EXECUTIVE. Lea N. Soupata is a native of New York City. She joined UPS in 1969 and during her 36 years with the company has managed a variety of human resources and customer service and operations functions. She also served as district manager in the New York area from 1990 until 1994.

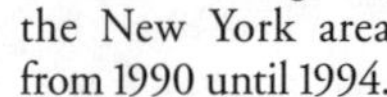

She serves as senior vice president for UPS and manages a human resources organization that serves 384,000 employees worldwide. She has been a member of the UPS Management Committee since 1995 and a member of the UPS Board of Directors since 1998.

Leslie Elaine South

JUDGE. Leslie Elaine South is a graduate of Chicago public schools and received her bachelor of Art degree with honors from Loyola University of Chicago in 1976. She earned her J.D. degree from Northwestern University School of Law in 1978.

She worked as an assistant prosecutor for the Cook County State's Attorney's office from 1978 to 1982 and as a staff attorney for the Chicago Transit Authority from 1984 to 1988. Judge South was appointed associate judge of the Circuit Court of Cook County in 1988 and was assigned to the Sixth Municipal District in Markham. She was elected to the Circuit Court of Cook County in 1992 and to the Appellate Court, First District, in 1996. She is serving as appellate judge for the First District, 3rd Division, for the state of Illinois.

Brenda S. Spears

JUDGE. Brenda S. Spears received her undergraduate degree from City College of New York and earned her Juris Doctor degree from the University of Pennsylvania Law School.

Her professional career includes serving as a law clerk, Eastern District of Pennsylvania; in private law practice; as the deputy bureau chief of the Real Estate Finance Bureau and as section chief of the Litigation Bureau with the New York State Attorney General's office; as the deputy general counsel and corporate secretary with the New York City Housing. Since May 1996, she has served as judge at the New York City Civil Court, Housing Part.

Kathleen M. Spencer

MILITARY. Kathleen M. Spencer is originally from Pittsfield, Massachusetts, and entered the Air Force through the Officer Training School in March 1977, receiving her commission in June 1977.

Her military and civilian education includes a Bachelor of Science in geology (cum laude) from the University of Massachusetts at Amherst, Massachusetts, in 1976; Squadron Officer School (distinguished graduate), Maxwell Air Force Base in Alabama; Air Command and Staff College; Air War College; the Industrial College of the Armed Forces at Fort McNair in Washington, D.C.; a Master of Science degree in international relations at Troy State University–Europe; and a Master of Science degree in national resource strategy from the National Defense University at Fort McNair, Washington, D.C.

She has held a variety of munitions and aircraft maintenance positions in several major commands at Air Staff and also served as an instructor at the Air University and military assistant to the executive secretary in the Office of the Secretary of Defense.

Her key command assignments include: in July 1990, commander, 6519th Component Repair Squadron, at Edwards Air Force Base in California; in July 1992, commander, 412th Logistics Test Squadron, Edwards Air Force Base, California; in November 1996, she was selected to serve as chief of logistics at Battle lab Integration Division at the Pentagon, in Washington, D.C.; in January 1999, she was selected to serve as the senior logistics representative, Quadrennial Defense Review at the Pentagon in Washington, D.C.; in August 1999, she was assigned as the deputy director at the Logistics Information System Program Office at Maxwell Air Force Base in Alabama; in July 2000, she was assigned as the commander, 355th Logistics Group at Davis-Monthan Air Force Base in Arizona; in August 2002, she was selected to serve as the deputy director, Logistics Management Directorate at Warner Robins Air Logistics Center at Robins Air Force Base in Georgia. She was promoted to colonel on March 1, 1999.

Loretta Spencer

ELECTED OFFICIAL. Loretta Spencer received a Bachelor of Science in elementary education from the University of Alabama. She is a former teacher in the Huntsville City School System. She was elected to her third term as mayor of Huntsville, Alabama, on September 14, 2004. She is the first woman to be elected and twice re-elected to the position.

Vaino Spencer

JUDGE. Vaino Spencer is a native of Los Angeles, California. She is a graduate of Los Angeles City College (summa cum laude), and earned her Juris Doctor degree from Southwestern University School of Law.

Her professional career includes serving in private law practice; as judge of the Los Angeles Municipal Court in 1961; and as judge at the Los Angeles Superior Court. Since 2001, she has served as presiding justice of the California Second District Court of Appeals. She was the first African-American female judge on the Los Angeles Municipal Court in 1961.

Linda Spilker

AEROSPACE. Linda Spilker is a native of Minneapolis, Minnesota. She received a Bachelor of Arts degree in physics and a Master of Science degree in physics from California State University at Fullerton. She earned a Ph.D. summa cum laude from the University of California at Los Angeles.

In 1977, she joined the Jet Propulsion Laboratory as a research assistant at the California Institute of Technology, helping to study meteorite samples to learn more about the birth of the solar system. In 1978, she joined the team of scientists and engineers who flew the Voyager 1 and 2 spacecraft on their historic explorations of Jupiter, Saturn, Uranus and Neptune. She worked for 13 years for the Voyager Infrared Team. She currently serves as deputy project scientist and a member of the Cassini Composite Infrared Team.

Linda M. Springer

GOVERNMENT OFFICIAL. Linda M. Springer received a Bachelor of Science degree cum laude from Ursinus College and attended the Executive Program in Managing the Enterprise at Columbia University Business School.

Her professional career includes serving in positions of increasing responsibility at Penn Mutual Life Insurance Company from 1979 to 1992. She served as vice president and controller of Provident Mutual, an insurance, annuity and financial services company. She

spent over twenty-five years in the financial services industry in executive positions responsible for general and financial management and strategic and operational planning. Ms. Springer was nominated by President George W. Bush to be the director of the United States Office of Personnel Management on March 18, 2005, and was unanimously confirmed by the United States Senate on June 24, 2005. She is the eighth director of the United States Office of Personnel Management.

Marlene Springer

EDUCATION. Marlene Springer received a bachelor's degree in English and business administration from Centre College in Kentucky and a Master of Arts in American literature at Indiana University in Bloomington. She earned her doctorate in English literature from Indiana University, Bloomington.

Her professional career includes having served as a member of the faculty, as acting associate dean, chair of the Department of English and as an associate vice chancellor for academic affairs and graduate studies at the University of Missouri in Kansas City.

Dr. Springer was appointed president of the College of Staten Island, the City University of New York, in 1994.

Carole Squire

JUDGE. Carole Squire is a native of Springfield, Ohio. She received a Bachelor of Arts degree in English from the Ohio State University in 1974. She earned her Juris doctorate degree from the Ohio Sate University College of Law in 1977.

Her professional career includes serving as a Franklin County Prosecutor's Juvenile Unit; as a staff attorney for the Ohio Legal Rights Services; and in private law practice for 25 years. She serves as a judge for the Ohio Franklin County Court of Common Pleas, Division of Domestic Relations and Juvenile Branch, in Columbus, Ohio.

Deborah Ann Stabenow

ELECTED OFFICIAL. Deborah Ann Stabenow is a native of Gladwin, Michigan, and a graduate of Clare High School. She received a Bachelor of Arts degree from Michigan State University in East Lansing, Michigan, in 1972 and earned her Masters of Social Work (magna cum laude) from Michigan State University in 1975.

Her professional career includes serving as a social worker and leadership training consultant; as an Ingham County commissioner from 1975 to 1978; as a member of the Michigan State House of Representatives from 1979 to 1990; as a member of the Michigan State Senate from 1991 to 1994. She was elected a United States Representative to the 105th and 106th Congresses (January 3, 1997, to January 3, 2001); she was elected to the United States Senate in 2000.

Renee Starghill

MILITARY. Renee Starghill is a native of Detroit, Michigan, and entered the United States Air Force in October 1983. She attended Basic Military Training at Lackland Air Force Base, Texas, and her Advanced Individual Training (Basic Personnel Course) at Keesler Air Force Base, Mississippi.

Her military and civilian education includes all the Noncommissioned Officer Education System Courses; Noncommissioned Officer Academy, Royal Air Force Upwood, England; the Senior Noncommissioned Officer Academy, Gunter Air Force Base, Alabama. She earned an associate degree in human resource management and personnel administration,

CCAF and holds a Bachelor of Science degree in business administration and management from the University of Maryland as well as a Master of Business Administration degree from Webster University.

Command Master Chief Sergeant Starghill's key military assignments include serving as the noncommissioned officer in charge of personnel orderly room, Galena Airport, Alaska; from May 1990 to May 1992, as noncommissioned officer in charge of classification and training, Rhein-Main Air Base, Germany; from May 1992 to May 1994, noncommissioned officer in charge of logistics officer assignments, Headquarters USAFE, Ramstein Air Base Germany; from 1994 to June 1995, noncommissioned officer in charge of evaluations and career enhancements, Osan Air Base, South Korea; from July 1995 to March 1997, superintendent, Military Personnel Flight, Bolling Air Force Base, Washington, D.C.; from March 1997 to May 2000, she served as the Air Force enlisted aide manager and superintendent for Air Force general officer matters office, Headquarters United States Air Force, Washington, D.C.; from June 2000 to November 2001, as superintendent, Secretary of the Air Force Military Personnel Division, Headquarters United States Air Force, Washington, D.C.; from November 2001 to July 2003, executive assistant to the vice chief of staff, Headquarters United States Air Force, Washington, D.C.; from August 2003 to January 2004, she served as superintendent, 86th Contingency Response Group, Ramstein Air Base, Germany.

In October 2004, she was serving as the command chief master sergeant, 86th Airlift Wing at Ramstein Air Base in Germany.

Bobbie L. Steele

ELECTED OFFICIAL. Bobbie L. Steele was born in Cleveland, Mississippi. She attended Alabama A&M College in Huntsville, Alabama, for two years.

In 1986, she was elected to the Cook County Board of Commissioners She served as a commissioner for the 2nd District of Cook County, Illinois, for 20 years. She is currently the longest serving African American woman in the history of Cook County. She is the first and only African American woman to serve as chairman of the Finance Committee of the Forrest Preserve District of Cook County. She serves as Cook County Board President, the first female board president in the 175-year history of Cook County. She was sworn in as the 32nd president of the Cook County Board of Commissioners on August 1, 2006.

Gail Steele

ELECTED OFFICIAL. Gail Steele received a Bachelor of Arts degree in sociology from the University of California at Berkeley in 1979 and earned a master of public administration from the University of San Francisco in 1989.

Her professional career includes serving as executive director of the Eden Youth Center from 1979 to 1992. In June 1992, she was elected as an Alameda County Supervisor, Oakland, California. She served as president of the Board of Supervisors in 1995 and 2003.

Toreaser A. Steele

MILITARY. Toreaser A. Steele received a Bachelor of Science degree in home economics education from Tennessee State University in Nashville, Tennessee. She earned a Master of Science degree in guidance and counseling from Central Michigan University at Mount Pleasant. Her military education includes Squadron Officer School at Maxwell Air Force Base in Alabama; Air Command and Staff College; Armed Forces Staff College; Industrial College of the Armed Forces at Fort Lesley J. McNair; Senior Executive Program at Columbia University in New York, New York.

She was commissioned through the Air Force ROTC program at Tennessee State University and began her career as a personnel officer. Her command and staff assignments includes being assigned in January 1986 as squadron commander, division chief and group commander at United States Air Force Academy in Colorado Springs, Colorado. From June 1990 to June 1992, she was assigned as command division chief and special assistant to the commander in chief, Strategic Air Command at Offutt Air Force Base in Nebraska. From June 1993 to January 1995, she was assigned as the assistant director for officer plans and programs in the Office of the Sec-

retary of Defense, Washington, D.C. She was promoted to colonel on January 1, 1995.

In January 1995, she was selected to serve as the military assistant to the principal deputy assistant secretary of defense for force management policy in the Office of the Secretary of Defense in Washington, D.C. From July 1996 to September 1998, she was assigned as commander of the 737th Training Group at Lackland Air Force Base in Texas. From September 1998 to August 2000, she served as the commander, 17th Training Wing at Goodfellow Air Force Base in Texas. From August 2000 to July 2002, she served as the director of personnel resources, and director of Air Force personnel operations agency in the Office of the Deputy Chief of Staff for Personnel at Headquarters United States Air Force in Washington, D.C. She was promoted to brigadier general on April 1, 2001.

In July 2002, she was selected to serve as the vice commander of the Army and Air Force Exchange Service in Dallas, Texas. AAFES is a $7.5 billion retail, food and services business that operates nearly 10,000 facilities in 29 countries and all 50 states. AAFES employs more than 52,000 associates, many of them military family members. In July 2002, she was selected to serve as vice commander of the Army and Air Force Exchange Service in Dallas, Texas.

Margaret O. Steinbeck

JUDGE. Margaret O. Steinbeck received a Bachelor of Science degree (summa cum laude) from the University of Georgia in 1978 where she was a distinguished military graduate of the Army ROTC program. She attended law school on an Army merit scholarship and received her Juris Doctor in 1984 from the University of Virginia School of Law. Later she was awarded a Masters' of Law degree with honors from the Army Judge Advocate General's (JAG) School.

She was commissioned as a second lieutenant into the regular Army and entered active duty in the Army Adjutant General's Corps. She served as a JAG officer from 1984 to 1990. Her military career included assignments as a criminal prosecutor in Germany, and as an environmental litigation attorney at the Pentagon in Washington, D.C. After leaving active duty, she continued her military service in the Army Reserve, and she is currently a lieutenant colonel assigned to the faculty of the Army JAG School at the University of Virginia in Charlottesville, Virginia.

Prior to Judge Steinbeck's judicial appointment, she was engaged in private law practice in Washington, D.C., and Naples, Florida. In 1995, Judge Steinbeck was appointed an assistant U.S. attorney for the Middle District of Florida. In 1998, she was appointed judge to the 20th Judicial Circuit, State of Florida. She was elected without opposition in 2000 to continue her service on the circuit bench. She is currently assigned to the Family Division of the Circuit Court in Lee County, Florida.

Connie Steinhelmer

JUDGE. Connie Steinhelmer is a native of Nevada. She received her undergraduate degree from the University of Nevada in Reno and earned her Juris Doctor degree from Willamette University in Salem, Oregon.

She was engaged in private law practice from 1984 to 1992. She was elected judge to the Nevada Second Judicial District Court in Washoe County, Nevada.

Elizabeth Guber Stephen

ENTERTAINMENT EXECUTIVE. Elizabeth Guber Stephen grew up in Miami, Florida, and received a bachelor's degree from Brown University. Her professional career includes working in feature films as a studio executive acquiring and developing hits such as Hollywood Pictures' *The Hand That Rocks the Cradle*, Eddie Murphy's *The Distinguished Gentleman* and Tristar Pictures' *Only You*, which was directed by Norman Jewison. She spent six years as executive vice president in charge of feature film development and production for the Avnet/Kerner Company.

Ms. Stephen was named president of Mandalay Television and executive vice president of motion picture production, Mandalay Pictures. She oversees all creative development and production for the group. She serves as executive producer on all network and cable television movies, mini-series and series.

Cynthia D. Stephens

JUDGE. Cynthia D. Stephens has served as a judge for the Michigan Third Circuit Court in Detroit for

more than 21 years. She was appointed judge in 1985. She has served as chief judge pro tempore and as chair of the Mediation Tribunal Association. She has taught trial advocacy at the University of Detroit Mercy School of Law since 1990. She is the former president of the Association of Black Judges of Michigan and is a member of the Academic Advisory Committee of the Michigan Judicial Institute.

Linda Stephens

JUDGE. Linda Stephens received a Bachelor of Arts degree (magna cum laude) from the University of South Carolina in 1973 and earned her Juris Doctor degree from the University of North Carolina School of Law.

Her professional career includes serving as a law clerk to the North Carolina Court of Appeals from 1979 to 1980 and as deputy commissioner at the North Carolina Industrial Commission from 1980 to 1984. She was engaged in private law practice from 1989 to 2006. In 2006, she was appointed judge to the North Carolina Court of Appeals.

Sherry K. Stephens

JUDGE. Sherry K. Stephens received her undergraduate degree in criminal justice from Arizona State University in 1977 and earned her Juris Doctor degree from Arizona State University in 1980.

From 1980 to 2001, she served as an assistant attorney general, Arizona Attorney General's Office. Since 2001, she has served as judge, Superior Court of Arizona in Maricopa County.

Anne Stevens

BUSINESS EXECUTIVE. Anne Stevens is a native of Reading, Pennsylvania. She received a bachelor's degree in mechanical and materials engineering from Drexel University in Philadelphia. She completed graduate work at Rutgers University in New Brunswick, New Jersey.

Ms. Stevens has held various engineering, manufacturing and marketing positions at Exxon Mobil Corporation. She joined Ford Motor Company in 1990 as a marketing specialist in the Plastic Products Division, Vehicle Exterior Systems. In 1992, she was named manager of the Quality Services Department at the division's Saline (Mich.) plant. In August 2001, she was named vice president of North America vehicle operations. In October 2003 she was named group vice president of Canada, Mexico and South America. She was responsible for business operations in each country, including purchasing, finance, sales and marketing. On November 1, 2005, she was named executive vice president of Ford Motor Company and chief operating officer, the Americas.

Joyce L. Stevens

MILITARY. Joyce L. Stevens received a Bachelor of Science degree in management, human resources from Park College and earned a Master of Science degree in strategic studies from the Army War College. She is a graduate of the Army Command and General Staff Course.

Brigadier General Stevens began her military service in April 1979. Her assignments include various command and staff position within the 49th Armored Division and the 71st Troop Command. She served as the commander of the 536th Forward Support Battalion where she was also the full-time battalion administrative officer; the assistant chief of staff, G-4 for the 49th Armored Division (Rear); the 71st Troop command assistant chief of staff and the commander of the 111th Area Support Group. She deployed to combat as a brigade level task force commander in support of Operation Enduring Freedom in Afghanistan. She assumed duties as the assistant adjutant general for the Army, Texas Army National Guard in May 2006. She was promoted to brigadier general on July 14, 2006.

Lisa Stevens

GOVERNMENT OFFICIAL. Lisa Stevens received a bachelor's degree in zoology and pre–veterinary medicine from Michigan State University. She attended the AZA School for Professional Management Development for Zoo and Aquarium Personnel.

Ms. Stevens has held positions as a field research assistant in pet and aquarium retail, veterinary clinic operations, insect zoo husbandry and interpretation and riding stable management. She has served as manager of the giant panda program for over 20 years. She became a familiar face and voice in 2005 when panda cub Tai Shan was born at the National Zoo in Washington, D.C. where she works as the zoo's curator of pandas.

Julia A. Stewart

BUSINESS EXECUTIVE. Julia A. Stewart received a bachelor's degree from San Diego State University. She has served in various key marketing positions with leading restaurant companies including Stuart Anderson's Black Angus/Cattle Company Restaurants, Spoons Grill & Bar, Burger King Corp. and Carl's Jr. Restaurants.

She served as national vice president of franchise and license and Western region vice president of operations with Taco Bell Corporation, a division of Yum! Brands, Inc. Ms. Stewart served as president of the domestic division of Applebee's International, Inc. She joined IHOP in December 2001, and was named chairman and chief executive officer of IHOP Corp.

Martha Stewart

BUSINESS EXECUTIVE. Martha Stewart is a native of Jersey City, New Jersey. She received a bachelor's degree in history and architectural history from Barnard College in New York City. While in college, she worked as a model to help pay her college tuition.

Her professional career includes serving in 1967 as a stockbroker; in 1973, she moved to Westport, Connecticut. In 1976, she began a catering business, which she ran from the basement of her home. Within 10 years, this had become a $1 million enterprise. She later expanded to a retail store where she sold entertaining supplies and specialty foods. In 1982, she published the book *Entertaining*, and in 1990 she began her own monthly magazine, *Martha Stewart Living*. Following a number of television appearances and specials, Martha also began her own television show that, like her magazine, was called *Martha Stewart Living*. In 1997, she created Martha Stewart Living Omnimedia, a conglomerate with branches encompassing publishing, broadcasting, direct mail, a radio channel on Sirius Satellite Radio Inc., home construction and other avenues.

Angela R. Stokes

JUDGE. Angela R. Stokes is a native of the greater Cleveland community and is the daughter of retired U.S. Congressman Louis Stokes. She graduated with honors from the University of Maryland in College Park, receiving a Bachelor of Arts degree in psychology. She earned her Juris Doctor degree from Howard University School of Law in Washington, D.C.

Her professional career includes serving in private law practice; as an assistant attorney general for the state of Ohio from 1984 to 1990 and again from 1993 to 1995. She was first elected judge to the Cleveland Municipal Court on November 7, 1995, to an unexpired term and was re-elected in 1999 to a full six-year term.

Terri J. Stoneburner

JUDGE. Terri J. Stoneburner received a Bachelor of Arts degree from Hanover College in Hanover, Indiana, and earned a Juris Doctor degree from the University of Washington School of Law.

Her professional career includes a staff attorney, State of Alaska Commission for Human Rights; in private law practice from 1980 to 1990. She was appointed judge to the Fifth Judicial District in New Ulm, Minnesota, in April 1990. She served as assistant chief judge for the Fifth Judicial District from July 1997 to April 2000.

On March 8, 2000, Governor Jesse Ventura appointed her judge on the Minnesota Court of Appeals and she was seated on April 28, 2000.

Janice D. Stoney

BUSINESS EXECUTIVE. Janice D. Stoney became a Northwestern Bell officer when elected vice president of personnel in January 1980; and then was named vice president, marketing in June 1983. In January 1984, she was named vice president, communications services. In July 1985, she was appointed executive vice president and chief operating officer. She served as president and chief executive office of Omaha, Nebraska-based Northwestern Bell Telephone Company. She was the executive vice president, total quality system, for US WEST Communications Group, Inc., from March 1991 until her retirement in December 1992.

She was elected a director of Whirlpool Corporation in August 1987.

Elinore Marsh Stormer

JUDGE. Elinore Marsh Stormer graduated from Davidson College with an undergraduate degree in history. She earned her Juris Doctor degree from the University of Akron graduating in the top of her class. She was elected to the bench in 1991.

Evelyn Lundberg Stratton

JUDGE. Evelyn Lundberg Stratton received her Juris Doctor degree from the Ohio State University College of Law. She began her legal career in the courtrooms of central Ohio as a trial lawyer. In 1989, she was the first woman judge elected to the Franklin County Court of Common Pleas in Ohio. She was appointed justice to the Ohio Supreme Court and later elected to the Supreme Court.

Ashley W. Stroupe

AEROSPACE. Ashley W. Stroupe received a Bachelor of Science degree in physics concentrations in astrophysics and anthropology from Harvey Mudd College and a Master of Science in electrical and computer engineering from George Mason University. She earned a Master of Science in robotics and a Ph.D. in robotics from Carnegie Mellon University.

She served as a staff engineer at the Jet Propulsion Laboratory since December 2003. Her research focuses on multi-robot teams in complex environments and behavior-based control with applications to exploration and mapping, dynamic target observation, and cooperative manipulation. Since October 2004, she has served as a member of the Mars Exploration Rovers Engineering Team.

Laura Stubbs

MILITARY. Laura Stubbs is a native of Philadelphia, Pennsylvania. She began her naval career in July 1980 when she was commissioned a lieutenant. Her first assignment was as a Naval Nuclear Power School instructor. She was the first African-American to become a Nuclear Power School instructor at the Naval Academy.

Captain Stubbs education includes a Bachelor of Science degree in engineering from the University of Pennsylvania in 1979; she received a Master's degree in me-

chanical engineering and applied mechanics from the University of Pennsylvania in 1980; she has also earned a Ph.D. in mechanical engineering from the University of Maryland at College Park, Maryland.

In 1983, she was assigned to the United States Naval Academy as an assistant professor in the Mechanical and Naval Systems Engineering Departments. She left active duty in 1986 and joined the Naval Reserve as a line officer. She served in numerous leadership assignments to include serving as chief learning officer for the Naval Surface Warfare Center and as a qualified engineering duty officer in the Naval Reserves.

Dianne B. Suber

EDUCATION. Dianne B. Suber is a native of Tallahassee, Florida. She received a Bachelor of Science degree in early childhood education at Hampton (Institute) University and a Master's of Education degree in curriculum development from the University of Illinois at Urbana. She earned a Doctorate of Education degree in education administration from Virginia Polytechnic Institute and State University in Blacksburg, Virginia.

Her professional career includes serving at Hampton University in Hampton, Virginia, in numerous positions of increasing responsibility from 1986 to 1990, as an adjunct professor in the Graduate College of Education; from 1992 to 1993, as dean of administrative services; from 1994 to 1995, as assistant provost; from 1996 to 1997, she served as assistant provost for academic affairs; from 1998 to 1999, served as vice president for administrative services.

Dr. Suber was the 10th president of Saint Augustine's College and assumed the presidency of the college on December 1, 1999. She is the first woman to lead the institution.

Betty Sutton

ELECTED OFFICIAL. Betty Sutton is a native of Ohio. She received a Bachelor of Arts degree from Kent State University in Kent, Ohio. She earned a Juris Doctor degree from the University of Akron in Akron, Ohio.

Her professional career includes serving in private law practice. She was elected a member of the Barberton City Council (1991–1992). In 1992 she was elected to the Ohio State House where she served until 2000. In 2006, she was elected a United States Representative from Ohio as a Democrat to the 110th Congress, and assumed her seat on January 7, 2007.

Anne Sweeney

ENTERTAINMENT EXECUTIVE. Anne Sweeney received a Bachelor of Arts degree in English from the College of New Rochelle and a master's of education degree from Harvard University.

Her professional career includes serving 12 years at Nickelodeon/NICK Television at Nite in various executive positions, most recently as senior vice president of program enterprises. In 1993, she was named chairman and chief executive officer of FX Networks, Inc. She joined the Walt Disney Company in February 1996 as president of Disney Channel and executive vice president of Disney/ABC Cable Networks.

In 2004, Ms. Sweeney was named co-chair of Disney Media Networks and president, Disney-ABC Television Group.

Pattie P. Swift

JUDGE. Pattie P. Swift received her Juris Doctor degree from the University of New Mexico School of Law in 1989. She was appointed judge, Colorado Judicial District, of Costilla County in 1989. She was appointed judge to the Colorado Twelfth Judicial District in September 2002.

Sheryl Swoopes

SPORTS. Sheryl Swoops is a native of Brownfield, Texas. She transferred to Texas Tech from South Plains Junior College (Texas) after being named the 1991 Junior College Player of the Year. She received a bachelor's degree from Texas Tech and during her two seasons (1992–93) at Texas Tech compiled a 58–8 record and participated in two NCAA tournaments, captured the 1993 NCAA title and won two Southwest Conference titles. She was named MVP of the 1993 NCAA Final Four after leading Texas Tech to the national championship and setting a NCAA record for points scored in the title game with 47 points in the Lady Raiders' 84–82 win over Ohio State. She was selected the 1993 and 1992 Southwest Conference (SWC) Player of the Year and finished in 1993 ranking as the NCAA's second leading scorer averaging 28.1 points per game. Her Texas Tech #22 jersey was retired on February 19, 1994.

She was a member of the 1994 USA Goodwill Games Team which won the gold medal and was a member of the 1994 USA World Championship Team that won a bronze medal. Ms. Swoop was a member of the gold medal–winning 1996 USA Olympic and the historic 1995–1996 USA Basketball Women's National teams that won a combined 60–0 record and were named the 1996 U.S. Olympic Committee and USA Basketball Team of the Year. She has won gold medals in the 1996, 2000 and 2004 Olympic Games and a gold medal in the 2002 FIBA World Championship. She signed with the Houston Comets of the Women's National Basketball Association (WNBA) in 1997. She helped the Houston Comets to four WNBA titles (1997, 1998, 1999, and 2000) and was a member of the 1997 WNBA All-Star team that toured Europe. In 2005, she led all WNBA scorers and was voted Most Valuable Player in 2000, 2002 and 2005. She played in the All-Star games of 1999, 2000, 2002, 2003, 2005 and 2006. She was the All-Star Games Most Valuable Payer in 2005 and named All-Defensive first team in 2006.

Gwendolyn Sykes

GOVERNMENT OFFICIAL. Gwendolyn Sykes is a native of Anchorage, Alaska. She received a bachelor's degree in accounting from the Catholic University of America and a master's degree in public administration from the American University. She is a certified government financial manager.

She served as a legislative correspondent for Senator Ted Stevens where she coordinated activities to protect Alaska's vital fishery industry during the *Valdez* oil spill; served with the Defense Contract Audit Agency; provided program and financial control support to the under secretary of defense (comptroller). In November 2002, she was selected as the deputy chief financial officer for financial management for the National Aeronautics and Space Administration (NASA). On July 1, 2003, she was nominated by President George W. Bush to serve as the chief financial officer for the National Aeronautics and Space Administration (NASA). On November 4, 2003, her appointment was confirmed by the United States Senate. AS the chief financial officer for NASA, she ensures the financial health of the organization, including responsibility for ensuring that NASA resources are effectively employed toward the achievement of NASA's strategic plan.

Joan Synenberg

JUDGE. Joan Synenberg is a graduate of Mayfield High School and received a bachelor's degree from Cleveland State University. Following law school she started her own law practice. In January 2005, Ohio Governor Robert Taft appointed her to the Cleveland Municipal Court to fill the seat vacated by the election of Judge Mary Eileen Kilbane to the Eighth District Court of Appeals.

Deanell Reece Tacha

JUDGE. Deanell Reece Tacha is a native of Goodland, Kansas. She received a Bachelor of Arts degree from the University of Kansas in 1968 and earned her Juris Doctor degree from the University of Michigan Law School in 1971.

After law school she served as a White House fellow, special assistant to the secretary, U.S. Department of Labor, from 1971 to 1972; served in private law practice; served as director, Douglas County Legal Aid Clinic, Lawrence, Kansas, from 1974 to 1977; served on the faculty of University of Kansas School of Law from 1974 to 1985; served as member, U.S. Sentencing Commission, from 1994 to 1998.

She was nominated by President Ronald Reagan on October 31, 1985, to a new seat created on the U.S. Court of Appeals for the Tenth Circuit. She was confirmed by the Senate on December 16, 1985, and received commission on December 16, 1985.

Julia Kurtz Tackett

JUDGE. Julia Kurtz Tackett is a native of Union County, Kentucky. Both her undergraduate and graduate degrees were received from the University of Kentucky. Before election to the Court of Appeals in 1999, Judge Tackett served six consecutive terms as district judge.

Prior to that, she served as Fayette County assistant commonwealth's attorney, federal public defender for the Eastern District, and law clerk for the chief justice of the then Court of Appeals.

Hope Taft

FIRST LADY (STATE). Hope Taft is a native of Camden, Arkansas. She received a bachelor's degree in business administration from Southern Methodist University in 1966. She and Governor Taft were married in 1967.

As first lady of Ohio, she focuses on promoting positive youth development, preventing drug and alcohol abuse and supporting community volunteerism. She is co-founder of Drug-Free Action Alliance and Ohio Alcohol and Drug Policy Alliance. She serves on the President's Council on Service and Civic Participation, the National Advisory Council on Alcohol Abuse and Alcoholism, and the National Conference of State Legislatures Advisory Committee on the Treatment of Alcoholism and Drug Addiction. She has made Ohio a national leader in its participation in National Make a Difference Day, the largest one-day national event to promote volunteerism.

She has helped build more than two dozen Habitat for Humanity homes and has launched "reading rooms" for children visiting parents in correctional facilities.

Ms. Taft is transforming the governor's residence into a living museum to preserve the property's rich heritage and create a showcase of artistic, industrial, political, geological and horticultural histories of Ohio for educational purposes.

Debra Linn Talley

GOVERNMENT OFFICIAL. Debra Linn Talley is a native of Cleveland, Ohio. She received a bachelor's degree in economics and earned her Juris Doctor degree from Case Western Reserve University.

Her professional career includes serving in the banking industry in both retail banking management and operations; she was engaged in private law practice; she served nine years as an assistant prosecutor with the Cuyahoga County Prosecutor's Office.

Ms. Talley serves as the director of the Office of Equal Opportunity, a position she has held since January 2006.

Elizabeth J. Yalin Tao

JUDGE. Elizabeth J. Yalin Tao received a Bachelor of Arts degree from George Washington University in 1982 and earned her Juris Doctor degree from New York University School of Law in 1985. Her professional career includes serving as a senior court attorney for the New York Unified Court System from 1986 to 1992 and as an associate court attorney, Trial Part of New York Unified Court System from 1992 to 1994. She was appointed judge to the Housing Court, Civil

Court of the City of New York, Bronx County and served from 1994 to 2003.

In 2004, she was appointed judge, Housing Court, Civil Court of the City of New York, Bronx County; her term expires in 2009.

Pauline Tarver

JUDGE. Pauline Tarver is a graduate of John Adams High School and John Carroll University. She earned her Juris Doctor degree from Cleveland-Marshall College of Law.

Her professional career includes serving in private law practice in 1992 and as an acting magistrate in East Cleveland Municipal Court. She was elected judge to the Cleveland Municipal Court on November 4, 2003.

Judy Marie Tate

AEROSPACE. Judy Marie Tate is a native of Hitchcock, Texas, and a graduate of LaMarque High School, just south of Houston, Texas. She received a bachelor's degree in biology from Southwest Texas State University in San Marcos and earned a master's degree in biology from the University of Houston–Clear Lake.

She began her career in 2000 with the Lockheed Martin Corporation, a NASA contractor. At NASA's Johnson Space Center, she planned the science experiments and cargo and called payloads that would eventually trail to the Space Station. She is the first African-American woman to support Space Station science activities as a lead increment scientist representative, called a "LIS" rep, acting as the liaison as the liaison between the lead increment scientist at NASA's Johnson Space Center in Houston and the Payload Operations and Integration Center at Marshall that plans Space Station science activities.

In November 2002, Ms. Tate was given the opportunity to work with the science research as it is being conducted on the station. She had to move to Huntsville, Alabama, to work at the Marshall Flight Center where she coordinates Space Station activities with scientists and ground teams.

Susan Tate

JUDGE. Susan Tate is a native of Monroe, Georgia, in Walton County. She received a Bachelor of Arts degree and a Juris Doctor degree from the University of Georgia in Athens, Georgia.

She began her legal career as a staff attorney for the U.S. Department of Energy in the Southeast region. She was promoted to deputy regional counsel in 1980, where she managed an office of attorneys under the direction of the regional counsel, providing legal support for 150 Department of Energy personnel. She moved back to Athens in 1982 and served in private law practice. She was elected probate judge of Athens–Clarke County in 1996 and took office in January 1997.

Dorothy Watson Tatem

MINISTRY. Dorothy Watson Tatem received a Bachelor of Arts degree in secondary education and a Masters of Education, both from Temple University. She earned a Masters of Divinity from Union Theological Seminary and a doctorate of ministry from Eastern Baptist Theological Seminary. She also holds an honorary doctorate from Albright College.

Dr. Tatem has served as a secondary English teacher in the school district of Philadelphia. She is the director of urban ministries for the Eastern Pennsylvania Conference of the United Methodist Church and is a devout member of the James Memorial United Methodist Church. She has also served as the former pastor of Camphor United Methodist Church. Her community outreach activities include working with the Mercy Hospice for Women, Metropolitan Christian Council of Philadelphia.

Beverly Daniel Tatum

EDUCATION. Beverly Daniel Tatum received a Bachelor of Arts in psychology from Wesleyan University

in Middletown, Connecticut. She earned a Master of Arts degree and a doctorate degree in clinical psychology from the University of Michigan. She also holds a Master of Arts degree in religious studies from Hartford Seminary.

Her professional career includes serving as an associate professor and assistant professor of psychology at Westfield State College, Massachusetts and as a lecturer in black studies at the University of California at Santa Barbara. She spent 13 years at Mount Holyoke College, serving in various roles during her tenure there as professor of psychology, department chair, dean of the college and acting president.

Dr. Tatum was appointed the ninth president of Spelman College in 2002.

Ellen O'Kane Tauscher

Elected Official. Ellen O'Kane Tauscher is a native of Newark, Essex County, New Jersey. She received a Bachelor of Science from Seton Hall University in South Orange, New Jersey, in 1974. She was engaged as an investment banker at the New York Stock Exchange from 1977 to 1979; founded the Child Care Registry, Inc., in 1992; and was elected as a United States Representative to the 105th and to the four succeeding Congresses (January 3, 1997–present).

Angela Taylor

Sports Executive. Angela Taylor is a native of Mountain Home, Idaho. She received a Bachelor of Arts degree in economics from Stanford University. While at Stanford she was a four-year varsity letter winner who helped guide the Stanford women's basketball team to two NCAA national championships (1990 and 1992). She earned a Master of Business Administration (with an emphasis on marketing and management) from New York University's Stern School of Business in May 2002.

She has served as an assistant coach for the women's basketball teams at Stanford University, Texas A&M University and the University of Arizona. As an assistant coach at Stanford, her Stanford teams went to back-to-back Final Fours in 1996 and 1997. While an assistant coach at Stanford, she had the opportunity to work with 1996 Olympic gold medal–winning head coach Tara VanDerveer and to coach two former Minnesota Lynx pioneers (Kristin Folki and Charmin Smith). She spent more than 9 years (10 seasons) with the Women's National Basketball Association (WNBA) league office based in New York City, most recently as senior director, player personnel. While at the league office, she was primarily responsible for all player-related matters and issues including collegiate and international player evaluation, player marketing, and player programs. She was promoted with the WNBA to manager in October 1999, senior manager in 2002, director in 2004, and senior director in 2005. Ms. Taylor was named vice-president of business development with the Minnesota Lynx in July 2006.

Anna Katherine Johnston Diggs Taylor

Judge (First). Anna Katherine Johnston Diggs Taylor is a native of Washington, D.C. She received a Bachelor of Arts degree in economics from Barnard College at Columbia University in New York in 1954. She earned her Juris Doctor degree (one of only five women in her class) from Yale Law School in 1957.

She served as an attorney in the Office of the Solicitor, United States Department of Labor, in Washington, D.C. She was the first African-American to serve in a subcabinet position. She served as assistant Wayne County prosecutor in Michigan from 1961 to 1962; in 1964, she went to Mississippi to defend civil-rights workers who were jailed for registering black people to

vote. She served as assistant United States attorney in Detroit, Michigan; from 1967 to 1970, she served as her husband's legislative assistant and Detroit office manager for U.S. Rep. Charles C. Diggs, Jr.; in 1970 she was engaged in private law practice; she served as an adjunct professor at Wayne State University School of Labor and Industrial Relations from 1972 to 1975; during this time she and Diggs divorced and she campaigned for Coleman Young helping him become Detroit's first black mayor; in 1975, she served as supervising assistant corporation counsel, City of Detroit, Law Department. From 1976 to 1977, she was an adjunct professor, Wayne State University Law School; during this time she married S. Martin Taylor, then director of the Michigan Employment Security Commission; in 1976, she campaigned for Jimmy Carter's presidential bid. On May 17, 1979, she was nominated judge by Jimmy Carter to the United States District Court, Eastern District of Michigan. She was confirmed by the United States Senate on October 31, 1979, and received her commission on November 2, 1979. Judge Taylor was the first black female federal district judge in the United States 6th Circuit, comprised of Michigan, Kentucky, Tennessee and Ohio.

Susan Taylor

MEDIA EXECUTIVE. Susan Taylor is a native of New York. Although she never attended college, she was a licensed cosmetologist who understood the specific needs and concerns of black women. She holds an honorary doctorate from Lincoln University in 1998 and an honorary doctorate from the University of Delaware in 1993.

She was the founder of her own company, Nequal Cosmetics, before becoming *Essence*'s fashion and beauty editor, and in 1981, its editor-in-chief. Under her guidance, the monthly readership passed the five million mark, reaching black women all over the world. In March 1986, Taylor was elected vice president of *Essence* Communications, Inc. and became senior vice president in 1993. She was the host and executive producer of *Essence,* the country's first nationally syndicated African-oriented magazine television show, the *Essence* Awards show and the *Essence* Music Festival. In 1999, she became the first African-American woman to receive the Henry Johnson Fisher Award, the magazine industry's highest honor. In 2002, she was inducted into the American Society of Magazine Editors' (ASME) Hall of Fame.

Ms. Taylor is currently the co-chair of a capital campaign with Danny Glover to raise money to build housing in the rural areas of South Africa. She serves on the board of the Joint Center for Political and Economic Studies in Washington, D.C. In addition, she serves on the Louisiana Recovery Authority at the request of Governor Kathleen Blanco to aid in the state's post–Katrina rebuilding.

Dorothy A. Terrell

NONPROFIT EXECUTIVE. Dorothy A. Terrell received a bachelor's degree from Florida State A&M University.

Her professional career included serving as a corporate officer at Sun Microsystems Inc. As president of SunExpress, the company's aftermarketing and on-line services business, she set benchmarks for customer satisfaction and asset management, and created a global intelligence system to integrate customer, product and competitor information. In 1996, she and her team pioneered Sun's ability to conduct business through electronic commerce. At NMS Communications (formerly Natural Microsystems Inc.) she served as president, platforms & services group, and senior vice president, worldwide sales. NMS is a pioneer in the delivery of innovative voice, video, and data services for wireless and wireline networks. She has also served as a partner at First Light Capital, a venture capital firm committed to identifying and funding early stage technology companies.

Ms. Terrell serves as president and chief executive officer of Initiative for a Competitive Inner City, a national not-for-profit organization whose mission is to promote economic prosperity in America's inner cities through private sector engagement.

Mary Jane Theis

JUDGE. Mary Jane Theis is a native of Chicago and received her Bachelor of Arts degree from Loyola University in 1971 and her J.D. degree from the University of San Francisco School of Law in 1973.

She was an assistant public defender in Cook County from 1974 to 1983, an associate judge from 1983 to 1988 and a circuit judge from 1988 to 1993. She was assigned to the Illinois Appellate

Court, First District, in 1993 and elected to the court in 1994. She serves as an appellate judge for the First District, 4th Division, for the state of Illinois.

Debi Thomas

MEDICINE. Debi Thomas received a bachelor's degree in engineering from Stanford University in 1991. She earned her Medical Doctor degree from Northwestern University in Evanston, Illinois. She completed her residency in orthopedic surgery at the Martin Luther King, Jr./ Charles R. Drew University Medical Center in Los Angeles and her surgical residency at a hospital in Arkansas.

Dr. Thomas was a champion figure skater prior to her medical career. In 1986, she won the United States and World Figure Skating Championships; in 1988, she won the bronze Olympic medal; she won the World Professional Figure Skating titles in 1988, 1989 and 1991. She is the first African American to win in women's singles in the U.S. National Figure Skating Championship competition. She was inducted into the United States Figure Skating Hall of Fame in 2000.

Dr. Thomas served as director of outreach, chief of obstetrics and residency director in the Department of Obstetrics and Gynecology and Reproductive Medicine at Lincoln Medical and Mental Health Center in the Bronx, New York.

Deborah A. Thomas

JUDGE. Deborah A. Thomas is a graduate of Cass Technical High School in Detroit, Michigan. She received a Bachelor of Arts degree from Western Michigan University in Kalamazoo, Michigan, in 1973 and received a Master's of Arts degree from the University of Detroit. She earned her Juris Doctor degree from Valparaiso University School of Law in 1977. She also was a graduate student in the master's program for public administration and urban planning at Wayne State University. She was selected to participate in the National Community Lawyer Fellowship for two years at Howard University School of Law.

Her professional career includes serving as a teacher and substitute teacher with Detroit Public Schools, teaching high school; as director of personnel and public relations administrator, International Telephone and Telegram, Detroit, Michigan; as a teaching assistant, Valparaiso University School of Law; as an attorney with Oakland County Legal Aid Society; as an attorney, U.A. W. Legal Services Plan; as an administrative law examiner for the state of Michigan, Department of Labor, Michigan Employment Security Commission; as an assistant general counsel for Southeastern Michigan Transportation Authority; in private law practice; as a mediator for the Wayne County Probate Court.

Since 1995, Judge Thomas has served as judge for the state of Michigan, Third Judicial Circuit Court, in Detroit, Michigan.

Jacqueline D. Thomas

MILITARY. Jacqueline D. Thomas is a native of Wilson, North Carolina. She received an associate's degree from Central Piedmont Community College and a bachelor's degree from Excelsior College. Her military education includes the First Sergeant Course and the United States Army Sergeants Major Academy.

She enlisted in the Army on September 17, 1984. She completed basic training at Fort Jackson, South Carolina, and advanced individual training at Fort Gordon, Georgia. Command Sergeant Major Thomas has held numerous assignments, to include serving as the command sergeant major of the 141st Signal Battalion.

Joyce A. Thomas

GOVERNMENT OFFICIAL. Joyce A. Thomas received a Bachelor of Arts degree in social work and earned a Master of Arts degree in counseling with a minor in Spanish, both from the University of Northern Iowa.

Ms. Thomas serves as the regional administrator for the Administration for Children and Families Region V in Chicago. The region comprises the six states including Illinois, Indiana, Michigan, Minnesota, Ohio and Wisconsin, and 35 tribal nations. She serves as the lead regional administrator for the Office of Community Service and the Faith Based and Community

Initiatives within the Administration for Children and Families.

Paula Hinson Thomas

JUDGE. Paula Hinson Thomas is a native of Sumter, South Carolina. She received a Bachelor of Science degree from the University of South Carolina in 1979 and received a masters' of education from the University of South Carolina in 1981. She earned her Juris Doctor degree from the University of South Carolina in 1986.

She was engaged in private law practice. In 1992, she was elected to the South Carolina House of Representatives. In May 1996, she was elected by the South Carolina General Assembly to the position of circuit court judge-at-large, Seat No. 1. In 1998, she was elected as a resident judge for the South Carolina 15th Judicial Circuit where she continues to serve.

Pamela Thomas-Graham

BUSINESS EXECUTIVE. Pamela Thomas-Graham received a bachelor's degree from Harvard University and a Masters of Business Administration from Harvard University. She also earned her Juris Doctor degree from Harvard University Law School where she served as an editor of the *Harvard Law Review*.

Her professional career includes serving as a director of Idenix Pharmaceuticals, Inc.; as a consultant at McKinsey & Company from September 1989 to September 1999; she served as an executive vice president of NBC and chief executive officer of CNBC.com from September 1999 to February 2001; from February 2001 to July 2001, she served as president and chief operating officer of CNBC; from February 2005 to September 2005, she served as chairman of CNBC and served as president and chief executive officer of CNBC. She stepped down as chairman of CNBC, the business news cable channel owned by NBC Universal, for a senior job at Liz Claiborne Inc., a major maker of women's apparel and accessories.

Ms. Thomas-Graham has served as group president of Liz Claiborne, Inc., since September 2005.

Lauren Thomasson

JUDGE. Lauren Thomasson is a native of Pittsburgh, Pennsylvania. She earned her Juris Doctor degree from the University of Pittsburgh. After law school she entered private law practice. She worked 13 years in the city attorney's office in Stockton, California.

On July 28, 2005, Governor Arnold Schwarzenegger appointed her judge on the San Joaquin County Superior Court. The appointment made her the first African-American judge to be seated on Joaquin County Superior Court in history.

Linda A. Thompson

JUDGE. Linda A. Thompson is a native of Chattanooga, Tennessee. She received a Bachelor of Arts degree and a Master's of Art degree in art history from Vanderbilt University. She earned her Juris Doctor degree from Mississippi College School of Law where she was production editor of the *Law Review*.

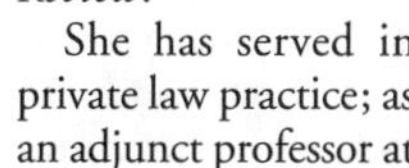

She has served in private law practice; as an adjunct professor at Mississippi College School of Law, teaching workers' compensation law; as president of the Hinds County Bar Association; as commissioner of the Mississippi Bar and president of the Mississippi Women Lawyers Association

She served as senior attorney for the Workers Compensation Commission from 1988 to 1992. She was appointed an administrative judge on the Workers Compensation Commission in 1992.

Thelma Thompson

EDUCATION. Thelma Thompson received a bachelor's degree in English cum laude and a master's degree in English, both from Howard University. She earned a doctorate degree in English literature from Howard University in 1978 and received a teacher's diploma from Bethlehem Teacher's College in Jamaica in the West Indies. She also holds an education certificate from London University.

Her professional career includes serving as a teacher at all levels of education, from elementary to graduate school; she served as the dean of the School of Arts and

Letters for eight years in the United Kingdom; she served for four years as vice president for academic affairs at Norfolk State University in Norfolk, Virginia.

Dr. Thompson was appointed the 13th president of the University of Maryland Eastern Shore in Princess Anne, Maryland.

Jannet M. Thoms

TECHNOLOGY EXECUTIVE. Jannet M. Thoms received a Bachelor of Science degree in business administration from the University of Memphis and a Masters of Science in business from Central Michigan University. She earned a Ph.D. from Nova Southeastern University in information systems.

Ms. Thoms has served as vice president of information technology at Technology Plus Corporation, an IT solutions staffing and consulting firm. She also served as director of Information Technology for Halo Solutions managing a critical multi-million dollar global account and team of software developers and as associate director of the BellSouth Corporation's E-Directory. She is the assistant general manager of technology and customer service delivery/CIO at the Metropolitan Atlanta Rapid Transit Authority (MARTA) in Atlanta, Georgia. As MARTA's chief information officer, Ms. Thoms is responsible for all technology programs and the overall management and direction of the authority's technology investments.

Leslie T. Thornton

GOVERNMENT OFFICIAL. Leslie T. Thornton received a Bachelor of Arts from the University of Pennsylvania and earned her Juris Doctor from Georgetown University Law Center.

Her professional career includes serving in private law practice. From 1992 to 1993, she served as associate counsel in the Office of the Presidential Transition and Vice Presidential Transition. In 1992, she was a member of the Clinton-Gore Crime and Drug Issues Task Force, the manager of the Alexandria, Virginia, Clinton-Gore campaign headquarters, and legal counsel for the Alexandria Democratic Committee and Election-day Counsel. She served as deputy chief of staff and counselor to the secretary of education from 1993 to 1996. In 1996, she served as deputy adviser for presidential debates to President Clinton in 1996 . She was appointed chief of staff to United States Secretary of Education Richard W. Riley.

Shirley M. Tilghman

EDUCATION. Shirley M. Tilghman is a native of Canada. She received a Bachelor of Science in chemistry from Queen University in Kingston, Ontario, in 1968 and earned her doctorate in biochemistry from Temple University in Philadelphia.

Her professional career includes serving as a secondary school teacher in Sierra Leone, West Africa; she served on the Princeton faculty from 1986 to 2001, first as the Howard A. Prior Professor of the Life Sciences. Two years later, she also joined the Howard Hughes Medical Institute as an investigator. In 1998, she took on additional responsibilities as the founding director of Princeton's multi-disciplinary Lewis-Sigler Institute for Integrative Genomics.

Dr. Tilghman was elected Princeton University's 19th president on May 5, 2001, and assumed office on June 15, 2001.

Jacquette M. Timmons

FINANCE. Jacquette M. Timmons received a Bachelor of Science degree in marketing from the Fashion Institute of Technology and earned a Master of Business Administration from Fordham University's Graduate School of Business.

She has worked in the investment industry for more than 20 years, dedicating the last ten to teaching investment management and financial coaching. She served for nine years with Bankers Trust Company (now Deutche Bank). Her media appearances include Bloomberg Radio, Fox TV's *Good Day New York*, WNBC's *Today in New York*, and BET Tonight's *Nightly News*. She is the founder of Sterling Investment Management.

Linda S. Titus

JUDGE. Linda S. Titus received a Bachelor of Arts degree from Morningside College in Sioux City, Iowa, in 1969; and earned her Juris Doctor degree from William Mitchell College of Law in 1978.

Her professional career includes serving as a secondary-level English teacher in Circle Pines, Minnesota (1969–1973); as an assistant city attorney for Worthington, Minnesota (1978–1984); in private law practice (1984–1990); as the Jackson County attorney (1988–1989). She was appointed judge, Minnesota Judicial District for Jackson County on March 1, 1990. She has won every election since her appointment.

Doreen A. Toben

BUSINESS EXECUTIVE. Doreen A. Toben received a Bachelor of Arts degree in political science from Rosemont College and earned her Masters of Business Administration in finance and marketing from Fairleigh Dickinson University.

Her professional career includes serving in 1983 at AT&T in treasury and in positions of increasing responsibility in the areas of finance and strategic planning there, and subsequently at Bell Atlantic — Pennsylvania, where she held a number of leadership positions in equipment engineering, operations, and small business and consumer market management. In 1992, she was named assistant vice president/comptroller at Bell Atlantic–New Jersey. Ms. Toben was appointed their chief financial officer in 1993.

In April 2002, Ms. Toben was appointed executive vice president and chief financial officer for Verizon.

Debra McCloskey Todd

JUDGE. Debra McCloskey Todd is a native of Ellwood City, Pennsylvania. She is a 1979 honors graduate of Chatham College and a 1982 Law Review graduate of the University of Pittsburgh School of Law. In 2004, she was awarded the LL.M. degree in the judicial process from the University of Virginia School of Law.

From 1982 through 1987, she was an in-house litigation attorney for U.S. Steel Corporation. She maintained a trial practice in the city of Pittsburgh from 1987 through 1999. Judge Todd was elected to the Superior Court in November 1999 and commenced service on the Superior Court in January 2000.

Lynda A. Tolen

JUDGE. Lynda A. Tolen received both her undergraduate degree (1973) and her Juris Doctor from the University of Michigan in 1977. She was appointed judge by Michigan's governor to the District Court in Berrien County in 1987, and served as the presiding judge of the Civil Division of the Berrien County Trial Court in October 1996.

Lynn Toler

JUDGE. Lynn Toler received a bachelor's degree from Harvard University and earned her Juris Doctor from the University of Pennsylvania Law School.

Her professional career includes serving from 1986 to 1994 as an arbitrator for the Cuyahoga County Common Pleas Court; she was elected judge in 1993 and from 1994 to 2001, she served as an administrative judge in Cleveland Heights Municipal Court, presiding over cases involving a wide array of issues, including small claims, domestic violence, negligent homicide, assault and stalking. She left the bench in 2001 after being chosen to act as a judge on the American syndicated television court show, *Power of Attorney*.

Judge Toler, former Ohio judge, took over television's *Divorce Court*, replacing Mablean Ephriam on September 11, 2006. Judge Toler is also the host on MyNetwork TV's new show *Decision House*, which premiered in September 2007.

Carol Tome

BUSINESS EXECUTIVE. Carol Tome is a native of Jackson, WY. She holds a bachelor's degree in communication from the University of Wyoming and a Master's degree in finance from the University of Denver.

She serves as the executive vice president and chief financial officer of the Home Depot. She is responsible for all corporate finance matters including financial reporting, financial planning and analysis, financial operations, divisional finance, internal audit, investor relations, treasury and tax. She joined the company in 1995 as a vice president and treasurer.

Michelle Tortolani

MEDIA EXECUTIVE. Michelle Tortolani received a Bachelor of Science degree and earned a Master of Science degree in electrical engineering from Boston University.

Her professional career included more than 15 years of experience in engineering management and terrestrial and satellite communications product and system design, development, and integration. She has managed the development and implementation of satellite-based mobile voice and data communications terminals for land mobile, aeronautical, fixed site and maritime application at American Mobile Satellite Corporation.

Ms. Tortolani was named senior director of repeater operations at XM Satellite Radio Inc., a satellite radio broadcasting company headquartered in Washington, D.C.

Frances Townsend

GOVERNMENT OFFICIAL. Frances Townsend received a Bachelor of Arts degree in political science cum laude and a Bachelor of Science degree in psychology from the American University. She received a Juris Doctor degree from the University of San Diego School of Law in 1984. In 1986, she attended the Institute on International and Comparative Law in London, England.

Her professional career includes serving in 1985 as an assistant district attorney in Brooklyn, New York; in 1988, she joined the United States Attorney's office for the southern district of New York where she focused on international organized crime and white-collar crime cases; in 1991, she worked in the office of the Attorney General to assist in establishing the newly created Office of International Programs, the predecessor to the Executive Office for National Security; in December 1993, she joined the Criminal Division where she served as chief of staff to the assistant attorney general; from November 1995 to November 1997, she served as director of the Office of International Affairs; in November 1997, she was appointed as acting deputy assistant attorney general, Criminal Division; in March 1998, she was appointed counsel for intelligence policy; after 13 years at the Department of Justice, she was assigned to the U.S. Coast Guard where she served as assistant commandant for intelligence.

Ms. Townsend was appointed Homeland Security advisor by President George W. Bush on May 28th, 2004. Ms. Townsend chairs the Homeland Security Council and reports to the president on United States Homeland Security policy and combating terrorism matters.

Julie Townsend

AEROSPACE. Julie Townsend received a Bachelor of Science degree in aero/astro from Massachusetts Institute of Technology and a Master of Science degree in aero/astro from Stanford University. She earned a Ph.D. in aero/astrophysics from Stanford University.

She joined the Jet Propulsion Laboratory in 2001 and for four years she worked on the Mars Exploration Rovers, first in development, integration, testing and later as a cruise and surface operator. She has now transferred to robotic technology development where she works as a systems engineer and software developer. Her work to date has focused primarily on multilimbed systems such as the LEMUR-lia and ATHLETE robotic platforms.

Sharon S. Townsend

JUDGE. Sharon S. Townsend received a Bachelor of Arts degree from the University of Connecticut and Juris Doctor degree from the University of Connecticut School of Law 1979. Her professional career includes serving as clerk for the Eric County Family Court and serving in private law practice. She was elected judge, William Village Court, in 1985; she was elected judge, Family Court, Erie County; the chief administrative judge appointed her acting justice, Supreme Court for Erie County; she was appointed by the chief administrative judge as supervising judge for Family Court, 8th Judicial District-wide in 1996; in 2004 she was elected Supreme Court justice, Erie County, New York.

Amy Trask

SPORTS EXECUTIVE. Amy Trask received a bachelor's degree from the University of California at Berkeley and earned a Juris Doctor from the University of Southern California.

She joined the Oakland Raiders as an intern while in graduate school and started to work for the team full time in 1987 in the team legal department. Team owner Al Davis appointed her to serve as the Oakland Raiders chief executive officer and she is the National Football League's first female [MSOffice1]chief executive. Ms. Trask was recognized by the *San Francisco Business Times* as one of the 75 Most Influential Bay Area Business Women.

Tracey Thomas Travis

BUSINESS EXECUTIVE. Tracey Thomas Travis' professional career includes serving in various management positions at Pepsi-Cola/Pepsi Bottling Group including market unit general manager and CFO, Michigan business unit; from 1999 to 2001, she served as chief financial officer of the Americas group of American National Can; from 2001 to 2002, she served with Limited Brands in Columbus, Ohio, first as chief financial officer of Intimate Brands Inc., and from 2001 to 2004, as senior vice president of finance for Limited Brands.

Ms. Travis has served as senior vice president of finance and chief financial officer at Polo Ralph Lauren since 2005, with responsibility for corporate finance, financial planning and analysis, treasury, tax and corporate compliance.

Judith R. Trepeck

JUDGE. Judith R. Trepeck received a bachelor's degree from the University of Michigan Business School. She is a Certified Public Accountant. Previously she was in public practice concentrating in the areas of tax, consulting, dispute resolution and board and executive management governance, She has served as the chief operating officer of the International Institute of Strategic Business Professionals and served as shareholder of Michigan Regional Public Accounting, a consulting firm. She was appointed to the Michigan Tax Tribunal in 2004.

Linda Copple Trout

JUDGE. Linda Copple Trout received a Bachelor of Arts degree from the University of Idaho in 1973 and earned her Juris Doctor degree from the University of Idaho College of Law in 1977.

Her professional career includes serving in private law practice. In 1983, she was appointed to the position of magistrate judge, later serving as acting trial court administrator for the five counties included in the Second Judicial District; in 1990, she was elected a district judge and handled cases in Nez Perce and Clearwater counties.

In August 1992, she was appointed by Governor Cecil Andrus to be the first woman justice on the Idaho Supreme Court. She was elected by the Supreme Court to the position of chief justice for a four-year term beginning February 1, 1997, and was re-elected to a second term ending September 1, 2004.

United States Supreme Court Chief Justice William H. Rehnquist appointed Justice Trout to the Judicial Conference Committee on Federal and State Jurisdiction in 2001 for a three-year term, and she was reappointed for an additional three-year term in 2004.

Shirley Troutman

JUDGE. Shirley Troutman is a graduate of Bennett Park School No. 32. She received a Bachelor of Science degree in business administration from the State University of New York at Buffalo and earned her Juris Doctor degree from Albany Law School of Union University.

She began her legal career in 1986 as an assistant district attorney at the Erie County District Attorney's office and as an assistant attorney general for the New York State Department of Law in 1989. She served as an assistant United States attorney, United States Department of Justice in New York from 1992 to 1994).

In 1994, she was appointed judge to Buffalo City Court and in the November election of 1994 she was elected to a full ten-year term.

Irene Trowell-Harris

MILITARY (FIRST). Irene Trowell-Harris received a Bachelor of Arts degree in health education cum laude from Columbia Hospital School of Nursing, Jersey City State College in New Jersey. She earned a Master of Science degree in public health from Yale University, New Haven, Connecticut. She earned a doctorate of health education, distinguished alumni, Columbia University in New York. She graduated from Columbia Hospital School of Nursing. Her military education includes the Air Command and Staff College; National Security Management Course, distinguished graduate; Air War College.

She was commissioned in the New York Air National Guard in April 1963 where she held the positions of chief nurse, nurse, administrator, flight nurse instructor and flight nurse examiner. She was appointed commander of the 105th United States Air Force Clinic in Newburgh, New York, in March 1986, becoming the first nurse in Air National Guard history to command a medical clinic. She subsequently served on active duty from July 1987 to February 1993 as Air National Guard advisor to the chief, Air Force Nurse Corps. She was promoted to colonel on June 16, 1988.

In February 1993, she served as Air National Guard assistant to the director, medical readiness and nursing services, in the Office of the Surgeon General at Headquarters United States Air Force in Washington, D.C. She was promoted to brigadier general on October 25, 1993, becoming the first African American female in the National Guard and Air National Guard to receive the general rank.

From September 1998 to September 2001, she served as the Air National Guard assistant to the director, Air National Guard for Human Resources Readiness in Washington, D.C. She was promoted to major general on September 1, 1998. She retired from the Air National Guard on September 29, 2001.

General Trowell-Harris became the first female in history to have a Tuskegee Airmen, Inc., chapter named in her honor, the Major General Trowell-Harris Chapter in Newburgh, New York.

Amy Tuck

ELECTED OFFICIAL. Amy Tuck is a native of Maben, Mississippi. She re-

ceived both a bachelor's degree in political science and a master's degree in public policy and administration from Mississippi State University. She earned her Juris Doctor degree from Mississippi College in 1989.

She began her career as a public servant in 1990 when voters elected her to the Mississippi State Senate. In 1999, she was elected lieutenant governor for the state of Mississippi and then re-elected in 2003.

Jeannine Turgeon

JUDGE. Jeannine Turgeon is a native of Ephrata, Pennsylvania, and graduated from Central Dauphin East High School in 1970. She received a Bachelor of Arts degree from Chatham College in 1974 and earned her Juris Doctor degree from the University of Pittsburgh School of Law in 1977 (class president).

Her professional career includes serving as a law clerk at the Commonwealth Court of Pennsylvania (1977–1979); she was engaged in private law practice (1979–1991). In 1991, she became the first woman elected to Pennsylvania's Dauphin County Court of Common Pleas and only the third Democrat since its inception over 200 years ago.

Carol I. Turner

MILITARY. Carol I. Turner is a graduate, with distinction, from both Purdue University and Indiana University School of Dentistry (1975). Upon completion of dental school, she practiced in Jacksonville, North Carolina until 1977. In September of that year, she was commissioned as a lieutenant in the Navy Dental Corps. She is a graduate of the Naval War College.

Her naval career includes serving in a variety of assignments of increased authority and responsibility to include in 1996, serving as commanding officer of the combined command 1st Dental Battalion, 1st Force Service Support Group/Naval Dental Center at Camp Pendleton, California; she served next as officer-in-charge, Naval Healthcare Support Office, Norfolk, Virginia; in July 2001 she assumed command of the National Naval Dental Center in Bethesda, Maryland; she served as the deputy chief for dental operations then subsequently health care operations for Navy medicine at the Bureau of Medicine and Surgery in Washington, D.C.

Rear Admiral Turner serves as commander, Navy Medicine Support Command, in Jacksonville, Florida; commander, Naval Medical Education and Training Command, Bethesda, Maryland; and chief, Navy Dental Corps.

Linda Edmonds Turner

EDUCATION. Linda Edmonds Turner is a native of Roanoke and Halifax County, Virginia. She was one of the first six black females to graduate from Virginia Polytechnic Institute and State University in Blacksburg, Virginia, with a bachelor's degree. She earned a Master of Business Administration and a Ph.D. in business administration from Virginia Polytechnic Institute and State University. She was a Harvard Administrative Fellow at Harvard University in Cambridge, Massachusetts.

Her professional career includes serving as a partner at Crewe & Turner Consulting in Washington, D.C. She was vice president and chief marketing officer at Dean College in Franklin, Massachusetts, where she provided marketing expertise and strategic support to the president and senior management staff. In March 2003, the Board of Trustees of the Urban College of Boston appointed Dr. Turner president of Urban College of Boston, Massachusetts.

Mary Ann Turner

JUDGE. Mary Ann Turner received a Bachelor of Arts degree from the University of Texas at Austin in 1976 and earned her Juris Doctor from the University of Houston in 1979. Her professional career includes serving in private law

practice and as the first female assistant district attorney in Montgomery County District Attorney's Office from 1980 to 1987.

She was appointed judge, County Court at Law No. 4, Montgomery County, and was elected to a full term on January 1, 2003.

Gail S. Tusan

JUDGE. Gail S. Tusan received a Bachelor of Arts degree in psychology from the University of California at Los Angeles. She earned her Juris Doctor from George Washington University National Law Center. She also attended the National Judicial College.

Her professional career includes serving as a law professor at Georgia State University School of Law and as a faculty member of the Georgia Institute of Continuing Judicial Education. She served the city of Atlanta as an administrative law judge. From 1986 to 1990, she served as a Fulton County magistrate. In August 1990, she was appointed a judge for the City Court of Atlanta. In July 1992, she was selected to serve as judge on the State Court of Fulton County in Atlanta, Georgia. In May 1995, she was elected as a judge on the Superior Court of Fulton County, Georgia.

Veronica Tutt

MILITARY. Veronica Tutt is a native of Augusta, Georgia, and entered the United States Navy TAR program in 1978 as a storekeeper seaman and attended Storekeeper "A" School at Naval Air Technical Training Center, Meridian, Mississippi.

Her key military assignments include: In 1990, she transferred to Inshore Undersea Warfare Group One in San Diego as the logistics supervisor chief petty officer. In 1993, she was selected to attend the United States Army Sergeants Major Academy at Fort Bliss, Texas. After completion of the academy, she transferred to Readiness Command Region Nineteen where she received her master's degree in human resource management and selected for master chief petty officer. In 1995, she requested sea duty onboard USS *John F. Kennedy* (CV 67). There she served in various divisions within the supply department, including being the supply department leading chief. During her tour at sea, she earned both her Surface Warfare and Air Warfare qualifications. In 1998, she was selected to the Command Master Chief program and attended the Senior Enlisted Academy in Newport, Rhode Island. She reported to Naval and Marine Corps Reserve Center, Jacksonville, Florida after completion of the academy as the command master chief.

Command Master Chief Tutt moved to New Orleans in February 2000 to serve as the senior enlisted advisor and assistant department director at the Naval Reserve Personnel Center. She assumed duties as Naval Reserve Readiness Command Southeast's command master chief in September 2003.

Jodi S. Tymeson

MILITARY. Jodi S. Tymeson received a Bachelor of Arts degree in elementary education from the University of Northern Iowa and a masters of public administration from Drake University. She is a graduate of the United States Army War College and the Harvard University Program for Research Fellows in National Security.

Brigadier General Tymeson began her military career in 1974 when she enlisted in the Iowa Army National Guard. She attended the Iowa Military Academy, Officer Candidate School. She was commissioned in 1982. During the past 25 years of military service she has held a variety of assignments to include serving as commander 67th Troop Command, as special projects officer and inspector general with the Iowa National Guard. She was appointed deputy commander of the Iowa Army National Guard, Camp Dodge, Johnston, Iowa, on September 24, 2002. As deputy commander, she is responsible for supporting the command guidance and to represent the Iowa National Guard in the community. She was promoted to brigadier general on October 20, 2003.

Lynn A. Tyson

TECHNOLOGY EXECUTIVE. Lynn A. Tyson received a bachelor's degree in psychology from the City College of New York and earned a Master's degree in finance/international business from the Stern School of Business, New York University.

Her professional career includes serving 12 years at PepsiCo holding various positions in treasury, international corporate finance and investor relations where she assisted in planning and execution of the spin-off Tricon from PepsiCo; she served as vice president of investor relations for Tricon Global restaurants (now YUMBrands).

Ms. Tyson joined Dell in April 2000 and serves as vice president of investor relations and global corporate communications.

Robin Bailey Umberg

MILITARY. Robin Bailey Umberg received a Bachelor of Science in nursing from Walter Reed Army Institute of Nursing and earned a Master of Business Administration in health care administration from the University of Northern Colorado. She is a graduate of the United States Army Command and General Staff College.

Brigadier General Umberg has over 30 years of military service in the Army Reserves, including serving as commander, 6253rd United States Army Hospital in Mesa, Arizona. From May 2000 to June 2003, she served as the commander, 4211th United States Army Hospital in San Diego, California. In May 2005, she was assigned as the chief nurse for the 3rd Medical Command in Forest Park, Georgia.

Lupe Valdez

LAW ENFORCEMENT. Lupe Valdez has earned a Master of Arts degree in criminology and criminal justice from the University of Texas at Arlington. Her professional career includes serving as a jailer in a county jail and then a federal prison and subsequently served as an investigator in multiple agencies. While serving as a U.S. Customs agent, she was sent to an array of assignments in large cities throughout the United States, as well as selected hot spots in Central and South America. She was selected as one of only seven officers to train officers in selected foreign law enforcement agencies. As a team leader in the federal Counter Smuggling Initiative, she implemented the highly effective public/private partnership known as the Business Anti-Smuggling Cooperative.

Ms. Valdez was elected sheriff of Dallas County, becoming the first woman in the history of Dallas County to serve as sheriff. She serves as the chief law enforcement officer of Dallas County. She acts as the executive officer of the county's district courts and supervises the Dallas County jails and all Dallas County prisoners.

Donna VanCleave

EDUCATION. Donna VanCleave received a Bachelor of Arts in communication studies from Virginia Tech and a Masters in Business Administration from the College of William & Mary.

Her professional career includes working to assist with the development and implementation of educational policies at the State Council of Higher Education for Virginia; in 1994, she was hired by Edward Mazur, former state comptroller and then vice president of finance and administration at Virginia State University; she was appointed Virginia Lottery director, she served in this position for six years directing lottery financial operations; more than $2 billion was raised for the lottery's beneficiary, public education K–12 in Virginia.

Ms. VanCleave was appointed vice president for finance at Radford University. She began her duties at Radford on August 15, 2006.

Sophie V. Vandebroek

TECHNOLOGY EXECUTIVE. Sophie V. Vandebroek received a master's degree in electro-mechanical engineering from Katholieke Universiteit, Leuven, Belgium, and earned her Ph.D. in electrical engineering from Cornell University in 1990. She is a fellow of the Institute of Electrical and Electronics Engineers and served as an elected member on the IEEE Administrative Committee. She is also a Fulbright fellow and a fellow of the Belgian-American Educational Foundation.

Her professional career includes serving from 1991 until 2000 she held a number of responsible roles at Xerox including technical advisor to Xerox's chief operating officer and director of the Xerox Research Centre of Canada; in 2002, she assumed the position of chief engineer of Xerox Corporation and vice president of the Xerox Engineering Center.

Dr. Vandebroek serves as the chief technology officer and president of Xerox Innovation Group for Xerox Corporation, Stamford, Connecticut. She was named to this position on January 2006, and a corporate vice president in February 2006.

Teresa Vanhooser

AEROSPACE. Teresa Vanhooser is a native of Johnson City, Tennessee. She received a bachelor's degree in industrial engineering from Tennessee Technological University and earned a master's degree in administrative science and project management from the University of Alabama in Huntsville.

She began her NASA career at the Marshall Center in 1980 as an engineer in the Ground Systems Analysis Branch. In 1987, she served in the flight projects office, where she was the assistant mission manager for the first ATLAS mission and later managed the second ATLAS mission. From 1994 to 1997, she was mission manager of Microgravity Science Laboratory-1, a mission in which a series of 29 experiments were performed in a pressurized Spacelab module onboard the shuttle. In 1997, she was named manager of the Space Station Utilization Office. In 2000, she was selected as a member of the federal Senior Executive Service. Ms. Vanhooser was named deputy director of the Engineering Directorate at NASA's Marshall Space Flight Center in Huntsville, Alabama.

Sheila Varnado

MILITARY. Sheila Varnado is a native of Cleveland, Ohio, and was commissioned into the United States Women's Army Corps at Fort McClellan, Alabama, after receiving her Master's degree from Syracuse University. After completing her basic military training, she was branched into the Adjutant General's Corps where she has served the full spectrum of command and staff assignments during her career.

In July 1997, Colonel Sheila Varnado became the first African American and first female to serve as a professor of military science and commander, University of Southern Mississippi Army Reserve Officer Training Corps Battalion. In July 1999, she was reassigned to the 3rd United States Army stationed at Fort Stewart, Georgia. She and her daughter were deployed in support of Operations Iraqi Freedom, mother and daughter working just a building apart at Camp Dohar in Kuwait. Colonel Varnado was assigned to Headquarters, Combined Forces Land Component Command in Camp Dohar, Kuwait.

Patti A. Velasquez

JUDGE. Patti A. Velasquez received her Juris Doctor degree from Yale Law School in 1980. She was engaged in private law practice in Chicago, Illinois (1980–1983) and West Palm Beach, Florida (1983–1990). She served as assistant county attorney, Palm Beach County (1991–1994). She currently serves as commission/general master in the 15th Judicial Circuit beginning in November 1994 at the main courthouse in the Family Division.

Vanessa Velasquez

JUDGE. Vanessa Velasquez received her undergraduate degree from the University of Houston and earned her Juris Doctor degree from South Texas College of Law. She served as a trial prosecutor in the Harris County District Attorney's office for 15 years. In 2005, she was appointed judge by Governor Perry to the Texas 183rd Criminal District Court in Houston, Texas.

Nydia Velazquez

ELECTED OFFICIAL. Nydia Velazquez received a bachelor's degree magna cum laude from the University of Puerto Rico. She earned a master's degree in political science from New York University.

In 1984, she became the first Latina appointed to serve as a member of the New York City Council. In 1986, she served as the director of the Department of Puerto Rican Community Affairs of the United States. In 1992, she was elected to the United States House of Representatives, representing New York's 12th District and became the first Puerto Rican woman member of Congress. She was still serving in Congress in 2007.

Ann M. Veneman

GOVERNMENT OFFICIAL. Ann M. Veneman is a native of Modesto, California. She received a bachelor's degree in political science from the University of California at Davis, and a master's degree in public policy from the University of California at Berkeley. She earned a Juris Doctor degree from the University of California, Hastings College of Law.

Her professional career began as a staff attorney with the general counsel's office of the Bay Area Rapid Transit District (BART) in Oakland, California, in 1976. In 1978, she returned to her hometown of Modesto where she served as a deputy public defender. In 1980 she served in private law practice. In 1986, she moved to Washington, D.C., to work at USDA. She served in various positions at USDA to include serving as deputy undersecretary of agriculture for international affairs and commodity program. She served as deputy secretary, the department's second-highest position. From 1993 to 1995, she was in private law practice in Washington.

Ms. Veneman was nominated by President George W. Bush to serve as the 27th secretary of the United States Department of Agriculture (USDA) and was sworn in as the first woman secretary of USDA on January 20, 2001. On May 1, 2005, she was appointed the fifth executive director to lead the United Nations Children's Fund (UNICEF) in its 60-year history.

Shirley Verrett

ENTERTAINMENT. Shirley Verrett is a native of New Orleans and was raised in Southern California. She graduated from the Juilliard School of Music in New York. She has received honorary doctorates from Holy Cross College in Worcester, Massachusetts, Northeastern University in Boston, and her alma mater, Juilliard School of Music in 2002.

She has performed the role of Nettie Fowler in Rodgers and Hammerstein's *Carousel* at the Vivian Beaumont Theater at Lincoln Center in New York City during the 1994–1995 seasons. In 1999, she was appointed the James Earl Jones Distinguished Professor at the University of Michigan. For several summers, she has taught at the Accademia Musicale Chigiana in Siena, Italy.

Ms. Verrett has also served on two White House commissions to preserve American antiquity under the Carter and Reagan administrations.

Christine S. Vertefeuille

JUDGE. Christine S. Vertefeuille is a native of Britain, Connecticut. She received a Bachelor of Arts degree in political science from the University of Connecticut in 1972 and earned her Juris Doctor degree from the University of Connecticut School of Law in 1975.

She was engaged in private law practice from 1975 to 1989. On September 13, 1999, she was appointed judge to the Connecticut Appellate Court. On January 3, 2000, she was associate justice on the Connecticut Supreme Court. She was also appointed administrative judge of the Appellate System on June 1, 2000, until July 31, 2006.

Rebecca Vigil-Giron

ELECTED OFFICIAL. Rebecca Vigil-Giron is a native of Taos, New Mexico. She received a bachelor's degree in French and social science from New Mexico Highlands University and is a graduate of the Senior Executives Program at the John F. Kennedy School of Government at Harvard University.

She has served as an elections observer in Nicaragua, Equatorial Guinea, and the Dominican Republic, and was a member state delegate with the Unites Nations in Angola during that country's presidential election in the early 1990s.

Ms. Vigil-Giron was elected New Mexico secretary of state. She is the first Hispanic woman to serve in this office and the highest ranking elected Hispanic woman state official in the nation. She served three terms as secretary of state through 2006.

Patricia K. Vincent

BUSINESS EXECUTIVE. Patricia K. Vincent received a Bachelor of Arts degree summa cum laude in journalism from Drake University and earned a Master of Business Administration degree from the Harvard Business School.

Her professional career includes serving as vice president of marketing and sales with Arizona Public Service Co.; she was in the strategic consulting group at Price Waterhouse and in brand management at the Quaker Oats Co.; in January 1999, she served as vice president of marketing at NCE (Xcel Energy's predecessor company). Upon NCE's merger with NSP to form Xcel Energy, she became vice president of marketing and sales; she served as vice president of retail services at Xcel Energy.

Ms. Vincent has served as president and chief executive officer, Public Service Company of Colorado since August 2003. She has responsibility for Colorado operations for 1.2 million gas and 1.3 million electric customers.

Lesley Visser

JOURNALISM. Lesley Visser is a native of Quincy, Massachusetts. She received a bachelor's degree in English from Boston College.

Her professional career includes serving 10 years as a sportswriter at the *Boston Globe*. She covered everything from basketball to baseball to the Olympics to Wimbledon, and also became the first female NFL beat writer where she covered the New England Patriots; in 1984, she joined CBS Sports and was a member of *The NFL Today* along with Greg Gumbel and Terry Bradshaw. She covered the Final Four, the NBA, the Olympics, Major League Baseball and the U.S. Open. In 1989, she covered the fall of the Berlin Wall, focusing on how sports would change in East Germany. In 1992, she became the first and only woman to handle the Super Bowl trophy presentation.

In 2000, Ms. Visser returned to CBS where she continues to work today covering the NFL and college basketball. In 2004, Visser became the first woman to carry the Olympic torch, where she was honored for being a "pioneer and standard-bearer." She was the first woman to receive the Pro Football Hall of Fame's Pete Rozelle Radio-Television Award. She was presented the award on August 5, 2006, at the Hall of Fame induction ceremonies.

Mary Ann Viverette

LAW ENFORCEMENT. Mary Ann Viverette received a Bachelor of Science degree in law enforcement/criminology from the University of Maryland and a master's degree in human resource management which she completed in 1998 from the University of Maryland. She is a graduate of the FBI National Academy in 1988.

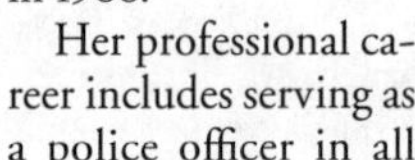

Her professional career includes serving as a police officer in all ranks with the Gaithersburg Police Department. In 1986, she was appointed chief of police of the Gaithersburg Police Department. She also serves as the president of the International Association of Chiefs of Police (IACP). Chief Viverette also serves as vice president of the National Association of Women Law Enforcement Executives and she was a founding member of that Association.

Gayle Nelson Vogel

JUDGE. Gayle Nelson Vogel is a native of Rockford, Illinois, and graduated cum laude from Rockford College in 1971. She earned a Juris Doctor degree from Drake University Law School. After law school she served in private law practice. In 1996, she was appointed judge to the Iowa State Court of Appeals.

Nora D. Volkow

MEDICINE. Nora D. Volkow received a Bachelor of Arts degree from Modern American School in Mexico City, Mexico, and earned her Medical Doctor degree from the National University of Mexico in Mexico City. She received her post-doctoral training in psychiatry at New York University.

Her professional career includes serving at the Brookhaven National Laboratory (BNL) as the associate director for life sciences and director of nuclear medicine. She served as a professor in the Department of Psychiatry and as an associate dean of the medical school at the State University of New York (SUNY)–Stony Brook. Since May 2003, she has served as the director of the National Institute on Drug Abuse. An international leader in drug addiction research and brain imaging, she was the first to use imaging to investigate neurochemical changes that occur in drug addiction.

Ann Wagner

GOVERNMENT OFFICIAL. Ann Wagner received a Bachelor of Science degree in business administration from the University of Missouri–Columbia. She served for nine years as a local committeewoman in Lafayette Township, Missouri; a position she retained even while working as both the Missouri chair and the RNC co-chair. She has served in management positions at Hallmark Cards in Kansas City, Missouri, and Ralston Purina in St. Louis, Missouri.

Nominated by President George W. Bush and confirmed by the U.S. Senate, Ann Wagner was sworn in as the 19th U.S. ambassador to Luxembourg by Secretary of State Condoleezza Rice on August 1, 2005, in Washington, D.C.

LaVonda Wagner

SPORTS. LaVonda Wagner is a native of Bristol, Virginia. She received a bachelor's degree in physical education with a minor in recreation from Mars Hill College, North Carolina, in 1986 and a master's degree in education with an emphasis in athletic administration from East Tennessee State University in 1988. A successful student-athlete, she earned National Association of Intercollegiate Athletics (NAIA) honors in basketball and volleyball in 1986 at Mars Hill College. On October 23, 1998, she was inducted into the Mars Hill Hall of Fame.

Her professional career includes serving from 1988 to 1994 as an assistant basketball coach and recruiting coordinator at East Tennessee State and as an assistant coach at the University of Illinois. After the completion of the 1998 to 1999 season, she was promoted once again to associate head coach; from 2002 to 2005, she served as an assistant coach at Duke University where she was heavily involved in recruiting, scouting, and working with the Blue Devils' post players. She posted 300 wins as an assistant coach and was involved in nine consecutive postseason appearances. She has coached in the NCAA Final Four, two NCAA Elite Eight games and two NCAA Sweet Sixteens.

Ms. Wagner was named the fourth women's basketball coach in Oregon State University history when she was hired on April 15, 2005.

Cheryl L. Waite

JUDGE. Cheryl L. Waite received her undergraduate degree from Youngstown State University (1982) and earned her Juris Doctor degree from Cleveland-Marshall School of Law (1985).

Her professional career includes serving as an assistant law director for the city of Youngstown in 1985; she served as the city's acting risk manager beginning in 1991 through 1996. She was elected judge to the Ohio Seventh District Court of Appeals in 1996 and reelected to that bench in 2002. She began serving as presiding judge of this court in February of 2003.

Kathleen Waldron

EDUCATION. Kathleen Waldron received her doctorate in Latin American history from Indiana University in 1977. She received a certificate in business from New York University in 1983.

Her professional career includes serving from 1977 to 1981 as an assistant professor at Bowdoin College in Maine; as a Fulbright Scholar at the Universidad Catolica-Andres Bello in Caracas, Venezuela, in 1981; from 1988 to 1991, she was director of Citibank's International Agencies Division; from 1991 to 1996, she was president of Citibank International in Miami where she managed a $25 million business and served on a transition team when Citicorp merged with Travelers Insurance to form Citigroup in 1998; she served as dean of the School of Business, public administration and information science of Long Island University Brooklyn Campus.

On August 2, 2004, Dr. Waldron was appointed the president of Baruch College, the nation's largest accredited business school.

Alice Walker

AUTHOR. Alice Walker is a native of Eatonton, Georgia. She attended Spelman College in Atlanta and received a bachelor's degree from Sarah Lawrence College in 1965. She served as a teacher in Mississippi and worked for the civil rights movement. She is an author whose work includes *The Color Purple*, which won her the Pulitzer Prize and was made into a film by Steven Spielberg. She is the first black woman to win the Pulitzer Prize.

Angelia Walker

AEROSPACE. Angelia Walker is a native of Phenix City, Alabama. She received a bachelor's degree in electrical engineering from Tuskegee University in Tuskegee, Alabama.

After receiving her degree she went straight to work as an electrical engineer supporting design and maintenance of manufacturing equipment for the Polaroid Film Division in Waltham, Massachusetts. In 1987, she joined the NASA Marshall Center as a quality engineer supporting the Solid Rocket Booster Project Office. At the time, NASA was preparing to return to flight following the loss of Shuttle *Challenger*. She now serves as the manager for safety, reliability and quality assurance policy assessment department, one of the primary offices of the Safety and Mission Assurance Directorate at NASA's Marshall Space Flight Center in Huntsville, Alabama. Her department ensures every engine system and hardware component that leaves Marshall for another NASA test stand or launch pad is ready to go safely into space.

Debra K. Walker

GOVERNMENT OFFICIAL. Debra K. Walker earned a bachelor of business administration degree in 1989 and a master of public administration degree in 1997 from Georgia College and State University. She received a masters in public affairs program from the Woodrow Wilson School of Public and International Affairs at Princeton University in Princeton, New Jersey, and graduated from the Air Command and Staff College.

She has served in various management positions throughout the Warner Robins Air Logistics Center at branch, division and directorate levels. She served as deputy director for depot maintenance, Directorate of Logistics, Headquarters Air Force Materiel Command, Wright-Patterson Air Force Base in Ohio. She was selected to serve as deputy director of resources, deputy chief of staff for installations and logistics, Headquarters United Sates Air Force, Washington, D.C.

Linda Walker

JUDGE. Linda Walker received a Bachelor of Science degree in biology from Southern University and earned her Juris Doctor from the University of Georgia School of Law. She was appointed as federal magistrate in 2000. She became the first and only African American woman to become a federal judge in the state of Georgia.

Carolyn Walker-Kimbro

GOVERNMENT OFFICIAL. Carolyn Walker-Kimbro received a Bachelor of Arts in languages/political science at Tougaloo College in Mississippi in 1973; she earned a master's in public administration from Tennessee State University, Nashville, Tennessee. Her military schools include the Disbursement Accounting Specialist Technical Training, Sheppard Air Force Base, Texas in 1975; Officer Training School, Lackland Air Force Base, Texas, in 1979; Professional Military Comptroller School at Maxwell Air Force Base, Alabama in 1990.

She entered the federal civil service in 1984. She has held a variety of positions in several comptroller disciplines, including disbursement accounting, budget and cost analysis and financial management.

In June 1992, she served as supervisory budget analyst chief, operations and maintenance division directorate of financial management, Headquarters Air Force Materiel Command, Wright-Patterson Air Force Base, Ohio; in February 1993, supervisory budget analyst, chief, Defense Business Operations/Cost Policy Branch; chief, Materiel Support Division Financial Management Branch, Air Force Working Capital Fund, Directorate of Financial Management Headquarters Air Force Materiel Command, Wright-Patterson Air Force Base, Ohio; in August 2000, chief, special project division, Directorate of Financial Management Headquarters Air Force Materiel Command, Wright-Patterson Air Force Base, Ohio. In January 2003, she was selected to serve as the director, comptroller directorate, Warner Robins Air Logistics Center, Robins Air Force Base, Georgia.

As director, she is responsible for the management and oversight of all appropriated and working capital funds. She oversees budgets, financial analysis, cost analysis/studies and assures fund distributions are accomplished in a timely manner and that financial execution is in accordance with public law. She is responsible for the commitment accounting and reporting of financial transactions. She serves as a focal point for determining funding propriety and directs the training assignments and career broadening/development for the financial management career field.

Barbara Wallace

JUDGE. Barbara Wallace received both a Bachelor of Arts degree in economics and her Juris Doctor degree from Washington University in St. Louis, Missouri. She was engaged in private law practice from 1976 until 1995 when she was appointed to the bench. On November 15, 1995, she was appointed circuit judge for Missouri's 21st Judicial Circuit, St. Louis County. She became the first woman to serve as a presiding judge in the 21st Judicial Circuit in January 2001.

Joy Wallace

BUSINESS EXECUTIVE. Joy Wallace's professional career includes serving key roles in finance, marketing, sales and product development at Pilgrim's Pride, Prepared Foods, Inc., and Uncle Ben's Inc. She served as senior director of national sales for the Pizza Hut Nontraditional Business Group. In her five years at Pizza Hut, she took the lead in developing new business opportunities previously untapped by the company. Among her many accomplishments was the development and implementation of the Pizza Hut Pizza Pack.

Ms. Wallace serves as president and chief executive officer of J.O.Y. Foods, Inc., which is the exclusive supplier of the Pizza Hut Pizza Pack, a pre-packaged, ready to assemble pizza kit to primary and secondary schools.

Barbara Walters

JOURNALISM. Barbara Walters is a native of Boston, Massachusetts. She received a Bachelor of Arts degree from Sarah Lawrence College.

She became the youngest producer with WNBC-TV, a local station in New York. She was hired as a writer for NBC's *Today* show and ended up being a co-host of the program without the official title, but in 1974 NBC officially designated her as the program's first female co-host.

She has interviewed every American president and first lady since Richard Nixon. She has also interviewed many world leaders including Russia's Boris Yeltsin, Great Britain's former Prime Minister Margaret Thatcher, and Iraq's former President Sadaam Hussein. She made journalism history by arranging the first joint interview with Egypt's

President Anwar Sadat and Israel's Prime Minister Menachem Begin in November 1977. Another first was an hour-long primetime conversation with Cuban President Fidel Castro.

Ms. Walters joined ABC News in 1976 as the first woman to co-host the network news. In 1984, she became co-host of the ABC newsmagazine *20/20*. She is co-owner, co-executive producer and co-host of *The View,* which premiered in August 1997 and is broadcast live from New York City.

Alice Louise Walton

BUSINESS EXECUTIVE. Alice Louise Walton received a bachelor's degree from Trinity University in San Antonio.

Her professional career includes served as owner of Liama Investment Company and as the first chairperson of the Northwest Arkansas Council. Her company Liama sold $79.5 million in airport revenue bonds for the new airport, Northwest Arkansas Regional, and for that effort she had a terminal named after her. The terminal has a bronze bust of Ms. Walton and an inscription that tells the airport's story. She moved to a 3,200-acre ranch in central Texas, Walton's Rocking W Ranch, to raise cutting horses full-time (including a mare named Walsmart).

Ms. Walton is the only daughter of Wal-Mart founder Sam Walton and Helen Walton.

Janice Warder

JUDGE. Janice Warder received a Bachelor of Science degree from West Virginia University in 1971 and received a Master of Arts degree from West Virginia University in 1976. She earned her Juris Doctor degree from Southern Methodist University School of Law in 1980.

She served as first prosecutor and later chief felony prosecutor for the Dallas County District Attorney's office in Dallas, Texas. She spent 12 years to the day beginning on December 1, 1980, and leaving the District Attorney's office on December 1, 1992. She was elected judge to the Texas Criminal District Court of Dallas County in Dallas, Texas, in December 1992.

Janis L. Ware

MEDIA EXECUTIVE. Janis L. Ware is a native of Atlanta, Georgia. She was educated in the Atlanta public schools and received a bachelor's degree in business administration from the University of Georgia in 1977. She began her career with the *Atlanta Voice* newspaper in entry-level positions and advanced to general manager. In 1978, she was licensed to sell real estate in the state of Georgia and she established a company to handle residential and commercial sales and property management.

For years, she worked alongside her famous father in the publishing business (the *Atlanta Voice* is the only black-owned print press operation in the Southeast) learning his style, understanding his dedication to excellence, and receiving inspiration from his passion for his people. His legacy has become her mission. She continues in the spirit of the high journalistic standards and commitment to the community passed on to her by her esteemed father. She serves as publisher of the *Atlanta Voice* newspaper.

Bette R. Washington

MILITARY. Bette R. Washington received her graduate degree in food marketing and distribution (agricultural economics) from Cornell University, Ithaca, New York, in 1989.

Her military education includes the Quartermaster Officer Basic and Advanced courses, the Combined Arms Service and Staff School, the Support Operations Course, the Command and General Staff College and the United States Army War College.

Colonel Washington served as group commander of the 501st Corps Support Group in 2002. She entered the Army Quartermaster Corps in 1980 after receiving a degree in economics from Alcorn State University, Lorman, Mississippi.

Linda Jacobs Washington

GOVERNMENT OFFICIAL. Linda Jacobs Washington is a native of Annapolis, Maryland. She received a bachelor's degree from Morgan State University and a master's degree from the University of North Texas.

Her professional career includes serving 12 years with Xerox Corporation holding various sales and marketing positions, the last of which was in management with Xerox Business Services. In 1994, she joined the Library of Congress as chief of the photo-duplication service. After serving nine years at the Library of Congress as the director of integrated support service, she was selected on May 19, 2003, to serve as deputy assistant secretary for administration at the United States Department of Transportation. She was responsible for the planning and relocation of the department to its new headquarters building in 2006. She has served as acting assistant secretary for administration since August 2005.

Tereasa H. Washington

LAW. Tereasa H. Washington is a native of Tuscumbia, Alabama. She received a bachelor's degree in economics from Alabama A&M University in Huntsville and earned a Juris Doctor from Vanderbilt University School of Law in Nashville, Tennessee.

After law school she joined the Marshall Center's Office of Chief Counsel as a legal research assistant. In 1983, she was appointed general attorney-advisor handling legal matters for the center's administration and technical operations. In 1988, she became associate chief counsel for issues related to personnel and labor relations. In 1992, she was appointed associate deputy chief counsel for the center. In 1995, Ms. Washington was named director of the Marshall Center's human resources and administrative support office. She led the office's evolution in January 1998 into the customer and employee relations directorate which today under her direction includes more than 250 civil service and contract employees. In 2002, President Bush honored Ms. Washington with the 2002 Presidential Rank Award, the highest honor for a civil servant.

Diana Wasserman-Rubin

ELECTED OFFICIAL (FIRST). Diana Wasserman-Rubin was born in Havana, Cuba, and came to the United States in 1960. She became a U.S. citizen in 1970 and received an honorary Juris Doctor from Nova Southeastern University Law School. In 1984, she was appointed by the governor of Florida to serve on the South Broward Hospital District Board of Commissioners. In 1988, she became the first Hispanic female elected countywide when she won a seat on the Broward County School Board. She was re-elected in 1992 and 1996. In 2000, she became the first Hispanic-American elected to the Broward County Board of Commissioners

and was the first Hispanic-American elected by the nine-member commission to serve as vice-chair in 2001. In November 2002, the voice of the people would forever change Broward County's governing charter and as a result Commissioner Diana Wasserman-Rubin would make history becoming the very first mayor of Broward County.

Maxine Waters

ELECTED OFFICIAL. Maxine Waters is a native of St. Louis, Missouri. She received a Bachelor of Arts degree in sociology from California State University in Los Angeles. In 1966, she served as an assistant teacher with the Head Start program in Watts. In 1976, she was elected to the California State Assembly. She was the first woman in California history to be elected by her colleagues to chair the assembly's Democratic Caucus. After serving for fourteen years in the California State Assembly in 1990, she successfully ran for a seat in the 29th congressional District of California.

In 1992, she successfully ran for a seat in the 29th Congressional District representing South Central Los Angeles, Inglewood, Gardena and Hawthorne.

Allison L. Watson

BUSINESS EXECUTIVE. Allison L. Watson received a Bachelor of Arts degree in economics from Stanford University and a Master of Business Administration from San Diego State University.

She joined Microsoft Corp. in 1993 as general manager for Microsoft's mid–Atlantic district and as chief of staff in support of Microsoft's platforms and services division. Ms. Watson was named corporate vice president of the worldwide partner group at Microsoft Corp.; she leads a global team of 5,000 Microsoft employees and is responsible for Microsoft's worldwide strategy for the more than 500,000 independently owned-and-operated partner companies.

Diane Edith Watson

ELECTED OFFICIAL. Diane Edith Watson is a native of Los Angeles, California. She earned a Bachelor of Arts degree from the University of California, Los Angeles, in 1956 and a Master of Science degree from California State University in Los Angeles in 1987. She is a graduate of the Kennedy School of Government at Harvard University at Cambridge, Massachusetts, and earned her Ph.D. from Claremont Graduate University in Claremont, California.

Her professional career includes serving as a member of the faculty of California State University at Los Angeles from 1969 to 1971; from 1971 to 1973, she served as a health occupation specialist, Bureau of Industrial Education, California Department of Education; from 1975 to 1978, she served as member of the Los Angeles, California, Unified School Board; served as a member of the California State Senate; from 1999 to 2000, she served as United States ambassador to the Federated States of Micronesia.

Dr. Watson was elected on June 5, 2001, as a Democrat to the 107th Congress by special election to fill the vacancy caused by the death of U.S. Representative Julian Dixon and reelected to the two succeeding Congresses.

Kyra Watson

ELECTED OFFICIAL. Kyra Watson is a 1987 graduate of Berkeley High School and a graduate of St. Louis University with a Bachelor of Science in business and administration. She is a veteran of the U.S. Air Force Reserve and currently works as a technical writer.

She was elected mayor of the city of Berkeley, California. She serves on the Information, Technology and Communications Policy Committee for the National League of Cities.

Faye Wattleton

NONPROFIT EXECUTIVE. Faye Wattleton received a Bachelor of Science degree in nursing from Ohio State University and a Master of Science degree in maternal and infant care with certification as nurse-midwife from

Columbia University. She holds twelve honorary degrees and is the 2004 recipient of the prestigious Fries Prize for service in improving public health.

Ms. Wattleton served from 1978 to 1992 as the president of the Planned Parenthood Federation of America. As the youngest person and first woman named to the chief executive officer position of the nation's oldest and largest family planning service provider, she played a leading role in shaping worldwide planning policies and programs. At the time of her departure, Planned Parenthood was the seventh largest charity in the United States.

Ms. Wattleton serves as president of the Center for the Advancement of Women, a research, education and advocacy think tank to advance women's equality and full participation in society.

Lisa D. Weatherington

MILITARY. Lisa D. Weatherington is a native of Petersburg, Virginia, and in 1978 earned a Bachelor of Arts degree from Saint Augustine's College. She received a Masters of Science degree in personnel management in 1983 from Troy State University.

Her military education includes the Army Medical Department Basic and Advanced courses; the Military Personnel Officer's Course; the Personnel Management Officer Course; the Staff Service School; the Army Command and General Staff College; Personnel Management for Executive Course and Fundamentals of Systems Acquisition Management.

She entered the Army as a Medical Service Corps officer in 1978. She graduated magna cum laude from St. Augustine's and was designated a distinguished military graduate upon graduation from ROTC. She has enjoyed a variety of assignments as battalion personnel officer, Fort Polk, Louisiana; hospital adjutant and company commander at Fort Rucker, Alabama; clinic administrator in Germany; medical department recruiter administrative officer in Washington, D.C.; personnel management officer and executive officer in Korea; deputy division chief, PERSCOM, Alexandria, Virginia; health policy analyst and force management officer, Falls Church, Virginia; chief operating officer , Rader Health Clinic, Fort Myers, Virginia; assistant chief of staff for personnel for the North Atlantic Regional Medical Command at Walter Reed Medical Center; deputy chief of staff for personnel, G-1 and troop commander, United States Army Medical Research and Material Command, at Fort Detrick, Maryland; in May 2004 she was assigned as the deputy chief of the Medical Service Corps, United States Army at Fort Detrick.

Renita J. Weems

MINISTRY. Renita J. Weems received a bachelor's degree from Wellesley College and earned her doctorate from Princeton Theological Seminary.

Her professional career includes serving from 1987 to 2004 as a professor of Hebrew Bible studies at Vanderbilt University Divinity School in Nashville, Tennessee. She served as the 2003–2005 Camille and William Cosby Visiting Professor in Humanities at Spelman College in Atlanta, Georgia. She is an ordained an elder in the African Methodist Episcopal tradition.

Dr. Weems has numerous academic books and articles to her credit and serves as a speaker at national religious, civic, and sorority gathering, local churches, community-wide events and on radio and television programs.

Yolanda Maria Welch

BUSINESS EXECUTIVE. Yolanda Maria Welch is the founder and CEO of Respira Medical, a successful respiratory and durable medical equipment home care company started in 2001. Through a women's business center, Women Entrepreneurs of Baltimore, she was able to learn the basic business skills necessary to start her business. In recognition of her Hispanic heritage, the company was named Respira Medical (respire means to breathe in Spanish).

Linda Ann Wells

JUDGE. Linda Ann Wells is a native of Independence, Louisiana. She received a Bachelor of Science degree from University of Florida in 1969. She earned her Juris Doctor degree in 1976 (with honors) from Florida State University.

Her experience includes serving in private practice from 1977 to 1999; in 1999, she served as chief district legal counsel, District 11, Florida Department of Children and Families; since 2003, she has served as a judge on the Third District Court of Appeal for the state of Florida.

Kathryn M. Werdegar

JUDGE. Kathryn M. Werdegar is a native of San Francisco, California. Justice Werdegar commenced her law studies at the University of California School of Law where she was first in her class and the first woman to be elected editor-in-chief of the *California Law Review*. She completed her law studies at George Washington University where she graduated first in her class. She received her Bachelor of Arts (with honors) from the University of California at Berkeley.

Before her appointment to the bench, her career highlights included service with the United States Department of Justice in Washington, D.C.; director of the criminal law division of California Continuing Education of the Bar; senior staff attorney with the California Court of Appeal and the Supreme Court; and professor and associate dean for academic and student affairs at the University of San Francisco School of Law; judge on the First District Court of Appeals in San Francisco.

She was appointed to the California Supreme Court by Governor Pete Wilson on May 3, 1994. In November 2002, she was re-elected to a new term of office which began on January 7, 2003.

Barbara A. Westgate

GOVERNMENT OFFICIAL. Barbara A. Westgate received a Bachelor of Science degree in general studies (summa cum laude) from New York Institute of Technology, Old Westbury. She earned a Master of Science degree in national resource strategy from the Industrial College of the Armed Forces, Fort Lesley J. McNair in Washington, D.C., and graduated from the Air Command and Staff College. She also completed a Program Management Course, Defense Systems Management College at Fort Belvoir, Virginia.

Her professional career includes serving as the deputy director, Directorate of Global Power Programs, Office of the Assistant Secretary for Acquisition in Washington, D.C.; as the associate director of programs, deputy chief of staff for plans and programs at Headquarters United States Air Force, Washington, D.C.; she serves as the director of plans, programs at Headquarters Air Force Materiel Command, Wright-Patterson Air Force Base in Ohio.

Michele Warholic Wetherald

BUSINESS EXECUTIVE. Michele Warholic Wetherald is a native of Cleveland, Ohio, and received her bachelor's of arts degree in business management from Hiram College. She received her Juris Doctorate from the University of Akron School of Law.

Ms. Wetherald has held several senior level administrative and instructional positions in higher education, including both public and private institutions. She practiced law in the private sector and served in significant management positions at several plant locations for the world's largest automobile manufacturer. With more than 30 years of professional experience, her areas of expertise include leadership, contract management, policy development and administration, human resources and labor relations,

Ms. Wetherald held the position of president of the AAUW Legal Advocacy Fund board of directors until its merger into the AAUW Education Foundation in April of 2005. Her AAUW leadership experience stems from serving in roles at the state and national level on all three national boards.

Ms. Wetherald holds the appointed position of executive director of the 100,000-member American Association of University Women.

Ann Wettersten

TECHNOLOGY EXECUTIVE. Ann Wettersten received a Bachelor of Science degree in mechanical engineering from Purdue University and earned a master's degree in business management from Santa Clara University.

Her professional career includes serving as senior director of systems and software marketing in Sun's computer systems group; she managed Sun's wireless excellence centers in Stockholm, Sweden, and Menlo Park, California; she served as vice president of business development for Sun's wireless, broadband and IP communications initiatives in the network service provider group. She now serves as vice president, systems software marketing, Sun Microsystems, Inc.

Belle S. Wheelan

EDUCATION (FIRST). Belle S. Wheelan received a bachelor's degree with a double major in psychology and sociology from Trinity University in Texas. She earned a master's degree in developmental educational psychology from Louisiana State University and a doctorate in educational administration with a special concentration in community college leadership from the University of Texas at Austin.

Her career spans 34 years and includes the roles of dean of student services at Thomas Nelson Community College, the provost of the Portsmouth campus of Tidewater Community College, the president of Central Virginia Community College and the president of Northern Virginia Community College, the second largest community college in the nation. She is the first black woman to serve as president of a two- or four-year public institution or higher education in the Commonwealth of Virginia. She has served as Virginia's secretary of education. She currently serves as president of the Commission on Colleges of the Southern Association of Colleges and Schools and is the first black American and the first woman of any race to serve in this capacity.

Pamela Wheeler

SPORTS EXECUTIVE. Pamela Wheeler received a bachelor's degree from Dartmouth College and earned her Juris Doctor from Boston University Law School. She has served in private law practice. She now serves as the first director of operations for the Women's National Basketball Association (WNBA) Players Association.

Deborah C. Wheeling

MILITARY. Deborah C. Wheeling received a Bachelor of Science degree in nursing from Columbia University and earned her Master of Science degree in nursing, adult oncology, from Duke University. She also earned a Master of Science in strategic studies from the Army War College.

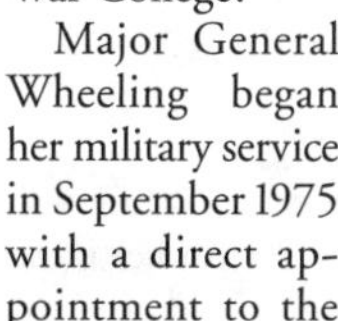

Major General Wheeling began her military service in September 1975 with a direct appointment to the Army Nurse Corps. Her experiences have encompassed a myriad of assignments within both active and reserve components, serving as the assistant surgeon general for mobilization, readiness and Army National Guard affairs prior to assuming the deputy surgeon general position in 2005.

Alice Wheelwright

BUSINESS EXECUTIVE. Alice Wheelwright received a Bachelor of Arts degree in English and American literature from Brown University. Her professional career includes serving as a manager with Coca-Cola Co, the Nabisco Brands, and Oglivy & Mather. She now serves as vice presi-

dent of industry marketing for Ecolab Inc. She has managed a series of product innovations and programs to help Ecolab customers simplify their operations, control costs, and improve food, employee and customer safety. She has been on the Women's Foodservice Forum's executive committee since 2000, having served as chair elect from 2003 to 2005.

Rachel H. Whipple

LAW ENFORCEMENT. Rachel H. Whipple received a Bachelor of Science degree from the University of Kansas and earned a Juris doctorate degree from the University of Missouri–Kansas City School of Law.

She joined the Kansas City, Missouri, Police Department on December 10, 1979. During her long career with the Kansas City Police Department, she has held every assignment in the police department from the patrol division, special investigations division, personnel development unit, field services bureau, street narcotics unit, employment unit and the investigations support division. In July, 2002, she was promoted to lieutenant colonel, deputy chief, and named commander of the investigations bureau of the Kansas City Police Department.

Jeannette Lee White

TECHNOLOGY EXECUTIVE. Jeannette Lee White was born in Seoul, South Korea. She moved with her family to Hawaii when she was 12 years old and to Bethesda, Maryland, at 14. She received a bachelor's degree from George Washington University in Washington, D.C., in 1983. She also has received executive education from Dartmouth and completed an YPO/MIT Presidents Seminar on eBusiness at MIT.

In 1987, she decided to open a company specializing in information technology services. The company, originally named Tasqe Inc., aimed to complete complicated data analysis for government and private-sector clients. She then provided IT training for a couple of years to keep the business going. In 1989, her new company Sytel qualified for the Small Business Administration's minority and women's business program. In 1991, the newly named Sytel turned a profit for the first time. Sytel opened its headquarters in Bethesda, later opening stores in Rockville, Maryland; Herndon, Virginia; and Palo Alto, California. White's company specializes in enterprise network services including network integration, network management, web integration, enterprise information portals and intranet.

Katherine E. White

EDUCATION. Katherine E. White received a Bachelor of Science degree in education from Princeton University in 1988 and earned her Juris Doctor degree from the University of Washington in 1991. She also earned an LL.M. degree from the George Washington University Law Center in 1996.

Her professional career includes serving as a judicial law clerk to the Honorable Randall R. Rader, circuit judge, U.S. Court of Appeals for the Federal Circuit; from 2000 to 2002, she was appointed by the secretary of commerce to serve on the United States Patent and Trademark Office Patent Public Advisory Committee; she was appointed to serve as a regent to the Regents University of Michigan; and she also serves as a major in the U.S. Army Reserves. She is currently assigned to the U.S. Army Judge Advocate General's School (JAG) at the University of Virginia, Charlottesville. In addition, she is a Fulbright Senior Scholar and a White House Fellow from 2001 to 2002.

Ms. White serves as a law professor at the Wayne State University Law School in Detroit, Michigan.

Maxine A. White

JUDGE. Maxine A. White received a master's degree in public administration from the University of Southern California and earned her Juris Doctor degree from Marquette University Law School.

Her professional career includes serving as an assistant United States attorney from 1985 to 1992. She has served on the faculty of both the Wisconsin and National Judicial Colleges and as an instructor at the University of Wisconsin Law School. She was appointed judge to the Wisconsin Circuit Court in Milwaukee County in 1992, elected in 1993 and re-elected in 1999. Judge Maxine Aldridge White was named the State Bar of Wisconsin's 2001 Judge of the Year.

Trudy White

JUDGE. Trudy White is a native of Baton Rouge, Louisiana. She graduated from McKinley High School in 1974 and received a bachelor's degree in business management from Howard University in 1978. She earned her Juris Doctor degree from Louisiana State University Law Center in 1981. She also completed studies at Harvard's John F. Kennedy School of Government and Kellog's School of Management.

Her professional career includes serving as deputy general counsel and general counsel to the Louisiana Department of Revenue and she was engaged in private practice. On December 6, 1999, Ms. White became the first African American female elected to Division "B" of the Baton Rouge City Court to fill an unexpired one-year term. Subsequently, she was unopposed for reelection and began serving a six-year term on January 1, 2001.

B. J. White-Olson

GOVERNMENT OFFICIAL. B. J. White-Olson received a Bachelor of Science degree in management from Wright State University in Ohio and graduated from the professional Military Comptroller School and the Air University at Maxwell Air Force Base in Alabama, 1992. She earned a master of public administration degree from Troy State University in 1994 and a master's degree in national resources strategy from the Industrial College of the Armed Forces, National Defense University, at Fort Lesley J. McNair in Washington, D.C.

Ms. White-Olson has held numerous positions of increasing responsibility to include serving from October 1994 to November 1996 as chief, Major Automated Information Systems Division, Air Force Cost Analysis Agency in Arlington, Virginia. From November 1996 to July 2000, she served as chief of the Space Programs Division, Air Force Cost Analysis Agency in Arlington, Virginia. In July 2000, she was appointed chief of the military construction division, Directorate of Budget Investment Directorate, Office of the Deputy Assistant Secretary for Budget in Washington, D.C. In July 2001, she served as technical director in the Office of the Deputy Assistant Secretary for Cost and Economics in Arlington, Virginia. In April 2002, she served as special assistant for financial management transformation in the Office of the Assistant Secretary for Financial Management and Comptroller in Washington, D.C. In January 2006, she was selected to serve as the director for budget management and execution in the Office of the Deputy Assistant Secretary for Budget in Washington, D.C.

Ruth Whiteside

GOVERNMENT OFFICIAL. Ruth Whiteside is a native of Texas. She received a Bachelor of Arts in history from Austin College. She earned a Master of Arts degree from the University of Texas in international relations and a Ph.D. from Rice University.

Her professional career includes serving as assistant director of the Southwest Center for Urban Research and the Institute for Urban Studies at the University of Houston. From 1997 to 2001, she was the deputy director of

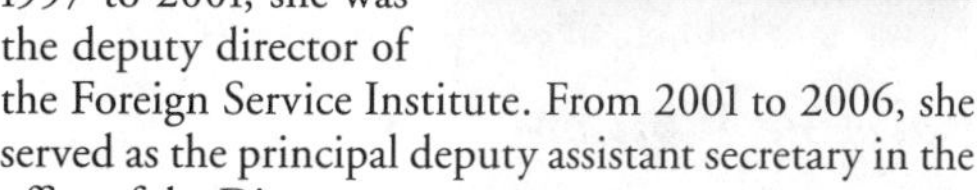

the Foreign Service Institute. From 2001 to 2006, she served as the principal deputy assistant secretary in the office of the Director General Bureau of Human Resources. On February 13, 2006, she assumed her duties as director of the Foreign Service Institute.

Christie Todd Whitman

GOVERNMENT OFFICIAL (FIRST). Christie Todd Whitman is a native of

Hunterdon County, New Jersey. She received a bachelor's degree in government from Wheaton College in Massachusetts in 1968.

Ms. Whitman was the 50th governor of New Jersey and its first female governor. She appointed New Jersey's first African American state Supreme Court justice, its first female state Supreme Court chief justice and its first female attorney general.

Mr. Whitman was sworn in as Environmental Protection Agency administrator on January 31, 2001.

Margaret C. Whitman

BUSINESS EXECUTIVE. Margaret C. Whitman is a native of Cold Spring Harbor, New York. She received a bachelor's degree in economics from Princeton University in 1977 and earned her Master of Business Administration from Harvard Business School in 1979.

Her professional career includes serving from 1979 to 1981 with Procter & Gamble and then eight years working for the consulting firm Bain and Company, eventually becoming a vice president. From 1989 to 1992, she served as the senior vice president of marketing for the Disney consumer products division. From 1992 to 1995 she served as president of the Keds Corporation's Stride Rite division. From 1995 to 1997, she served as president and chief executive officer of Florists Transworld Delivery (FTD). In 1997, she became the general manager of Hasbro Inc.'s preschool division. In February 1998, she became the president and chief executive officer of eBay Inc., the top consumer e-commerce site and one of the world's fastest-growing companies in reshaping online global commerce.

Caroline Whitson

EDUCATION. Caroline Whitson received a Bachelor of Arts degree, a Master of Arts degree and her doctorate degree in English from the University of Arkansas. She has also received a diploma in international relations from the London School of Economics.

Her professional career includes serving as a professor of English, a vice president for advancement and a provost and vice president for academic affairs. Dr. Whitson was appointed the 17th president of Columbia College in 2001.

Peggy A. Whitson

ASTRONAUT. Peggy A. Whitson is a native of Mt. Ayr, Iowa, and her hometown is Beaconsfield, Iowa. She graduated from Mt. Ayr Community High School in 1978; she received a Bachelor of Science degree in biology/chemistry (summa cum laude) from Iowa Wesleyan College in 1981 and a doctorate in biochemistry from Rice University in 1985.

Her professional career includes serving as a NASA–JSC National Research Council resident research associate in 1989; she was selected for Space Station Redesign Team (March–June 1993); in 1990, she gained the additional duties of research advisor for the National Research Council Resident Research Associate; from 1991 to 1993, she served as technical monitor of the biochemistry research laboratories in the Biomedical Operations and Research Branch; from 1991 to 1992, she was the payload element developer for Bone Cell Research Experiment (E10) aboard SL-J (STS-47) and was a member of the US-USAR Joint Working Group in Space Medicine and Biology; in 1992 she was named the project scientist of the Shuttle-Mir Program; from 1993 to 1996 she held the additional responsibilities of the deputy division chief of the Medical Sciences Division at NASA-JSC; from 1995 to 1996, she served as co-chair of the U.S.–Russian Mission Science Working Group; in April 1996, she was selected as an astronaut candidate and started training in August 1996. Upon completing two years of training and evaluation, she was assigned technical duties in the Astronaut Office Operation Planning Branch and served as the lead for the crew test support team in Russia from 1998 to 1999. In November 2003, she was appointed as deputy chief of the Astronaut Office.

She also served as an adjunct assistant professor in the Department of Internal Medicine and Department of Human Biological Chemistry and Genetics at University of Texas Medical Branch in Galveston, Texas. In 1997, she began a position as adjunct assistant professor at Rice University in the Maybee Laboratory for Biochemical and Genetic Engineering.

Carolyn Whittington

JUDGE. Carolyn Whittington received a Bachelor of Science degree in journalism from Northwestern University in Evanston, Illinois. She earned her Juris Doctorate degree from St. Louis University.

She served as an assistant county attorney for St. Louis County from 1980 to 1987.

She was engaged in private law practice from 1987 until 1992. She was appointed associate circuit judge in 1992 and was retained in 1994 and 1998. On January 19, 2002, she was sworn in as circuit judge, Missouri Judicial Circuit Court in St. Louis County, Division 7.

Lucy A. Wieland

JUDGE. Lucy A. Wieland received a Bachelor of Arts degree from Stanford University in 1972 and earned her Juris Doctor degree (magna cum laude) from William Mitchell College of Law.

She is the chief judge of the Fourth Judicial District serving Hennepin County, Minnesota. She was first elected chief judge in 2004 and re-elected in 2006. Prior to that, she was the assistant chief judge from 2000 to 2004 and the presiding judge of the Criminal Division from 1999 to 2001.

Benaree Pratt Wiley

NONPROFIT EXECUTIVE. Benaree Pratt Wiley received a bachelor's degree from Howard University and earned a master's degree from Harvard University Business School.

Her professional career includes serving as director of the Crispus Attucks Children's Center; she has served as a consultant with such corporations as Abt Associates, Contract Research Corporation and Urban Systems Research and Engineering.

Ms. Wiley has served as president and chief executive officer of the Partnership since March 1991. The Partnership's unique mission is to develop professionals of color in Boston, increase their representation in the Boston area businesses and institutions and enhance opportunities for their leadership potential.

Reba D. Wiley

MINISTRY. Reba D. Wiley is a native of Spartanburg, South Carolina. She graduated from Spartanburg Methodist Junior College in 1970 and received a bachelor's degree from Winthrop University in 1974; and graduated from the Candler School of Theology at Emory University in 1977.

The Rev. Wiley's professional career includes serving at Epworth United Methodist Church in Eufaula, Alabama; Campground-Petrey charge near Troy, Alabama; at St. Mark's United Methodist Church in Montgomery, Alabama; Flomaton United Methodist Church in Flomaton, Alabama; Gilbertown charge in Gilbertown, Alabama; and Grove Hill United Methodist Church in Grove Hill, Alabama. She served as an alternate delegate to General Conference in 1996 and was the first clergywoman elected from this conference to serve as delegate to General Conference in 2000 and was elected as a delegate to the General Conference of 2004. She served as a delegate to the Jurisdictional Conference in 1996, 2000, 2001 and 2004. She was appointed to the Demopolis District as the first woman to become a district superintendent in July 2001.

Rillastine R. Wilkins

ELECTED OFFICIAL. Rillastine R. Wilkins was first elected in 1977 as councilwoman to the city of Muskegon Heights. She has since served as mayor protem and as mayor of the city of Muskegon Heights, Michigan. She has also served as president of Women in Municipal Government for Michigan and as a member of National Black Caucus of Local Elected Officials.

Ann Claire Williams

JUDGE. Ann Claire Williams is a native of Detroit, Michigan. She received a Bachelor of Science degree from Wayne State University in 1970 and a Master of Arts degree from the University of Michigan in 1972. She earned a Juris Doctor degree from Notre Dame in 1975.

Her professional career includes serving as law clerk to Hon. Robert A. Sprecher, U.S. Court of Appeals, Seventh Circuit, from 1975 to 1976; from 1976 to 1985, she served as assistant U.S. attorney, Chicago, Illinois; from 1980 to 1983, she served as deputy chief, Criminal Receiving and Appellate Division; from 1983 to 1985 as chief, Organized Crime Drug Enforcement Task Force, Northern Central Region. Since 1979, she served as an adjunct professor and lecturer at Northwestern University Law School and at John Marshall Law School.

Judge Williams was nominated by President Ronald Reagan to serve as judge on the U.S. District Court for the Northern District of Illinois on March 13, 1985, to a new seat created by 98 Stat. 333; she was confirmed by the Senate on April 3, 1985, and received commission on April 4, 1985. Service terminated on November 17, 1999, due to an appointment to another judicial position. At the age of 35, she became the youngest judge ever appointed to the federal court.

Judge Williams was nominated by President William J. Clinton to serve as judge on the U.S. Court of Appeals for the Seventh Circuit on August 5, 1999, to a seat vacated by Walter J. Cummings, Jr. She was confirmed by the U.S. Senate on November 10, 1999, and received her commission on November 15, 1999. She is the only African American to serve on the Seventh Circuit.

Annalisa S. Williams

JUDGE. Annalisa S. Williams received a bachelor's degree in political science from Kent State University and received a master's degree in urban studies from Kent State University. She earned her Juris Doctor degree from the University of Akron Law School. She was elected judge to the Akron Municipal Court in November 2003.

Betty Smith Williams

EDUCATION. Betty Smith Williams received a Bachelor of Science degree in zoology from Howard University and a master of nursing. She earned her Doctor of Public Health from Case Western Reserve University, Cleveland, Ohio.

Her professional career includes serving in faculty and assistant dean positions in the School of Nursing at University of California at Los Angeles; she is former dean and professor, School of Nursing, University of Colorado; she is professor emeritus, Department of Nursing, California State University at Long Beach.

Dr. Williams is a founder, charter member and seventh president of the National Black Nurses Association. She co-founded the Council of Black Nurses Inc., Los Angeles, in 1968. She is president of the National Coalition of Ethnic Minority Nurse Associations and was elected a fellow of the American Academy of Nursing in 1980.

Carolyn Grubbs Williams

EDUCATION. Carolyn Grubbs Williams received a Bachelor of Science degree in sociology and a Master of Arts degree in urban planning from Wayne State University. She also earned her doctorate degree in higher education from Wayne State University in Detroit, Michigan. She has received numerous honorary degrees.

Her professional career includes serving as dean of student affairs at Highland Park Community College at Detroit Michigan; as acting vice president for academic affairs at Wayne Community College, Detroit, Michigan; as president of Los Angeles Southwest College from 1991 to 1996.

Dr. Williams was named the fourth president of Bronx Community College, a unit of the City University of New York, in June 1996. She is the first female to serve as the leader of Bronx Community College.

Darlene Williams

GOVERNMENT OFFICIAL. Darlene Williams received a Bachelor of Arts degree from Howard University and a Master of Business Administration degree from the University of Chicago. She earned a Master of Arts degree and a Ph.D. from Stanford University.

Her professional career includes serving with Pacific Bell and on the management teams of Eastman Kodak and Ryder Systems, Inc. In 1996, she joined TXU and served as a loaned lobbyist for TXU during the 77th Texas Legislative Session; she became the corporate policy manager in 2001; from 2003 to 2005, she served as the general deputy Assistant secretary for policy development and research at the Department of Housing and Urban Development.

Dr. Williams was confirmed by the U.S. Senate as the assistant secretary for policy development and research on October 7, 2005.

E. Faye Williams

BUSINESS EXECUTIVE. E. Faye Williams received a Bachelor of Science degree from Grambling State University of Louisiana and a master of public administration from the University of Southern California. She earned a Juris Doctor degree from Howard University School of Law and a doctorate degree in public administration from City University at Los Angeles, California.

Her professional career includes serving as a professor of international law at Southern University Law Center in Baton Rouge, Louisiana; she served as legislative counsel for the District of Columbia City Council; served as chief of staff to D.C. Councilmember Marion Barry; she was the first African American to run a viable political campaign for the U.S. Congress in Louisiana, narrowly missing victory after a mysterious "computer breakdown"; she served as a White House liaison to the U.S. Department of Energy during the first four years of the Clinton presidency.

Dr. Williams serves as president and chief executive officer of Natural Health Options of Washington, D.C. She has exclusive manufacturing, marketing and distribution rights to natural products created from the work of the scientific genius Dr. George Washington Carver. The flagship product of Dr. Williams' company is a peanut rubbing oil that was created by Dr. Carver more than 70 years ago for arthritis, gout, diabetic neuropathy, stress and various other pain relief.

Hattie Williams

MILITARY. Hattie Williams is a native of Norfolk, Virginia. She enlisted into the United States Army in December 1979 and attended Basic Combat Training and Advanced Individual Training at Fort Gordon, Georgia, under the One Stop Unit Program as an OSB radio operator.

Command Sergeant Major Williams' military and civilian education includes all the Noncommissioned Officer Education System courses; Drill Sergeant School; Instructor Training courses; Legal Clerk Course; First Sergeant Course; United States Army Sergeants Major Academy; Command Sergeants Major Course. She also holds a Bachelor of Science degree in liberal arts from Regents College.

Her key leadership assignments include serving as first sergeant and commo chief, 1st Armor Brigade, 2nd Infantry Division, Camp Casey, Korea; noncommissioned officer in charge, Net CECOM, Fort Monmouth, New Jersey; first sergeant, Joint Logistic Support Command (JLSC) for Operation Uphold Democracy in Haiti; first sergeant, D Company 122nd Signal Battalion, 2nd Infantry Division, Camp Casey, Korea; first sergeant/senior drill sergeant at Fort Dix, New Jersey; platoon sergeant/commo chief, 3/52nd ADA, Fulda, Germany; platoon sergeant/com section custodian/commo chief, 24th Aviation Brigade, Hunter Army Airfield, Georgia; command sergeant major, 125th Signal Battalion, 25th Infantry Division, Schofield Barracks, Hawaii.

Pearlene M. Williams

LAW ENFORCEMENT. Pearlene M. Williams received a Bachelor of Science degree in criminal justice from South Carolina State University and earned a master's degree in criminal justice from Georgia State University.

She joined the Atlanta Police Department in 1981. In 1993, she was promoted to sergeant and assigned as unit commander of the financial investigations unit.

She managed the processing of over one million dollars in seized assets (money, vehicles and real property) through the Dekalb County and Fulton County District Attorney's offices and the Drug Enforcement Administration. She was also supervisor of the intelligence/organized crime unit whose responsibility was to gather intelligence information on organized crime, police corruption and dignitary protection assignments. In 1999, she was promoted to lieutenant and was assigned as the unit commander of the license and permits unit. In April 2003, she was appointed as major of the major crimes section which includes homicide, sex crimes, robbery, burglary, larceny, fugitive, aggravated assaults/family violence, auto theft and the general investigations unit. Major Williams serves as the chief of staff for the Atlanta Police Department. The chief of staff serves as a link between the chief of police and the various departmental components.

Serena Jameka Williams

SPORTS. Serena Jameka Williams was born in Saginaw, Michigan. When she was four and a half, she won her first tournament and she entered 49 tournaments before the age of 10, winning 46 of them. At one point, she replaced her sister Venus as the number-one-ranked tennis player aged 12 or under in California.

In 1991 Serena was sent to Rick Macci's tennis school in Florida and became a professional in September 1995 at the age of 14. Because of her age, she had to participate in non–WTA events. Her first professional event was the Bell Challenge in Quebec and she was ousted in less than an hour of play. At the beginning of 1997 she was ranked number 304 in the world, but was ranked 99th by the end of that year. She was ranked number 20 in the World Tennis Association (WTA) in 1998 and won the mixed doubles titles at Wimbledon and the United States Open with Max Mirnyi, completing the Williams family's sweep of the 1998 mixed doubles Grand Slams. Ms. Williams won her first pro title in doubles at Oklahoma City with her sister Venus Williams, becoming the third pair of sisters to win a WTA tour women's doubles title. In 1999, she defeated Amelie Mauresmo in a final the same day her sister Venus won in Oklahoma City, marking the first time in professional tennis history that two sisters had won titles in the same week. She was ranked number 21 in WTA in 1999 before she defeated three top 10 players at the Indian Wells tournament and she finished the 1999 season as the fourth-ranked women's player in the world. In the fall of 2000, both Venus and Serena Williams represented the United States in the Olympic Games in Sydney, Australia, alongside Lindsay Davenport and Monica Seles. Continuing their winning streak, they won gold medals for the United States. In 2001, she lost to her sister Venus in the first meeting of sisters in a Grand Slam since 1884. The sisters won the doubles title at the Australian Open in 2001 marking their dominance in doubles in the year 2001. In 2002 she was victorious in eight out of the eleven tournaments she entered. At the NASDAQ-100 Open in Miami, Florida, she defeated the top three players in the world, including her sister, to win the singles title. This achievement marked one of many history-making wins; she and Steffi Graf are the only ones to defeat the world's three best players in one tournament. In 2002, Ms. Williams became one of only seven women in the history of the game to win three consecutive Grand Slam titles in a single year. In 2003, she defeated her sister Venus to win the 2003 Australian Open, her fourth straight Grand Slam singles title, becoming only the ninth woman ever to win all four Grand Slam events. At the end of 2006, she was ranked 95th in the world. In 2007, she defeated fifth-seeded Nadia Petrova of Russia to win the Australian Open.

On March 10, 2008, in Bangalore, Serena defeated fourth-seeded Patty Schnyder of Switzerland 7–5, 6–3, to win her first WTA Tour singles title of 2008 and her 29th career singles title. In April 2008 in Miami, Florida, Serena defeated fourth-seeded Jelena Jankovic of Serbia, Russia, in the final of the Sony Ericsson Open 6–1, 5–7, 6–3, to win her fifth Miami Singles title and 30th overall career singles title. On May 28, 2008, she lost to Mathilde Johansson in the French Open at Roland Garros stadium 6–4, 6–3. On July 5, 2008, Serena lost to her sister Venus in the Wimbledon final 7–5, 6–4, in London, England.

On September 7, 2008, Serena Williams won the 2008 U.S. Open title and regained her number one tennis ranking.

Venus Ebone Starr Williams

SPORTS (FIRST). Venus Ebone Starr Williams' father withdrew her from middle school in Delray Beach, Florida, so she could be home schooled. She began playing tennis as a child and on October 31, 1994, she turned professional. In 1998, she teamed up with Justin Gimelstob to win the mixed doubles title at the Australian Open and the French Open. In 1999, she won the tournament in Miami, defeating Jana Novotna, Seffi Graf, and her sister Serena in successive matches. Ms. Williams also won the tournaments in Hamburg, Rome, New Haven, and Zurich. Venus teamed up with her sister Serena to win the doubles titles at the French

Open and the U.S. Open, becoming the first sister team to win a Grand Slam doubles title in the 20th century. In 2000, Ms. Williams won the single title at both Wimbledon and the U.S. Open and two gold medals at the 2000 Summer Olympics in Sydney. The Williams sisters also won the Wimbledon doubles title for the first time. In 2001, she successfully defended her Wimbledon and U.S. Open singles titles. In 2002, she won the Gold Coast tournament and in February 2002 she became the number one ranked player in the world, the first black American tennis player ever to receive the top ranking. The Williams sisters won the Wimbledon doubles title for the second time in 2002.

In 2003, she won the Proximus Diamond Games in Antwerp, Belgium, for the second consecutive year. She advanced to her fourth consecutive Wimbledon final and lost the final to her sister Serena. In 2004, she won the Tier I Family Circle Cup in Charleston, South Carolina and she also won the Tier II tournament in Warsaw. In 2005, she won the Tier III title in Istanbul, defeating second-seeded Nicole Vaidisova in the final and defeated top-seeded Lindsay Davenport, winning the Wimbledon singles title in the longest Wimbledon final in history. This was the first time in 70 years that a player had won after being down match point during the women's final. In 2007, at the WTA Tier III Cellular South Cup in Memphis, Tennessee, she won the title, her first tournament since October 2006 and her 34th career singles title.

On July 5, 2008, Venus defeated her sister Serena in the Wimbledon Finals 7–3, 6–4, in London, England. The Williams sisters have met in seven of nine Grand Slam title matches from the U.S. Open in 2001 through Wimbledon 2008. Serena has won five of the seven matches. This was Venus's second consecutive title at Wimbledon and seventh major championship overall.

Ms. Williams is also CEO of her interior design firm, V Starr Interiors, located in Jupiter, Florida.

Margaret Chamberlain Wilmoth

MILITARY. Margaret Chamberlain Wilmoth received a Bachelor of Science degree in nursing and a Master of Science degree in nursing from the University of Maryland. She earned a doctorate degree in nursing from the University of Pennsylvania and a master's degree in strategic studies from the United States Army War College.

Brigadier General Margaret Chamberlain Wilmoth serves in the United States Army Reserves as commander, 332nd Medical Brigade in Nashville, Tennessee, since May 2005. She also serves as a professor, School of Nursing, College of Health and Human Services at the University of North Carolina–Charlotte in Charlotte, North Carolina.

Cindy Polk Wilson

JUDGE. Cindy Polk Wilson received a Bachelor of Arts degree from Mississippi State University in 1980. She earned her Juris Doctor degree from the University of Mississippi School of Law in 1986.

Her professional career includes serving in private law practice. She was appointed an administrative judge with the Mississippi Worker's Compensation Commission.

Debra A. Wilson

JUDGE. Debra A. Wilson received a Bachelor of Arts degree from Luther College in 1971 and received a Master's of Arts degree from the University of Minnesota in 1973. She earned her Juris Doctor degree from William Mitchell College of Law in 1981.

She served in private law practice before her appointment as a compensation judge at the Office of Administrative Hearing for Minnesota. She now serves as a judge for the Workers' Compensation Court of Appeals.

Heather Wilson

ELECTED OFFICIAL. Heather Wilson is a native of Keene, New Hampshire, and a graduate of Keene High

School. She received a Bachelor of Science degree from the United States Air Force Academy, Colorado Springs, Colorado, in 1982. She was a Rhodes Scholar, Master of Phil. at Oxford University, Oxford, England, in 1984 and earned her Doctorate of Phil. from Oxford University in Oxford, England, in 1985.

Her professional career includes serving in the United States Air Force from 1978 to 1989; serving as cabinet secretary of the New Mexico Children, Youth and Families Department from 1995 to 1998; as director for European defense policy and arms control, National Security Council from 1989 to 1991. She was elected a United States Representative to the 105th Congress by special election to fill a vacancy and was reelected to the four succeeding Congresses since June 23, 1998.

Janice Rose Wilson

JUDGE. Janice Rose Wilson received a Bachelor of Arts degree (cum laude) from Willamette University in 1976 and earned her Juris Doctor degree (summa cum laude) from Willamette University in 1979.

Her professional career includes serving as law clerk to the United States District Court for the District of Oregon and United States Court of Appeals for the Ninth Circuit from 1979 to 1981; she was engaged in private law practice from 1981 to 1991. In March 1991, she was appointed judge to the Oregon District Court in Portland. She was elevated to judge of the Circuit Court of Oregon.

Rosa L. Wilson

MILITARY. Rosa L. Wilson served as the command master chief for the legendary Black Knights of Helicopter Anti-Submarine Squadron Four at Naval Air Station North Island, San Diego, California.

The Black Knights returned from the 2002–2003 world record western Pacific deployment aboard the USS *Abraham Lincoln* (CVN 72) with accomplishments including military engagement with Pakistan, detachments in Kuwait and CSAR training in Australia, all in support of Operation Southern Watch and Operation Enduring Freedom. During Operation Iraqi Freedom, HS-4 supported Navy SEAL, British Commando and Polish GROM forces in Kuwait and Iraq and were the primary force protection for the USS *Abraham Lincoln* battle group. The nine-and-one-half month deployment (a record since World War II) included 1,283 sorties and 3,228 flight hours' flown — new records since the Vietnam War. With its current complement of six helicopters, 27 officers and 162 enlisted personnel, the Black Knights are the most decorated helicopter antisubmarine squadron in history.

Stephanie D. Wilson

ASTRONAUT. Stephanie D. Wilson was born in Boston, Massachusetts. After graduating from Harvard University in 1988 she worked for two years for the former Martin Marietta Astronautics Group in Denver, Colorado. As a loads and dynamics engineer for Titan IV, she was responsible for performing coupled loads analyses for the launch vehicle and payloads during flight events. She left Martin Marietta in 1990 to attend graduate school at the University of Texas. Her research focused on the control and modeling of large, flexible space structures. Following the completion of her graduate work, she began working for the Jet Propulsion Laboratory in Pasadena, California, in 1992. As a member of the attitude and articulation control subsystem for the Galileo spacecraft, she was responsible for assessing attitude controller performance, science platform pointing accuracy, antenna pointing accuracy and spin rate accuracy. While at the Jet Propulsion Laboratory, she also supported the interferometer technology program as a member of the integrated modeling team which was responsible for finite element modeling, controller design and software development.

She was selected by NASA in April 1996 and reported to the Johnson Space Center in August 1996. Having completed two years of training and evaluation, she is qualified for flight assignment as a mission specialist. She was initially assigned technical duties in the Astronaut Office Space Station Operations Branch. She then served in the Astronaut Office CAPCOM Branch working in mission control as prime communicator with on-orbit crews. She later served in the Astronaut Office Shuttle Operations Branch. She was assigned to the crew of STS-120.

Oprah Gail Winfrey

ENTERTAINMENT EXECUTIVE. Oprah Gail Winfrey is a native of Kosciusko, Mississippi. She learned to read at the age of two-and-a-half, and when enrolled in kindergarten, she wrote a note that pointed out in no uncertain terms that she belonged in the first grade; her astonished teacher had her promoted. After completing that academic year, she skipped directly to the third grade. At the age of six, she was sent to join her mother and two half-brothers in the Milwaukee ghetto. Her unmarried parents separated when she was very young and she later moved to Nashville to live with her father and his wife Zelma. Her father was a barber who became a member of the Nashville City Council. When she was 16 she won an Elks Club oratorical contest that guaranteed her a full scholarship to college. She received a bachelor's degree from Tennessee State University in 1976.

Her professional career includes serving as a newscaster at WVOL in Nashville while still in high school. During her freshman year at Tennessee State University, she became Miss Black Nashville and Miss Tennessee and in 1971 she was a contestant in the Miss Black America Pageant. She accepted a position with WTVF-TV, becoming Nashville's first African American woman to serve as co-anchor on the evening news. She served as a reporter and co-anchor on the six o'clock news at WJZ-TV, the ABC affiliate in Baltimore, Maryland. In January 1984, she moved to Chicago to become an A.M. anchor for WLS-TV on *A.M. Chicago*, which was later renamed *The Oprah Winfrey Show*. Her subsequent success led to a role in Steven Spielberg's film *The Color Purple* in 1985, for which she was nominated for an Academy Award. In 1986, *The Oprah Winfrey Show* entered national syndication and became the highest-rated talk show in Chicago and made her the third woman in the American entertainment industry to own her own studio. *The Oprah Winfrey Show* has remained the number-one talk show for 20 consecutive seasons. *The Oprah Winfrey Show* and *The Women of Brewster* Place were produced by her production company, Harpo Productions, Inc.

Ms. Winfrey's commitment to children also led her to initiate the National Child Protection Act in 1991, when she testified before the U.S. Senate Judiciary Committee to establish a national database of convicted child abusers. On December 20, 1993, President Clinton signed the national "Oprah Bill" into law.

Ms. Winfrey is co-founder of Oxygen Media, which operates a 24-hour cable television network for women that launched in 1998; she also created the Oprah's Angel Network in 1998; in 2002, she debuted *Oprah After The Show* and also in December 2002, she announced a partnership with South Africa's Ministry of Education to build the Oprah Winfrey Leadership Academy for Girls in South Africa.

In 2005, Ms. Winfrey made her Broadway debut as a producer for the musical *The Color Purple* which opened on December 1, 2005, at the Broadway Theatre in New York City. Through a joint venture, she announced the launch of *Oprah & Friends*, a new channel on XM Satellite Radio in 2006.

Cleta Winslow

ELECTED OFFICIAL. Cleta Winslow graduated from Tennessee State University with a bachelor's degree in social work. She received her master's degree from the Clark Atlanta University School of Social Work. She has worked at the Carrie-Steele-Pitts Children's Home and been housing director for the Atlanta Urban League. Ms. Winslow also worked for the city of Atlanta as a human service planner and as a neighborhood planning unit coordinator in the Bureau of Planning. She has served as president of the National Association of Neighborhoods.

Ms. Winslow has served on the Atlanta City Council, District 4, for over twenty years.

Terri Winstead-Wilfong

LAW ENFORCEMENT. Terri Winstead-Wilfong received a Bachelor of Science degree in justice administration from the University of Louisville and is a graduate of the Southern Police Institute.

She started her law enforcement career with the Jefferson County Sheriff's Department and as a Kentucky State Police trooper. In 1985, she joined the Jefferson County Police Department. She was promoted to lieutenant and served in the Adam District before becoming commander of the internal affairs unit. She was also assistant commander of David District. After being promoted to captain, she served as com-

mander of David District. She was promoted to lieutenant colonel on February 6, 2003, making her a member of the first command staff of the newly merged Louisville Metro Police Department. She has also served on the Jefferson County Crisis Negotiation team for 12 years.

Phyllis Wise

EDUCATION. Phyllis Wise received a bachelor's degree in biology from Swarthmore College in 1967 and earned a doctorate degree in zoology from the University of Michigan in 1972.

Her professional career includes serving from 1976 to 1993 as a faculty member at the University of Maryland, Baltimore, where she was promoted to the rank of full professor of physiology in 1987; from 1993 to 2002, she served as professor and chair of the Department of Physiology at the University of Kentucky in Lexington; from 2002 to 2005, she served as dean of the College of Biological Sciences at the University of California at Davis; she served a professor of physiology and biophysics, biology and obstetrics and gynecology at the University of Washington.

Dr. Wise serves as the provost for the University of Washington.

Lorna Wisham

GOVERNMENT OFFICIAL. Lorna Wisham is a native of Cleveland, Ohio. She received a bachelor's degree in business and organizational communication from the University of Akron and earned a master of public communication from American University in Washington, D.C.

Her professional career includes serving as an events manager; serving in the *Plain Dealer* Washington bureau as the editorial researcher, and for local public relations firms. She served as vice president for three years for Downtown Cleveland Partnership, downtown Cleveland's economic development group. Ms. Wisham was appointed chief public affairs officer for the city of Cleveland in February 2002. She was sworn in September 2002 as the first woman to head the Cleveland Community Relations Board and has since been asked to lead the public affairs cluster.

Sharon Bingham Wolfolk

MILITARY. Sharon Bingham Wolfolk is a native of Washington, D.C. She began her military career in 1983. She holds a bachelor of music from the Catholic University of Virginia. She is a past winner of the Friday Morning Music Club Student Concerto Competition and as the winner performed as a soloist with the McLean (Virginia) Symphony Orchestra.

An active freelance musician in the Washington, D.C., area, she has performed regularly as a violinist with the Fairfax and Prince George's symphonies, Landon, Beethoven ensemble Strings for Christ.

In 1985, she was awarded a scholarship to the renowned Aspen Music Festival in Colorado. She is a violinist with the United States Air Force Band at Bolling Air Force Base, Washington, D.C.

Andrea Wong

BUSINESS EXECUTIVE. Andrea Wong received a Bachelor of Science degree in electrical engineering from Massachusetts Institute of Technology in 1988 and earned her Masters of Business Administration from Stanford University Graduate School of Business in 1993.

Her professional career includes joining ABC News in August 1993 as a researcher for ABC News *Prime Time Live*; in June 1994 she was named executive assistant to the president of ABC Television Network; in November 1995 she was appointed executive assistant to the president, ABC, Inc.; in September 1997 she was promoted to vice president and executive assistant to the president, ABC, Inc.; by 1998 she was a appointed vice president, alternative series and specials for ABC Entertainment.

Ms. Wong was named executive vice president, alternative programming, specials and late-night,

ABC Entertainment, in May 2004. She brought the UK phenomenon *Dancing with the Stars* to the American audience in June 2005. Her programming won its second Emmy for ABC when *Extreme Makeover: Home Edition* picked up another statue for Outstanding Reality Program. In addition, the 2006-07 season saw two critically acclaimed and highly rated reality series enter their third years, *Wife Swap* and *Supernanny*.

Lisa Godbey Wood

JUDGE. Lisa Godbey Wood received a bachelor's degree as first honor graduate from the University of Georgia in 1985. She earned her Juris Doctor degree summa cum laude from the University of Georgia in 1990.

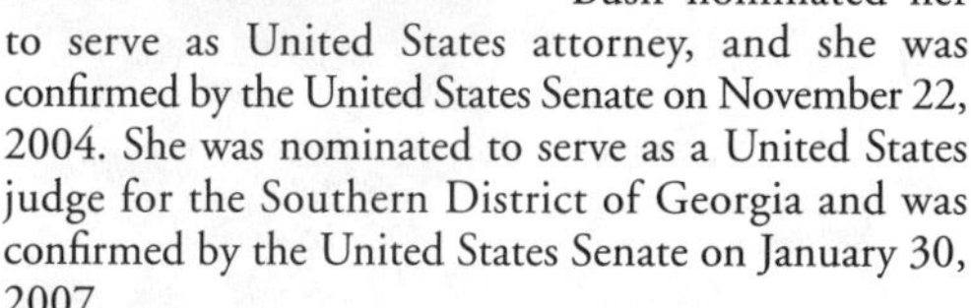

Her professional career includes serving as a law clerk for Judge Anthony A. Alaimo in Brunswick. She served in private law practice in Brunswick, Georgia. She served as a magistrate judge in Glynn County, Georgia. President George Bush nominated her to serve as United States attorney, and she was confirmed by the United States Senate on November 22, 2004. She was nominated to serve as a United States judge for the Southern District of Georgia and was confirmed by the United States Senate on January 30, 2007.

Ruth A. Wooden

BUSINESS EXECUTIVE. Ruth A. Wooden attended Lawrence University in Appleton, Wisconsin, and she received a Bachelor of Arts in sociology and history from the University of Minnesota. In 1994, she was awarded an honorary doctorate from Northeastern University.

Her professional career includes serving as a research branch analyst at the Ralston Purina Company in St. Louis, Missouri. and as an account supervisor, senior vice president and managing director at N. W. Ayer Advertising in New York. From 1987 to 1999, she served as president of the Advertising Council; she served as a volunteer president of the National Parenting Association; as executive vice president senior counselor at the international public relations firm of Porter Novelli. On August 4, 2003, she became president of Public Agenda.

Jacqueline Woods

BUSINESS EXECUTIVE. Jacqueline Woods received a Bachelor of Science degree from the University of California at Davis and a Masters of Business Administration with a concentration in marketing from the University of Southern California.

Her professional career includes serving in marketing management positions with GTE where she developed sales and marketing strategies for GTE's premier U.S. accounts; as director of product management for Ameritech's customer premise, equipment business.

Ms. Woods serves as vice president of global pricing and licensing strategy for Oracle Corporation Business Practices. She chairs Oracle's pricing committee for its global lines of businesses.

Lynn C. Woolsey

ELECTED OFFICIAL. Lynn C. Woolsey is a native of Seattle, Washington, and a graduate of Lincoln High school in Seattle, Washington. She received a Bachelor of Science degree from the University of San Francisco in San Francisco, California, in 1980.

Her professional career includes serving in numerous positions as human resource manager; personnel service owner; teacher at Marin Community College in Indian Valley, California; as an instructor, Dominican College of San Rafael, California. From 1984 to 1992, she served as a member of the Petaluma, California, City Council; from 1989 to 1992, she served as vice mayor of the city of Petaluma, California; in 1992, she was elected as a Democrat to the 103rd and to the seven succeeding Congresses (January 3, 1993, to present).

Renee L. Worke

JUDGE. Renee L. Worke received a Bachelor of Science degree (magna cum laude) from Minnesota State University in 1980 and earned her Juris Doctor degree from William Mitchell College of Law in 1983.

Her professional career includes serving as a law clerk for District Court Judge Urban J. Steimann at Faribault, Minnesota; as a contract administrative law judge for the Child Support Division, Office of Administrative Hearings; as a contract assistant public defender for the Third Judicial District; and in private law practice.

She was appointed to the Waseca County District Court in 1996 and elected in 1998. She was appointed judge on the Minnesota Court of Appeals in 2005.

Aldona Zofia Wos

GOVERNMENT OFFICIAL. Aldona Zofia Wos was born in Warsaw, Poland, but spent her childhood on Long Island, New York. She earned her medical degree at the Warsaw Medical Academy and completed her internship and residency in internal medicine and a fellowship in pulmonary medicine in New York.

Her professional career includes serving in private medical practice, in corporate medicine, as an attending physician, clinical care, teaching, and staff physician duties for both hospitals and private industry. She was sworn in on August 13, 2004, by Secretary of State Colin Powell as U.S. ambassador extraordinary and plenipotentiary of the United States of America to the Republic of Estonia. She is the fifth U.S. ambassador since Estonia regained its independence.

Carolyn Wright

JUDGE. Carolyn Wright is a native of Houston, Texas. After graduating from high school, she enrolled in a paralegal program at Strayer College in Washington, D.C. After receiving her degree, she worked for the Citizens Crusade against Poverty, the Equal Employment Opportunity Commission and the Office of Youth Advocacy. She earned a Juris Doctor degree from Howard University School of Law in 1978.

Upon graduation from law school, she moved back to Texas and began a private law practice. In 1986, she was elected state judge of the 256th District Court. She served in the 256th District Court until she was appointed by Governor Bush to fill a vacant seat on the Fifth District Court of Appeals. She has since been elected twice to the same seat.

Justice Wright has

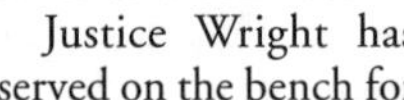

served on the bench for 20 years. She is the highest ranking African-American in the Texas State Judiciary.

Deborah C. Wright

FINANCE. Deborah C. Wright received a bachelor of business administration from Harvard University. She earned a Master of Business Administration degree from Harvard University and a Juris Doctor degree from Harvard University Law School.

Her professional career includes serving on the New York City Housing Authority Board and as a member of the New York City Planning Commission. From 1994 to 1996, she served as commissioner of the Department of Housing Preservation and Development. From 1996 to 1999, she served as president and chief executive officer of the Upper Manhattan Empowerment Zone Development Corporation. In 1999, she was named president and chief executive officer of Carver Bancorp, Inc. and Carver Federal Saving Bank. In February 2005, she was appointed chairman, president and chief executive officer of Carver Bancorp, Inc. and Carver Federal Savings Bank.

Doreen A. Wright

BUSINESS EXECUTIVE. Doreen A. Wright received a Bachelor of Arts degree from the University of Pennsylvania in 1979.

Her professional career includes serving at Merrill Lynch managing several retail client service and processing units; in 1984, she joined Bankers Trust Company as vice president, institutional trust and custody marketing; she served for 10 years in leadership positions as a managing director and senior vice president of numerous large-scale institutional customer service and technology groups; from 1995 to 1998, she served as senior vice president, operations and systems for Prudential Insurance Company's Prudential Investment Group; as executive vice president and chief information officer at Nabisco.

Ms. Wright was appointed senior vice president and chief information officer of Campbell Soup Company effective June 6, 2001. She leads the company's global information technology organization.

Karla F. Wright

JUDGE. Karla F. Wright received a Bachelor of Arts degree from Lincoln University in 1971 and received a Master's of Science degree in 1974. She earned her Juris Doctor degree from Northwestern University School of Law in 1983.

Her professional career includes serving in private law practice; as assistant public defender for the 10th Circuit; as assistant Hillsborough County attorney; as the senior attorney for the Department of Transportation; and assistant Polk County attorney.

She was appointed county judge in 2000 and was elected in 2002 to a full term. She received an appointment as circuit judge in 2005.

Sherry L. Wright

MILITARY. Sherry L. Wright is a native of Miami, Florida; she graduated from basic training at Fort Dix, New Jersey in 1981 and advanced individual training at Fort Gordon, GA. She has completed the United States Sergeants Major Academy (class 53). She attended Chaminade University and earned an associates degree in liberal studies. She holds a Bachelor of Science degree in business administration from Excelsior College. She is pursuing a master degree in human resource development and minor in management. She is a graduate of the Master Fitness Training Course and the Small Group Instructor Training Course.

Command Sergeant Major Wright's military assignments include serving three tours in the Federal Republic of Germany, first at 143rd Signal Battalion, then 101st Military Intelligence, and next with the 17th Signal Battalion. She served a short tour in 1991 in Saudi Arabia for Desert Shield/Desert Storm. She served as first sergeant for five consecutive years. In August 2004, she was serving as the command sergeant major for 141 Battalion, Wiesbaden, Germany.

She is a member of the prestigious Sergeant Audie Murphy and Sergeant Morales clubs.

Wilhelmina M. Wright

JUDGE. Wilhelmina M. Wright graduated with honors in literature from Yale University in 1986. She received her Juris Doctor degree from Harvard Law School in 1989.

After law school, she was a law clerk for the Honorable Damon J. Keith on the United States Court of Appeals for the Sixth Circuit. She served in private law practice in Washington, D.C. In 1995, she served as an U.S. attorney for the District of Minnesota at the United States District Court and the United States Court of Appeals for the Eight Circuit. She served as a trial judge on the Ramsey County District Court in Saint Paul, Minnesota.

She was appointed by Governor Jesse Ventura to the Minnesota Court of Appeals where she has served since September 3, 2002.

Merri Souther Wyatt

JUDGE. Merri Souther Wyatt attended Portland State University in 1966 and received a Bachelor of Arts degree from the University of Oregon in 1970. She earned her Juris Doctor degree from Willamette University College of Law in 1978.

Her professional career includes serving in private law practice from 1978 to 1989; from 1991 to 1993, she served as a Multnomah County Juvenile Court Referee and Special Prosecutor at Multnomah County Juvenile Court. She has served as judge, Multnomah County District and Circuit Court in Oregon.

May L. Wykle

EDUCATION. May L. Wykle received a Bachelor of Science degree in nursing from Case Western Reserve University and a diploma from the Ruth Brant School of Nursing, Martins Ferry in Ohio. She earned a Mas-

ter of Science degree in nursing and holds a Ph.D. from Case Western Reserve University.

Her professional career includes serving as a staff nurse with the Cleveland Psychiatric Institute; she has served as chairperson/director, psychiatric–mental health nursing, University Hospitals of Cleveland; she served as project director, Robert Wood Johnson Foundation Teaching Nursing Home; as an assistant professor of psychiatric nursing at Case Western Reserve University; she served as a visiting professor at the University of Zimbabwe, at the University of Michigan and at the University of Texas. She serves as president of Sigma Theta Tau International, the national nursing honor society.

Dr. Wykle serves as dean of the Frances Payne Bolton School of Nursing at Case Western Reserve University in Cleveland. She also serves as adjunct professor at Georgia Southwestern State University in Americus and was a Pope Eminent Scholar at the school's Rosalyn Carter Institute.

Nancy Wyman

ELECTED OFFICIAL. Nancy Wyman is Connecticut's first woman elected state comptroller. She acts as the chief fiscal guardian for state taxpayers. She was first elected statewide in 1994 and re-elected in 1998, 2002 and 2006.

From 1979 to 1987, she served on the Tolland Board of Education and was vice chairperson for four of those years. She has contributed to the local, state and national education debate and is known as an ardent champion of public education.

Prior to her election as state comptroller, she served as a state representative (1987 to 1995) from the 53rd District.

Dorothy Cowser Yancy

EDUCATION. Dorothy Cowser Yancy received a Bachelor of Arts degree from Johnson C. Smith University, a Master of Arts degree from the University of Massachusetts, Amherst, and a Ph.D. from Atlanta University (Georgia), with further study at a variety of universities. She is listed as an arbitrator with the Federal Mediation and Conciliation Services and the American Arbitration Association.

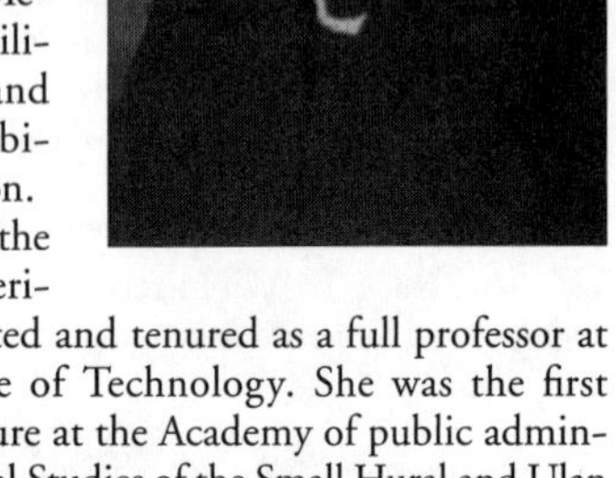

Dr. Yancy was the first African-American to be promoted and tenured as a full professor at Georgia Institute of Technology. She was the first American to lecture at the Academy of public administration and Social Studies of the Small Hural and Ulan Bator Mongolia in 1991. She has published over 40 articles and labor arbitration cases in academic journals.

She was the first African-American to be appointed special master for the Florida Public Employee Relations Commission. She also was a member of labor delegations to the Soviet Union and Europe in 1988 and 1990. Some of her other activities include president of the members of UNCF, Corporate Board and Executive Committee of UNCF, and vice-president of the North Carolina Association of Independent Colleges and Universities.

Dr. Yancy was appointed the first female president of Johnson C. Smith University.

Dr. Yancy has received numerous awards including Outstanding Teacher of the Year at Georgia Tech, Undergraduate Faculty Member of the year, and listings in various Who's Who publications. She was selected as "one of the Six Best Teachers in the U.S." by Newsweek on Campus in 1988. As president, Dr. Yancy has marshaled in phenomenal growth and progress. Heralded nationally as one of the best fundraisers, she helped raise $63.8 million for the Campaign of the 90s, more than doubling the university endowment to $40 million. In 2000, Johnson C. Smith University became the first HBCU "Laptop" university issuing IBM Thinkpads to all of its students.

In the July 2002 issue of nationally recognized *Savoy* magazine, she was listed as a "leader to watch." In 2004, she received the Delaney Award.

Linda Reyna Yanez

JUDGE. Linda Reyna Yanez received her Bachelor of Arts in inter–American studies from the University of Texas Pan American in 1970; her Master's of Law from the University of Virginia School of Law in 1998; and her Juris doctorate from Texas Southern University School of Law in 1976.

She taught at the Harvard Law School; she has been consulting attorney to the Mexican consul generals in Boston, Massachusetts, and Brownsville, Texas; she served on the Legal Advisory Committee to the United

Nations High Commissioner for Refugees; she has worked extensively with United Nations NGO's; she has served as a guest lecturer at the Law School at the University of Valencia in Spain.

She was appointed a justice on the Appellate Court of the State of Texas by Governor Ann Richards in 1993. She is the first Hispanic woman to serve on an Appeals Court in the history of the state of Texas.

Mamie L. Yarbrough

ELECTED OFFICIAL. Mamie L. Yarbrough is a graduate of Benton Harbor High School and attended Western Michigan University. She has several certifications in the field of housing administration.

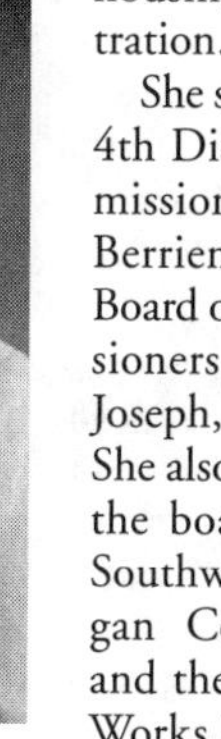

She serves as the 4th District commissioner on the Berrien County Board of Commissioners in St. Joseph, Michigan. She also represents the board on the Southwest Michigan Commission and the Michigan Works Board.

Mary Carlin Yates

GOVERNMENT OFFICIAL. Mary Carlin Yates is a native of Portland, Oregon. She received a Bachelor of Arts degree in English from Oregon State University and a master's degree in comparative East West humanities from New York University (NYU) where she pursed her doctoral studies in Asian affairs.

She is a career member of the Senior Foreign Service, Class of Minister Counselor who began her diplomatic career in 1980. She was assigned to the United States Embassy, Paris as senior cultural attaché, preceded by a tour as press attaché for Ambassador Pamela Harriman. She was nominated by President George W. Bush and confirmed by the United States Senate to serve as United States ambassador to the Republic of Ghana on November 15, 2002, and served as United States ambassador to the Republic of Burundi from 1999 to June 2002.

Ms. Yates assumed her duties as foreign policy advisor to the commander, United States European Command in September 2005. In this capacity, she helps formulate and recommend policy options and provides counsel to leadership on all European Command political-military affairs which pertain to United States forces operating across 92 countries in Europe, Eurasia, Africa and the Middle East.

Lea Ybarra

EDUCATION. Lea Ybarra received a bachelor's degree in 1970, a master's degree in 1972 and a doctoral degree in sociology from the University of California in Berkeley, California.

Her professional career includes serving in a variety of teaching and administrative positions at California State University in Fresno. From 1983 to 1992, she served as a professor in the Department of Chicano and Latin American Studies. From 1992 to 1993, she served as assistant to the provost and vice president for academic affairs. From 1993 to 1994, she was assistant to the president. From 1994 to 1996, she was acting associate provost for academic planning and student affairs. She served as senior research associate for Olmos Productions in Los Angeles, California. She was appointed executive director of the Institute for the Academic Advancement of Youth at Johns Hopkins University.

Pen-Shu Yeh

AEROSPACE. Pen-Shu Yeh received a Master of Science in electrical engineering from the University of Washington and a Ph.D. in electrical engineering from Stanford University.

She joined the National Aeronautics and Space Administration (NASA) in 1988. Prior to that she worked in both an academic environment and industry where she did research in computer /robotic vision, pattern recognition and data compression. Dr. Yeh is a co-investigator on the compression experiment to be flown on the SSTI/LEWIS spacecraft at the NASA Goddard Space Flight Center in Greenbelt, Maryland. For this experiment, both lossless and lossy algorithms are im-

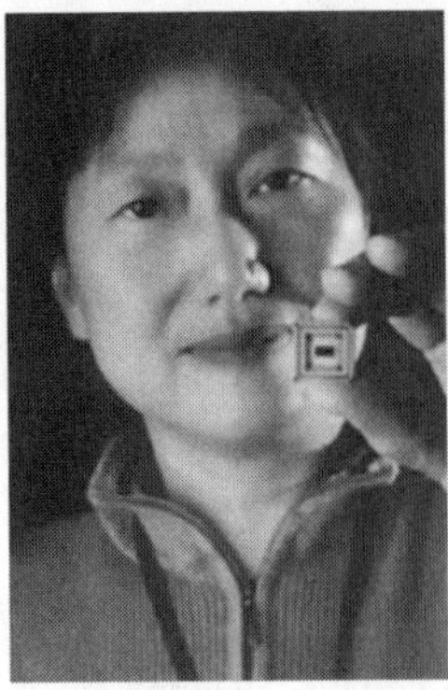

plemented. The lossless compression uses the VLSI hardware, whereas the lossy compression uses a combination of software and hardware. She is responsible specifically for the analysis, simulation and selection of data compression algorithms for further development into VLSI hardware. She served as group leader for advanced applications, Microelectronics and Signal Processing Branch, at NASA Goddard Space Flight Center, Greenbelt, Maryland. Dr. Yeh has invented new data compression methods that have improved processing of Hubble Space Telescope images and data from other missions.

Ying Yeh

BUSINESS EXECUTIVE. Ying Yeh received a Bachelor of Arts degree from the National Taiwan University.

Her professional career includes working for the U.S. government in 1970; she served as a journalist with the Times Groups in Singapore and NBC in New York; in 1982, she returned to the U.S. government to serve in the U.S. Foreign Service that included becoming the first female commercial officer to reach the rank of minister-counselor in 1995. She served in U.S. embassies in Burma, Guangzhou, Hong Kong, Taiwan and Beijing; she joined the Eastman Kodak Company in January 1997 as general manager for external affairs and vice president of the greater China region. In March 1999, her position was retitled as general manager, external affairs and vice president, greater Asia region. In January 2001, she was appointed vice chairman, China, to reflect her pivotal role in the execution of Kodak's growth strategy in China and in May 2002, the board of directors of Eastman Kodak Company elected her a vice president of the company.

Ms. Yeh was appointed chairman and president, North Asia region in October 2005.

Janet L. Yellen

FINANCE. Janet L. Yellen took office as president and chief executive officer of the Federal Reserve Bank of San Francisco on June 14, 2004. Prior to joining the bank, Dr. Yellen was the Eugene E. and Catherine M. Trefethen Professor of Business and Professor of Economics at the University of California at Berkeley where she has been a faculty member since 1980.

Dr. Yellen serves as vice president of the American Economic Association and as a research associate of the National Bureau of Economic Research. She is immediate past president of the Western Economic Association. She is a Fellow of the Yale Corporation and also is a member of the American Academy of Arts and Sciences.

Denise DeBartolo York

SPORTS EXECUTIVE. Denise Debartolo York received her bachelor's degree from Notre Dame. DeBartolo York's involvement in sports ownership branches out beyond the realm of professional football. When the DeBartolo Corporation owned the Pittsburgh Penguins of the National Hockey League (NHL) from 1981 to 1991), she was one of only a few female executives in the league. She was team president when the Penguins captured their first Stanley Cup title in 1991. She was instrumental in attracting the NHL All-Star game to the city of Pittsburgh for the first time ever on January 21, 1990.

Ms. DeBartolo York served as executive vice president of personnel and corporate marketing/communication for the San Francisco 49ers and was elevated to the position of vice chairman in April 1994. After the death of her father, Edward J. DeBartolo, in December 1994, she was named chairman. Ms. DeBartolo York serves as chairman of the DeBartolo Corporation and oversees the corporation's portfolio including the five-time world champion San Francisco 49ers.

Dona D. Young

FINANCE. Dona D. Young received a bachelor's degree and master's degree in political science from Drew University and earned her Juris Doctor degree from the University of Connecticut School of Law. In 2001, she

received the Outstanding Alumni Award from Drew University and in 2002 she received the Distinguished Graduate Award from the University of Connecticut School of Law.

Ms. Young joined Phoenix Wealth Management Company as an attorney in 1980. After advancing through several promotions in the law and reinsurance departments, she was named vice president and assistant general counsel in 1987. Ms. Young was promoted to senior vice president individual sales and marketing and general counsel in 1989. She was named executive vice president and general counsel in 1994 in charge of life insurance and annuity operations and corporate staff functions. She was elected a director of the company in 1998, president in 2000 and the following year added chief operating officer to her responsibilities. In mid–2002, Ms. Young assumed responsibility for the company's investment operations. She became president and chief executive officer on January 1, 2003, and in April of that year became chairman, president and chief executive officer.

Gwendolyn V. Young

GOVERNMENT OFFICIAL. Gwendolyn V. Young is a native of Hawaii and was raised in Southern California. She received a Bachelor of Science degree in elementary education and her master's in public administration from Brigham Young University in Provo, Utah.

She was selected as a presidential management intern and received an appointment to serve at NASA headquarters. Her career at NASA has included serving as the resources management officer responsible for all budget activities at NASA's Stennis Space Center in Mississippi. She worked in the Office of the International Space Station at both NASA Headquarters and in the Space Station Program Office in Reston, Virginia. During this time, she also completed a one-year detail as the NASA budget focal point in the Air Force/NASA's Joint Program Office of the National Launch System program at Los Angeles Air Force Base, California. She transferred to NASA Dryden in 1995 as chief financial officer responsible for overall financial and budget activities. At that time, she was only the second woman in NASA to hold this position. She was named associate director for management of NASA's Dryden Flight Research Center at Edwards, California.

Lynnette Young

GOVERNMENT OFFICIAL. Lynnette Young graduated from the University of Maryland, Baltimore County, with a degree in political science and completed the Certificate Program for Senior Executives in State and Local Government at the John F. Kennedy School of Government at Harvard University.

Her professional career includes serving as senior vice president with Camegie Morgan, a consulting firm headquartered in Maryland; for ten years she served under Baltimore Mayor Kurt L. Schmoke as chief of staff; prior to joining the city of Atlanta, she was a principal and senior consultant with Damespoint Partners. In 2006, she was serving as chief operating officer for the city of Atlanta. She is responsible for the day-to-day operation and management of city government. All operational departments of the city report to Mayor Shirley Franklin through Ms. Young. She has oversight and responsibility for service delivery and has operational accountability for all city services.

Patricia M. Young

GOVERNMENT OFFICIAL. Patricia M. Young received a Bachelor of Arts degree in communications from Wright State University in Dayton, Ohio, and earned a Master of Science degree in business and industrial relations from Wright State University in Dayton, Ohio.

Her federal service began in 1985 through the Palace Acquire Career Program with the Air Force Materiel Command at Wright-Patterson Air Force Base in Ohio. Her service includes serving in various assignments with the United States Transportation Command at Alexandria, Virginia, to include deputy chief, Mobility Systems Division, and chief, Business Center Division. She entered Senior Executive Service in 2002 as the deputy director logistics and business operation. She has served as deputy director for strategies and policy in the Strategies, Plans and Policies Directorate.

Ms. Young was appointed deputy to the commander, Military Surface Deployment and Distribution Command, United States Transportation Command, Alexandria, Virginia.

Deborah A. Yow

SPORTS. Deborah A. Yow is a native of North Carolina and received a bachelor's degree from Elon College in North Carolina.

Her professional career includes serving as women's basketball coach at the University of Kentucky in 1976, at Oral Roberts University, then at the University of Florida where she was coach of the Lady Gators basketball team; she served as associate athletic director and director of athletics at Saint Louis University.

Ms. Yow was named the athletic director for the University of Maryland in August 1994. She is the first woman to serve as athletic director at the University of Maryland. In 2001, she was elected president of the National Association of Collegiate Directors.

Sandra Kay Yow

SPORTS. Sandra Kay Yow is a native of Gibsonville, North Carolina. She received a Bachelor of Science degree in English from East Carolina University in 1964 and her master's degree in physical education from the University of North Carolina in Greensboro in 1970.

She has served as the coach for women's basketball at the University of North Carolina at Wilmington, Kansas State University, Drake University, East Tennessee State University and Providence College. She was named as an assistant coach with the WNBA Minnesota Lynx in 2006. On January 22, 2007, Yow returned as head coach for the University of North Carolina Wolfpack.

Paula Zahn

JOURNALISM. Paula Zahn received a bachelor's degree in journalism from Stephens College in Columbia, Missouri, attending on a cello scholarship.

Her professional career began when she joined WFAA-TV in Dallas.; in 1979 she moved to San Diego to work for KFMB-TV; she also worked at KPRC-TV in Houston; served at WNEV-TV (now WHDH-TV) in Boston; and served at KCBS-TV in Los Angeles before joining ABC News. She joined ABC in November 1987 as anchor of *The Health Show*; she served as primetime co-host of the 1992 Olympic Winter Games; she co-anchored the 1994 Olympic Winter games; she was host of *The Edge with Paula Zahn*, a daily news program on Fox News Channel; she joined CNN in September 2001; she anchored the CNN's network morning news program, *American Morning with Paula Zahn*, which she helped launch in fall 2001; in 2003, she anchored and provided the latest news on Operation Iraqi Freedom.

Ms. Zahn serves as anchor for CNN's weeknight primetime evening program, *Paula Zahn Now*, based in the network's New York bureau.

Debra Zedalis

GOVERNMENT OFFICIAL. Debra Zedalis holds a master's degree in strategic studies from the U.S. Army War College in Carlisle, Pennsylvania, a master's degree in business administration from Syracuse University and a Bachelor of Arts in managerial psychology from the University of Kentucky. She has attended many Army schools.

She is a Department of Army civilian who is currently the deputy garrison commander at West Point, New York.

Antoinette Zel

ENTERTAINMENT EXECUTIVE. Antoinette Zel is a native of New York and spent her high school years in Miami's Cuban part of the city. She received a Bachelor of Arts degree from Tufts University and earned her Juris Doctor degree from Columbia University School of Law.

Her professional career includes being engaged in private law practice in Manhattan at an entertainment law firm where she represented clients like Viacom and record label Def Jam and serving as president of MTV Network Latin America, Miami, Florida. She headed

MTV offices in Miami, Buenos Aires, Mexico City and Sao Paolo. She oversaw all long-time strategic business and creative aspects of Nickelodeon and MTV on air, online and for events.

Ms. Zel was named first as senior vice president of network strategy at Telemundo in November 2004 and then as senior executive vice president of the NBC-owned Telemundo Network Strategy in Miami, Florida.

Susan Tave Zelman

EDUCATION. Susan Tave Zelman received a doctorate in education from the University of Michigan. She also received an honorary doctoral degree in education from Baldwin-Wallace College, an honorary doctoral degree in public service from the University of Rio Grande and an honorary doctoral degree in humanities from Youngstown State University.

Her professional career includes serving as an associate professor of education and chair of the Department of Education at Emmanuel College in Boston while simultaneously holding a five-year appointment with the Education Technology Center of the Harvard Graduate School of Education; she served for six years in the Massachusetts Department of Education as associate commissioner of the Department of Education personnel; she served as deputy commissioner of the Missouri Department of Elementary and Secondary Education from 1994 to 1999.

Dr. Zelman has served as superintendent of public instruction for Ohio since 1999. Under her leadership, the Ohio Department of Education created a mission for the state's educational system that has brought sweeping change through standards-based reform. Ohio now has academic content standards in English language arts, mathematics, social studies, science, technology, foreign language and the arts.

Nancy Zimpher

EDUCATION. Nancy Zimpher is a native of Gallipolis, Ohio. She received a bachelor's degree, a master's degree and her doctorate degree, all from the Ohio State University.

Her professional career includes serving in various administrative positions and in research and development efforts concerned with improving the preparation of teachers, especially teachers for urban contexts; she held a faculty position in the School of Education at the University of Wisconsin; served as the executive dean of professional college and dean of the College of Education at the Ohio State University in Columbus, Ohio. In 1998, she was appointed the first female chancellor of the University of Wisconsin in Milwaukee.

On October 1, 2003, Dr. Nancy L. Zimpher was appointed the first woman to serve as president of the University of Cincinnati. She is the 25th president of the University of Cincinnati.

Andrea L. Zopp

BUSINESS EXECUTIVE. Andrea L. Zopp received both her bachelor's degree in history and science and earned her Juris Doctor degree from Harvard University.

Her professional career includes a legal career as a law clerk to U.S. District Judge George N. Leighton in the Northern District of Illinois. She served as the first assistant state's attorney in the Cook County's State's Attorney office in Illinois. She served in private law practice. She was appointed vice president and deputy general counsel in the law department of the Sara Lee Corporation.

Ms. Zopp was named senior vice president and general counsel, Sears Holding Corporation. In this position she has responsibility for legal affairs, public relations and compliance.

Appendix 1
Occupational Listing

Aerospace

Bingham, Nancy
Brown, Beth A.
Clark, Linda
Cobb, Sharon
Duncan, Elaine Flowers
Ennix, Kim
Ericsson, Aprille
Goodson, Amanda
Griner, Carolyn
Grymes, Rose
Jackson, Lorna Graves
Jernigan, Tamara E.
Johnson, Christyl
Kronmiller, Kate B.
Long, Irene Duhart
Lucid, Shannon W.
McGowan, Anna-Maria Rivas
Olsen, Kathie
Roe, Lesa B.
Sams, Jeneene
Spilker, Linda
Stroupe, Ashley W.
Tate, Judy Marie
Townsend, Julie
Vanhooser, Teresa
Walker, Angelia
Yeh, Pen-Shu

Artist

Lin, Maya

Astronaut

Baker, Ellen S.
Cagle, Yvonne Darlene
Caldwell, Tracy E.
Cleave, Mary L.
Coleman, Catherine G.
Collins, Eileen Marie
Currie, Nancy Jane
Davis, N. Jan
Dunbar, Bonnie J.
Fisher, Anna L.
Godwin, Linda M.
Higginbotham, Joan E.
Hire, Kathryn P.
Ivins, Marsha S.
Jemison, Mae C.
Metcalf-Lindenburger, Dorothy M.
Morgan, Barbara R.
Ochoa, Ellen
Whitson, Peggy A.
Wilson, Stephanie D.

Author

Angelou, Maya
Cheney, Lynne V.
Hawkins, Carol Hooks
Walker, Alice

Aviation

Anderson, Tina
Kennard, Lydia H.

Business Executive

Adams, Valencia
Adamson, Rebecca L.
Allen, Susan Au
Alseth, Becky
Anderson, Chandra Y.
Appolito, Collette
Armstrong, Mary
Arnold, Susan E.
Asefnia, Sepideh "Sepi"
Babrowski, Claire
Baldauf, Sari M.
Banks, Paula
Banse, Amy L.
Baranco, Juanita Powell
Barrett, Colleen C.
Barshefsky, Charlene
Beal, Maureen
Begley, Charlene
Bergman, Nomi
Black, Cathleen
Bland, Sharon Jackson
Boswell, Gina
Bowies, Barbara L.
Brewer, Rosalind
Brock, Roslyn McCallister
Brown, Adriane M.
Bruch, Ruth E.
Buckley, Mary Kate
Bucklin, Christine B.
Burns, Ursula M.
Calhoun, Essie L.
Calpeter, Lynn
Carranza, Jovita
Castagna, Vanessa
Cherng, Peggy Tsiang
Chow, Joan K.
Chowdhry, Uma
Clayton, Annette
Colucci, Marlene M.
Comstock, Beth
Conners, Ellen Engleman
Corvi, Carolyn
Counts, Millicent S.
Curby, Norma J.
De Alonso, Marcela Perez
Dillon, Mary
Duckett, Karen I.
Einhorn, Jessica P.
Eitel, Maria S.
Elam, Deborah
Elsenhans, Lynn Laverty
Epps, Evern Cooper
Fienberg, Linda D.
Fischel, Shelley
Folsom, Kim T.
Foster, Jylia Moore
Franklin, Barbara Hackman
Fudge, Ann
Fuller, Kathryn
Fulp, Carol
Gandara, Marilda Lara
Givans, Natalie M.
Gulyas, Diane
Hansen, Marka
Harriss, Cynthia
Hart, Cathy J.
Hart, Clare
Harvey, Keiko
Hayden-Watkins, Dorothy
Hellyar, Mary Jane
Henderson, Naomi
Herda, Larissa
Hill, Chris A.
Hooks, Tamara T.
Hooper, Michele J.
Hoskins, Michele
Hudson, Dawn
Inman, Pam H.
Jackson, Kathryn J. "Kate"
James, Gloria Schumpert
Jeon, Joori
Johns, Marie C.
Johnson, Sheila Crump
Johnson-Goins, Gloria
Johnson-Reece, Nicole
Jones, Elaine Hollan
Jung, Andrea
Katen, Karen L.
King, Gwendolyn
King, Karen
King, Reatha Clark
Koellner, Laurette
Kullman, Ellen J.
Lau, Constance H.
Lawrence, Gwendolyn H.
Lazarus, Rochelle B.

Lee, Esther
Lewis, Cynthia
Lloyd, Anne H.
Longaberger, Tami
Lopez, Shirlene
Lovett, Melendy
Lowe, Challis M.
Lucia, Marian M.
Madden, Teresa S.
Mallett, Lydia G.
Maloy, Frances
Manzi, Barbara
Mathews, Sylvia
Matthews, Candace
McCabe, Jewell Jackson
McCann, Renetta
McKissack, Cheryl Mayberry
Ming, Jenny
Moddelmog, Hala
Monsarrat, Nancy
Moore, Madeleine
Morrison, Denise
Moyers, Judith Davidson
Mulcahy, Anne Marie
Neal, Dianne
Newman, Andrea Fischer
Nicholson, Pamela M.
Nooyi, Indra K.
Palmer, Vicki R.
Parker, Jennifer J.
Perrin-Johnson, Tanya
Poon, Christine
Price, Anita
Provencio, Marla
Readon, Nancy A.
Reed, Wendy
Rees, Martha
Reid-Coleman, Desma
Reif, Debbie
Rhoades, Anne
Rice, Linda Johnson
Rickard, Lisa A.
Rodwell, Wanda Yancey
Russo, Patricia F.
Santona, Gloria
Scholly, Alison
Sclafani, Karen
Scott, Susan
Shavers, Cheryl
Simons, Renee V.H.
Sitherwood, Suzanne
Smalls, Marva
Soodik, Bonnie
Soupata, Lea N.
Stevens, Anne
Stewart, Julia A.
Stewart, Martha
Stoney, Janice D.
Thomas-Graham, Pamela
Toben, Doreen A.
Tome, Carol
Travis, Tracey Thomas
Vincent, Patricia K.
Wallace, Joy
Walton, Alice Louise
Watson, Allison L.
Welch, Yolanda Maria
Wetherald, Michele Warholic
Wheelwright, Alice
Whitman, Margaret C.
Williams, E. Faye
Wong, Andrea
Wooden, Ruth A.
Woods, Jacqueline
Wright, Doreen A.
Yeh, Ying
Zopp, Andrea L.

Chef

Garrett, Toba

Communications

Adams, Vickee Jordan
Campbell, Jill
Colony, Sandy
Cunningham, Andy
DeVard, Jerri
Douglas, Mae
East, Ellen
Hill-Ardoin, Priscilla
Phillips, Colette A.M.
Ruesterholz, Virginia P.

Community Activist

Carter, Majora
Edelman, Marian Wright
Obama, Michelle

Education

Ackerman, Arlene
Aldridge, Susan C.
Ambar, Carmen Twillie
Anderson, Belinda C.
Anderson, Michelle J.
Anderson, Tina
Austin, Debra
Baenninger, MaryAnn
Barazzone, Esther L.
Beck, Jill
Bell, Stephanie W.
Bell-Scott, Patricia
Bingham, Laura Carpenter
Bowman, Kathleen Gill
Bowman, Linda
Breckenridge, Cora Smith
Brehm, Sharon
Brown, Lisa L.
Bryan, T.J.
Bryant, Castell Vaughn
Buel, Sarah
Burmaster, Elizabeth
Cantor, Nancy
Cardenas, Blandina
Carr, Helen
Chan, Gwen
Cole, Johnnetta Betsch
Coleman, Mary Sue
Cureton, Deborah B.
de Macias, Carolyn Webb
DiCroce, Deborah M.
Easley, Mary
Frasier, Elizabeth
Gann, Pamela
Garcia, Juliet V.
Garcia, Mildred
Garrett, Sandy
Gast, Alice P.
Genshaft, Judy
Guinier, Lani
Hall, Beverly L.
Hall, Ethel H.
Harrington, Nicki (Virginia)
Harris, Gene T.
Harter, Carol C.
Hartford, Maureen A.
Hawkins, Carol
Haynes, Karen
Haysbert, JoAnn W.
Higginbotham, Eve J.
Hirsh, Sharon Latchaw
Hockfield, Susan
Hogan, Beverly Wade
Holbrook, Karen A.
Howard-Vital, Michelle
Hoxby, Caroline
Hughes, Marvalene
Jenkins, Sebeth
Johnson, Odessa
Kagan, Elena
Keizs, Marcia V.
Kelly, Susan
Kennedy, Yvonne
Kenny, Shirley Strum
Kimbrough, Marjorie L.
Kiss, Elizabeth
Lewis, Daree M.
Lewis, Shirley A.R.
Ma, Chung-Pei
McDemmond, Marie V.
Mellow, Gail O.
Merget, Astrid E.
Miller, Peggy
Natalicio, Diana S.
Newman, J. Bonnie
Nugent, Georgia
O'Leary, Hazel
Peruggi, Regina S.
Pippins, Shirley Robinson
Placide, Charlotte D.
Ponder, Anne
Powell, Dorothy L.
Presley, Vivian Mathews
Raab, Jennifer J.
Raines, Shirley C.
Ramaley, Judith A.
Ray, Sandra
Reed, Trudie Kibbe
Reid-Wallace, Carolyn
Rittling, Mary E.
Rodin, Judith
Roy, Loriene
Royster, Kay E.
Seurkamp, Mary Pat
Shalala, Donna E.
Shapiro, Judith R.
Sherman, Diane
Sias, Mary Evans
Skinner, Patricia A.
Smith, Jane E.
Springer, Marlene
Suber, Dianne B.
Tatum, Beverly Daniel
Thompson, Thelma
Tilghman, Shirley M.
Turner, Linda Edmonds
VanCleave, Donna
Waldron, Kathleen
Wheelan, Belle S.
White, Katherine E.
Whitson, Caroline
Williams, Betty Smith
Williams, Carolyn Grubbs
Wise, Phyllis
Wykle, May L.
Yancy, Dorothy Cowser
Ybarra, Lea
Zelman, Susan Tave
Zimpher, Nancy

Elected Official

Alvarado, Blanca
Alvarado, Carol
Ballard, Elizabeth
Balraj, Elizabeth K.
Barnes, Kay
Bean, Melissa L.
Bell, Ella B.
Bennett, Angela M.
Bergeson, Terry
Berkley, Shelley
Berry, Cherie Killian
Biggert, Judith Borg
Blackburn, Marsha
Blanco, Kathleen B.
Bono, Mary
Borders, Lisa
Boscola, Lisa M.
Boxer, Barbara
Bradley, Jennette B.
Brady, M. Jane
Brown, Corrine
Brown, Dorothy
Brown, Irma Hunter
Brown, Yvonne
Brown-Waite, Virginia
Burke, Yvonne B.
Bysiewicz, Susan
Cabral, Andrea J.
Campbell, Jane L.
Cantwell, Maria E.
Capito, Shelley Moore
Capps, Lois
Carnahan, Jean
Carnahan, Robin
Carson, Julia May
Castillo, Susan
Chapman, Beth
Chick, Laura
Clarke, Yvette Diane
Clayton, Eva M.
Clinton, Hillary
Cole, Sheryl
Coleman, Carolyn Quilloin
Collins, Barbara-Rose
Collins, Earlean
Collins, Susan Margaret
Cottrell, Carol
Cropp, Linda Washington
Cubin, Barbara L.
Davis, Jo Ann
Davis, Kathy L.
Davis, Susan A.
DeBerry, Lois M.
DeGette, Diana
DeLauro, Rosa L.
Denish, Diane
DiFiore, Janet
Dixon, Sheila
Dole, Elizabeth Hanford
Donohue, Mary O.
Drake, Thelma D.
Edwards, Ada
Emerson, Jo Ann
Eshoo, Anna Georges
Fallin, Mary
Feinstein, Dianne
Foxx, Virginia Ann
Frankel, Lois J.
Franklin, Shirley Clarke
Garcia, Sylvia R.
Gerard, Patricia
Gilbreath, Patricia
Gilmore, Marie
Goff, Mary
Gonzalez, Sara M.
Granholm, Jennifer M.
Gregoire, Chris
Hammond, Lauren
Handel, Karen
Harman, Jane F.
Harris, Kamala D.
Harris, Katherine
Hart, Melissa A.
Herrera, Carol
Herrera, Mary
Herseth, Stephanie
Hicks, Juanita
Hitchcock, Jeanne D.
Hooley, Darlene
Hughes, Teresa P.
Hunt, Lorraine T.
Hunter, Mattie
Hutchison, Kathyrn Ann Bailey
Iorio, Pam
Isaac, Teresa
Jackson, Edna
Jackson-Lee, Sheila
Jennings, Toni
Johnson, Beverly
Johnson, Carol D.
Johnson, Eddie Bernice
Johnson, Glorious
Johnson, Nancy L.
Jones, Patricia
Jones, Stephanie Tubbs
Jones-Ham, Wilmer
Kagan, Cheryl C.
Kassebaum, Nancy Landon
Katz, Vera
Kautz, Elizabeth
Kelly, Sue
Kilpatrick, Carolyn Cheeks
Kim, Donna Mercado
Kim, Jennifer
Klanderud, Helen
Klobuchar, Amy Jean
Kniss, Liz
Knoll, Catherine Baker
Krom, Beth
Krueger, Liz
Lacy, Mary
Land, Terri Lynn
Landrieu, Mary L.
Lautenschlager, Peggy A.
Lawrence, Brenda L.
Lawton, Barbara
Leahey, Jeanette
Lee, Barbara
Lincoln, Blanche Lambert
Lingle, Linda
Lofgren, Zoe
Loggins, Eugenia L.
Lowey, Nita M.
Madigan, Lisa
Mahan, Patricia
Maloney, Carolyn Bosher
Manross, Mary
Marshall, Elaine F.
Marshall, Helen M.
Martin, Leslie Baranco
Matsui, Doris Okada
McCarthy, Carolyn
McKinney, Cynthia Ann
McLin, Rhine
McMorris, Cathy
McTeer-Hudson, Heather
Meek, Carrie P.
Mikulski, Barbara Ann
Miller, Candice
Miller, Laura
Minner, Ruth Ann
Molina, Gloria
Molinari, Susan
Molnau, Carol
Moore, Gwendolynne (Gwen) S.
Morton, Lorraine H.
Mulder, Arlene J.
Murkowski, Lisa
Murray, Patty
Musgrave, Marilyn N.
Myrick, Sue
Napolitano, Grace F.
Napolitano, Janet
Nappier, Denise Lynn
Nobumoto, Karen S.
Northup, Anne Meagher
Norton, Eleanor Holmes
Pederson, Sally
Pelosi, Nancy
Perdue, Beverly Eaves
Pryce, Deborah D.
Radle, Patti
Rappaport, Margaret D.
Redd, Dana
Reed, Susan D.
Rell, M. Jodi
Rivers, Lynn Nancy
Roberts, Elizabeth H.
Ros-Lehtinen, Ileana
Sanchez, Linda T.
Sanchez, Loretta
Scarlett-Golden, Yvonne
Schakowsky, Janice D.
Schmidt, Jean
Schultz, Debbie Wasserman
Schwartz, Allyson Y.
Sebelius, Kathleen
Shea-Porter, Carol
Skillman, Rebecca
Slaughter, Louise McIntosh
Smith, Alma Wheeler
Snowe, Olympia Jean
Solis, Hilda
Spencer, Loretta
Stabenow, Deborah Ann
Steele, Bobbie L.
Steele, Gail
Sutton, Betty
Tauscher, Ellen O'Kane
Tuck, Amy
Velazquez, Nydia
Vigil-Giron, Rebecca
Wasserman-Rubin, Diana
Waters, Maxine
Watson, Diane Edith
Watson, Kyra
Wilkins, Rillastine R.
Wilson, Heather
Winslow, Cleta
Woolsey, Lynn C.
Wyman, Nancy
Yarbrough, Mamie L.

Entertainment

Allen, Debbie
Angelou, Maya
Banks, Tyra Lynne
Berry, Bertice

DeGeneres, Ellen Lee
Garel, Giana
King, Gayle
Lipper, Joanna
Lopez, Maria
Rhimes, Shonda
Verrett, Shirley

Entertainment Executive

Alonzo, Jenny
Ariyasu, Vicki
Arouh, Janice
Berman, Gail
Chau, Micheline
Currey, Gail
Deen, Paula
de Passe, Suzanne
Fili-Krushel, Patricia
Hall, Lisa Gersh
Hood, Lucy
Hudson, Dianne Atkinson
Jacobson, Nina
Koplovtz, Kay
Lansing, Sherry
Lawson, Kelli Richardson
Laybourne, Geraldine
McGrath, Judy
McHale, Judith A.
Panzer, Sue
Powell, Shirley
Ridgeway, Roslyn
Rocco, Nikki
Salhany, Lucille S. (Lucie)
Snider, Stacey
Stephen, Elizabeth Guber
Sweeney, Anne
Winfrey, Oprah Gail
Zel, Antoinette

Finance

Alemany, Ellen
Allen, Sharon
Ashley, Diane T.
Banta, Vivian
Biggins, J. Veronica
Bowen, Margretta Jeffers
Brown, Leilani
Desoer, Barbara J.
Cunningham, Paula D.
Dewey, Londa J.
Finucane, Anne M.
Isaacs-Lowe, Arlene
Johnson, Abigail
Johnson, Suzanne Nora
Joyner, Pamela J.
Krawcheck, Sallie L.
McColgan, Ellyn A.
McGetrick, Peg
Minehan, Cathy E.
Moss, Lesia Bates
Orman, Suze (Susan)
St. Claire, Dail
Sobbott, Susan
Timmons, Jacquette M.
Wright, Deborah C.
Yellen, Janet L.
Young, Dona D.

First Lady (State)

Bush, Columba
Henry, Kim
Holton, Anne
Pataki, Libby
Perdue, Mary
Perry, Anita
Rendell, Marjorie O.
Richardson, Barbara
Shriver, Maria
Taft, Hope

First Lady (U.S.)

Bush, Laura
Carter, Rosalyn

Government Official

Adams, Carolyn
Allen, Bernadette
Allen, Fannie L.
Alvarez, Aida
Alvillar-Speake, Theresa
Arsht, Leslye A.
Ayres, Judith
Baicker, Katherine
Bailey, Catherine Todd
Bailey, Darlyne
Ballard, Tina
Baskerville, Lezli
Blunt, Paula
Bodine, Susan
Braun, Carol Moseley
Bridgewater, Pamela E.
Brown, Gayleatha B.
Brownell, Nora
Bryan, Beth Ann
Buchan, Claire
Buckner, L. Gail
Burke, Sheila P.
Butenis, Patricia A.
Cabral, Anna Escobedo
Campbell, Phyllis C.
Caruso, Patricia L.
Castro, Ida L.
Chandler, Cassandra M.
Chao, Elaine L.
Chun, Shinae
Cino, Maria
Clarey, Patricia
Clark, Patrina
Clarke, Kathleen
Cloud, Rosemary R.
Coleman, Carolyn
Coler, Kate
Combs, Ann L.
Conlin, Linda
Dale, Shana
Davis, Audrey Y.
Davis, Ruth A.
Dawson, Diann
Dickerson, Terri A.
Dinkins, Carol E.
Dorbriansky, Paula J.
Dumas, Sharon A.
Duncan, Linda A.
Dunn, Karen-Sue
Earp, Naomi Churchill
Eissenstat, Janet Slaughter
Fields, Evelyn J.
Fields, Shirley L.
Finley, Julie
Fites, Jeanne
Fowler, Nuby
Freeman, Sharee
Gaines, Gay Hart
Gambatesa, Linda
Gardner, Janice
Gaskins, Kathern L.
Gercke, Sylvia
Gonzalez, Frances A.
Griffin, Patricia W.
Harris, Skila
Hayes-White, Joanne
Henney, Jane E.
Herman, Alexis M.
Hersman, Deborah A.P.
Higgins, Kathryn O'Leary
Holt, Karen E.
Hughes, Karen P.
Hutchens, Sandra
Immergut, Karin J.
James, Kay Coles
Jarrett, Valerie
Jenkins, Jo Ann C.
Johnson, Karen A.
Johnson, Katherine E.
Kelly, Suedeen G.
Kenney, Kristie Anne
Kicza, Mary Ellen
Kirk-McAlpine, Patricia
Lantz, Theresa C.
Leclaire, Margaret
Loston, Adena Williams
Lovelace, Gail T.
Loveland, Valoria H.
Madrid, Patricia A.
Marshall, Susan G.
Martinez, Carmen M.
Martinez, Shirley A.
Mathieu, Dennise
Mattingly, Rebecca Dirden
McBride, Anita
McCaw, Susan Rasinski
McMurray, Claudia A.
Michael, Jeanette A.
Miers, Harriet
Mishoe, Helena O.
Moller, Patricia N.
Monroe, Stephanie J.
Morella, Constance A.
Nason, Nicole
Newman, Constance Berry
Nuland, Victoria
Odom, Carmen Hooker
Olsen, Jody
Pack, Sandra L.
Perry, Cynthia
Perry, June Carter
Peters, Mary E.
Pinson, Tracey L.
Porter, Lisa J.
Radice, Anne-Imelda
Ragsdale, Marguerita
Render, Arlene
Rice, Condoleezza
Rice, Judith C.
Riley, Sandra R.
Rivera, Aurea L.
Rivera, Fanny
Robinson, Audrey
Rodriguez, Rose E.
Routen, Gina L.
Ryan, Mary Jean
Saar, Mary Ann
Sandberg, Annette M.
Sanders, Robin Renee
Sauerbrey, Ellen R.

Scarlett, Lynn
Scott, Beverly
Scott, N.H.
Seagren, Alice
Sharpe, Lisa Webb
Shelton, Barbara L.
Silverman, Leslie E.
Sison, Michele
Smith, Adrienne M.
Springer, Linda M.
Stevens, Lisa
Sykes, Gwendolyn
Talley, Debra Linn
Thomas, Joyce A.
Thornton, Leslie T.
Townsend, Frances
Veneman, Ann M.
Wagner, Ann
Walker, Debra K.
Walker-Kimbro, Carolyn
Washington, Linda Jacobs
Westgate, Barbara A.
White-Olson, B.J.
Whiteside, Ruth
Whitman, Christie Todd
Williams, Darlene
Wisham, Lorna
Wos, Aldona Zofia
Yates, Mary Carlin
Young, Gwendolyn V.
Young, Lynnette
Young, Patricia M.
Zedalis, Debra

Health

Brock, Rovenia
Ferretti, Charlotte
James, Barbara
Johnson, Melissa
Joyner, Donna Richardson
Maddox, Yvonne T.
Power, A. Kathryn

Journalism

Couric, Katie
Bundles, A'Lelia
Duron, Ysabel
Harnisch, Ruth Ann
Ifill, Gwen
Jordan, Karen
Mitchell, Andrea
Murphy, Frances
Sawyer, Diane
Visser, Lesley
Walters, Barbara
Zahn, Paula

Judge

Aaron, Cynthia
Aarons, Sharon A.M.
Ableman, Peggy L.
Abrahamson, Shirley S.
Adamson, Kim T.
Alexander, Pamela G.
Alexander, Yvette M.
Allen, Faye
Alshouse, Diane R.
Altonaga, Cecilia Maria
Armstrong, Saundra Brown
Asel, Jodie
Ash, Sylvia G.
Ashmann-Gerst, Judith
Atack, Sharon B.
Atherton, Judith S.H.
Atkins, Marylin E.
Babb, Ronda E.
Baker, Karen R.
Baldwin, Cynthia
Bamattre-Manoukian, Patricia
Barnes, Anne Elizabeth
Batchelder, Alice Moore
Battaglia, Lynne A.
Beier, Carol A.
Belfance, Eve
Benke, Patricia D.
Berger, Carolyn
Bernal, Margaret
Bernard, Marielsa
Bernes, Debra
Berry, Janet J.
Billings, Judith M.
Bishop, Patricia Martin
Black, Susan Harrell
Blackett, Carolyn Wade
Blackmon, Patricia Ann
Blechman, Deb S.
Blount, Nancy M.
Bowers, Kathleen M.
Boyden, Ann
Boyle, Edna J.
Boyle, Patricia Jean E.P.
Bradley, Ann Walsh
Bransford, Tanya Mozell
Brennan, Shirley M.
Bridges, Bobbe J.
Bromley, Rebecca Snyder
Brown, Janice Rogers
Brown, Kay Stanfield
Brown, Lucy Chernow
Brown, Yvette McGee
Browne, Kim A.
Bruner, Cindy H.
Brunson, Catherine M.
Bryant, Peggy
Bryant, Wanda G.
Bucklo, Elaine
Burke, Anne M.
Butz, M. Kathleen
Calabria, Ann Marie
Callahan, Lynne S.
Cannon, Evelyn Omega
Cantil-Sakauye, Tani Gorre
Caplinger, Nancy
Carey, Joan B.
Carlisle, Elaine
Carpenter, Christine
Carr, Dolores
Carrion, Audrey J.S.
Caswell, Susan P.
Chang, Shelleyanne W.L.
Chrzanowski, Mary A.
Chu, Regina M.
Clark, Nancy L
Clark, Nikki
Clarke, Cathleen B.
Clement, Edith Brown
Cobb, Kay Beevers
Coco, Gloria Grace
Coker, Mary Day
Cole, Brenda Hill
Collyer, Rosemary M.
Combs, Sara W.
Conlon, Patricia N.
Cooney, Colleen Conway
Cooper, Jessica R.
Cordell, LaDoris Hazzard
Cotter, Patricia O'Brien
Cowin, Judith A.
Crawford, Susan
Culley, Anna
Cunningham, Sheree Davis
Curley, Patricia S.
Dalianis, Linda Stewart
Davidson, Lisa
Davis, Laura Prosser
Davis, Marguerite H.
DeGenaro, Mary
Delgado, Katherine R.
Del Pesco, Susan C.
Dickey, Betty C.
DiMiceli, Elaine W.
DiPentima, Alexandra Davis
Dixon, Melba
Dolan, Colleen
Donald, Bernice B.
Douglas, Laura G.
Draganchuk, Joyce
Draper, Carol Enger
Draper, Judy P.
Druzinski, Diane M.
Duncan, Allyson Kay
Duncan-Peters, Stephanie
Dupont, Debra
Durham, Christine M.
Dyke, Ann
Earle, Elisabeth A.
Edlitz, Sandra B.
Edwards, Genine D.
Elliott, April Phillips
Elliott, Kate Ford
Emerson, Elizabeth Hazlitt
Ender, Elma Teresa Salinas
Ensor, Judith C.
Escher, Patricia G.
Espinosa, Carmen E.
Evans, Orinda Dale
Evans, Sue McKnight
Fairhurst, Mary
Falkowski, Colleen
Farmer, Nancy
Fisher, Fern A.
Flynn, Paulette K.
Francis, Nancy C.
Freeman-Wilson, Karen
French, Judith L.
Frossard, Margaret O'Mara
Fry, Cynthia A.
Fuerst, Nancy A.
Garcia, Jeanne
Garman, Rita B.
Garson, Robin S.
Gearin, Kathleen R.
George, Hulane
George, Kathryn A.
Gibbons, Julia Smith
Gilman, Shelley Ilene
Gilmore, Vanessa
Gonzalez, Lizbeth
Goodstein, Diane Schafer
Gottfried, Maureen
Graffeo, Victoria A.
Grant, Beverly G.
Graves-Robertson, Shauna
Gray, Karla
Green, Melvia B.
Greene, Deborah S.

Greene, Lillian J.
Greenwood, Pamela T.
Groves, Emanuella
Gurich, Noma D.
Gutierrez, Pamela C.
Hall, Diana R.
Hall, Shelvin Louise Marie
Haller, Judith
Hamilton, Joyce
Hamilton, Phyllis Jean
Hansen, Karla J.
Harper, Jane V.
Harthcock, Tammy
Hatchett, Glenda
Heard, Wanda Keyes
Hearn, Kaye G.
Heffernan, Pamela G.
Heller, Ellen M.
Henderson, Mary Jane
Hendon, Sylvia Sieve
Hill, Valarie A.
Hilliard, Ruth H.
Hinojosa, Leticia
Hoag, M. Jean
Holt, Cathy M.
Holtz, Judith A.
Hopkins, Vanessa
Hotten, Michele D.
Hudson, Natalie E.
Hutchinson, Susan F.
Huvelle, Ellen Segal
Irion, Joan K.
Jackman-Brown, Pam B.
Jackson, Carol E.
Jaffe, Barbara
Jefferson, Deadra L.
Johnson, Arlene
Johnson, Barbara Gilleran
Johnson, Norma Holloway
Johnson, Shelia R.
Jones, Edith Hollan
Jurden, Jan R.
Kapsner, Carol Ronning
Karpinski, Diane
Kauger, Yvonne
Kaye, Judith S.
Kearse, Amalya L.
Kelly, Marilyn J.
Kennard, Joyce L.
Kennedy, Cornelia G.
Keough, Kathleen Ann
Kessler, Gladys
Kessler, Joan F.
King, Carolyn Dineen
Kite, Marilyn S.
Kollar-Kotelly, Colleen
Kreeger, Judith L.
Lally-Green, Maureen E.
Lando, Maxine Cohen
Lane, Bensonetta Tipton
Lansing, Karen
Lanzinger, Judith Ann
Latimore, Alicia L.
Lawless, Janelle A.
Lee, Alison Renee
Lee, Sharon Gail
Lee, Sherry A.
Leesfield, Ellen
Leeson, Susan M.
Lewis, Leslie A.
Lias, Kay A.
Linder, Virginia L.
Littlejohn, Janet
Lott, Deneise Turner
Lott, Martha A.
Lynn, Barbara M.G.
MacKinnon, Cynthia
Madsen, Barbara A.
Malazzo, Beverly
Manning, Blanche M.
Manzanares, Sylvia A.
Maring, Mary Muehlen
Martin-Clark, Miriam B.
Matthews, Carolyn C.
Mayfield, Mabel Johnson
Mays, Anita Laster
McBeth, Veronica Simmons
McBride, Margaret Stanton
McCarty, Alison
McCleve, Shelia K.
McConnell, Judith
McDade, Mary
McDonald, Gabrielle Kirk
McDonald, Ysleta W.
McGee, Linda M.
McHugh, Carolyn B.
McNally, Colleen
McNulty, Jill K.
McVay, Jacque
McWhorter, Shirlyon J.
Meierhenry, Judith
Melvin, Joan Orie
Messerich, Kathryn Davis
Metzen, Leslie May
Meyer, Helen M.
Michael, Kathryn
Miles, Susan
Miles-LaGrange, Vicki
Milhouse, Donna Robinson
Milin, Maria
Millender, B. Pennie
Miller, Cylenthia LaToye
Miller, M. Yvette
Miller-Lerman, Lindsey
Mollway, Susan Oki
Moore, Carla
Moore, Frankie J.
Moore, Kimberly Ann
Moore, Thelma Wyatt Cummings
Mounger, Virginia Wilson
Mroz, Rosa
Munyon, Lisa
Murray, Dana Elizabeth
Myerscough, Sue E.
Nettles-Nickerson, Beverley
Newman, Sandra Schultz
Norman, Laureen K. Van
O'Banner-Owens, Jeanette
O'Brien, Sheila M.
O'Connor, Karen L.
O'Connor, Maureen
Ogden, E. Jeannette
O'Kane, Julie Hions
O'Malley, Denise M.
O'Neal, Elaine M.
O'Neill, Harriet
Ortega, Darleen
Ortiz, Maria D.
Owens, Susan
Pariente, Barbara J.
Parrish, Jill N.
Parrish, Patricia G.
Pasula, Angela M.
Peuler, Sandra N.
Pickard, Lynn
Pineda-Kirwan, Diccia T.
Plummer, Beverly
Ponder, Suzan S.
Pozza, Karen H.
Preska, Loretta A.
Provence, Tiffany
Quince, Peggy A.
Rappaport, Sheila A.
Read, Susan P.
Revilla, Ada Pozo
Reynolds, Penny Brown
Rhoades, Brenda T.
Richardson, Andra V.
Rivera, Gloria A.
Roberts, Victoria A.
Robertson, Vicki
Robinson, Deborah A.
Roche, Rene A.
Rodriguez, Julia I.
Rogers, Chase T.
Roggensack, Patience Drake
Roper, Ellen
Rosenbaum, Marilyn Brown
Rothenberg, Leslie B.
Rothstein, Barbara Jacobs
Roybal, Dianna R.
Royster, C. Lorene
Rykken, Miriam P.
Safford, Shirley Strickland
Sapp-Peterson, Paulette
Saris, Patti B.
Scarpulla, Saliann
Schafer, Diane
Schroeder, Mary B.
Schumacher, Deborah
Sears, Leah Ward
Serrette, Cathy H.
Siegal, Bernice D.
Singer, Arlene
Snelson, Teresa Guerra
Sotomayor, Sonia
South, Leslie Elaine
Spears, Brenda S.
Spencer, Vaino
Squire, Carole
Steinbeck, Margaret O.
Steinhelmer, Connie
Stephens, Cynthia D.
Stephens, Linda
Stephens, Sherry K.
Stokes, Angela R.
Stoneburner, Terri J.
Stormer, Elinore Marsh
Stratton, Evelyn Lundberg
Swift, Pattie P.
Synenberg, Joan
Tacha, Deanell Reece
Tackett, Julia Kurtz
Tao, Elizabeth J. Yalin
Tarver, Pauline
Tate, Susan
Taylor, Anna Katherine Johnston Diggs
Theis, Mary Jane
Thomas, Deborah A.
Thomas, Paula Hinson
Thomasson, Lauren
Thompson, Linda A.
Titus, Linda S.

Todd, Debra McCloskey
Tolen, Lynda A.
Toler, Lynn
Townsend, Sharon S.
Trepeck, Judith R.
Trout, Linda Copple
Troutman, Shirley
Turgeon, Jeannine
Turner, Mary Ann
Tusan, Gail S.
Velasquez, Patti A.
Velasquez, Vanessa
Vertefeuille, Christine S.
Vogel, Gayle Nelson
Waite, Cheryl L.
Walker, Linda
Wallace, Barbara
Warder, Janice
Wells, Linda Ann
Werdegar, Kathryn M.
White, Maxine A.
White, Trudy
Whittington, Carolyn
Wieland, Lucy A.
Williams, Ann Claire
Williams, Annalisa S.
Wilson, Cindy Polk
Wilson, Debra A.
Wilson, Janice Rose
Wood, Lisa Godbey
Worke, Renee L.
Wright, Carolyn
Wright, Karla F.
Wright, Wilhelmina M.
Wyatt, Merri Souther
Yanez, Linda Reyna

Law

Askew, Kim J.
Beasley, Teresa
Farber, Zulima V.
Shaw, Nina
Washington, Tereasa H.

Law Enforcement

Brooks, Fabienne
Bully-Cummings, Ella
Cuffney, Nancy
Dunham, Wanda
Kemp, Kathryn
McClain, Pamela
Nunn, Annetta W.
Robinson, Kathleen
Valdez, Lupe
Viverette, Mary Ann
Whipple, Rachel H.
Williams, Pearlene M.
Winstead-Wilfong, Terri

Librarian

Blake, Norma E.
Burger, Leslie

Media

Halpem, Cheryl
Norville, Deborah
Roberts, Robin

Media Executive

Boskin, Chris
Casiano, Kimberly
Chang, Lisa
Costantini, Lynne
Dangar, Jennifer
Dickerson, Lynn
Gatti, Rosa
Grant, Susan
Green, Peggy
Harrison, Patricia de Stacy
Heacock, Jessica
Hefner, Christie
Herman, Mindy
Hobson, Mellody
Huggins, Sheryl
Hughes, Catherine Liggins
Keever, Lynda
Madison, Paula
McAniff, Nora
McCall, Dawn L.
Perez, Anna M.
Rockefeller, Sharon Percy
Taylor, Susan
Tortolani, Michelle
Ware, Janis L.

Medicine

Allison-Ottey, Sharon
Bailey, Stephanie
Bath, Patricia E.
Beard, Lillian M.
Beckles, G. Valerie
Bondy, Melissa L.
Butler, Gloria
Caniano, Donna A.
Clancy, Carolyn M.
Cox, Darlene L.
Donze, Laurie Friedman
Elders, M. Joycelyn
Epps, Roselyn
Gaston, Marilyn Hughes
Gayle, Helene D.
Gerberding, Julie Louise
Hayes, Maxine
Hopson, Deborah Parham
Jemmott, Loretta Sweet
Lawrence, Deirdre M.
McGruder-Jackson, Sandra
Miladore, Dianne Bitonte
Moore, Lois Jean
Pace, Betty S.
Perez, Lucille C. Norville
Pinn, Vivian
Porter, Gayle K.
Reede, Joan
Ross-Lee, Barbara
Scantlebury, Velma
Sharma, Rajamalliga N.
Thomas, Debi
Volkow, Nora D.

Military

Adams, Cheryl
Adams, Karen S.
Adams-Ender, Clara
Anderson, Silvia Signars
Andrews, Annie
Aragon, LaRita A.
Bailey, Rosanne
Banks, Evelyn P.
Beldo, April D.
Benton, Valerie D.
Berg, Kathleen F.
Blakely, Shirley A.
Bolden, Barbaranette T.
Boney-Harris, Gwendolyn
Born, Dana H.
Bourbeau, Sheryl J.
Brannon, Barbara C.
Brault, Laurell A.
Breckenridge, Jody A.
Brice-O'Hara, Sally
Broadway, Rita Marie
Brooks, Janice M.
Brown, Nancy E.
Bruzek-Kohler, Christine M.
Burke, Rossatte Y.
Byrd, Cora
Carter, Normia E.
Ceaser, Deritha M.
Clark, Trudy H.
Clay, Patricia
Cleckley, Julia J.
Coaxum, Velva D.
Contres, Kathlene
Coogan, Cynthia
Crisp, Donna L.
Cummings, Angela M.
Cunningham, Pauline W.
Dacier, Donna Lee
Desjardins, Susan Y.
Diego-Allard, Victoria H.
Dixon, Althea Green
Eder, Mari Kaye
Edmunds, Jeanette K.
Emerson, Flora
Epps, Marry A.
Falca-Dodson, Maria
Farmer, Margrit Marie Anne
Farrisee, Gina S.
Fast, Barbara G.
Fetherson, Parisa Y.
Field, Marie T.
Fischer, Wendy
Flaherty, Karen
Flanders, Moira
Fleming-Makell, Rhonda
Forrest, Delores G.
Forster, Diane M.
Garrett, Tracy L.
Garrison, Marguerite C.
Green, Phyllis J.
Greene, Ellen Pfeiffer
Halstead, Rebecca S.
Harris, Marcelite J.
Harris, Stayce D.
Harris, Vera F.
Hart, Deborah L.
Hawley-Bowland, Carla G.
Hayes, Lou V.
Hemminger, Linda S.
Hodges, Adele E.
Hollis, Evelyn
Howard, Michelle J.
Hurd, Iris J.
Jackson, Patricia A.
Jackson, Sherry R.
Jenkins-Harden, Joyce R.
Johnson, Vickki
Jones, Carol A.
Jones, Michele S.
Joseph, Annette
Joseph, Phyllis R.

Keit, Patricia A.
Kennedy, Claudia
Kight, Mary J.
King, Teresa V.
Kirkland, Cynthia N.
Kraus, Julia A.
Krusa-Dossin, Mary Ann
Lescavage, Nancy J.
Loewer, Deborah A.
Malachowski, Nicole
Marks, Andrea R.
Martinez, Laura A.
Martinson, Wendy
McIntosh, Jeanine
McNeirney, Violet C.
McTague, Linda K.
Milligan, Pamela K.
Mitchell, Eithel P.
Morgan, Betty L.G.
Morris, Elizabeth M.
Murakata, Linda A.
Nero, Carrie Lee
Pinckney, Alma
Pinckney, Belinda
Pollock, Gale S.
Powell-Mims, Janie Mae
Prettyman-Beck, Yvonne J.
Quagliotti, Marilyn A.
Queen, Joan Renee
Ramble, Pamela M.
Redpath, Sharon H.
Reese, Andrea D.
Richardson, Sandra V.
Richardson, Velma L.
Richie, Sharon Ivey
Rivera, Margaret
Rivera, Sonya L.
Rondeau, Ann E.
Salinas, Angela
Saunders, Mary L.
Savage, Janice R.
Shanks, Mary Joe
Simmons, Bettye Hill
Smith, Melody D.
Smith, Mittie
Sobel, Annette L.
Spencer, Kathleen M.
Starghill, Renee
Steele, Toreaser A.
Stevens, Joyce L.
Stubbs, Laura
Thomas, Jacqueline D.
Trowell-Harris, Irene
Turner, Carol I.
Tutt, Veronica
Tymeson, Jodi S.
Umberg, Robin Bailey
Varnado, Sheila
Washington, Bette R.
Weatherington, Lisa D.
Wheeling, Deborah C.
Williams, Hattie
Wilmoth, Margaret Chamberlain
Wilson, Rosa L.
Wolfolk, Sharon Bingham
Wright, Sherry L.

Ministry

Allen, Carla H.
Davis, Sarah Frances
Dollar, Taffi L.
Flake, Elaine
Harris, Gayle Elizabeth
Harris, Mamie
Johnson, Wilma Robena
Kammerer, Charlene
King, Barbara L.
Long, Vanessa Griffin
McKenzie, Vashti Murphy
Schori, Katharine Jefferts
Tatem, Dorothy Watson
Weems, Renita J.
Wiley, Reba D.

Nonprofit Executive

Abernathy, Juanita Jones
Adolf, Mary M.
Bell, Diane L.
Bell-Rose, Stephanie
Brennan, Maria E.
Colaianne, Melonie
Davis, Lisa
Dorsey, Hattie B.
Gates, Melinda
Michel, Harriet R.
Terrell, Dorothy A.
Wattleton, Faye
Wiley, Benaree Pratt

Performing Arts

Austin, Debra
Butler-Hopkins, Kathleen
Jamison, Judith
Lowe, Melissa

Politics Executive

Brazile, Donna
CaHill, Mary Beth

Sports

Ackerman, Val
Ali, Laila
Cooper, Cynthia
Edwards, Teresa
Gore-Mann, Debra
Greene-Chamberlain, Lillian
Levick, Cheryl
Meyers-Drysdale, Ann
Miller, Cheryl
Palmer, Violet
Riley, Ruth Ellen
Rodriguez, Jennifer
Swoopes, Sheryl
Wagner, LaVonda
Williams, Serena Jameka
Williams, Venus Ebone Starr
Yow, Deborah A.
Yow, Sandra Kay

Sports Executive

Baird, Lisa
Bivens, Carolyn Vesper
Blackburn, Katie
Brown, Renee
Clark, Rena
Creer, Sharon
DeFrantz, Anita L.
Ferron, Jennifer
Fuller, Martha
Ng, Kim
Orender, Donna
Taylor, Angela
Trask, Amy
Wheeler, Pamela
York, Denise DeBartolo

Technology Executive

Archambeau, Shellye
Barton, Jacqueline K.
Bartz, Carol
Brown, Shona
Chan, Mary
Christy, Cindy
Curtis, Chandra
Davidson, Janet
Decker, Susan L.
Evans, Jane
Fike, Sherri
Fu, Ping
Gooden, Linda
Hoogen, Ingrid Van Den
Livermore, Ann M.
Lyons, Cathy
Maguire, Joanne M.
Sanford, Linda S.
Sheskey, Susan
Thoms, Jannet M.
Tyson, Lynn A.
Vandebroek, Sophie V.
Wettersten, Ann
White, Jeannette Lee

APPENDIX 2
GEOGRAPHICAL LISTING

United States

Arkansas

Ambar, Carmen Twillie
Baker, Karen R.
Bolden, Barbaranette T.
Brown, Irma Hunter
Clinton, Hillary
Dickey, Betty C.
Elders, M. Jocelyn
Epps, Roselyn
Joseph, Annette
Palin, Sarah Heath
Ramble, Pamela M.
Stoneburner, Terri J.
Sykes, Gwendolyn

Alabama

Abernathy, Juanita Jones
Aldridge, Susan C.
Bailey, Rosanne
Beasley, Teresa
Bell, Ella B.
Bell, Stephanie W.
Benton, Valerie D.
Brown, Janice Rogers
Butler, Gloria
Chapman, Beth
Clark, Linda
Clark, Trudy H.
Clay, Patricia
Clement, Edith Brown
Cobb, Sharon
Cunningham, Pauline W.
Davis, N. Jan
Duncan, Elaine Flowers
East, Ellen
Epps, Marry A.
Forster, Diane M.
Franklin, Shirley Clarke
Gaskins, Kathern L.
Goodson, Amanda
Griner, Carolyn
Hall, Ethel H.
Halstead, Rebecca S.
Hawkins, Carol Hooks
Haysbert, JoAnn W.
Henderson, Mary Jane
Herman, Alexis M.
Hire, Kathryn P.
Hughes, Marvalene
Hurd, Iris J.
Jackson, Lorna Graves
Jemison, Mae C.
Jenkins, Jo Ann C.
Jenkins-Harden, Joyce R.
Jones, Patricia
Kennedy, Yvonne
Kight, Mary J.
Kirk-McAlpine, Patricia
Lane, Bensonetta Tipton
Leclaire, Margaret
Loggins, Eugenia L.
McTague, Linda K.
Nunn, Annetta W.
Provence, Tiffany
Ray, Sandra
Reese, Andrea D.
Reid-Wallace, Carolyn
Rice, Condoleezza
Richardson, Sandra V.
Robinson, Audrey
Sams, Jeneene
Scantlebury, Velma
Smith, Mittie
Spencer, Loretta
Vanhooser, Teresa
Walker, Angelia
Washington, Tereasa H.
Weatherington, Lisa D.
Wiley, Reba D.

Alaska

Butler-Hopkins, Kathleen
Palin, Sarah Heath

Arkansas

Greene, Ellen Pfeiffer
Hartford, Maureen A.
Lincoln, Blanche Lambert
Moller, Patricia N.
Murkowski, Lisa
Taft, Hope
Whitson, Caroline

Arizona

Davis, Ruth A.
Elliott, April Phillips
Evans, Jane
Escher, Patricia G.
Fast, Barbara G.
Fleming-Makell, Rhonda
Garcia, Jeanne
Garcia, Mildred
Graves-Robertson, Shauna
Gutierrez, Pamela C.
Harris, Stayce D.
Hilliard, Ruth H.
Hoag, M. Jean
Holt, Cathy M.
Hudson, Natalie E.
Jenkins-Harden, Joyce R.
Lowe, Melissa
Manross, Mary
Matsui, Doris Okada
McNally, Colleen
McVay, Jacque
Mroz, Rosa
Napolitano, Janet
O'Connor, Karen L.
Peters, Mary E.
Robinson, Kathleen
Roy, Loriene
Stephens, Sherry K.
Umberg, Robin Bailey
Vincent, Patricia K.

California

Aaron, Cynthia
Ackerman, Val
Adams, Karen S.
Ali, Laila
Allen, Sharon
Alvillar-Speake, Theresa
Anderson, Michelle J.
Ariyasu,Vicki
Armstrong, Saundra Brown
Arouh, Janice
Ashmann-Gerst, Judith
Baicker, Katherine
Bamattre-Manoukian, Patricia
Banks, Tyra Lynne
Banta, Vivian
Barton, Jacqueline K.
Bath, Patricia E.
Beal, Maureen
Beck, Jill
Beldo, April D.
Benke, Patricia D.
Berkley, Shelley
Bernal, Margaret
Biggert, Judith Borg
Bingham,Nancy
Bono, Mary
Boskin, Chris
Boxer, Barbara
Brannon, Barbara C.
Brown, Adriane M.
Brown, Janice Rogers
Brown, Nancy E.

Bucklin, Christine B.
Bucklo, Elaine
Burke, Yvonne B.
Butz, M. Kathleen
Cabral, Andrea J.
Cabral, Anna Escobedo
Cagle, Yvonne Darlene
Caldwell, Tracy E.
Campbell, Jill
Cantil-Sakauye, Tani Gorre
Cantor, Nancy
Capps, Lois
Carr, Dolores
Castagna, Vanessa
Castillo, Susan
Chan, Gwen
Chandler, Cassandra M.
Chang, Shelleyanne W.L.
Chau, Micheline
Cherng, Peggy Tsiang
Chick, Laura
Clarey, Patricia
Cleckley, Julia J.
Coaxum, Velva D.
Collins, Eileen Marie
Colucci, Marlene M.
Contres, Kathlene
Coogan, Cynthia
Cooper, Cynthia
Cordell, LaDoris Hazzard
Creer, Sharon
Crisp, Donna L.
Cubin, Barbara L.
Cuffney, Nancy
Cunningham, Pauline W.
Cunningham, Andy
Currie, Nancy Jane
Dale, Shana
Davis, Ruth A.
Davis, Susan A.
De Alonso, Marcela Perez
DeFrantz, Anita L.
Del Pesco, Susan C.
de Macias, Carolyn Webb
Desoer, Barbara J.
Dixon, Althea Green
Donze, Laurie Friedman
Dunbar, Bonnie J.
Duron, Ysabel
Ennix, Kim
Escher, Patricia G.
Eshoo, Anna Georges
Evans, Jane
Feinstein, Dianne
Ferretti, Charlotte
Fischer, Wendy
Fisher, Anna L.
Folsom, Kim T.
Forrest, Delores G.
Gaskins, Kathern L.
Gast, Alice P.
George, Kathryn A.
Gerberding, Julie Louise
Gercke, Sylvia
Gilbreath, Patricia
Gilmore, Marie
Gooden, Linda
Goodson, Amanda
Gore-Mann, Debra
Granholm, Jennifer M.
Gray, Karla
Hall, Diana R.
Haller, Judith
Hamilton, Phyllis Jean
Hammond, Lauren
Hansen, Marka
Harman, Jane F.
Harrington, Nicki (Virginia)
Harris, Kamala D.
Harris, Marcelite J.
Harris, Stayce D.
Harriss, Cynthia
Hayden-Watkins, Dorothy
Hayes-White, Joanne
Haynes, Karen
Haysbert, JoAnn W.
Henderson, Naomi
Herman, Mindy
Hire, Kathryn P.
Hoogen, Ingrid Van Den
Hooks, Tamara T.
Hughes, Marvalene
Hughes, Teresa P.
Hunt, Lorraine T.
Hurd, Iris J.
Hutchens, Sandra
Immergut, Karin J.
Irion, Joan K.
Jackson, Patricia A.
Jacobson, Nina
Jarrett, Valerie
Jemison, Mae C.
Jernigan, Tamara E.
Johnson, Beverly
Johnson, Melissa
Johnson, Odessa
Johnson, Suzanne Nora
Johnson-Goins, Gloria
Jung, Andrea
Kelly, Suedeen G.
Kennard, Joyce L.
Kennard, Lydia H.
Kicza, Mary Ellen
Kight, Mary J.
Kirk-McAlpine, Patricia
Kniss, Liz
Krom, Beth
Lansing, Sherry
Lau, Constance H.
Lee, Barbara
Lescavage, Nancy J.
Levick, Cheryl
Lewis, Shirley A.R.
Lingle, Linda
Loewer, Deborah A.
Lofgren, Zoe
Lopez, Shirlene
Lucid, Shannon W.
Ma, Chung-Pei
Madison, Paula
Maguire, Joanne M.
Mahan, Patricia
Martin, Leslie Baranco
Matsui, Doris Okada
McBeth, Veronica Simmons
McCaw, Susan Rasinski
McConnell, Judith
McKinney, Cynthia Ann
McNally, Colleen
Meyers-Drysdale, Ann
Miller, Cheryl
Milligan, Pamela K.
Ming, Jenny
Molina, Gloria
Moore, Thelma Wyatt Cummings
Morgan, Barbara R.
Mulder, Arlene J.
Napolitano, Grace F.
Ng, Kim
Nobumoto, Karen S.
Ochoa, Ellen
Olsen, Kathie
Orman, Suze (Susan)
Ortega, Darleen
Palmer, Violet
Pelosi, Nancy
Perez, Anna M.
Porter, Lisa J.
Powell, Shirley
Provencio, Marla
Veneman, Ann M.
Verrett, Shirley
Waters, Maxine
Watson, Allison L.
Watson, Diane Edith
Watson, Kyra
Werdegar, Kathryn M.
Wettersten, Ann
White, Maxine A.
Wieland, Lucy A.
Williams, Serena Jameka
Williams, Venus Ebone Starr
Wilson, Stephanie D
Wong, Andrea
Woods, Jacqueline
Woolsey, Lynn C.
Ybarra, Lea
Yeh, Pen-Shu
Yellen, Janet L.
York, Denise DeBartolo
Young, Gwendolyn V.
Zahn, Paula

Colorado

Aldridge, Susan C.
Alvarado, Blanca
Bailey, Rosanne
Blakely, Shirley A
Borders, Lisa
Bowers, Kathleen M.
Bowman, Linda
Bromley, Rebecca Snyder
Brown, Lisa L.
Brown, Renee
Bruner, Cindy H.
Cheney, Lynne V.
Collins, Eileen Marie
Collyer, Rosemary M.
Conners, Ellen Engleman
DeGette, Diana
Delgado, Katherine R.
Desjardins, Susan Y.
Dunn, Karen-Sue
Gilman, Shelley Ilene
Greene-Chamberlain, Lillian
Hansen, Karla J.
Harris, Marcelite J.
Harris, Vera F.
Hart, Cathy J.
Hawley-Bowland, Carla G.
Hayden-Watkins, Dorothy
Herda, Larissa
Howard, Michelle J.
Ivins, Marsha S.
Jenkins-Harden, Joyce R.

Kapsner, Carol Ronning
Klanderud, Helen
Lacy, Mary
Lyons, Cathy
Madden, Teresa S.
Manzanares, Sylvia A.
Metcalf-Lindenburger, Dorothy M.
Murray, Dana Elizabeth
Musgrave, Marilyn N.
Pace, Betty S.
Rappaport, Sheila A.
Rice, Condoleezza
Rivera, Gloria A.
Roybal, Dianna R.
Swift, Pattie P.
Tome, Carol
Vincent, Patricia K.

Connecticut

Baicker, Katherine
Barton, Jacqueline K.
Beck, Jill
Belfance, Eve
Brehm, Sharon B
Brennan, Maria E.
Burger, Leslie
Burns, Ursula M.
Butler-Hopkins, Kathleen
Bysiewicz, Susan
Calpeter, Lynn
Capps, Lois
Davis DiPentima, Alexandra
DeFrantz, Anita L.
DeLauro, Rosa L.
Duckett, Karen I.
Edelman, Marian Wright
Epps, Marry A.
Eshoo, Anna Georges
Espinosa, Carmen E.
Flaherty, Karen
Gandara, Marilda Lara
Grymes, Rose
Guinier, Lani
Hilliard, Ruth H.
Hockfield, Susan
Hodges, Adele E.
Hood, Lucy
Huvelle, Ellen Segal
Jackson-Lee, Sheila
Jamison, Judith
Johnson, Nancy L.
Joyner, Pamela J.
Kagan, Elena
King, Carolyn Dineen
King, Gayle
Klobuchar, Amy Jean
Lane, Bensonetta Tipton
Lantz, Theresa C.
Lau, Constance H.
Lin, Maya
McBride, Anita
McGetrick, Peg
Mellow, Gail O.
Mulcahy, Anne Marie
Nappier, Denise Lynn
Nobumoto, Karen S.
Nooyi, Indra K.
Norton, Eleanor Holmes
Parrish, Jill N.
Reif, Debbie
Rell, M. Jodi
Rice, Judith C.
Rodin, Judith
Rogers, Chase T.
Stewart, Martha
Tatum, Beverly Daniel
Townsend, Sharon S.
Trowell-Harriw, Irene
Vandebroek, Sophie V.
Velasquez, Patti A.
Vertefeuille, Christine S.
White, Katherine E.
Williams, Betty Smith
Wright, Wilhelmina M.
Wyman, Nancy
Yanez, Linda Reyna

District of Columbia

Ackerman, Arlene
Adams, Karen S.
Allen, Bernadette
Allen, Debbie
Allen, Susan Au
Alvarado, Carol
Anderson, Silvia Signars
Andrews, Annie
Aragon, LaRita A.
Arsht, Leslye A.
Bailey, Rosanne
Baranco, Juanita Powell
Barshefsky, Charlene
Baskerville, Lezli
Bath, Patricia E.
Beard, Lillian M.
Belfance, Eve
Benton, Valerie D.
Bernard, Marielsa
Bivens, Carolyn Vesper
Black, Cathleen
Bland, Sharon Jackson
Blount, Paula
Bolden, Barbaranette T.
Boney-Harris, Gwendolyn
Born, Dana H.
Bourbeau, Sheryl J.
Brannon, Barbara C
Brazile, Donna
Brennan, Maria E.
Brock, Rovenia
Brooks, Fabienne
Brown, Beth A.
Brown, Gayleatha B.
Brown, Irma Hunter
Brown, Nancy E.
Bruzek-Kohler, Christine M.
Bryan, Beth Ann
Bryan, T.J.
Bryant, Wanda G.
Buchan, Claire
Bush, Laura
Butler, Gloria
Cabral, Anna Escobedo
CaHill, Mary Beth
Cannon, Evelyn Omega
Carlisle, Elaine
Carnahan, Jean
Carter, Rosalynn
Castro, Ida L.
Cheney, Lynne V.
Christy, Cindy
Cino, Maria
Clancy, Carolyn M.
Clark, King, Reatha
Clark, Patrina
Clark, Trudy H.
Cleave, Mary L.
Clinton, Hillary
Coker, Mary Day
Collyer, Rosemary M.
Colucci, Marlene M.
Combs, Ann L.
Conners, Ellen Engleman
Coogan, Cynthia
Crisp, Donna L.
Cropp, Linda Washington
Cunningham, Sheree Davis
Dale, Shana
Dangar, Jennifer
Davis, Audrey Y.
Davis, Lisa
Davis, Marguerite H.
Davis, Ruth A.
Dawson, Diann
Draper, Judy P.
Dunbar, Bonnie J.
Duncan, Elaine Flowers
Duncan, Linda A.
Duncan-Peters, Stephanie
Dunn, Karen-Sue
Duron, Ysabel
Earp, Naomi Churchill
Edelman, Marian Wright
Edmunds, Jeanette K.
Einhorn, Jessica P.
Eitel, Maria S.
Epps, Roselyn
Ericsson, Aprille
Espinosa, Carmen E.
Farmer, Margrit Marie Anne
Farrisee, Gina S.
Field, Marie T.
Fienberg, Linda D.
Finley, Julie
Fites, Jeanne
Fleming-Makell, Rhonda
Frankel, Lois J.
Franklin, Shirley Clarke
Freeman, Sharee
Gambatesa, Linda
Gardner, Janice
Garel, Giana
Gayle, Helene D.
Gottfried, Maureen
Hall, Shelvin Louise Marie
Halstead, Rebecca S.
Handel, Karen
Harman, Jane F.
Harris, Gayle Elizabeth
Harris, Kamala D.
Harris, Marcelite J.
Harris, Skila
Harris, Stayce D.
Harrison, Patricia de Stacy
Hart, Deborah L.
Hayes, Lou V.
Hemminger, Linda S.
Herman, Alexis M.
Herseth, Stephanie
Higgins, Kathryn O'Leary
Hill, Chris A.
Holt, Karen E.
Hooks, Tamara T.
Hopson, Deborah Parham
Hotten, Michele D.
Howard, Michelle J.

Hughes, Catherine Liggins
Hughes, Karen P.
Huvelle, Ellen Segal
Ifill, Gwen
Iorio, Pam
Isaacs-Lowe, Arlene
Jackson, Kathryn J. "Kate"
Jackson, Patricia A.
James, Barbara
Jenkins-Harden, Joyce R.
Johnson, Carol D.
Johnson, Karen A.
Johnson, Katherine E.
Johnson, Melissa
Johnson, Norma Holloway
Jones, Carol A.
Jones, Elain Hollan
Kagan, Cheryl C.
Kagan, Elena
Kennedy, Cornelia G.
Kenney, Kristie Anne
Kessler, Gladys
King, Gayle
King, Gwendolyn
Kollar-Kotelly, Colleen
Kraus, Julia A.
Kronmiller, Kate B.
Krusa-Dossin, Mary Ann
Lally-Green, Maureen E.
Lane, Bensonetta Tipton
Lantz, Theresa C.
Lawrence, Deirdre M.
Lawson, Kelli Richardson
Lee, Alison Renee
Lincoln, Blanche Lambert
Loewer, Deborah A.
Loston, Adena Williams
Lucid, Shannon W.
Martha Rees,
Martin-Clark, Miriam B.
Martinez, Laura A.
Martinez, Shirley A.
Martinson, Wendy
Mathews, Sylvia
Mathieu, Dennise
Matsui, Doris Okada
McBride, Anita
McDonald, Gabrielle Kirk
McGowan, Anna-Maria Rivas
McMurray, Claudia A.
McNeirney, Violet C.
Mellow, Gail O.
Merget, Astrid E.
Michael, Jeanette A.
Michel, Harriet R.
Miers, Harriet
Miles-LaGrange, Vicki
Miller, Peggy
Mishoe, Helena O.
Mitchell, Andrea
Mitchell, Eithel P.
Molina, Gloria
Moller, Patricia N.
Monroe, Stephanie J.
Morella, Constance A.
Morris, Elizabeth M.
Murakata, Linda A.
Murphy McKenzie, Vashti
Murphy, Frances
Nero, Carrie Lee
Newman, Andrea Fischer
Norton, Eleanor Holmes
Nuland, Victoria
Obama, Michelle
O'Connor, Maureen
O'Leary, Hazel
Pack, Sandra L.
Pariente, Barbara J.
Pelosi, Nancy
Perez, Anna M.
Peruggi, Regina S.
Pinckney, Belinda
Pinn, Vivian
Pinson, Tracey L.
Porter, Gayle K.
Powell, Dorothy L.
Prettyman-Beck, Yvonne J.
Quagliotti, Marilyn A.
Quince, Peggy A.
Richardson, Barbara
Richie, Sharon Ivey
Rickard, Lisa A.
Riley, Sandra R.
Robinson, Deborah A.
Rockefeller, Sharon Percy
Rondeau, Ann E.
Rosenbaum, Marilyn Brown
Ryan, Mary Jean
Salinas, Angela
Sanchez, Loretta
Sanders, Robin Renee
Serrette, Cathy H.
Spencer, Kathleen M.
Springer, Linda
Starghill, Renee
Steele, Toreaser A.
Steinbeck, Margaret O.
Stevens, Lisa
Stokes, Angela R.
Sweeney, Anne
Taylor, Anna Katherine Johnston Diggs
Taylor, Susan
Thompson, Thelma
Tortolani, Michelle
Trowell-Harriw, Irene
Turner, Linda Edmonds
Veneman, Ann M.
Wagner, Ann
Walker, Debra K.
Westgate, Barbara A.
White-Olson, B.J.
Williams, Betty Smith
Williams, E. Faye
Wolfolk, Sharon Bingham
Young, Dona D.

Delaware

Berger, Carolyn
Berry, Bertice
Brady, M. Jane
Chowdhry, Uma
Clayton, Annette
Coogan, Cynthia
Currie, Nancy Jane
Del Pesco, Susan C.
Griffin, Patricia W.
Jurden, Jan R.
Lias, Kay A.
Martha Rees,
Minner, Ruth Ann
Wright, Wilhelmina M.

Florida

Ackerman, Arlene
Ali, Laila
Allen, Faye
Altonaga, Cecilia Maria
Atack, Sharon B.
Austin, Debra
Ayres, Judith
Babb, Ronda E.
Banks,Evelyn P.
Barazzone, Esther L.
Beckles, G. Valerie
Bernes, Debra
Berry, Bertice
Black, Susan Harrell
Blechman, Deb S.
Boney-Harris, Gwendolyn
Brennan, Shirley M.
Brown, Corrine
Brown, Irma Hunter
Brown, Lucy Chernow
Brown-Waite, Virginia
Brunson, Catherine M.
Bryant, Castell Vaughn
Bush, Columba
Caldwell, Tracy E.
Carranza, Jovita
Clark, Linda
Clark, Nancy L.
Clark, Nikki
Clarke, Cathleen B.
Cobb, Sharon
Coker, Mary Day
Cummings, Angela M.
Cunningham, Sheree Davis
Curtis, Chandra
Davidson, Lisa
Davis, Lisa
Davis, N. Jan
Emerson, Flora
Epps, Marry A.
Fischer, Wendy
Fisher, Anna L.
Forrest, Delores G.
Frankel, Lois J.
Gaines, Gay Hart
Genshaft, Judy
Gerard, Patricia
Goodson, Amanda
Green, Melvia B.
Griner, Carolyn
Harris, Katherine
Hawkins, Carol
Hayes, Lou V.
Henderson, Mary Jane
Higginbotham, Joan E.
Hire, Kathryn P.
Holbrook, Karen A.
Holt, Karen E.
Hooks, Tamara T.
Hotten, Michele D.
Iorio, Pam
Jemison, Mae C.
Jennings, Toni
Johnson, Glorious
Johnson, Sheila Crump
Johnson-Goins, Gloria
Joseph, Phyllis R.
Kammerer, Charlene
Keever, Lynda
Kicza, Mary Ellen
King, Barbara L.
King, Karen

King, Teresa V.
Koellner, Laurette
Kreeger, Judith L.
Lando, Maxine Cohen
Latimore, Alicia L.
Leesfield, Ellen
Long, Irene Duhart
Lowe, Challis M.
Lucid, Shannon W.
Lynn, Barbara M.G.
MacKinnon, Cynthia
Manzi, Barbara
Martinez, Laura A.
Mattingly, Rebecca Dirden
McCall, Dawn L.
McDemmond, Marie V.
McDonald, Ysleta W.
McIntosh, Jeanine
McMorris, Cathy
McTague, Linda K.
McWhorter, Shirlyon J.
Meek, Carrie P.
Morris, Elizabeth M.
Morris, Elizabeth M.
Munyon, Lisa
Nason, Nicole
Nero, Carrie Lee
O'Kane, Julie Hions
Ortiz, Maria D.
Pariente, Barbara J.
Perdue, Beverly Eaves
Plummer, Beverly
Powell, Shirley
Provence, Tiffany
Quince, Peggy A.
Revilla, Ada Pozo
Rivera, Fanny
Rivera, Sonya L.
Robinson, Audrey
Roche, Rene A.
Roe, Lesa B.
Ros-Lehtinen, Ileana
Rothenberg, Leslie B.
Saunder, Mary L.
Scarlett-Golden, Yvonne
Schori, Katharine Jefferts
Shalala, Donna E.
Smith, Melody D.
Steinbeck, Margaret O.
Stephen, Elizabeth Guber
Suber, Dianne B.
Terrell, Dorothy A.
Turner, Carol I.
Velasquez, Patti A.
Waldron, Kathleen
Wasserman-Rubin, Diana
Wasserman-Rubin, Diana
Wells, Linda Ann
Wiley, Benaree Pratt
Williams, Hattie
Williams, Serena Jameka
Williams, Venus Ebone Starr
Wright, Sherry L.
Yancy, Dorothy Cowser
Young, Gwendolyn V.
Zel, Antoinette

Georgia

Adams, Cheryl
Adams, Karen S.
Adams, Valencia
Allen, Carla H.
Allen, Fannie L.
Anderson, Silvia Signars
Anderson, Tina
Andrews, Annie
Baranco, Juanita Powell
Barnes, Anne Elizabeth
Bell-Scott, Patricia
Bernes, Debra
Berry, Bertice
Biggins, J. Veronica
Black, Susan Harrell
Boney-Harris, Gwendolyn
Borders, Lisa
Braun, Carol Moseley
Brewer, Rosalind
Buckner, L. Gail
Bundles, A'Lelia
Carlisle, Elaine
Carter, Rosalynn
Clark, King, Reatha
Clay, Patricia
Clayton, Eva M.
Cloud, Rosemary R.
Cole, Brenda Hill
Cole, Johnnetta Betsch
Coleman, Carolyn Quilloin
Crawford, Susan
Davidson, Janet
Davis, N. Jan
Davis, Ruth A.
Deen, Paula
DeVard, Jerri
Diego-Allard, Victoria H.
Dixon, Althea Green
Dollar, Taffi L.
Dorsey, Hattie B.
Duckett, Karen I.
Dunham, Wanda
East, Ellen
Edelman, Marian Wright
Edwards, Teresa
Elam, Deborah
Emerson, Flora
Epps, Evern Cooper
Evans, Orinda Dale
Fowler, Nuby
Franklin, Shirley Clarke
Garel, Giana
Garrison, Marguerite C.
George, Hulane
Gerberding, Julie Louise
Goodson, Amanda
Gottfried, Maureen
Grant, Susan
Greene, Deborah S.
Hall, Beverly L.
Hall, Ethel H.
Handel, Karen
Harris, Katherine
Harris, Mamie
Harris, Marcelite J.
Hatchett, Glenda
Hawkins, Carol Hooks
Hayes, Lou V.
Hayes, Maxine
Haysbert, JoAnn W.
Heacock, Jessica
Hicks, Juanita
Higginbotham, Eve J.
Holbrook, Karen A.
Hooks, Tamara T.
Hurd, Iris J.
Jackson, Edna
Jackson, Lorna Graves
Jackson, Sherry R.
Johnson-Goins, Gloria
Jones, Carol A.
Jordan, Karen
Keit, Patricia A.
Kennedy, Claudia
Kimbrough, Marjorie L.
King, Barbara L.
King, Karen
King, Teresa V.
Kiss, Elizabeth
Lane, Bensonetta Tipton
Lawrence, Deirdre M.
Long, Vanessa Griffin
Lucia, Marian M.
MacKinnon, Cynthia
Maloy, Frances
Martinson, Wendy
McCall, Dawn L.
McDemmond, Marie V.
McKinney, Cynthia Ann
McTeer-Hudson, Heather
Miller, M. Yvette
Moddelmog, Hala
Moore, Thelma Wyatt Cummings
Morgan, Betty L.G.
Nero, Carrie Lee
Norville, Deborah
Perdue, Mary
Pinckney, Belinda
Pollock, Gale S.
Powell, Shirley
Price, Anita
Reynolds, Penny Brown
Richardson, Velma L.
Ridgeway, Roslyn
Rivera, Margaret
Roberts, Robin
Robinson, Deborah A.
Rodwell, Wanda Yancey
Scott, Beverly
Sears, Leah Ward
Sherman, Diane
Sitherwood, Suzanne
Smith, Jane E.
Smith, Mittie
Spencer, Kathleen M.
Tate, Susan
Tatum, Beverly Daniel
Thomas, Jacqueline D.
Thoms, Jannet M.
Tome, Carol
Tuson, Gail S.
Tutt, Veronica
Umberg, Robin Bailey
Varnado, Sheila
Walker, Debra K.
Walker-Kimbro, Carolyn
Ware, Janis L.
Weems, Renita J.
Wiley, Reba D.
Williams, Pearlene M.
Winslow, Cleta
Wood, Lisa Godbey
Wykle, May L.
Yancy, Dorothy Cowser

Hawaii

Allen, Sharon
Berg, Kathleen F.
Carter, Normia E.
Chang, Shelleyanne W.L.
Contres, Kathlene

Hawley-Bowland, Carla G.
Kim, Donna Mercado
Lau, Constance H.
Lescavage, Nancy J.
Lingle, Linda
McIntosh, Jeanine
Milligan, Pamela K.
Mollway, Susan Oki
Pollock, Gale S.
Prettyman-Beck, Yvonne J.
Young, Lynnette

Iowa

Allen, Bernadette
Alshouse, Diane R.
Bruch, Ruth E.
Coleman, Mary Sue
Garman, Rita B.
Hemminger, Linda S.
Lacy, Mary
Pederson, Sally
Tymeson, Jodi S.
Vogel, Gayle Nelson
White, Jeannette Lee

Idaho

Hart, Cathy J.
Lansing, Karen
Morgan, Barbara R.
Palin, Sarah Heath
Perry, Cynthia
Taylor, Angela
Whitson Peggy A.

Illinois

Adams, Carolyn
Adams, Cheryl
Babrowski, Claire
Banks, Paula
Beal, Maureen
Bean, Melissa L.
Biggert, Judith Borg
Bishop, Patricia Martin
Bowies, Barbara L.
Braun, Carol Moseley
Brown, Dorothy
Brown, Nancy E.
Bruch, Ruth E.
Buchan, Claire
Bucklo, Elaine
Burke, Anne M.
Cantor, Nancy
Carter, Normia E.
Chun, Shinae
Clark, King, Reatha
Clinton, Hillary
Coco, Gloria Grace
Coler, Kate
Collins, Earlean
Cooper, Cynthia
Crisp, Donna L.
Currey, Gail
Dewey, Londa J.
Dillon, Mary
Forrest, Delores G.
Foster, Jylia Moore
Frossard, Margaret O'Mara
Fu, Ping
Garman, Rita B.
Gilman, Shelley Ilene
Green, Melvia B.
Gulyas, Diane
Hall, Shelvin Louise Marie
Hamilton, Phyllis Jean
Hefner, Christie
Higginbotham, Eve J.
Higginbotham, Joan E.
Hirsh, Sharon Latchaw
Hobson, Mellody
Hooper, Michele J.
Hopkins, Vanessa
Hoskins, Michele
Howard-Vital, Michelle
Hudson, Dawn
Hudson, Dianne Atkinson
Hunter, Mattie
Hutchinson, Susan F.
Jarrett, Valerie
Jemison, Mae C.
Johnson, Barbara Gilleran
Johnson, Katherine E.
Johnson, Nancy L.
Johnson, Sheila Crump
Jordan, Karen
Kammerer, Charlene
Karpinski, Diane
Katen, Karen L.
Kenny, Shirley Strum
Klobuchar, Amy Jean
Krueger, Liz
Kullman, Ellen J.
Lansing, Sherry
Leclaire, Margaret
Madigan, Lisa
Manning, Blanche M.
McBride, Margaret Stanton
McCann, Renetta
McCarty, Alison
McDade, Mary
McNulty, Jill K.
Mitchell, Eithel P.
Molina, Gloria
Moore, Thelma Wyatt Cummings
Myerscough, Sue E.
Nason, Nicole
Ng, Kim
Norville, Deborah
Obama, Michelle
O'Brien, Sheila M.
O'Connor, Karen L.
O'Malley, Denise M.
Orender, Donna
Orman, Suze (Susan)
Perry, June Carter
Pippins, Shirley Robinson
Poon, Christine
Price, Anita
Rice, Linda Johnson
Roggensack, Patience Drake
Rosenbaum, Marilyn Brown
Royster, Kay E.
Schakowsky, Janice D.
Scholly, Alison
Shapiro, Judith R.
Shriver, Maria
South, Leslie Elaine
Steele, Bobbie L.
Theis, Mary Jane
Thomas, Joyce A.
Trout, Linda Copple
Velasquez, Patti A.
Vogel, Gayle Nelson
Whittington, Carolyn
Williams, Darlene
Winfrey, Oprah Gail
Wright, Karla F.

Indiana

Ackerman, Arlene
Anderson, Chandra Y.
Anderson, Silvia Signars
Bailey, Catherine Todd
Bailey, Rosanne
Bingham, Laura Carpenter
Breckenridge,Cora Smith
Brehm, Sharon B
Brown, Adriane M.
Cantwell, Maria E.
Carson, Julia May
Castagna, Vanessa
Coleman, Carolyn
Conners, Ellen Engleman
Davis, Kathy L.
Earp, Naomi Churchill
Farmer, Margrit Marie Anne
Foster, Jylia Moore
Freeman-Wilson, Karen
Gurich, Noma D.
Henney, Jane E.
Johns, Marie C.
Johnson, Eddie Bernice
Jones, Michele S.
Kapsner, Carol Ronning
Klanderud, Helen
Levick, Cheryl
Lowe, Melissa
Mayfield, Mabel Johnson
Merget, Astrid E.
Meyers-Drysdale,Ann
Miller, Peggy
O'Brien, Sheila M.
Pippins, Shirley Robinson
Riley, Ruth Ellen
Zopp, Andrea L.

Kansas

Armstrong, Mary
Ballard, Tina
Barnes, Anne Elizabeth
Beier, Carol A.
Benton, Valerie D.
Broadway, Rita Marie
Caplinger, Nancy
Coleman, Carolyn
Ender, Elma Teresa Salinas
Henney, Jane E.
Jenkins-Harden, Joyce R.
Johnson, Wilma Robena
Kassebaum, Nancy Landon
Kessler, Joan F.
Powell-Mims, Janie Mae
Riley, Ruth Ellen
Sebelius, Kathleen
Skillman, Rebecca
Smith, Melody D.
Stoneburner, Terri J.

Kentucky

Bailey, Catherine Todd
Carson, Julia May
Chao, Elaine L.

Coleman, Mary Sue
Combs, Ann L.
Combs, Sara W.
Eissenstat, Janet Slaughter
Harris, Skila
Isaac, Teresa
King, Teresa V.
Northup, Anne Meagher
Panzer, Sue
Perdue, Beverly Eaves
Pinckney, Alma
Raines, Shirley C.
Sawyer, Diane
Sias Mary Evans,
Tacha, Deanell Reece
Tackett, Julia Kurtz
Winstead-Wilfong, Terri
Yow, Sandra Kay

Louisiana

Abrahamson, Shirley S.
Alexander, Yvette M.
Allen, Carla H.
Banks,Evelyn P.
Baranco, Juanita Powell
Berry, Janet J.
Blanco, Kathleen B.
Brazile, Donna
Brown, Dorothy
Cannon, Evelyn Omega
Ceaser, Deritha M.
Chandler, Cassandra M.
Clement, Edith Brown
Dangar, Jennifer
Davis, Laura Prosser
DeGeneres, Ellen Lee
DeVard, Jerri
DiMiceli, Elaine W.
Elam, Deborah
Greene, Ellen Pfeiffer
Harris, Vera F.
Herman, Alexis M.
Hughes, Marvalene
Jackson, Sherry R.
Johnson, Norma Holloway
Kemp, Kathryn
Kenney, Kristie Anne
Landrieu, Mary L.
Lee, Alison Renee
McDemmond, Marie V.
McTeer-Hudson, Heather
Millender, B. Pennie
Perdue, Mary
Placide, Charlotte D.
Ponder, Suzan S.
Quagliotti, Marilyn A.
Roberts, Robin
Savage, Janice R.
Simmons, Bettye Hill
Taylor, Susan
Tutt, Veronica
Verrett, Shirley
Wells, Linda Ann
Wise, Phyllis
Zedalis, Debra

Massachusetts

Ableman, Peggy L.
Ariyasu,Vicki
Babb, Ronda E.
Baicker, Katherine
Banks, Paula
Banse, Amy L.
Barrett, Colleen C.
Baskerville, Lezli
Beck, Jill
Begley, Charlene
Bell-Rose,Stephanie
Berger, Carolyn
Bergeson, Terry
Bland, Sharon Jackson
Boswell, Gina
Brice-O'Hara, Sally
Brown, Adriane M.
Bryant, Castell Vaughn
Buel, Sarah
Bundles, A'Lelia
Burke, Sheila P.
Butler-Hopkins, Kathleen
Cabral, Andrea J.
Cabral, Anna Escobedo
CaHill, Mary Beth
Cardenas, Blandina
Casiano, Kimberly
Chao, Elaine L.
Chowdhry, Uma
Chun, Shinae
Clancy, Carolyn M.
Clarey, Patricia
Clark, Rena
Cleckley, Julia J.
Coleman, Catherine G.
Collins, Susan Margaret
Conlin, Linda
Coogan, Cynthia
Corvi, Carolyn
Cowin, Judith A.
Davis, Kathy L.
Davis, Susan A.
Decker, Susan L.
Desjardins, Susan Y.
Diego-Allard, Victoria H.
Dole, Elizabeth Hanford
Dorbriansky, Paula J.
Duncan, Linda A.
Elsenhans, Lynn Laverty
Emerson, Elizabeth Hazlitt
Epps, Evern Cooper
Ericsson, Aprille
Farmer, Margrit Marie Anne
Ferron, Jennifer
Field, Marie T.
Finucane, Anne M.
Fisher, Fern A.
Flake, Elaine
Franklin, Barbara Hackman
Freeman-Wilson, Karen
Fudge, Ann
Fulp, Carol
Garcia, Juliet V.
Gaskins, Kathern L.
Givans, Natalie M.
Gonzalez, Frances A.
Grymes, Rose
Guinier, Lani
Hall, Shelvin Louise Marie
Harman, Jane F.
Harris, Gayle Elizabeth
Harris, Katherine
Harris, Marcelite J.
Harrison, Patricia de Stacy
Hayes, Maxine
Haysbert, JoAnn W.
Hellyar, Mary Jane
Henney, Jane E.
Higginbotham, Eve J.
Hockfield, Susan
Holton, Anne
Hoxby, Caroline
Hughes, Marvalene
Huvelle, Ellen Segal
Ifill, Gwen
Jackson, Lorna Graves
Jamison, Judith
Johns, Marie C.
Johnson, Abigail
Johnson, Nancy L.
Karpinski, Diane
Kelly, Sue
Kennard, Lydia H.
Kessler, Gladys
Kirk-McAlpine, Patricia
Kiss, Elizabeth
Kniss, Liz
Lane, Bensonetta Tipton
Lawrence, Deirdre M.
Leclaire, Margaret
Lipper, Joanna
Lopez, Maria
Loston, Adena Williams
Lowey, Nita M.
Ma, Chung-Pei
Maddox, Yvonne T.
Maguire, Joanne M.
Manzi, Barbara
Mathews, Sylvia
McBride, Margaret Stanton
McColgan, Ellyn A.
McDemmond, Marie V.
McGetrick, Peg
McKinney, Cynthia Ann
Miller-Lerman, Lindsey
Minehan, Cathy E.
Mollway, Susan Oki
Moore, Kimberly Ann
Morella, Constance A.
Morrison, Denise
Mulder, Arlene J.
Obama, Michelle
Odom, Carmen Hooker
Olsen, Kathie
Pataki, Libby
Perez, Anna M.
Perry, Cynthia
Peters, Mary E.
Phillips, Colette A.M.
Pinn, Vivian
Ponder, Anne
Poon, Christine
Porter, Lisa J.
Power, A. Kathryn
Radice, Anne-Imelda
Ramaley, Judith A.
Reede, Joan
Richardson, Barbara
Rogers, Chase T.
Rosenbaum, Marilyn Brown
Roy, Loriene
Russo, Patricia F.
Rykken, Miriam P.
Saar, Mary Ann
Sandberg, Annette M.
Saris, Pattie B.
Seagren, Alice
Silverman, Leslie E.
Skinner, Patricia A.
Spencer, Kathleen M.

Spilker, Linda
Stoneburner, Terri J.
Tatum, Beverly Daniel
Taylor, Angela
Thomas-Graham, Pamela
Titus, Linda S.
Toler, Lynn
Tortolani, Michelle
Townsend, Julie
Turner, Linda Edmonds
Tymeson, Jodi S.
Vigil-Giron, Rebecca
Visser, Lesley
Walker, Angelia
Walters, Barbara
Watson, Diane Edith
Wheeler, Pamela
Wheelwright, Alice
White, Trudy
White, Trudy
Whitman, Margaret C.
Wieland, Lucy A.
Wiley, Benaree Pratt
Williams, E. Faye
Wilson, Debra A
Wilson, Stephanie D
Wong, Andrea
Worke, Renee L.
Wright, Deborah C.

Maryland

Aldridge, Susan C.
Allen, Bernadette
Altonaga, Cecilia Maria
Baenninger, MaryAnn
Beard, Lillian M.
Bell, Diane L.
Berman, Gail
Bernard, Marielsa
Bland, Sharon Jackson
Brannon, Barbara C.
Breckenridge,Jody A.
Brice-O'Hara, Sally
Bridgewater, Pamela E.
Brock, Roslyn McCallister
Brooks, Janice M.
Brown, Beth A.
Bruzek-Kohler, Christine M.
Bryan, T.J.
Burger, Leslie
Cannon, Evelyn Omega
Carrion, Audrey J.S.
Clark, Trudy H.
Cleave, Mary L.
Dacier, Donna Lee
Dickerson, Terri A.
Dixon, Sheila
Duncan-Peters, Stephanie
Einhorn, Jessica P.
Emerson, Jo Ann
Ensor, Judith C.
Ericsson, Aprille
Fast, Barbara G.
Forster, Diane M.
Fuller, Kathryn
Gayle, Helene D.
Gooden, Linda
Greene-Chamberlain, Lillian
Halstead, Rebecca S.
Harris, Marcelite J.
Heard, Wanda Keyes
Heller, Ellen M.
Higginbotham, Eve J.
Hitchcock, Jeanne D.
Ivins, Marsha S.
Jones, Michele S.
Katen, Karen L.
Kennedy, Yvonne
King, Gayle
King, Gwendolyn
Kraus, Julia A.
Lescavage, Nancy J.
Lovelace, Gail T.
Marks, Andrea R.
Martinez, Laura A.
Martinez, Shirley A.
McNeirney, Violet C.
Mellow, Gail O.
Mikulski, Barbara Ann
Miller, Laura
Monroe, Stephanie J.
Moore, Kimberly Ann
Morella, Constance A.
Murphy McKenzie, Vashti
Olsen, Jody
Pack, Sandra L.
Perez, Lucille C. Norville
Peuler, Sandra N.
Pinckney, Belinda
Pinson, Tracey L.
Pollock, Gale S.
Porter, Gayle K.
Power, A. Kathryn
Queen, Joan Renee
Rappaport, Margaret D.
Saar, Mary Ann
Salhany, Lucille S. (Lucie)
Sauerbrey, Ellen R.
Serrette, Cathy H.
Seurkamp, Mary Pat
Shanks, Mary Joe
Smith, Adrienne M.
Stubbs, Laura
Thompson, Thelma
Viverette, Mary Ann
Washington, Linda Jacobs
Weatherington, Lisa D.
Welch, Yoland Maria
Wiley, Benaree Pratt
Wise, Phyllis
Wright, Wilhelmina M.
Yow, Sandra Kay
Zelman, Susan Tave

Maine

Collins, Susan Margaret
Coogan, Cynthia
Hartford, Maureen A.
Yeh, Pen-Shu
Young, Lynnette
Yow, Deborah A.

Michigan

Atkins, Marylin E.
Austin, Debra
Baird, Lisa
Bergeson, Terry
Blount, Nancy M.
Boyle, Patricia Jean E.P.
Bridges, Bobbe J.
Brock, Roslyn McCallister
Brown, Beth A.
Brown, Kay Stanfield
Bruch, Ruth E.
Bryant, Castell Vaughn
Buchan, Claire
Bully-Cummings, Ella
Campbell, Jane L.
Cantor, Nancy
Caruso, Patricia L.
Chrzanowski, Mary A.
Clark, Nikki
Colaianne, Melonie
Coleman, Mary Sue
Collins, Barbara-Rose
Conlon, Patricia N.
Cooper, Jessica R.
Cottrell, Carol
Cox, Darlene L.
Cunningham, Paula D.
Davidson, Lisa
Donze, Laurie Friedman
Draganchuk, Joyce
Druzinski, Diane M.
Epps, Evern Cooper
Falca-Dodson, Maria
Farmer, Nancy
Francis, Nancy C.
George, Kathryn A.
Goff, Mary
Granholm, Jennifer M.
Gray, Karla
Green, Peggy
Green, Phyllis J.
Harrington, Nicki (Virginia)
Hartford, Maureen A.
Higginbotham, Eve J.
Holtz, Judith A.
Jackson, Carol E.
Jackson, Patricia A.
James, Barbara
Jarrett, Valerie
Johnson, Shelia R.
Johnson, Vickki
Johnson, Wilma Robena
Jones-Ham, Wilmer
Kagan, Cheryl C.
Kassebaum, Nancy Landon
Kearse, Amalya L.
Kelly, Marilyn J.
Kennedy, Cornelia G.
Kilpatrick, Carolyn Cheeks
Koplovtz, Kay
Land, Terri Lynn
Lando, Maxine Cohen
Lawless, Janelle A.
Lawrence, Brenda L.
Leahey, Jeanette
Lee, Sherry A.
Maguire, Joanne M.
Mallett, Lydia G.
Martin-Clark, Miriam B.
Mayfield, Mabel Johnson
McClain, Pamela
McDade, Mary
Meek, Carrie P.
Messerich, Kathryn Davis
Milhouse, Donna Robinson
Millender, B. Pennie
Miller, Candice
Miller, Cylenthia LaToye
Neal, Dianne
Nettles-Nickerson, Beverley
Newman, Andrea Fischer

Newman, Constance Berry
O'Banner-Owens, Jeanette
Ortega, Darleen
Pasula, Angela M.
Reid-Coleman, Desma
Richardson, Andra V.
Rivers, Lynn Nancy
Ross-Lee, Barbara
Royster, C. Lorene
Royster, Kay E.
Santona, Gloria
Sharpe, Lisa Webb
Simmons, Bettye Hill
Skinner, Patricia A.
Smith, Alma Wheeler
Snowe, Olympia Jean
Stabenow, Deborah Ann
Starghill, Renee
Stephens, Cynthia D.
Stevens, Lisa
Taylor, Anna Katherine Johnston Diggs
Thomas, Deborah A.
Tolen, Lynda A.
Travis, Tracey Thomas
Trepeck, Judith R.
White, Jeannette Lee
White, Katherine E.
Wilkins, Rillastine R.
Williams, Ann Claire
Williams, Serena Jameka

Minnesota

Adams-Ender, Clara
Alexander, Pamela G.
Alshouse, Diane R.
Bailey, Darlyne
Blackburn, Katie
Bowman, Kathleen Gill
Bransford, Tanya Mozell
Chu, Regina M.
Clark, King, Reatha
Coler, Kate
Cotter, Patricia O'Brien
DeVard, Jerri
Edwards, Teresa
Elders, M. Jocelyn
Flynn, Paulette K.
Fuller, Martha
Gearin, Kathleen R.
Goodson, Amanda
Heffernan, Pamela G.
Hellyar, Mary Jane
Hoag, M. Jean
Hudson, Natalie E.
Hughes, Marvalene
Johnson, Arlene
Kapsner, Carol Ronning
Kautz, Elizabeth
Kenny, Shirley Strum
Klobuchar, Amy Jean
Maring, Mary Muehlen
Martinson, Wendy
McDonald, Gabrielle Kirk
Messerich, Kathryn Davis
Metzen, Leslie May
Meyer, Helen M.
Miles, Susan
Milligan, Pamela K.
Williams, Carolyn Grubbs
Williams, Serena Jameka
Yarbrough, Mamie L.

Missouri

Ackerman, Arlene
Adams, Cheryl
Angelou, Maya
Asel, Jodie
Ballard, Elizabeth
Barnes, Kay
Bennett, Angela M.
Blackett, Carolyn Wade
Brown, Nancy E.
Carnahan, Jean
Carnahan, Robin
Carpenter, Christine
Caswell, Susan P.
Cherng, Peggy Tsiang
Coaxum, Velva D.
Curby, Norma J.
Dolan, Colleen
Draper, Judy P.
Fast, Barbara G.
Fowler, Nuby
Godwin, Linda M.
Harriss, Cynthia
Hill-Ardoin, Priscilla
Hollis, Evelyn
Hotten, Michele D.
Jackson, Carol E.
Joseph, Phyllis R.
King, Gayle
Laybourne, Geraldine
Levick, Cheryl
Lingle, Linda
Lott, Martha A.
Mitchell, Eithel P.
Molnau, Carol
Newman, Constance Berry
Nicholson, Pamela M.
O'Leary, Hazel
Poon, Christine
Price, Anita
Roper, Ellen
Schroeder, Mary B.
Springer, Marlene
Wagner, Ann
Wallace, Barbara
Waters, Maxine

Mississippi

Blackburn, Marsha
Blackmon,Patricia Ann
Brown, Yvonne
Butler, Gloria
Coaxum, Velva D.
Cobb, Kay Beevers
Davidson, Lisa
Dixon, Melba
Donald, Bernice B.
Edelman, Marian Wright
Harthcock, Tammy
Hayes, Maxine
Hockfield, Susan
Hogan, Beverly Wade
Jenkins-Harden, Joyce R.
Kennedy, Yvonne
Lott, Deneise Turner
Malachowski, Nicole
McTeer-Hudson, Heather
Mounger, Virginia Wilson
Murakata, Linda A.
Pinckney, Alma
Powell-Mims, Janie Mae
Presley, Vivian Mathews
Roberts, Robin
Royster, C. Lorene
Sias Mary Evans,
Steele, Bobbie L.
Thompson, Linda A.
Tuck, Amy
Varnado, Sheila
Walker, Alice
Watson, Kyra
Whipple, Rachel H.
Whittington, Carolyn
Wooden, Ruth A.

Montana

Walker-Kimbro, Carolyn
Washington, Bette R.
Wilson, Cindy Polk
Winfrey, Oprah Gail

North Carolina

Adams-Ender, Clara
Allison-Ottey, Sharon
Alseth, Becky
Angelou, Maya
Asefnia, Sepideh "Sepi"
Austin, Debra
Babrowski, Claire
Bergman, Nomi
Berry, Cherie Killian
Biggins, J. Veronica
Bingham, Laura Carpenter
Boney-Harris, Gwendolyn
Borders, Lisa
Brehm, Sharon B
Brown, Adriane M.
Bryan, T.J.
Bryant, Wanda G.
Bysiewicz, Susan
Calabria, Ann Marie
Cannon, Evelyn Omega
Capito, Shelley Moore
Clayton, Eva M.
Cole, Johnnetta Betsch
Coleman, Carolyn Quilloin
Coleman, Mary Sue
Coogan, Cynthia
Cotter, Patricia O'Brien
Cummings, Angela M.
Currie, Nancy Jane
Davis, Jo Ann
Davis, Susan A.
Dawson, Diann
Dole, Elizabeth Hanford
Douglas, Mae
Draper, Judy P.
Duncan, Allyson Kay
Easley, Mary
Elam, Deborah
Emerson, Flora
Fetherson, Parisa Y.
Fleming-Makell, Rhonda
Foster, Jylia Moore
Foxx, Virginia Ann
Frasier, Elizabeth
Fu, Ping

Gann, Pamela
Gates, Melinda
Goodstein, Diane Schafer
Gray, Karla
Griffin, Patricia W.
Hamilton, Joyce
Harper, Jane V.
Hartford, Maureen A.
Hawley-Bowland, Carla G.
Hicks, Juanita
Hockfield, Susan
Hopson, Deborah Parham
Howard-Vital, Michelle
Johnson, Karen A.
Johnson, Vickki
Kammerer, Charlene
King, Karen
Kiss, Elizabeth
Krawcheck, Sallie L.
Lawrence, Gwendolyn H.
Livermore, Ann M.
Lloyd, Anne H.
Malachowski, Nicole
Maloney, Carolyn Bosher
Marshall, Elaine F.
McCarty, Alison
McGee, Linda M.
Morton, Lorraine H.
Myrick, Sue
Odom, Carmen Hooker
Olsen, Kathie
O'Neal, Elaine M.
Owens, Susan
Parker, Jennifer J.
Perdue, Beverly Eaves
Ponder, Anne
Queen, Joan Renee
Radice, Anne-Imelda
Richardson, Velma L.
Scott, Susan
Sharma, Rajamalliga N. "Lee"
Stephens, Linda
Suber, Dianne B.
Thomas, Jacqueline D.
Turner, Carol I.

North Dakota

Wheeling, Deborah C.
Wilmoth, Margaret Chamberlain
Yow, Deborah A.
Yow, Sandra Kay

Nebraska

Anderson, Tina
Cubin, Barbara L.
Dunn, Karen-Sue
Hayden-Watkins, Dorothy
Hemminger, Linda S.
Higgins, Kathryn O'Leary
Hooley, Darlene
Hughes, Catherine Liggins
Kapsner, Carol Ronning
Kight, Mary J.
Klanderud, Helen
Maring, Mary Muehlen

New Hampshire

Adamson, Rebecca L.
Chao, Elaine L.
Dalianis, Linda Stewart
Hudson, Dawn
Joyner, Pamela J.
Miller-Lerman, Lindsey
Moore, Frankie J.
Norman, Laureen K. Van
Stoney, Janice D.

New Jersey

Ash, Sylvia G.
Baenninger, MaryAnn
Bartz, Carol
Blake, Norma E.
Bruzek-Kohler, Christine M.
Butenis, Patricia A.
Byrd, Cora
Carter, Normia E.
Castro, Ida L.
Conlin, Linda
Davidson, Janet
Dunn, Karen-Sue
Falca-Dodson, Maria
Farber, Zulima V.
Fleming-Makell, Rhonda
Forster, Diane M.
Gandara, Marilda Lara
Gerard, Patricia
Hall, Beverly L.
Hall, Lisa Gersh
Harris, Gayle Elizabeth
Hart, Clare
Heard, Wanda Keyes
Hobson, Mellody
Jackson, Sherry R.
Johnson, Wilma Robena
Johnson-Reece, Nicole
Jones, Michele S.
Jung, Andrea
Kagan, Elena
Kearse, Amalya L.
Keit, Patricia A.
King, Teresa V.
King, Teresa V.
Kiss, Elizabeth
Laybourne, Geraldine
Marks, Andrea R.
Mathieu, Dennise
McColgan, Ellyn A.
Mellow, Gail O.
Minehan, Cathy E.
Murakata, Linda A.
Newman, J. Bonnie
Ng, Kim
O'Leary, Hazel
Pariente, Barbara J.
Redd, Dana
Safford, Shirley Strickland
Sapp-Peterson, Paulette
Shea-Porter, Carol
Sobbott, Susan
Sobel, Annette L.
Soodik, Bonnie
Stevens, Anne
Stewart, Martha
Tauscher, Ellen O'Kane
Wheeler, Pamela
Wilson, Heather

New Mexico

Denish, Diane
Forrest, Delores G.
Fry, Cynthia A.
Henney, Jane E.
Herrera, Carol
Herrera, Mary
Kelly, Suedeen G.
Madrid, Patricia A.
Napolitano, Janet
Pickard, Lynn
Prettyman-Beck, Yvonne J.
Rhoades, Anne
Sobel, Annette L.
Tilghman, Shirley M.
Toben, Doreen A.
Whitman, Christie Tobb
Wright, Doreen A.

Nevada

Berkley, Shelley
Berry, Janet J.
Bromley, Rebecca Snyder
Brown, Renee
Butz, M. Kathleen
Campbell, Jill
Dixon, Melba
Harter, Carol C.
Hunt, Lorraine T.
Kirkland, Cynthia N.
Lane, Bensonetta Tipton
Lanzinger, Judith Ann
Malachowski, Nicole
McBeth, Veronica Simmons
Swift, Pattie P.
Vigil-Giron, Rebecca
Volkow, Nora D.
Wilson, Heather

New York

Aarons, Sharon A.M.
Abrahamson, Shirley S.
Alemany, Ellen
Alonzo, Jenny
Alvarez, Aida
Anderson, Chandra Y.
Anderson, Michelle J.
Ash, Sylvia G.
Ashley, Diane T.
Austin, Debra
Babb, Ronda E.
Bailey, Darlyne
Baker, Ellen S.
Barazzone, Esther L.
Barton, Jacqueline K.
Bath, Patricia E.
Battaglia, Lynne A.
Beck, Jill
Bell-Rose,Stephanie
Berger, Carolyn
Bergman, Nomi
Berkley, Shelley
Berman, Gail
Boxer, Barbara
Brown, Leilani
Brown, Lucy Chernow
Brown, Nancy E.
Brown-Waite, Virginia
Buckley, Mary Kate
Bundles, A'Lelia
Burke, Rossatte Y.
Burns, Ursula M.
Butler-Hopkins, Kathleen

Bysiewicz, Susan
Cagle, Yvonne Darlene
Calhoun, Essie L.
Caniano, Donna A.
Cantor, Nancy
Carey, Joan B.
Carrion, Audrey J.S.
Carter, Majora
Carter, Normia E.
Casiano, Kimberly
Castagna, Vanessa
Castro, Ida L.
Chan, Mary
Chao, Elaine L.
Chow, Joan K.
Clark, King, Reatha
Clark, Patrina
Clarke, Yvette Diane
Clay, Patricia
Cleave, Mary L.
Cleckley, Julia J.
Clinton, Hillary
Cole, Johnnetta Betsch
Collins, Eileen Marie
Collins, Susan Margaret
Colony, Sandy
Comstock, Beth
Costantini, Lynne
Couric, Katie
Cox, Darlene L.
Crisp, Donna L.
Culley, Anna
Davis, Sarah Frances
De Alonso, Marcela Perez
Decker, Susan
DeGeneres, Ellen Lee
DeGette, Diana
DeLauro, Rosa L.
de Passe, Suzanne
DeVard, Jerri
DiFiore, Janet
Donohue, Mary O.
Douglas, Laura G.
Draper, Carol Enger
Duncan, Linda A.
Duncan-Peters, Stephanie
Edlitz, Sandra B.
Edwards, Genine D.
Einhorn, Jessica P.
Emerson, Elizabeth Hazlitt
Ericsson, Aprille
Evans, Jane
Farmer, Margrit Marie Anne
Ferretti, Charlotte
Fienberg, Linda D.
Fili-Krushel, Patricia
Fischel, Shelley
Fisher, Fern A.
Flake, Elaine
Flanders, Moira
Fleming-Makell, Rhonda
Foxx, Virginia Ann
Frankel, Lois J.
Fudge, Ann
Fulp, Carol
Garcia, Mildred
Garel, Giana
Garrett, Toba
Garrison, Marguerite C.
Garson, Robin S.
Gatti, Rosa
Gayle, Helene D.
Genshaft, Judy
Gilmore, Marie
Gilmore, Vanessa
Gonzalez, Lizbeth
Gonzalez, Sara M.
Graffeo, Victoria A.
Grant, Susan
Graves, Barbara Kydd
Green, Peggy
Green, Phyllis J.
Hall, Beverly L.
Hall, Lisa Gersh
Halpem, Cheryl
Halstead, Rebecca S.
Harman, Jane F.
Harnisch, Ruth Ann
Harris, Gayle Elizabeth
Harris, Vera F.
Harrison, Patricia de Stacy
Hart, Deborah L.
Harter, Carol C.
Hayes, Maxine
Hockfield, Susan
Hood, Lucy
Huggins, Sheryl
Hughes, Marvalene
Hughes, Teresa P.
Hunt, Lorraine T.
Ifill, Gwen
Immergut, Karin J.
Isaacs-Lowe, Arlene
Jackman-Brown, Pam B.
Jackson-Lee, Sheila
Jaffe, Barbara
Jamison, Judith
Jemison, Mae C.
Johnson, Glorious
Johnson, Odessa
Johnson, Suzanne Nora
Jones, Carol A.
Kagan, Cheryl C.
Katz, Vera
Kaye, Judith S.
Kearse, Amalya L.
Keizs, Marcia V.
Kelly, Sue
Kelly, Suedeen G.
Kessler, Gladys
King, Carolyn Dineen
Koellner, Laurette
Krawcheck, Sallie L.
Krueger, Liz
Lane, Bensonetta Tipton
Lazarus, Rochelle B.
Leclaire, Margaret
Lee, Esther
Lewis, Daree M.
Lewis, Shirley A.R.
Lias, Kay A.
Lipper, Joanna
Lowe, Melissa
Lowey, Nita M.
Lynn, Barbara M.G.
Madison, Paula
Maloney, Carolyn Bosher
Maloy, Frances
Manzi, Barbara
Marshall, Helen M.
McAniff, Nora
McCabe, Jewell Jackson
McCarthy, Carolyn
McCaw, Susan Rasinski
McDemmond, Marie V.
McHale, Judith A.
McNeirney, Violet C.
McVay, Jacque
Mellow, Gail O.
Merget, Astrid E.
Michel, Harriet R.
Miles-LaGrange, Vicki
Milin, Maria
Miller-Lerman, Lindsey
Minehan, Cathy E.
Mitchell, Andrea
Molinari, Susan
Moore, Madeleine
Moss, Lesia Bates
Moyers, Judith Davidson
Napolitano, Janet
Ng, Kim
Nicholson, Pamela M.
Norton, Eleanor Holmes
Norville, Deborah
Nugent, Georgia
Ogden, E. Jeannette
O'Leary, Hazel
Olsen, Kathie
Orender, Donna
Pariente, Barbara J.
Parker, Jennifer J.
Pataki, Libby
Perez, Anna M.
Perez, Lucille C. Norville
Perrin-Johnson, Tanya
Peruggi, Regina S.
Pickard, Lynn
Pineda-Kirwan, Diccia T.
Pippins, Shirley Robinson
Placide, Charlotte D.
Pollock, Gale S.
Preska, Loretta A.
Raab, Jennifer J.
Read, Susan P.
Readon, Nancy A.
Reed, Wendy
Reede, Joan
Reid-Wallace, Carolyn
Richardson, Barbara
Rittling, Mary E.
Rivera, Fanny
Rivera, Margaret
Rivera, Sonya L.
Rocco, Nikki
Rodriguez, Julia I.
Rodriguez, Rose
Rondeau, Ann E.
Ross-Lee, Barbara
Rothstein, Barbara Jacobs
Ruesterholz, Virginia P.
St. Claire, Dail
Sanford, Linda S.
Scantlebury, Velma
Scarpulla, Saliann
Schori, Katharine Jefferts
Schultz, Debbie Wasserman
Schumacher, Deborah
Schwartz, Allyson Y.
Sclafani, Karen
Scott, Susan
Seurkamp, Mary Pat
Shalala, Donna E.
Shapiro, Judith R.
Shaw, Nina
Shea-Porter, Carol
Shelton, Barbara L.
Siegal, Bernice D.
Simons, Renee V.H.
Slaughter, Louise McIntosh
Sotomayor, Sonia
Soupata, Lea N.

Spears, Brenda A.
Springer, Linda M.
Springer, Marlene
Steele, Toreaser A.
Steinhelmer, Connie
Tao, Elizabeth J. Yalin
Tauscher, Ellen O'Kane
Taylor, Susan
Thomas, Debi
Timmons, Jacquette M.
Townsend, Frances
Townsend, Sharon S.
Troutman, Shirley
Trowell-Harriw, Irene
Tyson, Lynn A.
Velazquez, Nydia
Verrett, Shirley
Volkow, Nora D.
Waldron, Kathleen
Walters, Barbara
Washington, Bette R.
Whitman, Margaret C.
Williams, Carolyn Grubbs
Wooden, Ruth A.
Wos, Aldona Zofia
Zel, Antoinette

Ohio

Appolito, Collette
Arouh, Janice
Bailey, Rosanne
Balraj, Elizabeth K.
Batchelder, Alice Moore
Beasley, Teresa
Belfance, Eve
Berry, Bertice
Blackburn, Katie
Blackmon,Patricia Ann
Bono, Mary
Bowen, Margretta Jeffers
Bowers, Kathleen M.
Boyle, Edna J.
Bradley, Jennette B.
Bridgewater, Pamela E.
Brown, Yvette McGee
Browne, Kim A.
Bryant, Peggy
Calhoun, Essie L.
Callahan, Lynne S.
Campbell, Jane L.
Caniano, Donna A.
Cantwell, Maria E.
Clayton, Annette
Conlon, Patricia N.
Cooney, Colleen Conway
Counts, Millicent S.
Currie, Nancy Jane
DeGenaro, Mary
Duckett, Karen I.
Dumas, Sharon A.
Duncan, Linda A.
Dyke, Ann
Elam, Deborah
Emerson, Jo Ann
Falkowski, Colleen
Flake, Elaine
French, Judith L.
Fuerst, Nancy A.
Gardner, Janice
Gaston, Marilyn Hughes
Genshaft, Judy
Gerberding, Julie Louise
Greene, Lillian J.
Groves, Emanuella
Harris, Gene T.
Hart, Cathy J.
Hart, Deborah L.
Harter, Carol C.
Hendon, Sylvia Sieve
Hill, Chris A.
Hill, Valarie A.
Hilliard, Ruth H.
Holbrook, Karen A.
Hopson, Deborah Parham
Hudson, Dianne Atkinson
Hughes, Marvalene
Jones, Stephanie Tubbs
Jordan, Karen
Kammerer, Charlene
Karpinski, Diane
Kelly, Sue
Keough, Kathleen Ann
Lanzinger, Judith Ann
Lawson, Kelli Richardson
Leclaire, Margaret
Lewis, Shirley A.R.
Lin, Maya
Loewer, Deborah A.
Long, Irene Duhart
Longaberger, Tami
Mays, Anita Laster
McLin, Rhine
Merget, Astrid E.
Michael, Kathryn
Miladore, Dianne Bitonte
Milligan, Pamela K.
Moore, Carla
Murphy McKenzie, Vashti
Myrick, Sue
Nobumoto, Karen S.
Norton, Eleanor Holmes
O'Connor, Maureen
Parrish, Patricia G.
Ponder, Anne
Pryce, Deborah D.
Read, Susan P.
Reed, Trudie Kibbe
Rivera, Aurea L.
Ross-Lee, Barbara
Routen, Gina L.
Safford, Shirley Strickland
Salhany, Lucille S. (Lucie)
Schmidt, Jean
Sebelius, Kathleen
Shalala, Donna E.
Sheskey, Susan
Singer, Arlene
Skinner, Patricia A.
Sobel, Annette L.
Squire, Carole
Stokes, Angela R.
Stormer, Elinore Marsh
Stratton, Evelyn Lundberg
Sutton, Betty
Synenberg, Joan
Taft, Hope
Talley, Debra Linn
Tarver, Pauline
Toler, Lynn
Travis, Tracey Thomas
Varnado, Sheila
Waite, Cheryl L.
Walker, Debra K.
Walker-Kimbro, Carolyn
Wattleton, Faye
Westgate, Barbara A.
Wetherald, Michele Warholic
Williams, Annalisa S.
Wisham, Lorna
Wright, Deborah C.
Yeh, Ying
Zahn, Paula
Zedalis, Debra

Oklahoma

Adolf, Mary M.
Aragon, LaRita A.
Campbell, Jill
Caswell, Susan P.
Collins, Eileen Marie
Davis, Audrey Y.
Eissenstat, Janet Slaughter
Fallin, Mary
Garrett, Sandy
Gurich, Noma D.
Haysbert, JoAnn W.
Henry, Kim
Johnson, Arlene
Kauger, Yvonne
Lautenschlager, Peggy A.
Lucia, Marian M.
Wykle, May L.
Young, Patricia M.
Zelman, Susan Tave
Zimpher, Nancy

Oregon

Anderson, Tina
Ballard, Elizabeth
Bowman, Kathleen Gill
CaHill, Mary Beth
Castillo, Susan
Cherng, Peggy Tsiang
Hooley, Darlene
Immergut, Karin J.
Katz, Vera
King, Barbara L.
Leeson, Susan M.
Linder, Virginia L.
Lucid, Shannon W.
McMorris, Cathy
Miles-LaGrange, Vicki
Monsarrat, Nancy
Murkowski, Lisa
Ortega, Darleen
Parrish, Patricia G.
Robertson, Vicki
Roy, Loriene

Pennsylvania

Adams, Vickee Jordan
Anderson, Michelle J.
Archambeau,Shellye
Arnold, Susan E.
Baenninger, MaryAnn
Bailey, Darlyne
Baird, Lisa
Baldwin, Cynthia
Barazzone, Esther L.
Blount, Paula
Bodine, Susan
Born, Dana H.
Boscola, Lisa M.
Brown, Lisa L.
Brownell, Nora
Bryan, T.J.
Burke, Rossatte Y.

Butenis, Patricia A.
Butler-Hopkins, Kathleen
Calabria, Ann Marie
Campbell, Phyllis C.
Chow, Joan K.
Clancy, Carolyn M.
Cleckley, Julia J.
Contres, Kathlene
Cordell, LaDoris Hazzard
Cummings, Angela M.
Davidson, Janet
DeFrantz, Anita L.
Douglas, Laura G.
Eder, Mari Kaye
Elliott, Kate Ford
Fike, Sherri
Flaherty, Karen
Franklin, Barbara Hackman
Franklin, Shirley Clarke
Gaston, Marilyn Hughes
Gatti, Rosa
Grymes, Rose
Guinier, Lani
Harrison, Patricia de Stacy
Hart, Clare
Hart, Deborah L.
Hart, Melissa A.
Herman, Mindy
Hirsh, Sharon Latchaw
Hooper, Michele J.
Howard-Vital, Michelle
Huggins, Sheryl
Ivins, Marsha S.
Jackson, Kathryn J. "Kate"
Jamison, Judith
Jemmott, Loretta Sweet
Johnson, Christyl
Johnson, Karen A.
Johnson-Goins, Gloria
Johnson-Reece, Nicole
Jones, Carol A.
Jones, Edith Hollan
Jordan, Karen
Jurden, Jan R.
Knoll, Catherine Baker
Kronmiller, Kate B.
Lally-Green, Maureen E.
Laybourne, Geraldine
Lescavage, Nancy J.
Lewis, Cynthia
Lowe, Melissa
Lucia, Marian M.
Ma, Chung-Pei
Marshall, Susan G.
Matthews, Candace
McGrath, Judy
McGruder-Jackson, Sandra
Melvin, Joan Orie
Michel, Harriet R.
Mitchell, Andrea
Morris, Elizabeth M.
Newman, J. Bonnie
Newman, Sandra Schultz
Olsen, Kathie
Redpath, Sharon H.
Rendell, Marjorie O.
Richie, Sharon Ivey
Rickard, Lisa A.
Rodin, Judith
Schwartz, Allyson Y.
Shelton, Barbara L.
Snider, Stacey
Springer, Linda M.
Stevens, Anne
Stroupe, Ashley W.
Stubbs, Laura
Tatem, Dorothy Watson
Thomasson, Lauren
Todd, Debra McCloskey
Wagner, LaVonda
Wilson, Janice Rose
Wyatt, Merri Southern
Yate, Mary Carlin

Rhode Island

Beldo, April D.
Blackett, Carolyn Wade
Brault, Laurell A.
Cabral, Anna Escobedo
CaHill, Mary Beth
Contres, Kathlene
Crisp, Donna L.
Farmer, Margrit Marie Anne
Garrett, Tracy L.
Gatti, Rosa
Jackson, Patricia A.
Jacobson, Nina
Lane, Bensonetta Tipton
McGetrick, Peg
Powell-Mims, Janie Mae
Power, A. Kathryn
Queen, Joan Renee
Turgeon, Jeannine
Wright, Doreen A.
York, Denise DeBartolo
Zedalis, Debra

South Carolina

Bridgewater, Pamela E.
Brooks, Janice M.
Coaxum, Velva D.
Coleman, Catherine G.
Cureton, Deborah B.
Dawson, Diann
Farrisee, Gina S.
Fetherson, Parisa Y.
Fleming-Makell, Rhonda
Fowler, Nuby
Goodstein, Diane Schafer
Harris, Vera F.
Hayes, Lou V.
Haysbert, JoAnn W.
Hearn, Kaye G.
Hollis, Evelyn
James, Gloria Schumpert
Jefferson, Deadra L.
Jones, Michele S.
Joseph, Phyllis R.
Keit, Patricia A.
Kenney, Kristie Anne
Krawcheck, Sallie L.
Lawrence, Gwendolyn H.
Lee, Alison Renee
Marks, Andrea R.
Matthews, Carolyn C.
McDade, Mary
McNeirney, Violet C.
McNeirney, Violet C.
Meierhenry, Judith
O'Neill, Harriet
Pinckney, Alma
Pinckney, Belinda
Provence, Tiffany
Reed, Trudie Kibbe
Reede, Joan
Richardson, Velma L.
Roberts, Elizabeth H.
Schafer, Diane
Sharma, Rajamalliga N. "Lee"
Sherman, Diane
Smalls, Marva
Tutt, Veronica
Wheelwright, Alice

South Dakota

Stephens, Linda
Thomas, Paula Hinson
Whitson, Caroline

Tennessee

Askew, Kim J.
Bailey,Stephanie
Banks,Evelyn P.
Bell-Scott, Patricia
Bingham, Laura Carpenter
Blackburn, Marsha
Blackett, Carolyn Wade
Brown, Irma Hunter
Clayton, Annette
Coleman, Carolyn Quilloin
DeBerry, Lois M.
Donald, Bernice B.
Ennix, Kim
Evans, Sue McKnight
Flake, Elaine
Gibbons, Julia Smith
Harnisch, Ruth Ann
Harris, Skila
Hayes, Maxine
Hemminger, Linda S.
Herseth, Stephanie
Holt, Karen E.
Inman, Pam H.
Jackson, Kathryn J. "Kate"
Jamison, Judith
Jernigan, Tamara E.
Johnson, Odessa
Jordan, Karen
Kennedy, Claudia
Kennedy, Yvonne
Lee, Sharon Gail
Lewis, Shirley A.R.
Miller, Peggy
Mitchell, Eithel P.
O'Leary, Hazel
Palmer, Vicki R.
Raines, Shirley C.
Reid-Wallace, Carolyn
Scott, Beverly
Sherman, Diane
Thompson, Linda A.
Thoms, Jannet M.
Vanhooser, Teresa
Wiley, Reba D.

Texas

Adams, Cheryl
Allen, Debbie
Alvarado, Carol
Arsht, Leslye A.
Askew, Kim J.
Baker, Ellen S.
Barrett, Colleen C.
Beldo, April D.

Bivens, Carolyn Vesper
Bondy, Melissa L.
Brannon, Barbara C.
Bryan, Beth Ann
Buel, Sarah
Bundles, A'Lelia
Bush, Laura
Cardenas, Blandina
Carr, Helen
Ceaser, Deritha M.
Clarey, Patricia
Cole, Brenda Hill
Cole, Sheryl
Cooper, Cynthia
Cunningham, Pauline W.
Currie, Nancy Jane
Dale, Shana
Dinkins, Carol E.
Dixon, Althea Green
Dunbar, Bonnie J.
Dunn, Karen-Sue
Dupont, Debra
Earle, Elisabeth A.
Edwards, Ada
Edmunds, Jeanette K.
Eissenstat, Janet Slaughter
Ender, Elma Teresa Salinas
Forrest, Delores G.
Forster, Diane M.
Fuller, Kathryn
Garcia, Juliet V.
Garcia, Sylvia R.
Gates, Melinda
Gilmore, Vanessa
Gonzalez, Frances A.
Hall, Shelvin Louise Marie
Harris, Marcelite J.
Harris, Vera F.
Hawley-Bowland, Carla G.
Haynes, Karen
Hill-Ardoin, Priscilla
Hinojosa, Leticia
Hooks, Tamara T.
Hughes, Karen P.
Hutchison, Kathyrn Ann Bailey
Ivins, Marsha S.
Jackson-Lee, Sheila
Jenkins, Sebeth
Johnson, Eddie Bernice
Jones, Carol A.
Jones, Edith Hollan
Joseph, Annette
Joseph, Phyllis R.
Joyner, Donna Richardson
Keit, Patricia A.
Kenny, Shirley Strum
Kim, Jennifer
King, Barbara L.
Krom, Beth
Kronmiller, Kate B.
Krusa-Dossin, Mary Ann
Leclaire, Margaret
Lee, Barbara
Lescavage, Nancy J.
Littlejohn, Janet
Loston, Adena Williams
Lovett, Melendy
Lucia, Marian M.
Lucid, Shannon W.
Lynn, Barbara M.G.
Madison, Paula
Malazzo, Beverly
Martinez, Shirley A.
Martinson, Wendy
McDonald, Gabrielle Kirk
McIntosh, Jeanine
McTague, Linda K.
Miers, Harriet
Miller, Laura
Moore, Lois Jean
Moore, Thelma Wyatt Cummings
Morgan, Barbara R.
Morgan, Barbara R.
Moyers, Judith Davidson
Napolitano, Grace F.
Natalicio, Diana S.
O'Neill, Harriet
Pace, Betty S.
Palmer, Vicki R.
Panzer, Sue
Perry, Anita
Perry, Cynthia
Powell-Mims, Janie Mae
Pozza, Karen H.
Prettyman-Beck, Yvonne J.
Radle, Patti
Reed, Trudie Kibbe
Rhoades, Brenda T.
Riley, Ruth Ellen
Rondeau, Ann E.
Saunder, Mary L.
Schroeder, Mary B.
Scott, Beverly
Shanks, Mary Joe
Sias Mary Evans,
Simmons, Bettye Hill
Snelson, Teresa Guerra
Steele, Toreaser A.
Stevens, Joyce L.
Swoopes, Sheryl
Tate, Judy Marie
Taylor, Angela
Turner, Mary Ann
Valdez, Lupe
Velasquez, Vanessa
Wagner, LaVonda
Wallace, Joy
Walton, Alice Louise
Warder, Janice
Washington, Tereasa H.
Wheelan, Belle S.
Whiteside, Ruth
Wilmoth, Margaret Chamberlain
Winfrey, Oprah Gail
Winslow, Cleta

Utah

Adamson, Kim T.
Atherton, Judith S.H.
Billings, Judith M.
Boyden, Ann
Campbell, Phyllis C.
Clarke, Kathleen
Cleave, Mary L.
Davis, N. Jan
Davis, Sarah Frances
Dickerson, Lynn
Diego-Allard, Victoria H.
Durham, Christine M.
Graves-Robertson, Shauna
Greenwood, Pamela T.
Hansen, Karla J.
Harris, Stayce D.
Heffernan, Pamela G.
Whitson Peggy A.
Williams, Darlene
Wright, Carolyn
Yanez, Linda Reyna
Zahn, Paula

Virginia

Ackerman, Val
Adams, Karen S.
Adamson, Rebecca L.
Anderson, Belinda C.
Beldo, April D.
Billings, Judith M.
Black, Susan Harrell
Bourbeau, Sheryl J.
Bowman, Kathleen Gill
Brault, Laurell A.
Breckenridge,Jody A.
Bridgewater, Pamela E.
Brock, Roslyn McCallister
Brock, Rovenia
Bromley, Rebecca Snyder
Brown, Janice Rogers
Capito, Shelley Moore
Carnahan, Robin
Chang, Lisa
Clay, Patricia
Cleckley, Julia J.
Coleman, Catherine G.
Couric, Katie
Cummings, Angela M.
Dacier, Donna Lee
Davis, Jo Ann
Davis, Laura Prosser
Del Pesco, Susan C.
Dickerson, Terri A.
DiCroce, Deborah M.
Drake, Thelma D.
Duncan, Allyson Kay
Dunn, Karen-Sue
Earp, Naomi Churchill
Farrisee, Gina S.
Fetherson, Parisa Y.
Fields, Evelyn J.
Fields, Shirley L.
Flanders, Moira
Fleming-Makell, Rhonda
Forrest, Delores G.
Forster, Diane M.
Gambatesa, Linda
Gibbons, Julia Smith
Gulyas, Diane
Hall, Shelvin Louise Marie
Haysbert, JoAnn W.
Hearn, Kaye G.
Hersman, Deborah A.P.
Hodges, Adele E.
Holt, Karen E.
Holton, Anne
Jackson, Sherry R.
Jackson-Lee, Sheila
James, Gloria Schumpert
James,Kay Coles
Jemmott, Loretta Sweet
Jenkins, Jo Ann C.
Jenkins-Harden, Joyce R.
Jeon, Joori
Johnson, Christyl
Johnson, Sheila Crump
Jones, Elain Hollan

Joseph, Phyllis R.
Kammerer, Charlene
King, Teresa V.
Kirk-McAlpine, Patricia
Kraus, Julia A.
Landrieu, Mary L.
Lane, Bensonetta Tipton
Lewis, Leslie A.
Lynn, Barbara M.G.
Maddox, Yvonne T.
Manning, Blanche M.
Marks, Andrea R.
Martinson, Wendy
McCleve, Shelia K.
McDemmond, Marie V.
McGowan, Anna-Maria Rivas
McHugh, Carolyn B.
McNeirney, Violet C.
Miller, M. Yvette
Mitchell, Eithel P.
Moss, Lesia Bates
Napolitano, Janet
Nappier, Denise Lynn
O'Leary, Hazel
Olsen, Jody
Pace, Betty S.
Panzer, Sue
Parrish, Jill N.
Perdue, Beverly Eaves
Pinn, Vivian
Pippins, Shirley Robinson
Pollock, Gale S.
Porter, Lisa J.
Powell, Dorothy L.
Powell-Mims, Janie Mae
Prettyman-Beck, Yvonne J.
Quagliotti, Marilyn A.
Queen, Joan Renee
Quince, Peggy A.
Ragsdale, Marguerita
Ramaley, Judith A.
Rell, M. Jodi
Render, Arlene
Roberts, Elizabeth H.
Roe, Lesa B.
Salinas, Angela
Sanders, Robin Renee
Saunder, Mary L.
Scott, N.H.
Shelton, Barbara L.
Sison, Michele
Smith, Adrienne M.
Steinbeck, Margaret O.
Stroupe, Ashley W.
Suber, Dianne B.
Thompson, Thelma
Thornton, Leslie T.
Turner, Linda Edmonds
VanCleave, Donna
Wagner, LaVonda

Vermont

Weatherington, Lisa D.
Wheelan, Belle S.
White-Olson, B.J.
Williams, Hattie
Young, Gwendolyn V.
Young, Patricia M.

Washington

Alseth, Becky
Armstrong, Mary
Barrett, Colleen C.
Begley, Charlene
Bergeson, Terry
Bishop, Patricia Martin
Bridges, Bobbe J.
Brooks, Janice M.
CaHill, Mary Beth
Cantwell, Maria E.
Capps, Lois
Chang, Shelleyanne W.L.
Clancy, Carolyn M.
Corvi, Carolyn
Dunbar, Bonnie J.
Evans, Jane
Fairhurst, Mary
Farrisee, Gina S
Fuller, Martha
Garrett, Tracy L.
Grant, Beverly G.
Gregoire, Chris
Hartford, Maureen A.
Hayes, Maxine
Heffernan, Pamela G.
Hill-Ardoin, Priscilla
Holbrook, Karen A.
Kelly, Marilyn J.
Kight, Mary J.
Kim, Donna Mercado
King, Barbara L.
Lansing, Karen
Loveland, Valoria H.
Lowe, Melissa
Madsen, Barbara A.
McKissack, Cheryl Mayberry
McMorris, Cathy
Metcalf-Lindenburger, Dorothy M.
Murakata, Linda A.
Murray, Patty

Wisconsin

Abrahamson, Shirley S.
Barshefsky, Charlene
Bartz, Carol
Bowies, Barbara L.
Bradley, Ann Walsh
Burmaster, Elizabeth
Capps, Lois
Carranza, Jovita
Cheney, Lynne V.
Cureton, Deborah B.
Curley, Patricia S.
Dewey, Londa J.
Genshaft, Judy
Hansen, Karla J.
Hill, Valarie A.
Holbrook, Karen A.
Kelly, Susan
Kessler, Joan F.
Koplovtz, Kay
Lautenschlager, Peggy A.
Owens, Susan
Pace, Betty S.
Rothstein, Barbara Jacobs
Ryan, Mary Jean
Sandberg, Annette M.
Wise, Phyllis
Woolsey, Lynn C.

West Virginia

Lawton, Barbara
Mattingly, Rebecca Dirden
Moore, Gwendolynne (Gwen) S.
Murphy, Frances

Wyoming

Brannon, Barbara C.
Cubin, Barbara L.
Kite, Marilyn S.
Pace, Betty S.
Roggensack, Patience Drake
Tome, Carol
White, Maxine A.
Zimpher, Nancy

Other Areas

Africa

Perry, June Carter
Render, Arlene
Sanders, Robin Renee
Tilghman, Shirley M.

Antigua

Phillips, Colette A.M.

Asia

Rhoades, Brenda T.
Richardson, Sandra V.
White, Jeannette Lee
Williams, Hattie
Yeh, Ying

Australia

Born, Dana H.

Bahamas

Brault, Laurell A.

Brazil

Martinez, Carmen M.

Canada

Allen, Bernadette
Brown, Shona
de Alonso, Marcela Perez
Garrett, Toba
Granholm, Jennifer M.
Haynes, Karen
Tilghman, Shirley M.

Central America

Vigil-Giron, Rebecca
Chile
de Alonso, Marcela Perez

Colombia

Martinez, Carmen M.

Cuba

Gandara, Marilda Lara
Lopez, Maria
Ros-Lehtinen, Ileana

Wasserman-Rubin, Diana

Europe

Quagliotti, Marilyn A.
Reese, Andrea D.
Wos, Aldona Zofia
Yate, Mary Carlin

Finland

Baldauf, Sari M.

France

Pataki, Libby
Yate, Mary Carlin

Germany

Katz, Vera
Ramble, Pamela M.
Richardson, Sandra V.
Sears, Leah Ward
Shanks, Mary Joe
Starghill, Renee
Wright, Sherry L.

Great Britain

Kiss, Elizabeth
Marks, Andrea R.
Mathews, Sylvia
McHale, Judith A.

India

Balraj, Elizabeth K.
Chowdhry, Uma

Iran

Asefnia, Sepideh "Sepi"

Iraq

Banta, Vivian

Italy

Lyons, Cathy
Radice, Anne-Imelda

Jamaica

Hall, Beverly L.
Keizs, Marcia V.
Marks, Andrea R.
McIntosh, Jeanine

Japan

Gardner, Janice
Harvey, Keiko

Korea

Chun, Shinae
Jeon, Joori

Kuwait

Ragsdale, Marguerita

Mexico

Bush, Columba

Palestine

Sison, Michele

Puerto Rico

Alvarez, Aida
Carrion, Audrey J.S.
Castro, Ida L.
Espinosa, Carmen E.
Gonzalez, Lizbeth
Rivera, Aurea L.
Rivera, Margaret
Velazquez, Nydia

Qatar

Ragsdale, Marguerita

Trinidad

Babb, Ronda E.
Beckles, G. Valerie
Dixon, Althea Green
McGowan, Anna-Maria Rivas

Venezuela

Martinez, Carmen M.

Virgin Islands

Dixon, Althea Green

West Indies

Gilmore, Marie
Reese, Andrea D.

Zambia

Martinez, Carmen M.